Instrumental Music Education

Instrumental Music Education: Teaching with the Musical and Practical in Harmony is intended for college instrumental music education majors studying to be band and orchestra directors at the elementary, middle school, or high school level. This textbook presents an extensive look at the topics most vital to running a successful instrumental music program, balancing musical, theoretical, and practical approaches. A central theme is the compelling parallel between language and music, including "sound-to-symbol" pedagogies. Understanding this connection improves the teaching of melody, rhythm, composition, and improvisation.

Key Topics

- **Effective repertoire selection**—choosing (and score studying) the most appropriate music
- **Planning effective rehearsals**—communicating with the ensemble and solving common musical problems
- **Classroom management**—exploring a wide spectrum of philosophies and approaches
- **The history of instrumental music education**—learning the philosophical and practical roots of our current system
- **Administrative issues**—managing recruitment, fundraising, budgets, communication, sound levels, copyrights, and concert planning

Multimedia Features

The CD contains over 50 tracks of acoustically pure drones and demonstration exercises for use in rehearsals, sectionals and lessons.

The companion website includes:

- Over 30 rehearsal videos of high school, college, and community concert bands and orchestras
- Pedagogy videos for instruments, performed by professional players and teachers
- More than 220 rhythm flashcards, plus letters and forms discussed in the text
- "Tartini" intonation training software, which tracks the pitch of multiple tones in real time, charts vibrato, and illustrates the complete overtone series of any sounding pitch.
- Additional topics: "The Rehearsal Toolkit" and "The Job Search"

Evan Feldman is Conductor of the Wind Ensemble and Assistant Professor of Music at the University of North Carolina at Chapel Hill.

Ari Contzius is the Wind Ensemble Conductor at Washingtonville High School, Washingtonville, NY.

Mitchell Lutch is Assistant Professor of Music and Director of Bands at Central College in Pella, Iowa.

Instrumental Music Education

Teaching with the Musical and Practical in Harmony

Evan Feldman
Ari Contzius

With contributions by Mitchell Lutch
Foreword by Frank L. Battisti

Routledge
Taylor & Francis Group

NEW YORK AND LONDON

Please visit the companion website at
www.routledge.com/textbooks/9780415992107

First published 2011
by Routledge
270 Madison Avenue, New York, NY 10016

Simultaneously published in the UK
by Routledge
2 Park Square, Milton Park, Abingdon, Oxon OX14 4RN

Routledge is an imprint of the Taylor & Francis Group, an informa business

Typeset in ACaslon by Keystroke, Tettenhall, Wolverhampton
Printed and bound in the United States of America on acid-free paper by Sheridan Books, Inc.

Library of Congress Cataloging-in-Publication Data
Feldman, Evan, 1970-
   Instrumental music education : teaching with the musical and practical in
   harmony / by Evan Feldman, Ari Contzius, with Mitchell Lutch.
      p. cm.
   Includes bibliographical references.
   1. School music—Instruction and study. 2. Instrumental music—Instruction and study.
   I. Contzius, Ari, 1971- II. Lutch, Mitchell. III. Title.
   MT1.F42 2011
   784.071—dc22   2010008244

ISBN 13: 978-0-415-87990-3 (hbk)
ISBN 13: 978-0-415-99210-7 (pbk)
ISBN 13: 978-0-203-84892-0 (ebk)

Table of Contents

Foreword

Frank L. Battisti

Conductor Emeritus, New England Conservatory Wind Ensemble

Music and the Arts are important! They encourage individuals to feel, think, and solve problems creatively, and to arrive at conclusions and answers in unique ways. Collaborative music making experiences magnify the common denominators and diminish the differences between people—it brings them closer together. Music, like reading, math and science, should be part of every young person's education and life.

Effective and inspiring music teachers combine a love of music with a passion for sharing it with others. Their love of music compels them to select and use music that is "truthful"—the real thing—not surrogate mediocre, uninspired pseudo-music pieces. The performance of excellent quality music offers the best means by which students can discover and feel the awesome power of music—to become "music lovers."

The mission of the music teacher is to assist students in discovering music. In order to do this they must inspire, impart knowledge, teach skills, and guide students to an understanding and appreciation of music. Only if music is taught as "an art," where students learn, create and express in a unique manner (different than in other curricular subjects), can it be considered a necessary component in a student's education and development.

Evan Feldman, Ari Contzius and Mitch Lutch in their new book, *Instrumental Music Education: Teaching with the Musical and Practical in Harmony*, examine factors involved in teaching instrumental music—specifically, practical musical and pedagogical knowledge and skills, a "sound to symbol" teaching system, basic musicianship training, selection of music, rehearsal and classroom procedures and management, student assessment and evaluation, administrative responsibilities, and personal and professional development of the teacher.

There are many fine publications about teaching instrumental music. However, none are as comprehensive as *Instrumental Music Education: Teaching with the Musical and Practical in Harmony*. All teachers, both young and experienced, will find this book very valuable.

Preface

One of the most bracing realizations many teachers have when entering the profession is that being a good musician does not automatically make one a good teacher. It's a prerequisite, to be sure, but ultimately the finest virtuoso in the world will fail in front of a large group of students if he doesn't know how to translate his expertise into effective teaching. For many teachers, even when they feel prepared—after they have studied child psychology, learned how to conduct, given recitals on their primary instrument, and learned how to play every other instrument—their first job rarely mirrors their expectations.

There is an irony to this, for once you combine the significant demands of a music degree with education classes and the training needed to teach multiple instruments, you create a music education degree bursting at the seams with requirements. We mean this not as an indictment of teacher preparation programs, but rather as a recognition that music teaching (any teaching, for that matter) is a complex discipline. Not only is there much to learn, but there is a classic tension between theory and practice. After absorbing as much as we can as students, many of us enter the "real world" and find that some of the techniques and philosophies we practiced in school fit awkwardly into the realities of our new job.

Our intent in *Instrumental Music Education* has been to strike a balance among pedagogy and "in the trenches" practicality. Our approach is to show future educators what research and theory says they should do, and then provide the tools for how to do it. In some cases we present more than one perspective on the same issue, a way to recognize the hubris in insisting there is only one way to succeed, or that one viewpoint is inherently superior to another. Teaching the arts can only thrive with open-mindedness and introspection.

Our Teaching Philosophy

In many of the pedagogical sections of *Instrumental Music Education*, we emphasize the commonalities between music and spoken language. One of our impetuses for this was the gradual realization, through our own teaching, that the process of learning language reflects how students naturally learn music. Research shows compelling parallels between music and language[1]—not only neural and cognitive ones, but also in conceptual and pedagogical ways. Put simply, the most effective way to learn music is the same way one learns to speak one's native tongue.

What are the implications of this conclusion for teaching music in schools? With spoken language, children achieve fluency in speaking and understanding before they even enroll in school. Formal schooling then builds upon their fluency. It develops the ability to express oneself, increases their vocabulary, provides the structure of grammar and rules, and teaches reading and writing. In contrast, the conventional approach to instrumental music education teaches the same topics, but in reverse order. Most notably, reading (notation) and theory are taught first; everything else then follows, sometimes immediately, sometimes far behind.

By this process one teaches the symbol before one teaches what the symbol represents. As a broad example, we must avoid telling our students, "A quarter note looks like this" before we know they can perform and understand a basic melody. It would be akin to teaching a toddler how to recognize and recite the alphabet before she has spoken her first word. In writing this book we were interested in a linguistic-influenced approach—a band/orchestra pedagogy that emphasized "speaking" and understanding music before "spelling" and notating it. Sound (and its meaning) is taught first, followed later by the symbol that represents the sound: sound–to–symbol. Much of the pedagogy we present is an adaptation and hybridization of educational theorists such as Suzuki, Kodály, and Gordon, among others. Beyond the recognition of music's relationship with spoken language, their crucial insight was how to extract the tenets and mechanism of learning language, and then simulate and accelerate the process in the music classroom.

Features

Instrumental Music Education's twenty-five chapters cover a wide variety of topics, beginning with the issues raised by Sound–to–Symbol philosophies. These pedagogical topics include:

- a discussion of the connection between music and language, with an eye toward showing how this affects the teaching of music fundamentals
- an introduction to some of the pioneers of Sound–to–Symbol, including Kodály, Suzuki, Dalcroze, and Gordon
- a template for teaching rhythm, tonality, and reading with comprehension to beginning instrumental students
- suggestions for applying these ideas to a traditional method book
- strategies for teaching improvisation and composition in the instrumental classroom

We also include a section on classroom management, one of the most difficult subjects to master for any teacher, not least because experienced master teachers often make it look effortless. Yet though experience may be the best teacher, having a plan accelerates the learning process. One of our goals in writing this text was to provide teachers the concrete theory and tools with which to prepare themselves, especially since it's difficult to simulate a public school scenario in a college classroom or during student teaching and other in-the-field internships. We discuss a variety of philosophies and techniques, and we encourage every teacher to be thoughtful in their approach to disciplining and managing students in the same way they would be choosing repertoire and teaching musicianship.

Of course, being a music teacher involves much more than just teaching music and managing a classroom. Students must be recruited, programs advocated for, funds raised, budgets balanced, concerts managed, repertoire chosen, scores learned, parents communicated to, new jobs sought, and new skills attained. Often these skills are learned on-the-job, and indeed our text cannot replace years of first-hand experience. Still, we have tried to provide detailed primers for some of these crucial activities.

Organization

Instrumental Music Education is divided into three units:

Unit 1: The Process of Teaching Instrumental Music—includes: An Introduction to Sound–to–Symbol, Teaching Rhythm and Rhythm Reading, Tonality, Melody, and Singing, Teaching Improvisation and Composition, The History of Instrumental Music Education and Philosophy, and Two Models of Instructional Design.

Unit 2: Directing Bands and Orchestras—includes: Classroom Management, Curriculum, Assessment and Grading, Repertoire, Score Study, Large Ensemble Set-Up, Rehearsals (in three parts), Intonation, Directing Other Ensembles, and Motivation.

Unit 3: Administrative Issues—includes: Recruiting, Organizing, and Starting the Band and Orchestra, Planning and Managing a Concert/Concert Etiquette, Promotion and Advocacy, Communication, The Music Budget, Copyrights, Managing Sound Levels, Leadership, Mentors, and Professional Development.

A set of questions serve as the bookends for the beginning and end of each chapter. The introductory "To Guide Your Reading" questions quickly preview the goals of the chapter. The "Activities/Assignments for Further Exploration" offer suggestions for class assignments, discussion, and individual projects.

Multimedia Features

Instrumental Music Education provides robust multimedia materials, which include numerous teaching and learning tools for instructor and student. The enclosed CD contains over 50 tracks of acoustically pure drones and demonstration exercises for use in rehearsals, sectionals and lessons. Look out for the CD icon as these exercises are discussed.

The Companion Website, www.routledge.com/textbooks/9780415992107 has several special features:

- Instructional videos filmed with high school, college, and community concert bands. The instructional videos were born from our frustration with the inevitable disconnect between reading about a technique and trying to imagine how it would work in real-life. Having a description in a prose is important, but we knew we could write at great length and still never achieve the clarity of a four-minute video on the same subject. We have provided various methods for addressing musical issues that arise in rehearsal, though we also feel it is important to develop variations, extensions, and additions of these methods:
- Over 100 pedagogy videos for instruments, performed by professional players and teachers
- More than 220 rhythm flashcards, plus letters and forms discussed in the text
- "Tartini," intonation training software, courtesy of its primary author, Philip McCleod, which tracks the pitch of multiple tones in real time, charts vibrato, and illustrates the complete overtone series of any sounding pitch.
- Additional topics on *The Job Search and Interview Process* and *The Rehearsal Toolkit*, which includes "How to Practice," presented by Dr. Lynn Hileman (West Virginia University) and "Rhythmic Alteration and Practice Planning," presented by Matthew McClure (University of North Carolina at Chapel Hill)

- Look for the Companion Website icon throughout the text.

The process of writing this text has been an incredibly rewarding experience. As we worked to refine our ideas and philosophies we were enriched by the incredible wealth of experience and wisdom from our colleagues and from our profession. We hope you enjoy reading it, and we look forward to continuing the discovery process.

Best wishes, musically and otherwise,

Evan Feldman
Chapel Hill, NC
February, 2010

Ari Contzius
Middletown, NY
February, 2010

Mitchell Lutch
Pella, IA
February, 2010

Acknowledgments

The authors are indebted to a long list of colleagues, friends, and family, all of whom made it possible to complete this text. Among them:

Lynn Hileman—Assistant Professor of Bassoon and Music Theory, West Virginia University—for her peerless writing and editing abilities, vast experience with the philosophies of Renée Longy and Marianne Ploger, and consistent insight into the musical and pedagogical issues covered in this text. Her influence appears, overtly and subtly, in nearly every chapter. We are especially indebted to her for allowing us to use her original worksheets regarding melodic patterns, enrhythmic patterns, and subdivision.

Karey Sitzler—Orchestra Director, Lakeland High and Forest Glen Middle Schools; Conductor, String Orchestras, Williamsburg Youth Orchestra; Adjunct Professor, Paul D. Camp Community College— for the invaluable contributions generated by her passionate teaching, effervescent creativity, and years of experience, especially in the area of string and orchestra pedagogy.

Daniel Huff—Clinical Associate Professor of Music Education, University of North Carolina-Chapel Hill—for his assistance in defining major pedagogical issues and refining the text's approach to them, all enhanced by his ability to look at a problem from multiple perspectives.

Constance Ditzel—Senior Editor, Routledge Publishing—for her support and guidance throughout this project.

Sarah Stone—Production Editor—for her patience and counsel during the final stages of editing.

Denny Tek—Editorial Assistant—for all the behind-the-scenes work she did that we didn't even know about.

Matthew McClure—Assistant Director of Bands, University of North Carolina-Chapel Hill—for his musicianship, and his insight and belief in the power of drones.

Jeffrey Fuchs—Director of University Bands, University of North Carolina-Chapel Hill—for his consummate ability to balance the musical and practical while wearing six different hats.

Merida Negrete—Clinical Assistant Professor of Music Education, University of North Carolina-Chapel Hill—for her words of wisdom and encouragement throughout the process of thinking, writing, and editing.

Marianne Ploger—Senior Artist Teacher of Musicianship, Blair School of Music, Vanderbilt University— for her patient and passionate approach to teaching musicianship.

Alan and Judith Feldman—for their love and support throughout this entire process, even when they didn't understand what we were writing about.

Gabe Feldman—Associate Professor of Law and Director, Sports Law Program, Tulane University—for serving as a sounding board, and for providing the objective non-musician's perspective on organization and design (FMTPO!).

Morton and Cynthia Lutch—for their unending love, encouragement and support for this book and all of my interests, including all the MBL stories.

Mike, Larry, Steve, Cindy, and Josh Lutch—for their love, support, and healthy humor in all things Lutch.

Ashley Contzius—Director of Bands, Walkill High School—for her seemingly endless patience, support, beauty both inside and out, and unconditional love as this book consumed our lives.

Erik, Monica, and Jacob Contzius—for their unconditional love and support throughout this entire process.

Martin and Janet Contzius—for their lifelong support of music making, unconditional love, and support throughout this entire process.

Gail Waimon—for her lifelong support of music making, unconditional love, and support throughout this entire process.

Alex, Mo, Supera, and Leia Contzius—for their warmth and fuzziness, no matter that they do not know what instrumental music is, much less a book.

Richard Grunow, Professor of Music Education, Eastman School of Music—for first showing us about this crazy stuff called MLT.

Frank Battisti—Conductor Emeritus of the New England Conservatory Wind Ensemble—for his long-standing inspirational mentorship.

Michael Votta—Professor of Music, Director of Wind Studies, University of Maryland—for the influence brought on by his overall musicianship, which infuses everything he says and writes.

Rodney Winther—for his sense of humor and musical convictions.

Donald Hunsberger—for his contributions both subtle and dramatic, to our professional lives, and indeed, the entire profession.

Amy Noll—Director of Orchestras, Hicksville High School, NY—for over ten years of unflinching support and relentless excitement for playing and teaching strings.

Michelle Monty—Band Director, Washingtonville Central School District—for sharing her detailed approach on the art of elementary recruiting.

Laura Giorgio—Band Director, Washingtonville Central School District; Peter Giorgio—Orchestra Director, Monroe Woodbury Central School District; Christine Wegrzyn—Greenville Central District, New York; and Angelo Marcialis—Band Director, Washingtonville Central School District—for their expertise on elementary and middle school teaching.

Al and Jo-An Smukala—Band Directors, Orange County, NY—two master teachers that provided an immeasurable amount of band directing experiences and never-ending friendship.

Vic Izzo—Band Director, Wallkill Central School District and Ulster County Community College—for his mentorship, endless experience as a master teacher, and demonstration of how to think way outside the box.

Dick Redman—Band Director, Pella Community Schools—for his consultation on color guard units, despite his allegiance to the New York Yankees.

Peter Loel Boonshaft—Professor of Music, Director of Bands, Hofstra University—for sharing his endless wealth of knowledge on the art of teaching and making music.

Jeremy Bouteiller and Timothy Takagi—Student Teachers, Washingtonville High School—for serving as sounding boards and guinea pigs for many of the approaches outlined in this text.

Adam Fontana—for his generous contributions of annotated repertoire lists.

Nichole and Chris Jones—for their invaluable flute and clarinet expertise.

Sybil Kaphan and Larry and Jeannie Waimon—for their endless and unconditional love.

Jim Briggs—Washingtonville High School, Band Director—for his vast professional expertise and friendship.

Jen and Ralph Wagner—for their vast knowledge of high school and middle school band directing, brass and woodwind expertise, computer upkeep so work could continue, and never-ending friendship.

The UNC-Chapel Hill Wind Ensemble—for making great music, even with a Blue Devil standing on the podium.

Washingtonville High School Band students—for providing the joy of teaching and the reason this book needed to be written.

Central College music education majors—for their passion and dedication to be among the ranks of music teachers—an ongoing source of inspiration for this book.

The Process of Teaching Instrumental Music

Chapter 1

An Introduction to Sound–to–Symbol

To Guide Your Reading

What is "sound–to–symbol" and how does it differ from other teaching approaches often used in the music classroom?

What are the connections between music and language?

Why are these connections important when considering an approach to teaching music?

How does treating music as a language affect the way we teach it?

What are the fundamental concepts of Suzuki, Kodály, and Gordon?

In what ways can competing sound–to–symbol theories co-exist and support each other in the classroom?

What are the common questions, confusions, and misconceptions people have concerning these teaching approaches?

How can sound–to–symbol principles be integrated with non–sound–to–symbol curriculums and method texts?

Consider the structure of most beginning instrumental music programs: After students choose their instrument, the first lessons cover how to hold it, how to shape an embouchure, where to place the fingers, how to produce an initial tone, how to read simple rhythms, and how to apply correct fingerings. Students are shown a whole note, told it contains four quarter notes and gets four beats, and are then asked to play that note, usually on the easiest tone to produce. More rhythms and notes are introduced until students are prepared for simple melodies, which they read using their newly learned knowledge about notation and fingerings.

Conservatories and professional orchestras are filled with exceptional musicians who are products of this system. Nevertheless, traditional method books may not reflect the way people naturally learn music, which many educational theorists argue parallels language learning. This is a process that begins with learning to speak and only then moves on to learning to read. This approach is often called "sound–to–symbol," or "sound before sign," because it emphasizes aural recognition and understanding as precursors to theoretical knowledge and notational skills.

As we will see in Chapter 5, "sound–to–symbol" is not a new concept. Johann Heinrich Pestalozzi (1746–1827), the Swiss educational reformer, Hans Georg Nägeli (1773–1836), Pestalozzi's disciple, and John Curwen (1816–1880), the English minister and inventor of the tonic sol-fa system, all advocated similar philosophies. Yet somehow, at least in American public school instrumental music education, it remains on the periphery of teaching technique.

In the twentieth and twenty-first centuries, at least four music education philosophies reflect the sound–to–symbol approach: Kodály, Suzuki, Gordon's Music Learning Theory, and Dalcroze Eurhythmics (which will be discussed in detail in Chapter 2). These music philosophies rely on three basic assumptions, all of which are connected in some way to spoken language:

1. Nearly everybody acquires the ability to speak without the benefit of formal training and method books.
2. The processes of acquiring language and music parallel each other in key ways.
3. One of the most important steps in learning language or music is experiencing it and doing it.

The Connection between Language and Music

Despite Henry Wadsworth Longfellow's observation that it is the universal language, music is not technically classified as one. But perhaps it does not have to be a language in order to act like one. This is why "sound–to–symbol" philosophies assume a strong connection between language and music. This seems like common sense to many musicians, and the fields of linguistics, cognitive evolutionary science, and neuroscience are finding increasing evidence to support the connection.

Famed linguist Noam Chomsky was inspired by children's innate ability to learn complex linguistic skills on their own, a process he called "linguistic competence."[1] Marveling over their ability to produce grammatically correct sentences they had never before heard, he postulated that all children are born with "formal universals"—genetically encoded rules that operate in all languages (Bernstein, 55).

Leonard Bernstein seized upon this idea and makes a case for a musical version of it in his 1973 lecture series at Harvard, *The Unanswered Question*. In searching for a musical grammar that explains how we innately hear music, Bernstein painstakingly shows how Chomsky's grammatical rules apply to musical analogues, a process he admits is only "quasi-scientific" (Bernstein, 56–65).

Bernstein's Musical–Linguistic Analogs

musical motive ⇨ noun
chord or harmony ⇨ adjective
rhythm ⇨ verb

Though they may break down if we dig too deeply, Bernstein's analogies are food for thought as we work to establish a meaningful language–music connection. Fortunately, cognitive evolutionary research and brain research pick up the argument where Bernstein's poetic reasoning leaves off. Although the brain's music and language systems seem to operate independently, they share neurobiological origins in the same regions.[2] This helps explain why music shares several features with speech. Among them:

1. A set of grammatical and syntactical rules that govern a hierarchy of how structures (words, notes, etc.) are ordered and arranged

2. Memorized "representations"—in the case of language, these representations are words and their meanings; in the case of music, the representations are melodies.

Music and language share important brain processes that interpret rhythmic structure.[3] For example, both speech and music group sound into patterns called phrases. There is also evidence of overlap in how the brain processes the boundaries between phrases (Patel, 174).

As described by Aniruddh D. Patel in his book, *Music, Language, and the Brain*, the brain seems to process melodic contours in music and language similarly as well (Patel, 234–237). If we examine the makeup of those contours closely, we find that both music and language share a predominance of small intervals between pitches (Patel, 219), something that could be explained by the physiological limitations of the human voice. But studies by Patel, Iversen, and Rosenberg (2006) reveal characteristics in the music of countries that reflect the tonal patterns of those countries' languages.[4] The study found that English speech patterns appear in English music and French speech patterns appear in French music[5]—and these are differences that cannot be explained by physical characteristics of the French and English people. One explanation could be that composers regularly borrow text from their native language, and the text's patterns naturally find their way into their music (i.e., folk music). But Patel rejects this, pointing out that speech is reflected in many musical works that are not connected to folk music. Instead, he suggests that the connection could be more direct, that "implicit learning of prosodic patterns in one domain (ordinary speech) influences the creation of rhythmic and tonal patterns in another domain (instrumental art music)" (Patel, 224).

What about grammar and syntax? With language, rules and memory are controlled by different parts of the brain.[6] Recently, neuroscientists Robbin A. Miranda and Michael T. Ullman discovered that musical rules (defined as notes that stay properly within a given tonality) and memory show the same dichotomy. They found that memory for words and melodies share one part of the brain, and rules for language and music share another (Miranda and Ullman, 331).

Cognitive scientist Steven Pinker would probably dismiss these as happy coincidences. He famously dismissed music as "auditory cheesecake"[7]—something that developed without any clear evolutionary basis. Music, he argued, was a "spandrel," a byproduct of other evolutionary forces. It just happened to exploit pleasure channels that likely developed to reinforce linguistic communication. Pinker writes:

> As far as biological cause and effect are concerned music is useless. It shows no signs of design for attaining a goal such as long life, grandchildren, or accurate perception and prediction of the world. Compared with language, vision, social reasoning, and physical know-how, music could vanish from our species and the rest of our lifestyle would be virtually unchanged.[8]

But Pinker's assessment has been disputed. Some argue that rather than being a byproduct of language, music actually helps prepare the mind for cognitive and social activities. Neuroscientist Daniel Levitin writes:

> The fact that music lacks specific referents makes it a safe symbol system for expressing mood and feelings in a non-confrontational manner. Music processing helps infants to prepare for language; it may pave the way to linguistic prosody, even before the child's developing brain is ready to process phonetics. Music for the developing brain is a form of play, an exercise that invokes higher-level integrative processes that nurture exploratory competence, preparing the child to eventually explore generative language development through babbling, and ultimately more complex linguistic and paralinguistic productions. (Levitin, 262)

A child's first exposure to spoken language comes from all around them—from their parents, siblings, television, radio, stories that are read to them, and more. A baby utters her first words even though no one formally taught her how to say anything. The child simply imitates something she has already heard. She experiences it and then does it herself. Soon she associates these sounds with specific objects and people. "Dada" becomes a way to reference the father, "Mama" refers to the mother, and so on. The child communicates with her limited vocabulary, eventually combining words into phrases and sentences. Using the building blocks of vocabulary and phrases acquired from her parents, she soon speaks sentences she has never heard before. The child also extracts rules from what she has acquired and applies them to new sentences and additional vocabulary. After spoken language acquisition, the child begins to associate words with printed symbols, enabling reading and writing.

The memory children use to acquire vocabulary is powerful. In their first ten years children learn to recognize and understand an average of 2,000 words a year (over five each day).[9] What makes this feat of memorization possible is context. Children learn words by relating sounds to their meaning. As noted reading theorist Frank Smith writes, "Only nonsense is difficult to memorize" (Smith, 50).

Notice what is absent from this process: Parents do not teach their children to read and say the alphabet in order to speak. (Imagine a mother exhorting her child: "This is a 'b.' Say 'buh'!" OR "Say 'c' with a soft sound. Now with a 'k' sound!")

Surely it would be ridiculous to expect a toddler to learn how to read and write before he learns how to speak! Yet this is exactly how most music method books teach. Students learn to read notation before they can "speak" music by creating simple melodies, and they learn the musical alphabet (i.e., individual notes and scales) before they learn musical words and sentences (i.e., melodies and phrases). This approach effectively teaches students to read music before they understand what they are reading.

Emphasizing musical "words" rather than letters (individual notes) has advantages from a reading point of view, too, for there is a limit to how much the brain can absorb at one time. In written language the limit is four or five random characters per second, which hardly seems sufficient for reading until one realizes we rarely read random individual letters (Smith, 19). Rather, we read words comprised of individual letters. And words are not usually grouped randomly, either. For example, in "Boys peanut crowded skim", each word is easy to read, but the entire phrase takes time to absorb because the words are unrelated. "Boys eat peanuts quickly" has the same number of words, but is easy to comprehend because it makes sense—there is a context for each word.

Music works the same way:

- Notes are grouped into words, i.e. rhythmic and melodic patterns.
- Words are grouped into sentences with grammatical structure and context: rhythm words are given meaning by pulse and meter; melodic words are given meaning through tonality and harmonic function.

Though this analogy may be apt, it is incomplete. Music teacher and author Eric Bluestine observes there is an extra step in learning music: "Children build a language vocabulary by associating words with things that they see, hear, touch, taste, and smell. On the other hand, children build a music vocabulary by hearing patterns, then singing or chanting them—and then naming them."[10] This extra step is one of the keys to the Kodály, Suzuki, and Gordon approaches to teaching music.

Though an exhaustive discussion is beyond the scope of this text, the sections below present an introduction to each of these three approaches. In later chapters we present a more in-depth discussion of how to use sound–to–symbol teaching in the music classroom.

An Introduction to Kodály

Zoltán Kodály's philosophy of music education grew out of a study of Hungarian folk music that he undertook in 1905, when he began collecting and analyzing samples of traditional music. Examples of these soon appeared in Kodály's own compositions—from the direct quotations in his folk song arrangements with piano and children's choral music, to the harmonic—language and style that infused his instrumental music.

This authentic, high-quality folk music is central to Kodály's philosophy. After studying their linguistic forms he realized that the entire tradition of Hungarian peasant music was in danger of becoming forgotten amidst urbanization. He believed music education was a way to protect the long-term survival of the Hungarian musical tongue and provide a gateway into other music traditions. As noted Kodály educators Houlahan and Tacka write, "When children gain knowledge of different musical repertoires beginning with music of their own community and expanding to include music of other communities as well as art music they are in a position to become stewards of their cultural legacy."[11]

Kodály also believed folk music supports the physical, developmental, and psychological needs of children, and for over forty years he worked with other researchers and educators to develop a system for Hungary's teachers. Since then, teachers in many countries, including the United States, have adapted these ideas to fit their own culture.[12]

The classic principles that tie Kodály to the sound–to–symbol approach include the following:

- Experience comes before notation.
- Students should be grounded in the folk music of their culture.
- Melodic and rhythmic patterns are employed to teach the musical language that appears in folk music.
- Singing games and movement exercises aid musical development.

Other principles include:

- Use only the highest quality music.
- Music belongs to everyone, not just the elite.
- Musical experiences should begin in early childhood.
- Children should regularly listen to music and engage in activities that help them make connections between folk music and art music.
- A cappella singing is the foundation of any music learning, even instrumental.
- Literacy is the primary means for musical independence.
- Use of relative solfege syllables.
- Use of rhythm syllables. (Unlike the solfege syllables, the original Kodály rhythm syllables are not relative; instead, each syllable referred to a specific notational duration. For example, "tah" refers to a quarter note. Today, some Kodály teachers use syllables that adapt to the beat pulse, no matter how it is notated. Chapter 2 contains a more thorough discussion of these variations.)
- A child-centered learning sequence.[13]

An Introduction to Suzuki

Though he did not use the term "sound–to–symbol," Shin'ichi Suzuki nevertheless championed a system of music education that embodies many of its principles. After developing his philosophies in 1940's Japan and introducing them to the United States in the 1950s and 1960s, the Suzuki method became synonymous with private string music education. Yet it made few inroads into most American public school music classrooms.

Trained as a classical violinist, Suzuki believed music education should parallel language acquisition. Indeed, he called his method the "Mother Tongue Approach."[14] The impetus for his ideas were Chomsky-like observations: that young children learn to comprehend and speak complex languages without formal training. Suzuki observed that nobody corrects the grammar of a toddler's first sentences; nobody restricts what a toddler first utters to conform to a preset curriculum; nobody asks a toddler to practice speaking on his own; and nobody expects a toddler to write and read before he can talk. Instead, Suzuki believed parents should encourage their child's ability to speak, and do so without judging.

Suzuki believed the same lessons should apply to teaching music. Initially, he used his ideas only with violin, but they are transferable to every instrument. Called "Talent Education," the basic tenets of his philosophy include:

1. Begin music study early: Suzuki suggests children should begin playing violin at age three, but says they should start listening to recordings and other performers even earlier.
2. Listen regularly and often to the music that is being studied and will be studied. Suzuki firmly believed that listening is an essential part of acquiring language and music skill.
3. Take private lessons, and have parents directly involved with daily practicing—guiding, encouraging, and even playing. In the same way that students still use their first words even when practicing advanced ones, Suzuki also believed students should keep practicing their first pieces even when they have progressed to more difficult literature.
4. Everything the child plays should be memorized, and no notation should be introduced for up to three years. Again, Suzuki sets up an analogy to language acquisition: Children do not learn to read or write for many years after they have begun speaking and understanding. Everything a child says is memorized!
5. Learning notation is a process of association: A child should first see the written music after the piece has been memorized, and at that point will begin to associate the sound with its notation.[15]

Suzuki was a pioneer in recognizing and encouraging children's innate musical abilities. More recently, a growing body of research pioneered by Edwin Gordon in the 1980s expanded upon his ideas and linked "Talent Education" to contemporary educational psychology.

An Introduction to Music Learning Theory

Sound itself is not music. Sound becomes music through audiation, when as listening in language you translate sounds in your mind and give them meaning[16] (Gordon, *Buffalo Music Learning Theory*, ix).

If Suzuki is the philosopher of sound–to–symbol instruction, concerned as much with children's personal development as he is their musical development, and Kodály is the historically minded sociologist, dedicated to children's musical and psychological development through the preservation of their ancestor's musical traditions, then Edwin Gordon is the scientist. His approach is based on his own extensive research on how American children learn. In his seminal work, *Learning Sequences in Music*, Gordon outlines the stages through which children progress when they learn music. Like Suzuki, Gordon emphasizes that the ability to read is not the same as the ability to comprehend.[17]

Gordon proposes a musical counterpart to language comprehension: *audiation*. Audiation takes place when we assimilate and comprehend in our mind music that we have just heard or have heard performed in the past. We also audiate when we assimilate and comprehend in our mind's ear music that we may or may not have heard but are reading in notation or are composing or improvising.[18]

As the quote at the beginning of this section suggests, Gordon stresses the importance of audiation and comprehension over just reading (or "decoding"). His research, along with work by Richard Grunow and Christopher Azzara, has been influential in showing how the traditional approach to teaching does not reflect how children learn music. Gordon writes:

> We audiate music and we read and write notation. Unless we can audiate what we read and write in notation, we cannot give musical meaning to notation. We are "faking" as we are reading notation. If we cannot audiate, at best all we can do is try to decode notation. Reading notation should not be an act of decoding, it should be an act of audiation. For many young pianists who cannot audiate, for example, the piano keyboard represents nothing musical. The keys become another set of musically meaningless symbols which activate the decoding process. Without audiation, notation can reveal little. Notation is intended only to assist us in recalling in audiation what we have already perceived and audiated (Gordon, *Learning Sequences*, 59).

Here is a linguistic analogy: An English speaker can "read" Spanish by sounding out the words but will still have no idea what the words mean—i.e., he will not audiate their meaning. For Gordon, audiation is a fundamental skill students must have before learning "executive skills" (e.g., embouchure, fingerings, articulations) or theoretical concepts (e.g., reading printed note names and rhythmic patterns) (Gordon, *Buffalo*, 7).

Gordon describes two types of learning: *discrimination* and *inference*. Discrimination learning is the ability to "discriminate among pitches and durations" (Gordon, *Buffalo*, ix)—not simply individual notes, but tonal (melodic) and rhythmic (durational) patterns. In discrimination learning students are aware they are being taught but do not fully understand what they are learning. Imitation is a crucial component. Inference learning usually begins later, when students essentially teach themselves. They use their vocabulary from discrimination learning to understand—or infer—the meaning of unfamiliar tonal and rhythmic patterns (Gordon, *Buffalo*, ix).

Echoing Suzuki's method, but breaking the process down into more detail, Gordon proposes five stages of learning.

Aural/Oral—Students learn to recognize a pattern by hearing it (aural) and performing it (oral). Teacher presents (sing and play) patterns to students, who repeat those patterns (sing and play).

Verbal Association—Students connect the sound patterns they learned in the aural/oral stage with syllables, essentially naming the patterns to give them external meaning. Teacher presents the same patterns as before, but now with syllables. Students repeat the patterns with the syllables.

Partial Synthesis—Students connect sounds with their syntax and meaning and begin to hear individual patterns as part of meaningful series. At this stage the goal is not for students to recognize the individual patterns themselves, but rather to recognize the tonality and meter of patterns when they are grouped together. By doing so, students begin to demonstrate they understand the musical meaning of these patterns in tonal and rhythmic contexts.

Symbolic Association—Students associate sounds and syllables with visual symbols (i.e., notation). Teacher presents the previous patterns and syllables along with the corresponding notation. Students do not read, but rather learn to associate a symbol with what they are already performing.

Composite Synthesis—Students audiate tonality and meter at the same time they read or write series of tonal and rhythmic patterns. Teacher presents the notation of familiar patterns, with and without syllables. Students read and perform these patterns without the syllables (sing, then play).
(Adapted from Gordon, *Learning Sequences in Music* (2007), 90).

Sequence is crucial in Music Learning Theory. For example, if a student has not mastered aural/oral for a specific pattern or concept, he should not progress to verbal association. However, students can be at different stages for different patterns. They might be symbolically associating some patterns while first learning a new batch in the aural/oral stage.

To some, Music Learning Theory seems inflexible in its strict sequencing. In practice it is easily combined with other philosophies and adapted for classroom teaching.

A Contemporary Approach to Kodály

Recently, Micheál Houlahan and Philip Tacka re-examined Kodály's traditional teaching in the context of educational psychology and learning models. They took contemporary research questions (i.e., What teaching sequence best reflects the way people naturally learn music?) and combined it with the well-developed curriculum of traditional Kodály. Their model includes three phases: cognitive, associative, and assimilative.

Cognitive Phase

This is based on research and Gestalt principles that show students initially perceive music in patterns rather than individual notes. The cognitive phase involves teaching songs that contain essential melodic and rhythmic patterns. These patterns are later "extracted" and used as the basis for singing other songs and learning more complex patterns (Houlahan and Tacka, 146). Repetition, performance without notation, and movement activities strengthen musical memory and prepare for literacy. Houlahan and Tacka also suggest some of the following kinesthetic activities (Houlahan and Tacka, 147):

1. Conduct while singing.
2. Clap or pat the extracted pattern while performing it.
3. Perform a song while pointing to an image of the rhythm.
4. Clap the rhythm while singing in the "inner ear."
5. Perform a song while pointing to an image of its melodic contour.
6. Use hand motions to show the direction of a melodic line.

The next step is to use questions to develop students' aural awareness about the songs and patterns they learn (Houlahan and Tacka, 148):

1. On which beats does the target rhythm appear?
2. How many articulations appear on beat 3?
3. Where is the highest part of the phrase?
4. On which beats does the target melody occur?

Next, a visual element is introduced, though not through traditional notation. Students write personal representations of the sounds they hear and perform. This allows teachers to gage the class' understanding of the material and gives students time to make connections between what they hear and what it looks like (Houlahan and Tacka, 149). For example:

1. Write the rhythm using rhythm syllables.
2. Write a visual representation using horizontal lines, vertical lines, and shapes; encourage students to develop a personal system that accounts for pulse, duration, and the number of sounds per beat (e.g., eighth notes = 2, sixteenth notes = 4).
3. Write the solfege symbols for a melodic pattern.
4. Write a visual graph of the duration and contour of each note in a melody (Houlahan and Tacka, 150).

For beginners, these activities precede regular notation. Students are taught patterns using rhythmic and solfege syllables, and eventually they recognize the patterns in familiar songs without the syllables. The three-pronged approach recognizes there are different types of learners in the classroom: kinesthetic, aural, visual, and mixed (Houlahan and Tacka, 150).

Associative Phase

In this phase the teacher guides students to associate the pattern with its rhythm or solfege syllables, and then with its regular notation.

Assimilative Phase

This final phase is separated into three stages:

1. Students aurally and visually recognize the new pattern in familiar and new contexts.
2. Students practice the new pattern with old ones.
3. The instructor assesses understanding of the new pattern (Houlahan and Tacka, 152).

In many ways Gordon's Music Learning Theory and Houlahan/Tacka/Kodály are kindred spirits, as they share a Pestalozzian sound–to–symbol heritage. There are notable differences, however. For example, Gordon and Kodály use rhythm syllables that reflect conflicting philosophies about the structure of rhythm (to be discussed in Chapter 2).

Music Learning Theory and Kodály also emphasize different melodic patterns (though both use examples that are easy to sing and have no semitones). Music Learning Theory's patterns revolve around primary harmonies. Gordon bases this on research that suggests children learn pitches in relation to tonality and syntax. As noted educator Eric Bluestine puts it, students audiate syntax rather than phonology (Bluestine, 35).

The Kodály system is less concerned with tonality and harmony. Instead, it employs pentatonic patterns of the kind found in folk music, the idea being that these patterns are easy to sing and are the building blocks of children's music from around the globe. Kodály would teach do-mi-sol-la-sol, while Music Learning Theory would avoid the mixture of mi, sol, and la (at least initially) because it implies both tonic and subdominant harmony. Kodály himself writes:

> Nowadays it is no longer necessary to explain why it is better to start teaching music through the pentatonic tunes: First, it is easier to sing in tune without having to use semitones, second, the musical thinking and the ability to sound the notes can develop better using tunes which employ leaps rather than stepwise tunes based on the diatonic scale often used by the teacher.[19]

For Kodály, pentatony is an important introduction to world literature: It is the key to many world musics, from ancient Gregorian chant to Chinese folk music to Debussy.[20]

Kodály and Gordon also have different perspectives about when to first introduce notation. Kodály introduces it systematically as students learn patterns and develop their ears, in the firm belief that reading and writing music are absolutely central to music literacy. Music Learning Theory, on the other hand, holds that notation should initially be used in the same way we use written language with children who cannot read. Just as a child might follow along with the pictures and text of a bedtime story, a student might watch sheet music while they echo the teacher's singing.

Eclecticism and Hybridization

All three philosophies emphasize singing before playing, a structured learning sequence, the use of pitch and rhythm syllables as a precursor to notation, the introduction of notation after students are comfortable performing patterns and songs, and the development of the mind's ear (Gordon calls it "audiation"; Kodály calls it "inner hearing."). Kodály and Gordon also share a belief on the importance of learning to sing melodies, whether it be folk music (for Kodály) or well-known tunes (for Gordon). Indeed, in the big picture, Suzuki, Kodály, and Gordon agree more than they disagree. As John M. Feierabend, Professor of Music at the Hartt School of Music, writes, "Whether a teacher attempts a thorough integration or adapts only the learning sequence activity aspects of Music Learning Theory into a Kodály approach, the students will benefit" (Feierabend, 287). Moreover, though Music Learning Theory is often considered a rigid teaching method, in reality it is a tightly structured teaching theory. The method is a flexible reflection of that theory. Eric Bluestine observes, "Since there's no one right way to design a method based on Music Learning Theory, a music curriculum may take one of many possible forms. One can, for instance, write a music curriculum that combines Music Learning Theory with Orff and Kodály activities" (Bluestine, 260).

In *The Eclectic Curriculum in American Music Education*, Polly Carder writes that American music educators have long borrowed from diverse sources:

> From Lowell Mason's course of musical instruction based on theories of Pestalozzi (who in turn had been influenced by Rousseau), to the present complex music curriculums in schools and universities, Americans have seen fit to adopt or adapt and develop any useful educational concept . . . The basic ideas on which successful teaching methods are built seldom are entirely new, nor do good ideas, as a rule, come to only one person . . . The fact that an idea has recurred again and again in educational practice indicates that it is worthy of our consideration. New and different approaches to persistent problems may result from creative application of an old idea.[21]

Modeling and the Sound–to–Symbol Approach

Various studies show that teachers model about 10–25 percent of the time in rehearsals.[22] Perhaps this low percentage is because they do not feel comfortable demonstrating for their students, especially on secondary instruments, or perhaps it is because of modeling's negative association with rote teaching.

The flip side of this stereotype is modeling's positive association with the sound–to–symbol approach. Humans learn naturally by imitating, using implicit knowledge to shape their performance until it matches the original (Haston, 29). Though it is true that poor modeling inhibits creativity and musical growth, as we will see in later chapters, modeling is a powerful tool to teach melodic and rhythmic patterns.

Modeling can also help teach expression and style. The key is to make a distinction between spoon-feeding and conceptual demonstration. Musical spoon-feeding teaches "how the music goes"—i.e., the teacher performs a passage during rehearsal so students can quickly copy it. This is an effective short-term solution, but it teaches little that can be transferred to other contexts, and a similar passage in another piece will likely stump them again.

In conceptual demonstration, the teacher models rhythm patterns, tonal patterns, articulations, styles, and dynamics that appear in the music being rehearsed, but does so without making reference to the specific measure and its notation. By teaching and reinforcing a concept away from a specific occurrence, students can better transfer their understanding of it to new scenarios. Students listen, and then immediately imitate (Haston, 27).

The process:

1. Teacher demonstrates a concept (e.g., crescendo on a long note).
2. Students imitate.
3. Teacher evaluates, offers minimal verbal feedback.
4. More demonstration and imitation.
5. Teacher explains the "theory" behind the concept (e.g., "use more air, but keep the embouchure set").
6. Teacher shows what a crescendo looks like in notation, followed by more demonstration and imitation.
7. Students look for similar examples in their music.

On Adopting Sound–to–Symbol in the Instrumental Class

Because sound–to–symbol is so different from traditional instrumental music education, it is bound to generate questions and skepticism from teachers, parents, students, and administrators.

Recognize that sound–to–symbol is in near complete contradiction to most music curriculums. Combine this with a resistance to the unfamiliar ("That's not how I learned to do it!"), a perceived pressure from parents and administrators to see students perform as soon as possible, and a lack of support at the middle school and high school level (who may view the beginning level as their feeder), and we may find it is very difficult to adopt a new paradigm.

To those weaned on traditional method books, strict sound–to–symbol instruction may seem confusing because there is no five-line staff in the initial stages of learning. Remember, the goal is to delay the introduction of notation so students can develop audiation skills and musical vocabularies.

In addition, some may argue that time spent on audiation, singing, and pattern acquisition could be better spent on embouchures and technique. Yet research shows that developing the musicianship skills associated with sound–to–symbol learning improves the mechanics of instrumental performance.

In her 1987 study, Patricia Ann Grutzmacher showed that:

> the use of harmonization and vocalization activities improved the melodic sight-reading skills of beginning band students significantly more than a traditional method in which notes are individually identified directly from notation and without harmonization and vocalization activities. [Emphasizing] a tonal conceptual approach in the instruction of beginning instrumental music students did not delay the development of technical skills as demonstrated by improved melodic sight-reading skills and by observations made by the researcher.[23]

Further, researchers generally agree that developing a sense of tonality contributes to the ability to read music (Grutzmacher, 171).

In response to the question, "How will Music Learning Theory help my students?" music educator Scott Shuler writes:

> A clarinetist who fails to notice that he is flatting "ti" in major tonality lacks the tonal skills necessary to hear his mistake; a trumpeter who transforms duple meter patterns into triplets lacks a clear sense of duple meter; a saxophonist who cannot sight-read a technically simple melody lacks the ability to generalize from tonal and rhythm patterns he has already learned to the new patterns encountered in the melody. Those problems are therefore appropriately classified as tonal, rhythm, and notational generalization problems, respectively. If Music Learning Theory is truly the process through which persons most efficiently learn tonal, rhythm, and notational skills, then it follows that the application of Music Learning Theory to instruction will enable the conductor to solve those problems most rapidly.[24]

Becoming a better singer may not be the most direct path to becoming a trombonist, but it may be the most effective. The key with all of these strategies is to regularly incorporate them into the curriculum. Audiating, singing, etc., should not be treated as "special" topics to be introduced once and then never addressed again.

Sound–to–symbol instruction gives students the ability to recognize and correct their own mistakes. Though this requires an upfront investment in time and energy, as audiation improves teachers will have less need to micromanage what students play. Director-centered learning thus becomes student-centered learning, as these examples show.

Director-centered—Teacher tells John he is sharp; John adjusts his tuning slide.
Student-centered—John audiates the sound of in tune playing and recognizes that he is out of tune. He adjusts his slide until he is in tune.

Director-centered—Teacher catches Jennifer playing a B♮ instead of a B♭ and asks her to correct the note.
Student-centered—Jennifer recognizes that the B♮ does not fit the tonality of E♭ Major, notices her error and plays the correct note.

Still, it may be difficult to combat the assumption that it is impossible to play music without reading it first from the printed page. A compelling counter-argument is to explain the analogy between music and spoken language and observe that we would not expect students to read aloud from a book before they could speak on their own. Some parents and administrators mistakenly assume that without printed music there can be no concerts during the first semester. Assure them that concertizing is still part of the curriculum. Help them understand that sound–to–symbol instruction gives students the same fundamental skills that allow jazz musicians to play an entire concert without looking at music.

As with the introduction of any new idea or methodology, accept the reality that some folks will object no matter how persuasively we argue, but that eventually the "revolutionary" methodology will become the "traditional" one.

An instant break away from the traditional approach is thus not recommended, especially if we are not the only teacher in the district. If the beginning instrumental program uses sound–to–symbol but the high school program does not, students may seem unprepared for high school, when in reality they are simply prepared for a different set of expectations. To be successful, change requires the cooperation of music administrators and teachers at all levels. Further, it should be phased-in over several years so teachers, students, and parents can acclimate to new teaching approaches and expectations.

An increasingly extensive body of methods and materials is available to support a sound–to–symbol teaching approach:

• For a Kodály-based approach to high school theory classes: Houlahan and Tacka, *From Sound to Symbol: Fundamentals of Music*.

- For Music Learning Theory-based general music recorder instruction: Grunow, Gordon and Azzara. *Jump Right In: The Instrumental Series—For Recorder*. Chicago: GIA Publications, Inc., 1999.

- For Music Learning Theory-based wind, percussion, and string instruction: Grunow, Gordon and Azzara. *Jump Right In: The Instrumental Series—For Winds and Percussion*. Chicago: GIA Publications, Inc., 2001. Froseth, James and Molly Weaver. *Do It!* Chicago: GIA Publications, 1997. Grunow, Gordon, Azzara, and Martin. *Jump Right In: The Instrumental Series—For Strings*. Chicago: GIA Publications, Inc., 2002.

It is also possible to incorporate sound–to–symbol techniques within a traditional approach. Though the overall sequence is important, the realities of teaching allow flexibility. As Bluestine writes: "In theory, learning should proceed sequentially; but real life doesn't work that way. There is, after all, a difference between Music Learning Theory and music learning reality" (Bluestine, 57).

In other words, Music Learning Theory presents a sequential theory but does not define an absolute method. The overall tenets of sound–to–symbol can thus be integrated into nearly any method book, including *Standards of Excellence* (Kjos), *Essential Elements* (Hal Leonard), and similar books. Richard Grunow, Professor of Music at the Eastman School of Music and co-author of the *Jump Right In* series, offers the following suggestions:

Suggestions for Applying Principles from *Jump Right In: The Instrumental Series to Instrumental Music Instruction*, by Richard F. Grunow, Michael E. Martin, and Christopher D. Azzara (reprinted with permission)

Musicianship Skills for Teachers:

1. Sing and perform on your instrument by ear 30–40 melodies and bass lines for tunes commonly associated with beginning instrumental music instruction. Sing and play the tunes at musical tempos, with characteristic rhythms, and with connected and separated styles of articulation.
2. Develop skills with a system of tonal syllables and rhythm syllables based on function, as opposed to note names or note values.
3. Develop functional skills on a harmonic instrument (e.g., piano, guitar, and/or autoharp) to perform accompaniments and to establish tonality, meter, and style for the students.
4. Improvise to the melodies you have learned by singing and performing them on your instrument.

When Teaching Students:

5. Teach students to sing and perform on instruments many melodies and bass lines by ear.
6. Sing and play for students, not with students. Observe the students when they sing and play their instruments.
7. Sing tonal syllables and chant rhythm syllables; do not speak tonal syllables or rhythm syllables.
8. Play recordings that demonstrate exemplary musicianship and characteristic tone quality.
9. Establish tonality and/or meter before singing or playing.

10. Remind students to audiate what they are going to perform before they sing or perform on their instrument.
11. Listen to each student sing and play something alone in each lesson.
12. Spend the first three to six months playing by ear, before introducing music notation.
13. Spend the beginning of every lesson or rehearsal playing by ear.
14. Present the first concert without notation.
15. Make comparisons by teaching songs in both duple meter and triple meter. Also learn songs with other measure signatures (e.g., $\frac{5}{8}$ and $\frac{7}{8}$).
16. Make comparisons by teaching songs in both major tonality and minor tonality. Also learn songs in other tonalities (e.g., Dorian and Mixolydian).
17. Teach students the proper names of tonalities (e.g., major/minor), meters (e.g. duple/triple), and functions (e.g. tonic/dominant/macrobeats/microbeats), and how to recognize them by ear.

Students Should:

18. Sing first and then perform on their instruments.
19. Move their bodies in a variety of ways to the music they are learning.
20. Audiate the harmonic context of the music (e.g., resting tone, bass line, and harmonic functions).
21. Audiate the rhythmic structure of the music (e.g., macrobeats/large beats and microbeats/small beats).
22. Take the preparatory breath in the tempo of the music before performing.
23. Develop a vocabulary of tonal and rhythm patterns that they can recognize by ear, perform, read, and write.
24. Demonstrate proper posture, hand position, embouchure, and instrument position.
25. Sing while placing fingers for the correct pitches on the instrument.
26. Develop musical independence right from the start. It is each student's responsibility to play in tune and stay in tempo.
27. As much as possible, avoid placing tapes or dots on the fingerboards of string instruments. They may assist hand position; they do not assist audiation.
28. Play the same song in many keys; play the same song in many tonalities (major, minor, Dorian, Mixolydian, etc.).
29. Play the same song in many meters (duple, triple, $\frac{5}{8}$, $\frac{7}{8}$, etc.).
30. Improvise.

It is in the spirit of this pedagogical flexibility that we offer an approach for teaching rhythm, melody, tonality, and harmony in subsequent chapters—ideas that do not adhere strictly to a single viewpoint but rather are hybrids of other well-documented methods.

Activities/Assignments for Further Exploration

1. How do you view the relationship between music and language? Do some of the connections seem stronger than others?
2. If music can be taught in ways that are similar to a language, do you think there are other disciplines that could benefit from a similar approach?
3. The poet Longfellow famously said, "Music is the universal language of mankind." Do you agree? If so, how can we account for the cross-cultural difference in musical styles?
4. Kodály insisted on the use of folk music as a way to learn one's own musical culture. What are examples of folk music from our country? Is this repertoire familiar to children? Do you think it matters?
5. Suzuki believed that students should always revisit and practice materials from the early levels. Why do you think this is so?
6. Suzuki emphasized the importance of parent involvement in practicing. In what ways can this be achieved in public school instrumental settings?
7. According to Gordon, what stage(s) of learning would the following activities fall under?

   Learning a rhythm for the first time
   Reading a piece of music for the first time
   Improvising
   Writing in the counts to a rhythm
   Figuring out a melody successfully "by ear"

8. What are the potential advantages of "hybridizing" different learning approaches? Potential disadvantages?

Further Reading

Gordon, Edwin. *Buffalo Music Learning Theory: Resolutions and Beyond*. Chicago: GIA, 2006.

Gordon, Edwin. *Learning Sequences in Music: A Contemporary Music Learning Theory*. Chicago: GIA Publications, 2007.

Houlahan, Mícheál, and Philip Tacka. *Kodály Today: A Cognitive Approach to Elementary Music Education*. Oxford: Oxford University Press, 2008.

Kendall, John D. *The Suzuki Violin Method in American Music Education: What the American Music Educator Should Know about Shinichi Suzuki*. Washington, DC: MENC, 1973.

Kodály, Zoltán, and Ferenc Bónis. *The Selected Writings of Zoltán Kodály*. New York: Boosey & Hawkes, 1974.

Patel, Aniruddh D. *Music, Language, and the Brain*. New York; Oxford: Oxford University Press, 2008.

Suzuki, Shinichi. *Nurtured by Love: The Classical Approach to Talent Education*. Secacus, NJ: Suzuki Method International, 1983.

Suzuki, Shinichi, Elizabeth Mills, and Therese Cecile Murphy. *The Suzuki Concept: An Introduction to a Successful Method for Early Music Education*. Berkeley, CA: Diablo Press, 1973.

Walters, Darrel L., and Cynthia Crump Taggart, eds. *Readings in Music Learning Theory*. Chicago, Il: GIA Publications, 1989.

Chapter 2

Teaching Rhythm and Rhythm Reading

Audiation, Pulse, Pattern, and Meter

To Guide Your Reading

What is the connection between movement and rhythm?

How can we use movement to help our students internalize, feel, and understand rhythm better?

What is the difference between viewing rhythms as patterns ("words") rather than individual notes ("letters")?

How can the theories of sound–to–symbol be applied to teaching rhythm?

How can flashcards be used to teach students rhythmic patterns (i.e., rhythm words)?

What is the role of learning the theory behind rhythmic notation?

What are the common problems students have regarding rhythmic notation and time signatures?

With what techniques can we strengthen one's internal sense of subdivision?

What role do patterns have in developing reading abilities?

How do rhythm syllables help students learn rhythm?

What are the characteristics of an effective rhythm syllable system?

> Education does not consist in creating faculties which the pupil does not possess, but rather in enabling him to obtain the utmost possible benefit from those he does possess.[1]
>
> Muscles were made for movement, and rhythm is movement. It is impossible to conceive a rhythm without thinking of a body in motion.[2]
>
> Émile Jaques-Dalcroze

Having good rhythm is crucial for all musicians. Indeed, professional orchestral players often report that it is the primary characteristic they look for during auditions. Without it, it is impossible to function effectively.

Teaching rhythm to beginning instrumentalists is challenging, because to do it properly one must teach more than just the theory behind the notation. Understanding the proportional relationships between rhythmic values does little on its own to promote audiation and accurate performance of those rhythms. If the processes of calculating and notating rhythmic values are to have musical meaning for students, we must first connect them kinesthetically to meter and rhythmic patterns, and only then develop their ability to audiate and read. The sound–to–symbol process is a powerful ally in this since it stresses the importance of experiencing before doing; of "speaking" a language before learning to read it. Many of the techniques and strategies in this chapter are particularly suited for beginning band and orchestra students, but they are equally effective with more advanced players.

Some of these strategies may be viewed as mere rote teaching, often derided for stunting learning by the way it removes the burden of students figuring something out for themselves. But as with language, students must learn rhythm by the way it feels and sounds, not by the way it looks. The role of notation then becomes clear: It is a symbolic representation and organization of what one already experiences.

Rhythm and Movement

Physical movement as a means to internalize rhythm was passionately advocated by Émile Jaques-Dalcroze (1865–1950). While teaching at the conservatory in Geneva, Switzerland, Dalcroze developed his theory of "eurythmics." Underlying eurythmics is the principle that all music-making comprises three types of activities:

1. those that utilize the body/muscular system to perceive rhythm
2. those that utilize the ear to perceive sound
3. those that utilize the voice to reproduce what we perceive

Dalcroze believed that mature music making involves all three elements, but that early on each has to be developed separately.

> No schoolmaster would set a child to draw something with which he was not familiar, and before he knew how to handle a pencil. Nor would he begin to teach him geography before, having learnt to walk and gesticulate, he had acquired an elementary sense of space; nor direct him to draw a map until he could not only handle a pencil and trace lines, but had also acquired both a sense of space and an idea of the lie of the country. No one can exercise several faculties at the same time before he has acquired, however crudely, at least one faculty. (Dalcroze, 80)

Dalcroze insisted that instrumental study should not precede rhythmic study and ear training.[3] He believed the first faculty that develops is the muscular system's perception of rhythm; that the body is naturally rhythmic—from the beating of the heart, to the pace of the breath, to the meter of walking, to the conscious motion of limbs and fingers. But he found that "heredity, environment, and maladjustment had buried or restrained" these instinctive forms of rhythm.[4]

Eurhythmics emphasizes a fundamental connection between rhythmic motion and physical motion. "Rhythm is movement," Dalcroze wrote (Dalcroze, 83), and the physical experience of that motion is a prerequisite for musical consciousness. Jo Pennington explains it this way: Instead of saying, "I know," students must first say "I have experienced" (Pennington, 7).

Neuroscience and Rhythm

Science backs up Dalcroze's connection between rhythm and movement. Research has shown that the part of the brain that guides movement is the same part that regulates timing and tracks the beat[5]: the cerebellum.[6] The cerebellum is one of the oldest structures in the brain, and in fact it is often called the "reptilian brain." Neuroscientist Daniel J. Levitin points out that it also plays a role in reward, motivation, and emotion, and suggests there is a compelling evolutionary reason movement, rhythm, and emotion are neurally connected.

> Not all emotional activities lead to motor movements, but many of the important ones do, and running is prime among them. We can run faster and far more efficiently if we do so with a regular gait—we're less likely to stumble or lose our balance . . . And the idea that emotions might be bound up with cerebellar neurons makes sense too. The most crucial survival activities often involve running—away from a predator or toward escaping prey—and our ancestors needed to react quickly, instantly, without analyzing the situation . . . In short, those of our ancestors who were endowed with an emotional system that was directly connected to their motor system could react more quickly, and thus live to reproduce and pass on those genes to another generation (Levitin, 183).

> Interestingly, tonality and melody seem to be controlled by a different brain area—the cerebral cortex. One of the fascinating features about the brain is that the ear simultaneously sends neural information to both areas. Our perception of music—physically, emotionally, intellectually—is then created by how they process this information and bridge themselves together (Levitin, 263).

The concepts of rhythm and movement permeate music beyond the durational patterns we typically think of as rhythms: Harmonic rhythm, melodic flow, phrasing, rhythm created by text, duration/rhythmic nuances created by dynamics and articulations, even musical motion created by form and structure are all concepts for which students must say, "I have experienced!" (Landis and Carder, 13).

Eurhythmic exercises encourage students to move freely and individualistically in a way that evokes the sounds to which they listen. In traditional Dalcroze, the teacher improvises the music so as to encourage spontaneous movements. "The mastery of muscular energy being essential for the perfect realization of rhythm, the muscles should be subjected separately and simultaneously to dynamic exercises, involving gradations of force, successive transitions, and sudden contrasts—likewise contrasting simultaneous contrasts" (Dalcroze, 90).

Dalcroze developed his theories at a time when free-form interpretative dance was developing as a response to classical ballet. His ideas would influence a generation of world-class dancers, including Martha Graham. However, his goal was not to homogenize students' movements (Landis and Carder, 17–18). As Dalcroze himself writes:

> A striking phenomenon in lessons in eurhythmics is the extreme diversity of individual movements on the part of those who do the same exercises together, to the same music. In other words, there are great differences of interpretation of the same musical rhythms by different persons. This variety corresponds exactly to the personal characteristics of the various pupils . . .[7]

To those that argue traditional instrumental education offers the same value, Dalcroze counters:

> [I]t can be proved that a purely digital acquaintance with rhythmic values is inadequate. Movement is not simply a matter of time, but also of accent and direction . . . If you leave it entirely to the fingers to create motor images in the mind, these images will inevitably remain feeble and incomplete (Dalcroze, 109).

The entire body must become a musical instrument, moving through space in representation of pulse, direction, subdivision, and flow (Pennington, 8). Exploring the biological connection between rhythm, timing and movement is more than a "touchy feely" teaching technique. It has significant implications for the way we teach rhythm and notation. Method books usually teach rhythmic notation from the start, treating it as a mathematical process. But if we consider the connections between movement and rhythm, experience and knowing, and language and music, it becomes clear that this approach is counterproductive.

Most students engage in at least a minimal amount of movement: foot tapping. On its benefits, Daniel L. Kohut, the author and respected music educator, writes:

> The wind player, of course, cannot count aloud while playing. If he does not tap his foot, his only recourse is to count to himself. With beginners this usually results in their not counting at all. The teacher needs tangible proof that the student feels the beat. Foot tapping provides this evidence . . . The teacher can read the results of the foot; he cannot read the student's mind.[8]

Foot tapping also provides students a way to keep track of upbeats and downbeats. Pedagogical usefulness aside, however, foot tapping supplements but does not replace other movement exercises. Tense or fatigued foot muscles often create an unsteady pulse, and since the foot only moves up and down there is no expression of meter. Further, recent research suggests that movements larger than just the foot are needed for the body to develop a connection with rhythm. Indeed, observe the foot tapping of young musicians: notice that their movement does not synchronize with the pulse. Now watch the feet of professional musicians: They rarely move at all because their sense of internal rhythm is so well-developed.

Even so, as long as it (or its less obtrusive cousin, toe-tapping within the shoe) is not the "sole" way we ask students to move, it may help them externalize and strengthen their internal pulse. At the very least, tapping shows the teacher that the student is focusing on the issue.

But to truly internalize a sense of rhythm students must fully experience the analogy between musical time and physical space. Physically moving to rhythm allows students to feel a constant pulse (the "beat"), create context and connections among individual durations (rhythmic patterns, or words), and experience those patterns within a hierarchical framework of strong and weak beats (the meter) (Kohut, 2–3).

Using Movement in the Instrumental Music Classroom

A full-blown eurhythmics program is impractical for band and orchestra classes. First, Dalcroze suggested a eurhythmic education for students before they turn nine (Dalcroze, 109), which is before most students begin school-based instrumental instruction. Second, eurhythmics' full-body, dance-like movements are unwieldy for rehearsal spaces filled with chairs, stands, and instruments. However, in his description of Music Learning Theory, Gordon shows that meaningful movement is feasible if it involves upper body motions—head, shoulders, arms, wrist, and upper torso.[9] Instead of improvised music he suggests melodies that students already know, whether these be popular tunes, melodies from method books and concert literature, or tunes that we teach students in preparation for these exercises. He recommends against using text with the melodies, even if it is available, because it diverts focus away from feeling the rhythm. Instead, use a neutral syllable such as doo, mah, or lah (Gordon, 4).

Here are a few strategies to incorporate these techniques into the instrumental music curriculum:

1. Take baby steps when incorporating eurhythmics into the rehearsal—Try only a few minutes at a time, and no more than once per session.
2. Incorporate movement into the body of the rehearsal, not just for warmups—Whether fairly or not, students often treat warmup activities as chores divorced from real music.
3. Mix large and small group settings—Some students respond to the psychological security of moving in a large group; others prefer the relative privacy of a lesson or sectional, when they do not perceive that their peers are judging them.
4. Have a rehearsal (or part of one) without instruments, music stands, and chairs—This removes the distraction and bulkiness of equipment and frees space for uninhibited movement.

Conducting as a Movement Exercise

Rhythmic movement exercises are not the same as conducting. The goal is not to articulate every pulse in an organized manner, but instead to experience the continuous flow of musical time. Gordon writes:

> The model students observe does not include or even suggest "keeping time" by pausing between macrobeats or accenting macrobeats . . . Musical expression occurs between macrobeats, not on them . . . If anything, ballet motion is the rule, reference never being made to counting beats or musical time (Gordon, 9).

In spite of Gordon's warning, conducting can be used as a gateway exercise into expressive movement. Conducting can be framed as an athletic activity, and just as students enjoy moving in the context of baseball and basketball, conducting patterns are a non-threatening way of moving expressively under the guise of technique. Once the basic patterns are learned, encourage students to use them expressively, varying the size and intensity of the patterns depending on the dynamics and articulations of the rhythms being performed. Eventually we "bait and switch," and ask students to conduct without beating, much in the same way conducting students are often asked to do: Take the right hand away, and just conduct the phrase, not only the beats. Gradually we can progress to full body movement, almost as a sort of stationary upper body dance.

Beyond Exercises—Expressive Moving While Performing

Motion is an effective way to externalize internal expressiveness. In fact, it is difficult to *be* expressive without *moving* expressively. It is natural for a sports fan to throw his hands in the air while cheering a touchdown or for a debater to gesticulate with his hands when he makes an urgent point. We must draw similar expressiveness from musicians.

The lessons of Dalcroze and Gordon thus need not be confined to audiation and eurhythmics. Encourage students—even beginners—to move while they play, just as professional chamber players do: Use the upper body to show breath, phrasing, and releases; move through a phrase; punctuate articulations, etc. Essentially we want students to move as in eurhythmics, but to channel that movement into the upper body, since their hands and arms will be otherwise preoccupied with the instrument!

- Model for students ways to move expressively and retain good posture and technique while doing it.
- Show students any number of examples from pop culture. Music videos and live performances from today's pop musicians are filled with examples of musicians moving while they perform.

Choosing a System of Rhythm Syllables

As we have seen with Gordon's Music Learning Theory, one of the links between hearing a pattern and being able to read its notation is "verbal association," which provides an aural label for a sound. For example, we may choose to label the rhythmic pattern, "doo-doo-doooooooo" as "Ti Ti Ta" or "1 and 2". Whichever system of syllables we use, that label applies whenever that pattern appears. In a sense, it becomes that pattern's "name" and a way to apply structure to rhythmic sounds. As we will see later in this chapter, rhythm syllables are also used to decode unfamiliar rhythms that one does not already know.

There is no ideal system of rhythm syllables. Bruce Dalby outlines four attributes of appropriate systems, and we have added a fifth:[10]

1. It is based on how the rhythm sounds, not on how it is notated. Since enrhythmic figures sound identical to each other, they mean the same thing and should receive the same syllables (e.g., $\frac{4}{4}$, $\downarrow$ = 60 – $\downarrow\downarrow$ $\sqcap$ $\sqcap$ sounds identical to $\frac{6}{8}$, $\flat$ =60, $\sqcap$ $\sqcap$ $\sqcap$).
2. Each unique metrical subdivision receives a unique syllable. For example, the syllable for the second of three subdivisions should be different than the syllable for the second of two subdivisions. Triple subdivision means something different from duple subdivision, and the syllables should reinforce that.
3. Its syllables are easy to say, chant, or sing.
4. The system can express simple and complex rhythms.
5. The system is suitable for use at multiple levels of education.

Here are four of the most common systems in use today:

The Classic Kodály Syllables

The Classic Kodály syllables (Figure 2.1) are most appropriate for elementary school settings and do not display the level of sophistication required for complex rhythms. In this system, each syllable represents a specific note value rather than a relative relationship between notes and beats. For example, "ta" refers to a quarter note, regardless of whether or not the quarter note receives the beat. This is useful for developing reading and dictation skills but is less compatible with a contemporary "sound–to–symbol" approach.

FIGURE 2.1 The Classic Kodály Syllables (for sustained notes the vowel sound is elongated until the next consonance articulation)

ta   ta   ti ti ta   tri-o-la ta   ta-a ti   ti ka   ti ka tim ka   ti ka ti ta   ta-a   ta-a   ta-a-a-a

Takadimi

Proposed by Richard Hoffman, William Pelto, and John W. White, Takadimi syllables are beat-oriented rather than notation-oriented. No matter what note value is actually use in notation, "ta" always refers to the macrobeat and "di" always refers to a bisection of that macrobeat. Thus, $\frac{4}{4}$ ♩♩ ♫ ♫, with ♩ getting the pulse, $\frac{2}{2}$ ♩♩♩♩♩, with ♩ getting the pulse, and $\frac{6}{8}$ ♩♩ ♫♫ all receive the syllables *ta ta ta di ta di*. Why? Because they are enrhythmic with each other. (Enrythmic refers to rhythms that are notated differently but sound the same.[11]) The use of the same syllables reinforces the fact that they sound and feel alike even if the notation looks different. (See Figure 2.3.)

FIGURE 2.2 Takadimi

FIGURE 2.3 Takadimi—Enrhythmic One-Beat Patterns in Simple Meters (the note value that receives the pulse changes, but the rhythm syllables stay the same because the rhythmic relationships stay constant)

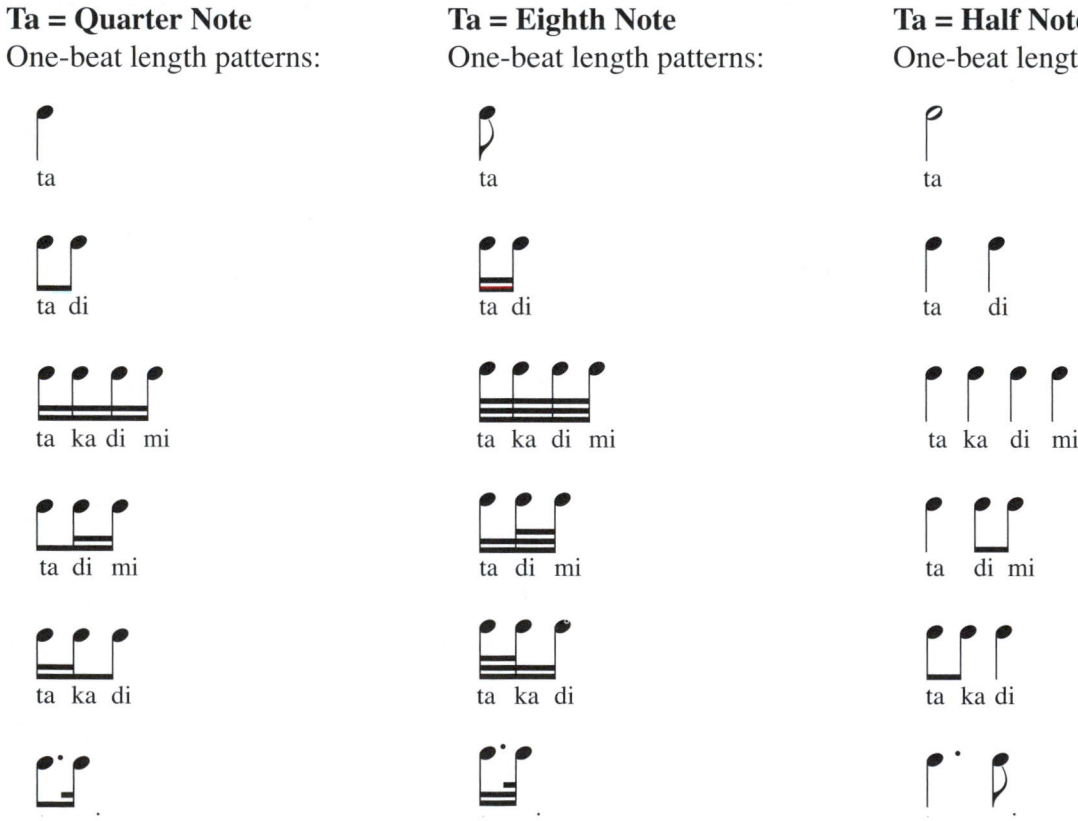

FIGURE 2.3 continued

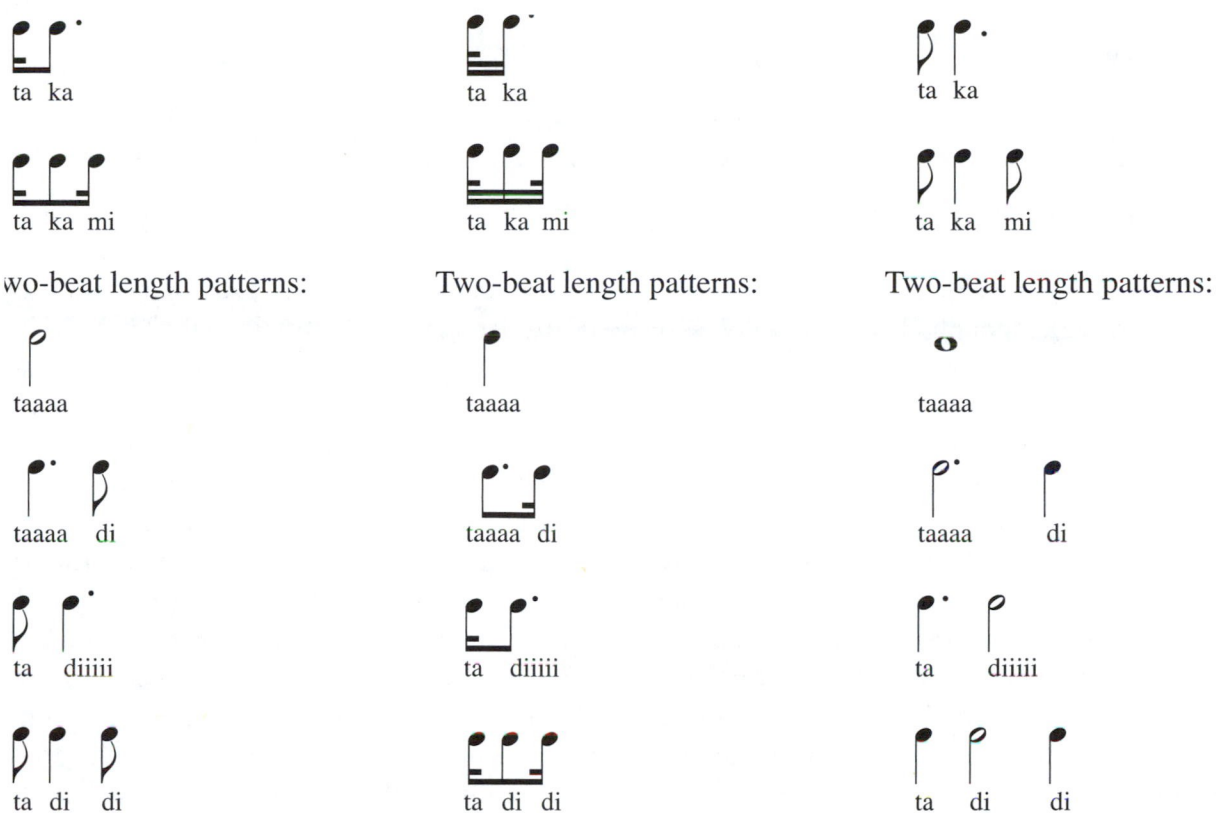

Both Kodály and Takadimi systems are relatively easy to say clearly and quickly.[12] They provide strong consonants for each articulation, mimicking the way wind players use their tongue when single and double tonguing, and are flexible enough to use with simple or complex rhythms. Takadimi differentiates simple and compound beat divisions with a unique syllable for each one, but provides a common syllable for subdivision points where the two systems align (i.e., the downbeat of simple and compound beat both sound "ta"; the midpoint of each beats sound "di.")[13] Also, the use of non-numeric sounds makes it appropriate for young students. However, for those that also want to allow beat counting, Don Ester, John Scheib, and Kimberly Inks suggest replacing "ta" with the proper number.[14] For example, see Figure 2.4.

FIGURE 2.4 Replacing "ta" with the Proper Number

Counting System

FIGURE 2.5 Counting System

Like the Takadimi system, the Counting System, sometimes referred to as the "Eastman Counting System," is beat flexible, though "1e+a" is usually associated with sixteenth notes. But it could just as easily be applied to straight eighth notes in a 2/2 measure (with 𝅗𝅥 receiving the pulse), or any number of enrhythmic variations. Counting syllables are easy to say quickly, and the numbers help students keep track of their place in the meter. The numbers also facilitate communication between conductor/player and the rest of the ensemble. However, the use of numbers makes it less appropriate for very young students and a sound–to–symbol approach in which meter has yet to be formally defined. Also, because there are few consonants with which to articulate, the subdivisions are often blurred together. Another major criticism of the Counting System is how it deals with triple subdivisions. Some advocate "1 e ah" for triplets, which we advise against because it obscures the distinction from "1 e + a" used for subdivisions of the microbeat. Compound duple meters such as 6/8 present further challenges. In 6/8 with the eighth note receiving the beat, "1 2 3 4 5 6" and "1 + 2 + 3 + 4 + 5 + 6 +" are viable. But 6/8 with ♩. receiving the pulse presents problems since "1 2 3 4 5 6" gives no sense of the duple nature of the meter, and there is no way to express the subdivision of the microbeat (e.g., sixteenth notes in 6/8). A common solution is to borrow the Kodály system's "tri-o-la." Other options are "tri-puh-let" and "1-trip-let," the latter of which retains the numbering of each beat.

Gordon Rhythm Syllables

The Gordon system predates Takadimi and shares several crucial characteristics with it. Enrhythmic figures receive the same syllable, no numbers are involved, and downbeats share a syllable ("du"), all of which contribute to its usefulness in a sound–to–symbol approach. But unlike Takadimi, all subdivisions in simple and compound receive different syllables—even the mid-point subdivision of simple and compound receive different sounds ("de" versus "ta"). This is partially a reflection of Gordon's overall philosophy of meter. In Gordon's view, though macrobeats can be divided into two or three (e.g., each ♩ in 4/4 or each ♩. in 6/8), macrobeats themselves can only be grouped as duples. For 2/4, 4/4, 6/8, etc., this is consistent with other systems. But in 3/4, for example, one measure equals one macrobeat; the quarter notes are microbeats of the dotted half-note macrobeat, and the true meter is a duple combination of two full measure macrobeats. In other words, Gordon maintains we may perform a 3/4 figure with quarter note as the pulse but that we actually feel that pulse as a division of a larger macrobeat. However, critics question Gordon's assertion that all meter is essentially duple. They observe that slow 3/4 music is difficult to feel in two and that many movement activities, especially dances, are organized in threes.

FIGURE 2.6 Counting System, Takadimi, and Gordon Rhythm Syllables Compared

The Takadimi System, the Counting System, and Gordon Rhythm Syllables are all viable systems. Some educators use more than one system in their teaching, often the "Counting System" and one other. This allows flexibility and variety but still equips students to use the "Counting System," which is the most commonly used one outside the classroom. Whichever is adopted, we recommend using the same system(s) at all levels of education, elementary through high school. This prevents the time-consuming inconvenience of practicing one system for several years and then re-learning another, somewhat akin to learning an entirely new set of note names. It may be possible to convert to a new one in the middle of one's studies, but it is not worth postponing other learning simply because the district could not agree on a standard.

Teaching Rhythm Words

The four-stage process presented on pages 29–32 is designed to teach a rhythmic vocabulary that helps prepare students for reading. We intend it primarily for beginning instrumentalists during the first years of instruction. However, the basic process can be used at any level, particularly the use of flashcards for rhythm reading.

Sound–to–symbol holds that students should learn music the way everybody learns language: by hearing it, experiencing it, imitating it, feeling it, and speaking it. This mimics the way a child learns to speak—with words and sentences rather than letters and rules—before reading.

Music students are often encouraged to analyze the counting theory behind each rhythm before performing it. It becomes a mathematical exercise—subdivide this, add this note value to that one, and presto, the rhythm is read. From a certain perspective this is a perfectly reasonable approach. Armed with these skills students can decode any rhythm they encounter. Though this method works it is not as effective as using a sound–to–symbol approach, and it does not reflect how literate musicians decode music. They do not use counting skills any more than they use phonics to break down every word heard or read in the newspaper. In both cases, musician and newspaper reader see individual notes and letters grouped together as words, just as they are heard and perceived without the notation. Rhythm "counting" comes into play only for unfamiliar or complex rhythms, similar to the way a newspaper reader sounds out or looks up the pronunciation for unfamiliar words.

For example, we hear or see "house" and instantly know how to say it and what it means. It would be ludicrous if every time we saw those letters we painstakingly sounded them out à la Sesame Street: H-O-U-S-E. If we hear "d-o-g" we instantly say, think, and picture a dog—no phonetic calculation needed.

Experienced musicians approach a rhythm word like ♩♪♪♩ in the same way: They see it and instantly know what it sounds like. Since it is a familiar rhythm word there is no need to think 1-EE-AND-A each time.

Since this is how musicians hear rhythm, it is also the most effective way to teach rhythm. In this method, instead of teaching what an eighth note sounds like (a rhythm "letter"), we teach what several notes sound like when combined into a pattern (a rhythm "word"). The goal is to make students familiar with as many rhythm words as possible and train them to instantly recognize these patterns in notation. Rhythm words are part of a musician's vocabulary. With an English vocabulary, as a student learns more words he can speak and read with greater sophistication. With a musical vocabulary, as a student learns more rhythm words he can play and read more complex music.

As suggested by sound–to–symbol philosophies, rhythm words should first be learned by ear, without any notation. Put simply, students must be able to perform and recognize rhythms before they see the notation. Otherwise our teaching is akin to showing how to spell "dog" at the same time we teach what a dog is! Obviously, by the time teachers introduce the word dog students already know what one is, and they can instantly recognize, comprehend and bring meaning to it well before they write it down. By the same token, the notation for each rhythm word should only be introduced when students have internalized it. By performing it, recognizing it, and naming it, they experience it with comprehension and immediate meaning.

For beginning students rhythm words can be as short as one beat, though we recommend adding a second beat so students can better feel the rhythm in the context of a pulse, much as how in geometry one point has no context until it can be related to a second point. If two points are required to create a geometric line, then two beats are required to create a musical one. The additional downbeat also helps one feel how the first beat ends. For more advanced students, the words can be as long as one measure.

Using Flashcards

 Oversized flashcards are an ideal way to present rhythm words to a large class. On the Companion Website which accompanies this book we have included Microsoft Word files with over 220 rhythms at various levels preformatted for 8.5 inch × 11 inch paper. After printing them out, hand-notate the rhythm on the back of the sheet in small print—large enough for you to see but small enough so students cannot read it from their seats. Try laminating the sheets to make them stiff and durable. Create additional patterns by using a black marker to write in ties.

The basic progression for teaching rhythm words with flashcards is as follows:

Stage 1: Learn what the word sounds like and be able to repeat it.
Stage 2: Attach an aural label (or name) for the word (e.g., rhythm syllables).

Stage 3: Learn to recognize a word by ear and then perform it with its appropriate label.
Stage 4: Associate visual notation with the aural word.

These four stages are suitable for individual and group practice of rhythm.

For any given rhythm word (or set of rhythm words), do not move to the next stage until students have mastered the last one. This may take days or weeks—be patient! As their vocabulary increases, students will be working with various sets of words in various stages.

To chant rhythms without syllables, use a consistent and easy to say syllable, such as "doo" or "da." When syllables are introduced in Stage 2, substitute your chosen system of rhythm syllables for the neutral syllable.

Stage 1: Learn What the Word Sounds Like and be able to Repeat It

1. Students externalize the pulse and meter (e.g., patting, tapping, or clapping.)
2. Teacher performs a rhythm word.
3. Students immediately echo the pattern, first by singing on a neutral syllable, then playing on their instrument using a repeated note.

Sample Script

Teacher says: "Today we're going to meet some new rhythm words. Let's first establish a meter. Now, please chant after me." (See Figures 2.7, 2.8, and 2.9.) *Note*: We suggest whispering the chant or pausing during the rests.

FIGURE 2.7

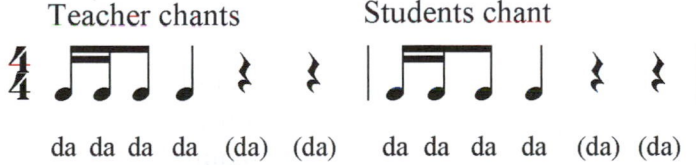

FIGURE 2.8

FIGURE 2.9

Stage 2: Attach an Aural Label (or Name) for the Word (e.g., Rhythm Syllables)

1. Students externalize the pulse.
2. Teacher performs the same words as Stage 1, but now uses the appropriate rhythm syllables.
3. Students immediately chant the pattern using the rhythm syllables.

Beyond giving the pattern a name, the association of syllables with the rhythm serves two other functions. First, it reflects the rhythm's structure, which aids in audiation and understanding. Second, it provides a memory anchor during reading and dictation exercises. ("Remember, John, that's a 'ta ka' on beat 2."; "Let's all chant the rhythm in m. 34 using syllables.")

Sample Script

Teacher says: "Let's do some rhythm words. First, let's establish a pulse and meter. Now, please chant after me." (See Figures 2.10, 2.11, and 2.12.)

FIGURE 2.10

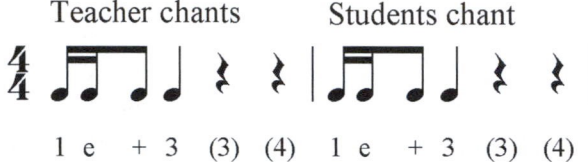

FIGURE 2.11

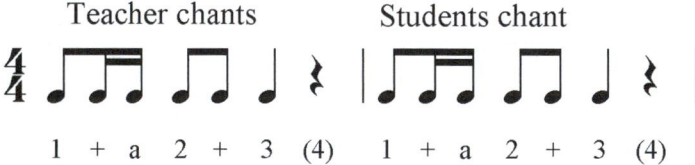

FIGURE 2.12

Stage 3: Learn to Recognize a Word by Ear and then Perform it with its Appropriate Label

1. Students externalize the pulse.
2. Teacher performs the words on a neutral syllable (i.e., no rhythm syllables).
3. Students immediately echo the pattern using the appropriate rhythm syllables.

Teacher says: "Let's do some rhythm words. First, let's tap a pulse. I'll chant a word, and you chant it back with rhythm syllables." (See Figures 2.13, 2.14, and 2.15.)

FIGURE 2.13

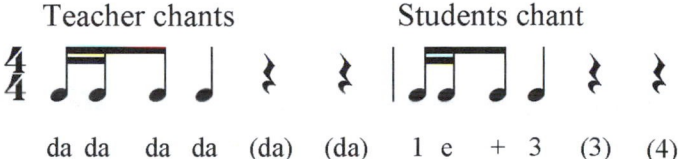

FIGURE 2.14

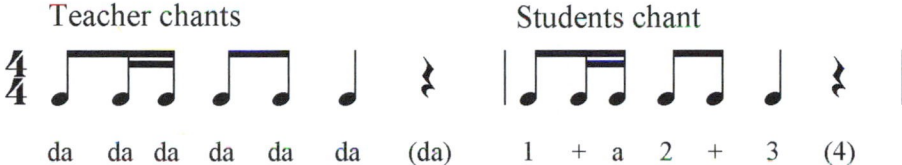

FIGURE 2.15

Stage 4: Associate Visual Notation with the Aural Word

This stage involves performing a rhythm word that has already been learned and associating the sound with its notation. This is the point that rhythm flashcards come into play.

1. Establish a pulse and meter.
2. Teacher performs a rhythm word in meter while pointing to a flashcard notation of that pattern.
3. Students echo the pattern back while looking at the flashcard.

Sample Script

Teacher says: "Let's do some rhythm words. First, let's tap a pulse. Now, please echo me." (See Figures 2.16, 2.17, and 2.18.)

FIGURE 2.16

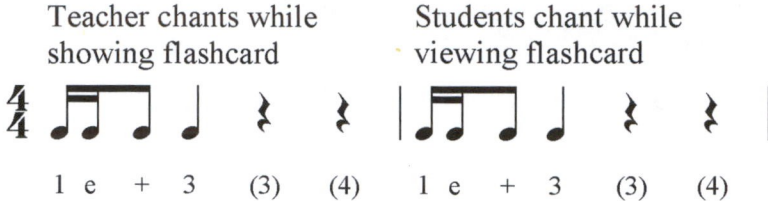

FIGURE 2.17

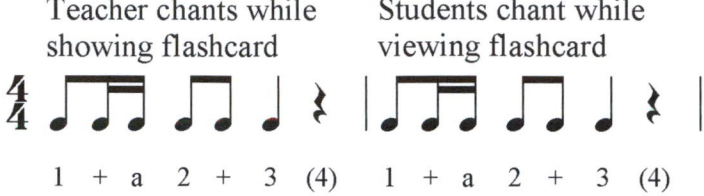

FIGURE 2.18

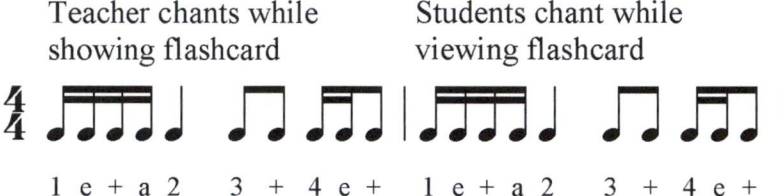

David Newell, author of *Teaching Rhythm*,[15] offers a variation of this process that is a combination of Stages 2, 3 and 4. (See Figure 2.19.)

FIGURE 2.19

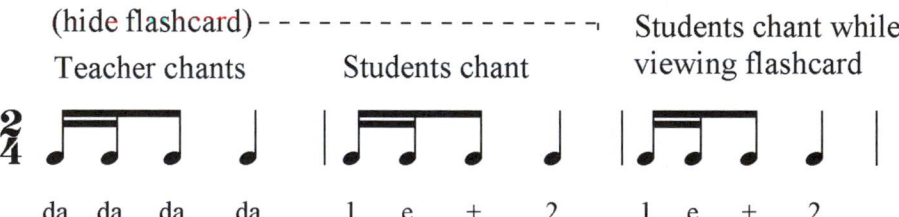

Always randomize the order the words are presented so students learn each word independently without trying to predict which comes next. However, feel free to repeat words if students have trouble, or "stack the deck," so the same difficult word appears more often. An effective way to do this is to present the difficult word in a sort of mini-rondo form (A = the difficult word): ABACADA, etc.

Introduce enrhythmic variations on a regular basis by changing the note value that receives the pulse; it doesn't always have to be the quarter note. For example, ♩ = pulse, ♪ ♫ sounds and feels identical to ♩ = pulse, ♩ ♩ ♩

Rhythm Words and Reading

Our discussion so far has focused on the relationship between the acquisition of language and the acquisition of a rhythmic vocabulary. But what about reading? Are there similarities between reading language and reading musical notation? Several studies showing a "positive correlation between language reading and music reading abilities" suggest a qualified "yes."[16] While these studies demonstrated that students who were proficient in music reading tended also to be proficient in language reading, others have noted that such a correlation does not guarantee a causal relationship. We cannot assume that skills in one discipline translate to another; perhaps proficient readers tend to be motivated in whatever they study.

Additional research has sought to identify a direct causal relationship. A 1972 study by Diana Nicholson looked at the effect music study has on language reading among slow reading learners. It set up an experimental group of 50 students who received special music instruction for a year and a control group of students who received no music instruction. At the end of the year the experimental group improved significantly in attention span and discrimination for paired groups of letters.[17] Other studies, including those by Hurwitz, Wolff, Bortnick, and Kokas (1975)[18] and Moritz (2007)[19], found that daily Kodály training improved reading skills in young children. But still other research, including a 2000 study by Butzlaff,[20] disputes these conclusions. And it is difficult to show that musical training is more effective than non-musical training in improving reading skills.

Beaming and Reading

The relationship between reading language and reading rhythms is reflected in the way letter groupings and beaming rules are both important for accurate reading. For example, sentence (a) below is difficult to read because the letters are improperly "beamed"—i.e., the spaces are in the wrong places. In sentence (b) the letters are grouped properly, making the words easier to identify.

(a)   Th eco wjum pedover thef ence.
(b)   The cow jumped over the fence.

Similarly, a rhythm (a) (see Figure 2.20) becomes much more difficult if the beaming obscures the pulse and rhythm words. Beam the notes properly to reflect the meter and the rhythm words become clear (b) (see Figure 2.21).

FIGURE 2.20 Rhythm (a)   **FIGURE 2.21** Rhythm (b)

In both cases, our ability to read is aided by our ability to see (or discriminate) groupings we find familiar and instantly know their meaning.

Beyond Stage 4—Using Flashcards to Improve Reading Skills

Once students are familiar with discrete, properly beamed rhythm words through Stage 4, we can use flashcards to practice recognizing and reading them. The basic process: Ask the group to perform each flashcard on the first beat of the meter. This allows time to read the next card, process its information, and perform it.

1. Establish a pulse and meter.
2. During the first measure of pulses, teacher shows the flashcard and clicks a pulse but does not chant the rhythm on the card.
3. Students sing/perform the rhythm back during the second measure.
4. Repeat!

FIGURE 2.22

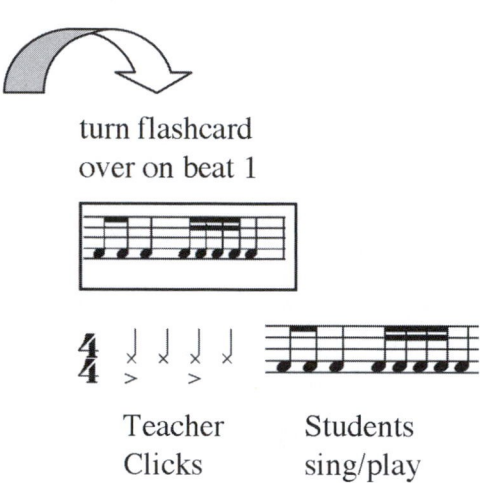

This process is viable at any age level, assuming the students have already learned the rhythm words being "flashed." A few wildcards mixed in are fine, but generally, if students do not know/understand the patterns, they are just guessing.

Sample Script

Teacher: "Let's practice reading some rhythms using flashcards. I'll show you the rhythm, and then you chant it back." (See Figure 2.22.)

Once students get the hang of this, we can decrease the time they have to process by either increasing the tempo, putting rhythms on multiple beats in a measure (e.g., 1 and 3 in $\frac{4}{4}$), choosing a meter with fewer beats (e.g., $\frac{2}{4}$ instead of $\frac{4}{4}$), or delaying the reveal of the flashcard. David Newell calls this "putting the flash into flashcards." (See also Figure 2.23.)

FIGURE 2.23

turn flashcard
over on beat 3

Teacher chants   Students sing/play

Sample Script

Teacher reveals card on beat 3. Students perform on beat 1. Reveal on beat 3. Students perform on beat 1.

Initially, the rhythm words used during flashcard reading should be the same ones taught in the aural/oral (sing and echo) and verbal association phases (sing and echo with syllables). After students master a variety of patterns they will be ready for inference learning, in which the flashcards may introduce unfamiliar rhythm words (based on the familiar ones).

Incorporating a Sound–to–Symbol Approach to Rhythms in Traditional Student Method Books

Keep in mind that traditional method books will likely not present their material using rhythm words, but instead use the mathematical "phonetic" counting method. Instead of asking students to "count out" each rhythm, encourage them to parse their part in terms of rhythm words. Admittedly, rhythm words do not always appear exactly as they do on the flashcards, and so we must point out words that have been modified with ties and rests (analogous to abbreviations and plurals) or combined (as in compound words). David Newell suggests a more proactive approach: Mark the teacher's edition with reminders to begin teaching rhythmic patterns before they are introduced with notation in the student's text. For example, if ♪♪♩ first appears on page 17, begin the four-stage process on page 14 or 15 so students are completely familiar with the sound and look of the rhythm before they encounter it in context (Newell, 54).

Learning Beyond the Beginning Stages—Constantly Building a Vocabulary

A common reason rhythm reading breaks down is due to a limited vocabulary of rhythm words. Imagine trying to read the *New York Times* if you knew only five words of English. It would be an impossibly tedious process of constantly stopping to look up unfamiliar words in the dictionary. Trying to read music with a vocabulary of five rhythmic patterns would be just as disheartening.

The advantage of a large vocabulary is two-fold. First, it decreases the chance of encountering an unfamiliar pattern. Second, it increases the chance of discovering an unfamiliar pattern's meaning. When we encounter a rhythm we have not seen before we subconsciously relate it to rhythms we already know.

Most rhythms, familiar or not, share a great deal in common. Say we have never seen the rhythm ♫ ♩ ♫. But we have seen ♫ ♫. And we have also seen ♩ ♫. It requires only a bit of insight to infer the meaning of the new rhythm from the two related ones. (In Gordon's system this is called *inference learning*. It describes our ability to infer the meaning of new patterns based on our familiarity with other ones.) From a linguistic perspective we do this constantly when we read. For example, the reader may never have seen the word "doorknob," but perhaps she has seen "door" and "knob" separately. Previous knowledge enables her to infer the meaning of the unfamiliar compound word.

Even though the four stages may seem pedantic for high school students, keep in mind that students at this level do not necessarily hear and perform musical patterns with an understanding of their rhythmic and tonal contexts, regardless of how the ensemble sounds in performance. Most teachers experience this regularly: A student will easily identify how many sixteenth notes and eighth notes are in a quarter note and still confuse the distinction while playing. Additional reminders have little effect, and teachers often resort to singing the rhythm to the student as a reminder. This usually works until the next time the student encounters that rhythm, and still, the fact he can calculate the relationship has little effect on his ability to play it. Even for students who read well, that ability is not, in and of itself, an indication of audiation and comprehension.

Whereas the four stages can comprise large segments of beginning instrumental lessons and rehearsals, in a high school setting it makes more sense to use them during warmup activities or as breaks during long rehearsals.[21] For example:

1. Review rhythm words students already know using the flashcard reading exercises discussed after Stage 4.
2. Introduce variations of familiar rhythm words into the flashcard mix.
3. Introduce new, more complex rhythm words (write your own if necessary) using Stages 1–4.
4. Consult the growing body of literature that applies sound–to–symbol teaching to a variety of contexts and learners:

> Houlahan, Micheál, and Philip Tacka. *From Sound to Symbol: Fundamentals of Music*. New York; Oxford: Oxford University Press, 2009.
>
> Krueger, Carol J. *Progressive Sight Singing*. New York: Oxford University Press, 2007.
>
> Runfola, Maria, and Cynthia Crump Taggart. *The Development and Practical Application of Music Learning Theory*. Chicago: GIA Publications, 2005.
>
> Walters, Darrel L., and Cynthia Crump Taggart. Readings in *Music Learning Theory*. Chicago, Il: G.I.A. Publications, 1989.

Teaching the Theory behind Rhythm Notation

Theoretical understanding of rhythm is inarguably important, but its primary role is not to facilitate reading. Instead, rhythm theory is important for analyzing rhythmic structure and decoding unfamiliar or complex patterns.

As sound–to–symbol philosophies suggest, the theory behind rhythm and its notation should be taught after students understand and can perform the rhythms they will learn about. Yet many method books teach rhythm theory from the start, using what we call "rhythm by division." This approach introduces the whole note and shows how to keep a steady pulse while sustaining a long tone. We usually see a variation on the "down–up" method of tracking pulses in which students sustain a long tone while internalizing the subdivision and tapping their foot. Smaller rhythmic values are subsequently introduced as subdivisions, and eventually students relate all note values to that whole note.

"Rhythm by division" does have several advantages. First, it integrates long tones into rhythm learning. Second, it teaches subdivision early in the process and prepares students to articulate smaller duration values, but not before they learn proper tonguing and bow-change technique. Third, it makes clear the symmetrical, mathematical relationship among durational values—e.g., ♫ = ♪; ♫ = ♩; ♩♩ = ♩; ♩♩ = o, etc. This relationship is efficiently portrayed as a rhythm "family tree," with the whole note as the father of increasingly smaller rhythmic children. (See Figure 2.24.)

FIGURE 2.24

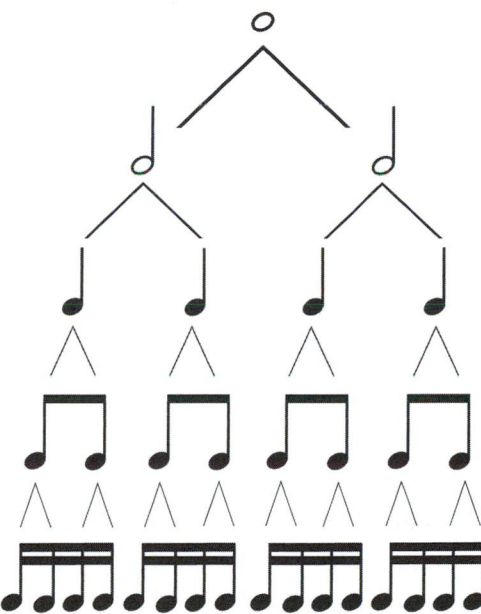

However, though most method books teach some variation of "rhythm by division" and the rhythm tree, it is important for students to realize that these are only notational relationships—i.e., according to this notational system, a whole note contains four quarter notes. But this reveals nothing about the pulse, beat, or count. And knowing what "gets the beat" is extremely important information in order for students to read and perform. Below we present two possibilities (Technique 1 and Technique 2) for teaching students the relationship between notation and pulse.

Technique 1: David Newell's Musical Algebra

In his excellent text, *Teaching Rhythm*, David Newell shows how to present rhythmic notation and time signatures as a problem of musical calculation (Newell, 91). Once students understand the formula they can write-in rhythm syllables to familiar and unfamiliar rhythms and use those as a tool for performing them.

Most students simply assume that a whole note always receives four beats, and a quarter note always receives one. These conclusions are reinforced by what the rhythm tree shows and the fact that most music students encounter works exactly that way. The most common variation from "whole note gets four beats" is *alla breve*, or cut time, in which the whole note receives two beats.

It is our responsibility to show students that in reality the whole note can receive any number of pulses/beats/counts. For argument's sake, let us say that the whole note gets 10 beats. Students who have learned that a whole note receives four will object that this is impossible. "Just look at the rhythm tree," they might say. "A whole note has four quarter notes, not 10. So it's impossible for a whole note to have 10 beats!" But the truth is that the rhythm tree only illustrates proportional durational relationships between note lengths (whole = 2 halves = 4 quarters = 8 eighths, etc.). It says nothing about the pulse itself, which is largely dependent on the tempo, style, and feel of the music. A whole note has two half notes in it regardless of whether the whole note receives one beat, four beats, ten beats, or 356 beats. So, if a whole note receives 10 beats there are still two half notes in it, each one receiving five beats—exactly one-half of the whole.

The proportional relationships of the rhythm tree hold true in all cases and resonate with what students learn in math class.

- ○ notes receive any number of counts.
- ♩ notes receives half the number of counts as ○ notes.
- ♩ notes receive one-quarter the number of counts as ○ notes.

For example:

	Example 1	Example 2
○ note =	8 counts	4 counts
♩ note =	4 counts	2 counts
♩ note =	2 counts	1 count
♪ note =	1 count	½ count
♬ note =	½ count	¼ count

Once students understand this concept, rhythmic calculations are easily practiced with worksheets, or in performance using the simple melodies found in beginning method books. For example, ask students to count and perform the following example three different ways:

(a) ○ = 4 counts

(b) ○ = 2 counts

(c) ○ = 8 counts

Understanding simple meter time signatures becomes a logical extension of this algebra. The top number describes the number of counts in a measure; the bottom number indicates the number of counts in a whole note (Newell, 107).

Examples:

$\frac{3}{4}$ = 3 counts in a measure, 4 counts in a whole note

$\frac{5}{4}$ = 5 counts in a measure, 4 counts in a whole note

Newell does not suggest using this approach for compound meter. He believes it is unmusical to teach $\frac{6}{8}$ "in six"—i.e. eighth note gets the pulse (Newell, 147). As noted earlier in this chapter, Newell's approach is rooted in sound–to–symbol, stressing the importance of internalizing rhythm before, or at least, *as* we teach the notation. Accordingly, he suggests teaching compound meters using rhythms students already know, such as those of common nursery rhymes. Indeed, any well-known poem or melody that easily flows in compound meter can be used. These rhythms are used as aural hooks before students see them in notation.

In compound meter the above system of musical algebra is modified (basically by adding a dot to each note value), but the important thing is for students to understand that with dotted notes, three notes "live" inside them. With non-dotted notes, two notes "live" inside them (Newell, 167). Once students recognize what a compound time signature looks like they can learn to group the note value indicated by the bottom number in groups of three (⁶⁄₈ = 2 groups of three; ⁹⁄₈ = 3 groups of three; ¹²⁄₈ = 4 groups of three, etc.).

Technique 2: Time Signatures as Musical Rulers

Another way to approach the problem is to focus on the time signature itself and show how the numbers themselves do not necessarily convey what note value gets the beat. For example, in ⁴⁄₄ time, the quarter note does not always get the beat, and in ⁶⁄₈ time the dotted quarter note does not always get the beat. True, they usually do, but by over-emphasizing this convention we put students at a disadvantage when they encounter scenarios. This is one reason why inexperienced musicians often struggle with simple compound meters (e.g., ⁶⁄₈), or when they are asked to count meters in a way that does not reflect the bottom number of time signature (e.g., counting ⁴⁄₄ in 8, or ⁶⁄₈ "in 6" or "in 2").

Gerald Eskelin summarizes it this way:

> American music students invariably begin their music reading lesson with meters in which the quarter note is the beat unit, and learn to perform a good deal of music in these meters. The problem is that many people discontinue their music studies believing that a quarter always gets one beat.[22]

The first way to avoid this quandary is to properly teach what a time signature means. Contrary to popular opinion, the top number of the time signature does not necessarily tell how many beats are in a measure, and the bottom number does not necessarily tell what kind of note value represents a beat. That approach typically works because the majority of music follows it. But we should not teach it as an absolute rule, lest we reinforce an incorrect assumption. We make ⁴⁄₄ counted "in 8" seem like a grotesque inconvenience rather than a completely reasonable possibility.

A time signature is a tool of measurement. Its two numbers simply indicate how long each measure is before the next bar line appears:

4—top number—Whatever the rhythmic value indicated by the bottom number, this number tells how many of that note value are contained within each measure.
4—bottom number—The rhythmic value used to measure the length of a bar.

Thus, ⁴⁄₄ indicates only that we measure bars in quarter notes and that each bar contains the equivalent of four of them. In and of itself it gives no information about what rhythmic value "gets the beat," only that the total rhythmic value of a bar is four quarter notes long. Even as we show students that, generally speaking, there are usually four beats in ⁴⁄₄, two beats in ⁶⁄₈, etc., we must also impress upon our students that any note value can become "the beat."

The best way for students to learn this is to experience it. Whenever possible, choose concert and lesson literature with a variety of meters in a wide variety of tempos. Particularly for ⁴⁄₄, ³⁄₄, ²⁄₄, and ⁶⁄₈ passages, vary the tempos and vary the durational value of the beat. If students routinely pulse to the eighth note, quarter note, and half note, they will no longer assume there are four beats in a ⁴⁄₄ measure.

Sample Script for Teaching Time Signatures as Rulers

(See Figure 2.25.)

1. Make an analogy between time signatures and rulers.

   "What do time signatures do? They measure exactly how long a bar is. They're just like rulers, but instead of measuring distance, they measure time."

   "Some rulers measure things in feet. For example, I can measure that these floor tiles are each 1 foot long. I can also measure that they are 12 inches long. What are some other units of measurement that rulers use?"

   Students: *Centimeters . . . Millimeters . . .*

2. Explain what the numbers in a time signature mean.

   "Good. Now, time signatures are similar to rulers in other ways, too. They can measure how long a bar is using different kinds of note values."

   (Teacher explains Figure 2.25.)

   "Instead of distance, we're measuring time. In this diagram we see how we can measure the length of the bar in quarter notes ($\frac{4}{4}$), eighth notes ($\frac{8}{8}$), or sixteenth notes ($\frac{16}{16}$)—though we can use any note value, and any of them can become the 'beat.'"

3. Check for understanding.

   "Let's try another example. If a measure is written in $\frac{6}{8}$, that means that each bar has a total of 6 eighth-notes in it. It's 6 eighth-notes long. You try now: If the time signature is $\frac{6}{4}$, what does that mean?"

   Student: *The measure is six quarter notes long.*

4. Show how pulse is independent of the time signature.

   "Good! The next step is to figure out what rhythmic value will get the pulse. This is the main beat we'll think in our head and tap with our foot. Unfortunately, the time signature doesn't tell us what gets the beat. We have to figure that out depending on how fast the music is, and what the style is. Let's try Line 2 with the quarter note getting the beat."

   Count off in quarter notes; group sings the example; group plays the example.

5. Vary the note value that receives the pulse, but use the same example.

   "Now let's try it with the eighth note getting the beat."

   Count off in eighth notes; group sings the example; group plays the example.

FIGURE 2.25

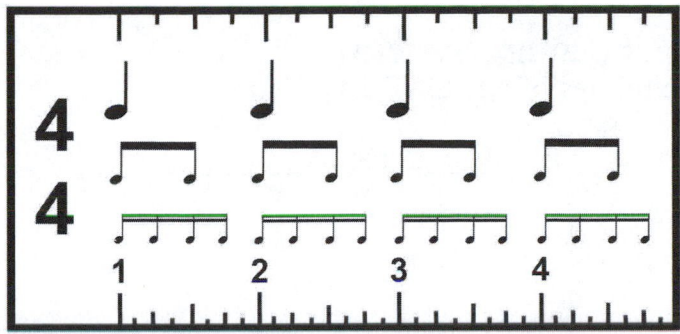

Teaching Students to Feel Internal Subdivision

To insure accuracy while playing rhythmic patterns, and also to aid students in understanding unfamiliar patterns, they need a strong sense of the pulse's internal subdivision. Having a strong sense of subdivision is like having an internal ruler on which to overlay and lock-in the rhythm (see Figure 2.25). Think of the benefits of an actual ruler: It is much easier to make precise measurements using millimeters rather than centimeters. Likewise, it is easier to play with rhythmic precision if we measure in sixteenth notes rather than quarter notes.

How many times have music teachers implored their students: "Make sure you're subdividing!"? One reason we do this is because, as Daniel Kohut previously observed, counting occurs in the mind's ear, hidden from our view. We can employ various strategies to develop these skills.

- Constant reminders and reinforcement, thus emphasizing its importance.
- Externalizing the subdivision (See "The Rehearsal Toolkit" on the Companion Website).
- The Longy Rhythm Sheet.

The Longy Rhythm Sheet (Figure 2.26) was developed by Renée Longy (1897–1979), distinguished ear-training teacher at the Juilliard School of Music. It is a deceptively simple sequence of numbers which can be used to improve rhythm skills. The sheet's columns are read top to bottom, with no pause or extra beat between lines. In other words, they are read exactly as one would read measures, except these "measures" are stacked vertically. Printed numbers should be spoken aloud, while the dots should be mouthed or spoken silently. Beats and subdivisions are tapped on the lap using one of two approaches, both of which are appropriate for lessons or ensembles (see Figure 2.27).

(In addition to Mme. Longy, who designed the original sheet, we are grateful to Professor Marianne Ploger, Senior Artist Teacher of Musicianship at the Blair School of Music, Vanderbilt University, for her mentorship in using this method.)

FIGURE 2.26 The Longy Rhythm Sheet

Rhythm Practice Chart (Longy System)
Based on the various division possibilities of any ONE BEAT unit

Two (2) equal parts

```
1  2
.  .
1  .
.  2
```

Three (3) equal parts

```
1  2  3
.  .  .
1  2  .
1  .  3
.  2  3
1  .  .
.  2  .
.  .  3
```

Four (4) equal parts

```
1  2  3  4
.  .  .  .
1  2  3  .
1  2  .  4
1  .  3  4
.  2  3  4
1  2  .  .
1  .  3  .
1  .  .  4
.  2  3  .
.  2  .  4
.  .  3  4
1  .  .  .
.  2  .  .
.  .  3  .
.  .  .  4
```

Five (5) equal parts

```
1  2  3  4  5
.  .  .  .  .
1  2  3  4  .
1  2  3  .  5
1  2  .  4  5
1  .  3  4  5
.  2  3  4  5
─────────────
1  2  3  .  .
1  2  .  4  5
1  .  3  4  .
.  2  3  4  .
1  2  .  .  5
1  .  3  .  5
.  2  3  .  5
1  .  .  4  5
.  2  .  4  5
.  .  3  4  5
─────────────
1  2  .  .  .
1  .  3  .  .
1  .  .  4  .
1  .  .  .  5
.  2  3  .  .
.  2  .  4  .
.  2  .  .  5
.  .  3  4  .
.  .  3  .  5
.  .  .  4  5
─────────────
1  .  .  .  .
.  2  .  .  .
.  .  3  .  .
.  .  .  4  .
.  .  .  .  5
```

Six (6) equal parts

```
1  2  3  4  5  6     .  .  .  .  .  .
1  2  3  4  5  .     .  .  .  .  .  6
1  2  3  4  .  6     .  .  .  .  5  .
1  2  3  .  5  6     .  .  .  4  .  .
1  2  .  4  5  6     .  .  3  .  .  .
1  .  3  4  5  6     .  2  .  .  .  .
.  2  3  4  5  6     1  .  .  .  .  .
────────────────────────────────────
1  2  3  4  .  .     .  .  .  .  5  6
1  2  3  .  5  .     .  .  .  4  .  6
1  2  .  4  5  .     .  .  3  .  .  6
1  .  3  4  5  .     .  2  .  .  .  6
.  2  3  4  5  .     1  .  .  .  .  6
────────────────────────────────────
1  2  3  .  .  6     .  .  .  4  5  .
1  2  .  4  .  6     .  .  3  .  5  .
1  .  3  4  .  6     .  2  .  .  5  .
.  2  3  4  .  6     1  .  .  .  5  .
1  2  .  .  5  6     .  .  3  4  .  .
1  .  3  .  5  6     .  2  .  4  .  .
1  .  .  4  5  6     .  2  3  .  .  .
.  2  3  .  5  6     1  .  .  4  .  .
.  2  .  4  5  6     1  .  3  .  .  .
.  .  3  4  5  6     1  2  .  .  .  .
────────────────────────────────────
1  .  .  .  5  6     .  2  3  4  .  .
1  .  .  4  .  6     .  2  3  .  5  .
1  .  3  .  .  6     .  2  .  4  5  .
1  2  .  .  .  6     .  .  3  4  5  .
.  2  3  .  .  6     1  .  .  4  5  .
.  2  .  4  .  6     1  .  3  .  5  .
.  2  .  .  5  6     1  .  3  4  .  .
.  .  3  .  5  6     1  2  .  4  .  .
.  .  3  4  .  6     1  2  .  .  5  .
.  .  .  4  5  6     1  2  3  .  .  .
```

Sometimes SIX parts stem from two basic parts:

```
1  .  .  2  .  .
```

OR

from three basic parts:

```
1  .  2  .  3  .
```

FIGURE 2.27 Hand patting motions in $\frac{4}{4}$ and $\frac{3}{4}$

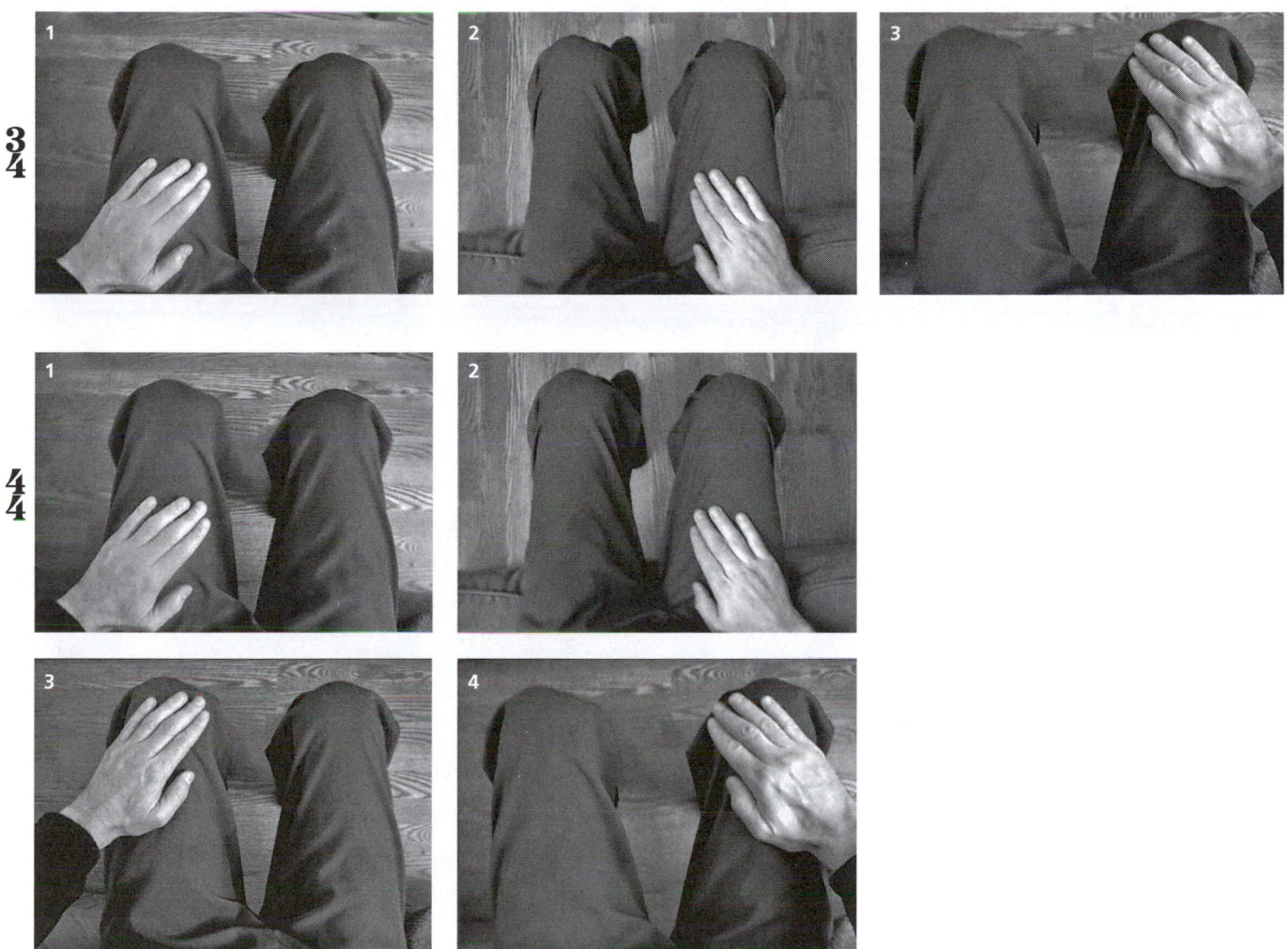

We recommend two approaches to using the Longy Rhythm Sheet: the first improves one's ability to subdivide; the second improves one's ability to track pulses within a meter.

Approach 1

Tap macrobeats, chant microbeats (each number or dot represents an individual subdivision of the beat).

Goal: This exercise develops one's ability to audiate microbeat subdivisions and accurately perform an articulation on any part of the macrobeat.

(a) Externalize the macrobeat organized into a meter (see Figure 2.27): Pat the left thigh with the left hand for the strong beats and the right hand on the right thigh for the weak beats. For measures with a secondary strong beat (i.e., beat 3 in a 4 macrobeat measure), the left hand pats closer to the knee in a different spot than the first strong beat. This is essentially an elaborate version of clapping or tapping one's feet, except now we have a tactile *and* visual representation of the meter.

(b) Using the numeric patterns on the Longy Rhythm Sheet, chant aloud the numbers that are printed and whisper the dots. The goal is to feel the subdivision even if it is not outwardly articulated. For example, if the line says:

1 2 3 ➝ Chant "1 2 3 " during one macrobeat pat

Microbeat:	1	2	3
Chant:	1	2	3
Macrobeat Pat:	X		

1·3 ➝ Sing   "1 (2) 3" during one macrobeat pat

Microbeat:	1	2	3
Chant:	1	(2)	3
Macrobeat Pat:	X		

( ) = whisper the number instead of saying it aloud.

Approach 2

Tap macrobeats, chant macrobeats (each number or dot represents a beat within a meter).

Goal: This exercise develops one's ability to track the pulses within a meter and accurately perform on any macrobeat.

(a) Externalize the macrobeat as above with pats, claps, or heel taps.
(b) Using the patterns on the Longy Rhythm Sheet, say aloud only the numbers that are printed and whisper the numbers that are replaced with dots. Each number or dot receives one macrobeat pat. For example, if the line says:

1 2 3 4 ➝ Chant "1 2 3 4" while tapping the macrobeat for each number

Macrobeat (Meter):	1	2	3	4
Chant:	1	2	3	4
Pat:	X	X	X	X

1··4 ➝ Chant "1 (2) (3) 4" while patting the macrobeat

Macrobeat (Meter):	1	2	3	4
Chant:	1	(2)	(3)	4
Pat:	X	X	X	X

( ) = whisper

Dr. Lynn Hileman, Assistant Professor of Music at West Virginia University, suggests another variation on the entire process. She uses Takadimi rhythm syllables in addition to the numbers, which are easier to say more quickly. (See Figure 2.28: dark syllables are chanted aloud; shaded syllables are whispered.)

For all of these exercises, begin at a slow tempo and increase the speed after students achieve mastery. Avoid adding an accelerando! For Approach 2, once a fast enough macrobeat tempo has been achieved, transition to Approach 1: treat the macrobeat chanting (one pat per number) as microbeats.

FIGURE 2.28 The Longy Rhythm Sheet, another variation

Rhythm Practice Chart (Longy System)
Based on the various division possibilities of any ONE BEAT unit
Adapted with rhythm syllables by Lynn Hileman

Keep a steady beat by tapping on your lap. Enunciate each syllable clearly, speaking aloud the syllables in bold, and whispering the syllables printed in gray.

Duple Subdivision
ta di
ta di
ta di
ta **di**

Triple Subdivision
ta ki da
ta ki da
ta ki da
ta ki **da**
ta **ki** da
ta ki **da**
ta ki da
ta ki **da**

Quadruple Subdivision
ta ka di mi
ta ka di mi
ta ka di mi
ta ka di mi
ta ka di mi
ta ka di mi
ta ka **di mi**
ta ka **di** mi
ta ka di mi
ta **ka di** mi
ta **ka** di mi
ta ka **di** mi
ta ka **di** mi
ta ka **di mi**
ta ka **di** mi

Quintuple Subdivision
ta ka di mi ti
ta ka di mi ti
ta ka di mi ti
ta ka di **mi** ti
ta ka di mi ti
ta ka di mi ti
ta ka di mi ti
ta ka di mi ti
ta ka di mi ti
ta ka di mi ti
ta ka di mi ti
ta ka di **mi** ti
ta ka di **mi** ti
ta ka di **mi** ti
ta ka di mi ti
ta ka di mi ti
ta ka di mi ti
ta ka di mi **ti**
ta ka di mi ti
ta ka di mi ti
ta ka di mi **ti**
ta **ka** di mi ti
ta ka **di** mi ti
ta ka di **mi ti**
ta ka **di** mi ti
ta ka **di** mi **ti**
ta ka **di** mi ti
ta ka **di mi** ti
ta ka di **mi** ti
ta ka di mi **ti**

Sextuple Subdivision
ta va ki di da ma   ta va ki di da ma
ta va ki di da ma   ta va ki di da **ma**
ta va ki di da **ma**   ta va ki di **da** ma
ta va ki di **da ma**   ta va ki **di** da ma
ta va ki **di da** ma   ta **va** ki di da ma
ta va ki di da ma   ta **va** ki di da ma
ta **va** ki di da ma   **ta** va ki di da ma
ta va ki di da ma   ta va ki di **da ma**
ta **va** ki di da ma   ta va ki **di** da ma
ta va ki di da ma   ta va **ki** di da **ma**
ta va ki di da ma   ta **va** ki di da **ma**
ta **va** ki di da ma   ta va ki di da ma
ta va **ki di da** ma   ta va ki di da ma
ta va ki **di** da ma   ta va ki di **da** ma
ta va ki di da ma   ta **va** ki di **da** ma
ta va **ki** di da ma   ta va ki di da ma
ta va ki di da ma   ta va **ki** di da ma
ta va **ki** di da ma   ta va ki di da ma
ta va **ki** di da ma   ta va ki di **da** ma
ta va **ki** di da ma   ta va ki di da ma
ta va **ki di** da ma   ta va **ki di da** ma
ta **va** ki di da ma   ta va ki **di da** ma
ta va **ki** di da ma   ta va ki **di da** ma
ta va **ki di da ma**   ta va **ki di da** ma
ta va ki **di** da ma   ta va ki di **da** ma
ta va ki **di da** ma   ta va ki **di** da ma
ta va ki **di da** ma   ta va ki di **da** ma
ta va ki di **da ma**   ta va ki **di da** ma
ta va ki di **da** ma   ta va ki di **da** ma
ta va ki **di da ma**   ta va ki di **da** ma

Sometimes the sextuple subdivisions stem from two basic parts:
ta va ki **di** da ma

Or from three basic parts:
ta va **ki** di **da** ma

Activities/Assignments for Further Exploration

1. Discuss the relative advantages and disadvantages of the rhythm syllables presented in this chapter. Which would you choose for your own teaching, and why?
2. Write five original rhythm flashcards and perform them for the class using each of the rhythm syllable systems discussed in this chapter.
3. Take five rhythm flashcards and teach them to the class using sound–to–symbol. Try changing the value of the pulse (i.e., what gets the beat, not the speed of the pulse) and teach them again.
4. Think back to your own experiences learning how to read music while also learning an instrument. What approach to teaching rhythm was used? How effective was it in learning how to understand and read rhythms?
5. Practice the exercises involving the Longy Rhythm Sheet. What are potential ways to use this during warmups?
6. Given the limitations of instruments and equipment, what are some strategies we can use to incorporate movement into the instrumental classroom? Be creative!

Further Reading

Daniel, Katinka Scipiades, Zoltán Kodály, and Barbara Gross Davis. *Kodály Approach: Method Book.* 2nd ed. Champaign, IL: M. Foster Music Co., 1979.

Findlay, Elsa. *Rhythm and Movement; Applications of Dalcroze Eurhythmics.* Evanston, IL: Summy-Birchard Co., 1971.

Forque, Charles E., and James Thornton. *Harmonized Rhythms for Concert Band: Progressive Melodic Rhythm Studies.* San Diego, CA: Kjos Music Co., 1994.

Gordon, Edwin. *Learning Sequences in Music: A Contemporary Music Learning Theory.* 2007 ed. Chicago: GIA Publications, 2007.

Houlahan, Micheál, and Philip Tacka. *Kodály Today: A Cognitive Approach to Elementary Music Education.* New York: Oxford University Press, 2007.

Jaques-Dalcroze, Émile. *Eurhythmics, Art, and Education.* New York: Arno Press, 1980.

Jaques-Dalcroze, Émile. *Rhythm, Music and Education.* London: Dalcroze Society, 1967.

Kodály, Zoltán, and Ferenc Bónis. *The Selected Writings of Zoltán Kodály.* New York: Boosey & Hawkes, 1974.

Lisk, Edward S. *The Creative Director: Alternative Rehearsal Techniques.* Ft. Lauderdale, Fla: Meredith Music Publications, 1991.

Mattingly, Rick. *The Drums and Percussion Cookbook: Creative Recipes for Players and Teachers.* Galesville, MD: Meredith Music Publications, 2008.

Newell, David. *The Simple Rhythmatician.* San Diego, CA: Neil A. Kjos Music Co, 2007.

Newell, David. *Teaching Rhythm: New Strategies and Techniques for Success.* San Diego, CA: Neil A. Kjos Music Co., 2008.

Pennington, Jo. *The Importance of Being Rhythmic; A Study of the Principles of Dalcroze Eurythmics Applied to General Education and to the Arts of Music, Dancing and Acting.* London; New York: G.P. Putnam's Sons, 1925.

Chapter 3

Tonality, Melody, and Singing

To Guide Your Reading

Why is an understanding and awareness of tonality important?

How can we help students understand tonality and sing with tonal awareness?

As compared to the rhythm words of the previous chapter, what are common "melodic words" used by Kodály and Gordon? What process can be used to teach them to students?

Why is it important for students to sing in rehearsal?

How can we encourage students to be comfortable singing in rehearsal?

What strategies can we use to teach melodies to students by ear?

How can we use these exercises to improve our students' ear training?

The Importance of Tonal Understanding

To a certain extent instrumentalists can feign their understanding of tonality simply because it is possible to produce a tone if one places his fingers in the proper place and blow, bow, or strike the instrument properly. But producing a tone is not the same as understanding it, just as sounding out the words in an unfamiliar language does not constitute speaking it.

With rhythm, we saw it was important to hear patterns in relation to a pulse and a meter. For melody and harmony, we must hear sounds in relation to tonality, for without tonal context notes are difficult to audiate (i.e., mentally hear and understand, even if no sound is present). For even greater tonal understanding students need to audiate groups of notes (melodic words) and recognize them in a tonal context. Eric Bluestine explains:

> Asking a child to sing a pitch—even a series of pitches—out of context is like asking a man in a lifeboat, adrift at sea, to find the mainland without a compass. It makes no sense to play a series of notes on the piano for a child and then ask her to "pick them out of the air." Pitch matching, in and

of itself, is a pointless activity; but asking a child to audiate and sing a resting tone after you've established tonality—now that's meaningful![1]

Here is a basic way to establish tonality and develop our students' ability to audiate it:

1. Play a simple I-V-I progression on the piano, OR Sing scale degrees $\hat{1}$-$\hat{5}$-$\hat{1}$-$\hat{7}$-$\hat{1}$, OR Teach the ensemble to perform simple I-V–I progressions.
2. Ask the class to sing the tonic pitch before playing a particular passage during rehearsals.

After a little practice students will have little trouble hearing the pitch center. For example, after cutting off a section, ask the group to sing the pitch center. Initially do this after an authentic cadence, then after a half cadence, and eventually after random points within a phrase. Another important way to develop this skill—one practiced by many professional wind and string players—is through the use of drones to practice scales, arpeggios, and other patterns (as discussed in Chapter 13). An added benefit of the ability to audiate tonic is that students can better sense pure intervals in relation to the pitch center, leading to better intonation.

Teaching "Melodic Words"

Figure 3.1 shows a variety of melodic words (patterns). Though these mostly emphasize tonic harmony (some with a pentatonic flavor), the melodic "vocabulary list" should eventually be expanded to include patterns that reflect dominant and subdominant harmonies. For the process described below we recommend making melodic flashcards.

As mentioned above, it is essential to first establish the tonality and pitch center against which the patterns will be understood and performed. Gordon recommends playing a I-V-I pattern on a keyboard as preparation, while Kodály advocates performing against a pitch-center drone (e.g., tonic drone). Both are effective.

The process for teaching tonal patterns/melodic words is similar to that of rhythm words. Be sure to have students sing the patterns before playing them.

Stage 1

1. Teacher establishes tonality.
2. Teacher sings the melodic word to the students on a neutral syllable.
3. Students immediately echo on a neutral syllable.

Stage 2

1. Teacher establishes tonality.
2. Teacher sings the melodic word using solfege syllables (or substitute solfege with scale degree numbers).
3. Students immediately echo using the solfege syllables.

Stage 3

1. Teacher establishes tonality.
2. Teacher sings a melodic word using solfege syllables while pointing to the notation of the word.
3. Students echo using solfege syllables, either pointing to the corresponding notation in their text, or by looking at the notation on the board.

FIGURE 3.1 Sample Melodic Patterns

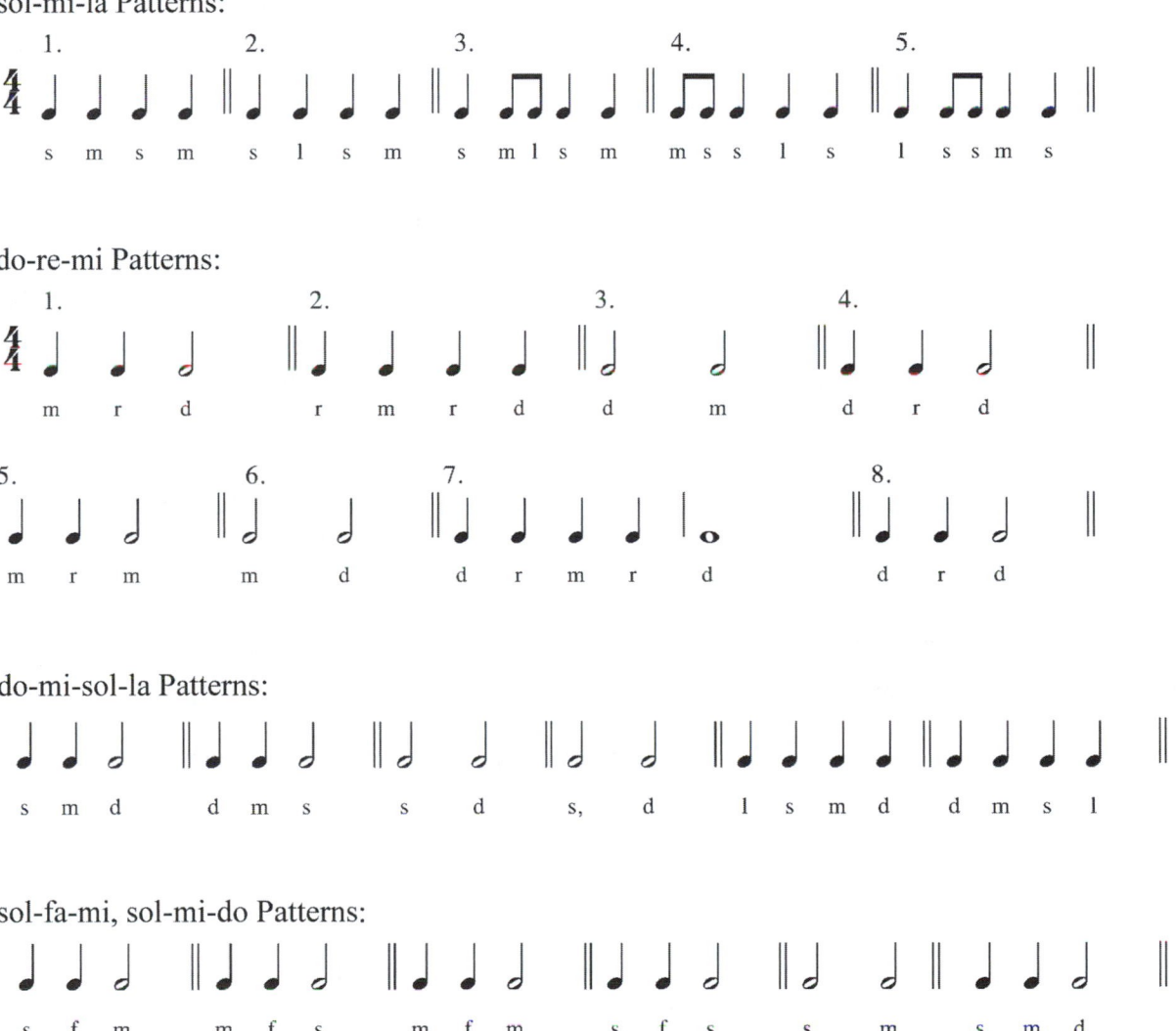

Melodic Patterns

sol-mi-la Patterns:

do-re-mi Patterns:

do-mi-sol-la Patterns:

sol-fa-mi, sol-mi-do Patterns:

As with rhythm words, once students aurally learn the patterns, use flashcards to introduce notation and reading. For example, post each flashcard on the board and improvise melodies by pointing to cards in an unfamiliar order, but locked into a steady pulse. Begin by putting two or more pulses between the performance of each melodic word. Eventually have each melodic word performed back to back, without a pause. Encourage students to look ahead while they read by pointing to the next card before it is performed (and show them how this is similar to how they should read printed language).

Eventually, students should improvise their own melodies—first with familiar melodic words, and later with variations on those words (i.e., new melodic words, melodic words with rhythm, etc.). By beginning early we can make improvisation a regular part of "classical" music, rather than a mystical activity only practiced by jazzers.

Singing in Rehearsal

Beyond the goals of developing tonal understanding, we should make singing a regular part of rehearsals. Among its advantages, singing:

1. It helps players experience a kinesthetic connection to the intervals they must play, which in turn helps note accuracy. This is especially true for brass players. (Encourage students to sing in a comfortable octave.)
2. It improves intonation. Regular vocalization has been shown to improve one's sense of pitch.[2] Often the instrument itself creates intonation challenges, either through a mental disconnect between pitches that are sung and played, or from a lack of physical skills needed to adjust the pitch. Singing in tune pitches, melodies, and chords imprints them in the mind's ear and improves chances of duplicating them on instruments.
3. It provides a vehicle to practice articulation, style, and phrasing. Once students move beyond their inhibitions about singing, the voice is an infinitely flexible and expressive instrument, especially since they have, in a sense, "practiced" their voices all their lives! First sing melodies together as an ensemble, and then transfer to instruments.
4. It offers a tool to keep the entire ensemble involved. Even if certain sections rarely play the melody (e.g., tubas!), singing it gives them a chance to participate with the main tune. Further, experiencing how to phrase the melody will inform them how their non-melodic parts need to be phrased (i.e., "Tubas, phrase your line exactly as if you had the melody.")

When to Use Singing in the Rehearsal

- During the tuning procedure—oboe sounds the reference pitch, group sings it, then plays it.
- During warmups, on chorales or chorale melodies.
- During rehearsal:

  - for out of tune notes
  - for out of tune chords
  - for melodies—have the entire group sing the melody (for intonation work, sing against a tonic drone)

Jump-Starting Non-Singing Ensembles

It is quite common for students to resist singing in band and orchestra. They may protest, "If I wanted to sing I would have joined the choir!" But with a little encouragement and some careful strategizing groups will sing confidently and effectively. Here are a few techniques to try:

- *Hum* first—Humming with the lips together allows the sound to resonate more strongly in one's ear. Start out by having the ensemble play, and then hum the same passage. During the humming have several members play softly as a reference. Then repeat, but now sing with mouths open.
- *Safety in numbers*—At first, avoid asking individuals or small groups to sing.
- *Sing* sustained notes during warmups (e.g., tuning pitches)—it's an easy and non-threatening way to get used to singing.
- *Use* songs students know—Whether it be "Happy Birthday", a song from a pop star, or a popular film soundtrack, students will feel much more comfortable singing something they already enjoy.
- *Kazoo Ensemble*—At first everybody will giggle, but for many students singing into a kazoo removes inhibitions. The buzzing of the kazoo hides their voice, thus making students less self-conscious, and then it is an easy transition from singing into a kazoo to singing without it. (One caveat: keep in mind that low notes will not buzz). Kazoos can be purchased in bulk for less than $1 each.

Teach Lots of Melodies!

Sound–to–symbol philosophies value the incorporation of songs and melodies into regular activities, as it is crucial for developing awareness and understanding of music's language. Thus, don't limit ensembles to singing melodies only from the repertoire in their folders. Teach additional melodies by rote and then have students transfer them to their instrument by ear.[3] Try this process:

1. Find a familiar melody in a clearly defined key. Choose melodies that:

   - use a variety of modes and meters
   - the students enjoy
   - contain the same patterns we have been teaching as melodic words
   - can be accompanied mostly with primary harmonies.

   Contemporary folk songs may be appropriate for very young students, though some band-aged students find them trite, and once students feel the exercise is beneath them it is doomed. Additional choices include pop songs, commercial jingles, and T.V. and movie themes (particularly if they employ patterns with which students will be familiar.) Collections of appropriate melodies are also available for purchase through several publishers.
2. Establish the tonality, and confirm students can audiate the pitch center by asking them to sing it back.
3. Sing the entire melody to the students on a neutral syllable. For longer and less familiar tunes, teach phrase by phrase. Sing one phrase and ask the class to echo it back. Work through the entire melody and then put everything together in one large chunk.
4. Have students sing or audiate (e.g., sing it in their mind's ear) the melody while we sing its accompanying bass line. Then teach students the bass line. As Kathy Liperote, Adjunct Professor of Music Education at the Eastman School of Music points out, the bass line "helps to solidify the melody, adds interest for the students, and encourages them to anticipate and predict what comes next in the music—necessary skills for improvisation and reading and writing with comprehension" (Liperote, 48).
5. Divide the ensemble into groups and practice singing the accompaniment and the bass line.

Extensions of this exercise include:

- bass line singers improvise rhythms on their notes (as groups or individuals)
- a group of students create a rhythmic accompaniment to the melody and bass line.

Using Songs for Melodic/Harmonic Dictation

Once tunes are learned by ear, the next step is to figure out the melody and bass line on instruments. This is essentially melodic and harmonic dictation disguised as a game, though in this case the transfer is from ear to instruments instead of from ear to page. Though we often think of dictation as a chore subjected upon college theory classes, the goal here is to strengthen and measure students' ability to audiate melodic and harmonic material (i.e., to be able to hear music in their head and understand it in a tonal context). Choose a comfortable pitch area and provide the starting pitch; for tricky melodies give the first few notes. Be sure to have students figure out the bass line, too. Assign this as homework or work simultaneously as a band (which may be cacophonous but it gives students the opportunity to use each other for guidance.) Invite individuals to model their "dictations" for the class ("Let's try a duet with flutes and trombones!").

Activities/Assignments for Further Exploration

1. Choose one or two melodic words from Figure 3.1 and teach them to the class.
2. What might be the advantages and disadvantages between using drones and I-V-I progressions to establish tonality?
3. Try teaching the class a familiar melody. Now teach an unfamiliar melody. Did you notice a difference in the class' reaction? When would each be appropriate, and what are the relative advantages and disadvantages of each?

Further Reading

Dalby, Bruce. *Tune Assistant: The Complete Tune Resource*. Chicago: GIA Publications, 2006.

Froseth, James. *Melodic Flashcards for Recorder*. Chicago: GIA Publications, 1984.

Froseth, James. *Performance Based Ear-Training*. Chicago: GIA Publications, 1994.

Krueger, Carol J. *Progressive Sight Singing*. New York: Oxford University Press, 2007.

McClung, Alan C. *Movable Tonic: A Sequenced Sight-Singing Method*. Chicago: GIA Publications, 2008.

<h1 style="text-align:center">Chapter 4</h1>

Teaching Improvisation and Composition

To Guide Your Reading

How does setting limits enable beginners to experiment with composition and improvisation?

Why is it important to give students a musical vocabulary with which to write or improvise?

In what ways can familiar styles and conventions be used to facilitate composition and improvisation?

Why is form an important parameter?

How can we use speaking and writing as analogies for musical improvisation?

Incorporating Improvisation and Composition into the Rehearsal

As we have seen in discussions of constructivist teaching and curriculums, composition and improvisation have important roles in instrumental music education. Performance skills are a large part of what we teach, but by themselves they do not develop complete musicians who "speak," understand, and create music in addition to being able to read and perform it.

Given that the paradigm of most instrumental music classrooms strongly emphasizes teaching and learning activities that are directly related to performance, *when* do we teach composition and improvisation, and *how* do we teach them? Making time to incorporate the strategies discussed in this chapter requires foresight, patience, and a willingness to experiment, as shown in these examples:

- Program one fewer piece on each concert, or for one piece program a grade level easier than you normally would, thus freeing time for other activities during class.
- On a weekly or bi-weekly basis, set aside one rehearsal or part of one rehearsal for non-performance activities.
- Schedule activities directly after a concert, when the pressure to prepare for a concert is at a minimum.
- For warmups, instead of focusing exclusively on instrumental technique, engage the ensemble with improvisation and composition activities, even if just for 5–10 minutes once or twice per week.
- Find ways to collaborate as an ensemble on improvisation and composition activities. This is especially useful for younger students who need guidance creating their own music.

- Program pieces that incorporate or allow opportunities for improvisation (e.g., jazz arrangements, aleatoric works, etc.).
- Program student compositions.

No matter how we approach it, some students may resist at first, especially those who have never had composition and improvisation in their band or orchestra class. Still, it is important that we engage in these activities regularly and treat them as a meaningful part of our curriculum and a normal part of playing an instrument.

Teaching Improvisation

The thought of playing music without being able to read it is enough to paralyze some folks, and the prospect of teaching it to others is worse. However, if we accept sound–to–symbol's "music as language" analogy, improvisation is a natural, integral, and essential part of music-making. Quite simply, before it is written or read, language is spoken. If someone asks you what you did last night, you might say, "I came home after school, made dinner, and did some house chores. Then a friend of mine called on the phone and we talked for a while before I went to bed." Chances are quite good, too, that you will not be reading this description from a book. You will be improvising it! You make it up as you go, though there is still structure, grammar, and content to your improvisatory statement. And yet you would never expect someone to be impressed ("My word, you are a terrific improviser when you speak!")

This chapter's discussion of improvisation is written primarily from a jazz perspective, mainly because that style is familiar to most students and is supported by a wide range of literature and repertoire. However, recognize that improvisation appears in a variety of classical, rock, folk, and world music traditions, and the below strategies can be successfully applied to many of them.

Most jazz improvisation methods teach a combination of scales, chords, and patterns as the tools for improvising. All of these are useful, though in and of itself, playing scales and chords does not constitute improvising anymore than reciting the alphabet or reading the words in a dictionary constitutes speaking. In either case we are merely speaking gibberish without meaning.

For language, speaking with meaning involves combining letters into words; words into phrases; phrases into sentences; sentences into paragraphs, etc. For music it means combining notes into motives; motives into themes; themes into sub-phrases; sub-phrases into phrases, etc.

At a basic level it is certainly possible to "sound good" simply by playing appropriate scales and chords over a progression (for example, pentatonic scale over a blues progression); in the same way we can make pretty sounds at the piano by only playing the black keys. Generally speaking, however, this becomes boring rather quickly, and only speed and unusual technical proficiency can hide, at least temporarily, a lack of musical meaning or structure.

A lack of meaning also explains why many young students fear improvising. Imagine we teach you the Russian alphabet. You practice speaking it, memorize it, and perfect your accent and pronunciation. You can even recite the alphabet out of order, and at random. And yet if we put you in front of a room of people *you still cannot speak coherently*. Quite literally, you have nothing to say. Non-improvisers in music often feel the same way. Even when outfitted with an array of scales and chords they still have nothing to "say" beyond quasi-random recitations of the musical alphabet.

The solution is to teach students musical "words" before we teach them the musical "alphabet" in the same way we teach children to say "Mama" and "Dada" years before they know anything about spelling. As we will see in "Teaching Composition," this approach sets limits, which ironically makes it easier to improvise, rather than harder.

Teaching Improvisation with Musical Patterns

Musical words need not be jazzy or complicated. In fact, the first ones should be the same patterns taught with the flashcard method described in Chapter 3. Additional musical words (e.g., jazz patterns, patterns with chromaticism, etc.) can be taught aurally.

Here is a step-by-step strategy for introducing improvisation with musical words to beginning improvisers:

1. By rote, teach the ensemble two or three simple musical words. Use words with:

   - 2–4 notes, preferably from a major scale, pentatonic scale, or blues scale
   - mostly stepwise motion; one leap at the end or beginning is also effective
   - repetition of rhythm or pitch.

2. As with melodic and rhythmic words, first have the students sing the patterns and then transfer them to their instruments. Eventually ask each individual student to play the word back to you.

3. Present improvisation as a game of musical dialogue: The teacher plays a short phrase, which is then answered by a student. It is important to emphasize the analogy between improvisation and spoken language. The student's answer may be an imitation (agreement), a variation (agreement with more information), or a contradiction (disagreement, or question). Be sure to engage individual students— direct each "sentence" at an individual and rotate around the room. Be expressive, and coax students to be the same. Instead of speaking in a musical monotone, speak:

   - excitedly
   - haltingly
   - questioningly
   - angrily
   - happily
   - repetitively
   - thoughtfully
   - hyperactively, etc.

   This exercise can be done a capella or with accompaniment. Students need not know many music words to participate in the musical dialogue—even a single note with a rhythmic pattern or a two-note diatonic pattern is appropriate. *It is essential the teacher model these techniques on patterns students can imitate.*

4. Teach how to construct a musical "sentence" using the learned vocabulary. Demonstrate the following.

   - *Repetition*—Repetition is among the most common compositional strategies of composers and improvisers in all musical traditions. Repetition creates desirable familiarity (though too much turns this comfort into boredom).
   - *Tempo and rhythmic variation*—Playing a word slower, faster, or with a slightly altered rhythm is an excellent way to combine the satisfying predictability of repetition with the excitement of change.
   - *Dynamic changes*—Another way to balance repetition and variation, dynamic changes help modulate intensity, emphasis, and surprise.
   - *Motivic variation*—Musical words are easily modified with chromatic alterations (e.g., turn Major into minor, play the first or last note up/down a half step), or split into smaller words.

- *Ornamentation*—Musical words can be decorated with mordents, trills, chromatic grace notes, etc.
- *Meter/Inflection/Emphasis*—Our perception of a musical phrase is easily altered by changing the meter, or which notes are emphasized.
- *Dissonance and "wrong notes"*—A huge challenge with beginning improvisers is convincing them to enjoy and appreciate dissonance rather than fear it (and consequently play timidly to avoid it). Show students how dissonance creates the tension necessary to balance and set-up consonance. Teach beginners to introduce dissonance with simple chromatic inflections (e.g., blues notes). Develop their ability to hear the relative dissonance of scale pitches in relation to the tonality or underlying harmony (drones are a wonderful tool for this).

Though at first it will be counterintuitive, insist that dissonance be played *more strongly* than consonance. In this sense, "wrong notes" should be viewed as accidental dissonances that are best embraced. Repeat the wrong note, play it strongly, and resolve it to consonance. Demonstrations by the teacher are particularly helpful in showing how one can "sell" even the worst wrong note and make it sound like brilliant improvisation. (For example, play a dissonant note with a snappy rhythm to signal to the listener it is something interesting.)

Using Other Linguistic Analogies

It is important students understand that they are applying the same techniques expressive speakers use when they talk, albeit in this case with a comparatively limited vocabulary of musical words.
    Here are some examples:

Repetition and dynamics: "John, I need you to come here. I need you to come here right now!"
Rhythmic variation: "Please pass the salt. Puhleeeze pass the salt . . . Thank you!"
Dynamics: "I'm so happy. I'M SO HAPPY!"
Motivic variation: "The bus driver is very friendly. In fact, the driver of that bus is a good friend."
Meter/Inflection: "It is really GREAT to see you. It is really great to see YOU. It IS really great to see you."
Ornamentation: "The king lives in a castle. The very pompous king lives in an ornate castle."
Wrong notes: "John cheated on his guest. Guest! Ha! Guest! I mean, John cheated on his test!"

---

5. Challenge students to construct their own musical sentences using only the "words" they recently learned. Use a simple accompaniment (e.g., recorded blues progression or drone) as background. For the first few attempts, have the entire class improvise simultaneously. The resulting cacophony provides a safe environment for students to experiment without being judged.

   Note: When asking students to compose or improvise something for the first time, give them a chance to plan some ideas before putting them on the spot. Remember, even great improvisers do not make everything up as they go along. Rather, they combine melodies, rhythms, and patterns they already know in new and interesting ways. Before they are asked to manipulate it through improvisation novice improvisers must be comfortable with their vocabulary, however limited. Again, this is best done as a group activity, with the entire class playing together.

6. Now we can begin to introduce longer musical sentences. Continue the analogy with spoken language to help students understand how to expand their "sentences" into paragraphs. Though it may seem a bit ridiculous, we can learn a lot from how toddlers "speak." All but perhaps the most precocious toddler only know a few words, and so their attempts at speaking in paragraphs might take the following form: "Mama. Mama! Waaaaa . . . Mama . . . ball. Ball! . . . waaaaaa . . . Ball . . . giggle . . . giggle . . ." This isn't really a coherent paragraph, of course, but the babble provides a useful model for how to extend few words into a long statement. For the musical improviser, the child's cries, giggles, and burbles are replaced with simple sustained tones, scales, and arpeggios. This analogy serves as a useful place to introduce scales and arpeggios because it treats them as connecting material rather than as meaningful thematic information. Thus, the improviser's model becomes: "Word 1 . . . Scale . . . Word 1 . . . Scale . . . Word 1 and Word 2 . . . Sustained note . . . Arpeggio . . ." (see Figure 4.1).

FIGURE 4.1 Example of Improvisation Using the Above Language Model

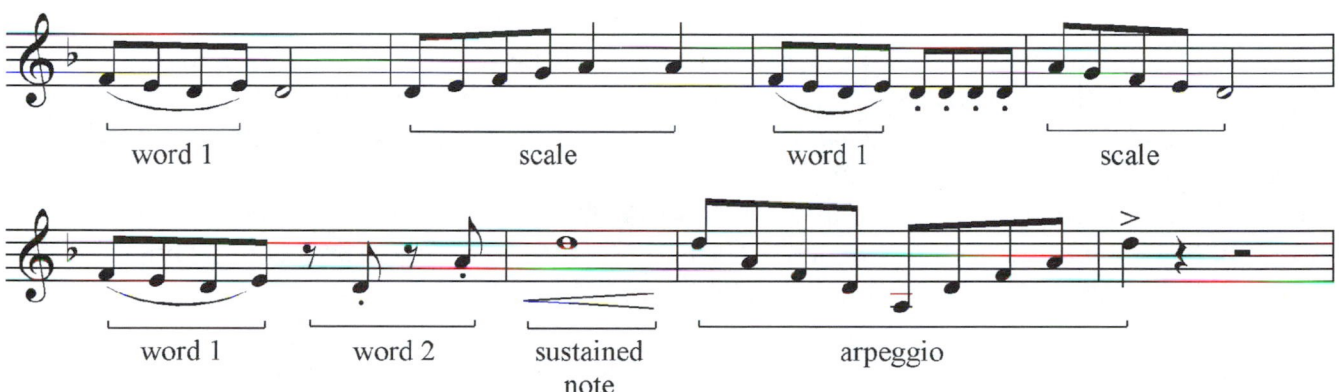

For a more sophisticated approach we can turn to basic paragraph construction, as follows.

Topic sentence
Transition to ⇨ Details about that topic
Transition to ⇨ Concluding sentence

Translated into musical terms, the improviser's model becomes:

Word 1 and/or Word 2
Scale/Sustained note/Arpeggio
Variation or new combination of Word 1 and Word 2
Scale/Sustained Note/Arpeggio
Word 1 and/or Word 2

More sophisticated expressions of these models develop as we expand our vocabulary (learn i.e., additional musical words), develop our ability to manipulate those words (apply variations such as transposition, sequence, augmentation, diminution, etc.), and master more sophisticated transitional material (additional scalar and chordal patterns). Indeed, once students approach improvisation as speaking with expression (Step 3), meaning (Steps 4 and 5), and structure (Step 6), the possibilities are endless.

Caveat emptor: Teaching improvisation is a long-term project, and depending on the complexity we create and the amount of time we spend in each lesson, we should expect these steps to take months to complete. Be patient, and let students become comfortable with one step before moving to more sophisticated techniques.

Using Improvisation to Teach Other Musical Fundamentals

Improvisation is an excellent vehicle for teaching a host of music fundamentals.

1. *Aural skills*—Instead of the printed music, students must rely on their ears to tell them what to play. A simple way to develop this is to use imitation and call-and-response activities. These exercises are particularly well suited for warmups. For example, teacher/student sings or plays a 2–5 note melody, and the group repeats it.[1] Limits are important. Start with two notes and expand to pentatonic scales and diatonic scales. Also incorporate rhythm imitation, initially on a repeated pitch.
2. *Form*—Using a form such as ABA may seem to complicate the exercise, but as before, limits and repetitions ease the improviser's burden to invent new material while also improving melodic memory. Even lengthy forms such as Theme and Variations and Rondo provide templates to practice the techniques discussed earlier.
3. *Layers*—Jazz improvisers generally improvise melodically while the rhythm section takes care of the rest. Jeffrey Agrell, author of *Improvisation Games for Classical Musicians*, points out that improvisation in the classical context introduces additional roles. He writes:

> The contemporary classical improviser will need to be able to switch quickly in and out of foreground/background roles (i.e., solo and accompaniment) in the performance of pieces where the "script" is invented in the moment, which requires sensitivity and skill. Players learn to be selfless for the sake of the piece and to make their playing partners look good. Those who insist on hogging the limelight are soon at a loss for playing partners (Agrell, 31).

For example, try a non-jazz version of "trading fours." Instead of one player sitting tacit while the other solos, have the two players trade solo and accompaniment roles (Agrell, 39). At least at first, provide archetypes for the students to imitate:

- oompah bass
- drones (spice them up with re-articulations and bagpipe-like scoops)
- ostinati
- simple scalar figures ($\hat{1}$-$\hat{2}$-$\hat{1}$, $\hat{1}$-$\hat{2}$-$\hat{3}$-$\hat{2}$-$\hat{1}$, $\hat{1}$-$\hat{2}$-$\hat{3}$-$\hat{4}$-$\hat{5}$-$\hat{4}$-$\hat{3}$-$\hat{2}$-$\hat{1}$)
- imitation (repeat part of the soloist's rhythm and/or melody)
- musical punctuation—play a musical period, exclamation point, question mark, etc., and the end of a soloist's phrase.

Teaching Composition

The Importance of Placing Limits

The challenge of teaching composition parallels that of teaching improvisation. Most students stumble because they simply do not have a language with which to express themselves. Giving a student a piece of manuscript paper and asking him to write a piece is fundamentally the same as asking him to compose a poem in French, Italian, or some other language in which he knows no words or syntax. For any composition activity we should give students:

- vocabulary and syntax (or, the musical building blocks)
- form (or, the blueprint to follow/modify)
- limits

Limits are important. A blank slate—"Compose whatever you'd like!"—can be overwhelming, as students spend most of their energy simply making choices about what resources to use. Instead, free them to explore by limiting their palette. In his book *Composing Music*, William Russo takes precisely this approach.[2] His first assignments involve using only one note and a few rhythmic values, and gradually more variables are introduced. (This is an exercise practiced by some of the most accomplished composers. Ligeti famously employed it in his *Musica Ricerta* in which the first movement uses only two notes (albeit with free rhythm and multiple octaves), the next movement three notes, and so on. It is a classic example of how limitations enhance expressiveness rather than suppress it.)

Other General Strategies for Teaching Composition

- Make time to teach to students' individual differences. Each student is unique and likely to approach the challenges of composition differently, and thus need our experience to facilitate their progress.
- Allow students time to develop their compositional skills.[3] This is not something that can be taught in one class period. Even the greatest composers famously tortured themselves working and re-working their processes.
- Show students how to draw upon the skills and experiences they already have. Explain how all composers appropriate what they know and shape it in new ways. (e.g., Mozart and Haydn were likely influenced by Austrian folk song; Bartok and Kodály by Hungarian folk song.) A straightforward way to do this is to use the rhythms and melodies from concert literature as raw materials for new pieces.
- Encourage collaboration. Students should be allowed to "share in the evolution of their own musical thinking, discoveries, influences, and day–to–day progress," along with their peer composers and the teacher, too (Lapidaki, 109).

Some specific approaches to teaching composition include the following:

Medieval Parody Technique/Repertoire-Based Composition

Composers in the Middle Ages and Renaissance wrote sacred contrapuntal works using other pieces and popular melodies as the starting point. They began these so-called "Parody Masses" with the original melody, and then spun it into new material. Band and orchestra students can use the same principle in their compositions. Instead of asking students to compose original melodies from scratch, borrow melodies from the current ensemble repertoire, as described below.

1. Students separate into small groups.
2. Each group chooses 2–3 melodies from the repertoire (or segments of melodies).
3. Each group writes a piece of pre-determined length using the chosen melodies.

Introduce a variety of compositional techniques that can be applied. For example:

- *sequence*—repeat the melody at different pitch levels
- *modal switch*—put the melody into a different mode (major into minor, etc.)
- *inflection*—add or subtract accidentals to the original melody
- *retrograde*—reverse the sequence of notes in the melody
- *inversion*—a mirror image of the original melody's intervals
- *rhythmic displacement*—putting a melody into a different meter, or starting on a different part of the measure (e.g., different beat, offbeat instead of onbeat, etc.); this procedure is most effective with an accompaniment to make the displacement clear (Russo, 33)
- *ornamentation*—add trills, chromatic decorations, etc.
- *addition/subtraction*—add new notes to the figure (e.g., pickup notes, small runs to fill in leaps, etc.) (Russo, 36)
- *augmentation/diminution*—play the melody at half the speed or twice the speed
- *counterpoint*—juxtapose melodies in a canon (same melody) or as a quodlibet (different melodies at the same time)
- *repetition*—repeat entire phrases or just fragments/motifs
- *melodic harmonization*—harmonize the melody at a parallel interval above or below the original (e.g., thirds, sixths, fifths, seconds, etc.)
- *chordal harmonization*—add a bass line and/or accompaniment

It is incumbent upon us to illuminate these and other compositional techniques in the literature we program. Thus, instead of simply drilling the music we must describe how it is constructed. The point is to demystify the creative process by demonstrating that good composition is part inspiration and part technique. Once students have the raw materials of inspiration (whether they composed it themselves or "borrowed" it from another source), composition is simply creative application of techniques in their compositional toolkit.

A few more strategies:

- Especially with novices, it is important to put limits on the exercise.
- Initially students should work out their compositions by ear and then put the results into notation.
- Provide a list of forms, preferably simpler ones such as:

> Binary
> Ternary
> Rondo
> Theme and Variations

Write Your Own Theme

Ask students to compose a personal theme melody, and use this melody as the basis for a composition. See above for techniques and procedure.

Isomelody and Isorhythm

The idea here, as suggested by William Russo, is to free creativity by systematically limiting options. Melodic isorhythm is similar to melodic serialism. Students write a tone row (or generate one randomly) and then use it as the basis for a composition. (Unlike 12-tone serialism, the row need not be all 12 chromatic pitches, and a tone may be repeated in the row (Russo, 67). In others words—B D F D G♯ is a legitimate isomelody as long as those notes are used in their original order before cycling to the beginning.) *In isomelody only the rhythm need be composed.*

In isorhythm one composes a repeating rhythmic figure. Note that this is similar to an ostinato except the rhythm does not have to fit neatly within a measure —a five quarter note isorhythm may be used in $\frac{4}{4}$ time, with the understanding being that the fifth note of the pattern will bleed into the next bar. *In isorhythm only the pitches need be composed.* Russo points out that isomelody and isorhythm may be combined (Russo, 69).

Onomatoepeia Composition

Ask students to compose a work that translates non-musical sounds into the musical ones. For example, consider the sounds of:

- nature
- the city
- a birthday celebration
- a factory
- a busy office

In this exercise orchestration and timbre are an essential part of the process; melody and form are suggested by the sounds that are imitated. We can even encourage a combination of traditional and non-traditional instruments (perhaps household objects commandeered as instruments). Opportunities for exploration abound in the percussion family. (Admittedly, this might involve students tapping vigorously on everything in sight, but it will encourage them to find unique solutions!)

Arranging Familiar Tunes (Advanced Project)

Develop a list of popular tunes the marching band or pep band would like to play at football and basketball games and assign each one to a different student. Orchestras can make this a piece to be played on the final concert of the year. Or, assign as a senior group project, with the teacher serving as consultant for orchestration and notation. This type of activity offers several advantages:

- Pep band arrangements are designed to be short, and so even 30–60 seconds of music serve as a stand-alone piece.
- With the melody already composed, students may concentrate on tonal center, transpositions, introductions, harmonization, accompaniments, counter-melodies, and endings.
- Experiencing the *art* of orchestration: Young musicians do not always understand how the arrangement is as integral to a work's success as the notes and rhythms.
- Experiencing the *science* of orchestration: Marching bands have fewer parts than wind ensembles and orchestras, and for reasons of expediency their pieces generally follow clear conventions. Orchestra arrangements can be approached as pieces for SATBB string ensemble. These limits make arranging more manageable for novices.
- Gives students an opportunity to create a musical "legacy."

Activities/Assignments for Further Exploration

1. Beyond the ones listed in this chapter, what other compositional and improvisational techniques can be added to the student's palette that would help them manipulate a musical vocabulary in an expressive way?

2. Develop a list of forms that are useful for composition and improvisation. What well-known musical compositions can be used to demonstrate them?

3. Design a warmup that teaches elements of improvisation.

4. Design a composition activity that a band or orchestra can work on as a group.

5. Find examples in the orchestra and band literature that illustrate common compositional and improvisational techniques/strategies.

6. This chapter is written from the perspective that it is important to include composition and improvisation in the instrumental music classroom. Do you agree with this perspective? Why or why not? What would a possible counterargument be?

Further Reading

Agrell, Jeffrey. *Improvisation Games for Classical Musicians: A Collection of Musical Games with Suggestions for Use: For Performers, Instrumental Teachers, Music Students, Music Therapists, Bands, Orchestras, Choirs, Chamber Music Ensembles, Conductors, Composers, Pianists, Percussionists, and Everybody Else (Even Jazz Players).* Chicago: GIA Publications, 2008.

Azzara, Christopher D., and Richard F. Grunow. *Developing Musicianship Through Improvisation, C Instruments (treble clef).* Chicago: GIA Publications, 2006.

Bailey, Derek. *Improvisation: Its Nature and Practice in Music.* New York: Da Capo Press, 1993.

Baker, David. *David Baker's Jazz Improvisation: A Comprehensive Method For All Musicians.* Van Nuys, CA: Alfred Pub. Co., 1998.

Berg, Shelton G. *Jazz Improvisation: The Goal-Note Method: A Comprehensive, Programmed Guide to Jazz Theory and Improvisation.* Delevan, NY: Kendor Music, 1998.

Coker, Jerry. *Patterns for Jazz.* 3rd ed. Lebanon, Ind: Studio Publications, 1970.

Copland, Aaron. *Music and Imagination.* Cambridge: Harvard University Press, 1980.

Copland, Aaron. *What to Listen for in Music.* San Francisco: McGraw-Hill, 1988.

Hickey, Maud. *Why and How to Teach Music Composition: A New Horizon for Music Education.* Reston, VA: MENC, 2003.

Kaschub, Michele, and Janice Smith. *Minds on Music: Composition for Creative and Critical Thinking.* Lanham, Md: Rowman & Littlefield Education, 2009.

Russo, William, Jeffrey Ainis, and David Stevenson. *Composing Music: A New Approach.* Chicago: University of Chicago Press, 1988.

Wine, Toby. *1001 Blues Licks.* New York: Cherry Lane Music, 2003.

Chapter 5

The History of Instrumental Music Education and Its Philosophy

A Brief Introduction

To Guide Your Reading

How did the music education philosophies of the Greeks and Romans influence music education today?

What have been the various goals of music education over the years that have been used to justify its importance?

What did America's first European settlers view the purpose of music education to be?

How did the growing popularity of orchestras and bands during the nineteenth and twentieth centuries influence their acceptance into public education?

How did economic forces shape the development of music education in America?

How did the philosophy of music education evolve during the twentieth century through the ideas of Britton, Reimer, and Elliott?

To understand the philosophies and pedagogies of instrumental music education in the United States, it is necessary to examine them in the context of the 2,000 years of music educational tradition that preceded them. This examination must begin with the ancient Greeks and Romans, who left behind an educational and philosophical legacy that remained influential from the Middle Ages to the twentieth century.

Music was an integral part of Greek education, whose main purpose was to develop citizens capable of fully participating in society. In his first account of the subject in Republic, Plato presents an ideal of moral education designed to shape character by training both the body—through gymnastics—and the soul—through music. Of the two, "Education in music is most sovereign, because more than anything else, rhythm and harmony find their way to the innermost soul and take strongest hold upon it, bringing with them and imparting grace, if one is rightly trained."[1] This training included instruction in both vocal and instrumental music, as well as in poetry and rhetoric. The goal of musical education was to develop an idealization of community life through singing tales that promoted love of justice and hatred of injustice. This idea of musical study as a form of moral education to develop model citizens expressed a utilitarian philosophy that would dominate music education philosophy for over 2,000 years.

The ancient Romans also recognized music's power to shape an individual's relationship to society, but regarded its main value as scientific. As one of the seven liberal arts, music—along with arithmetic, geometry, and astronomy—was part of the *quadrivium*, four subjects whose study revealed the physical and spiritual realities of the universe. The Roman view of music was stated most powerfully by statesman and scholar Boethius in *De Institutione Musica*, a work that preserved Greek music theory and was studied in Europe from the Middle Ages through the nineteenth century. In it, he described music as a representation of the cosmic harmonies of the universe, which were to be perceived through the intellect, not the senses. The difference between the Greek and Roman approaches illustrates the tension inherent in music's dual nature as something both apprehended aesthetically by the senses and understood abstractly by the mind.

The scientific and artistic aspects of music were both subjects of study in the Middle Ages, when the invention of notation led to further developments in music theory, and the development of reading as a subject of musical study. For most outside the highest levels of the monastic schools, however, music still existed as a force for moral education, used this time by the Carolingian Empire to exert religious influence and reinforce the role of the individual in society. Seven hundred years later, Martin Luther advocated teaching music on the same grounds, as did John Amos Comenius, who led the drive to educate the newly formed middle class in the seventeenth century.

Against this backdrop, the first European settlers came to America. The Anglicans, Catholics, Lutherans, Mennonites, Moravians, Pietists, and Quakers who made up the early Pennsylvania immigrants brought sophisticated European music with them and taught it in their schools. As before, the focus of this education was not on the music itself, but on the effect it would have on those who studied it. According to one Moravian educator, "That the youth should become musicians is by no means a necessary result, not even a desirable one; we would only insist that music should have its sway in the whole formation and refinement of mind and heart" (Mark 2008, 9).

It was the much less diverse New England colonists, however, who had the greatest and most widespread influence on the future music education system in America. Unlike the economically stratified society of the southern colonies, where European secular music was popular but only available to the upper classes, theocratic New England offered musical experience to all through worship in church. But though the access to musical participation was greatly increased, the variety of music available to a New Englander of the seventeenth and eighteenth centuries was severely limited: The Calvinist Puritans and Pilgrims viewed the singing of Psalms as the only appropriate form of music in their services. Psalmody was thus a vital part of religious practice, and maintaining the quality of singing became a major concern of the New England clergy. Two singing styles were practiced by different congregations: The "Old Way," a call and response technique in which a deacon sang or read each line, which was repeated by the congregation, and the "Regular Way," in which congregations read music from books. Psalms sung in the Old Way were unstandardized by nature, as they were dependent upon the skill of the deacon and were prone to variation and embellishment. By 1721, the state of congregational singing among those practicing the Old Way had degenerated into what Rev. Cotton Mather described as "an odd noise," and a movement began to root out the method and replace it with the Regular Way by promoting music literacy among the general populace (Mark 2008, 13).

One of the first to take action was Rev. John Tufts (1689–1750) of Newbury, Massachusetts, who published the first American music textbook in, *An Introduction to the Singing of Psalm Tunes* (1721). Tufts sought to simplify music reading, developing his own systems of both pitch and rhythmic notation, but it was his promotion of "singing schools" that laid the groundwork for teaching music on a mass scale and established him as the most significant figure in American music education of the next hundred years. These singing schools met in homes or classrooms one to five nights a week for anywhere from a few weeks to six months. They were most often taught by itinerant singing masters, who traveled from town to town and might also serve as peddlers, carpenters, tanners, masons, or wheelwrights during their time in a community.

As singing schools flourished in both the north and the south throughout the eighteenth into the early nineteenth centuries, cultural and economic changes were taking place in America's cities that would lead to the downfall of singing schools and their transformation into the prototype of today's public music education. The industrial revolution brought an influx of immigrants—both from Europe and from the American countryside—into the nation's cities after 1820. The buzzword of the early nineteenth century was "progress," and for the first time, many people were exposed to and had the economic means to partake in European culture. In comparison with the new music being heard in the cities, the traditional psalmody of the singing schools seemed archaic and provincial, and was reviled as "Yankee" music by contemporary critics and historians (Mark 2008, 26–27). The latest generation of music educators agreed, and began a movement in the 1830s, led by Lowell Mason (1792–1872) and Elam Ives, Jr. (1802–1864), to replace the traditional repertoire of psalm tunes with the music of less prominent European composers and European influenced pedagogical music composed specifically for use in teaching.

Teachers composing their own music was nothing new; many early American composers, such as William Billings, were singing masters who counted teaching pieces and texts among their works. The wholesale discarding of an extant repertoire and its replacement by newly composed works, however, represented a major change in the teaching of music. According to music historian Michael L. Mark, it also represented an economic opportunity for Mason and Ives, who stood to profit considerably by establishing a need for new music that only they could fill (Mark 2008, 53). Moreover, this music has been criticized in recent times for its poor quality, described by Mark as a "bland innocuous genre with no obvious redeeming characteristics," in which the immediate artistic experience of the student is sacrificed for the sake of gaining skill. He continues, "Children's interest in fine music was expected to come later, when they had learned to read and could participate in performances of European oratorios. . . . It is interesting to think what might have been accomplished . . . if a more musical genre of literature had been selected as the foundation for educational music" (Mark 2008, 53). (Note the similarities between this argument and the one Stephen Budiansky raises about contemporary educational music—see Chapter 9.)

Repertoire was not the only aspect of Lowell's reforms influenced by Europe, nor was it the most important. The reformers had a larger goal: to incorporate music into the Boston public schools. Universal education had existed in New England since 1642, but music education had been a private affair. To justify including music in the public school curriculum, reformers needed a convincing educational philosophy, which they found in the works of influential Swiss educator Johann Heinrich Pestalozzi (1746–1827) and his colleague and disciple Hans Georg Nägeli (1773–1836).

Pestalozzi believed that education could improve the economic and social conditions of the impoverished, and, like Plato, that it should aim to build citizenship by developing the student's moral, physical, and mental faculties. His reforms replaced the tradition of strict discipline and memorization with a concern for the understanding of individual children and a focus on relating education to life activities. Though Pestalozzi valued music, he did not teach it; it was Nägeli who first applied Pestalozzi's educational principles to music instruction. The American minister, geographer, and educational reformer William Channing Woodbridge (1794–1845) witnessed Nägeli's methods firsthand during a trip to Europe, and became convinced that his approach was better than that of the American singing masters. The principles behind this approach were as follows:

1. To teach sounds before signs—to make the child sing before he learns written notes or their names.
2. To lead the child to observe, by hearing and imitating the sounds, their resemblances and differences,

their agreeable and disagreeable effects, rather than explaining these things to him. By this principle, the child was to be an active, rather than passive, learner.

3. To teach but one thing at a time—rhythm, melody, expression are taught and practiced separately before the child is called to the difficult task of attending to all at once.
4. To make children practice each of these divisions, until they master it, before passing to the next.
5. To give the principles and theory after practice, and as an induction from it.
6. To analyze and practice the elements of articulate sound in order to apply to them to music.
7. To have the names of the notes correspond to those used in instrumental music (Mark 2008, 33).

It is interesting to note how today's sound–to–symbol philosophies still bear the strong imprint of these original Pestalozzian principles.

Charles Ives became the first American music teacher to apply Pestalozzi's principles in two important works, *American Elementary Singing Book* (1830), and *The Juvenile Lyre* (1831), which was written with Mason. The preface of *The Juvenile Lyre* was crafted as a weapon in the effort to include music in the Boston public schools. According to Mark, it formed a utilitarian manifesto of music education and provided justification for music instruction that would be used for nearly a century: the belief that music would aid the moral, intellectual, and physical development of children (Mark 2008, 40). It took nearly a decade for Mason, Ives, and Woodbridge to succeed, but in 1838, vocal music was adopted as a curricular subject, and Mason was appointed Superintendent of Music. In the same year music was incorporated into Cincinnati, Ohio's public school curriculum, and several other programs were established in the years before the Civil War.

As vocal music's importance was being recognized by its inclusion in school curricula, interest in instrumental music was growing in America's towns and cities. Military and militia bands were organized starting around 1800, and town bands began appearing across the country in the 1820s. Professional bands toured with minstrel troupes in the years before the Civil War, bringing music to communities that might not have heard it otherwise. Interest in orchestral music was especially strong in urban centers where symphony orchestras were established (beginning with the New York Philharmonic in 1842), European touring musicians performed, and European immigrant musicians and teachers had settled.

Two touring ensembles played key roles in the rise of instrumental music in mid-nineteenth century America: the Theodore Thomas Orchestra and Gilmore's Band. The Theodore Thomas Orchestra, led by German-born violinist Theodore Thomas, later conductor of the New York Philharmonic and founder of the Chicago Symphony, toured the country from 1862 to 1888, visiting both large and small communities and providing many Americans with their first experience of good orchestral playing.

As significant as the Thomas Orchestra was, it was Gilmore's Band, led by Irish immigrant Patrick S. Gilmore, that became a nationwide phenomenon, sparking an explosion in the number of bands throughout the country. As bands served a different social function from orchestras—providing popular entertainment rather than maintaining old world traditions—Gilmore entertained with an eye toward spectacle and helped create several icons of American civic life. In 1855 he held the first Promenade Concert in America, the forerunner of today's Boston Pops concerts on the Esplanade; he created Gilmore's Concert Garden in New York City, which later became the first Madison Square Garden; and he began the tradition of celebrating the new year in Times Square in 1888. He was also the music director for the both the July 4th centennial celebration in 1876 in Philadelphia and the dedication of the Statue of Liberty in 1886.

Gilmore did not restrict himself to high-profile national events. Perhaps his most important performances occurred on tours his band undertook every year from 1876 until his death in 1892. Their arrangements of works by Wagner, Liszt, Mendelssohn, Berlioz, and Verdi provided the first opportunity for many audience members to hear such works. The concerts also influenced the development of town bands, encouraging them to increase the number of woodwinds, as Gilmore had earlier done in emulating European bands, and to perform the same types of repertoire. After Gilmore's death, John Phillip Sousa took over his legacy, touring the world and bringing the Sousa Band's performances to new levels of accomplishment.

This golden era of the professional band reached its height at the beginning of the twentieth century, which coincided with the first public school instrumental music programs. It would be simplistic, however, to say that the immense popularity of the touring orchestras and bands led directly to the adoption of instrumental music into public school curricula. To understand the social and economic forces that made the inclusion of instrumental music possible, we must answer the question: If there were so many instrumental ensembles in the mid and late nineteenth century—one source estimates there were 10,000 adult and youth bands in 1889—where did these musicians learn their craft?[2]

Nineteenth-century instrumental music education was, like eighteenth-century vocal music education, largely a private matter. It was taught in homes and music academies, and unlike the traditional teaching of singing to groups of students, it mostly occurred in private lessons. Two early schools of instrumental music were significant for their development of group classes in addition to private instruction: the Howell brothers of Cotton Plant, Arkansas, and the Benjamin family of New York and Philadelphia.

James and Joseph Howell were active from 1849–1861 as teachers and instrument dealers, two businesses that would surely have reinforced each other. They both attended singing schools (which persisted in the south longer than in the north, due to the south's lack of public education), and their teaching methods, preserved in Joseph's 1859 *New Class Book*, show the influence of the old institution. Violin instruction was given in group classes, and musical selections followed the traditions of southern hymnody (Keene, 272).

The Benjamin family's influence on music education began in 1847 when Lewis A. Benjamin, Sr., organized a musical academy in New York City, offering classes in violin and private lessons for other instruments, including guitar, pianoforte, and accordion. His sons, Lewis A. Jr. and Frank, opened Benjamin Brothers Musical Academy in the 1880s, offering free violin classes in the hopes of selling instruments, music, and private instruction. They organized annual Benjamins' Children's Carnivals, massed performances that grew from an orchestra of 300 students in its first year to 2,000 children performing in orchestra, chorus, fiddling contests, and solos by 1889. A year earlier, Frank and his wife Ida organized free violin schools in Philadelphia, attracting more than 500 students. Their 1891 Carnival was attended by the Pennsylvania governor, the Philadelphia school superintendent, and many school principals. More than 2,500 students participated, and its success may have inspired the reintroduction of vocal music into the Philadelphia schools after 22 years of absence (Keene, 273–278).

While the Benjamins were developing free violin schools, another movement was underway to establish a European-style conservatory system in the United States. The Leipzig Conservatory, founded by Mendelssohn in 1843, was the most emulated by Americans. Many German musicians and teachers trained there before immigrating to the United States, and likewise, Americans had gone to Leipzig to study music and returned home eager to teach in the European style. Though others tried to establish conservatories in the United States around the same time, the music dealer and teacher Eben Tourjée's efforts were the first to achieve significant and lasting results. After two failed attempts at establishing conservatories in Massachusetts in the 1850s, he traveled to Europe to study the continental conservatories in person. Upon returning, he founded the Providence Conservatory of Music, and in 1867, the New England Conservatory of Music (Keene, 280). Like the Benjamins, Tourjée was a proponent of class instruction, but not because he hoped to trade the students up to more expensive private lessons. Class instruction was the norm at the Leipzig Conservatory, where small groups of students performed masterclass-style, and was used in American conservatories until instrumental music education became established in the public schools in the twentieth century.

This network of private and group instruction supported youth bands and orchestras, which were increasingly becoming affiliated with public schools, though still outside the curriculum. This escaped the attention of most public school music educators of the time, who were still focused on vocal music. Public school orchestras—and, less commonly, bands—began forming in the late 1890s, but actual instrumental instruction was largely left to conservatories, academies, and private teachers.

Meanwhile, the first large-scale, systematic implementation of class instrumental instruction in public schools was taking place not in the United States, but in Britain. In 1898, the Murdock Company, a London instrument dealer, began offering violin classes at the All Saint's School in Maidstone, providing the necessary instruments, music, and equipment. Classes occurred under the supervision of the school, and payments were accepted in weekly increments so that poorer students could participate. This arrangement benefited the Murdock Company greatly—in the first five years of the "Maidstone Movement", almost 500,000 violins were sold and the program expanded to 5,000 schools. Massed performances demonstrated the program's effectiveness, growing from 700 students in the 1st Annual Festival of the National Union of School Orchestras in 1905 to 6,800 at the 10th Annual Festival in 1914 (Keene, 281–282).

World War I ended the Maidstone Movement in England, but the idea was carried to America by Charles Farnsworth, Albert Mitchell, and Paul Stoeving, each of whom witnessed the program's results. In particular, Boston school Music Supervisor Mitchell traveled to England to study the Maidstone Movement. He later organized classes based on its techniques, which ran after school for three years before being incorporated into the school day. Mitchell claimed that Boston was the first city in America to have systematic violin class instruction in its public schools.

The significance of the Maidstone Movement was not its direct influence on American pedagogy, but rather its demonstration that it was possible to create a program of group instrumental instruction that would train students as an ensemble from the beginning of musical study. This was a new concept, one that freed the ensemble from reliance on outside instruction and allowed the teacher to establish a balanced instrumentation from the very start. John W. Wainwright was one of the first teachers to apply this method to band instruments, and his Oberlin, Ohio High School band toured extensively in 1914, performing in New York City, Philadelphia, and Washington D.C., as well as throughout northern Ohio. They became ambassadors through their high level of performance, demonstrating the effectiveness of teaching instruments during the school day and inspiring other schools to organize bands (Keene, 286–287).

This was a critical time for instrumental music education. Now that class instruction had been proven effective, school music supervisors were paying attention to instrumental music, and began searching for justification for including bands in the curriculum. The orchestra needed no artistic rationale, as it reflected a professional symphonic model, and the chorus had a long history dating to colonial times. The band, however, in the words of Keene, was "always closer to show business than to rarified artistic pursuits" (Keene, 288). Nevertheless, the growing demand for bands could not be ignored, and the ensemble's proponents turned to an old idea to prove its worth to the teaching profession: that performing in a band would develop democratic and egalitarian principles by promoting community thinking and community consciousness. W. Otto Miessner also argued that teaching all of music's branches—not just a rarified few—would democratize the art and allow students greater access to musical participation (Keene, 288–289).

World War I marked a major change in the status of school bands, as their numbers increased and they began supplanting school orchestras at functions like graduations, assemblies, meetings, and concerts. The war itself influenced the rise of bands in two ways: First, by stimulating the desire for the patriotic music that bands often played, and second, by providing training for bandmasters who became the next generation of teachers. Regimental bands were omnipresent during the war, and there were not enough well-trained band directors to lead them. General John Pershing, dismayed at the quality of American military bands, asked conductor Walter Damrosch to devise a plan to improve the bands in 1918. In response, Damrosch formed a bandmasters school, hiring some of France's top musicians as teachers. After the war these bandsmen returned to civilian life, many finding their niche in the schools (Keene, 192).

As public school bands were on the rise, the professional bands that had inspired them were declining. Society was evolving rapidly during the first two decades of the twentieth century, and professional bands could not keep up with changing tastes. Dances popular with the previous generation—the polka, schottische, waltz, and two-step—were replaced by the Charleston, jitterbug, and foxtrot, and dance bands began displacing concert bands as the favored form of musical entertainment (Mark 2008, 124–125).

The automobile also played a role in the professional band's demise. Many bands performed at "trolley parks," amusement parks so named because of their location at the end of a city's trolley line. These parks offered music, dancing, gambling, roller coasters, and food to millions of Americans looking for a weekend destination. With the arrival of the automobile and the increased mobility of everyday Americans, trolley parks no longer had a monopoly on the entertainment market. As their fortunes waned, so did those of the professional bands (Mark 2008, 125).

The musicians themselves were not the only ones affected by the decline of bands. With fewer professionals to count on as customers, instrument manufacturers' sales decreased, and their drive to expand the market for band instruments became a centralized effort to create a national movement in school instrumental music. Like the British instrument dealers who created the Maidstone Movement twenty years earlier, American instrument manufacturers helped create the phenomenon of band competitions, which provided a huge stimulus to the movement and helped cement the school band in American culture. It is a testament to the popularity of these contests that only three years after the first competition, sponsored by the Holton Band Instrument Company in 1921, the National Bureau for the Advancement of Music advocated for educators, not manufacturers, to control the contests. National contests were held until World War II, but their influence remains in today's state-level competitions.

Orchestras and choirs joined the contest movement in 1929, the same year that the National Research Council of Music Education published "High School Credit Courses in Music" in the *Music Supervisors Journal*.[3] The report describes curricular music courses and suggests guidelines for their implementation, indicating the diversity of public school music programs of the time, with courses in theory, appreciation, and history; choral music; and instrumental music, including orchestra, band, chamber music, and applied music.

The report's educational objectives also reflect a purpose broader than the singing and reading-oriented music programs of 25 years earlier, and included the following:

1. Developing an appreciation of good music through vocal and instrumental performance, listening to beautiful music, and studying literature, history, and form.
2. Developing technical power through rhythmic, aural, vocal, instrumental, and compositional training.
3. Developing "the spirit of cooperative service, thereby reënforcing [sic] spiritual values" through altruistic service projects and the unity of group experience (NRCME, 30–31).

The authors take special care to emphasize the interdependence of these objectives, writing, "The acquirement of technique should be motivated and directed by musical feeling and on the other hand genuine appreciation is dependent upon the acquirement of technical knowledge and power" (NRCME, 31).

This was a marked departure from post-Civil War educational philosophy, which emphasized strict pedagogy, technical knowledge, and preparation for future work over instruction for beauty or enjoyment's sake (Mark 2008, 54). The new emphasis reflected the influence of progressive education, a movement that began at the turn of the twentieth century, and whose goal was to educate the whole child through self-generated activity. Frances W. Parker, the father of progressive education, held that while music has important intellectual and disciplinary aspects, its true value lies in its ability to affect us emotionally, and advocated replacing "joyless drill" with "deeply moving musical experiences" (Mark 2008, 74–75).

Though progressive education never gained widespread acceptance, its ideas remained prevalent during the first half of the twentieth century. In 1945, Frank L. D'Andrea called upon instrumental music teachers to embrace progressive ideas in his essay, "Music Education Looks Back."[4] He encouraged educators to look beyond drill-based technical training, and ask:

> Am I reserving enjoyable musical experience through the instrument until some distant date? Am I making arduous technical training a dogmatic prerequisite to that future happy day? Or am I permitting the instrument to contribute to the total personal growth of the student here and now through pleasurable participation and through having easily perceived and attainable objectives? (D'Andrea, 30)

D'Andrea also notes fundamental educational changes being brought about by the "current world upheaval"—World War II—and declares that it is time to reconsider traditional ways of teaching that persist in "emphasizing the technical and reflecting a confined interpretation of the import and influence of the aesthetic in education" (D'Andrea, 34).

Neither the social upheaval that D'Andrea spoke of, nor the drive to bring greater emphasis on the aesthetic into music education, ended with the war. As the United States emerged as the world's leading military, industrial, and economic power, a transformation began that would turn it from an industrial society into a technological one. With this transformation, education's priority became producing the engineers and scientists whose skills would maintain America's superior position in the face of the growing Soviet threat (Mark 2008, 138). This new attitude—which devalued "non-essential" subjects—was a threat to music's position in the curriculum, and a movement began to develop a new philosophy of music education that would replace the utilitarian arguments that had prevailed since antiquity, and would instead be based upon the music itself: aesthetic education.

Aesthetic education was first articulated by Allen Britton in *Basic Concepts in Music Education*, the publication of MENC's 1954 Commission on Basic Concepts, the first attempt to establish guidelines for a profession-wide philosophy of music education (Mark 2008, 151). According to Mark, Britton's philosophy was "characterized by total emphasis on the aesthetic development of the child and rejection of extramusical values as part of the philosophical justification of music education."[5] Charles Leonhard, another early proponent of aesthetic education and the author (with Robert House) of the first textbook on the subject, 1959's *Foundations and Principles of Music Education*, explained this rejection as eliminating a potential weakness in the argument for music education:

> While the reliance on statements of the instrumental [utilitarian] values of music may well have convinced some reluctant administrator more fully to support the music program, those values cannot stand close scrutiny because they are not directly related to music and are not unique to music. In fact, many other areas of the curriculum are in a position to make a more powerful contribution to these values than is music.[6]

Leonhard also suggested that utilitarian philosophy contributed to low musical standards: "If one is teaching music for citizenship, health, or recreation, it matters little what kind of music one teaches or how well he teaches it" (Leonhard, 59).

If Britton and Leonhard laid the philosophical foundations for aesthetic education, it was Leonhard's student Bennett Reimer who turned it into, in the words of Mark, "an intellectual basis for the profession that still serves as the belief system for many music educators" (Mark 2008, 152). In his 1970 work, *A Philosophy of Music Education*, Reimer discussed the concept of "absolute expressionism," which holds that the arts are essential and unique in what they offer children, and that musical meaning exists entirely within a work itself, without reference to anything outside of it.[7]

Though Reimer's articulation of aesthetic education would become the prevailing philosophy for the next 25 years, concerns about its narrow focus were being raised as early as the late 1970s by Abraham Schwadron and Douglas Lemmon, who argued that it could not account for the wide range of musical practices in a multicultural society (McCarthy and Goble, 22). When the early 1980s brought a decline in arts education funding, music's curricular importance was questioned again, and some worried that the "purposelessness" of music inherent in the philosophy posed a danger to the music education profession (McCarthy and Goble, 22). This, combined with a greater acceptance and appreciation of cultural differences, sparked a renewed interest in philosophy among music educators that led to the development of alternative philosophies.

The most important of these was presented by David Elliott, who emphasized music as a practice rather than an object in his 1995 work, *Music Matters: A New Philosophy of Music Education*. His philosophy is known as praxial education, after the Greek praxis, which refers to action rooted in practice rather than in theory. The essence of Elliott's objections to aesthetic education is that its conception was too limited and that its assumptions about the nature of musical experience were mistaken. First, he objected to the focus on music as a fixed object independent of performance, which he argued led to a narrow concept of both music and music education, and to a curriculum that emphasized listening at the expense of performing. His second objection was on the grounds of musical perception. Elliott held that focusing solely on aesthetic perception restricted one's understanding of the full range of musical experiences, ignoring all non-musical aspects, imposing an archaic, Eurocentric ideology, and homogenizing the diversity of musical activities by attributing a single purpose, motivation, and mode of response to them all. Lastly, he objected to the very notion underlying aesthetic education: that the musical experience is primarily an aesthetic one.[8]

Elliott defined all musical activity as "musical practice," a four-dimensional concept in which (1) a doer (the "musicer") (2) undertakes an activity ("musicing"), (3) that accomplishes something ("music"), (4) within a cultural context, and which interlocks with listening, in which a "listener" listens to "listenables," within a context of listening (Koopman, 3–4).

The significance of Elliott's philosophy lies in the doing of it—when musicians engage in musical practice, they engage in what psychologist Mikhail Csikszentmihalyi called "flow experiences," characterized by the complete absorption and enjoyment that comes from deep concentration (Mark 2008, 153). As musicians tackle challenges they face in the course of "musicing," they enter the state of "flow," which can, according to McCarthy and Goble, "bring order to their own consciousness, engendering personal self-knowledge, and raised self-esteem" (Mark 2008, 23). It was on the basis of this transformation of consciousness that Elliott affirmed and defended the value of music.

The debate between aesthetic and praxial education continues today, as Riemer and Elliott publish new variations on their work. Though the two approaches approach educational philosophy in very different ways, both have positively influenced music education. In emphasizing Western art music as a distinctive art form, aesthetic education helped validate it as a subject with content that was unique and important on its own grounds, rather than one whose worth was based on utilitarian considerations. It provided a profession-wide conceptual basis for music education, allowing teachers, administrators, and parents to develop a vocabulary for discussing the importance of music in our educational system at a time when the prevailing philosophy was becoming less relevant to modern life. Praxial education, by challenging the concept of music as an object, brought new focus to the varied forms of musical activity, emphasized their significance in everyday life, and challenged teachers to consider and respond to the multitude of musical traditions that students bring with them into today's schools. The debate between the two highlights different aspects of music's essential character and demonstrates the current spirit of inquiry, causing McCarthy and Goble to surmise, "If controversy is an indication of vitality, the dialogue now taking place among these thinkers would seem to bode well for the future of music education" (25).

Activities/Assignments for Further Exploration

1. Of the major music education philosophies (e.g., ancient, utilitarian, aesthetic), which resonates most with you, and why? Which do you think is reflected in the way public schools currently teach instrumental music?

2. Write a personal philosophy of music education. Consider questions such as: What is the goal/purpose of music education? Should music be studied for its aesthetic, social, or utilitarian value? Why? What sorts of learning activities should be involved in its study? What role should schools have in this process? Should everyone study it?

Further Reading

Elliott, David James. *Music Matters: A New Philosophy of Music Education*. New York: Oxford University Press, 1995.

Hansen, Richard K. *The American Wind Band: A Cultural History*. Chicago, IL: GIA Publications, 2006.

Jorgensen, Estelle Ruth. *Transforming Music Education*. Bloomington, IN: Indiana University Press, 2003.

Mark, Michael L. *Music Education: Source Readings from Ancient Greece to Today*. New York: Routledge, 2002.

Mark, Michael L., and Charles L. Gary. 1992. *A History of American Music Education*. New York: Schirmer Books, 1992.

Reimer, Bennett. *Seeking the Significance of Music Education: Essays and Reflections*. Lanham, MD: Rowman & Littlefield Education, 2009.

Reimer, Bennett. *A Philosophy of Music Education: Advancing the Vision*. Upper Saddle River, NJ: Prentice Hall, 2003.

Chapter 6

Special Topics: Two Models of Instructional Design

On the one hand teaching is an art, informed by our experiences and our personality. On the other hand it is a science, and we can identify effective strategies for teaching nearly anything. Let us briefly examine two pillars of instructional design: teacher-centered instruction and *constructivism*. In the classroom these are often applied side by side, each borrowing strategies from the other. Sound–to–symbol philosophies reflect this dichotomy, too. Teacher-centered instruction is featured in the systematic way Kodály and Music Learning Theory teach their sequence of rhythmic and melodic patterns; Constructivism, in which students essentially create, or "construct" knowledge for themselves from a combination of what they already know and new interactions with their experiences, is reflected in the way Kodály, Suzuki, and Music Learning Theory:

(a) immerse learners in a culture of songs and performing
(b) model music learning on the way children naturally acquire language during social interactions.

Teacher-Centered Approaches—Direct Instruction and Expository Teaching

Cognitive theories dominate most classroom teaching. Its principles influence the basic procedure used to teach everything from how to tie shoelaces to the meaning of the Declaration of Independence; from changing oil in a car to forming a proper embouchure. One of the most well-known applications of teacher-centered instruction is Madeline Hunter's seven element plan, which is meant to be used as a flexible model for presenting new material. Though the elements are often referred to as "steps," Hunter points out that not every lesson will include every element, because complex learning occurs over time through a series of lessons.[1]

Hunter's Seven Elements

* *Anticipatory Set*—A "hook" to prepare students for the new lesson, often by relating it to previous lessons or something in the student's experience; may also include a review of previous lessons.
* *Statement of Objective or Purpose*—What the outcome of the lesson will be, or what students will be able to accomplish at the end.
* *Input*—The skills students will need and the plan for teaching the objectives.

- *Models and Demonstrate*—Demonstration of the process and final product.
- *Check for understanding*—Students demonstrate that they have the knowledge and skills necessary to achieve the learning outcome (e.g., students explain the process themselves and demonstrate it for the teacher or the class).
- *Guided practice*—Students practice individually under the teacher's guidance.
- *Independent practice*—Students practice individually in class or at home without the teacher's guidance (homework)

(adapted from Hunter, 3).

Hunter's method, which is often referred to as *direct instruction* or *expository teaching*, is especially conducive for teaching physical techniques and concepts that involve muscle memory. Though its general principles can be applied effectively to nearly every topic, it is not the most effective way to stimulate classroom discussion, reward student curiosity, or encourage self-exploration. And its pervasiveness does not guarantee its effectiveness. Some educational theorists argue that learning can only occur when students respond to something which can be observed and then reinforced. Expository instruction, they maintain, treats students passively: They listen, they read, they watch, but they do not respond and learn. The counterargument says students who listen to lectures, read explanations, etc., are mentally active,[2] and thus the key to making expository learning work is to engage students and enable them to rehearse and store new information, organize it, and elaborate upon it. Even so, some theorists prefer an approach to learning and teaching that is less programmed and didactic.

Constructivism and Discovery Learning

Discovery-learning is an inquiry-based method of learning famously advocated in the 1960s by the learning theorist Jerome Bruner. Discovery learning takes a constructivist approach. It posits that humans use their prior knowledge and experience to teach themselves, regardless of how they are taught, formulating questions and answering them via experimentation. Thus, they "discover" new knowledge for themselves.

In his seminal article, "The Act of Discovery," Bruner writes:

> Mastery of the fundamental ideas of a field involves not only the grasping of general principles, but also the development of an attitude toward learning and inquiry, toward guessing and hunches, toward the possibility of solving problems on one's own . . . For if we do nothing else we should somehow give to children (students) a respect for their own powers of thinking, for their power to generate good questions, to come up with interesting informed guesses . . . [to make] study more rational, more amenable to the use of mind in the large rather than memorizing.[3]

Discovery Learning in the Music Classroom

Though one might suspect discovery learning is more useful in science labs where students can formulate questions about chemical reactions or the physical properties of specific compounds, the music room is actually fertile with opportunities for its application, as these examples show.

1. *Learning Fingerings*—Beginning instrumentalists who have a basic (but still limited) knowledge of fingerings can be encouraged to figure out how to play familiar melodies on their own, without reading from sheet music or relying on the teacher's help. As an ear training exercise, of course, this is an

excellent activity for all musicians. For beginners, the ear training challenge encourages an exploration of the instrument itself to "discover" new fingerings. (Example: "I know I need to create a sound above G; now I must figure out what combination of fingerings can achieve that.")

    Note: Students will need a base level of knowledge to complete this—e.g., for woodwinds, this means knowing enough fingerings to understand the basic concept of the more holes closed, the lower the pitch; for brass, this means knowing the basic pattern of valve combinations.

2. *Learning melodic, rhythmic, and tonal patterns*—Sound–to–symbol philosophies suggest students learn unfamiliar patterns by relating them to familiar patterns. In other words, students encounter something new and then infer (or discover) its meaning. Again, a minimum level of knowledge is needed to make this work.

3. *Composition projects*—Discovery-learning and other inquiry-based procedures are part of the natural process composers use. Eleni Lapidaki, founder of C.A.L.M. (Community Action in Learning Music), writes:

> The abstract adventure of the conception of an initial musical or non-musical idea or image has the capacity to generate a whole range of possibilities, choices, and problems, which may, consequently, open up to the composer a new perspective for discovery. Indeed, for most composers this problem-solving and choice-making process is one of discovery. . . [4]

Given that many aspects of learning an instrument do not afford such opportunities, composition projects thus allow students to learn based on the choices they make about melody, rhythm, harmony, form, and texture.

4. *Ear training exercises*—Jazz musicians frequently transcribe well-known solos in an effort to improve their ear and answer the question: "What is that soloist doing in that phrase which makes it sound so cool?" The same exercises, albeit with simpler models, can be used for beginning instrumentalists. Give students recorded music examples (jazz, pop tunes, movie themes), and ask them to figure out the melody on their own instrument. Notating the melody is useful but not essential. Add another challenge by asking them to analyze specifics: "Why does the end of the melody sound like a surprise?"; "What is the character of this melody? How does the composer create this character?" Ask students to transpose the melody to another key (give them the starting note, or the pitch-center note).

Activities/Assignments for Further Exploration

1. Using direct instruction, teach the class how to do something. For example:

   - How to tie your shoes
   - How to juggle (or some other activity that only you know how to do)
   - How to hold a violin
   - How to play a scale on a keyboard instrument
   - How to play a szforzando piano
   - How to determine what key a piece is in
   - How to play a phrase expressively.

2. What might be the potential pitfalls of using discovery learning? Potential benefits?

3. As a class, brainstorm some ways to use discovery learning in the music classroom. Make a distinction between activities that are appropriate for small groups and large groups and those that are best for large groups.

4. Choose a topic and design two separate lesson plans—one that uses a teacher-centered approach and one that uses a constructivist approach. Now design a lesson plan that integrates elements from both.

Further Reading

Bruner, Jerome S. *The Process of Education*. Cambridge: Harvard University Press, 1977.

Gardner, Howard. *The Mind's New Science: A History of the Cognitive Revolution*. New York: Basic Books, 1987.

Hunter, Madeline. *Enhancing Teaching*. New York: Macmillan, 1994.

Larochelle, Marie, Nadine Bednarz, and James W. Garrison. *Constructivism and Education*. Cambridge: Cambridge University Press, 1998.

Marlowe, Bruce A., and Marilyn L. Page. *Creating and Sustaining the Constructivist Classroom*. Thousand Oaks, Calif: Corwin Press, 2005.

Piaget, Jean. *The Psychology of Intelligence*. Routledge Classics. London: Routledge, 2001.

Skinner, B. F. *About Behaviorism*. New York: Knopf, 1974.

Vygotskii, L. S., and Michael Cole. *Mind in Society: The Development of Higher Psychological Processes*. Cambridge: Harvard University Press, 1978.

Vygotskii, L. S., and Alex Kozulin. *Thought and Language*. Cambridge, Mass: MIT Press, 1986.

Winch, Christopher, and John Gingell. *Key Concepts in the Philosophy of Education*. London: Routledge, 2008.

Unit 2

Directing Bands and Orchestras

Chapter 7

Classroom Management

To Guide Your Reading

Why are the first days of school important in developing good classroom management?

How can positive reinforcement be used to strengthen good behavior?

What is the difference between rules and procedures?

What are natural, logical, and progressive consequences? How can they be used to enforce rules?

What types of behaviors do procedures cover?

How are procedures taught and enforced?

How do pacing, engagement, giving instructions, literature, and room set-up affect discipline?

The thought of standing before a room filled with students can be daunting for any new teacher, but music teachers face special challenges: class sizes are two to three times larger than most core classes; instead of neatly organized desks, rehearsal rooms are set up to allow more movement; and students hold a delicate, valuable musical instrument that is designed to make sound! It may be no surprise, then, that teachers cite problems in classroom management (CM) as a major factor when leaving the profession.[1]

Regrettably, unlike many topics music education students study—conducting technique, score study, budget skills, instrumental proficiencies, etc.—CM cannot be developed in a practice room. During lesson planning, our hypothetical class always behaves beautifully, and most attempts to simulate the actions of grade students in college classes are unreliable simulations of the real thing. Thus, the first time most teachers practice in front of "real students" is during pre-service field experience or student teaching. Even these experiences are a mirage, as student teachers often enjoy a "halo" effect from the cooperating teacher's authority.

Classroom management is not one-size-fits-all. The strategies we need to employ depend on our own strengths and weaknesses, the age of our students, and the dynamic of the specific students in our class. Every teacher brings unique personality traits, and every class reacts differently to each personality. Although teachers must adopt traits that support effective classroom management—confidence, patience, consistency, wisdom—they must not change their inherent nature. Our credibility suffers if students sense we put on an act to occasionally play the role of authoritarian or manager.

The key is to not rely solely on strength of personality, but also on five strategies:

1. Logical, clear, and fair rules that define expectations for student behavior.
2. Consequences based on whether students follow the rules and procedures.
3. Procedures which describe desired behavior and explain how specific activities should be completed.
4. Motivational techniques and strategies to reinforce and encourage appropriate behavior.
5. Consistent, insistent, and persistent behavior on the part of the teacher.

Setting the Tone/The Importance of the First Weeks of School

Classroom management is an ongoing process, but what we do in the first week, and especially the first day, is crucial. Students take an immediate inventory of a teacher's approach and determine for themselves where their limits lay. Where they see none, they impose their own. Use the first few days of class to set a tone, especially amidst the hectic energy of the beginning of the year. Be firm, patient, and in control. Explain your expectations to the class. What are the class rules? What are the consequences for breaking them? What procedures must the students be aware of? If we commit to teaching these things properly, consistently, and right from day one, it will pay huge dividends in the long run, even if it means we forfeit time early on.

Beware of the temptation to give short shrift to teaching discipline during the first week in order to proceed directly to music-making. The assumption that students will learn procedures once they get into the flow of the semester is wishful thinking. We may think, "Yes, they are rowdy today. But they're excited to see their friends after the summer. I'll emphasize the discipline stuff after things settle down. I'm not worried." You should worry, though. The students are likely to never settle down, and as we start feeling the pressures of performances and competitions we are less likely to spend time dealing with non-curriculum issues.

Accept that the first week of class will be an investment in the future efficiency of the classroom. Accept that we may have a rehearsal when most of the time is spent enforcing rules and rehearsing procedures, not the music. Accept the fact we will need to be uncompromising and unwavering to establish our own credibility. And accept the fact that even though students will learn rules, procedures, and expectations, we still need to be consistent, insistent, and persistent throughout the year.

Behaviorism and Operant Conditioning in the Music Classroom

At the most basic level, behaviorists argue that environmental stimuli control behavior. Behaviorist techniques involve the management of stimuli through *operant conditioning*, which includes positive reinforcement, negative reinforcement, and punishment. Technically speaking, reinforcement involves an increase in a behavior in response to the appearance or removal of a stimulus. For example, if Johnny arrives early to rehearsal in order to warmup, and we praise him for that, we attempt to positively reinforce his behavior. If we are successful, our praise increases the frequency of his early arrivals.

A common misconception occurs in cases when the student's behavior and our reaction are negative. If Johnny arrives late to rehearsal and we verbally scold him or assign detention, is this considered negative reinforcement? Actually, it is not, because our reaction is meant to decrease the frequency of Johnny's lateness. (In fact, it is considered punishment). In operant conditioning theory, negative reinforcement occurs when we *remove* a stimulus and behavior *increases* as a response. In this scenario, imagine if Johnny's section mates put constant peer pressure on him by giving dirty looks each time he walks in after the bell. If Johnny arrives on time and his section mates smile at him, the removal of the unpleasant stimulus (the peer pressure) may negatively reinforce (e.g., increase) the desired behavior (arriving to class on time).

Operant conditioning is a powerful CM tool because it preemptively strengthens good behavior before undesirable behavior begins through the use of positive reinforcement. Its application can be summarized as "catch students being good." Rather than wait for someone to do something wrong and then dole out punishment, we find examples of good behavior and immediately reinforce them, thus increasing their frequency. (Remember, negative reinforcement is the removal of a stimulus that consequently *increases* a behavior.)

Operant conditioning comes in many flavors, and most people practice it without even realizing it. Here are some examples:

Verbal praise—Assuming students like praise (and most do!), we positively reinforce behavior with verbal comments about rehearsal attitude, practice habits, and cooperation, etc.:

- "Bravo! Very hard working and productive rehearsal today everyone."
- "Thank you for working out that tricky part, Sarah."
- "Sam, I'm very proud of you for staying focused and not talking during the entire class."
- "Thanks for the great attention you gave our guest conductor at yesterday's rehearsal."

Concrete reinforcers—These are reinforcements that involve actual things (Ormrod, 389), e.g.:

- giving stickers for achieving certain performance levels
- awarding certificates and medals at end-of-the-year ceremonies.

Non-verbal signals—These are more subtle than verbal and concrete reinforcers, but they also indicate approval:

- Signal "thumbs up" to the trumpet section if they have all brought their mutes and use them properly during a piece.
- Nod approvingly to a student who follows the proper procedure for putting away her instrument.

Implied approval—Demonstrating approval and praise without explicitly stating the approval:

- Have an individual and/or section model the correct articulation for the entire ensemble.

Group contingencies—Some reinforcement strategies can be applied to the entire class by tethering reinforcement to achievement or appropriate behavior by the entire group (Ormrod, 389):

- Offer special privileges to the section that practices most during a week. (The privileges positively reinforce the home practice, and are only attained if the entire section contributes.)
- Allow the group to play its favorite piece at the end of a rehearsal only if the entire ensemble was on-time for class and followed proper procedures. (The opportunity to play a favorite piece at the end of class positively reinforces the on-time behavior at the beginning.)
- Allow the ensemble to vote between two works of similar style that you are considering for the following concert, if everyone participated in a group fundraiser.

It is important to realize that not all strategies are effective for all students. High schoolers will likely react negatively to receiving gold stickers and other tangible items they perceive as patronizing. Younger students may enjoy modeling their achievement for the entire class, but older students may feel embarrassed. Verbal praise needs to be used differently, too. Most people enjoy receiving it, but older students will see it as insincere if they perceive the encouragement and praise to be directed towards unchallenging or uninteresting goals.

Admittedly, operant conditioning is not an efficient strategy to shape some behaviors, such as when to enter and exit the classroom, when it is appropriate to talk, etc. In these cases we need to explicitly define good behavior. Instead of simply catching students being good, we proactively tell students what our expectations are through carefully chosen rules and procedures. It's almost as if we tell one of Pavlov's dogs, "I'd like you to salivate!" rather than finding a stimulus that provokes it. Even with rules and procedures, however, it is crucial to reinforce good behavior when it occurs, even if it is simply a case of someone following instructions and doing what they are "supposed" to do.

Wait for Silence before Continuing

An extremely effective group contingency is called "waiting for silence." This involves making the following promise to the ensemble: "So we can have the most focused, efficient, and musical rehearsals, I promise to wait for every student's attention before I continue to rehearse. I promise to wait for complete silence."

This technique makes a powerful yet reasonable assumption: The vast majority of students would rather play their instruments than sit waiting to play. Initially the procedure may seem like a colossal waste of time. "Why wait for absolute silence and attention when I can rehearse effectively with a few people talking quietly?" we might ask. Unfortunately, once the class learns that we are willing to work with distraction, more and more students will discover that they, too, can talk. The consequence? Perhaps an occasional lecture or scolding.

Instead, if we insist on waiting for silence and attention—every last drop of it—students learn that if they want to play (and most of them do), the only option is to offer quiet attention to the teacher. We must not yell; we must not holler "Quiet please!" or "SShhhh!" Rather, merely wait for silence and offer the occasional reminder that we will keep our promise: "Flutes—my apologies. I'd like to rehearse but we need to wait for complete silence from the trumpets." "Janice, I'm sorry but we need to wait for your attention before we continue." If we remain consistent the class learns that playing only results from agreeing to be attentive, and thus the former positively reinforces the latter.

What about those few students who value the attention they receive from disrupting the class over playing? Some evidence suggests peer pressure will encourage these students to behave appropriately, at which point peer "approval" positively reinforces them (Ormrod, 390).

Rules, Consequences, and Punishment in the Classroom

In the simplest terms classroom rules communicate expectations about behavior. If a rule is broken, consequences are the actions we take as a means to encouraging that they are met in the future. But before we write rules and procedures we need to define what good student behavior is. First, read all school-wide rules, regulations, procedures, and consequences. Then, ask yourself how you want your students to:

- enter and leave the classroom
- behave during class/rehearsal
- care for equipment and the classroom space
- work/cooperate with others
- demonstrate respect towards peers and faculty

Designing Classroom Rules

Consider the following:

1. Err on the side of simplicity—e.g., "Be in your seat with your instrument ready to play when the bell rings" rather than "When you arrive to rehearsal, sign the attendance sheet, remove any hats, tune your instrument, and then move to your seat using the most direct route. . .").
2. State in a positive way whenever possible–Avoid rules that sound like warnings (e.g., "Bring your pencil and music to every rehearsal" rather than "Do not arrive to rehearsal without a pencil and music.")
3. Prioritize—Choose between three and five rules (an excessive list confuses students and dilutes each rule's importance).
4. At the beginning of the school year, verbally explain the rationale for each rule and how following it benefits the entire group.
5. Write rules that cover subjects different from school-wide rules. In fact, many schools require teachers to post school-wide rules, anyway, which frees us to design rules to meet the music class' specific needs.
6. Rules are adjustable. We may later find that some are unnecessary and new ones are needed. For example, if you did not anticipate that students would consistently leave small pieces of trash on the floor after rehearsal, consider a new rule about cleaning up after oneself. If cell phone texting is not a problem, consider removing it as a rule to emphasize other issues.
7. Only write rules we are willing to police and enforce. Otherwise, the rules are meaningless.
8. Post the classroom rules and consequences in a location the students pass by often. Also include them in the ensemble handbook.
9. Heed all district and school rules. Our classroom policies must support those that exist outside our classroom.

Types of Rules

We can write rules to describe any behavior, though generally they fall under the following categories:

Rules that Describe General Behaviors

General rules cover many behaviors with one statement. However, they become toothless if they are *too* general, such as "Behave well," or "Be prepared."

EXAMPLES OF EFFECTIVE GENERAL RULES

Respect the property of others.
Respect the personal space of others.
Use polite and respectful speech and body language.
Treat others with respect.

Treat others the way you would like to be treated.
Attend to personal needs before coming to class.
Stay on task.
Always do your best.

Rules that Describe Specific Behaviors

Specific rules target behaviors about which we are particularly concerned. Use specific rules only for behaviors that are crucial for classroom management, or for misbehavior that becomes acute later in the year.

EXAMPLES OF EFFECTIVE SPECIFIC RULES

Listen quietly/carefully while others are speaking.
Raise your hand and wait to be called upon.
Play instruments only when instructed to do so.
Follow directions immediately.
Remain in your seat unless given permission to leave it.
Come to class prepared with music, a properly working instrument, and necessary supplies.
Attend to personal needs before coming to class.
Be in your seat ready to play at 9:06am.

"Do Not" Rules

Generally we recommend putting rules in the positive, but occasionally "Do not" rules are effective.

EXAMPLES OF "DO NOT" RULES

No gum, hats, or lewd clothing.
No horsing around.
Do not interfere with the rights of others to teach and learn.
Do not disrupt the rehearsal.
Do not play out of turn.

Five Sample Rules for Posting

1. Treat others with respect.
2. Come to class prepared with music, a properly working instrument, and supplies.
3. Be in your seat ready to play at 9:06 am.
4. Use polite and respectful speech and body language.
5. No food, drinks, or gum in class.

Progressive Generic Consequences

Many of us are reluctant to discipline a typically good student for a minor offense, especially when other students break the rules more often. Thus, a progressive system of generic consequences affords the teacher consistency and fairness. Progressive generic consequences become more severe with each successive transgression. For example:

Progressive Consequences (in Order of Increasing Severity)

- Visual warning
- Verbal warnings
- Daily grade is reduced/demerits
- Loss of privileges (e.g., last to leave classroom after dismissal)
- Detention
- Phone call
- Student/Parent conference
- School referral

Visual warnings are usually our first line of attack, though they are not usually posted. Most teachers post four or five consequences:

Examples

First time a rule is broken: Verbal warning
Second time: Grade for the day is reduced
Third time: Phone call made to parents
Fourth time: School referral and phone call to parents

Natural and Logical Consequences

Some research suggests that consequences are most effective when they are consistent, not progressive. But the noted educational psychologist Rudolf Dreikurs argues that the generic nature of both progressive and consistent consequences will be resented by students as punishments forced upon them. Instead, Dreikurs suggests logical consequences, which flow directly from the misbehavior. Logical consequences operate from the humanistic, democratic perspective that students choose their own actions and must learn to accept the results of their behavior. Logical consequences, which are imposed by people, are an outgrowth of natural consequences, which occur on their own. Dreikurs writes, "When an adult forgets to take an umbrella to go shopping on a day that the weather forecaster predicted rain, and the adult consequently gets very wet, this is an example of 'natural consequences.'"[2] After all, most real-life punishments are "natural," and they are often powerful behavioral modifiers. For instance:

- Speed repeatedly or drive drunk ⇨ get into an accident
- Miss an application deadline ⇨ application not considered; end up unemployed or with an undesirable job

- Act meanly/poorly/thoughtlessly towards friends ⇨ lose the confidence, support, and companionship of those friends
- Treat personal belongings poorly ⇨ lose the benefit of using those belongings

Natural consequences also exist in the music classroom:

- Student does not practice ⇨ he sounds bad during rehearsals; he is embarrassed in front of his peers; the entire ensemble sounds bad
- Student does not maintain good reeds ⇨ she squeaks a lot during rehearsal
- Percussionists do not maintain instruments ⇨ instruments break and players are forced to participate on inferior equipment, or no equipment at all
- Bow is left too tight ⇨ the stick can warp and hair can break
- Pegs are turned too fast or too far ⇨ strings will break

Natural consequences reinforce two key concepts of living: (1) A poor decision has an outcome that is directly related to that decision; and (2) An individual has a choice over the decisions he makes. In *The Confident Child*, Terri Apter explains that it is important a child understand that behavior has consequences:

> If a child sees that she is making amends for poor behavior, then she sees herself as behaving responsibly, rather than simply being punished. This can take the humiliation out of "punishment," and bring it under a child's own control. If something has been damaged by her, then that thing has to be replaced or mended. If someone's feelings have been hurt, or if someone has been insulted, then she must make amends in some way. If she is disrupting a class . . . then she must find a solution to her problematic behavior so that it will cease and not be repeated.[3]

Natural consequences can make a difference, but they do not always change the initiating behavior. People usually speed soon after receiving a ticket; some convicted criminals become repeat offenders after serving time; many students do not practice even after a "train-wreck" of a performance; students who vandalize find other things to damage.

But "manmade" logical consequences can follow the same logic. In assigning logical consequences, the goal is to guide students to choose appropriate behaviors. For example, if a student litters in the instrument storage room, instead of a demerit or detention, the logical consequence is to have the student clean the instrument storage room. Unlike direct commands, logical consequences give students a choice, albeit a limited one. To highlight that the future is in the student's hands they should be expressed without anger. Here are some examples:

"If you damage the percussion equipment (or forget to put it away), you will lose the privilege of playing that instrument and your part will be reassigned."
"If you bring food into the rehearsal room you will be asked to clean the room of trash and wrappers/asked to serve as monitor at the beginning of rehearsals to prevent others from making the same mistake."
"If you miss the sectional rehearsal you will need to schedule a make-up session."

Admittedly, not every situation has an appropriate or feasible logical consequence. And we should avoid using them when students misbehave in an attempt to engage us in a power struggle. But unlike predetermined, arbitrary punishments, logical consequences teach valuable lessons about real life and still hold students accountable for their actions.

Using Band/Orchestra Handbook and Acknowledgment Forms

In addition to on-the-job training about rules and procedures, we should provide students with a written copy of the most important things we ask of them. This list can be posted at the front of the room, but should also be part of the band/orchestra handbook. Require students to share this information with their parents and acknowledge their understanding by signing a statement at the back of the handbook. (e.g., "I have read the band/orchestra handbook, and I understand the obligations, privileges, and expectations of being in the Acme High School Orchestra.") Regardless of whether this is a legally enforceable document it at least gives us some leverage if a student becomes disruptive, and it provides legitimacy with our administration should we need their support.

Procedures—Moving Beyond the Right and Wrong of Rules

The bell rings and some students walk in late. Others stand around and talk to their friends instead of getting their instruments and music ready. The room is filled with noise. When it is time to start, the teacher raises his voice to get the attention of the class, and yet it takes 30 seconds for the chatter to settle down. Even still, some students converse with their friends.

Classroom situations like this yearn for a collection of procedures that describe how students should behave at the beginning of class. Classroom procedures are routines that make classes run smoothly. Unlike rules, which clarify *what* must or must not be done, procedures describe specifically *how* we expect classroom actions to be completed.

Procedures are part of everyday life. Without them regular activities would be chaotic.

1. Purchasing popcorn at the movie theater—The procedure is to stand in line and wait your turn. You cannot jump ahead. Line jumpers are met with glaring stares and public admonishments by those on the line.
2. Negotiating a four-way stop intersection—The procedure is to give the right-of-way to the person who arrives first. In the case of a tie we allow the person to our right to proceed. Ignoring this procedure is a recipe for a fender-bender.
3. Speaking during class—Most students learn at an early age that the proper procedure for talking in class is to raise one's hand and wait for the teacher to recognize it. Otherwise, class participation becomes a shouting match.

Designing Classroom Procedures

Procedures can cover nearly every aspect of running a class, but they need to balance general and specific expectations. If they are too general students will fill in the blanks with their own procedures and behaviors. If they are too specific we choke off the possibility for reasonable variation and the unexpected.

Music class procedures fall into three categories:

1. Pre- and post-rehearsal
2. Rehearsal etiquette
3. Administrative.

As ensemble directors we need to decide how we want every aspect of our class to run and then establish procedures that govern student behavior from the moment they walk into the classroom until the moment they leave. Design procedures by role-playing: Pretend you are a student and think about you can potentially do, and why. For any area that you discover too many options, consider writing a procedure. It is also useful to consider each procedure as an answer to a specific question: For example:

What do we want students to do when . . . ?
What should students do if . . . happens?

Generally speaking, procedures for middle school students mostly cover the same range of activities as those for high school students. The prime difference between the two levels is how the procedures are taught. The younger the student, the more important it is to have organized explanations, reviews, and rehearsals of the procedure. In some cases, especially with older students for procedures we expect them to already know, a streamlined explanation may suffice.

Pre- and Post-Rehearsal Procedures

These procedures explain what students need to do before and after the rehearsal.
  Students should know the answers to questions such as:

- What am I expected to do prior to the first downbeat?
- What am I expected to do during the tuning process?
- As a percussionist, how should I organize my equipment at the end of rehearsal?

Below are sample procedures to consider:

Entering the Room

- Enter the rehearsal room by the time the late bell rings.
- Check for any handouts on the table in the front of the room.
- Unpack your instrument and leave the case in the designated area.
- Organize your music into the rehearsal order that is written on the chalkboard.
- Take out your pencil and put it on your stand.
- Sit with your instrument in rest position until the director begins the warmups.
- Be completely ready to play three minutes after the late bell.

Tuning

- Principal tuba player sustains B♭ concert.
- Everyone hums concert B♭.
- While everyone else hums, all principals play and sustain concert B♭.
- Entire ensemble joins on the concert B♭.

End-of-Class Dismissal

- Listen for any final instructions.
- Check the board for assignments.
- Leave your seat when instructed to do so.
- Remove all music and papers from your music stand.
- Woodwind players: Swab out your instrument.
- String players: Wipe off excess rosin from instrument and strings; loosen bow hair.
- Percussionists: Return instruments to proper place in rehearsal room.
- Woodwinds, Brass, and Upper Strings: Return instruments in cases to storage lockers.
- Cello and bass players: Carefully place instrument on storage racks.
- For students with a locker in the instrument storage room, return to the rehearsal room after putting the instrument away.
- Remain in the rehearsal room until the passing bell rings.

Note: If there is no rack for cellos and basses, a buddy system for re-packing these instruments can be very helpful to ensure their safety. These instruments are deceptively large and quite fragile, and students need to be taught proper storage habits from the onset.

Percussion Section's End-of-Class Dismissal (Assignments)

Devin: Cover the xylophone and orchestra bells.
Jack: Turn off snare(s) and return all mallets to Wind Ensemble stick bag and percussion cabinet.
Jeremy: Put all auxiliary equipment away and return to proper area on stage.
Heather: Make sure all music is accounted for and not left on stands after rehearsal.
Ashley: Release tension on timpani pedals and cover all heads.
Ryan: Cover absentee assignments, including covering parts.

All jobs will rotate at the end of each quarter.

Rehearsal Etiquette Procedures

These procedures address every aspect of how a rehearsal is managed. Present these procedures as elements of good "Rehearsal Etiquette"—the music classroom's equivalent of table manners. When proper etiquette is not followed, the rehearsal of the procedure first involves a reminder: "Class, remember, the proper etiquette for switching to the next piece is. . ."

Our students should know the answers to questions such as:

- What is everyone expected to do when the conductor first steps on the podium at the beginning of the rehearsal or after a break?
- What is everyone responsible for doing when the conductor gives instructions to add to or change the music?
- What is everyone expected to do after the conductor cuts the ensemble off to give instructions?
- What should every member do when the conductor's baton comes up to the ready position?
- What is the responsibility of each player during an extended multi-measure rest during a rehearsal?
- What is each player expected to do when the conductor is not rehearsing their section?
- How should students react if a player beautifully performs a solo written in the ensemble literature?
- What should students do if they arrive late/tardy for class?

The following are sample rehearsal procedures:

Tardy Students

- Sign-in at the clipboard by the door.
- Pin the tardy pass to the wall above the clipboard.
- Proceed quietly to your seat without disrupting the class.

Coming to Playing Position

- When the conductor raises the baton, stop all conversations and bring your instrument to playing position.

Stopping After a Cut-off

- In order to keep the rehearsal running efficiently and effectively, watch the conductor for cut-offs.
- If the conductor keeps the baton up after the cut-off, keep all instruments in the playing position and listen attentively.
- If the conductor puts the baton down, put all instruments at "rest position" and listen attentively.

Administrative Procedures

Administrative procedures tell students how to do non-musical activities. Our students should know the answers to questions such as:

- How does one request a bathroom pass?
- When and how does one obtain a new reed?
- What happens if I break a string during rehearsal?
- When is it appropriate to rosin my bow?
- What should I do if my instrument goes out of tune?
- To where do we return concert folders after a rehearsal or performance?
- How does one turn in paperwork (e.g., written assignments or signed permission slips)?
- How does one sign-up for activities, such as solo/ensemble competition and field trips?

The following are sample rehearsal procedures to consider:

Turning in Paperwork (e.g., written assignments or signed permission slips)

- All paperwork is to be submitted prior to warmups via the "Inbox" located at the front of the classroom.

Obtaining a New Reed

- In the rare instance when a student may have run out of their supply, purchase one from the band director outside of class time.

Maintaining and Enforcing Procedures

When students properly follow procedures, use positive reinforcement to strengthen their good behavior. But if students fail to properly follow procedures we must continually enforce them using rehearsal, repetition, and practice. Note how this process differs from that for rules, which relies more on punishment and other negative consequences. (However, if a procedure becomes a chronic problem for the class, it may be worth converting it into a rule.)

Phase 1 (first or second occurrence): Remind
"What is the procedure for . . . ?"

Phase 2 (third or fourth occurrence): Explain, Review, and Practice
"Remember, we have this procedure because . . . "
"Let's review the steps together."
"Now show me . . . "

Phase 3: Drill
"Let's practice this procedure a few times so we're confident we remember it."

Phase 4 (sixth offense): Meet Separately
"John, we need to meet after school to practice this procedure together."

Phase 5 (seventh and beyond): Apply Logical Consequences
"Jennifer, you can either follow the procedure for putting your instrument away after rehearsal or you will not be allowed to participate the next time."
"Frank, because you have not properly put your instrument away you will need to stay after school to help me organize the equipment in the band room."
"Cindy, because you mistreated the timpani you will lose the privilege to play it next week. You'll have an opportunity to show me that you can be more responsible the week after."

Addressing Students about Discipline Issues

How we address students is nearly as important as the rules, procedures, and policies themselves. Use the wrong approach and we reinforce the behavior we are trying to extinguish. If our consequence involves an extended personal conversation with a student, meet with them privately. For some, public admonishments embarrass; for others, it improves the aggressor's status with his peers. In either case, few people like being scolded in front of others. Whenever we speak to students, Beverley H. Johns and Valerie G. Carr[4] suggest we avoid the following tactics:

1. Raising one's voice and becoming agitated—If we cannot stay calm, we cue students to act similarly.

2. Ridiculing a student—It creates insecurity, puts students on the defensive, and does nothing to modify the behavior.

   Example: "It was incredibly stupid to leave the bassoon there on the floor."

3. Forcing a student to confess and admit lies—It gives the student a chance to deny wrongdoing, and frequently begins a more heated argument.

   Example: "John, admit to me now that you were cheating on the theory exam. I know you did it."

4. Asking students why they act out—Unless this is done using a non-confrontational method meant to root out the student's base motivation, asking students rarely improves the behavior, and it risks eliciting a comically obvious response.

   Example: "I took the reeds without asking because I needed them!"

5. Making disapproving comments—It calls attention to the negative behavior, and research has shown this actually exacerbates the problem (Johns & Carr, 20).

   Example: "Melanie, I'm very disappointed that you forgot your instrument at home. It's extremely irresponsible."

6. Comparing a student's misbehavior with other children's good or bad behavior—Both damage self-esteem, and the latter creates a self-fulfilling prophecy: If Dave is told he is as bad as John, he has nothing to lose by acting that way.

   Example: "Dave, your attitude is as poor as John's. Is that really how you want to behave?"

7. Yelling and trying to win verbal battles. In rare cases yelling may shock a timid student into compliance, but more often it puts the student on the defensive and intensifies the argument.

8. Making unrealistic threats. Teachers rarely follow through on threats made in the heat of the moment, and students quickly learn to ignore them.

   Example: "Sarah, I'm not going to let you march for the entire season."

Behavior Specific Dialogue

For most behaviors, we recommend "behavior specific dialogue." This involves the use of an "I" request, followed by a five-second pause (Johns and Carr, 65–67). Note the difference between behavior dialogue, which stresses "I," and rehearsal dialogue, which uses "we":

1. Teacher gives the "I" request: "I need you to put your instrument away in the storage room."
2. Wait five seconds.
3. If the student complies, reinforce their behavior: "Good, John, thank you. . ."
4. If the student does not comply, repeat the "I request" and wait another five seconds.
5. If the student now complies, reinforce as in point 3.
6. If the student does not comply, apply the appropriate consequence.

Put Your Money Where Your Mouth Is

Rules, consequences, and procedures relieve us from constantly acting as classroom judge. If a student breaks a rule, we apply a consequence, not because we are tyrannical, but because this is the process explained clearly and fairly at the beginning of the school year. If a student does not follow a procedure, we rehearse it. We do not yell, and we do not strike out in frustration. We simply do it again until the procedure is learned. Raising our voice only raises the level of tension in the classroom.

Yet it is important to remember that rules, consequences, and procedures must be enforced and rehearsed immediately, consistently, and relentlessly. If we play favorites we create resentment. Further, behavior that is only occasionally reinforced is the most difficult to eliminate.[5] As Clifford Madsen and Charles Madsen point out, one only has to look at casinos to see an example of how an occasional reinforcement (such as the jackpot payout) sometimes strengthens the gambler's habit to the point of addiction (Madsen and Madsen, 74).

Consider how few people follow posted speed limits. Many people drive at least 5–10 mph over the limit simply because they know the police lack the manpower to monitor every road. But drivers typically slow down when they pass an officer on the side of the road giving someone else a ticket. We should expect students to behave identically. As with speed limits, if we relax enforcement and allow violations to slide, students will take advantage of our indifference.

The Importance of Knowing Our Students

As much as we would like to believe our class is the center of each student's day, the reality is that music is only one of a student's many obligations and interests. Increasingly, students are pushing themselves to take more advanced classes and participate in more after-school activities. Thirty years ago it may have been easy to pigeon-hole students based on their interests (e.g., "He's a football player. She's in the chess club. He's in the band.") Today, these same children are "Renaissance students," with a variety of interests they pursue passionately.

If we appreciate and respect students' lives outside the rehearsal hall we will be better equipped to understand their behavior and motivate them to succeed inside of it. The direct way to achieve this is simply to talk to them–before class, after class, when we see them in the lunchroom, on the bus to a competition, and before school and after school. Even brief encounters are enough to show we care about them as people, and not simply as clarinetists and trombonists. Another strategy: At the beginning of the school year, in addition to their schedule, contact information and musical vitals, ask students to write down their main school interests, favorite subjects, and activities. It's a bit of a cheat sheet, but it's worth reading every so often as a reminder of who our students are.

Over time we may find that certain students confide in us about a variety of personal situations (e.g., struggles in other classes, conflicts with peers, troubles at home, break-ups with their boyfriend or girlfriend, etc.). As their teacher, while we should be steadfast in our support and concern, we must take care not to cross the line from supportive teacher to trusted friend. Even if we feel comfortable advising we must remember that psychology and therapy are beyond our area of specialty. If a student starts spending too much time confiding serious personal issues, refer him to the appropriate party—guidance counselor, school psychologist, nurse, administrator, etc.

In fact, we should be proactive and share our concerns with these colleagues in case the student neglects to do so. Sometimes it is appropriate to meet with school nurses, guidance counselors and/or psychologists to identify issues about which we should be aware. Most likely, the district will offer orientation sessions regarding proper protocol for such situations. If questions remain be sure to ask a colleague, union representative, or administrator.

Other Factors that Affect Classroom Management

Pacing

Lesson pacing directly affects student behavior. Students can stay on task for any individual activity for only a limited amount of time before they become disinterested, and thus more likely to disengage and disrupt. Generally, the older the student, the longer he can focus. Kindergarten and early elementary classroom teachers are acutely aware of these tendencies. They know a single period's lesson plan must contain up to ten different activities per hour.

Even experienced learners have limited focus. A.H. Johnstone and F. Percival observed that adult learners in a lecture environment experienced a lapse in attention after 10–18 minutes, and as the lecture progressed, attention spans fell to as low as 3–4 minutes.[6] Put simply, students who are distracted are less likely to learn, and much more likely to become disruptive.

One solution is to change activities before attention spans wane, thus "resetting" the clock.[7] Fortunately, ensemble rehearsals are particularly conducive to this. We must be sensitive to students' limits, build variety into our rehearsal plan, and be prepared to move to another activity if we sense their attention fading. Lingering on any objective too long sows the seeds of discipline problems.

Much has been speculated about how television, video games, modern movie editing techniques, and popular culture have decreased today's attention spans compared to those of 50 years ago. Certainly we are not suggesting that we completely submit to these trends, turning our rehearsals into a rush of frenetic activity with little substance. Rather, we suggest exploring, pushing, and exercising the limits of student productivity while recognizing that fatigue and distraction are normal, predictable reactions. This will occasionally mean leaving an activity even if it is not completed. Simply say, "We need to spend more time on this, but let's move on." Or, "This section needs more work, but let's revisit it tomorrow after some home-practicing."

The Lessons of Muzak

In spite of the jokes made about Muzak for its saccharine renditions of popular and classical standards, the original goal of so-called "elevator music" was to maximize office-worker productivity. Rather than simply serving as innocuous background sound, the music piped into offices was based on careful research. Called "Stimulus Progression," the concept was to "combat monotony and offset boredom at precisely those times in a work day when people are most subject to these onslaughts."[8] Organized in 15-minute segments, the music increases in intensity to counteract the natural lag in worker energy and productivity over time. This was found to be more effective than playing random selections without regard to how people feel (Lanza, 49).

Though students in our ensemble are not "workers," they are as susceptible to fatigue as everybody else. "Stimulus progression" and "restarting" teach that we can compensate for fatigue and distraction by increasing the speed, pace, and intensity of our rehearsal. For example:

- Move to a new piece, or a completely different section of piece.
- Use the "Quick Drill" rehearsal (see Chapter 12).
- Involve the full group, especially if a large chunk of time has been spent with individual sections.
- Do a run-through.
- Vary the rehearsal technique (musical versus technical issues).

Engagement

Consider a rehearsal where students listen to us talk more than they play. Once they become passive the learning process stagnates and the opportunities to create classroom disruption multiply. If students are not participating in the class, what else is there to do? Unfortunately, simply asking students who are not playing to "pay attention" is insufficient. Instead, there is a variety of techniques we can use in rehearsal to engage students even if we are not directly rehearsing their parts. For example:

- Ask students to hum and finger their own parts while another group is playing.
- Ask students to clap their own parts or tap the rhythm on their knees.
- While other groups are being rehearsed, have strings "shadow bow" their parts by bowing wood-side down on the inside of their elbows.
- Have students subdivide the beat with clapping or using their mouth on a "tss" sound.
- Ask questions that require students to actively listen to the section that is being rehearsed.

Giving Instructions

Even if we have well-established rules and procedures we still need to proactively manage the classroom when transitioning between activities or giving instructions. Often we merely need to remind them of an established procedure; other times we must improvise instructions.

Since students often interpret new activities as a cue to talk we should give instructions clearly and specifically. For instance, if the group is on a trip in an unfamiliar environment, instructing: "Class, please put your instruments away and return to your seats" is potentially inadequate. As with pre-rehearsed procedures, we need to create structure and set limits.

Design instructions so they answer the following questions:

- *Who are the instructions for?* As with the basic WHO–WHERE–WHAT rehearsal technique (see Chapter 12), addressing specific students focuses their attention. Also, consider the group's prior history. If, for example, they habitually talk inappropriately, provide stricter guidelines during transition activities.
- *What should the target group of students do?* Give specific information. Familiar tasks require very little guidance, but unfamiliar ones need more detail, such as when to start the task, what to do, how to do it, how to behave while performing it, and when to complete it.
- *What are the benefits of following these instructions?* This legitimizes the activity beyond "Because I SAID so."
- *In what order should the students complete the activity?* This creates efficiency and avoids bottlenecks, particularly with large groups of students.
- *How long will the activity last?* Providing a deadline motivates students to complete the task without undue distraction.
- *When are the students supposed to start and end the transition time?* Give students an idea of what to expect.

Sample Script for Giving New Instructions

Scenario:

The day after the high school band concert; the students listen to and critique a recording of their performance, after which they need to turn in their music.

Instructions

"When I say to, first everyone will give their music to their section leader. Next the section leader will organize each piece by first, second, and third parts."
"Then the section leader will alphabetize the pieces by title. Once your section's music is organized, the section leaders will line up in reverse score order; please raise your hand to tell me that you are ready for turning in your sections folder. Place each piece onto the stands located in the front of the room. At 10:25 I will raise my hand to tell you we are going to start. At 10:45 everything needs to be finished."
"During this activity everyone must stay in their seats without talking (expectation of behavior)."

Literature Selection

One characteristic that defines the best composers for school ensembles is their ability to write interesting parts for all instruments, not just the lead players. But inevitably there are inequalities. Imagine the bass drum player who has only quarter notes for an entire piece. After the ensemble has rehearsed it for two months, has that player really had the same musical education as the flute players? Would we be surprised if that percussionist is more often bored and disruptive than the flutist sitting in the front row? In choosing appropriate, quality literature, we should consider more than just the overall sound of the piece. We should ask whether we have chosen a work that challenges our low reeds, tubas, and percussionists. How can we give them more to do than just "ooom-pahs" and suspended cymbal rolls?

Sample Strategies for Turning Uninteresting Parts into Interesting Ones

- Create variety for the percussionists. Rotate parts from rehearsal to rehearsal. This also ensures every student is exposed to every instrument.
- Manufacture interesting melodic percussion parts by giving the oboe part to the mallet player.
- Transpose the first trumpet part for the low brass and low woodwinds to play during warmups and, on occasion, rehearsals of the melody.
- Even if just for rehearsal, have an entire section of instruments play the first part, especially if certain passages need reinforcement.
- Advanced string players can take parts up an octave as an exercise in ear training and as a challenge for their upper register techniques.

Room Set-up and Proximity

Design the room set-up so you can move easily throughout the room. One reason students in the back of the ensemble often misbehave is because the teacher is so far away! Make a point to vary where you stand during the rehearsal. Do this while working with an individual section, or even just to monitor everyone's progress when the full group is playing. Sometimes our mere proximity is enough to prevent discipline problems.

When students enter the rehearsal room, all chairs, stands and percussion equipment must be in their proper place, and music and other instructional materials should be organized. First impressions of the classroom environment send a strong message to students. Visual cacophony begets behavioral cacophony: If the room looks disorganized it signals to students that *we* are disorganized. If extra music is stacked haphazardly, it encourages students to treat their music poorly. If chairs and stands are carelessly placed it encourages students to enter the room without consideration for their peers and our equipment.

Other Considerations

- When students are absent, remove their chairs and stands for that particular rehearsal. This creates the feeling of a full, unified ensemble and helps prevent morale problems caused by empty chairs and incomplete sections (Let the students in the adjacent chairs know of the adjustment as they get to their row).
- Place the clock behind the percussion section (i.e., facing the conductor). Remember "a watched pot never boils!"
- Eliminate physical distractions. For example: poles; large instruments blocking main walking or teaching areas; glaring sunlight; poor lighting; uncomfortable temperatures; electrical buzzing sounds or noises from the ventilation system; poor air quality or distraction odors; chairs in poor condition; loose stand heads or legs.
- When setting up stands, raise and angle the top to the desired height for good eye contact with the conductor. This gives the room an organized, professional look and encourages good eye contact during rehearsal. (However, beware of letting students place their stands too high so that we cannot easily see their face.)

Involving Parents in Classroom Management

When a student consistently disregards procedures, the classroom's consequences policy may indicate it is time to contact a parent. Before doing so, think carefully about what your goal is, and be sure to call at a time when you are not apt to be interrupted. Find at least one positive quality about the student, and share that first during the conversation. For instance, begin by saying how much you have appreciated their child's membership in the program and note any specific contributions. Then, segue into your concern and desire to make the parent aware of the problem before it escalates. Briefly discuss what steps you have already taken (e.g., making the student aware of the relevant policies, speaking with the student, etc.). Most of the time parents will volunteer to intervene, but if not—and depending on the severity of the problem—it might be wise to suggest they speak to their child. Or, we can simply keep them informed.

Be prepared for a variety of reactions: some parents are surprised, some indignant, some skeptical, and some concerned and accepting. Listen patiently to their reaction without interrupting, and never become argumentative. If the parents do not understand, believe, or accept the problem, walk them through the situation again: the discipline policy, how the child has struggled to meet it, why this matters, and the steps you have taken to affect a change.

Avoid comparing one student to another (e.g., "I wish Johnny would behave more like his stand partner Billy"; "If Johnny could just follow the example set by his sister"). Keep comments focused on how Johnny's behavior affects his own classroom achievement and disrupts the learning environment of others. At the end of the call, thank the parent for their time and concern, and keep a log of the conversation for future reference.

Activities/Assignments for Further Exploration

1. How might some of the following factors affect one's approach to classroom management? What other factors might be important?

   - The teacher's inherent personality
   - The teacher's experience
   - Age level of the class
   - Size of the class

2. Discuss ideas for each type of positive reinforcement.

3. Write five rules for the ensemble you play in now.

4. How might we be able to tell if the rules we choose for our class are appropriate?

5. Some teachers advocate involving students in the creation of class rules, thus giving the class ownership and a greater sense of accountability. What do you think are the pros and cons of this approach?

6. What procedures might be more important to teach younger students? Older students?

7. Each of the classroom management approaches in this chapter relies on certain assumptions about human psychology. Discuss these. Do you see problems in each? Can several of them co-exist in the classroom?

8. Beyond those discussed in this chapter, what other factors might affect student discipline?

9. Think back on teachers you have had who have maintained well-managed classrooms. Identify specific strategies they used. What influence did their personality have?

10. Discuss possible ways to handle the following situations:

   • Jennifer consistently talks during rehearsal.
   • Fred regularly curses in front of the entire class.
   • Sarah arrives to class on time, but takes too long to take her instrument out and sit down.

   More: Have each student in the class make up a scenario and assign it to someone.

Further Reading

Apter, T. E. *The Confident Child: Raising Children to Believe in Themselves*. New York: W.W. Norton, 2007.

Dreikurs, Rudolf, Pearl Cassel, and Eva Dreikurs Ferguson. *Discipline Without Tears: How to Reduce Conflict and Establish Cooperation in the Classroom*. Mississauga, ON: Wiley, 2004.

Haugland, Susan L. *Crowd Control: Classroom Management and Effective Teaching for Chorus, Band, and Orchestra*. Lanham, MD; Reston, VA: Rowman & Littlefield Education, 2007.

MacKenzie, Robert J. *Setting Limits in the Classroom: How to Move Beyond the Dance of Discipline in Today's Classrooms*. Roseville, CA: Prima Publishing, 2003.

Medhus, Elisa. *Hearing is Believing: How Words Can Make Or Break Our Children*. Novato, CA: New World Library, 2004.

Moore, Marvelene C., Angela L. Batey, and David M. Royse. *Classroom Management in General, Choral, and Instrumental Music Programs*. Reston, VA: MENC, the National Association for Music Education, 2002.

Wong, Harry K., and Rosemary T. Wong. *The First Days of School: How to be an Effective Teacher*. Mountain View, CA: Harry K. Wong Publications, 2005.

Chapter 8

Curriculum, Assessment, and Grading

To Guide Your Reading

How can curriculums guide our teaching?

How do today's music curriculums reflect Jerome Bruner's concept of a "spiral curriculum"?

What are the National Standards?

What are some of the controversies surrounding state and national standards?

What are observable behaviors, and how can they guide curriculum and assessment?

What is the difference between assessment and grading?

What is "authentic assessment"?

What is the difference between summative and formative assessment? How can we use both in the classroom?

In what ways can we assess individuals during an ensemble rehearsal?

What strategies can be used to assess performance skills? Non-performance skills (theory, history, composition, improvisation)?

How can we test declarative, procedural, and conceptual learning?

What is a rubric, and how can it be used to assess achievement?

What issues often complicate grading in music classes?

What are some common grading systems?

Issues Concerning the Curriculum

Curriculums can be conceived in multiple ways, though educators rarely agree on an exact definition.[1] What a teacher chooses to teach over the course of any given year is a "curriculum," just as an articulated, multi-year, district-wide body of knowledge and skills is one too. Both conceptions are important, for before we can assess and grade student achievement, we must first know what we should be teaching them. For our purposes let us define curriculum as something that provides guidance about a set of subjects, a sequence of topics, a set of objectives, a course of study, and the range of experience students will experience during their study of music. Colleen Conway, Assistant Professor of Music at the University of Michigan, offers the following list of features a curriculum should have (Conway, 55):

- Philosophy for the music program—one or two paragraphs
- Goals and beliefs for the overall program—list of beliefs about music and teaching
- List of developmental skills or benchmarks
- Required resources—teaching spaces, staffing needs, equipment, and budget
- Sample teaching strategies—lesson plans
- Sample assessment strategies—checklists, rating scales, and rubrics
- Suggested curricular resources—including method books and ensemble literature

Well-developed curriculums offer several advantages:

1. By setting learning goals for each level, curriculums insure students transition to their next grade with a certain set of skills and comprehension upon which the next teacher will build.
2. The learning goals of curriculums guide repertoire decisions rather than allowing repertoire decisions to dictate learning goals.
3. Curriculums create useful continuity between grade levels regarding issues of terminology, teaching strategies, counting systems, etc. For example, if one Elementary teacher uses the "counting system," another uses Gordon's rhythm syllables, and the Middle school teacher uses "Takadimi," students must relearn a set of skills simply to pick up where they left off before switching levels. A curriculum keeps everyone on the same page.

Teachers in successful music programs usually adhere to a well-developed curriculum, though admittedly, some perceive it constricts control of what and how to teach. The reality is that most music curriculums are no more constrictive, and possibly less so, than those in math or science. In fact, music affords considerable creativity in regards to the vehicle (the repertoire) used to teach it.

The Spiral Curriculum

The "what" of today's curriculums is strongly influenced by Jerome Bruner's concept of a "spiral curriculum."[2] In a spiral curriculum, concepts and skills are "context independent," meaning they can be taught in some intellectually honest way at every level. Along the continuum between elementary through high school, concepts become more complex in degree, but essentially unchanged in kind. The "spiral" aspect refers to the process of circling back to topics taught previously. Though the curriculum keeps building upon its core, what does change is the context in which those skills reside.[3] In a spiral curriculum we cannot say, "I don't have time to teach intonation now. They'll have time for that in middle school," because every level is responsible for teaching, in some way, the concepts from which the spiral is constructed.

Even though a spiral curriculum, in a sense, repeats back onto itself, it does not release students from higher and higher levels of achievement. Rather, it emphasizes that they should achieve excellence at whatever level is appropriate. But how do we define "appropriate"? Professor Robert Duke, Director of the Center for Music Learning at The University of Texas at Austin, writes, "If students are performing repertoire at the brink of their current technical capacity, for example, what is the likelihood that they will play beautifully, expressively, artistically? What if instead of deciding a priori that students must play or sing repertoire at a given level of difficulty, we insist that students play or sing only repertoire that can be performed beautifully, expressively, fluently?" (Duke, 81–82). This definition emphasizes the quality of music making, not the difficulty of the repertoire (Duke, 82). The goal is for students to perform with good rhythm, tone, intonation, style, and musicality rather than stumble through repertoire in which they have reached none of our musical expectations. Students' technical skills will still improve by virtue of the performance habits and skills associated with beautiful music-making.

National and State Standards

So, how do we define the topics, skills, concepts, and activities that populate a spiral instrumental music curriculum? Standards provide a possible answer. Long an educational buzzword, standards provide a template of knowledge and skills which students should be able to demonstrate after a given period of instruction. In effect, by identifying what knowledge is valued and considered important, standards of competency imply, if not dictate, what the curriculum should include. Introduced in 1994 as an extension of the National Arts Standards, MENC's National Music Standards were intended to insure that music students throughout the nation achieve a minimum level of proficiency at all grade levels in a broad range of skills. The standards support three dimensions of learning:

1. *Declarative learning*, or "what students should know"—includes information acquisition, fact learning, and the demonstration of knowledge:

    - musical notation
    - rhythmic and melodic patterns
    - musical terms
    - historical, social, and contextual information about composers, pieces, and styles.

2. *Procedural learning*, or "what students should be able to do"—includes "how-to knowledge," demonstrated through completing skills and procedures:

    - individual performance technique—e.g., posture, embouchure, hand and body position, bow technique, breathing, playing with dynamics/articulation
    - ensemble performance technique—e.g., rehearsal procedures, playing rhythms together, beginning and cutting off as an ensemble, listening to others.

3. *Conceptual understanding*, or "what students should understand"—includes the ability to form a concept (or idea) so that meaning and prior knowledge can be transferred to new experiences:

    - speaking and writing critically about music
    - composing
    - improvisation
    - analysis.

MENC's National Standards[4]

1. Content Standard: Singing, alone and with others, a varied repertoire of music.
2. Content Standard: Performing on instruments, alone and with others, a varied repertoire of music.
3. Content Standard: Improvising melodies, variations, and accompaniments.
4. Content Standard: Composing and arranging music within specified guidelines.
5. Content Standard: Reading and notating music.
6. Content Standard: Listening to, analyzing, and describing music.
7. Content Standard: Evaluating music and music performances.
8. Content Standard: Understanding relationships between music, the other arts, and disciplines outside the arts.
9. Content Standard: Understanding music in relation to history and culture.

The Standards divide achievement into four levels: ages 2–4, Grades K–4, Grades 5–8, and Grades 9–12. Central to the Standards are the ideas that music should be taught for its intrinsic value, that performance is only one component of musical learning, and that students must make connections between musical concepts and across subjects (MENC, Introduction). MENC's standards are interdependent, meaning that the ability to meet one standard facilitates meeting another. For example, Standard 5 aids Standard 4; Standard 1 improves ones proficiency of Standard 2; Standard 6 helps Standard 4, etc.[5] As with a spiral curriculum, the standards operate under the assumption that any topic can be taught in some intellectually honest way at any level of development.[6] Each level builds upon the previous one's expectations.

National music standards are not the only set of standards available. Many states, including New York, California, Virginia, and Texas, have their own content standards. Though not identical to MENC's standards, they generally display a similar balance of declarative, procedural, and conceptual learning. For example, Virginia's standards cover four areas, with increasingly advanced tasks for each standard as instrumental music students progress from Beginner level (Grade 1–2 music), Intermediate level (Grade 2–4), Advanced level (Grade 4–5), and Artist level (Grade 5–6).

Virginia's Music Standards of Learning (2006)
Performance and Production
Cultural Context and Music Theory
Judgment and Criticism
Aesthetics

Further Reading on the National Standards

Bennett Reimer: *Performing with Understanding: The Challenge of the National Standards for Music Education* (Rowman and Littlefield Education)
MENC: *Performance Standards for Music: Strategies and Benchmarks for Assessing Progress Toward the National Standards, Grades PreK-12* (Rowman and Littlefield Education)
MENC: *Opportunities-to-Learn Standards for Music Instruction: Grades PreK-12* (Rowman and Littlefield Education)
MENC Task Force for National Standards in the Arts. *The School Music Program: A New Vision.* Lanham, MD: Rowman and Littlefield Education, 1994.

Critics of National Standards

Standards do have their detractors. The influential philosopher of music education, David Elliott, criticizes them as an ineffectual form of *summative assessment* in which we test, examine, and judge students' efforts removed from the efforts themselves. He argues that standards reduce music-making and music-listening to a fragmented set of skills and facts that we distill into numbers, grades, and percentiles.[7] He derides policy makers, too—in this case, MENC—for releasing standards that guide teacher actions without having consulted the teachers themselves. Elliot argues that although most teachers

> see assessment as a means of supporting their students' growth and development, many administrators, school boards, and test designers do not. They care more about using summative assessments to iden-tify "failing" students and "failing" schools in order to determine state and local budgets (Elliott, 42).

Summative assessment refers to the process whereby students study a unit for a certain amount of time and then take a test to assess what they have learned. This assessment "summarizes" what the students have learned. In contrast, *formative assessment* is more fluid exchange between teacher and student that takes place during the learning process. In formative assessment, teacher and student alike evaluate understanding and make adjustments in the process to achieve learning goals.

Renowned music educator Richard Colwell observes that policy makers, politicians, and school admin-istrators parade standards as proof of proactive change. But he suggests that for all their political attrac-tiveness they are essentially toothless and have had minimal impact upon the classroom.[8] Partly this is because the standards have been more or less imposed upon schools without the tools that would enable their implementation, akin to a new computer operating system being released without the software and hardware needed to take advantage of its features. Let's consider the "hardware" perspective: Content standards have changed, but class sizes and contact time have not, and it can be daunting to teach skills that are considered individual activities —for example, composition and writing—to a large class that typically functions as a group. From the "software" side of the equation: Some content standards require a significant modification to the ingrained rehearsal-performance paradigm, and many teachers do not know how to adapt them to what they already do. Even if they were so inclined, they have few strategies to integrate singing, composition, improvisation, writing, and analysis into the traditional instrumental classroom. Instead, it is easier to simply retrofit what they already do in ways that meet the standards and satisfy administrators.

Daniel Huff, Clinical Associate Professor of Music Education at the University of North Carolina at Chapel Hill, suggests that Elliott's real objection to standards may be that, in the hands of teachers with limited musical imagination or skill, the push to teach them can cause all musical instruction to devolve into declarative knowledge. Thus the real core of music and music making is not taught, assessed, or even acknowledged or advocated.

Elliott subversively but provocatively coaches teachers to "walk-the-walk and talk-the-talk" about teaching to the Standards, fill out whatever paperwork about standards that administrators require, and then, well, *ignore* them inside the classroom. "The fact is," he writes, "if we are teaching music well (in a caring, holistic, artistic, and humanistic way), then we are already exceeding any 'standard' the writers of the MENC standards had in mind" (Elliott, 54).

So, perhaps standards can provide a useful template for those who understand the benefits of teaching holistically and humanistically. It may be inaccurate to assume, however, that good teachers will understand exactly how to teach this way in the classroom, even teachers versed in Elliott's theories. Further, it is worth noting that both the Standards and Elliot's perspective may fail to account for the seemingly contradictory expectations of some administrators and community members, which sometimes pressure teachers to offer a broad music curriculum and still field award-winning marching bands. Seen in this light, even administrators may support Elliot's conscientious objector approach to standards.

Whether or not they are the ultimate solution to music education's challenges, standards are indeed filled with powerful ideas and exciting possibilities. But to build an effective curriculum, their guidelines must be developed into specific objectives, skills, and behaviors.

What to Teach—Curriculum Guides, Component Skills, Observable Behaviors

In and of themselves, content standards, even with the performance and achievement guidelines that supplement them, are too general to guide everyday teaching. But curricular specificity is needed in music, just as it is in other subjects. The science teacher knows exactly what concepts, theories, and lab skills a student should have at the end of the semester; the history teacher knows exactly what events students should understand for a given time period; the language teacher knows exactly what vocabulary and grammar is needed to comprehend conversation at the next level. These subjects rely on a textbook to guide students through a curriculum. In music, method books initially fill this role, and later the repertoire we choose supplements and reinforces the same topics.

Curriculum Guides

So in addition to standards it is useful to have a specific list of benchmarks with which to measure student progress. One example is the *ASBDA Curriculum Guide*. Though the details may be debated and each school may devise their own variations, the guide is an excellent resource for activities, projects, and rehearsal techniques, especially those that emphasize declarative and procedural knowledge.

Primary Performance Outcomes of Instrumental Music Study (from the ASBDA Curriculum Guide)[9]

1. Demonstrate the language art of reading and interpreting music notation.
2. Perform music independently and with others.
3. Describe, analyze, and create music.
4. Evaluate music by using critical thinking and listening skills.
5. Demonstrate a knowledge of music history and cultural heritage.
6. Participate in cultural/musical life of the community through involvement in local and regional music/arts opportunities.

Demonstrate the Language Art of Reading and Interpreting Music Notation (ASBDA, 28)

The student will:

1. Identify and notate the following interpretive symbols: accents, marcato, staccato, tenuto, dynamic markings, crescendo, decrescendo.
2. Write the key signatures for the following major scales in treble and bass clefs: Concert C, F, G, B♭, D♭, E♭, A♭.
3. Identify all pitches on the grand staff.
4. Perform at sight rhythms containing the following notes and rests, including dotted notes and rests: whole note and rest; half notes and rest; quarter note and rest; eighth note and rest in the following meters: $\frac{4}{4}, \frac{3}{4}, \frac{2}{4}, \frac{6}{8}, \frac{3}{8}$.
5. Demonstrate legato, tenuto, staccato, marcato patterns as required in given pieces of music.
6. Interpret and perform dynamic changes as notated in given music selections.
7. Interpret given tempo markings and alternations as notated in appropriate music selections.
8. Interpret (and perform) music containing first and second endings, measure rests and repeats, D.C. and D.S. indications, and codas.
9. Interpret and count (orally and in written form) given rhythms from Grade II+ and III levels music using a counting system.
10. Interpret and perform at sight music at the Grade II level.

Perform Music Independently and With Others (ASBDA, 30–31)

The student will:

1. Demonstrate correct fingerings, including alternate fingerings, for all notes within the practical range of his/her instrument.
2. Perform major scales (2 octaves where possible) in eighth notes at a metronome marking of ♩ = 100 for all keys appropriate to music being studied. The following scales should be included: Concert C, F, G, B♭, D♭, E♭, A♭.
3. Perform natural and harmonic minor scales (2 octaves where possible) appropriate to the music being studied. The following scales should be included: Concert a, d, g, c, f. These scales will be performed in eighth notes, at a metronome marking of ♩ = 100.
4. Perform a chromatic scale within the ranges listed below:

TABLE 8.1 Performing a Range of Chromatic Scales

	E♭1 to F3
Clarinet	small E to B♭2
Saxophone	C1 to C3
Oboe	D1 to A2
Bassoon	great F to F1
Trumpet	small F♯ to A2
French Horn	small F to G2
Trombone/Euph	great F to F1
Tuba	low F to small F

This scale will be performed in eighth notes at a metronome marking of ♩ = 100.

5. Identify standard preparatory conducting beats, release motions, entrance cues, and expressive gestures.
6. Demonstrate vibrato, as it relates to tonal enrichment, for instruments where vibrato is characteristic.
7. Adjust the pitch of his/her instrument to a given standard during actual performance and with the use of a tuning device.
8. Demonstrate the attack and release of a tone in accordance with the needs of given music selections at Grade II and III levels.
9. Demonstrate appropriate playing position for his/her instrument(s).
10. Demonstrate a tone quality characteristic of his/her instrument in the middle register and in the middle dynamic levels.
11. Perform music with rhythms that contain the following notes and rests, including dotted notes and rests: whole, half, quarter, eighth, sixteenth.
12. Perform music selections containing the following time signatures: $\frac{4}{4}, \frac{3}{2}, \frac{3}{4}, \frac{2}{4}, \frac{6}{8}$.
13. Perform from the following compositional periods with characteristic interpretive elements: Baroque, Classical, and Twentieth Century (educational music).
14. Perform with other instrumentalists to achieve a refined ensemble sound, including volume, timbre, balance, and blend.
15. Demonstrate appropriate care of his/her instrument(s).

(Reprinted by permission of the publisher.)

Component Observable Behaviors

In contrast to MENC and state achievement standards, Professor Duke takes a different approach in his book, *Intelligent Music Teaching*. Rather than general benchmarked standards, Duke's outline breaks achievement into "component observable behaviors." The idea is that large-scale goals of the standards are actually the culmination of smaller skills and achievements, each one of which can be measured by observing specific student behaviors. (See Companion Website for the complete outline, reprinted by permission.)

Each part of the outline can be broken into context-independent learning outcomes as advanced by a spiral curriculum. For example:

Perform independently with a pulse as given by the director—This skill is expected from elementary through high school students; the difference is that the repertoire in elementary school is much easier than that in high school.

Perform louder or softer as indicated by the director or the notation—We can expect beginners to play with some dynamic range, and we expect high school students to play with even more.

Define musical terms as indicated in performance repertoire—We should expect beginners to learn basic terms such as "Allegro" and "Andante," and expand the vocabulary as students advance.

Improvise an accompaniment to a well-known melody—As with everything else, this skill is attainable at all levels, even if the beginner's accompaniment is rhythmically and harmonically simplistic compared to that of an advanced player.

Cultural Reproduction

It should be noted that a list of observable behaviors can be viewed as being a form of what educational theorist Michael Apple calls "cultural reproduction," in which the values, traditions, and norms of one generation are transmitted to another. In the case of Duke's list of specific observable behaviors, one may note that there are relatively few that fall outside the parameters of western music and what is typically associated with "polite" middle class standards of conduct. Thus, the list may be seen as inherently biased, comprising a small part of what Apple calls a "hidden curriculum" that "serves ideologically to buttress and naturalize structurally based social and economic inequalities."[10] Apple writes, "the language of learning tends to be apolitical and ahistorical, thus hiding the complex nexus of political and economic power and resources that lies behind a considerable amount of curriculum organization and selection."[11] The danger of cultural reproduction, regardless of whether the "hidden curriculum" is knowingly and intentionally prioritized, is that it is designed to exclude rather than broaden, thus recreating society's inequalities.

One strategy to insure against cultural reproduction is to expand Duke's list to include specific observable behaviors that characterize the style, performance practice and levels of skill for a variety of repertoires and musical traditions. For example, the component observable behaviors of playing a proper crescendo on a string instrument may include:

- starting at the tip of the bow to crescendo towards the frog
- using more bow speed as the crescendo increases
- using more bow weight as the crescendo increases
- maintaining a good sense of pulse through the crescendo
- maintaining tone quality and pitch through the crescendo.

The component observable behaviors of playing proper "marcato" articulations on a woodwind instrument may include:

- using more air at the beginning of the note
- using a light tongue to begin the note
- quickly tapering the strength of the note after the initial attack
- stopping the air flow between notes to create separation
- using embouchure to maintain good tone quality and pitch during the beginning of the note.

The component observable behaviors of playing an open tone on a conga may include:

- tipping the drum slightly by lifting the drum with the heels of one's feet
- striking near the edge with an open hand
- contacting the head in the upper part of the palm, opposite where the fingers meet the knuckles on the back of the hand
- allowing the fingers to spring back to a straight position with the back of the hand.

Although it is possible to assess accurately without these specifics—e.g., it's easy to recognize an effective crescendo without knowing how it was made—it is nearly impossible to teach methodically, diagnose problems and offer solutions to those who struggle. By carefully defining these behaviors we synchronize teaching, diagnosis, and assessment.

Assessment

Assessment and grading go hand-in-hand. Whereas assessment is the measurement of student performance, grading is the way we communicate the information provided by assessment. As Duke observes, assessment is "finding out", while feedback and grading are "communicating what you've found out" (Duke, 51).

Compressing the Assessment Cycle

Ensemble music activities are usually assessed as a group. We critique the *ensemble's* playing during rehearsal, and we critique it after a performance. Indeed, the performance is often sold as the culminating "test" of the rehearsal process. Moreover, we go to state *ensemble* festivals and receive a score with detailed comments about the *ensemble's* performance. And we travel to festivals to receive feedback and measure our worth by competing against other *ensembles*. Unfortunately, none of these activities provide data about the achievement of *individual* students.

If we accept that our responsibility as educators goes beyond getting the ensemble to sound good on a concert, it becomes clear we must assess more than just the group. But how? One common way is through periodic playing tests (a summative form of assessment).

Duke points out the problem of relying exclusively on this approach:

> I have often heard teachers express that they "wonder how the students are going to do on this next exam." Why do they wonder? Why don't they know? The answer, of course, is that there have been few opportunities for these teachers to observe individual students doing the kinds of tasks that they will be required to do on the examination . . . (Duke, 57).

Duke's comment raises two crucial assessment issues. The first is that not all assessment should be summative. Also important is assessment that reveals information to teachers about the areas in which their students are struggling *during the learning process* and provides critical feedback for students. This type of assessment is called *formative assessment*. Consider it as part of a cycle:

FIGURE 8.1 The Assessment Cycle [12]

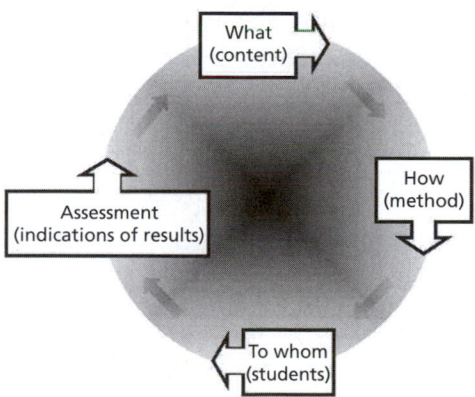

In this model, assessment is not merely an end-game; it is an ongoing process that connects back to the beginning of the cycle. What teachers learn from assessment affects the content of what they teach next . . . and then the cycle repeats.

This regularly manifests itself in the music classroom. We wonder if students will be able to phrase something beautifully on their own. We wonder if students remember and understand the musical concepts we discuss during rehearsal. We wonder how well the individuals in a section know their music. We wonder if students have the confidence to play musically on their own. And so, in order to *not* wonder, we use formative assessment to compress the Assessment Cycle into a much tighter circle by evaluating individuals on a regular, daily basis.

The second important issue is that assessment—both formative and summative—should be *authentic*. In authentic assessment we ask students to perform tasks and apply concepts in real-life situations that reflect the manner of their instruction.[13] For example, if we teach students to play musically by rehearsing how to follow a melody's contour, we should test students' ability to (a) play those phrases musically in that manner, and (b) apply that concept to new melodies. If we simply ask students to describe what to do through a written test (e.g., Question: "How do we typically shape melodies?" Answer: "With a crescendo or decrescendo that follows the contour of the line."), the assessment is not authentic. Why? Because it is not consistent with the context in which the skills were taught. For this type of skill, a traditional written test does not recreate a real-life situation: "Real-life" music-making involves actually playing phrases, not talking about playing phrases.

A notable feature of authentic assessment is that it involves "planning backward" for curriculum design. In this model, teachers design the real-life tasks they wish students to perform and then formulate instructional methods to teach those tasks.[14] (Contrast this with traditional curriculum design, in which a body of knowledge is organized into a curriculum, and then assessments are designed to determine if that knowledge has been delivered to students.)

With the concept of authentic assessment in mind, let us revisit the opening discussion about assessing music students in groups. Though we want our students to perform musically on their own, the goal of the ensemble experience is not solely to develop high-achieving individuals. Indeed, good ensembles embody a brand of music-making that is more than the sum of their parts. Among other things, playing successfully in an ensemble involves listening for blend, balance, and intonation; the ability to interface one's individual playing into a small group (section) and then into a larger group (full ensemble); an understanding of how one's individual part fits into the whole, etc. If we indeed value the "task" of performing musically in group, then authentic assessment of the group's performance is a legitimate goal. Athletic teams offer an illustrative analogy. We evaluate players not only on their individual skills—how many points they score—but also on their skills as a member of the team—their ability to make those around them better. We value both sets of skills because the activity is a team sport. The star player may set a record for home runs, but how much does this matter if the team fails to win a game?

We believe there is a place for both individual and group assessment in the instrumental classroom, but for the purposes of our discussion we will focus on the challenges of assessing individuals.

Formative Assessment: Regular and Individual

Rehearsals, lessons, and concerts only go so far in measuring individual student achievement in performance. It is not uncommon for a student who can seemingly play their part in a group context to fail on their own. The student may rationalize, "I can do it fine when I'm in the section!" or "I was able to play it in rehearsal. I'm just nervous because I'm being put on the spot." But we know the reality is that she only *thinks* she can play it with the group. Or, she really can but has little experience doing it in isolation, and unfortunately anxiety takes over. In both cases our assessment process has failed, either because group assessment gives her credit for skills she does not have, or because we do not provide opportunities for her to individually develop and demonstrate those skills before we test her on them.

Again, we must compress the assessment cycle. In formative assessment we assess regularly and individually rather than intermittently and collectively. The point is to give students an opportunity to demonstrate their understanding and provide immediate feedback. Formative assessment is often (but not always) informal, meaning we do not assign a grade. Some strategies to make it work (Duke, 61–63):

- *Not every individual every day*—With limited contact time, it is not practical for every student to perform or respond during every meeting. Spread the opportunities around; choose students under the pretense of identifying good models for the ensemble and those that need some extra practice.
- *Make it non-threatening*—To assess who can perform a musical selection accurately we can quickly have each student play it one at a time. The challenge is to make students feel comfortable playing alone so they consider it a regular aspect of music-making. Avoid "going down the line" as a sign of frustration to suddenly embarrass students that cannot play their parts or do not know the answer.
- *Ask questions that test declarative, procedural, and conceptual learning, e.g.:*

  "Which measure has a rhythmic problem?"
  "Which instrument played the softest?"
  "What's the strongest note the violins just played?"
  "What do you think should be the strongest note?"
  "What are some ideas for shaping this phrase?"
  "What does D.C. al Coda mean?"
  "In what part of the piece have we heard this theme before?"
  "Who can model the proper articulation for this section?"

- *If one student answers a question properly it does not mean everyone also knew the answer*—This is obvious in performance situations—just because the principal player performs something does not mean the last chair player can—but it is often forgotten with non-performance questions. Two effective strategies to combat this problem: (1) Always vary the respondents so as to take a broad sample of the class' knowledge; and (2) Find opportunities to have every individual respond simultaneously.
- *When appropriate, get responses from everybody, not just volunteers*—When we ask for volunteers we favor the students who (a) are confident they know the answer, (b) seek attention, or (c) know that they need help (Duke, 62). We inadvertently single out students who (a) do not realize they need help, or (b) are too shy to volunteer. Make it non-threatening, create a culture where everyone is expected to participate, and do not ignore the excited student who wants to volunteer everything!
- *Form students into small groups to hear individuals*—Instead of asking one student to play by himself, create mini-chamber groups within the ensemble. Students will feel comfortable playing with others and there will be few enough playing that we can still assess each individually, e.g.:

  - 2nd clarinets only
  - one player from each section (i.e., ask second desk/inside string players to play a passage)
  - just the boys, followed by just the girls
  - just 9th graders, followed by just 10th graders
  - every other person
  - just the people on the right side of the room, followed by those on the left side
  - just one row at a time
  - ad-hoc string quartets, brass quintets, and woodwind quintets (i.e., ask one flute, one oboe, one clarinet, one horn, and one bassoon to play a passage)
  - students wearing blue shoes

- *Assess the large group while the small group performs*—Solicit reactions, responses, and suggestions from the large group to keep them focused and engaged. For efficiency, use hand-signs and individual dry-erase boards to quickly see everyone's answers. If large-group responses are inappropriate, make a point to call on students who would not normally volunteer.

- *Tell students that they will be tested on the material they are learning!*—"Teaching to the test" is bad only if the test does not reflect what we want students to know. But if the curriculum is a way to get students to perform the real-life skills of the assessment, why wouldn't we tell them what is on the test? Telling students what they will be tested on is also a motivational tool to hold them accountable (Duke, 68).

Summative Assessment: Detailed and Systematic

As a culminating experience, summative assessment provides a diagnostic of learning for a longer period of time than formative assessment. It is often (but not always) a type of "formal" assessment, which means we assign a grade. Summative assessment helps hold students accountable for knowing and understanding a variety of topics:

- ensemble music
- passages from method/lesson books
- solo literature studied in group lessons
- parts from duets, trios, and other chamber music
- scales and technical exercises
- proper care of instrument
- music history
- music theory

Consider the following techniques to evaluate student performance:

Live Playing Assessments

Administered in rehearsal, during lessons, or after-school, these test each student individually. To focus student practicing and save time, do not test every measure of every piece.

For beginning string players, Karey Sitzler, veteran teacher at Lakeland High School and Forest Glen Middle Schools in Virginia, and conductor of the Williamsburg Youth String Orchestra, suggests assessing certain skills with a bit of flexibility to avoid confusing talent and strength with prior knowledge and experience. To do this, identify the list of skills that are needed by the end of the year. On a midterm examination, ask not that students perform a *specific set* of activities from this list, but rather that they demonstrate a certain *number* (e.g., half) of their choice. Thus, on the way to complete proficiency, a student's achievement will be determined by a combination of his individual strengths and his perseverance and practice. Keep track of the entire class' progress. This will provide a reference during conferences with students and parents, and also aid us in selecting music that reflects the strengths and weaknesses of the entire class.

Whereas live, in-class playing assessments are time consuming, technology offers several workarounds, as outlined below.

Recorded Playing Assessments

Have students record their playing tests on their computer, save it as a standard sound file (mp3, WMA, WAV, etc.) using *Audacity* or other software, and submit it via CD, email, USB flash drive, or online dropbox. Many computers have built-in/internal microphones, and external microphones for older laptops and desktops cost less than $10.

Two advantages of take-home assessments are that they minimize performance anxiety and induce the "word processor effect": when turning in papers written with a word processor, students are more reluctant to turn in sloppy work than if they were asked to turn it in by hand. The same holds for recorders, since the ability to re-record the test as needed encourages proof-reading (or proof-listening!)

Computer-aided Evaluations

SmartMusic, published by MakeMusic, is software that evaluates student performance—including note, rhythm, and tempo accuracy—without a teacher having to be present. Teachers select exercises from the *SmartMusic* library, including rhythm and melody exercises, play-by-ear exercises, jazz improvisation, concert band and orchestra music, solo literature, and popular method books. After the teacher programs the criteria on which the software should evaluate, students perform the passage with an inexpensive clip-on microphone. *SmartMusic* gives instant feedback to the student, saves the results, and lets the teacher listen to the student's original performance and respond with comments. It is a tremendous time-saver, creates an anxiety-free environment for students, and like many computer-assisted education programs, is an attractive and entertaining way for students to complete assignments. A peripheral benefit is that it insures our grading is consistent and objective from student to student.

Beyond its uses for assessment, *SmartMusic* is also a powerful practice tool, allowing students to play along with flexible accompaniments, transpose music to new keys, record their playing, create practice loops, listen to a digital recording of their piece, access a range of exercises and fingering charts, and use a digital metronome and tuner.

Using Rubrics for Assessment

Consider the grading sheet shown below. It is a perfectly feasible method, but the use of generic categories and point ranges gives no indication about how points are to be assigned within each one. This open-endedness increases the likelihood the teacher will score inconsistently from student to student. Further, the points for each category tell the student very little about his performance.

A STANDARD NON-RUBRIC EVALUATION FORM

Acme School Music Department

Playing Evaluation

Name _____ Date _____ Instrument _____

Year in school _____

Excerpt (title and composer)_____

Technical facility (20 points)_____

Rhythmic accuracy (20 points) _____

Intonation accuracy (15 points) _____

Dynamics (10 points) _____

Articulation and expression marks (10 points) _____

Phrasing (10 points) _____

Interpretation (5 points) _____

Comments: _____

_____

_____

_____

_____

Teacher signature _____

It may seem that students want the results from assessments as quickly as possible (they will often pester us "When are we getting back our tests?") but our desire to return grades quickly should not cause us to undermine the value of feedback with generic comments such as "Good work," "Sloppy," or "Nice improvement." Feedback is most effective when it contains specific information rather than merely a summary of the level achieved.[15] In other words, students often *want* the general feedback grades given to them, but they really *need* specific feedback. If we use authentic assessment to design tasks that require problem-solving, critical thinking, and the demonstration of "real-life" skills, then students need to know what comprises a good performance of that task.

An extremely powerful tool for this is a *rubric*. A rubric systematically states the expectations for a task and defines acceptable and unacceptable performances. By doing so students can understand exactly how they will be graded. The expectations are often grouped into categories, and each category represents a percentage of the overall grade. In some ways rubrics are merely an ultra-explicit version of how many teachers believe they are already grading, even if they do not use an explicit list of guidelines. Effective rubrics consist of the following components:

1. What task the rubric is measuring
2. A list of the components that comprise the task
3. A description of what successful completion of each component entails—This should describe the highest achievement level and 4–5 lower levels (e.g., excellent, good, fair, satisfactory, unsatisfactory). More than five levels can be confusing for students and difficult to grade. Fewer than four gives insufficient guidance and hampers our ability to make distinctions in achievement
4. A scoring key that assigns points (or percentages) to each component and converts point totals into a grade

Throughout this chapter we will present sample rubrics for performance, composition, improvisation, and writing. Keep in mind that rubrics are not the "answers to the test". Rather, they guide students to develop the skills and comprehension needed to complete real-life tasks, and so we should share them during the teaching process.

Sample Rubric: Performance Test

In the basic rubric for performance tests (see Table 8.2), notice that the criteria is generalized and context independent. Instead of specific measures, it identifies performance expectations that apply to all levels. Thus, as the repertoire changes over time and, say, rhythms become more complex, the skill descriptions stay consistent.

TABLE 8.2 Basic Rubric for Performance Tests

Points	Criteria/Component
Pitch	
3	Each note is consistently in tune relative to all other pitches.
2	Occasionally there are isolated intonation errors.
1	The pitch is sometimes stable but a majority of notes are sharp or flat.
0	The pitch constantly shifts between sharp and flat throughout the performance.
Articulation	
3	All articulation markings (staccato, accent, tenuto, marcato, slur, etc.) are accurately performed.
2	Most articulation markings are accurately performed.
1	Some of the articulation markings are performed inaccurately or lack clarity.
0	Most of the articulation markings are performed inaccurately or lack clarity.
Rhythm	
3	Rhythms are accurate through the entire performance.
2	1–3 rhythmic errors occur, but they do not detract from the overall performance.
1	4–7 rhythmic errors occur, somewhat detracting from the overall performance.
0	8 or more rhythmic errors occur, seriously detracting from the overall performance.
Tempo	
3	The tempo is within the range of the printed markings and contains no hesitations or accelerations.
2	Compared to the printed tempo, the performance is 10–15 beats per minute too fast or too slow and/or contains 1–4 hesitations or accelerations.
1	The tempo is more than 10–15 beats per minute too fast or too slow and/or contains 5 or more hesitations or accelerations.
0	Incorrect tempo and repeated tempo hesitations/accelerations make it difficult to perceive the intended rhythm.
Note accuracy	
3	There are 0–2 note errors.
2	There are 3–5 note errors, but they do not detract from the overall performance.
1	There are 6–10 note errors, somewhat detracting from the overall performance.
0	More than 10 note errors occur, significantly disrupting the flow of the music.

TABLE 8.2 continued

Points	Criteria/Component
Dynamics and Expression Markings	
3	All dynamic/expression markings are clearly executed with a noticeable distinction among each.
2	Most dynamic/expression markings are clearly executed with a noticeable distinction among each.
1	A majority of dynamic/expression markings are improperly executed.
0	Nearly all dynamic/expression markings are improperly executed.
Tone Quality	
3	The tone has a characteristic sound in all registers and a focused core to each note.
2	The tone is generally characteristic and focused in all registers, but is occasionally any of the following: thin, shrill, weak, blatty, spread, or unfocused.
1	The tone is characteristic in some registers, uncharacteristic in other registers, and is often any of the following: thin, shrill, weak, blatty, spread, or unfocused.
0	The tone is uncharacteristic in all registers.
Expression/Musicianship	
3	Student plays with excellent musicianship, including the addition of expressive features that are implied or suggested by the notation on the page.
2	Student plays with good musicianship, but not necessarily with the addition of expressive features that are implied or suggested by the notation on the page.
1	Student adds expressive features that are implied by the notation on the page, but does not present them musically.
0	Student does not play musically or with ideas that are implied or suggested by the notation.

Evaluations of Conceptual Understanding

Perhaps because it is the system with which we are most familiar, many teachers find it difficult to move beyond written tests, auditions, and performances as assessment tools. But to insure conceptual understanding we cannot assume students understand things just because they have memorized facts and practiced musical skills (Hartenberger, 73). Douglas C. Orzolek suggests teachers should push students to "solve musical problems much like those that real composers, performers, or listeners might be required to solve" by building upon their previous experiences as musicians.[16] For example, when students participate in chamber music they need to solve the problem of how to coherently build an interpretation using skills learned in large-ensemble settings and lessons. (See Chapter 14 for a discussion of chamber music.)

Other activities that develop conceptual understanding, many of which are explicitly encouraged by the National Standards, include:

- rehearsal evaluations
- composition
- improvisation
- program note assignments

Rehearsal Evaluations

Rehearsal evaluations put students in the role of adjudicator. Provide a copy of the adjudicator form used for competitions and have students evaluate the group's progress. For better perspective, invite a few students to listen to the rehearsal from the front of the group, or record a run-through and post it as an mp3. Rather than give numerical scores for each category, ask students to write specific comments about tempo, precision, balance, intonation, expression, etc. (e.g., Which section is out of tune? Where in the music?) Or, create a rubric for students to use.

Practice Charts

Practice sheets, such as the one below, are a tool for students, parents, and teachers to track practice progress throughout the semester. Student accountability is built into the system: The weekly signature from the parent verifies to the teacher that the students are practicing; the weekly signature from the teacher shows parents their children are attending lessons and reminds them to encourage daily practice.

Use this sheet to correlate a student's achievement with the amount of time he spends practicing. For a student who performs poorly and logs very little practice time, simply point out the deficiency in time. But if a student performs poorly and practices adequately we need to diagnose the problem. Here are some of the possibilities:

- The amount of material was too much for the amount of time available to prepare it.
  Solution: Reduce the size of future assignments.

- The student did not understand aspects of the assignment.
  Solution: Spend time explaining, demonstrating, modeling, and practicing with students to ensure they know *how* to play their assignments, not just *what* to play.

- The student's practice habits are ineffective and/or inefficient.
  Solution: Take the time to teach effective practice strategies.

- The material is beyond the student's present ability level.
  Solution: Modify the material to match the student's present level—give the student an opportunity to succeed and make beautiful music.

Sometimes we can question struggling students to get to the root of the problem:

1. Did you understand what the assignment was?
2. Did you understand how to play it (e.g., rhythms, fingerings)?
3. Are you using the proper practice techniques?

If the student answers "yes" and still presents a signed sheet filled with practice minutes, we must consider the possibility that a parent is lying to help the student or not paying attention to what she is signing. In any case, it is time to contact the parent to resolve the situation.

Composition and Improvisation Projects

Music teachers are generally more adept at evaluating student performance than student composition, probably because composition assessment involves seemingly subjective criteria.[17] We perceive good performance as a reflection of work and dedication, but good composition as the result of inspiration and talent. How can we criticize someone, one might argue, who works hard but simply isn't very talented?

FIGURE 8.2 Sample Filled-Out Practice Chart (See Companion Website for a blank, editable version of this form)

Name: *Jenn Wagner*

Assignment Sheet + Practice Chart

Assignment 1 - Week of: September 7 - 13

1. **Scales:** A-flat Major, one octave, in 8th notes, quarter note = 100 — Grade (0-4) **3**
2. **Rhythms:** Rhythm Packet A, Page 1, lines 1 - 5 — Grade (0-4) **4**
3. **Music:** Sarabanda and Gavotta, A. Corelli, arr. Clarence Hurrell, line 1 - 3 — Grade (0-4) **4**
4. **Conceptual Learning:** Improvise over B-flat 12 Bar Blues — Grade (0-4) **4**
   melodic motive = first two notes of the B-flat Blues scale
   rhythmic motive = quarter + 2 eighths

Overall grade and comments: ← Watch Descending [15] A ☺

Date:	Monday	Tuesday	Wednesday	Thursday	Friday	Saturday	Sunday	Total Minutes
Practice Minutes	30	30	45	Ø	30	30	25	190

Parent's Signature: _____ Teacher's Signature: _____

Assignment 2 - Week of: September 14 - 20

1. **Scales:** D-flat Major, one octave, in 8th notes, quarter note = 100 — Grade (0-4) **4**
2. **Rhythms:** Rhythm Packet A, page 1, lines 6 - 10 — Grade (0-4) **4**
3. **Music:** Sarabanda and Gavotta, A. Corelli, arr. Clarence Hurrell, line 4 - 6 — Grade (0-4) **2**
4. **Conceptual Learning:** Improvise over B-flat 12 Bar Blues — Grade (0-4) **4**
   melodic material = B-flat Blues scale
   rhythmic motive = quarter + 2 eighths

Overall grade and comments: [14] A ☺ ← Work Rhythm at Rehearsal B.

Date:	Monday	Tuesday	Wednesday	Thursday	Friday	Saturday	Sunday	Total Minutes
Practice Minutes	30	30	30	35	30	45	30	260

Parent's Signature: _____ Teacher's Signature: _____

Assignment 3 - Week of: September 21 - 27

1. **Scales:** D Major, one octave, in 8th notes, quarter note = 100 — Grade (0-4) **4**
2. **Rhythms:** Rhythm Packet A, page 2, lines 1 - 5 — Grade (0-4) **4**
3. **Music:** Sarabanda and Gavotta, A. Corelli, arr. Clarence Hurrell, line 7 - 9 — Grade (0-4) **4**
4. **Conceptual Learning:** Improvise over B-flat 12 Bar Blues, — Grade (0-4) **4**
   melodic material = B-flat Blues scale
   rhythmic motive = quarter + 2 eights and half note + 2 quarter notes

Overall grade and comments: [16] Bravo! A

Date:	Monday	Tuesday	Wednesday	Thursday	Friday	Saturday	Sunday	Total Minutes
Practice Minutes	Ø	30	30	30	30	30	30	180

Parent's Signature: _____ Teacher's Signature: _____

GRADING KEY: A (16-13) = extremely accurate   B (12-9) = very accurate with small error(s),   C (8-5) = moderately accurate   D (4-1) = many inaccuracies   F (0)= completely unprepared

Perhaps there is a fundamental difference between the arts and other disciplines in that music has quantifiable *and* qualitative measures of success. Since there is no single "correct" answer to a composition assignment, and no absolute "correct" way to shape a phrase, there are multiple answers worthy of an "A."

Still, not *every* answer deserves an "A." The goal is not rampant relativism, in which we somehow justify excellence in every student, but rather a clearly articulated rubric to define the specific criteria of a good composition. Note that some of the grading categories still allow for subjectivity.

Sample Rubric for Composition

Unlike the general performance test rubric, this rubric is context *dependent* because it describes tasks specific to this assignment (see Table 8.3).

TABLE 8.3 Sample Rubrics for Composition and Improvisation

Melody

4	Melody shows required arc shape and is 6–8 measures long.
3	Melody shows arc shape but is longer than 8 measures.
2	Melody shows some arc shape but is shorter than 6 measures.
1	Melody is 6–8 measures long but shows no arc shape.
0	Melody has no discernible shape and is not within the required length.

Phrase Structure

4	Antecedent/consequent phrase is clearly expressed (two balanced phrases, thematic/rhythmic relationship between the two, implied half-cadence at the end of the antecedent phrase, implied authentic cadence at the end of the consequent phrase).
3	Antecedent/consequent phrase contains proper cadential and thematic elements, but length is unbalanced.
2	Two elements missing from the phrase structure (balance, thematic relationship, first cadence, second cadence).
1	Three elements missing from phrase structure.
0	All elements missing from phrase structure.

Overall Form

4	ABA form is complete (including: A presents theme 1, B presents contrasting material, A returns, balanced length between A and B sections).
3	Form is missing one element (e.g., A does not return; B does not contrast; inappropriate overall length; imbalance among sections).
2	Form is missing 2–3 elements.
1	Form is missing more than 3 elements.
0	No recognizable form.

Rhythm

4	♫♩ rhythm appears at least four times.
3	♫♩ rhythm appears three times.
2	♫♩ rhythm appears two times.
1	♫♩ rhythm appears once.
0	♫♩ rhythm does not appear.

TABLE 8.3 continued

Expression Markings

4	Dynamics match the contour of the phrase; articulations are used consistently and effectively to enhance the expressive effect of the melody.
3	One of the elements is used effectively, another moderately well.
2	Both elements are used moderately well.
1	One element is used effectively, another needs work.
0	Neither element used effectively.

Length

4	Melody is 8 or more measures long.
3	Melody is 6–7 measures long.
2	Melody is 4–5 measures long.
1	Melody is 2–3 measures long.
0	Melody is 1 measure long.

Creativity

4	Melody is enjoyable to listen to and makes a strong artistic impression with its musical ideas.
3	Melody is somewhat enjoyable to listen to, with a few good ideas that make a coherent musical statement.
2	Melody has a few good ideas, but generally does not hold together as an artistic statement.
1	Melody has a few good ideas, but does not hold together as an artistic statement.
0	Melody makes little impression and has no ideas that engage the listener.

Idiomatic

4	Melody is idiomatic to play; range is appropriate for 10th graders; takes advantage of the instrument's strengths and avoids its weaknesses.
3	The melody has one or two notes that go beyond the normal 10th grade playing range of the instrument.
2	Melody is awkward to play; more than two notes in an inappropriate range; does not highlight instrument's strength's or avoid its weaknesses.
1	Melody is awkward to play; many notes in an inappropriate range.
0	Melody is inappropriate for the level for which it is written.

Notation

4	Notation is professional, easy to read, and includes all appropriate markings.
3	Notation is somewhat hard to read, but all appropriate markings are present.
2	Notation is easy to read but important markings are missing.
1	Notation is difficult to read and important markings are missing.
0	Notation is difficult to read and all important markings are missing.

Improvisation Rubric Tonality

4	Plays harmonically appropriate notes within the changes, with appropriate excursions to non-harmonic tones.
3	Plays harmonically appropriate notes within the changes, but no excursions into non-harmonic tones.
2	Plays a few wrong notes around the changes, but does play one or more appropriate non-harmonic tones.
1	Plays several notes outside the changes of the tune, none of which are appropriate non-harmonic tones.
0	Plays many notes outside the changes of the tune.

Rhythm

4	Rhythm locks into the groove well and shows a variety of speed and density (including mixing duple and triple figures).
3	Rhythm locks into the groove well but shows only slight variety in speed and density.
2	Rhythm falls out of the groove at several spots but shows variety of speed and density.
1	Rhythm falls out of the groove at many spots and shows little variety.
0	Rhythm is frequently out of the groove or never in the groove.

Phrasing

4	Phrasing is balanced and well-paced, with effective use of silence.
3	Phrasing is balanced and well-paced, but silence is not used effectively (e.g., too much or too little).
2	Phrasing begins effectively but never develops.
1	Phrasing ends well but shows little connection to the opening.
0	Phrasing is poorly paced and unbalanced throughout.

Motives, Patterns, and Licks

4	Effectively incorporates at least 3–4 of the assigned patterns or licks into the solo.
3	Incorporates at least 3–4 of the assigned patterns, but not always effectively.
2	Effectively incorporates 1–2 of the assigned patterns, or ineffectively incorporates at least 3–4 patterns.
1	Incorporates 1–2 of the assigned patterns, but not effectively.
0	Does not incorporate any of the assigned patterns into the solo.

(Note: The below category may be substituted for the above one.)

Arpeggios and Scales

4	Plays all changes with the correct scale or arpeggio, and in a stylistically appropriate way.
3	Plays most changes with the correct scale or arpeggio, and most in a stylistically appropriate way.
2	Plays 2–3 changes with the incorrect scale or arpeggio.
1	Plays more than 3 changes with either an incorrect arpeggio or scale, or in a stylistically inappropriate way.
0	Plays most changes with incorrect scale/arpeggio, or in a stylistically inappropriate way.

Melody and Ornamentation

4	Melody is played effectively over the changes along with examples of effective melodic ornamentation.
3	Melody is played effectively over the changes but includes no effective melodic ornamentation.
2	Melody is played somewhat effectively over the changes and includes examples of melodic ornamentation.
1	Melody is played somewhat effectively over the changes but contains no effective melodic ornamentation.
0	Melody is not played effectively over the changes.

An Alternate Way of Writing Rubrics

Instead of the format in Table 8.3, another way of constructing rubrics is to calculate the number of points achievable for each category and then list the elements that would earn each point. Then, the teacher just needs to circle (or check) the elements the student achieves in order to calculate the student's score.

For example, in an improvisation rubric, the "Rhythm" category might be constructed as shown in Table 8.4.

TABLE 8.4 Example of an Improvisation Rubric

Rhythm
(4 points total)

Locks into the groove of the rhythm section.
Shows a variety of speed (small rhythmic values and long rhythmic values).
Has at least one change from duple to triple feel.
Uses *rests* or *long* tones to vary the pace.

For descriptions that contain more than one possibility, circle each one that is achieved to provide specific feedback for the student.

Writing Assignments

A well-known aphorism about pop music criticism says, "Talking about music is like dancing about architecture." Still, by requiring students to articulate their understanding through descriptive language, writing pushes them to organize and refine the way they perceive musical concepts. In addition, writing serves as a summative assessment tool we can use in conjunction with the formative assessment of oral discussion.

Program Notes and Concert Reviews

Have students take the role of music critic and write a review or a program note for something being rehearsed. Challenge them to move beyond simplistic statements such as "I don't like it," or "I like the way it sounds," and instead be specific about how the work's musical elements (melody, harmony, rhythm, form, style, etc.) shape their opinion. Students can also write constructive performance reviews, either of their own concerts and rehearsals (e.g., an analysis of the ensemble's current progress, which can later be shared with the rest of the students), or outside events (mini-reviews of professional pop, classical, and jazz concerts).

As with other potentially open-ended activities, provide guidelines, structure, and limits. Dee Hansen suggests brainstorming appropriate vocabulary in preparation for assignments.[18] For example, words that describe texture include:

full, thin, contrapuntal, homophonic, tutti, soloistic, range, tone color, timbre

Another tactic is to frame the assignment as a series of questions students must answer through their writing. Below each is an example:

Sample Guidelines for Program Note Assignment

- **Brief discussion about the composer**—Try to find an angle that relates to the piece at hand. Answer questions such as:

Where is the composer from?
When did he/she live?

Why is this composer significant?
For which pieces is he/she most remembered?
Where does this piece fit into the composer's life?

Born in Beaumont, Texas in 1932, John Barnes Chance studied composition at the University of Texas with Clifton Williams, another well-known composer for bands. Chance is best remembered for his tuneful, rhythmically active, and well-crafted works for school ensembles, including Incantation and Dance, Blue Lake Overture, and Variations on a Korean Folk Song.

- **Background of the work.**

What is the form? How many movements?
Why and when was it written? For whom or what?
Is there an extra-musical background?
Notable instrumentation?

Variations on a Korean Folk song uses as its source material the Korean folk song "Arrirang." Though written in 1965, Chance first became interested in this melody while serving in the 8th U.S. Army Band in Seoul from 1958–59. The work includes a straightforward statement of the main theme and five variations. Percussion instruments, especially the pentatonic temple blocks, are featured prominently, something we might expect from a former percussionist with the Austin Symphony orchestra.

- **Narrative**—What should the listener expect to hear? Encourage students to use a combination of writing techniques, e,g,:

Play-by-Play: Describe what happens and when. Describe things literally, but avoid bogging down in every detail.
Theory Explanations: Don't be pedantic, but use and define technical terms when appropriate.
Metaphor: Use descriptive adjectives, metaphors, and analogies to help readers understand the music without sophisticated musical jargon.
Big picture: What is the overall effect of what listeners will hear?
Editorialize: Occasionally it is appropriate to draw a conclusion or express an opinion about the work, assuming it is qualified as such.

Chance takes us on a musical journey in which a simple, unassuming folk melody experiences a series of character transformations. Each character is like an elaborate disguise, but if we listen closely we can always hear the original melody beneath the costume. The work begins with a soft, solemn folk melody played by the clarinets in their lower register, soon joined by the flutes. As with much folk music, this melody is pentatonic, meaning it only uses five notes (as in the black notes on a piano). The full ensemble soon enters to accompany the melody with rich, sustained harmonies. A gong hit announces the end of the lyrical opening and the beginning of the first variation. Now the folk song turns into a frenetic version of itself. It is heard in a canon in which the second voice quickly follows after the entrance of the first voice, almost like a dog chasing its own tail. After a unison burst by the entire ensemble, a melancholy waltz takes over for Variation 2, with a plaintiff oboe melody playing another variation of the theme. Variation 3 takes the form of a bouncy march in $\frac{6}{8}$. A slightly ominous accompaniment in the horns sets the stage for the trumpets to virtuosically carry the melody. The woodwinds join in the fun, too, punctuating the melody with quick exclamations. The fourth variation turns the melody *into a chorale, but the energy of the march is ever-present in the insistent rhythm of the timpani. The final variation begins with gong, triangle, temple blocks, and vibraphones layering rhythms on top of each other. By the time the vibraphone and woodwinds join, we hear a kaleidoscope of sound, and we realize that every layer forms an elaborate accompaniment for a bold, final statement of the original theme by the brass.*

In addition to program notes and concert reviews, try using other "prompts" to motivate students (Hansen, 29):

- Craft a letter of recommendation for why a work should win an award.
- Write a short story, movie treatment, or mini-screenplay inspired by a specific work.
- Be a critic. Take two pieces of similar styles or about similar topics, and make an argument why one is more effective than the other.

Tests of Declarative and Procedural Knowledge

Written Evaluations of Knowledge

In contrast to authentic assessment, written evaluations that include multiple choice, short answers, matching questions, etc. are a type of traditional assessment. They are useful for testing the declarative and procedural information that is included on rehearsal "Study Sheets" (See Chapter 9). Written evaluations need take only 5–10 minutes of class time, perhaps during the middle of a concert cycle or directly after a concert.

Sample questions

1. Briefly define the following musical terms:

   Slancio
   Allegro non troppo
   con rubato.

2. For each of the following meters, write one properly beamed measure using only eighth notes, dotted eighth notes, sixteenth notes, and dotted sixteenth notes.

   Beat = ♩ $\frac{2}{4}$ Beat = ♩. $\frac{6}{8}$ Beat = ♪ $\frac{4}{4}$ Beat = ♪ $\frac{3}{8}$

---

3. In $\frac{12}{8}$, which of the following is usually considered the beat unit?[19]

A.   B.   C.   D.

4. Why did Andrew Boysen, Jr. compose the piece "I Am"? What was the inspiration for its commissioning?

5. In "I Am" who has the primary melody at Letter C?

6. The form of Charles Carter's "Overture in C" most closely resembles which of the following?

AAB
ABACABA
ABA2
ABCD

7. What is hemiola? What section of "Festival March" uses it prominently?

8. After Letter D, how many times does the main theme repeat? Who plays it last?

9. What contrapuntal compositional device appears at Letter H?

10. For the below example, add bar lines in the proper places according to the printed meter.

11. Listen to the melody performed during this test and answer the following questions:

Is the tonality major or minor?
Is the meter in duple or triple? What could be the time signature?
Using your answer from above, how many measures long is this melody?
Write the rhythm of the first measure using two different time signatures.
Does the melody begin and end on the same note?
Does the melody end on tonic?

12. Which of the following four rhythms is being performed?

         A.   B.   C.   D.

13. Error detection: Listen to the following rhythm and circle the beat that is incorrectly played.

14. Error detection: Listen to a performance of the following scale and circle note played incorrectly.

The Value of Student Self-Assessment

Regular self-assessment is as useful for students as it is for the teachers trying to help them. Inexperienced musicians are notoriously poor at evaluating themselves. For example, studies have shown that school-age students overrate their performances compared to expert evaluators.[20] Generally speaking, middle schoolers overrate more than high schoolers. Melody and rhythm are the most accurately evaluated, while tone, intonation, and technique/articulation are the least accurate (Hewitt 2005, 159). It's not that middle schoolers are arrogant about their abilities; they simply lack the requisite awareness or experience needed to evaluate, highlighting why assessment must do more than measure attendance and attitude.

Part of the problem goes back to how often we assess and give students opportunities to perform on their own. As Robert Duke points out:

> Many novice performers judge the level of their readiness to perform based on their ability to follow someone else's instructions to play a difficult passage; that is, "If I can follow the teacher's step-by-step instructions that lead me to a beautiful performance of this clumsy passage today in my lesson, then I can play this." OK, so now it's time for the student to perform the piece on his own in front of an audience . . . (Duke, 59).

What happens? The student struggles because he has little experience performing on his own. Exacerbating the issue is that inexperienced players tend to evaluate themselves based on their best previous performance, even though it probably happened only one time (and under less stressful circumstances). Or, the student perceives he is ready because he has played every part of the passage well at some point in time, though never in the same run-through.

Ways to combat these problems include:

1. Provide multiple performance opportunities to develop confidence during stressful situations.
2. Instill good practice habits so as to make accurate run-throughs a regular occurrence rather than a happy fluke.
3. Teach students to assess themselves accurately: We can refine students' self-assessment skills by providing regular "expert" feedback so they are not surprised by their performance on formal playing tests. This pays dividends far down the line, as some research suggests accurate self-assessment is highly correlated with performance success at the college level.[21]
4. Record student performances and listen as a group. Show students what we listen for when we evaluate performances and have them practice these skills.
5. Play a professional recording and point out the features that distinguish it. Also, play examples of *poor style*, even if you record them yourself. Not every professional example must be held as an ideal, and contrasting approaches are a useful catalyst for discussion and debate. (e.g., "How does this performer's approach to articulation alter the effect of the piece?")
6. Share rubrics with students before an evaluation so they understand exactly how they will be assessed.

Grading Systems

Fairly or not, grades have become currency in an academic economy in which high marks are traded for educational opportunities and poor ones cast a shadow on other achievements. As a teaching tool, however, grades are first and foremost a way to improve learning, and they are essentially useless unless they:[22]

- describe unambiguously the worth, merit, or value of the work accomplished
- improve the capacity of students to identify good work, that is, to improve their self-evaluation or discrimination skills with respect to work submitted
- stimulate and encourage good work by students
- communicate the teacher's judgment of the student's progress
- inform the teacher about what students have and haven't learned.

In Chapter 7 we discussed the effect positive reinforcement has on student behavior. Any stimulus that increases a corresponding behavior is considered positive reinforcement, and thus one way to shape student behavior is to identify the stimuli to which they respond. Grades often have this effect. Many students want an "A" for virtually the same reasons they want verbal praise, and thus receiving a good grade positively reinforces the behaviors that earned it in the first place. Unfortunately, the same effect applies for those students who prefer "Ds" and "Fs." Receiving them may reinforce the originating behavior (poor performance).[23]

On Assessing Behavior, Participation, and Attendance

What behaviors should grades be based upon? Sometimes music teachers link grades to participation and cooperation—i.e., if students come to class regularly, arrive on-time, and obey rules and procedures, they are likely to receive an "A" or "A−." A 1988 study about grading music students showed that these types of criterion were more common than actual musical criterion; a 1991 study found that school principals put more emphasis on basic performance technique than did band and choral directors.[24] Yet some research shows the opposite—that music teachers do indeed use musical criterion as the basis for grading. The author of the above studies, Claire Wehr McCoy, suggests the following explanation for the discrepancy:

> [Directors] have two sets of objectives: an ideal set, and a pragmatic set against which they evaluate students. Ensemble directors have many demands placed on them and, in the rush to prepare for concert performances, they may feel they have no time to devote to music listening, theory, or history. They undoubtedly find grading by attendance much easier and less stressful than evaluating actual performance (McCoy 1991, 189).

Another reason music teachers commonly assign a disproportionately high percentage of A's is a tendency to value effort over quantifiable achievement. Consider: Johnny does not play well, but he practices, comes to lessons, and tries his hardest. Consequently, he receives an A. Does he deserve it? Is "trying hard" a reasonable criterion for a good grade? Perhaps it is one factor, but should it be the crux? One problem with this approach is the lack of an effective, valid, and reliable way to measure effort, attitude, and behavior.[25] Observation is too subjective, and though practice sheets are useful, they are difficult to validate and do not measure *quality* of effort.[26]

Some teachers grade on improvement, arguing that variable aptitudes make it difficult to hold everyone accountable to the same scale. Aptitude measures the *potential* for achievement, but is not a measure of *actual* achievement. Theoretically speaking, one's achievement may not fulfill one's aptitude, but neither can it surpass it. Thus, the justification is that it is unfair to penalize Frank simply because he has low aptitude. Instead, we should compare Frank's improvement to what is reasonable to expect from him.

This is why parents and administrators sometimes expect uniformly high grades in music (Grading Practices, 40). "How can you penalize Johnny just because he doesn't have the same natural-born talent as Frank?" Sounds reasonable, but would anyone take a math teacher seriously if he gave a high grade and justified it because the student did not have a "talent for math"? Ironically, rewarding progress penalizes high performing students because progress is easier when achievement is low (Lehman, 23).

Grading based on progress also assumes we have measured our students' aptitude. It is inaccurate (not to mention unfair) to infer aptitude through subjective assessments—e.g., how a student dresses, behavior, performance in other classes, and previous musical achievement. Using poor behavior as an indicator is particularly insidious because it is likely correlated with low *achievement*, not low aptitude. By assuming poor performers have low potential or that poor behavior is correlated with low potential, we risk creating self-fulfilling prophecies. Worse, grading on attendance and effort borders on fraud, which might explain why other educators believe music education lacks substance, and why college admissions officers often disregard music grades (Lehman, 23).As Paul R. Lehman, former president of MENC, writes:

> The problem with these criteria is that they have nothing to do with music itself. Anyone reading a transcript has a right to assume that a good grade indicated knowledge and skill in the subject matter. A grade is not just misleading, it's dishonest if it means merely that the student has come to class, or tried hard—or, more accurately, given the appearance of trying hard. No student who does poorly in algebra or biology can expect a good grade solely because she tried hard or came to class. Why should music be different? (Lehman, 23).

Before we judge too harshly the teachers who use these criteria, consider that many feel compelled to employ grades as a retention tool. However unfairly, many music programs are considered luxuries, so teachers sometimes fear too many Bs, Cs, and Ds will drive students away from the program, lower their enrollment numbers, and place the program in jeopardy. Another reason is practical: too many students and not enough time. Classes are far too large for intensive individual assessment during class time, and schedules are too crowded to absorb significant overloads (Hoffer, 31).

But even if one uses the assessment methods discussed earlier in this chapter, Lehman admits that ensemble classes will likely have more high grades than other academic classes. Why? Because band and orchestra are electives that select for motivated, experienced students. Further, many students come to class with prior training from private lessons and outside groups (Grading Practices, 38).

Attendance Grades and Consequences

Though good behavior and attendance are not in and of themselves educational objectives, they are necessary to achieve our *actual* objectives. Particularly in an ensemble class, in which individual participation and cooperation are essential for the success of other individuals, it may be reasonable to make attendance and behavior a limited component of the grade. Ensembles are sort of like musical "teams," and students need to understand their role in the music-making of the whole. This includes being held accountable for bringing to class a working instrument, ensemble music, lesson books, pencil, and instrument-specific items such as valve oil, rock stop, good reeds, rosin, neck strap, reed cases, swabs, cleaning rods, etc. If a student arrives unprepared they create a *de facto* absence for the group, and this can be reflected in their daily/semester grade.

It should be noted that many districts employ school-wide policies to monitor attendance, releasing (and in some cases prohibiting) us from the need to factor it into our grading. In other cases, especially extra-curricular marching bands, the onus is on us to assign grades and/or administer consequences for attendance. Absences are usually categorized as being either excused or unexcused. Excused absences usually include:

- school-sponsored field trips
- illness
- family emergency

It is necessary for teachers to verify excused absences. For example, for school-sponsored trips, students should present a permission-slip at least one week in advance. For other absences, a signed letter from a parent or doctor should be presented immediately after returning, or even in advance of the absence. All other absences are generally considered unexcused unless the student made special arrangements in advance. Directors should make clear that work commitments, vacations, homework, alarm clock malfunctions, etc., are not excusable absences.

Possible methods to calculate attendance grades include the following:

1. Direct reduction of final grade—Create an equation between absences/tardies and grade reductions. For example: 2 tardies = 1 unexcused absence; 2 unexcused absences=1/2 letter grade reduction.
2. Indirect reduction using points—Use a demerit system and assign a value for each absence, each tardy, etc. For example, unexcused absence = 2 point reduction; tardy = 1 point reduction, etc.

Excused absences often carry a penalty analogous to accidentally damaging someone's property—the person must apologize and repair the damage. *Unexcused absences* are treated like intentional vandalism—the perpetrator must repair the damage and accept the punitive consequences of the law.

For excused absences, directors sometimes allow students to make up the missed time, or earn back points (depending on the grading system they use.) If possible, avoid using non-musical activities to earn back missed performance activities and behavioral demerits. Instead, use logical consequences (see Chapter 7). For example, cleaning the rehearsal hall is not a substitute for attending rehearsal. First, it does not compensate for the musical loss, and second, it signals to the rest of the ensemble that taking care of the rehearsal hall is the responsibility of the delinquent, when in reality it is a collective obligation, like learning music and attending rehearsals. A more appropriate and logical consequence is to require the student to practice during a free period or after school, or to complete an assignment on *SmartMusic*. Some directors do not allow students to make-up any absences, or their schedule prohibits them from supervising the make-up practice sessions.

There are two types of consequences for unexcused absences: an activity so students make up missed responsibilities (e.g., practicing), and a grade reduction or demerit to serve as disincentive for further problems. Again, we recommend that students repay their missed time through musical activities, not office work.

In all cases, for both participation and behavior, the system of consequences must be clear and predictable. We cannot ask one student to stay after school for missing rehearsal and later absolve another student for the same violation.

Whichever grading system we implement, students should be able to track the status of their grade during the semester. For example, keep an online average so a student can log-in to check their grade, or make their semester's grades available for review upon appointment. For students with chronic problems, it may be necessary to call home or send a progress report to the parents.

Merit and Demerit Grading Systems

Grading systems usually reflect a balance between two philosophies: merits and demerits (or point-counting and per-infraction). Neither one is sufficient on its own, but together they measure student performance by balancing rewards (for desired behaviors—playing achievement, good attendance, etc.) with punishment (for undesired behaviors—tardiness, absences, disrupting the rehearsal, being unprepared, etc.). Ultimately, clear, thorough, and authentic assessment and grading emphasizes that students *earn* grades rather than being given them by teachers. In other words, a student's grade should not come as a surprise to him. An important caveat: Though clarity in our expectations is important, beware of excessively micromanaging grades to the point that the system's complexity confuses students and distracts us from teaching.

Demerit (Per Infraction)

The demerit system assumes all students achieve highly unless they prove otherwise. Accordingly, each student starts with the highest possible score at the beginning of the semester and loses points based on deficiencies in performance, behavior, attendance, etc. The demerit system makes grade adjustments very clear because each scenario is a simple equation: Action X = Grade adjustment Y.

Examples (Every 5 points lost is a $\frac{1}{3}$-letter grade reduction):

- Tardy = 2 points
- Unexcused absence = 4 points
- Disciplinary action (e.g., call home, referral to Principal, etc.) = 2 point reduction for each action

- Arriving at class unprepared (without instrument, music, pencil, etc.) = 1 point reduction
- Instrument left in school over night three times or more (per day) = 1 point reduction
- Chewing gum = 1 point reduction
- Equipment/Music not put away = 2 point reduction
- Improper dress for performance = 10 point reduction (and student will not be allowed to perform)
- Disruptive in rehearsal or performance = at the discretion of Director, depending on the disruption/situation

As in other classroom management scenarios, we must not compromise when applying demerits. If students discover we are inconsistent they are more likely to test the system and gamble we will not penalize them. Inconsistency also exposes us to the criticism of playing favorites (e.g., "Johnny did the same thing, why didn't you give *him* demerits?")

Keep in mind that the size of the point reduction signals how important an item is to us. The key is to make the punishment fit the crime. We might try to eradicate all talking in class by making any infraction a full letter grade reduction, but this strategy quickly becomes unwieldy. Instead, uses rules and procedures, implement a proportional consequence, and be immediate and consistent in their application.

Merit (Point Counting)

In contrast to the demerit system, merit (point counting) asks students to earn their grade from the bottom up. Instead of penalizing infractions with point reductions, students gain points based on positive achievement and behavior. This system is built upon the classroom management motto "catching students being good." A common approach gives each student a daily grade, worth a maximum of, say, five points. Students earn those points by doing what we expect of them during rehearsal.

For example:

Musical preparation = 2 points
Arriving on time = 1 point
Being prepared (instrument, music, pencil, etc.) = 1 point
Good behavior and attitude = 1 point

The more "good" we observe, the more points students earn. And the more points they earn, the higher their grade. For example, if there are 90 days in a semester, based on five points per day the maximum score for the daily grades would be 450. Other components of the semester grade can receive similar point totals.

Daily grade = 450 points total for the semester
Playing tests = 100 points total
Written tests = 100 points total
Concert attendance and performance = 200 points (100 per concert)
Total: 850 points

With this system, calculating grades on 4.0 scales, letter scales, or 100-point scales is a matter of simple ratios and percentages.

Extra Achievement Points (Extra Credit Points)

Some directors use their grading system to reflect special recognition and musical opportunities outside of school. These extra credit points provide an opportunity to catch students being good for achievement that goes beyond the base level of what we expect.

Examples (Every five points earned is half-letter grade increase):

• Receiving a "Good" or higher at solo/ensemble contests = 5 points
• Practicing more than 2 hours per week (as verified by practice cards signed by parents) = 1 point
• Perfect attendance for the semester = 5 points
• Attending a concert at another school (and writing a concert report) = 2 points
• Writing program notes for a concert = 3 points

However, though attractive, the merit system raises some philosophical questions. First, if we allow students to earn grades higher than an A, do we send the message that we no longer require good behavior once a student reaches 100 percent? Are we tacitly giving students permission to misbehave and skip class, since they know they can make up points with other activities? Are we doing a disservice to our educational goals by turning special achievement into a sort of grade system currency? Thus, instead of grades, some directors link achievement points to band/orchestra letters, varsity pins, or other awards at the end of the year.

For example:

Band/orchestra letter = 100 points
Band/orchestra pin = 75 points
Band/orchestra "Certificate of Dedication" = 50 points

Activities/Assignments for Further Exploration

1. Make a list of five things you have learned in the past year and determine whether each is an example of declarative, procedural, or conceptual learning. Were the teaching methods different for each type of learning?

2. What are the potential advantages and disadvantages to using Standards in our teaching? Among other things, consider the following:

   • Who gets to write the standards?
   • Do they change over time?
   • Would they change based on the country, culture, or era they are used in?
   • Should every discipline have standards?

3. For each of MENC's National Standards, choose a grade level and discuss five activities that would satisfy the standard. Be sure to determine the age level for which you are striving.

4. Robert Duke views learning objectives in terms of their component observable behaviors. With your professor and/or classmates, choose a learning objective that is not on Duke's list and work out its component observable behaviors. How would these behaviors affect the way we teach the objective? How would they affect assessment?

5. The *ASBDA Curriculum Guide* offers a detailed list of benchmarks for each level. Discuss the challenges involved in teaching these benchmarks through method books and repertoire.

6. Write a sample rubric. Use the following activities as a starting point.

   - Basic marching technique
   - Performing a D-Major scale with two notes per bow
   - Performing a solo from memory for the class
   - Sightreading a melody or rhythm
   - Writing program notes

7. For a piece of music you are studying in methods class, conducting class, or ensembles, write a written evaluation of knowledge that tests the concepts you would teach if leading the class.

8. Besides an inaccurate perception of their own ability, can you think of other ways in which students' self-assessment problems might reveal themselves? Do you think these problems apply to their perception of the group's performance? To other individuals? Do these problems appear in other subject areas?

9. Develop your own philosophy on the issue of music grading: How important is attendance? Effort? Achievement?

10. Design logical consequences that could be applied to various contingencies. For example:

    - missing a rehearsal
    - missing a concert
    - arriving late to a rehearsal
    - arriving unprepared.

11. What strategies can a teacher use to insure he is grading accurately, fairly, and consistently?

Further Reading

Duke, Robert A. *Intelligent Music Teaching: Essays on the Core Principles of Effective Instruction*. Austin: Learning and Behavior Resources, 2005.

Farrell, Susan R. *Tools for Powerful Student Evaluation: A Practical Source of Authentic Assessment Strategies for Music Teachers*. Ft. Lauderdale, FL: Meredith Music Publications, 1997.

Garofalo, Robert Joseph. *Blueprint for Band: A Guide to Teaching Comprehensive Musicianship Through School Band Performance*. Ft. Lauderdale, FL: Meredith Music, 1983.

Garofalo, Robert Joseph. *Instructional Designs for Middle/Junior High School Band*. (*Guides to band masterworks*). Ft. Lauderdale, FL: Meredith Music, 1995.

Kimpton, Paul, and Delwyn L. Harnisch. *Scale Your Way to Music Assessment: The Ultimate Guide to Creating a Quality Music Program*. Chicago: GIA Publications, 2009.

Labuta, Joseph A. *Teaching Musicianship in the High School Band*. Fort Lauderdale, FL: Meredith Music, 2000.

MENC, the National Association for Music Education (U.S.). *Spotlight on Assessment in Music Education*. Spotlight series (Reston, Va.). Reston, VA: MENC, 2001.

Odegaard, Denese. *Music Curriculum Writing 101: Assistance with Standards-based Music Curriculum and Assessment Writing: For Band, Choir, Orchestra, and General Music*. Chicago, IL: GIA Publications, 2009.

O'Toole, Patricia Ann. *Shaping Sound Musicians: An Innovative Approach to Teaching Comprehensive Musicianship Through Performance*. Chicago, IL: GIA Publications, 2003.

Chapter 9

Repertoire

To Guide Your Reading

Why is choosing appropriate repertoire important?

How can we define "musical quality"?

What are some ways to achieve appropriate balance in programming?

What templates can we use to design a printed concert program?

How can our repertoire choices support our curricular goals?

What are some strategies to incorporate music history, form, theory, and other arts into a "regular" rehearsal?

How can "study sheets" be used to hold students accountable for the concepts we teach through repertoire?

What resources are there for finding quality literature?

How do we accurately evaluate the difficulty of a work?

What should we consider when programming transcriptions and pop music?

In what ways can we consider student opinion when making repertoire choices?

Curriculua tend to be stable: the history of the American Revolution does not change; the basic concepts of algebra remain the same; the vocabulary of the Spanish language is well-codified. Likewise, a well-designed music curriculum guides us to teach certain melodic, harmonic, rhythm, theoretical, and historical concepts consistently from year to year. What changes, more so than other classes, however, is the vehicle with which we teach them: the repertoire. Some directors never use the same "textbook" twice, while others regularly revisit masterworks every few years.

Abraham Lincoln reportedly once said, "If I had eight hours to chop down a tree, I'd spend six hours sharpening my ax." The time and effort we devote to selecting music will pay off in the quality of our rehearsals and concerts and the success of our students in meeting curriculum goals. To choose effectively, however, we must balance a host of related, unrelated, and often conflicting variables. Appropriate repertoire does the following:

1. Provides the means to learn essential musical concepts
2. Keeps the entire ensemble engaged, which reinforces classroom management
3. Gives the ensemble a chance to perform successfully, which in turn improves motivation and morale
4. Offers a vehicle to perform art.

This fourth criterion is particularly crucial, but it presumes we can find and recognize quality literature. But is it even possible to measure artistic quality?

On Musical Quality

"Quality" is a relative term, its meaning complicated by the influences of relativism, multi-culturalism, and context. It is perfectly possible, and eminently reasonable, to prize one work for its harmonic elegance, another for its melodic beauty, and still another for its rhythmic inventiveness, even if none of the three works embody the best of all three elements. The question is further complicated in our role as music educators. What criteria should we consider? Playability? Technical challenges? Compositional techniques? Pedagogical value? Historical significance? Cultural significance?

In his 1978 study on wind band literature, Acton Eric Ostling proposed ten criteria by which to judge any work's quality[1]—from ballet music to film medleys; American folk music to world music; classical transcriptions to contemporary works. Even though the answers to these questions are subjective, the sheer act of confronting them guides us to consider a work's artistic merit.

Acton Ostling's Criteria for Determining Serious Artistic Merit

1. *The composition has form—not "a form," but form—and reflects a proper balance between repetition and contrast.*
    The important point here is not that music must follow standardized forms such as theme and variations or rondo, but rather that it must create some type of logical and satisfying shape, even if the shape is appropriate only for that piece.
2. *The composition reflects shape and design, and creates the impression of conscious choice and judicious arrangement on the part of the composer.*
    As an extension of the first criterion, this describes the tools the composer uses to create shape and form, including phrasing, harmonic rhythm, cadences, and the pacing of music events.
3. *The composition reflects craftsmanship in orchestration, demonstrating a proper balance between transparent and tutti scoring, and also between solo and group colors.*
    By now we can sense a theme that binds these criteria together: balance. The point is not to prescribe a certain amount of solo, group, and tutti, but rather to recognize that too much of one texture, without relief or contrast, is musically unsatisfying. Even full-blast heavy metal songs use this; head banging only works if it balances with sections in which the head may (relatively) rest!
4. *The composition is sufficiently unpredictable to preclude an immediate grasp of its musical meaning.*
    Unsaid but implied here by Ostling is that the composition must also be sufficiently *predictable*. Gordon's Music Learning Theory (See Chapters 1 and 2) is an obvious analog: musicians use familiar (i.e., predictable patterns) as a reference to understand unfamiliar (unpredictable) ones. Without having the familiar as context, the unfamiliar is incomprehensible.
5. *The route through which the composition travels in initiating its musical tendencies and probable musical goals is not completely direct and obvious.*

Again, the converse is also true: The route through which the composition travels should not be completely indirect and obscure. Something which is entirely unpredictable is no more satisfying than something entirely predictable. The gratuitously random (e.g., a haphazard collection of melodies with no connection) is as problematic as the overly obvious (e.g., music that dutifully and unimaginatively fulfills conventions).

6. *The composition is consistent in its quality throughout its length and in its various sections.*
   Certainly it is frustrating to encounter a work that shows flashes of quality but fails to sustain it. However, sometimes it is reasonable to program these pieces anyway; after all, we don't throw out a piece of fruit simply because of a bruise on its skin. Our decision may depend on how much musical "sweetness" a work offers in relation to its "bitterness."

7. *The composition is consistent in its style, reflecting a complete grasp of technical details, clearly conceived ideas, and avoids lapses into trivial, futile, or unsuitable passages.*
   Inevitably, conductors, performers, and listeners will judge certain passages of a work to be "better" than others. But this quality standard is less about personal preference, and more about the composer's intent to be true to the style of his work. For example, if the work is an arrangement or medley themes, are transitions used effectively to connect disparate ideas? For works of any style, does every section appear to be there for an artistic reason, or are there passages that seem gratuitously added or superfluous to the work?

8. *The composition reflects ingenuity in its development, given the stylistic context in which it exists.*
   Great composers often embrace established conventions without treating them as formulae. But note Ostling's stylistic clarification: Whereas string quartets and symphonies were the experimental playgrounds of the eighteenth century, there is a limit to how much ingenuity a ceremonial march can endure before it no longer fulfills its function (think constantly shifting meters and tempos, etc.). Predictability and a lack of ingenuity can be comforting and pleasing. (Think of a movie sequel that reprises the main theme from the original. In this context the return of the original is powerful in its nostalgia.)

9. *The composition is genuine in idiom, and is not pretentious.*
   As in point 8, even as it innovates, we want a march to respect, or at least recognize, the conventions of the march form. We want a symphony to honor the traditions of symphonic form. Yet all the while we respect the composer's right to purposefully thwart certain aspects of an idiom. The operative word is balance, in this case between tradition and innovation.

10. *The composition reflects a musical validity which transcends factors of historical importance, or factors of pedagogical usefulness.*
    Sometimes we study and program these pieces as musicological exercises— e.g., "Patriotic Music from the Civil War." But though history is a factor in evaluating a work's merit, it cannot be the overriding one. One's perception of a poor composition is only slightly mitigated if it were commissioned for a landmark event, or if it holds a unique place in a composer's oeuvre.

Ostling's list is an extremely useful guide, though admittedly few pieces would receive perfect scores across the board. The goal, however, is not to find one "perfect" piece of music, but rather to maximize the quality of the works we choose to put in front of our students.

The Debate about "Educational Music"

During his 2009 talk at the WASBE (World Organization of Symphonic Bands and Ensembles) conference in Cincinnati, OH, Stephen Budiansky, journalist and historian, took an aggressive stance on the general quality of music played in educational settings. In comparing the style of Gunther Schuller's work *Nature's Way* to that of many "educational band pieces," Budiansky remarked:

> I thought how remarkably ironic, that a real composer with a reputation outside of the school music racket is writing a piece not only with more artistic merit but more educational value than the stuff produced by the writers who specialize in the education market. And of course what that really underscores is that the writers for the ed [education] market don't really care about education. They care about marketability, and that's come down to getting "superior" ratings at contests with pieces that sound harder than they are; it comes down to pieces that are "safely cross cued" to cover up mistakes; it comes down to not challenging students with something that might expose their flubs; it comes down to appealing to the lowest common denominators of ignorance and surface flash to produce pieces with built in applause lines at the end and lots of percussion activity in the middle.[2]

Whether the practice of cross-cueing and doubling is as pernicious as Budiansky believes is open to debate. The other side of the argument maintains that it is folly to play a piece with a prominent bassoon part with an orchestra that does not have a bassoon player, or to play music with difficult horn parts with a band with young horn players who lack the technical facility to play the part. Perhaps there is a difference between putting students in a position to fail as individuals and as a group, even in the name of great music, and challenging them in ways that might cruelly expose their faults. One goal of effective cross-cueing is to allow ensembles—with their various shapes, sizes, and imperfections—to play good music well, in spite of their weaknesses.

Mr. Budiansky's larger point concerns his perception of the lack of quality in educational music, or what he calls "that piece"—music that "exists nowhere in the known music universe—except for the twilight zone of school music performance" and is written by a composer who is only known within the world of educational music.[3] Budiansky summarizes this music as such: "Much of the music composed specifically for school band is formulaic, emotionally superficial, monotonously alike, dull, and didactic; that it fails to inspire students; and that by being removed from any genuine living musical tradition, classical or popular, it fails to provide students with a true musical education or the basis for further independent exploration of music, either as a performer or a listener." [4]

Perhaps the solution is: When in doubt, program great music. Allen Britton (as quoted by Budiansky), summarizes it this way:

> Should not our music curriculum consist, first of all, of the world's most beautiful music? Should a child be able to sing in a high school choir or play in a high school band or orchestra for several years and still not have come to know at least a fair sample of the best there is in our musical heritage? . . . To construct curriculums with music of lasting beauty would by no means exclude the use of new music or even of the teaching pieces now so widely available. It would, however, ensure that music of the greatest worth would be presented to our students in larger quantities than is now the case, and that they would know some of it when they get out of school (Britton 1991, p. 180).[5]

A common argument in favor of educational music is its pedagogical value: "That piece" may not be a work by Beethoven, but it could still be quality music that is also designed to further the curricular needs and practical requirements of public school music making. But Budiansky rejects this justification, arguing that an English teacher would not substitute an inferior play for something written by Shakespeare just because the new play provided great opportunities to teach sentence structure, or alliteration, or any number of other pedagogical objectives.

Mr. Budiansky largely blames music publishers, and there is something compelling about his argument that they "rig" the system to sell new, but inferior, music for educational purposes through the use of relentless marketing and manipulation (Budiansky, WASBE, 26)—a tactic that echoes the efforts of the pharmaceutical and food industries.

But seen in this light, any complaints about educational music also echo the fast food/obesity argument. Should we blame McDonald's for hawking the latest supersized hamburger, or should we blame the customer who buys it even though he knows it is no good for him? Composers and publishers are an easy target, but we as teachers own much of the blame, too. If we demand quality (however we choose to define it) and only buy quality, then publishers will produce quality.

Using Categories and Dispositions: Programming with Balance and Variety

Once we understand the concept of quality in music, we are ready to consider a host of other factors as we construct our concert program.

Balance—Are we providing a balanced and varied musical experience for our students, encompassing a range of composers and styles?

Difficulty—Have we chosen a program that the group can learn in time for the concert?

Presentation—Does our program provide a satisfying overall experience for our audience?

Technical considerations for the ensemble—Have we chosen repertoire that is attainable by the less-accomplished players but does not bore the advanced members, and vice-versa?

If only to help satisfy these considerations it is useful to view works in terms of categories. Then, rather than blindly choosing from a large pool of repertoire we can work from a program template and adjust it to our tastes and needs.

Common Categories

Openers—Generally 2–5 minute works that grab an audience's attention; fanfares and overtures are the most common examples.

Expressive works—Generally slow pieces, though the entire work does not have to be slow; preludes, chorales and elegies are common examples.

Multi-movement works—Usually the longest works with the most depth and greatest variety. Suites, symphonies, concerti, and divertimenti are common examples.

Features—Works that feature a soloist, small group, or section; concerti are the most common example.

Standalones—Single movement works, though separate movements may be implied within the form. Standalones are generally 5–15 minutes long and have more depth and variety than short openers. Fantasies and Overtures are common examples; many contemporary works are standalones.

Closers—The musical coda at the end of the concert. Often 2–5 minutes of virtuosic music that showcases the ensemble. Marches, Dances, and Paso Dobles are the most common examples.

Project pieces—Any work that will use the largest percentage of rehearsal time and might be worked on over a longer period of time than other pieces; usually a work of high quality that challenges musically and technically.

Note: Project pieces can come from any category, though we usually recommend a standalone, expressive piece, or multi-movement work. If the project piece is an opener or closer it may mean we've chosen to spend the most rehearsal time on the least amount of music, or that we've missed an opportunity to program something more substantial. There is nothing wrong with working hard on a short, exciting piece, provided we are not valuing flash over depth.

Wildcards—Works that don't easily fit into a category.
Double agents—Works that fill more than one category at the same time (i.e., an expressive work or multi-movement work that is also a project piece).
Thorny works—Whereas project pieces usually stretch technical ability, thorny works stretch musical understanding. Thorny works are often contemporary pieces that provide the opportunity to teach new compositional techniques, harmonic languages, and formal structures.
Novelties—Generally short works that feature a comic gimmick, unusual soloist or instrumentation, or are otherwise light and audience-friendly (e.g., Leroy Anderson's *The Typewriter*).

Categories are the building blocks of a program template. For example, a typical professional orchestra concert often has three slots in its template:

Overture (opener)
Concerto (feature)
Intermission
Symphony (multi-movement/Project piece).

The typical school band/orchestra concert usually contains at least four slots, for example:

1. Opener
Multi-movement
Feature
Closer

2. Standalone
Feature
Multi-movement work

3. Standalone
Expressive work
Multi-movement
Closer

4. Standalone
Multi-movement
Expressive work
Standalone
Closer

The paint-by-numbers approach with categories does not guarantee a balanced program. There are other, more abstract aspects we should balance besides genre. Style is one possibility, though what constitutes a balance of styles is difficult to describe. Does it mean a piece from each historical period? Loud, soft, fast, slow? Neither of these is completely satisfactory. Instead of genre or style, perhaps we should strive for a balance of disposition. For example, in his book *The World in Six Songs*, Daniel Levitin argues there are six essential types of music, each of which played a role in human development:

> [Music] is not simply a distraction or a pastime, but a core element of our identity as a species, an activity that paved the way for more complex behaviors such as language, large-scale cooperative undertakings, and the passing down of important information from one generation to the next.[6]

Levitin's six song archetypes are:

- friendship
- joy
- comfort
- knowledge
- religion
- love

It is easy to debate whether his categories can account for all music (What about war songs? What about absolute music?). But even if we choose to expand his list, the important point is that music always has a point of view and an underlying motivation, even if, as with absolute music, that point of view is simply the music itself. When we construct a program, we should try evaluating how many "songs" are represented. Six works of joy may entertain our students and audience, but the homogeneity offers no balance, variety, depth, or perspective. If Ostling's list teaches us what great music has in common, Levitin's list highlights its diversity.

Teaching the Curriculum through Repertoire—Comprehensive Musicianship through Performance

The process of teaching musical concepts beyond performance readiness is often called "Comprehensive Musicianship Through Performance." As a philosophy, Comprehensive Musicianship was an outgrowth of the "Contemporary Music Project," which was conceived and chaired by the composer Norman Dello Joio. Its aim was to use creative, contemporary techniques to direct a more substantial and inclusive study of the musical arts, allowing students to discover for themselves the process involved in composing a work.[7] Through a series of seminars and workshops in the 1960s, the Contemporary Music Project evolved into "Comprehensive Musicianship Through Performance (CMP)." Essentially an extension of the original CMP project, this revamped incarnation was a reaction to what was viewed as a compartmentalized approach to teaching music—especially performance. In the CMP model, ensemble music-making incorporates music theory, analysis, critical thinking, appreciation, and performance as the means to teach history, style, composition, and improvisation (Fitzgerald, 57). CMP seeks to make connections among these areas in order to make every topic more meaningful. It also employs "discovery learning"—i.e., students learn about music by writing, creating, and performing it for themselves.

In the sections below we offer a brief introduction to the process of incorporating CMP into the ensemble rehearsal. For an excellent in-depth discussion, we recommend Patricia O'Toole's *Shaping Sound Musicians* (GIA).

Music History and Style

The concert band's repertoire resides almost exclusively in the twentieth- and twenty-first-century music of the United States and England. This makes it crucial to seek repertoire from other time periods and cultures. In contrast, the orchestra's core repertoire includes a broader variety, including Baroque, Classical, Romantic, and Contemporary works.

Among the styles and techniques we should seek are:

Historical Styles

- Medieval
- Renaissance
- Baroque
- Classical
- Romantic
- Twentieth century
- Twenty-first century

Cultural Styles

- American
- European
- Latin-American
- Asian
- African
- Middle-Eastern, etc.

Compositional Styles and Techniques

- Contrapuntal
- Tutti textures
- Contrast between tutti and chamber textures
- Expressive works (regardless of tempo)
- Programmatic
- Absolute/Non-programmatic
- Solo with ensemble
- Polymeter/Mixed meter/Uneven meter
- Tension-release
- Tonality
- Polytonality
- Triads/Extended harmonies
- Atonality
- Motivic development
- Improvisation

Programming music by a great composer presents an obvious opportunity to learn about the life and work of a great artist. "Beethoven struggled with depression while writing the *Fifth Symphony*" becomes more than just an interesting factoid if students are actually performing his music. Moreover, performing a piece by a Brahms, Beethoven, Copland, etc., or pieces in a similar style, becomes a doorway to explore other masterworks.

Beyond facts and concepts, a few strategies to incorporate music history and style directly into the ensemble rehearsal include the following:

1. Isolate notable passages during rehearsal; if possible, "rescore" the section to highlight effective compositional decisions the composer has made. For example, if a chord contains an expressive dissonance, temporarily remove it from the orchestration. Then, restore it so students can appreciate the difference. This is particularly effective to answer questions such as: What compositional techniques define the composer's style?
2. Play recordings, or read works in a similar style and draw comparisons.
3. For classical works or arrangements, discuss how the style compares to the norm of the era. Is it significant because it introduced a new form or technique? Then play recordings (or read) works that came before and after it. Create an aural timeline of stylistic development.

Admittedly, many composers we perform are contemporaries. We can explore their history while it is still being written:

a) Composer-in-residence
b) Meet-the-composer via speaker-phone, Q and A conference
c) Meet-the-composer via video conference

Form, Structure, and Theory

Without a working knowledge of form, students are doomed to constantly view the trees—specific notes on their specific part—without ever seeing the forest—how their part fits into the architecture of the entire work. Though directors easily perceive ABA, theme and variation, rondo, fugue, sonata form, etc., for many students these forms are unfamiliar. With some guidance, however, classical forms become a toehold to appreciating the big picture.

An easy way to incorporate the study of form into the rehearsal is simply to use the terminology. For example, introduce the work by using the proper terms—sonata, rondo, theme and variations etc.—and have students label each theme and section in their parts as they are identified. Then, refer to sections of the piece by their role in the form (e.g., "Let's start at the recapitulation." "Trumpets, let's hear you play theme number 2 where it first comes in.") This pushes students to be aware of their musical surroundings.

One advantage of incorporating theory into the rehearsal is that it allows us to relate the occasionally abstract constructs of music theory to actual music being performed. Triads, non-chord tones, progressions, etc., become more than just mathematical relationships; they become compositional tools with practical applications and expressive results.

To facilitate rehearsal-based theory, we need to teach the ensemble a minimum of basic skills and terminology, as below:

1. Ability to transpose their part to and from transposed pitch
2. Basic structure of a chord—root, third, fifth, seventh
3. Basic concepts of consonance, dissonance, preparation, tension, and release

4. The concept of tonal center or key area (*Note*: This is *not* the same as key signatures.)
5. Basic chord progressions (I-IV-I; I-IV-V^7-I)
6. The concept of modulation

We can use this basic knowledge to incorporate theory into the rehearsal:

1. Play condensed excerpts from the score at the piano. Illustrate how the composer's melodic, harmonic, and rhythmic vocabulary create the "sound" of the work (e.g., chord structure, unexpected rhythms). Use this technique to answer questions such as: How does the composer manipulate rhythm, melody, tonal centers, and chord structures to create interesting music? Be sure to identify which instruments have which role (Who plays the dissonance? Who plays the parallel triadic progression?)
2. Address sections using concert pitch. (e.g., "Everybody who has a concert G on beat 2 . . .")
3. Balance harmonies using chord terms. (e.g., "We have a C Major chord on beat 1. Everybody who has the third of the chord, please play . . .") Even better, ask students to identify their role in the chord for themselves ("Everybody who has the root of the chord in m. 23, please play and sustain it.")
4. Illustrate examples of dissonance (e.g., "Trombones, your A♭ is the dissonance in this E♭ major triad since it is not in the chord.)
5. Point out suspensions and resolutions (e.g., "Trombones, bring out your D♭ so we hear the suspension," or "Flutes, stress the G, then decrescendo as it resolves.") Even better, ask students to identify these pitches for themselves. ("Let's just hear the folks who have the suspension in the last measure.")

Interdisciplinary Topics

Social and Economic History, Language, Law and the Sciences

Even in this age of interdisciplinary studies, history, especially at the secondary school level, tends to be compartmentalized. Scientific history is taught separately from political history; music history is isolated from economic history. How many students have ever made the connection that the American Revolution happened at the same time Mozart wrote the *Paris Symphony*? Or that Charles Ives was writing his nostalgic homages to American folk music at the same time thousands of Americans were fighting and dying in World War I? Historical connections and parallels are more than just interesting trivia—they create meaning through contextualization. Research sponsored by MENC suggests that teachers often shy away from integrating music and other disciplines because they are uncomfortable or lack confidence in how to do it. But their attitudes changed after participating in collaborative workshops.[8] Be proactive: Approach other teachers, express your interest in collaborating, and come prepared with ideas to stimulate discussion.

Below are a few ways to incorporate social and economic history into the rehearsal:

1. Discuss the political, social, and economic climate that existed while the piece was written.
2. Discuss any programmatic or cultural significance a work has (e.g., LoPresti—*Elegy for a Young American* and President Kennedy; Sousa—*Stars and Stripes Forever* and America's Independence Day; Camphouse—*A Movement for Rosa* and the Civil Rights Movement).
3. Collaborate with a classroom teacher:

   • Music and Physics: Acoustics
   • Music and Math: Intervals, Basic set-theory

- Music and History: Social, historical, and cultural influences on music composition
- Music and Foreign Language: Music of other cultures; lyrics
- Music and Business Law: musicians' contracts, musicians unions, copyrights, intellectual property

Analogies to Other Arts

Form, structure, theory, dissonance, color, and blend are terms shared by most art forms, including visual art, dance, architecture, and theatre. Make connections to these other forms by examining their masterpieces. By noting common aesthetics and conceptual approaches, we strengthen students' understanding of all artistic disciplines.

Here are a few suggestions:

1. Display examples of artwork by master painters throughout the rehearsal hall. Use these as examples of color, blend, and shading and refer to them when discussing music.
2. Illustrate how aesthetic principles in the same stylistic period manifest themselves in different art forms. For example:

- Baroque music and Baroque architecture
- Renaissance music and Renaissance sculpture
- Minimalistic music and Minimalistic art
- Melody/Harmony in music to Foreground/Background in art

Study Sheets: Holding Students Accountable for What We Teach through the Repertoire

Study sheets help us avoid the "it-won't-be-on-the-test" syndrome, in which a good teacher brilliantly covers musical topics but fails to hold students responsible for knowing and understanding them. As Joseph Labuta recommends in *Teaching Musicianship in the High School Band*, study sheets outline what we wish students to learn from a piece and facilitate the integration of music rehearsing and classroom teaching.[9] Since it is awkward for students to take notes while they hold an instrument, a study sheet provides a reference outline of everything for which they will be held accountable. It is incumbent upon us to analyze each piece we program for its non-performance related elements, and identify topics that need to be covered later.[10]

Study sheets are often a gateway to further exploration, including (Labuta, 21):

- outside reading assignments that expand upon ideas discussed in rehearsal
- outside listening that familiarizes students with the piece they are performing and other related works

What to Include on a Study Sheet

1. Biographical information about the composer and work, and the circumstances surrounding its composition
2. A form diagram

3. Key concepts about the historical period in which it was written
4. Musical concepts students will experience through rehearsing and performing the work
5. Specifically how students should focus their listening while performing the piece
6. Stylistic information—How should the following be performed:

  • articulations
  • dynamics
  • balance
  • tone color

7. Required readings (e.g., biographical essays about the composer, introductions to the time period, reviews of the work's premiere, program notes by the composer, etc.).

Successful integration of this type of learning requires very little change in a traditional rehearsal routine (Labuta, 200).

• Allot a few minutes at the end of every other rehearsal to review topics on the study sheets, outside readings, etc.
• At the first or second rehearsal after a concert, or midway through the rehearsal process, dedicate some rehearsal time teaching concepts from the study sheet.
• Spend one rehearsal period directly after the concert for assessment.

Resources for Finding Quality Literature

Be proactive in seeking out quality literature. Take advantage of opinions you respect, but don't allow others to make judgments for you. Seek out as much information as you can find, and don't settle for mediocrity. And for better and for worse, don't judge a book by its cover. We recommend these strategies for finding good literature:

Patronize your own school's ensemble library—Last year's ensemble music is often treated like yesterday's toys: played with once or twice and then forgotten. But some things never go out of fashion. Don't let faded parts and dull covers distract you from rediscovering good literature the school already owns. Many publishers commission new works based on what was previously successful, so it is likely that some pieces in the library are the original archetypes of the sequels that currently fill catalogs. Take the time to peruse these scores and uncover forgotten gems.

Patronize someone else's library—Ask a colleague at a neighboring school if you can browse their library. Even they may not know what forgotten gems are hidden in old file cabinets.

Past programs—Discover what works your predecessor found were successful.

Get on publishers' mailing lists—Make sure you are receiving information from the best sources. Most publishers have a "Request a Catalog" link on their websites. Below is a non-comprehensive list of important publishers for school band and orchestras.

  Alfred Publishing
  American Composer's Forum BandQuest
  Amstel Music

BandQuest (Hal Leonard)
Brolga Music (Australia)
C. Alan Publications
Carl Fischer (including Wind Band Select)
C.L. Barnhouse
Daehn Publications
DeHaske Publications (Netherlands)
G. Schirmer, Inc.
Grand Mesa Music Publishers
Kendor Music
Ludwig Music Publishing Company, Inc. Manhattan Beach Music
Meredith Music Publications
Neil A. Kjos Music Company
Oxford University Press
Shawnee Press, Inc.
Southern Music Company
Theodore Presser, Inc.
Tierolff Muziekcentrale (Netherlands)
Windependence Series (Boosey & Hawkes)
Wingert-Jones Music, Inc.

Use, but don't overuse, promotional recordings—Judge a work on its musical merits, not how it sounds on a professionally produced CD. The majority of these recordings are performed by advanced college groups and professional ensembles. Publishers want us to buy their wares, and eliciting the reaction, "Wow, that piece sounds great, I want my orchestra to sound like that!" reflects the same tactics that television commercials employ every day. As with score study, recordings should be a tool, not a crutch. Professional recordings easily hide technical and scoring problems that may make a work inappropriate for your ensemble (e.g., brass ranges, inner parts, lack or preponderance of doublings, etc.) A more useful evaluation requires analysis of the score itself, and at a more thorough level than allowed by the one or two page samples available on many websites. Look at a complete score whenever possible.

Order music on approval—Many retailers allow music to be ordered "on approval," meaning they will send a full set but allow its return within one-two weeks as long as it is sent back in pristine condition.

Scores only—Particularly for large, expensive works, consider ordering a separate full score first.

Visit your dealer—On a semi-regular basis, take a pilgrimage to the nearest music retailer that specializes in ensemble repertoire. Discuss repertoire with the salespeople and browse their entire inventory.

Don't exclusively program from the catalog—It's easy to receive a shiny new catalog in the mail and build the year's repertoire based only on new releases. Not only is this expensive, but it allows the publishers to dictate their definition of quality. A new release catalog is like a box of new reeds. Most of them will play, but only a few are worth using in a concert!

Go to conventions—Most people know that publishers and retailers usually bring boxes of scores and recordings to conventions. Less known is that many MENC and state associations set-up listening rooms with a plethora of scores and recordings waiting to be browsed. Use both resources.

Solicit the opinion of your colleagues and fellow directors—Get in the habit of asking, "What have you programmed recently? Anything notable?"

Consult a repertoire text—See the list of resources at the end of the chapter.

Keep a repertoire log (See below).

Repertoire Logs

Composers do not write music that is "one size fits all." Each piece has its own set of challenges and rewards. That makes life exciting for performers, but it means that not every piece is appropriate for every ensemble. Even within an overall grade level some pieces are more or less appropriate for a specific group, and directors should be sensitive to these subtleties.

This is why directors regularly ask each other questions such as, "Do you know a good slow piece for my band that doesn't need strong French horns?" or "Can you recommend a Grade 4 work that features trombones?" or "Do you know good Grade 3 Renaissance pieces?" Email listservs, online bulletin boards, and repertoire textbooks are invaluable resources for answering these questions. We can create our own resources, too. Consider keeping a personal "repertoire log" that is essentially an annotated list of works. Populate the list with works from any source, and add a work even if you have no immediate plans to program it. The information might be of help to a colleague, and it might solve a programming challenge down the line. Some tips for keeping the repertoire log:

- Create lists for each category—opener, multi-movement work, etc.
- Create special lists—For example: Good Renaissance pieces; works that don't require strong horns; expressive works that involve multiple percussionists.
- Assign a grade level for each work (or create a list of "Grade 3 Closers," "Grade 4 Project Pieces," etc.).
- Write brief notes to remind yourself of important details for each work (e.g., "beautiful harmonies, extended oboe solo"; "overture that includes a fugue in the middle, limited mallet percussion").

Evaluating the Difficulty of a Work

Band and orchestra literature is usually graded by difficulty on a scale from 1 to 6 (where 1 = easiest; 6 = most difficult). Lists published by states are used to pick approved music for contest and festival. Those in GIA's *Teaching Music Through Performance* series and Manhattan Beach Music's *Best Music for Band* books are excellent references for any situation. Keep in mind, however, that though most rating scales evaluate on a combination of technical and musical factors, there is no universal standard. A Grade 3 piece on one list might be a Grade 2 or Grade 4 on another list. Adding to the confusion are publishers, who generally rate according to their own scale, one which occasionally underrates difficulty in an effort to sell more copies. The most accurate way to evaluate the true level of a work is to examine the score to determine how it fits the relative strengths and weaknesses of our ensemble. Examine the following aspects:

Ranges

Professional recordings make every piece sound playable, but the reality is that our students, especially the brass players, have range limitations. First, check the highest note in the lead parts. Then see how long these part stays in the highest tessitura. Will fatigue be an issue? Examine the range of the lower parts. Experienced educational composers often assume a wide level of ability from the top of the section to the bottom and write accordingly. Do the lower parts match the ability of the players?

For string music, attention must be given to range and clef changes. As students approach upper intermediate to advanced playing, it is our responsibility to broach these issues. Except for beginners, do not automatically avoid tenor clef for cello/bass players, treble clef for viola, or passages that go above fifth position in the first violin. We must present these techniques methodically and teach them through appropriate literature of high quality.

Interest of Parts

In professional ensembles the players are contractually obligated to be there, so there is little pressure to involve the entire orchestra. However, in educational ensembles we have an obligation to engage every player according to their abilities. Are the lower parts active, or do they passively accompany the lead parts? Scoring roles are easily typecast—horns on offbeats, tubas on root position downbeats, etc. This may be acceptable for marches and dances, but not as a rule. Determine whether all instruments—including low brass, low woodwinds, and percussion—have a chance to take the lead.

Contrapuntal Density

It is important to understand how counterpoint challenges young players. Put simply, the more independent lines there are, the harder it is for less mature players to play confidently and accurately. Don't shy away from challenging your students, but recognize that "independence" is a skill that must be rehearsed alongside technique and musicality. The length of a section is a key factor. Even inexperienced students are generally able to grasp short sections of contrapuntal writing.

Another effective way to introduce counterpoint is to seek out scores with fugal writing that employ direct canons instead of suggestions of imitation. These pieces are easier to digest for inexperienced students and let everyone "get the tune." Likewise, look for literature that uses short, idiomatic riffs in imitation. Even if it requires students to break away from the comfort of homorhythmic playing for only a few measures, these experiences prepare them for more advanced counterpoint.

Voicing Density (Thickness Versus Transparency)

Voicing density often involves harmony in rhythmic unison—i.e., multiple voices play the same rhythm, but with different pitches. High density (thickness) creates richness, but once again, independence is an issue. Although mature players have the confidence to balance and project multiple voices, younger players may struggle. As with melodic counterpoint, what looks simple in isolation is a challenge in context. Generally, a density of more than four voices creates a challenge for young players.

Doubling

Many works contain a good deal of cross-cueing, in which lines are doubled in several voices. This helps strengthen those voice parts and serves as insurance against an unbalanced ensemble, or one in which certain players are weak (e.g., many horn parts are doubled in the saxophone section, which tends to be stronger, or at least numerous, in most bands.) Generally speaking, the more doubling a piece contains, the more flexibly it can be adapted to any ensemble. But excessive doubling limits a composer's ability to explore counterpoint, color, and texture.

Adjusting Scores to Fit the Characteristics of Your Ensemble

It is rare that a school band or orchestra has perfectly balanced instrumentation with uniform ability levels within each section and across the ensemble. When faced with a work that is *mostly* appropriate for our ensemble, we have three choices:

1. Program it and hope for the best on the difficult sections.
2. Reject it because it is not completely appropriate.
3. Adjust the score to fit the characteristics of our ensemble.

Choice 1 is clearly undesirable. Challenges do not solve themselves, and we do our students a disservice if we knowingly put them in a position to fail. Choice 2 follows the aphorism, "Discretion is the better part of valor," and it is a wise option when the needs of the work far outstrip the abilities of the ensemble (e.g., Grade 5 clarinet parts with Grade 3 clarinet players; seven mallet percussion parts with only two percussionists in the ensemble, etc.).

But it would be foolish to reject quality music from our program if we can effectively adapt it without betraying the work's form and spirit. The most common alterations include:

- re-score solo passages for another instrument
- bolster the strength of one section in the ensemble by re-scoring the passage
- simplify rhythms and technical passages
- adjust/displace octaves (e.g., flutes down an octave at certain passages; or, half of the section down the octave)
- supplement the ensemble with outside players (other students or adults)
- supplement the ensemble with electronics (but be tasteful: don't use an electric bass in a Holst Suite or Beethoven Symphony!)
- rewrite sections with clef changes in the usual clef for each instrument (e.g., tenor clef passages in bassoon, trombone, and cello converted into bass clef)—although it will add dreaded ledger lines players may find this more comfortable; once the section is learned, return to the original clef to develop its use.
- double high alto/tenor voice parts in another voice—e.g., double cello parts in viola, high horn parts in trumpet, etc. This strategy adds richness to the sound and gives young players confidence with difficult technique without sacrificing the integrity of the work.

Caveat: Many of these changes will be unacceptable according to the rules at festivals and contests. Always check with the organizers and judges to confirm what is allowed.

On the Use of Transcriptions and Arrangements

Whether or not to use transcriptions is one of the most oft-debated topics in programming, especially for winds. The purist asks: Why program a piece that has been altered from the composer's original vision—one that makes compromises in order to become playable by wind instruments? The pro-transcription advocate counters: As long as the transcription maintains the spirit of the original, why not extend the wind band's repertoire into the huge realm of orchestral masterworks?

The morass thickens in regards to simplified arrangements. Should an orchestra or band play a simplified version of, say, a Mozart overture, thus exposing younger students to great music, or do arrangements remove the essence of a work, reducing it merely to a collection of great melodies?

Arrangements are often seen as a perversion of great literature. But great melodies are just that: great melodies, composed by great composers. We recommend the following guidelines when choosing transcriptions:

1. Look for arrangements that simplify technically difficult passages without distorting other elements of the piece, particularly harmony and form. The younger the target group, the more accepting we can be of compromises—e.g., Mark Williams appropriately abridges the *1812 Overture* in his Grade 4 band arrangement (Alfred).
2. Seek out works (even slow, lyrical ones) originally for voices—e.g., Robert H. Reynolds' wind setting of Morten Lauridsen's *O Magnum Mysterium*. Since voices are essentially a type of wind instrument, these works often employ phrasing that translates well to woodwinds and brass. Further, brasses, clarinet, and saxophone are adept at imitating the blended sonority of a choir.
3. For band transcriptions, favor works whose original instrumentation is wind-centric, even if strings are in the mix—e.g., the orchestral version of Shostakovich's *Festive Overture*, with its brass fanfares and woodwind solos, predisposes it for an effective transcription (as Donald Hunsberger's arrangement bears out).
4. Seek out transcriptions in which the original source material is not a large ensemble, but rather a keyboard, à la Mussorgsky's *Pictures at an Exhibition*. Keyboard works allow arrangers to be creative when using the colors of the band.
5. Seek transcriptions completed or approved by the composer. This is the strongest indication we have that the composer's intent has been retained in the transcription—e.g., Bernstein specifically approved Clare Grundman's 1986 transcription of *Overture to Candide*; John Zdechlik himself arranged *Chorale and Shaker Dance II* (simplified version of the original *Chorale and Shaker Dance*).
6. Be wary of slow, lyrical works originally written for strings—e.g., Samuel Barber's *Adagio for Strings*. Wind instruments have great difficulty matching string instruments' ability to sustain indefinitely, and so these works often translate awkwardly.

On Programming Pop Music

At some point or another most music teachers hear questions from students, parents, or administrators along the lines of: "Why can't we play more . . .

"music that we like!"
"music that we know!"
"popular music!"
"movie music!"

From the parent and student perspectives, these are reasonable questions. After all, music provides entertainment for most people; shouldn't school music do the same? But from our perspective, it is a frustrating question. Do students ask the history teacher, "Why can't we study the history of candy and movies?" Do they ask English teachers, "Why don't we read more *Harry Potter* and *X-Men*?" Of course not!

An excellent answer to these questions—so long as it isn't phrased as a retort—is: "We don't play pop music for the same reason we don't read comic books in English class." Point out that this decision is not a value judgment, and it has nothing to do with disliking pop music. Rather, it is a recognition that school is a place for studying, experiencing, and performing music that: (1) is often not heard at home; and (2) requires guidance in order to fully appreciate its beauty and perform at a high level.

Even so, we can and *should* make room for student- and audience-pleasers. But we suggest the following guidelines:

1. Program *no more than one pop piece per concert*.
2. Regardless of the piece, *choose only quality arrangements*. If the medley of the new blockbuster movie is rubbish or poorly arranged, do not consider it no matter how popular.
3. Treat it with *the same respect and attention as for "serious" works*. Model to students that playing popular music does not absolve us from our responsibility as the composer's advocate. Our message should be consistent: Promise them, "Anything I put on your music stand is worth playing because it has something to offer us. And if it's worth playing, it's worth playing well. No matter why the piece was written, we must determine and convey the composer's wishes/designs."
4. *Have fun!* Conducting a movie score might be the classical music equivalent of a sweet dessert, so enjoy it, and show that enjoyment to your students.

When choosing a pop work, try asking students to name some of their favorite songs that are on the radio or heavily downloaded. Then ask everyone to go home and listen to them with a new ear. Guide them to pay attention to melody and content and see if they can discern which ones would "sound good" on wind and string instruments. After compiling a list of ten or twelve pieces, discuss each song's merit as a class. Ask the following questions:

- Would this melody stand on its own, void of lyrics?
- Does the content lend itself to a string/wind sound?
- Is there enough harmonic interest to sustain one's attention without the lyrics?

If the piece is not available for purchase, consider arranging it as a class project. Guide collaborative decisions regarding accompaniment, orchestration, key, etc. Depending on the age and experience of the group, much of the arrangement can be generated, notated, and premiered by the ensemble itself. (Be sure to investigate copyright implications of performing these arrangements, however.)

Teaching Music through Pop Selections

Béla Bartok, Percy Grainger, and Zoltán Kodály taught us that folk music is filled with variety, intricacy, and tradition. Many of the wind and orchestral world's greatest masterpieces are based on this philosophy. In *Lincolnshire Posy*, for example, Grainger arranged standard folk tunes but retained the unpredictable phrasing and rhythms of native folk singers. In Bartok's *Music for Strings, Percussion, and Celeste*, the melodies are Bartok's own, but flavored throughout with his beloved Hungarian music.

Folk music's influence is not limited to musicologically-inclined composers. Mozart and Haydn incorporated the style of Austrian folk music—the eighteenth century's popular music—into their string quartets, symphonies, and operas. Today's mainstream folk music canon, which includes rock, pop, and musical theatre (in addition to rural folk music and nursery rhymes), does not serve as the same grist for contemporary composers, but it displays some of the same musical subtleties.

If we program pop music, teach students what makes it interesting. Help them become more informed consumers, and perhaps in the process appreciate the same features in other music.

Using Popular Music as a Gateway for Teaching Musical Concepts

In *What to Listen for in Rock*, Ken Stephenson explores rock music from the theorist's perspective. Here are some of the features he points out:[11]

Phrasing

Stephenson observes how in both folk and pop music, the hypermeter[12] does not necessarily synchronize with the vocal phrase (e.g., a four measure hypermeter phrase does not always contain a four measure vocal melody). Instead, we often see the following.

- 3:1 ratios—A three measure vocal phrase that ends on the fourth measure of the hypermeter, letting the instrumental accompaniment carry the music into the next hypermeter.
- 2:2 ratios—A two measure vocal phrase that cadences on the third hypermeter downbeat (this pattern of two measures of melodic activity followed by two measures of rest, or two measures of call followed by two measures of response, has its roots in blues, another type of contemporary folk music).

  Examples: Chuck Berry's "Roll Over Beethoven"
  Sting's "If I Ever Lose My Faith in You"

- 4 + phrases—A four measure vocal phrase that ends on the downbeat of the next hypermeasure (i.e., overlapping with the beginning of the next four measure phrase).

  Examples: Neil Young's "Harvest Moon"
  The Eagles' "Take It to the Limit"

- Shifting hypermeter—In spite of its stereotype, folk music does not always fall into neat four measure phrases. A four measure pattern is often interrupted by a two, three, or four measure hypermetric phrase. In other words, the second, third, or fourth measure of a phrase also serves as the first measure of a new hypermetric phrase.

  Examples: Elton John's "Goodbye Yellowbrick Road"
  Doobie Brothers' "China Grove"

- 1 + 1—Two short melodic phrases within a four-measure hypermeter; the first begins near the first downbeat and ends on the second downbeat; the second begins near the third downbeat and ends of the fourth downbeat.

Examples: Bob Dylan's "All Along the Watchtower"
The Doors' "Light My Fire"

Pitch Centers

We usually teach students to recognize a pitch center based on the key signature and the beginning/ending harmonies. This works nicely for common practice music, but not always for rock and contemporary classical music. Their complexities offer a teaching opportunity to develop students' ability to recognize pitch centers by sound, not notation. How? Use drones! After playing through a passage or listening to a recording, ask the group to sing the pitch center (i.e., tonic). If the group sings the wrong pitch, or more than one, indicating some confusion, help them test their hypotheses. Establish one of the candidates as a drone, either by singing, on instruments, or through a recording, perform the passage again and have the group evaluate it. Ask these questions:

• How well does the piece work with this pitch as a drone accompaniment?
• Does the melody sound stable in relation to the drone, or is there tension?

Then test the next candidate. Notational clues provide a useful cross-reference. Stephenson offers the following strategies for rock music, though the same principles apply to nearly any genre (Stephenson, 37):

1. Identify the root and quality of the first chord and assume that the chord is the tonic harmony.
2. Confirm or question this assumption by noting one of more of the following features:

   (a) the first harmony initiates phrases persistently
   (b) structural pitches are P4 or P5 apart in the melody
   (c) the last melodic pitch in major sections is the same as the first.

In some music a case can be made for two different pitch centers, and we should celebrate these ambiguities with our students. Explore how our perception of a piece changes based on how we hear its notes relating to each other, much as an object looks different as we view it from different angles.

Listening to Students and Giving Them Input

Choosing appropriate literature is one of our greatest responsibilities as a band or orchestra director. Choose wisely, and we put our ensembles in a position to perform well and learn the concepts outlined in our curriculum. Yet, even as we exercise our autonomy in programming, we should also value student opinion. Obviously, if we are going to program pop music partially to meet student interest, they ought to like our choices. What's the point of offering a dessert of apple pie if nobody likes apples or pie?

In other cases there may be room for flexibility, particularly if we begin rehearsing more literature than we can program on one concert. If we are considering two works that present the same benefits, and we must ultimately cut one of them, why not involve students in the final decision?

Taking a vote quickly gages class preferences, but it is not always the best method, especially with a public vote. Only one side can win the election, and so an exercise intended to give students ownership becomes an instant disappointment for the losing minority. Instead, gauge interests more casually, perhaps outside the rehearsal. Poll a random sample, or ask students you trust who have the pulse of the ensemble. Usually this reveals the same preferences as the full vote.

Do not avoid votes all the time; it is healthy for students to participate in the democratic process and learn how to handle its triumphs and disappointments. For example, at the end of a long rehearsal, when there is enough time to run-through a short work, give the students two choices and take a vote. Or, choose two similar works to sightread and let the ensemble vote on which one. Be careful of ceding too much "power" to the ensemble, however. Ultimately the final decision rests with the music educator, and the students must be made aware of this from the beginning.

Even if students are not involved in the decision making process it is useful simply to listen to their opinions. What do they enjoy? What works frustrate them? Understanding student likes and dislikes helps us discover how to teach the literature we need to program. Put yourself in their shoes. Would you enjoy playing the third clarinet, tuba, or bass drum part in the music you selected? These discussions may be in the full ensemble setting, or even informally, before and after rehearsal. In any case, challenge students to think critically about their beliefs and preferences. Push them for answers that reveal "why." "Beside the fact that it's fun to play, *why* do you like this piece? *Why* is it fun to play?" "What's your favorite section of this piece? Why?" "*Why* do you think the group dislikes this piece?"

Remember, these conversations are two-way streets, and thus perfect opportunities for us to share our own likes and dislikes. We can help students understand why we program certain works and why we avoid others. Disagreeing with students and respecting their opinions are not mutually exclusive, and even the perception we understand their perspective offers the group an important degree of ownership in the ensemble.

Another way to incorporate student opinion regarding literature is to designate a concert in which students choose one of the works. For example, begin a tradition where seniors choose a "farewell" piece for their final concert, either from a list the director provides, or perhaps a favorite from past concerts. Allow students to make the decision, but reserve veto power and serve as an adviser during their discussions. As a variation, incorporate the entire ensemble, or form a committee of students who have earned the privilege to choose a piece (for good behavior, most improved, strong performance, etc.).

As long as we provide guidelines, an entire program could be effectively designed by students. Provide a list of works (with recordings and scores) for each category and guide students through the process we use:

- Create a balance between repertoire that challenges and purely entertains.
- Find music that is technically interesting but achievable; playable but not boring.
- Select works that fit together well.
- Take into account considerations about rehearsal schedule and concert length.
- The director has veto power!

Activities/Assignments for Further Exploration

1. Discuss Ostling's attempt to define musical quality. Does he succeed? Are there any criteria missing from his list? Any that should be removed?

2. One might argue that quality, like beauty, is in the eye of the beholder. Do you agree? How do your conclusions affect your view of Ostling's list?

3. Write your personal definition of musical quality. Give at least one specific example that embodies your definition.

4. Daniel Levitin describes six types of "songs." Are there other ways to categorize music?

5. Make a list of the most memorable or meaningful pieces you have performed. What made them so?

6. Make a list of the pieces you have played in the last few years and separate them into repertoire categories. Now, create a new concert program using these pieces.

7. Write a study sheet for a piece of music you are currently rehearsing.

8. Using your state's rating system, evaluate three works from your school's library that are NOT on the state list and assign them a grade level from 1–6. Be able to justify your grading.

9. Read Stephen Budiansky's January 30, 2005 article, "The Kids Play Great. But that Music," from *The Washington Post*. Discuss his argument and conclusions.

10. Discuss the design for an interdisciplinary collaboration between yourself and a teacher in another field. Choose at least one appropriate piece of repertoire to work with and a non-musical topic to connect to it.

Recommended Resources

Best Music for Beginning Band: A Selective Repertoire Guide to Music and Methods for Beginning Band, by Thomas L. Dvorak, Richard L. Floyd, Bob Margolis, and Frank L. Battisti (Manhattan Beach Music).

Best Music for Chorus and Winds, by Keith William Kinder (Manhattan Beach Music).

Best Music for High School Band: A Selective Repertoire Guide for High School Bands and Wind Ensembles, by Thomas L. Dvorak, Robert Grechesky, and Gary M. Ciepluch (Manhattan Beach Music).

Best Music for Young Band: A Selective Guide to the Young Band/Young Wind Ensemble Repertoire, by Thomas L. Dvorak (Manhattan Beach Music).

Blueprint for Band: A Guide for Teaching Comprehensive Musicianship through School Band Performance, by Robert Joseph Garofalo (Meredith Music).

Canadian Band Music: A Qualitative Guide to Canadian Composers and Their Works for Band, by Michael Burch-Pesses (Meredith Music).

A Composer's Insight, Vol. 1–4, ed. Timothy Salzman (Meredith Music).

Great Music for Wind Band: A Guide to the Top 100 Works in Grades IV, V, VI, by Chad Nicholson (Meredith Music).

Instructional Literature for Middle Level Band, edited and compiled by Edward J. Kvet (Rowman and Littlefield).

The Jazz Ensemble Companion: A Guide to Outstanding Big Band Arrangements Selected by Some of the Foremost Jazz Educators, by Michele Caniato (Rowman and Littlefield).

Shaping Sound Musicians, Patricia O'Toole (GIA).

Teaching Music Through Performance in Band, Vol. 1–7, by Larry Blocher, Ray Cramer, Eugene Corporon, and Tim Lautzenheiser (GIA).

Teaching Music through Performance in Beginning Band, Vol. 1–2, by Thomas Dvorak (GIA).

Teaching Music Through Performance in Jazz, by Richard Miles and Ronald Carter (GIA).

Teaching Music Through Performance In Orchestra, Vol. 1–3, by Michael Allen, Louis Bergonzi, Jacquelyn Dillon, and Robert Gillespie (GIA).

The Wind Band and Its Repertoire: Two Decades of Research As Published in the CBDNA Journal, ed. Michael Votta (Alfred).

The Wind Band Masterworks of Holst, Vaughan Williams and Grainger, by Willis M. Rapp (Meredith Music).

The Winds of Change: The Evolution of the Contemporary American Wind Band/Ensemble and its Conductor, by Frank Battisti (Meredith Music).

Chapter 10

Score Study

To Guide Your Reading

Why is score study important?

How does the concept of Macro–Micro–Macro apply to the score study process?

What shorthand can we use to notate harmonic information in the score?

What strategies can we use to realize the sound of the full score?

How can we use our knowledge of the score to shape an interpretation?

How can we develop conducting gestures appropriate for the work we are studying?

How can we best use recordings during the score study process?

What are some effective ways to mark a score for use in rehearsal and performance?

A musical phrase may lack the specific meaning, the immediacy of words or pictures, but it also escapes their limitations.[1]

Jan LaRue

One might question the necessity of score study amidst a music teacher's myriad responsibilities. After all, particularly at beginning levels, the music is technically, harmonically, and formally quite simple. Wrong notes and rhythms stand out pretty clearly. It is easy to "wing it"—to bring the score into rehearsal and deal with problems as they are detected, using only our musical instincts and casual familiarity with the piece. But even in these cases score study will repay the time we put in. A detailed knowledge of the score allows us to anticipate problems before they occur, detect errors quickly, develop a coherent interpretation, and teach a work's structure and inner workings to the ensemble. Indeed, winging it fails more often than it succeeds and leads to minimally productive rehearsals. Score study is the type of activity whose value will become most clear after you try it.

Earlier in this text we have discussed music's parallels with language. But unlike language, which is designed for specificity, music often communicates through ambiguity. This is partly what makes it attractive—its meaning is flexible and subjective. It also places burdens on those that seek to explain it—i.e., us! How can we describe something in constant motion whose meaning is influenced and interpreted by the conductor, performer, and listener? The theorist Jan LaRue points out that the analyst's solution is to "freeze" music's motion, allowing each moment to be studied individually (LaRue, 2). This type of analysis enhances our appreciation of the composer's creative process, the materials he uses, and the methods with which he presents his argument. Our understanding of the "frozen" music complements our subjective reaction to it when it is unfrozen. For the conductor/educator, this process is a major component of score study. It informs our interpretation, illuminates the musical elements we share with students, and equips us to guide the ensemble efficiently through the learning process.

Proper score study mimics the Macro–Micro–Macro technique we use during rehearsals.

Some may worry that the whole process is overwhelming. "Do I really have the time? Does it really matter if I do it?" It definitely matters, and the positive effect it has on your rehearsals will be clear once you try it. Still, completing the entire study process on every piece before we put in front of students may be a challenging goal, and there will be scenarios when we only have time to complete Phase 1 (Macro) before the first read-through. In these cases, complete the process in the days afterward.

Phase 1—Macro

Score study is not simply a technical exercise of learning the notes and rhythms in order to teach them to students. The process is really like studying a screenplay: There is a cast of characters, a context and environment in which those characters live and interact, and a narrative which shapes their destiny. The Macro stage (or Phase 1) of the process is a cover-to-cover overview of the work before we freeze it, break it down and scrupulously analyze every aspect. These first steps are also the most superficial: Absorb everything the composer explicitly reveals—the title, when it was written, for whom it was written, and why it was written. Read any of the composer's or publisher's program notes at the beginning of the score and throughout it, and then supplement it with more research. Do we know anything about this composer besides his/her name? What other significant works has the composer written? If the piece refers to an historic event, can we speak intelligently about that event?

This prepares us to experience the "Cliffs Notes" version of the work, except in this case we write our *own* summary. First, survey the architecture of the piece: Are there multiple movements, or multiple movements implied within a single movement? Identify the major characters (themes and motives). Then sing through and trace them through the work. Identify significant pitch centers and architecturally significant transitions, keys, meters, and tempo changes. What is the work's form (sonata, theme and variations, etc.)? Make a chart for unfamiliar and unpredictable ones. Be sure to look up any unknown terms!

Once we meet the musical protagonists we can examine the context in which they live. Are the textures constructed as melody and accompaniment, as counterpoint, or as a combination of the two? What is the texture of the accompaniment (e.g., sustained chords, oompah, block harmony articulated with rhythmic ostinati, etc.)? How does the composer use counterpoint? Are there notable orchestrations (e.g., flute and tuba duets, extensive solos, thick tutti passages, etc.)? The goal here is to construct a melodic, harmonic, rhythmic, timbral, and formal template in our mind's ear.

Phase 2—Micro

After the Phase 1—Macro overview we enter the Phase 2—Micro portion of score study. Phase 2—is a thorough deconstruction of the piece on every level: melody, rhythm, harmony, orchestration, and form. Ideally we want to audiate the score to create a complete recording in our mind's ear. Though this is difficult in harmonically complex works, it is a skill we develop over time.

The first step is to establish the work's tonality in our mind's ear and then sing its melodies. For example, if a work is in the concert key of F Major, play a I-V-I chord progression on a keyboard to establish the pitch center. Next, play the prevailing chord of each measure and use solfege/aural skill training to hear and sing as many of the parts as possible while the harmony is ringing. Start with the most prominent melodies and work through the other parts.

Analyzing the Harmony

A harmonic analysis is the most commonly skipped step, but it is crucial in order to audiate the piece and prepare effective rehearsals. A notational shorthand must be developed for those unable to audiate instantly by reading the score, or who do not have the piano skills to play multiple staves simultaneously. The most common method is a Roman numeral analysis, which is superb at reflecting the functional relationships among harmonies but is too abstract for showing what the actual notes on the page are (i.e., "IV" efficiently tells us the chord has subdominant function but gives no direct clue as to whether it is a C Major chord, F Major chord, etc.) When audiating, playing at the piano, or rehearsing, we want to quickly and efficiently read the notes, chords, *and* function.

Notating Harmonic Information

Most conductors notate the analysis in the bottom margin and use the inner spaces of the score sparingly. For study purposes, consider making a separate copy of the score. Notate with jazz-style notation supplemented by Roman numeral analysis (the latter to show key changes and applied dominant relationships (e.g., V7 of ii)). Why is this important? The better we know what we are supposed to hear, the better we can detect problems and bring out interesting details.

The goal is to distill the work's harmony down to an easily readable format that conveys the following information:

1. *Chord Root and Quality*
   Use capital letters for Major chords (optional: Add a triangle to show Major), lower case for minor, capital with "+" for augmented, lowercase with "o" for diminished, lowercase with "Ø" for half-diminished.

   For extended harmonies, use superscript numbers to show seventh, ninth, and eleventh chords. Show modifications in parentheses either with the numbers (e.g., $\sharp 5$ = sharp fifth of the chord) or with the name of the note itself.

   - Remember, neither our students nor the audience will see what we mark on the score, so ultimately the important thing is that it communicates detailed information to us in a compact, consistent, and easily understood way.
   - Develop a system to differentiate between triads, extended harmonies (7, $\flat 9$, etc.), unison pedals (e.g. G ⇨), and open fifths (e.g., C-G).

2. *Chord Inversion*

Use traditional figured bass notation (e.g., C^6) or jazz slash chords, which quickly conveys the note in the bass.

3. *Non-chord Tones and Dissonances*

Again, use traditional notation (e.g., "4–3" to show suspension and resolution) or explicitly show pitch names and their voice leading (e.g., G ⇨ F). For triadic harmonies that are decorated with non-chord tone dissonances, show the added tone in parentheses (e.g., C (F♯) is a C Major triad with an F♯ also sounding).

- Keep a special look-out for dissonances of a second! Teach ensembles to embrace the tension/release of this interval will enable them to play them with better intonation and musicality.
- As with any theoretical analysis there may be more than one interpretation for a harmony or non-chord tone. Make a decision that resonates with the way you hear it. If it looks like a b minor seventh chord but you hear it as D Major with an added sixth (B), the latter should be your answer. (Or notate both).
- Circle important notes in the score for quick visual reminders (for use in pre-rehearsal planning and in-rehearsal diagnosis). For example, perhaps circle the root of the chord or an important dissonance, especially if it is buried in only a few instruments. For groups of instruments that play self-contained chords (e.g., in a polytonal context) notate the harmony directly next to those instruments. This helps remind our ear what is expected and helps us determine what is wrong if we hear something different.
- For complex harmonies, use a rubber stamp to imprint a blank five-line staff on the bottom margin to notate the chord and its voicing. (Custom rubber stamps are available inexpensively at most print shops. Simply bring in a 2–4 inch piece of manuscript paper and ask for it to be converted into a stamp.)
- Rely on your solfege/aural skill training to hear as much as possible. Keep a keyboard nearby for reference.
- Notate important doublings in the margin. (e.g., primary melody = flute 1, clarinet 2, trumpet 1 and 2; countermelody = flute 2, clarinet 2, euphonium, etc.). This allows us to quickly announce what instruments we wish to rehearse without fumbling through each stave.
- Examine the score for clef changes and significantly high ranges in the string parts. These areas will need extra rehearsal and should be notated in the margins for easy identification.

By completing this type of analysis we examine every line and essentially create a "lead-sheet" version of the full score to audiate, sing, or play the piece at the keyboard. Develop a system that works for you! At this point in the process consider the orchestration but do not focus on its details. Once the mind's ear absorbs the essential melody, rhythm, and harmony we will add subtleties of texture and color.

Realizing the Sound of the Score in Our Mind's Ear

Now we're ready to combine singing the melodic line with the analysis of the harmony. Experiment with the following exercises:

1. Play the harmony with the left hand (from the new "lead sheet') and the melody with the right (reading and transposing off the score).

2. Play the harmony and sing the melody.
3. Sing the bass line (or inner voice) while playing another.

Determine the length of each phrase. Are they consistent and predictable? Are there moments when the composer contracts or extends a pattern?

Other Strategies for Realizing the Sound of the Score

Even non-pianists can use play-and-sing techniques. Experiment with some of the following strategies:

1. *Play the score as a lead sheet*—Use the chordal notation from the margins to "comp" the prevailing harmony in the left hand and play the melody in the right hand.
2. *Highlighting*—Sorting through twelve or more staves can be difficult. However, since many scores use heavy doublings use a highlighter to mark essential melody, bass line, and accompanimental parts. Ignore octave doublings and choose non-transposing instruments whenever possible. The goal is to create a condensed score through the highlighting. Once the basic sound of the piece is mastered, switch to the full score, sans highlights.
3. *Artificial intelligence*—For complex contrapuntal scores, use notation software or a sequencer to input lines with real-time entry. The process of entering every note ensures we hear and play each line, and now if we want to hear only the 2nd clarinet and 3rd horn parts, we simply select them. The bland MIDI payback is a perk, as it challenges us to substitute our own interpretative ideas. As with the highlighter technique, use AI as a temporary crutch.
4. *Using Instruments to Play Lines*—Play through each voice on your "native instrument." Or, play each part on its proper instrument. This is a terrific way to practice secondary instruments and anticipate what problems students will encounter.

Realizing the Orchestration—Adding Color and Nuance

As we construct a piece in our mind's ear we should work to crystallize our conception of the orchestration. Strive to audiate specific instrumental combinations and textures. For example, at the beginning of Gustav Holst's *First Suite in E flat*, do we hear the opening euphonium and tuba duet—the octaves, the mellowness of the conical instruments, perhaps a slight vibrato in the euphonium? Later on, do we hear the change in color as the horn passes the chaconne to the saxophone?

Analysis—Deconstructing the Composer's Intent

At this point the goal is to examine how the composer treats melody, harmony, rhythm, etc., and identify which elements carry the primary musical interest at any given point in the work.
    Consider:

- intervals/motives/melodies
- harmonies
- rhythms
- cadences
- scales/modes
- orchestration

- form
- style

Also consider how the composer balances "tension and release," which is the lifeblood of a work's expressive power. "Tension and release" takes several forms:

- expectation and surprise
- consonance and dissonance
- ebb and flow

Far more than suspensions and seventh chords, these variations on a theme manifest themselves at every level of a work's construction, and in any of the eight elements listed above—from the minutia of note-to-note progressions to the overall flow of the form's architecture; from the unexpected manipulation of stylistic conventions to the comfort of forms we already know; from the directness of unison rhythms to the complexity of overlapping ones; from the insistent repetition of a theme to the dramatic withholding of a recapitulation until the very end of the piece.

How well the composer employs these techniques influences a work's effectiveness. Too much expectation, consonance, or release and the music becomes trite and predictable. Too much surprise, dissonance, and tension and the effects lose their punch. (Think of a horror film: If skeletons jumped out of the shadows in every scene they would scare no-one. If people were always happy in dramas they would be excruciatingly boring.)

Like the twists and turns of a great movie, these techniques influence our emotional reaction and inform our analysis. Score study is the process through which we tease it all out. This is also the point to look for connections and transformations—the compositional strategies through which a good composer weaves a cohesive piece. The most obvious connections are melodic. How are themes developed? If there are multiple themes, do they relate to each other? Look also for connections *between* thematic, harmonic, and rhythmic elements (e.g., perhaps the composer treats a pitch set, say [F-B♭-C] as both a melody and a harmony) Does a motive appear in more than one guise? Is the same motive expressed through different rhythms? With notes in a different order?

Finding these relationships does not occur in one study session. Be patient and refine your interpretation over time. Certainly music for beginning ensembles has fewer layers of complexity than a Beethoven symphony. But if we choose quality literature by quality composers, even so-called "simple" works will repay our study and that of our students.

What Do We Do With This Information?

- *We serve as the composer's advocate!*—In his seminal book *The Composer's Advocate*, conductor Erich Leinsdorf highlights the conductor's role as a representative of the composer's musical wishes and intentions.[2] By highlighting significant motives, clarifying harmonies, emphasizing important rhythms, etc., we are able to shape a performance that compellingly reflects the internal logic of its construction.
- *We share important conclusions and connections with students!*—When students understand how their part connects to another we make performance meaningful and collaborative. Do not pontificate; choose information that will help students better understand and perform the work.
- *We use it to rehearse effectively and efficiently!*—Diagnosing problems is easy if we know exactly how the piece "should" sound. Hear a wrong note? Our lead-sheet analysis directs us to the solution. Working

on expression and musicality? Our understanding of the phrasing contributes to the interpretation we share with the ensemble. Which leads us to . . .

Phase 3—Macro-Redux

Hearing a work in the mind's ear is the prerequisite for this next phase. Indeed, merely knowing what the correct notes and rhythms sound like provides only a generic, characterless version of the music. To be prepared to stand up in front of an ensemble we must make interpretative decisions for every note. Michael Votta, Professor of Music and Director of the Wind Orchestra at the University of Maryland, College Park, refers to this as the transformation of "instructor ears" into "conductor ears."[3] Conductor ears ask, "Yes, there are eighth-notes in m. 4. but how sort should they be? What voice is the most important in m. 12? What is the character of the music at letter B, and how should that translate into articulation? How long is the phrase starting at letter C? What is its direction?" Leave no note unturned! The more specific our inner-recording is the easier it becomes to rehearse effectively.

Fortunately, developing conductor ears is not a guessing game; it is a direct result of the detailed analysis we completed in Phase 2. If we discovered a recurring motive embedded within the melody and accompaniment we may choose to bring that feature to the foreground. If we notice the harmony progresses from major to minor, we may choose to highlight the chromatic motion of the third of the chord.

The Interpretive Dance—Warning: You Must Give Yourself Permission to Look Foolish!

Now comes the time to turn interpretive ideas into conducting gestures. It is not necessary to choreograph every move, but it is important to have a vocabulary of gestures that reflect our inner-recording of the music. When in the privacy of your home or office, sing the piece and create an expressive, uninhibited, interpretative dance. Do as much of the score from memory as possible, or have it handy for reference while you dance. Avoid patterns and time-beating, and instead move à la eurhythmics. Accents, syncopations, and huge arrival points will involve preparations and downbeats, but at least initially the dance should not resemble conducting at all: Move your feet, walk across the room, swing your arms, crouch, spring, make expressive facial gestures—do whatever it takes to physically manifest the sound. What's important is the flow, style, and energy of the movement as you sing the *melos*. The *melos*, as coined by Richard Wagner, refers to the melody as it transfers its way through different voices, orchestrations, themes, and ranges. Matthew McClure, Assistant Director of Bands at the University of North Carolina, Chapel Hill, calls it "the thing." Every measure has a "thing"; it's the guiding aspect of the music, whether it be a single line or a composite of several lines. Be free, take chances, and give yourself permission to move outside your comfort zone. Remember, nobody is watching . . . yet!

The next step is to convert the dance into conducting. Plant your feet and conduct through the piece as you would in front of the ensemble, vocalizing the *melos* as you go. Work to transfer as much as possible of the interpretive dance into the framework of standard conducting patterns. Assimilate as much as you can:

- face and eye gestures
- body posture

- arm and shoulder motions
- hand positions (*very* useful for left-hand gestures)

Frank Battisti, Conductor Emeritus of the New England Conservatory Wind Ensemble, insists that sitting at a desk and beating time while following the score is *not* score study. So instead, get out into some open space and move!

On Using Recordings

To use or *not* to use recordings! That is the age-old, much-debated, oft-controversial, and difficult-to-answer question. It is completely reasonable to listen to them when choosing literature. We consider this "pre-score study listening." So, what should we do when we actually sit down to learn a new score? Some argue we should let technology work for us and listen to recordings as needed, particularly when our unmanageable schedules preclude intensive score study. Others argue recordings are a crutch that restrict the development of the mind's ear, stagnate one's creative juices, and obscure a score's inner workings. Our position is a hedge between these extremes. We recommend the following:

- *Right after Phase 1*—Listen to a recording—one time only—to get a sense of the piece and its sound world.
- *After Phase 2*—Listen again—once or twice only—after the in-depth analysis. This crystallizes difficult-to-hear harmonies, counterpoint, and orchestrations. Read the score as you listen to strengthen connections between what you have analyzed and what you actually hear. Avoid beating time during this process, which feels satisfying but falsely represents what it feels like to conduct a group. Instead, conduct to the recording in your mind's ear.
- *Now put the recordings away*—Though tempting, repeated listenings harbor two dangers:

  1. They unduly influence our interpretation. Consider our idealized inner-recording of a piece we already know (say, Beethoven's *Fifth Symphony*, or one of the Holst *Military Suites*). Chances are our interpretation is similar to our first experience with the work, whether as performer or listener. Thus, if our first experience with a work is immersive listening to a recording, we imprint someone else's interpretation before we have formed our own.
  2. Recordings hide inner lines and harmonic subtleties. Just because we cannot hear it distinctly on the recording does not mean it is not worth hearing clearly. In addition, some inner voices affect the overall texture without jumping to the foreground. Make these decisions through the process of score study, and do not allow recordings to dictate what is and is not important!

- *Revisit the recordings after Phase 3*—Listening to recordings—especially different performances of the same work—can help fine-tune interpretations.

Marking the Score for Conducting

Score marking is a very personal process; what works for one person may not work for another. One school of thought eschews marking anything, arguing:

1. Any marks are an admission the score has not been thoroughly learned.
2. If we put them in the score we will surely look at them, to the detriment of good eye contact with the ensemble.

Another school of thought prescribes a detailed, systematic process for marking (or highlighting, if it is already printed) nearly every dynamic, expression, tempo, and entrance. Taken to the extreme, this results in a color-coded score that allows the eye to quickly find essential information. But the overload of color also runs counter to the point of marking in the first place—everything looks highlighted and so nothing looks highlighted. (As mentioned earlier, some conductors prefer to study from a heavily marked score and then substitute a blank one for rehearsals. Much like the artificial intelligence form of score study, tracing every mark ensures that every detail is read.)

Score *marking* is not a substitute for score *studying*. Rather, it should be shorthand for information we have already studied, but which:

• is crucial for conducting the piece (e.g., entrances, transitions, etc. we CANNOT miss)
• is confined mostly to the margins so as not to disproportionately call attention to itself
• reflects details that are not worth memorizing, but which we need to know (e.g., mute in, details about harmony, "wait for page turn," etc.

What to Mark—Creating a Quick-Read Road Map

With an effectively marked score we should only periodically glance at the page to glean important information, or perhaps remind ourselves of things we consistently forget (after consistently trying to remember!). Avoid marking every dynamic, articulation, and expression mark, but do mark cues, meter changes, and transitions that could cause a "train-wreck" if missed. We suggest the following strategies, easily adaptable to fit one's own style. Again, mark as needed, but *only* as needed.

Materials
Regular pencil, or red/blue pencil (red on one end, blue on the other; available through most educational supply stores: Crayola "Twistables").

Cues
Using a blue pencil, put a square "open bracket" at the beginning of the entrance and write the abbreviated instrument name to the left, or slightly above and to the left (e.g., Fl, Ob, Cl, Tpt, Tbn, etc.). Avoid putting the abbreviation above, below, or to the right of the bracket, as the point is to alert us *before* we make the cue.

Bowings
For string instruments, make sure all bowings that are in the parts are also in the score.

Meter

Use large numbers to show meter changes when the prevailing macrobeat stays constant—e.g., $\frac{3}{4}$ to $\frac{4}{4}$ time, ♩ note keeps the pulse. Draw the number two to three inches high and one to two inches wide near the middle of the system. Or, place two numbers in the same system (one in the top half, one in the bottom half). For asymmetric meters such as $\frac{5}{4}$, use tall and short slashes to help show where the strong beats fall.

- Be consistent. Avoid using large numbers to show a shift from $\frac{2}{4}$ to $\frac{3}{8}$ because it is easy to mistake the large "3" as a three macrobeat pattern rather than as a temporary change in the number of microbeats in one macrobeat (from ♫ to ♫♪). For mixed meters (2 + 3, 3 + 2, etc.), show duples using slashes (or Ls, or squared-off upside-down Us) and triples using triangles. If the pattern and macrobeat shift constantly, show the number of macrobeats as a large number above the first slash/triangle symbol.
- Avoid marking every measure. Mark only the changes.
- If the meter changes at the beginning of a new system or after a page-turn, "preview" the new meter in the margin.

Transitions

Emphasize fermatas, breath marks, and caesuras by tracing them over with a colored pencil, or reproducing them at triple-size.

Stringendo = arrow pointing to the right; *Ritardando* = wavy line.

Releases

Create visual reminders about when sustained notes release—e.g., a release on beat 4 could be notated "-4".

Phrases

At the very top of the score (to avoid confusion with meters or harmonic analysis), mark the beginning of each phrase by indicating the number of measures it contains. This provides confidence for the conductor to make eye contact, and also serves as a reference during rehearsals. Another option: use a regular pencil to mark the borders between phrases with a thick vertical line.

FIGURE 10.1 Sample Score Marking (*Battlestar*, by Kees Vlak, Tierolff Muziekcentrale)

FIGURE 10.2 Sample Score Marking (*Three Famous Cathedrals*, by Charles Michiels, Tierolff Muziekcentrale)

FIGURE 10.3 Sample Score Marking—Mixed Meter

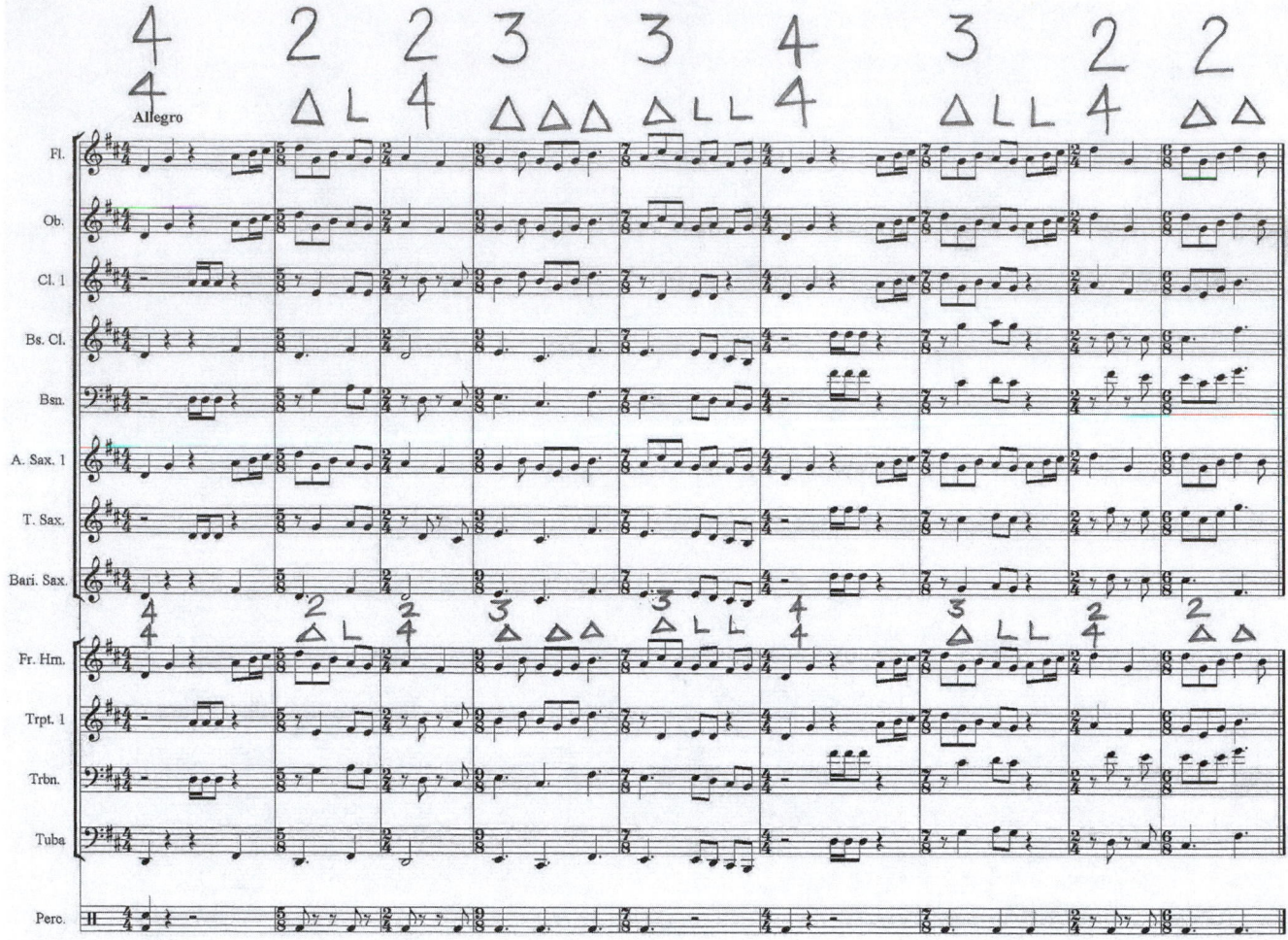

Activities/Assignments for Further Exploration

1. Score study involves striking a balance between determining the composer's intentions (i.e., being the "composer's advocate") and adding one's own interpretation. Discuss some of the challenges involved in deciding what can be interpreted and what must be taken at face value. Are dynamics fair game? Tempos? Rhythms? Notes? Orchestration? Are your conclusions absolute, or do they change based on the situation?

2. One might argue that performing a piece as a player takes the place of studying it as a conductor. (i.e., "I already know this piece because I've played it before.") What do you think?

3. Practice playing and singing passages from a full score. Start with two lines and expand from there, using chordal notation shorthand as needed.

4. Discuss the advantages and disadvantages of:

- using recordings in the score study process
- rehearsing with a marked-up score
- performing with a marked-up score
- conducting from memory
- winging it on a Grade 1–2 level piece.

5. Discuss strategies a band or orchestra director can use to make time for score study.

Further Reading

Battisti, Frank L., and Robert Joseph Garofalo. *Guide to Score Study for the Wind Band Conductor*. Ft. Lauderdale, FL: Meredith Music Publications, 1990.

Blum, David. *Casals and the Art of Interpretation*. London: Heinemann, 1977.

Boonshaft, Peter Loel. *Teaching Music with Passion: Conducting, Rehearsing, and Inspiring*. Galesville, MD: Meredith Music, 2002.

Green, Elizabeth A. H., Mark Gibson, and Nicolai Malko. *The Modern Conductor: A College Text on Conducting*. Upper Saddle River, NJ: Pearson Prentice Hall, 2004.

Hunsberger, Donald, Roy E. Ernst, and Allan Schindler. *The Art of Conducting*. New York: McGraw-Hill, 1992.

Leinsdorf, Erich. *The Composer's Advocate*. London: Yale University Press, 1982.

Meier, Gustav. *The Score, the Orchestra, and the Conductor*. Oxford: Oxford University Press, 2009.

Schuller, Gunther. *The Compleat Conductor*. New York: Oxford University Press, 1998.

Chapter 11

Large Ensemble Set-Up

To Guide Your Reading

What considerations should we make when measuring the useable set-up space of the room?

How should the strengths and weaknesses of our ensemble affect its set-up?

What general strategies and principles should we consider when designing a set-up?

What set-up guidelines should we consider for each instrument?

It is not a stretch to say that ensemble set-up influences nearly every aspect of our teaching. Want your students to be able to hear each other better while they play? Need to improve classroom management? Want to make classroom procedures more efficient? Need to fit more students in the same space? Change the set-up!

Measuring the Physical Space

Before designing a set-up that suits the group's musical, educational, and disciplinary needs, consider that every classroom and rehearsal space has a unique set of dimensions and characteristics—leveled rows (built-in risers), ramps, support beams, etc. Measure the set-up dimensions laterally (from side to side) and medially (front to back). Figure out the number of rows and chairs that can fit in each row.

Calculate the following:

1. Maximum number of rows front to back
2. Ideal number of rows front to back
3. Maximum number of chairs per row
4. Ideal number of chairs per row
5. Number of players per instrument

• Remember to calculate the space stands will take up and the extra room trombones and cellos need in front of them.

- Allow an extra bit of lateral room for flutes and violas. Seats that are too close will encourage bad posture and embouchure.
- Allow enough space for easy traffic flow as students go to and from their seats.
- Leave room for the teacher to freely move around the room. It is important to observe posture, technique, and discipline players from all angles. A few set-up strategies for this include:

  - Create an aisle that lets the conductor walk "through" the ensemble, from the front to the back.
  - Leave enough space between the front of the room and the first row of players so the conductor can walk around the ensemble.
  - Leave room between the end of each row and the side wall.
  - Leave adequate space between rows so the conductor can move over to any player in any row.

Keep in mind that the more rows there are the further away the students will be from the conductor, which may exacerbate discipline problems. On the other hand, extremely wide rows make it challenging for students on the edges to see the conductor and hear the other side of the ensemble.

Evaluating the Ensemble

The set-up we choose depends on the strengths and weaknesses of our ensemble. Consider the following questions.

1. *How many players are there within each section relative to the rest of the ensemble?* All factors being equal, place smaller sections that are difficult to hear towards the front of the ensemble, even if that entails an unorthodox placement.
2. *What is the caliber of each player within each section?* Especially in sections with a range of abilities, the placement of the strongest players should help support the weakest—e.g., With the trumpets, try placing the firsts between the second and third part players.
3. *Are there particularly inexperienced string players with technique, position, or posture problems?* For rehearsal purposes, consider seating them in the second row so they see the section leader and use him as a model, but are close enough to the podium so the teacher can offer direct help.
4. *What is the overall caliber of each section relative to the caliber of the rest of the ensemble?* In ensembles with unevenness among sections, we improve the overall ensemble sound if we "feature" the stronger sections by placing them towards the front of the set-up, or if we feature stronger players by placing them towards the front or ends of the set-up.
5. *What are the specific needs of each work we are performing?* Adjust the set-up as needed! For instance, in a work with a critical bassoon soli, place that section closer to the audience.

Ten Basic Principles of Set-Up

Though none are absolute, the following ten principles are extremely useful when designing a set-up.

1. *Proximity effects volume*—The closer an instrument is placed to the audience the easier it can be heard. This is true whether the instrument is placed towards the front or on the edges of a row. Though this may be obvious, think beyond a conventional set-up. If, for example, the trombone section in our young band only has two players, considering moving them into the second row.

2. *Proximity of players within a section affects their ability to hear each other*—This includes side–to–side and front–to–back proximity. If a large section is seated all in one row the players towards the ends will struggle to hear each other. Two adjacent rows would bring them closer together. Additionally, placing the strongest players in the middle of the section allows proximity to a larger number of weaker players.

3. *Proximity of sections within the ensemble affects their ability to hear each other*—e.g., clarinets and trumpets will hear each other better if they are placed in adjacent rows rather than opposite ends of the same row. This principle also applies to soloists. If a bass clarinet and piccolo play important passages together, consider sitting them next to each other for that piece, even in the front row.

4. *The direction of the bell is the direction its sound travels*—This affects the dynamics and blend of the entire ensemble.

5. *Bell-front instruments (trumpet, trombone) are easiest to hear when sitting in front of them.*

6. *Players feel more secure when similarly scored parts are placed near each other*—e.g., trombone and bassoon, horn and alto saxophones.

7. *The amount of space between chairs and stands affects the sound of the group and students' ability to hear each other*—The closer players sit to each other, the easier it is to for them to hear each other. The further players sit from each other, the more space there is between chairs for sound to project through the ensemble.

8. *The placement of individual sections within the set-up affects the sound blend*—Create separation between similarly ranged sections for more transparency and appreciation of individual tone colors. Group similarly ranged sections together for security and blend.

9. *The physical make-up of the facility may dictate changes in the set-up.*

10. *The set-up is always adjustable.*

Though professional and premiere college groups keep the same set-up year-to-year, we should be prepared to experiment, tweak, and overhaul. And the next year, given a new set of variables, we'll likely start the process over again. Rather than blindly heeding convention, consider first what suits the needs of the students and matches your style of directing.

Considering the Placement of Specific Instruments

Note: Unless otherwise noted, "left" and "right" are from the conductor's perspective

Concert Bands and Wind Ensembles

- With six or fewer *flutes*, it is probably best to put them in the first row. Piccolo is often on the outside, but another option is to place it in the center to help it match the pitch of other principal players. Large flute sections are often split between the first and second rows.
- *Oboes* are usually placed in the center of the first or second rows (if placed further back, the rest of the ensemble will overwhelm their sound.)
- *French horns and saxophones* are typically placed near each other since they frequently have similar parts. Beyond this, there are several approaches:

  1. Horns in front of the saxophones so their bells essentially face each other (improves the ability to hear each other).

2. Horns in the same row as saxophones, with horns on the right side so their bells face into the center of the ensemble (allows the saxophones to tune to the horns, and helps the horns blend into the rest of the band).

3. Horns on the left side of a row so their bells project directly into the audience (improves projection of the horns, but highlights imperfections).

4. Horns in the center (a compromise between points 2 and 3).

5. Separate horns and saxophone so their individual timbres can be appreciated.

- *Trumpets* are typically placed towards the center of a row, with weaker players on the outside. To help projection, try reversing this, thus placing stronger players on the outside where they can project into the audience more easily.
- *Trombone* projection is often improved if they are slightly elevated with risers.
- A common tactic for *tubas* is to make them part of a bass voice "spine" that runs through the entire group (i.e., low reeds and low brass placed down the center of the ensemble.) This puts the tubas in the center of the back row, a tactic that works if a shell reflects their sound forward. Otherwise, their sound may be lost in the fly space of the stage. Without a shell, consider placing tubas in the back row, stage-left, or in front of the proscenium (second or third row).
- The *brass section* is sometimes set up in a single row behind the woodwinds, often on risers. This set-up requires a very wide stage. The advantage is that it allows all the sections to be heard clearly by the audience. The disadvantage is that the brass will have a harder time hearing each other.

    Always consider how the brasses' *bell direction* affects their sound. If bells face the center of the group it improves blend; if bells face the audience it maximizes sound projection. Consider the latter strategy for outdoor performances.[1]
- For *extra-large trumpet and trombone sections*, some directors use a double row to focus the sound and allow players to hear each other more easily. Others believe this set-up makes it difficult for young players to evaluate their own sound, since someone else is playing into their ear (Bollinger, 70).
- *Orchestra wind sections* generally use the standard set-up seen in Figures 11.7 and 11.8. The Eastman Wind Ensemble set-up (Figure 11.6) is essentially an orchestral set-up augmented with saxophone, euphonium, and percussion.

Orchestra and Band Percussion Sections

- Give the *percussion section* room to easily walk to and from either side of the set-up. This enables quick part changes without crashing into instruments.
- Place *snare, crash cymbals,* and *bass drum* in the back/center to help the ensemble stay together.
- *Mallet instruments* work well behind the back left row, which brings them closer to the audience. Place the instrument that needs to be the strongest on the very outside. Since they often share parts, place the bells behind the woodwinds.
- *Tubular bells* are effective on the edge of the stage (behind the bells or marimba) where the audience can see them and hear their unique timbre.
- The head of the *bass drum* should not face the audience (unless the music requires a special timbre).
- *Auxiliary percussion instruments* (triangle, maracas, clave, etc.) should be held high to help their sound project. (Plus audiences appreciate seeing special, unfamiliar instruments.)
- *Avoid sound reflectors directly above the percussion section* on stage, for they may make their sound too loud.

- The *string bass* is notoriously difficult to hear in the band. Ideally, place it next to the tuba, unless the tubas are far back in the set-up, in which case it's better to place the string bass next to the low woodwinds. If resources allow, consider having multiple string basses, or some tasteful amplification, with the speaker facing the group to help the sound blend.
- Arguments exist for placing the *piano* on either side of the ensemble. With a grand piano, stage left allows the open end of the lid to face the ensemble, which of course makes it easier for the group to hear it. Stage right puts it near the mallet instruments, with which it often shares parts. It also lets the open end project towards the audience. The directional considerations for an upright piano are less important, though an upright's smaller sound output may require placement towards the front of the set-up. With any keyboard instrument, experiment with its angle so the player can easily see the conductor.
- Place the *harp* on the left side of the ensemble, in front of the mallet instruments.

Full Orchestras and String Ensembles

The standard set-up for *strings* places them, from left to right: Violin 1, Violin 2, Viola, Cello, with double basses behind the celli.

Examining Sample Seating Charts for Band and Orchestra

FIGURE 11.1 Percussion Set-up for Band

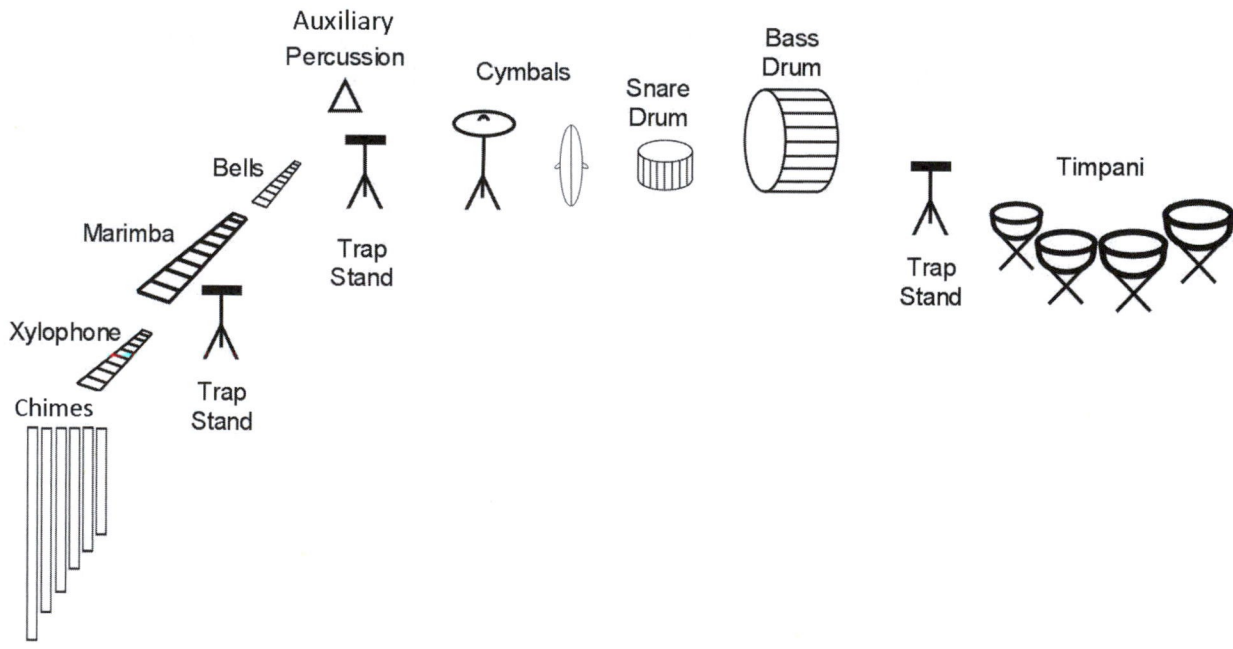

Analysis

1. Timpani near low brass and low winds.
2. Snare and bass drum in center to help keep ensemble together.
3. Cymbal next to snare because they share music and their parts are often related.

4. Mallet instruments near clarinets.
5. Small auxiliary instruments near cymbals because they often share parts.

- Entire percussion set-up is flexible based on the music and number of players available.

FIGURE 11.2 Large Concert Band Set-up #1

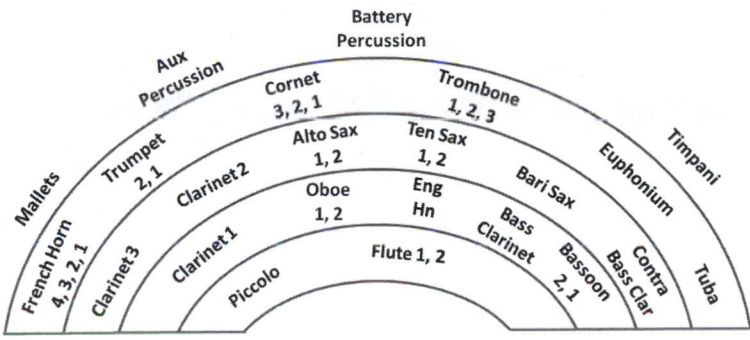

Analysis

1. Principal players/soloists placed near each other: flute/piccolo/clarinet/oboe.
2. Tuba and bassoons placed on outside right for better projection.
3. Horns placed on outside left so their bells project directly into audience.
4. Instruments with similar parts placed near each other: bass instruments (including timpani); flute/clarinet/trumpet/oboe/mallets; tenor saxophone/trombone.

FIGURE 11.3 Large Concert Band Set-up #2

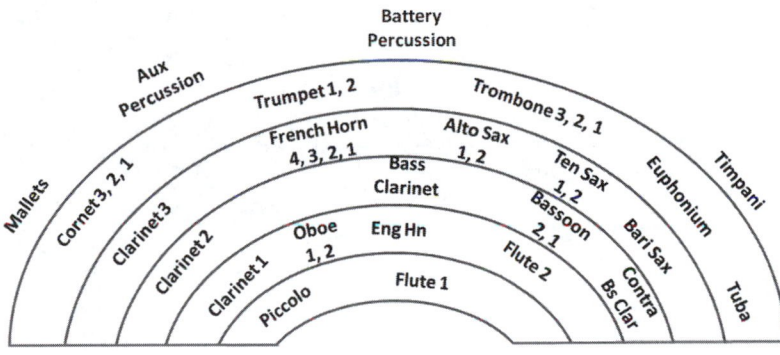

Analysis

1. Principal players/soloists placed near each other: flute/piccolo/clarinet/oboe; alto saxophone/horn.
2. Bass instruments grouped together and placed on the outside for ensemble precision and projection.
3. Instruments with similar parts placed together: bass instruments (including timpani); flute/clarinet/trumpet/oboe/mallets; horns/saxophones; saxophones/trombones.

FIGURE 11.4 Large Concert Band Set-up #3

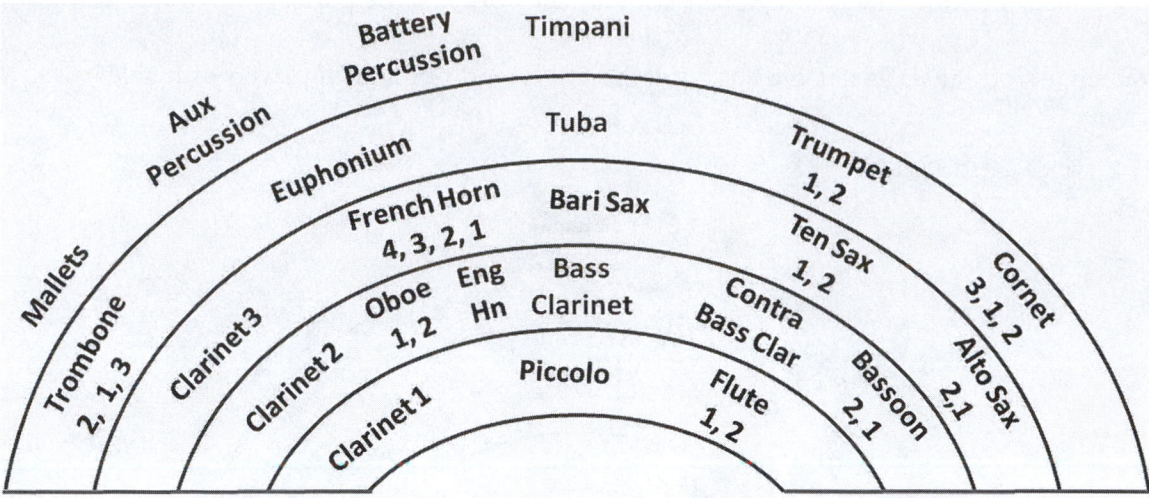

Analysis

1. Principal players/soloists placed near each other: flute/piccolo/clarinet/oboe; alto saxophone/bassoon.
2. Bass instruments towards the center of the set-up (including timpani).
3. Trumpet and trombone sections: first-part players in the center to anchor weaker players.
4. Saxophones separate from horns so their individual tone colors are appreciated.

FIGURE 11.5 Small Concert Band Set-up

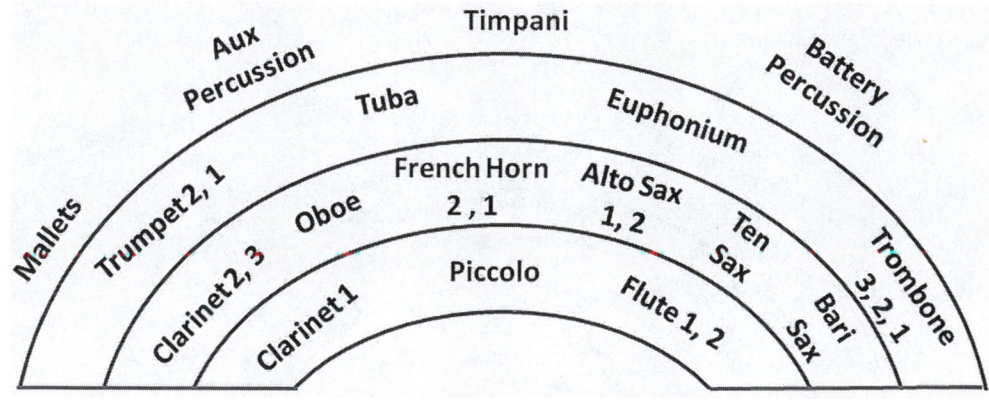

Analysis

1. Horns in second row for better projection (as opposed to a third row entirely of brass).
2. Instruments with similar parts placed together: alto saxophone/horn/trombone/euphonium.

FIGURE 11.6 Eastman Wind Ensemble Set-up

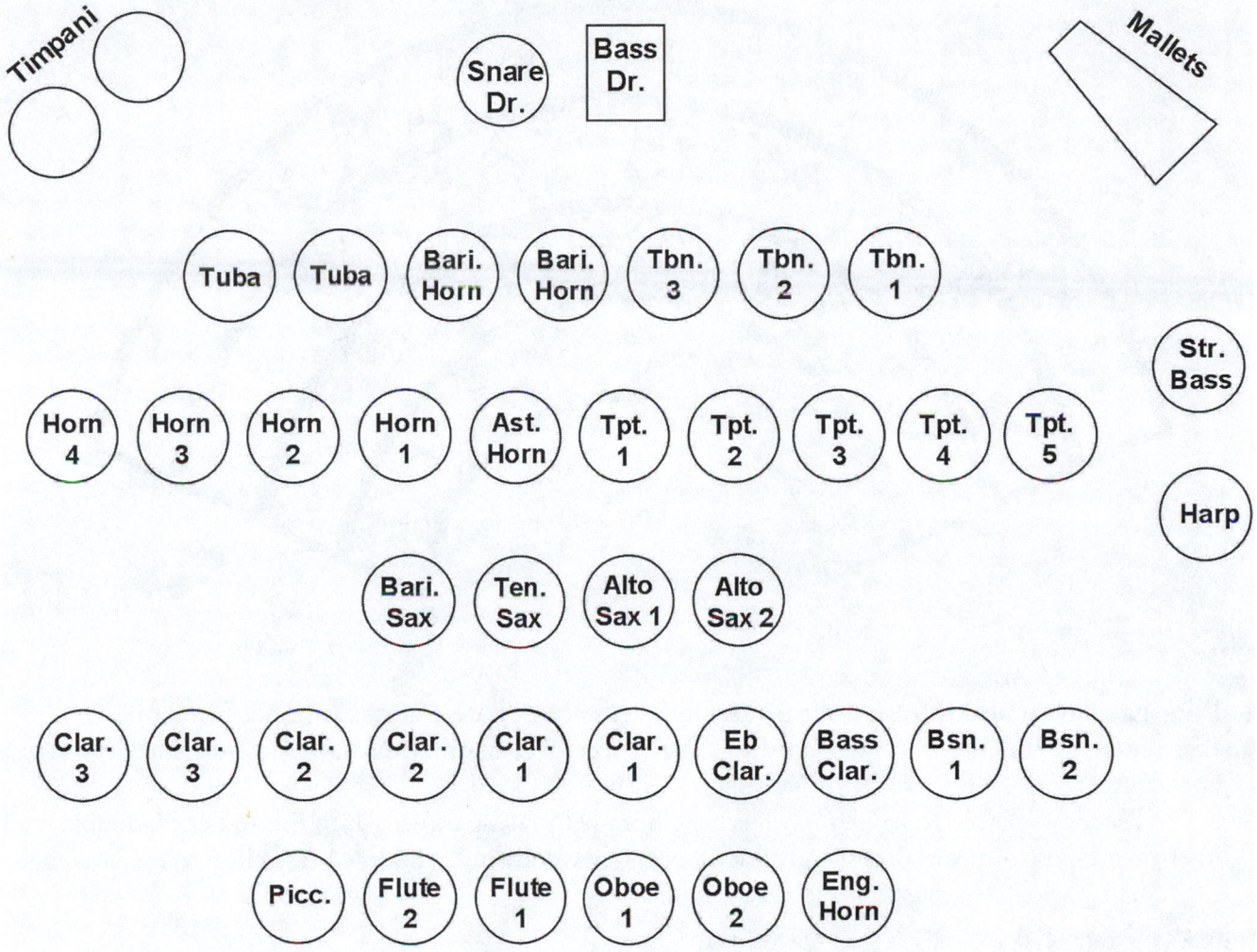

Analysis

1. Set-up mimics orchestral wind section (with an additional row for saxophones).
2. Principal players grouped in the center.
3. Instruments with similar parts placed together: low brass (back row); bass clarinet and bassoon.
4. Alto saxophones and horns separated so their tone colors are appreciated.

FIGURE 11.7 Dallas Wind Symphony Set-up

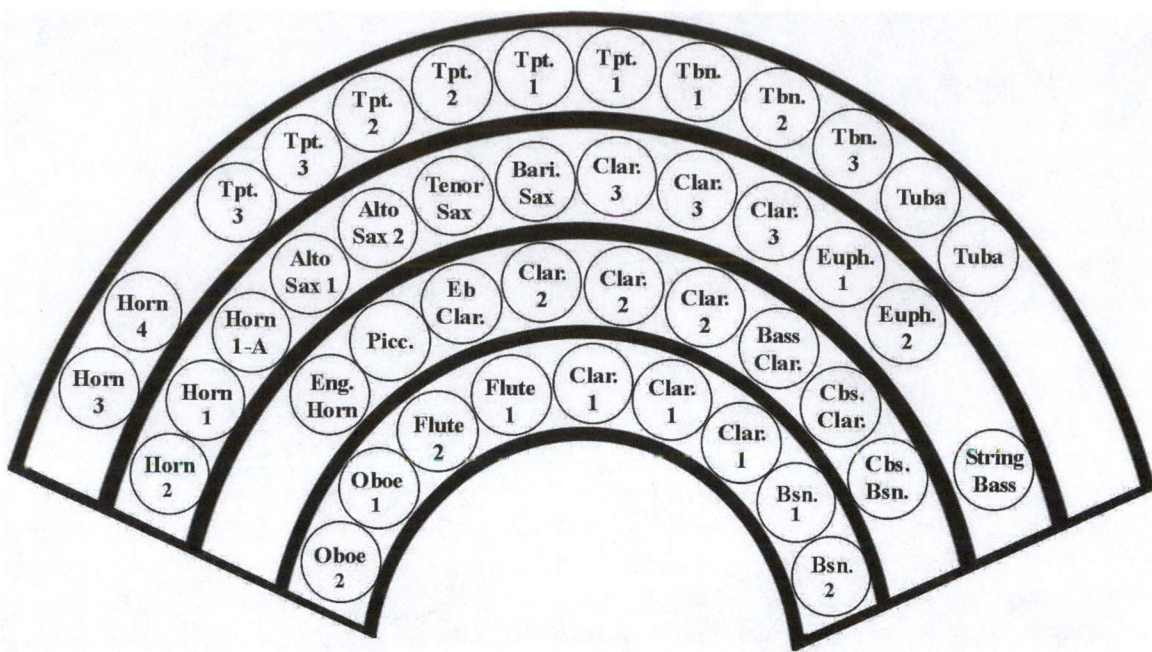

Analysis

1. Principal players placed toward the center of the ensemble: flute/clarinet/trumpet/trombone.
2. Instruments with similar parts placed together: piccolo/E♭ clarinet; bassoon/bass/clarinet/low brass; horns/alto saxophone.
3. Several sections placed to facilitate projection: horn bells facing directly into the audience; double reed instruments in front row closest to the audience; low woodwinds and low brass close to the audience.

FIGURE 11.8 Large Concert Band in a Small Space Set-up

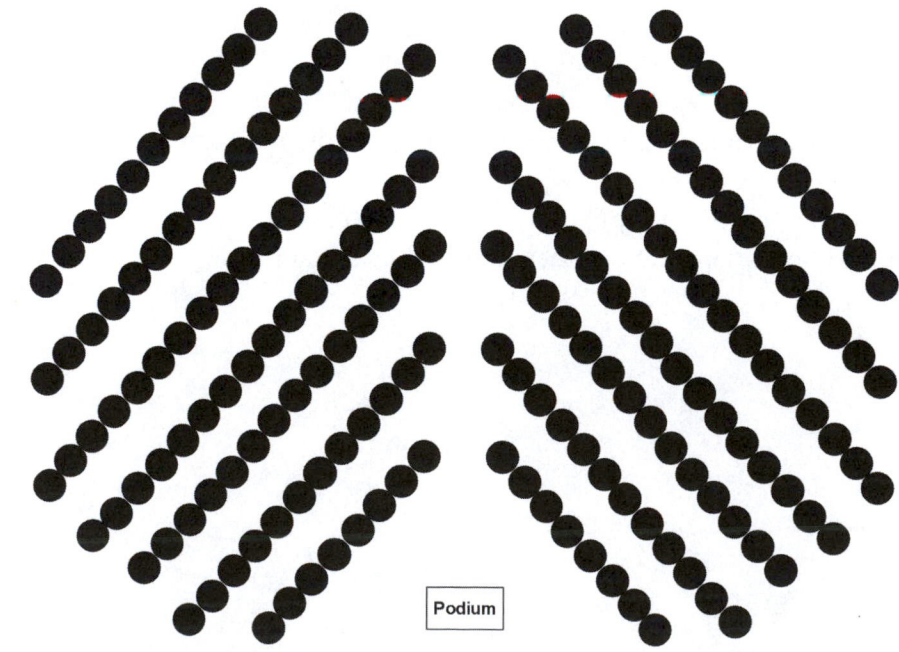

Analysis

Though a bit unusual, this set-up is designed for fitting large numbers of players in a relatively small space.

1. Completely straight lines in the V-shape maximize the number of chairs in each row. (Conventional curved rows have added space between chairs.)
2. Aisle down the center gives students and conductor easy access to any row and either side of the ensemble.

FIGURE 11.9 Full Orchestra Set-up

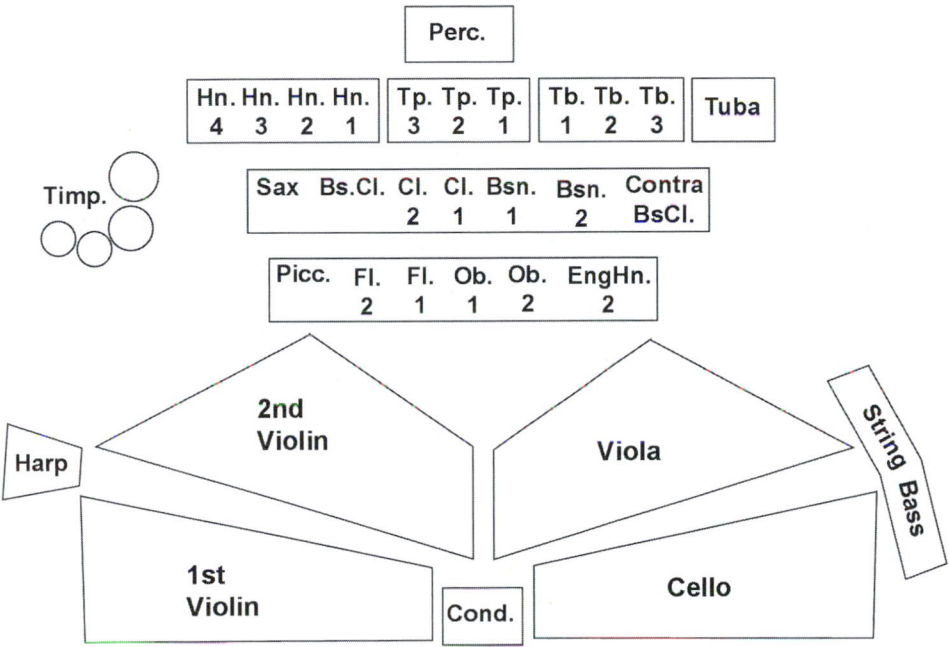

FIGURE 11.10 String Ensemble Set-up

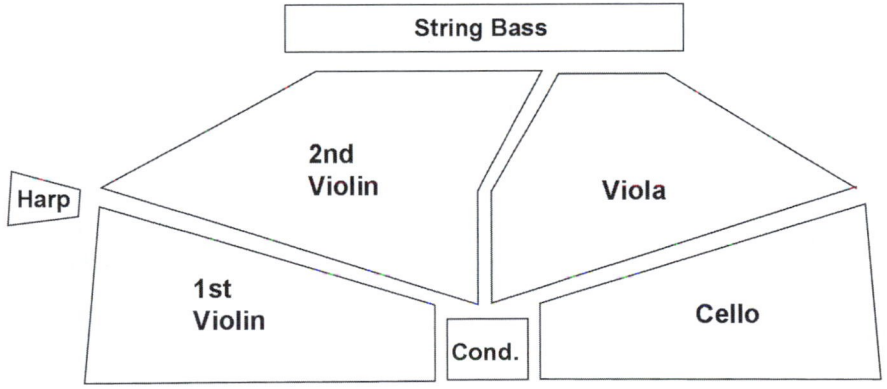

Activities/Assignments for Further Exploration

1. Create a seating chart for each instrument below (use the blank template in Figure 11.11; also included on the enclosed Companion Website).
2. For each set-up you create, explain your reasoning for the placement of each section.

FIGURE 11.11   Seating Chart Template

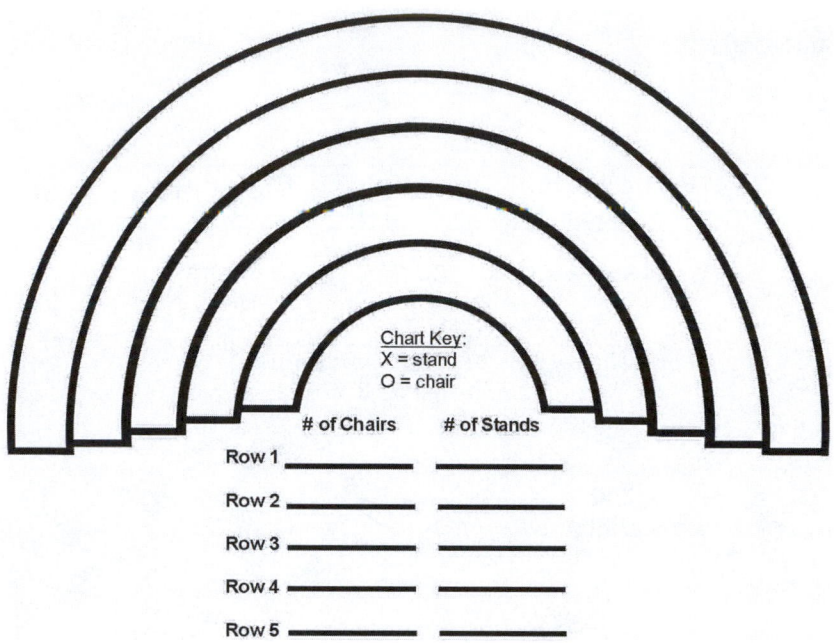

Chart Key:
X = stand
O = chair

	# of Chairs	# of Stands
Row 1	_____	_____
Row 2	_____	_____
Row 3	_____	_____
Row 4	_____	_____
Row 5	_____	_____

Medium-sized Ensemble—51 Wind Players

Players per instrument

1—Piccolo	1—Baritone saxophone	Xylophone
3—Flute 1	1—Bassoon 1	Marimba
3—Flute 2	1—Bassoon 2	Vibraphone
1—Oboe 1	3—Trumpet 1	Tubular bells
1—Oboe 2	3—Trumpet 2	Bass drum
3—Clarinet 1	3—Trumpet 3	Snare drum
3—Clarinet 2	4—French Horn	Crash cymbal
4—Clarinet 3	2—Trombone 1	Suspended cymbal
2—Bass clarinet	2—Trombone 2	Timpani
1—Alto saxophone 1	2—Trombone 3	Wind chimes
2—Alto saxophone 2	1—Euphonium	Tam tam
1—Tenor saxophone	3—Tuba	

Large Ensemble—113 Wind Players

Players per instrument

1—Piccolo	1—Bassoon 1	4—Tuba
9—Flute 1	3—Bassoon 2	Xylophone
13—Flute 2	4—Cornet 1	Marimba
2—Oboe 1	5—Cornet 2	Vibraphone
8—Clarinet 1	5—Cornet 3	Tubular bells
9—Clarinet 2	2—Trumpet 1	Bass drum
9—Clarinet 3	2—Trumpet 2	Snare drum
3—Bass clarinet	6—French horn	Crash cymbal
4—Alto saxophone 1	3—Trombone 1	Suspended cymbal
5—Alto saxophone 2	4—Trombone 2	Timpani
2—Tenor saxophone	4—Trombone 3	Wind chimes
2—Baritone saxophone	3—Euphonium	Tam tam

Small Ensemble—29 Wind Players

Players per instrument

1—Piccolo	1—Baritone saxophone	Marimba
2—Flute 1	1—Bassoon 1	Vibraphone
2—Flute 2	2—Trumpet 1	Tubular bells
1—Oboe 1	2—Trumpet 2	Bass drum
2—Clarinet 1	2—Trumpet 3	Snare drum
2—Clarinet 2	1—Trombone 1	Crash cymbal
2—Clarinet 3	1—Trombone 2	Suspended cymbal
1—Bass clarinet	1—Trombone 3	Timpani
1—Alto saxophone 1	1—Euphonium	Wind chimes
1—Alto saxophone 2	1—Tuba	Tam tam
1—Tenor saxophone	Xylophone	

Unbalanced Ensemble—57 Wind Players

Players per instrument

1—Piccolo	1—Baritone saxophone	Vibraphone
8—Flute 1	1—Bassoon 1	Tubular bells
9—Flute 2	5—Trumpet 1	Bass drum
1—Oboe 1	6—Trumpet 2	Snare drum
2—Clarinet 1	1—French horn	Crash cymbal
2—Clarinet 2	1—Trombone 1	Suspended cymbal
3—Clarinet 3	2—Trombone 2	Timpani
1—Bass clarinet	1—Euphonium	Wind chimes
4—Alto saxophone 1	1—Tuba	Tam tam
5—Alto saxophone 2	Xylophone	
2—Tenor saxophone	Marimba	

<h1 style="text-align:center">Chapter 12</h1>

Rehearsals

Part I: Basic Rehearsal Technique

To Guide Your Reading

How can the concept of Macro–Micro–Macro be applied to the rehearsal process in the short term and long term?

What is the most efficient way to address the ensemble and provide feedback?

How can we involve the entire group while rehearsing an individual section of the ensemble?

How can we use lesson plans to structure rehearsals?

Like most creative endeavors, rehearsing is an art and a craft, and directors must arrive prepared, organized, and able to demonstrate good technique. Recently the challenges have intensified: National standards and multi-cultural initiatives have brought composition, improvisation, history, and theory to the fore of our curriculums. Further, the pressure to justify music programs has increased the need to demonstrate, evaluate and measure student achievement, particularly skills and knowledge beyond performance ability.

Given that contact time with students has not increased, efficiency and organization has never been more important.

This unit is thus organized into three parts: (1) Basic rehearsal technique, (2) Components of an effective rehearsal, and (3) Diagnosis and Prescription of Common Problems.

Basic Rehearsal Technique—Macro–Micro–Macro

"Macro–Micro–Macro," or "Big–Small–Big" is the most basic rehearsal technique directors must master. Imagine you are an auto mechanic: Before fixing a car, you must first run the engine and look for faults and peculiar sounds. Once you have diagnosed these problems, you stop the engine, open the hood, start removing components, and then examine, repair or replace them. Finally, you restart the engine and evaluate its performance again.

This is the same approach effective conductors take in rehearsal. First they run a segment of the piece and listen for faults by comparing what they hear to their inner interpretation—their idealized version of the music. Once problems are identified, they break the piece down by isolating and repairing individual components—e.g., melody only, trumpet part only, woodwind part only, etc. Finally, they place the components back together, run the section again, and re-evaluate.

Macro–Micro–Macro: Zoom-in (Example 1)

(This technique involves becoming more and more specific until the exact problem is isolated, solved, and then put gradually back into context. Notice how some trial and error is common before the root problem is identified.)

Group plays from Rehearsal A to Letter B.
Conductor identifies general problem: there seems to be a wrong note.
  "Let's hear just the people with the accompaniment."
Accompaniment plays, but sounds fine.
  "OK, let's hear just the melody people."
Melody plays, and conductor hears a wrong note in the clarinets in measure 25.
  "Let's have just the clarinets play measure 25. Watch the B♮ on beat 3."
Clarinets play; it improves but is still not perfect.
  "Clarinets, just play beat 2 to beat 3, slowly. Remember to use the left hand B♮ after the D♯."
Clarinets play; it gets better.
  "Good. Please mark 'LH' in your parts. Let's try the whole measure now."
Clarinets play the measure accurately.
  "Good, clarinets! Now let's combine all the melody folks from measures 24–28."
Melody plays.
  "Excellent. OK now let's put the entire section back together. And let's see if we can make more crescendo to the end of the phrase."
Everyone plays rehearsal A to B.

Macro–Micro–Macro: Zoom-In (Example 2)

(Conductor hears a wrong note while the group is playing a passage.)

  "OK, 2nd violins, let's isolate a pitch in measure 3. Notice that the second finger on your E string should be playing a G♮. We need to use our minor tetrachord finger placement."
All violins play and hold their open E together.
  "Now, all violins play F♯."
Violins play and hold the note.
  "Now, FREEZE! OK, all violins, without moving your bow, place the second finger on the G♮. GREAT! Now on my downbeat, sound the G♮ with your bows. Violas, celli, and basses, play your open G with them for support. Remember, violins, we must always hear the lowest sound and adjust the left hand accordingly."
Group plays.
  "Now, 2nds, go back to measure 3. Let's all play slowly together through the measure and hold the G to be sure we land in tune when it is in the passage."
Students play and sustain the G.

"Great! OK, orchestra, everyone at measure 3, playing at a slower tempo."

The ensemble plays measure 3, all together, under tempo.

"Great, that sounds much better."

"Now let's have only the 2nd violins play the entire passage."

2nds play the entire passage.

"Excellent, 2nds! Let's add everyone else and play the passage one more time."

Ensemble plays.

Terrific—problem fixed!

Macro–Micro–Macro: Process of Elimination

(Breaking a section down into separate voice parts—e.g., melody/accompaniment/bass; melody/counter-melody/rhythmic accompaniment—allows us to hear issues more readily than we can when everyone is playing. In the scenario below the conductor senses something is wrong but cannot identify the exact problem. The solution is to systematically work through each line in the texture and then recombine them.)

Group plays from measure 72 to 83.

Conductor hears rhythmic problems across the ensemble.

"Let's hear just the bass line."

Bass line plays without any problems.

"OK. Let's hear the upper woodwinds. Anyone who has three-sixteenth notes starting on beat 1."

Upper woodwinds play; conductor hears a small problem, but not the major one.

"Good. Be careful not to rush the sixteenth notes. Let's try it again."

Woodwinds play again but this time without any problems.

"Excellent. Now let's hear the saxophone, French horn, and trombone line."

They play, with a distinct problem on beats 3 and 4.

"Let's make sure to release the tie together on beat 3 and play the ♪♪♩ rhythm staccato. Let's try it again."

Group plays, but there is no improvement.

"Let's all sing and count the rhythm of that measure."

Group sings the rhythm and style accurately; conductor repeats the exercise for reinforcement.

"Good, now let's play it."

Group plays the measure.

"Excellent. Now let's try the entire passage."

Group plays.

"OK. Now let's put it back together. Everybody at measure 72."

Macro–Micro–Macro Process: Breaking into Micro to Show How the Music is Put Together

(Sometimes breaking things down from macro to micro and building it up again gives students the chance to hear how their part fits with the others.)

Group plays from Letter B to Letter C.

"We're having some balance issues. Let's make sure we all understand the role of everyone's parts."

"Let's just hear the bass line."

Bass line plays; conductor makes some suggestions and repeats.

"Now let's add the eighth-note line in the trombones and saxophones. Make sure you feel the downbeats from the bass line so you know exactly where to put the offbeats."

Eighth-note line joins; conductor makes suggestions.

"Good. Now let's add the half-note line in the French horns and saxes. So as not to cover the lines we've just heard, put a little decay on each half note."

French horns and saxophones join.

"Finally, let's layer the melody on top of it all. In contrast to all the rhythm behind you, be as lyrical as possible by crescendoing through the line."

Melody joins in; now the entire group plays.

The basic approach of Macro–Micro–Macro can be applied to any aspect of the rehearsal:

- short term—a small part of an entire rehearsal (as described above)
- medium term—the shape of one complete rehearsal
- long term—the progression from initial read-through to concert performance.

In the medium term, for example, the first part of a rehearsal on a specific piece is spent running large segments, the second part rehearsing those sections in detail, and the final part reviewing and revisiting the large segments, thus solidifying and contextualizing improvements.

For the long-term rehearsal process, when an ensemble first receives a piece, the initial rehearsals are spent working on the big picture—notes, rhythms, form, tempo, etc. The middle rehearsals are spent on the details—ensemble precision, intonation, balance, technique, style, etc. Finally, as the performance approaches, rehearsals revisit the big picture for consistency and flow.

Communicating with the Ensemble

Rehearsal Instructions—Who! What! Where!

There are few things more frustrating than repeating oneself because students are not paying attention. Sometimes, the problem originates from the podium. In order to make instructions clear, use the following order when rehearsing something specific:

1. WHO you are addressing
2. WHERE in the music you are directing them
3. WHAT you would like them to do

For example, "Trumpets—at Letter A play the eighth notes staccato," or "Woodwinds—at measure 34 don't forget the crescendo," or "Everybody who has half notes in measure 24—don't rush!" Certainly, we should encourage students to listen to every instruction. They are bound to learn something from the musical challenges of other players, and they must learn to hear their part in the context of the entire ensemble.

If we wish to emphasize that all students should listen to every instruction, alter WHO–WHERE–WHAT, and instead begin with WHERE.

Addressing Players Within the Ensemble

There are four levels of specificity when addressing a group:

1. **Identify the large group of students.**
   "Everybody, we need to arrive at rehearsal on time."
   "Woodwinds, thank you for arriving early enough to warmup."
   Obviously, this technique is useful for giving general announcements and instructions. But be aware that because it is general, it holds no individual accountable.

2. **Identify smaller groups by name.**
   "Trumpets, at measure 42, everyone should be using mutes."
   "Violins, bravo for practicing this passage over the weekend!"
   "Saxophones, at measure 25, be sure you can hear the flute melody."

3. **Identify individuals using their instrument name.**
   "Third trumpets, at measure 39, your eighth notes need to be much shorter."
   "Second flutes, at measure 12 be sure to provide enough breath support to protect the end of the phrase."

4. **Identify individuals using their proper name.**
   "Frank, beautiful solo!"
   "Sandra, please stop talking."

The use of individual names can be extremely effective when giving positive comments. *"Jennifer and Bob—Thank you for the excellent eye contact."*

For better or worse, critical feedback is the most common way to communicate with the ensemble. After all, we feel pressure to make improvements, and this is often done by pointing out what is wrong. However, if we publicly point out an individual's problems, we should publicly tell the student when things are better, too. Otherwise the student will just play softer next time and hope not to be heard. (e.g., "Anna, look at your hand: Are you really reaching a whole step between fingers one and two? Finger the A, now finger the B♮. Excellent! That sounds much better now.") Remind students, "No hard feelings—it's just my job to fix the issues you can't quite hear when playing in a group."

Indeed, positive feedback should be used regularly. For example, after stopping the group, but *before* launching into a new list of problems, point out what has improved. It takes only a few seconds to say, "Trumpets, thank you for that excellent crescendo," and it goes a long way towards fostering a positive rehearsal environment.

An efficient way to communicate the positive is while conducting—a simple "OK" sign, head-nod, or thumbs-up directed at a section or individual offers welcome approval. When offering praise to the individual, section, or ensemble, be specific. Saying, "That was better" is not meaningful; say *exactly* what has improved. Specificity is equally important when providing constructive criticism. If the flutes are playing out of tune, saying "Flutes, be sure to listen" usually results in more questions than answers; the flutes need to know for *what* they should be listening.

In a healthy rehearsal dynamic, feedback is a two-way street between the conductor and the ensemble. For example, after giving an instruction such as, "Trumpets, at Letter A, please play stronger," the section should be encouraged to "check-in" with the conductor the next time through. By using eye contact to essentially ask, "Was that better?" students create a window through which to receive more feedback.

Giving Multiple Instructions

Conductors with astute ears often compile a list of issues they would like to address and in the name of efficiency offer them all at once, laundry-list style. However, too many suggestions at once can overload students' capacity to concentrate and retain the information. (*Note*: An important exception to this is the "Sticky Note" rehearsal; see below.) Instead, put a cap on multiple comments to individuals (or sections) and distribute comments around the group—e.g., one for the trumpets, one for the flutes, etc.

"We" versus "I"

The use of the pronouns "I" and "We" has different effects. Use "I" to exercise authority or to communicate non-musical instructions—e.g., "I need everybody to stack the stands after rehearsal." For musical issues, however, "I" suggests an adversarial relationship between conductor and ensemble. Students feel more fully invested and more collaborative when the pronoun "We" is used. (See Table 12.1.)

TABLE 12.1 The Effects of Using the Pronouns "I" and "We"

"I" – centered/adversarial	"We"– inclusive
I want to hear the flutes at Letter B.	Can we hear the flutes at Letter B?
I want the dotted-half to be held for its full duration.	We need the dotted-half to be held for its full duration.
Can I hear more crescendo?	Can we hear more crescendo?

Also effective are:

1. State the request as a simple command.
   Example: "Release the sustained note on beat 3."
2. Substitute the composer's name for "I" or "We."
   Example: "Persichetti calls for more marcato at the beginning of the recapitulation."

Engaging the Entire Ensemble During the Rehearsal

It is easy to act as if we are wearing aural blinders in rehearsal, treating one section as the only people in the room. To insure everyone participates, even while focusing on a specific section, speak globally but rehearse locally. For example, while rehearsing an intonation issue, first ask, "Can we all hear the beats within this unison line? Is the pitch tendency sharp or flat?"; We thus rehearse a specific group while still involving everyone.

Many teachers seek to engage students by asking questions to the ensemble and then calling upon a single student to answer. This is an extremely inefficient way to engage students or test knowledge. Only one student participates at a time, and it is usually someone who does not need the practice in the first place; they raise their hand precisely because they are confident they know the answer. If the teacher calls upon someone who is not volunteering, that student often stammers until the teacher steps in to help.

The Questions/Instant Feedback Technique

An alternative to the traditional hand-raising procedure is *response cards,* which significantly increase the number of students responding to teacher questions and improves test scores based on those questions.[1] It also makes the rehearsal atmosphere collaborative, rather than establishing the conductor as a dictator who constantly berates the group (e.g. "Trumpets too loud; Clarinets, pitch is sharp; Basses, don't rush").

In the response card procedure, each student uses a personal dry erase board to write their answer. Then, the entire class simultaneously shows their boards to the teacher, who can quickly scan the responses and offers feedback (Cipani, 12). It is incredibly simple and remarkably effective. Admittedly, for an ensemble setting, where music stands offer limited desk space in close quarters and students negotiate bulky, fragile instruments, adding a dry erase board may be unwise (instead, try using them in smaller settings, such as lessons and sectionals). An alternative is to ask the entire ensemble to provide feedback using simple hand signs. For example:

Question: "What dynamic were the trumpets actually playing? With a show of fingers: 1 = piano; 5 = fortissimo."

Question: "Was Clarinet 1 flatter or sharper than Clarinet 2?" *Handsign:* thumbs up = sharper; thumbs down = flatter; thumbs sideways = in tune.

Hands signs are more efficient than awaiting verbal responses from each player. A quick scan of everyone's hand position gives the feedback we need and strengthens the critical listening skills of the ensemble. Our students can offer each other instant feedback, too. For example, pair each student with the person sitting next to him. While one student plays the other watches his posture and offers critique with positive and negative feedback. It's helpful to give each student two or three chances to play so he can make adjustments.

If we plan on rehearsing a small section of the ensemble for an extended period, consider asking the other students to work on independent activities:

- Number their measures
- Write in rhythm counts
- Finger their parts
- Update their music with special notes which are provided for them on a handout—e.g., reminders about dynamics, articulations, style, etc. as in the "Do-It-Yourself" rehearsal (see Part II)

Other ways to keep everyone involved include:
(*see the "Rehearsal Toolkit" on the Companion Website, for detailed explanations*)

- Strength in numbers
- Numeric dynamics
- Percentage dynamics
- The human metronome
- One ensemble, one pulse
- Hum the countermelody or other inner voice
- Ensemble music critics
- Interpretation through democracy.

Strategies to Keep the Percussion (and String Basses) Involved

Most conductors would probably hate to admit it, but it's easy to overlook the percussion section during rehearsal. With diverse wind parts struggling with pitch, rhythm, and tone color, and percussion parts that are usually less active, it's certainly explainable though not altogether excusable. Consider the following tactics to keep those percussionists involved:

- For music with minimal percussion parts, have some percussionists play the oboe part on mallet instruments. Use soft mallets to preserve the overall balance.
- Have percussionists who are not playing double on drum pads.
- Have percussionists rotate parts every several days (especially when the music is easy enough to do so).
- Assign percussionists to help sections of the ensemble who are having rhythmic difficulties. Sit the percussionists next to the section that needs help and have them clap the rhythms while the section plays. (Or, give a copy of the part to the snare drummer and have her play along.)

In the string ensemble, if we find that a section, such as the string basses, is frequently waiting while we rehearse other sections, use the following strategies to involve them.

- Have them search for alternate fingerings—this needs only a quick comment but engages them to find a new solution to a fingering problem.
- Ask them to pluck their part for support as other strings play theirs.

Lesson Planning—Structuring the Rehearsal

If you fail to plan, you have planned to fail.

(traditional adage)

Music ensemble lesson plans should reflect the interplay between the introduction of new concepts and the continual review and refinement of old ones. We may want the clarinets to learn measures 23–24, but we must recognize that the complete learning process may take several rehearsals, during which time technique improves and subtleties of phrasing, pitch, and color are gradually added.

Admittedly, it is far easier for conductors to improvise a plan during class than it is for, say, the physics teacher. After all, conductors are encouraged to listen and react. An organized lesson plan, however, ensures that directors pace learning through the rehearsal process, place reasonable limits on per-rehearsal progress, and focus on high priority musical issues, rather than just reacting to the first sounds the ear encounters.

Announcements/Music Order

When our students walk into the room, have announcements, warmups, and the music order already written on the board. This allows students to begin organizing before the period officially begins. Advance notice of the rehearsal order is particularly important to the percussion section.

There are always things that need to be announced, and it is important that students hear them with their full attention. Keep them short and to the point, and decide the best time to give them: Giving announcements at the beginning of class takes advantage of students' freshest attention, but it starts the rehearsal with a slow pace. Announcements in the middle are effective if the class needs a change of pace, but they can also bring a flowing rehearsal to a screeching halt. Announcements at the end leave them fresh on students' minds as they leave, but if they are anxious to pack up we may not have their undivided attention. Beyond giving verbal announcements, try posting them on a bulletin board, website, or printed handout.

Warmup (Skill-building and Tuning)

In some ways ensemble warmups are the musician's version of the stretching and drills an athletic team does before practice. Warmups are also an opportunity to develop the musicianship and fundamental skills musicians need to perform individually and collectively.

It can be tempting to eliminate skill-building exercises and tuning in favor of more music rehearsal time, but the short-term gains from this will eventually be offset by long-term losses in group intonation, blend, and listening skills. We recommend cutting this activity only on rare occasions.

Specific skills that warmups address include:

1. *Ear training*—e.g., aural recognition of pitch patterns, harmonic progressions, modes, intonation, and singing); singing/humming the tuning pitch, singing/playing I-IV-V-I progressions, discrimination of pitch tendencies (especially when tuning).
2. *Musicality*—e.g., exercises for balance, articulation, phrasing, hearing intonation, rhythmic exercises, chorales, long tones.
3. *Technique building blocks*—e.g., scales, arpeggios, interval exercises, and rhythms.
4. *Physical Skills*—e.g., breathing exercises, adjusting pitch with embouchure, tonguing/double-tonguing, finger speed, range, air speed, breath support, phrasing/when to breathe, long tones, vibrato technique.
5. *Sightreading*—e.g., solfege patterns, flashcards, ensemble music, rhythmic exercises.
6. *Ensemble Intonation*—e.g., unisons, harmonies, melodic intervals.

Warmup activities should be balanced between familiar and unfamiliar activities. Several publishers offer books devoted to warmup and skill-building exercises. Among the most popular are these:

Michael Allen and Don Hanna, *Daily Warm-ups for Full Orchestra*, Hal Leonard
Quincy Hilliard, *Chorales for Beginning and Intermediate Orchestra*, KJOS Music
Ed Lisk, *The Creative Director*, Meredith Music Publishing
Roger Maxwell, *Fourteen Weeks to a Better Band*, C.L. Barnhouse
James D. Ployhar, *I Recommend*, Belwin Publishing
Rom C. Rhodes and Donald Bierschenk, *Symphonic Band Technique*, Southern Music Co
Claude T. Smith, *Symphonic Techniques for Band*, Hal Leonard Publishing Corp
Leonard B. Smith, *Treasury of Scales for Band and Orchestra*, Alfred Publishing
Richard Williams and Jeff King, *Foundations for Superior Performance, Warm-ups & Techniques for Band*, KJOS

Warmup method books are a tremendous resource for scales, arpeggios, and rhythmic exercises. Besides their comprehensiveness, their greatest advantage may be that everyone participates in every exercise. Most ensemble music, especially for young players, tends to typecast: woodwinds play the difficult melodies and rhythms; low brass sustain, rarely receive the melody, and even more rarely play difficult licks. Method books are the great equalizer. Low reeds and low brass practice the same rhythms, scales, technique, and articulation as the rest of the ensemble.

But exercises themselves do not automatically improve student performance in phrasing, blend, balance, pitch, and sightreading. If chosen effectively, excerpts from the literature offer the same benefit and are much more satisfying to play. A 1982 study by Linda Morehouse concluded that ensembles with supplementary materials fared no better in sightreading than groups who just used concert literature (Morehouse, 1982). Similarly, in "Effects of Two Instructional Methods on High School Band Students' Sight-Reading Proficiency, Music Performance, and Attitude," Regena Turner Parrish compared the sightreading performance of two groups: one used a traditional skill-building book, and another used excerpts from literature that emphasized the same components of pitch, rhythm, and expression.[2] The conductor of each ensemble used the same teaching techniques. The results showed that the students using music excerpts:

- were no weaker in sightreading ability than those using drills
- had higher performance achievement
- indicated more positive attitudes.

These studies suggest that just as important as the music students play is what we ask them to do with it. One key is to avoid turning warmup exercises into a routine that the ensemble does without even thinking or paying attention. While creating routines is an important component of classroom discipline, and scale, arpeggio, articulation, and rhythm exercises concisely reinforce concepts that appear in the literature, too much predictability causes students to view the process as an empty ritual. To prevent this, regularly rotate at least some exercises and liberally expose the group to as much unfamiliar music as possible, even in small doses and sections.

Related to this is the benefit of using materials that transfer to the concert repertoire. If we treat warmups as isolated exercises, students cannot apply what they have learned to actual music. To be sure, many exercises—scales and articulation—apply to virtually all music. But it is worth tailoring the warmup to reflect what needs work during the rest of rehearsal. For example, take a piece you are about to rehearse and design warm-up exercises that:

1. Are in the same overall key.
2. Tune chords in the same tonality.
3. Ask the entire band to practice a tricky rhythm together.
4. Has a type of articulation that needs attention.
5. Practise scales/modes that appear within challenging passages.
6. Allow all instruments to play the main melody in unison (write it out for all transpositions and clefs).

After the warmup, don't assume students will make connections themselves. Point out similarities and rehearse the same concepts in the concert literature.

To maximize their effectiveness, avoid using warmup/skill-building as a time to handle other activities, such as taking attendance, collecting forms, speaking with students individually, fetching reeds, or repairing instruments. Rather, be proactive in evaluating the ensemble's performance. If articulations are not clean, stop and address them. If the group plays well, offer specific complements—e.g., "Trombones: Excellent crescendo during the E♭ scale!" If students perceive that the director is not listening, they will in turn treat the warmup as tedium and become less focused for the rest of the rehearsal.

Rehearsing the Music

When planning a rehearsal, consider the following:

1. *Prioritize notes and rhythm versus musicality*—We cannot add details of musicality to a piece when students do not have a reasonable grasp of its notes and rhythms. Certainly we can address the big picture of style and phrasing while we woodshed, but realize that students will not be able to fully incorporate these details until they know their parts. Priorities shift during the rehearsal cycle; early in the process notes and rhythm occupy the majority of our attention, though we still must find opportunities to teach phrasing and musicianship. Towards the end of the cycle musicality is our focus, even though we still may be "cleaning" notes (See Figure 12.1).

FIGURE 12.1 Pyramid of Rehearsal Priorities

Pyramid of Priorities

2. *Calibrate your ears for specific musical issues*—Anticipating problems is important, but avoid scripting the entire rehearsal. We suggest writing two to three objectives per work, and then allowing your "conductor ear" to detect issues as they arise. *Calibrate* your ears to the sorts of issues that need prioritizing. Define these as the musical issues you will stop to rehearse on that particular day—e.g., remind yourself, "I will be listening especially to articulation, and stop as necessary to work on these details. Share these objectives with the students so they understand your priorities and intentions for the rehearsal—e.g., "Let's play from Letter A to B and then rehearse in detail. I'm especially interested in how the accompaniment parts are fitting together"; "We'll begin at Letter D and start and stop as necessary. Pay extra attention to your dynamic markings!"
3. *Don't over-schedule*—In an effort to create continuity between rehearsals it is tempting to schedule each piece every day. Doing so, however, runs the risk of making the rehearsal superficial and wastes valuable time while the percussionists reset for the next piece. For those that have 40 minute periods, we recommend scheduling one or two works per rehearsal. (Exceptions: "Overview" rehearsals, "Spot-Check" rehearsals," and run-throughs before a concert.)
4. *Begin and end with success*—Whenever possible, begin and end rehearsals with music that allows students to experience success. In the middle of the period, when student focus is optimized, schedule music that requires intense rehearsal but that may end short of mastery.

5. *Anticipate*—By thoroughly studying a work and using our knowledge of instrumental pedagogy we can anticipate many problems students will encounter.
6. *Prevent "chop" burnout*—Especially with young brass players, embouchure endurance is an issue even in a 40-minute rehearsal. Avoid scheduling works with extended ranges immediately after the warmup, and be sensitive to fatigue when repeating a difficult passage.
7. *Know when to move on*—Directors with an acute "conductor ear" will always find *something* that needs attention, but eventually we have to move to the next rehearsal objective. Moreover, remember that learning technical facility is a gradual process. Be sensitive to when the group has reached its limit and revisit the passage another day. Use phrases such as "This has made improvement today," and "Practice this at home and let's revisit it during the next rehearsal."

Assignments/Homework

The most common homework we give is "Practice!", which is made more effective if we (1) give specific goals, and (2) hold the students accountable for achieving them. A general demand for practicing encourages poor practice habits, as students face a folder full of music without any direction. Also, remember that assignments need not only be performance-based (e.g., writing assignments).

Post-Rehearsal Evaluation

After a rehearsal, take the time to evaluate the ensemble's progress. For each piece, take notes on what has improved and what still needs work. This list will be the basis for writing the next rehearsal plan.

Lesson Plan Format

There are many ways to express and format a lesson plan. The sample plan shown in Figure 12.2 is designed to reflect the way we present learning goals in rehearsal: Who will the activity involve? What part of the music? What is our objective? How will we achieve that objective? How can the completion of that objective be assessed? The clock-timings in the left column guide our pacing and keep us on task. Be flexible, however; if an activity takes longer than anticipated, it may be best to reschedule part of the plan for another rehearsal.

Allotting Time for Each Part of the Lesson Plan (Class Length Matters)

For 40–60 Minute Classes

Class periods under an hour place extra demands on our ability to be organized and efficient. Once we subtract the time needed for warmups, announcements, and putting instruments away, there may be only 30-35 minutes of solid rehearsal time. The typical 40–60 minute rehearsal can be broken down into the following activities:

Announcements and administrative matters—3–5 minutes.
Warmup/skill-building and tuning—5–7 minutes.
Music rehearsal—30–35 minutes.
Assignments/Homework—3–5 minutes.

FIGURE 12.2 Sample Lesson Plan Format

November 15, Symphonic Band, Period 2 –– Lesson Plan

<u>Materials</u>: Baton, metronome, tuner, permission slips, Mozart Rondo recording

Time	Piece	Instrument	Measures	Objective	Method	Assessment
9:00 - 9:05	Warm-ups: Evaluation Intonation training	Group	---	Developing intonation, ear training	2 trumpets play together a whole note	Band evaluates intonation using thumb signs
9:05 - 9:15	Student-led call and response improvised rhythms	Tutti	---	Students are able to improvise rhythms in 8th and 16th rhythms	8 volunteers, one for each note of the Bb scale, 4 beats of improvised rhythm on each note	---
9:15 - 9:25	The Constance March	Trombones Trumpets	Second Strain m.16 – 32	note and rhythm clarity	"slow and accurate" to "fast and accurate"	---
		Tutti	Dog fight	Contrast of dynamics, accents, and staccato	Parody/Satire Tech. "tool kit"	---
9:25 - 9:40	Routledge Rondo	Tutti	Entire piece	Students construct form diagram chart of Routledge Rondo	1. Review rondo form using Mozart Rondo 2. Play each section of Routledge Rondo separately 3. After each section students write "A" for refrain or "B, C, D" for episodes	Students check work with stand partner
9:40 - 9:55	Hileman Hoedown	Tutti	A section	Lightness of articulation	Sing correct style then play and imitate that style	Listen to students in quintets
		Woodwinds & Brass	Run m. 132-142	Transition to Coda	Break layers down and put back together	Perform accurately 3 times in a row.
		Tutti	Run piece	To provide a performance for evaluation	Play and record	Homework – student assessment of recording "posted mp3"
9:55 – 9:59	Announcements	permission slips due Friday				

For 60–90-Minute Classes

Whereas 40–60-minute classes may meet every day, 60–90-minute classes usually meet on alternating days as part of a block schedule. This makes rehearsal–to–rehearsal continuity more of a challenge, but provides more time for substantial music rehearsal and more intensive skill-building activities.

> ## Activities/Assignments for Further Exploration
>
> 1. Examine any portion of a score and discuss how it could potentially be rehearsed using Macro–Micro–Macro techniques.
> 2. Practice addressing the ensemble using "We"-centric, composer-centric, or direct commands.
> 3. Practice WHO–WHERE–WHAT: Using any score, randomly point to a measure and practice identifying to WHOM you are pointing (which staves), WHERE you are pointing (which measures) and WHAT you might need to rehearse (anticipate an issue with articulations, dynamics, or style).
> 4. Write a sample lesson plan for a work you are conducting or studying.

Part II: Components of an Effective Rehearsal

To Guide Your Reading

What strategies can we use to vary the pace, intensity, and detail of our rehearsals?

Why is sightreading a misnomer?

Types of Rehearsals—Balancing Pace, Intensity, and Detail

The key to pacing rehearsals is to balance low-energy, small group (e.g., working on intonation with one section) with high-energy, full-group, engaging activities (e.g., playing a large section to work on phrasing and dynamics). Running a rehearsal partly involves responding to what the ensemble is doing, but the pace and detail of our response must modulate, lest rehearsals become monotonous.

Below are several rehearsal styles, each with their own pace, flow and level of detail. The one feature they share is a high play to talk ratio. We should always strive to play far longer than we talk.

The Step and Go Macro–Micro–Macro Rehearsal

The "Bread and Butter" rehearsal incorporates the classic Macro–Micro–Macro approach. This is the technique where we do the bulk of our rehearsing and accomplish the nitty-gritty, in-the-trenches detail work that only Macro–Micro–Macro can achieve. The essential concept to remember is to break the music down—by melody/accompaniment, by section, by voice part, etc. Without isolating these specifics, it is difficult to hear the details needed to diagnose and resolve problems. This rehearsal approach requires a disciplined classroom, for not everyone will be playing all the time.

The "Overview" Rehearsal

This approach is most useful at the beginning of a rehearsal cycle, when a piece is new to the group. The main goal is to experience the big picture and answer the following questions for the students:

What is the overall style of the work?
What is the form?
Where are the musical peaks and valleys?

To answer these questions we should attempt to play through the entire work, stopping only to correct complete breakdowns, explain transitions, and teach recurring rhythms and themes. As with discovery learning, asking questions encourages students to discover the answers themselves.

At times it is more effective to introduce a work by starting some place other than the beginning—perhaps at the work's most accessible section—thus "hooking" the students before they face unfamiliar and challenging sections.

The "Quick Drill"

Nothing saps energy and morale more than slow-paced rehearsals with excessive talking by the teacher. Ironically, directors tend to talk more (and play less) when trying to achieve the most. An effective way to inject energy into a rehearsal is the "Quick Drill" technique. This is a high-paced technique with constant playing interspersed with quick comments—e.g., play—quick talk—play—quick talk—play, etc. Often, the "talk" involves a brief suggestion about what was just played, followed by an immediate repetition of that passage. Have students keep their instruments in playing position during the entire process. Minimize instructions to 5–10 seconds each and keep the students in playing position to minimize delays before starting up again. In the "Quick Drill" we essentially jettison Macro–Micro–Macro in favor of high-paced intensity. Note, however, that it can easily become draining and frenetic, and thus we recommend using it only for 2–5 minutes at a time.

The "Sticky Note" Rehearsal

A "Sticky Note" rehearsal is an extremely detailed lesson plan that targets issues we already know exist. This direct approach allows us to plan the rehearsal without waiting to react to what we hear. Either attach sticky notes to the score to use as tabs or make a single list of measures and issues to be tackled. Write specific issues or approaches to fix the problem directly on the sticky notes for quick reference. Some examples:

> m. 23—Trumpets need to be short
> Letter A—Pitch in the melody instruments
> m. 55—Transition into the waltz section

"Sticky Note" rehearsals are particularly effective (1) before concerts, to "spot check" transitions and difficult passages; (2) when time is in short supply; or (3) as review of an earlier rehearsal.

The "Self-Study" Rehearsal

On certain occasions it is possible to rehearse without talking at all, but rather by allowing students to make adjustments from a list of rehearsal points the director supplies. This "Self-Study" document should be user-friendly, using WHO–WHERE–WHAT to present each suggestion with a direct statement—e.g., "Trumpets, m. 23: Drop the tie!" The list should be distributed at the beginning of rehearsal so students may mark their part before class begins. (Consider writing instructions in terms of what students should actually write in their parts. Instead of "trumpets, measure 56, play forte," write "trumpets, measure 56, circle forte symbol.") For younger groups, use a shorter list over the course of several rehearsals; more mature ensembles can handle a longer list. The "Self-Study" approach is particularly effective before a performance, perhaps at a dress rehearsal, when there is limited time for detailed work. It is also useful to convey reminders or adjustments students can make on their own without practicing as a full ensemble.

A brief example (notice the use of the WHO–WHERE–WHAT):

Gustav Holst, "Jupiter" (from *The Planets*)
Everyone: In general the entire beginning is too loud!
Clarinets/Euphonium: m. 1–5, tongue
    m. 6–12—highlight slur marking
    m. 13–15—tongue all notes
    m. 16–21—slur
Everyone: 3 m. before rehearsal 1—add a slight crescendo into rehearsal 1
Violas: 4 m. after rehearsal 1—must be strong because nothing else is going on—play forte
Cornets: 9 m. before rehearsal 1—cut off the eighth note; do not hang over!
Flute and Oboe: 5 m. before rehearsal—excellent playing last rehearsal.
    Bravo!

(Sight)Reading

"Sightreading" is an unfortunate name for an activity that should be a regular part of rehearsals. When we pick up the morning newspaper we do not say, "I'm going to sightread the headlines." Instead, we simply *read* them, something achieved easily because we understand the rules of grammar, remember a large vocabulary of words, and apply a wealth of experience that helps us comprehend new sentences constructed from those words. Music learning is similar. We infer new words, phrases, sentences, and concepts from the ones we already know.

Reading unfamiliar music should be approached with the same regularity, pleasure, and joy of discovery with which we read everything else. Much of what we read in books and newspapers is a one-time activity—i.e., we never intend to revisit them after we "sightread." Encourage your students to approach music the same way. Thus, some of the music we read and rehearse need not be intended for performance. Instead, the goal can be to experience new sounds, increase one's musical vocabulary, and play for the sheer pleasure of it.

Strategies for Successful (Sight)Reading in Rehearsal

1. Soon after reading a new work, play a recording. This is the musical version of "A picture is worth a thousand words." Put another way: Imagine you are an art teacher. If you want your students to paint like Picasso, you do not simply describe his use of color, brush-stroke technique, etc. Instead, you show a Picasso painting to the class. Recordings work the same way. Unless it is a work with contemporary techniques or unconventional style, we suggest allowing students at least one chance to make sense of it on their own before playing a recording.
2. Before they play challenging passages, have students hum or sing the material.

Activities/Assignments for Further Exploration

1. Record yourself rehearsing and calculate how many minutes were spent playing and how many were spent talking. Did you achieve a high playing to talking ratio?
2. Design two exercises for each type of warmup/skill-building.
3. Write a "Self-Study" rehearsal document for a work you are currently rehearsing (either as player or conductor).

Part III: Diagnosis and Prescription of Common Problems

To Guide Your Reading

What is an efficient process to teach notes and rhythms?

What is the "conductor ear" and how can it be developed?

What types of performance problems should the conductor listen for?

What is differentiated instruction, and how can it be applied in the instrumental music classroom?

What is the role of repetition in rehearsals? How can it be used effectively?

How can metaphor and analogy be used to convey musical goals?

What are rehearsal "tools," and how can they be combined with other strategies?

What mistakes do students often make during practicing?

Which practice strategies do students often use? What are the most effective techniques?

What strategies can teachers use to encourage regular and efficient practicing?

Correcting Basic Rhythm and Note Issues in the Rehearsal

Building the Foundation of the Priority Pyramid

Before we address issues such as dynamics, phrasing, and style, the foundation of notes and rhythms must be in place. Without the foundation, the basic intent of the composer is altered, and interpretive details are meaningless. Although we certainly do not want to make rehearsals a substitute for individual practicing, often we cannot avoid rehearsing difficult passages for which students need guidance before tackling the challenge themselves. The basic way to practice technique is the time-honored process of slowing down the tempo and gradually increasing it as facility improves. We suggest the following method: "'Slow and Accurate' to 'Fast and Accurate'".

1. Isolate the notes and rhythms in question.
2. Slow down the passage to a tempo at which the notes and rhythm are played accurately.
3. Gradually increase the tempo while maintaining the level of accuracy. *Never go faster than what the students can perform accurately and musically.*
4. Place the passage back into context. Play from the beginning of the section.
5. Be prepared to isolate and master even the smallest details, and insist on proper technique even at a slow tempo. For example, in string playing, remind players to use the appropriate bow stroke and length of stroke so as not to add a problem later when the tempo is fast. Also, recognize that sometimes the issue can be as small as a leap to one note or the placement of a single grace note. And beware of misdiagnoses: often the problem is the transition from one passage to another, and thus isolating subsequent sections is ineffective.

Admittedly, constantly playing something under tempo can be seen as drudgery. First, be sure to play a recording so students know what they are working to create. Also, try working one section up to performance tempo and let students experience the satisfaction of the end product, even if just for a small chunk of music. But even if something is not ready it can be useful to occasionally play something at regular speed so students understand what the final product will feel like.

In addition to "Slow and Accurate-to-Fast and Accurate," other strategies for correcting rhythm and pitch include the following:

1. Use a "human metronome" to establish an audible beat. (For example, a snare drummer playing strong downbeats or subdivisions.)
2. Vamp the passage (i.e., ask students to add an imaginary "repeat bar").
3. Remove grace notes or other ornaments and have students learn the essential melody first (i.e., "make sure the Christmas tree is stable before adding the ornaments").
4. Remove the rhythm altogether and play note-by-note to isolate fingerings and pitch (or partials).
5. Demonstrate, using a student who can model the passage correctly.
6. Have students blow air through their instruments and execute articulations, rhythm, and fingerings/slide positions without pitch.

Note: Emphasize to the group that these are the same tactics individuals should use when practicing. (See the "The Rehearsal Toolkit," included on the Companion Website.)

Developing Your "Conductor Ear" (Score Study, Audiate, and Make Interpretative Decisions)

Even with a detailed lesson plan, the conductor must be able to diagnose problems on the spot and prescribe solutions.

A crucial prerequiste for this is being able to audiate the score. This is akin to a physician understanding what a healthy patient looks like. For the conductor, it involves having an idealized inner-recording of the work in which everything—every note, every rhythm, every phrase—has been considered. This is the "healthy" version of the music. It includes a precise concept of how the correct notes and rhythms sound, as well as decisions about interpretive issues such as phrasing, tempo, and style. Inexperienced conductors often fear facing an ensemble and having nothing substantial to say. The antidote? Know thy score and make every decision before the first rehearsal! Once we achieve this (and, admittedly, that takes time and effort), rehearsing fundamentally involves listening to the group and comparing it to the sounds we have playing in our mind's ear.

The ability to recognize the distinction between the two (i.e., what we *wish* to hear and what we *actually* hear) is another characteristic of a strong conductor ear. The key is to know what problems to listen for and what they sound like. Most of us can diagnose musical issues on a very general level—i.e., we know *something* is not quite right. But truly efficient conductors—those with good "conductor ears"—focus on the exact problem. Indeed, the main difference between a novice conductor and a seasoned professional is the level of detail with which they listen. Do they hear a problem with dynamics, or do they hear a problem with the violins making a crescendo too quickly compared to the celli?

As briefly discussed in Chapter 10, this is the difference between "instructor ears" and "conductor ears."[3] "Instructor ears" listen for mistakes that require little or no specific knowledge of a specific score, including the following:

- Time: Steady pulse, accurate rhythms, coordinated attacks and releases
- Pitch: Correct notes, centered pitches, good intonation

- Dynamics
- Expression markings (e.g., allargando, marcato, etc.)
- Articulations
- Quality of sound (balance, blend, intonation)

By using instructor ears, a good musician can listen to a performance of a piece he barely knows and still hear intonation problems, poor tone quality, inconsistent tempos, and sloppy rhythmic precision. And just looking at the score reveals unperformed notes, rhythms, dynamics, expression markings, and articulations. In other words, if the score says staccato, and one doesn't hear staccato, there's a problem—no score study is even necessary!

"Conductor ears" listen more specifically, more creatively, and more musically. They are the difference between "winging" a rehearsal by staying barely one step ahead of the ensemble and striving for a higher standard, even if the group has not yet reached it. When we listen with conductor ears our standards are crystalline and performance errors pop out like red flags. We anticipate what we wish to hear and we react to discrepancies. "Conductor ears" only develop with score study, and they listen for:

- color/timbre
- phrasing
- weight
- character
- energy
- "feel"
- "spirit"
- harmonic texture and balance
- motivic/thematic unity and connections
- priority of balance among contrapuntal textures
- tempo relationships

Of course, we should not underestimate the importance of actually *seeing* problems. We may use our ears to hear musical issues, but we can use our eyes to diagnose them. Here are some examples:

- *Intonation*—String players missing the correct place on the fingerboard; trumpet players not pushing out their third valve slide.
- *Phrasing*—Wind players breathing at the wrong time; string players using the wrong bowing.
- *Articulation*—String players using the wrong bow technique (e.g., on-string versus off-string); percussionists using improper mallets (e.g., yarn versus rubber) or poor technique (not dampening pitches on timpani, etc.).

Listening for Common Problems

Though it may not be possible to listen for everything simultaneously, we should calibrate our ears to listen specifically rather than generally. Consider the following list of common problems:

Notes

- Wrong fingerings
- Wrong partials on brass instruments
- Missed key signatures
- Horn transposition incorrect when playing stopped
- Error in printed part

Rhythms

- Students playing incorrect rhythms.
- Lack of precision throughout the ensemble (e.g., dotted-eighth to sixteenth rhythms played as triplets).
- Syncopated figures are ambiguous.
- Long notes and long rests end too late or too soon.
- Quarter-note triplets are uneven or drag.
- Phasing among sections in the ensemble.
- First notes of the piece not together.
- Anacrusis not together.
- Notes are late after rests (e.g., ♪♫ is late off the downbeat).
- Notes after tied rhythm are late.
- Repeated upbeat eighth notes are unsteady (drag or rush).
- Mixed-meter subdivisions unsteady.

Tempo and Timing

- Unsteady tempo (speeds up, slows down, or fluctuates).
- Ritardando/accelerando not gradual.

Dynamics and Balance

- Not enough contrast in dynamics.
- Overall dynamics are too loud or too soft.
- Forte/piano markings played as mezzo forte/mezzo piano.
- Phrase peaks too early or too late.
- Dynamic range is limited (no use of very soft or very strong levels).
- Individual students are too prominent or need to be heard more.
- Sections of the ensemble are too prominent or need to be heard more.
- Specific chord tones are too prominent.
- Dynamics are "top heavy" (too much first part and too little third part) or bottom heavy.
- Percussion section is too loud.
- Accompaniment lines overpower melodic lines (or vice versa).

Intonation

- No clear pitch center in the ensemble.
- Individual instruments or sections out of tune.

- Chords out of tune.
- Ensemble's overall pitch is sharp or flat.

Tone and Blend

- Distorted tone (blatty).
- Pinched tone (weak).
- Quality diminishing in very soft or very loud sections.
- Individuals or sections of the ensemble are too prominent.

Articulation

- Students do not play the printed markings.
- Articulations do not sound clear.
- Short articulations lack precise or crisp sound.
- Staccato notes are too long.
- Legato notes are too short.
- Marcato notes are not well-spaced.
- Slurred parts lack clarity.
- Style not well-defined.
- Articulations not consistent.

Misdiagnosing-Understanding the Underlying Problem

As we listen in detail for performance problems we must beware of "misdiagnoses." Misdiagnoses, or "misreads," are confusions over what is causing a problem in the ensemble's performance. Basic misdiagnoses occur when students are still learning a work's notes and rhythms, which creates a host of problems, including poor precision, balance, blend, and intonation. It is important to address the underlying sources of these problems by solidifying the base of the Priority Pyramid (see "Rehearsals": Part I). Then we calibrate our "conductor ear" to detect other problems, many of which will have been solved by virtue of the correct notes and rhythms.

For many issues the underlying problem may be physical, not musical. Students may be playing staccato with no separation because they are tonguing improperly. Dynamic ranges might be limited because students take small breaths and exhale with low air speed. Intonation problems could be caused by a host of problems, including embouchure and air speed (wind instruments) or hand and instrument position (string instruments). Indeed, poor technique will almost never allow for good intonation.

Differentiated Instruction

One of the challenges of teaching large ensemble classes is the variety of students it brings together. Of course, every class, regardless of the subject area, reflects this to some degree. An eighth-grade Spanish class, for example, may be comprised of 13 year olds at similar levels, but the reality is that each student is a unique combination of social, cultural, intellectual, developmental and emotional factors, filtered through gender and economic background. Some will learn faster than others; some will respond to aural comprehension and dialogue, others to the written language; some will come with some basic vocabulary and grammar, others will know not a word. The process of teaching to all students by acknowledging their diversity and providing for instruction that maximizes potential even as it accommodates difference is often called, *differentiated instruction*, or *differentiated learning*. Differentiated learning (teaching) is based on assessment, both initial, in terms of what students already know, and formative, considering what they are learning as instruction progresses. On the basis of these assessments, teachers employ a variety of instructional models and strategies to interface with as many permutations of student needs as possible.[4]

An instrumental music classroom is one of the best possible examples of a situation in which differentiated instruction is necessary, for in addition to multiple ability levels we must contend with multiple grade levels and multiple instruments.

Differentiated instruction can manifest itself in several ways, as outlined below.

Small-Group Versus Large-Group Instruction

By definition, "the band" is a large organization, but each section represents a sub-group of a specific type—trumpets, trombones, clarinets, etc.—with common problems, timbral qualities and arguably, social and cultural characteristics. Also, music is commonly written so that the function of each instrument varies. For example, a tuba is low, rarely plays melodic or rapid passages, is pivotal to the success of the whole, often functions in the background and arguably attracts a different kind of player than a clarinet or a trumpet. Indeed, music is often written so that rapidly moving notes are reserved for instruments which can readily play them well— trombonists rarely play sixteenth notes at presto, while flutes do so all the time.

Small-group music-making allows us to adapt the level of instruction to the needs of a specific type of instrument or individual ability level. The most common small groups in the setting of instrumental music are chamber music/small ensembles, sectionals, and group lessons by skill level (advanced players, intermediate players). For example:

- *Percussion ensemble*—In large ensemble repertoire the percussionists' role is often to provide rhythmic support and tone color. Percussion ensemble affords them opportunities to take the primary melodic and harmonic role.
- *Trombone sectional*—Trombonists and other low brass instruments have technical challenges other brasses do not face. Sectionals allow these special techniques to be addressed.
- *Lessons for advanced clarinetists and intermediate clarinetists*—Variations in ability exist even within a section. In dividing by achievement the pace and level of instruction can be accurately synchronized with the needs of the group (i.e., fewer students bored, fewer students left behind).

Models of Instructional Design

As discussed in Chapter 6, direct instruction and constructivism offer two models of teaching.

Spiral Curricula

One of the beautiful aspects of the spiral curriculum, in which all concepts can be taught in some legitimate form at all levels of achievement, is that it naturally supports differentiated learning. For example, phrasing can be taught to all musicians, including beginners, even if advanced players also receive a more detailed and subtle version of the same lesson. We can apply this in several ways in the instrumental classroom.

- *Present different versions of the same lesson during rehearsal.*

> Phrasing Level 1—*"Let's start this phrase softly and gradually crescendo through the downbeat of m. 34."*
>
> Phrasing Level 2—*"Let's shape this phrase so it follows the natural contours of the melodic line as it ascends to the climax in m. 34."*
>
> Intonation Level 1—*"Clarinets, let's hold the concert F; Keep adjusting until you hear the beats disappear."*
>
> Intonation Level 2—*"Clarinets, make sure you remember your natural tendency on that concert F and anticipate the necessary adjustment. As we play the passage again, evaluate whether our pitch improves."*

In each of these cases (and many other instances), both lessons are appropriate whether they are presented consecutively or at different rehearsals. The crucial point is that we present the same concept in multiple ways to account for multiple ability levels.

- *Choose literature with differentiated parts for the same instrument*—Most literature written for school ensembles has this feature built-in, since 1st parts are usually more technically difficult than 2nd parts. This allows the entire ensemble to learn lessons about form, style, history, and compositional technique while working at a level suitable for their technical proficiency. The real challenge for educators is to choose repertoire that is differentiated but still interesting for all voice parts. The third trumpet part may have a lower range than the first part, but it should still be satisfying to play.

Creative Repetition

Sometimes, merely pointing out a problem will improve it, for it focuses attention on something specific. This is especially true with advanced collegiate players and professionals. They have enough control over their instruments to allow them to achieve physically what their ear tells them to do musically. Simply remind them they are not together, or that they need to play something more legato, and they can comply. Inexperienced players, however, work harder to develop technical proficiency and musicality, and they are likely to do so at different paces. They have less control over their instruments, and thus it is the director's responsibility to facilitate improvement.

An effective solution is to employ "creative repetition," in which the same passage is played several times (often consecutively, but not necessarily), each time with a different set of announced objectives and suggestions. This effectively "hides" the repetition. In the below example, even though we may repeat the same section, creative repetition differentiates learning objectives for several sets of learners.

Instruction— *"Let's try Letter A to B again to really capture the light style Offenbach is after. Trombones, please exaggerate the crescendo in m. 34. Saxophones, make a mental note of which of your pitches is out-of-tune. Upper woodwinds, lock your rhythm into the percussion ostinato."*

This instruction carries four discrete objectives at four discrete levels:

Objective 1: *Trombones*—have technical mastery, but now focus on a subtle issue of phrasing.
Objective 2: *Saxophones*—have a relatively uninteresting part, but are now challenged to refine it.
Objective 3: *Upper woodwinds*—are struggling with technical precision, but are provided with a strategy and another chance to improve.
Objective 4: *Entire ensemble*—has enough technical mastery to consider general style issues.

Creative repetition need not include a long list of extra suggestions. Even one additional differentiation is effective. For example, if our primary objective is to work on a technical aspect in a part by slowing the tempo, we further differentiate by:

- giving musical objectives to the rest of the group (style, phrasing, dynamics, balance)
- asking other sections to clap a steady pulse or sing an in tune reference drone
- adding new challenges—conduct and sing the rhythm; swap parts with another player in the section (i.e., so everyone experiences something new).

Repetition may seem unimaginative, but it reinforces progress toward mastery by strengthening mental and muscle memory. Play a section once and the progress may or may not be maintained; play it several times and those improvements will solidify and endure. We recommend playing a passage at least two or three times *beyond* the first accurate performance.

Repetition also creates continuity between rehearsals (i.e., review). Something learned in Monday's rehearsal can easily become "unlearned" by Tuesday. To counter this, repeat the passage at the beginning of the next rehearsal for stable, long-term results.

Multiple Intelligences

In his seminal book *Frames of Mind: The Theory of Multiple Intelligences*, Howard Gardner argues that human intelligence is expressed through a variety of abilities, not simply the skills tested through traditional IQ tests.[5] The implication for educators is that students have a variety of intelligences, and so teaching methods must use a variety of approaches. Not only does variety help avoid monotony, but it also increases the chances our instructions connect with all students. Here are Gardner's original categories of intelligence and a few examples of teaching strategies to relate to students who may be strong in each area:

- *Musical*—Use modeling and "call and response" techniques to aurally demonstrate musical concepts.
- *Visual–spatial*—Relate musical tone to visual color, or draw diagrams to illustrate a rhythm, phrasing, and form; relate musical concepts to painting, sculpture, and architecture; use documentary films to teach about theory and history; hold videoconferences with guest composers and conductors.
- *Bodily kinesthetic*—Use Dalcroze movement techniques to internalize the meter and pulse; ask students to conduct as they chant rhythms.
- *Verbal–linguistic*—Use sound–to–symbol techniques as described by Kodály and Gordon; use metaphor and analogy to describe musical concepts; ask students to describe form in narrative terms (e.g., stories) rather than strictly formal terms (e.g., sonata, rondo); have the ensemble brainstorm descriptive words and ask students to write the best examples in their parts rather than strictly musical terms such as crescendo, piano, etc.; provide readings about the composer, the piece, the compositional style, and the historical period.
- *Logical–mathematical*—Describe rhythmic relationships through ratios and fractions; discuss a work's form; incorporate theory lessons into rehearsal (e.g., intervals, triads, overtones, etc.); analyze music.
- *Intrapersonal*—Ask students to record and evaluate their own solo performances; provide opportunities for solo performance, improvisation, and composition; give writing assignments (journals,concert reviews, program notes, etc.).
- *Interpersonal*—Involve students in running sections and small chamber ensembles; create student leadership positions; engage in classroom discussions.

Experienced educators can have a personal "rehearsal thesaurus"—i.e., a variety of teaching strategies for the same concept that maximizes students' potential and allows them to engage in a collective musical experience at a level consistent with their pre-existing knowledge.

Developing Your Rehearsal Thesaurus

Here are a few strategies to develop your "Rehearsal Thesaurus":

1. Keep a notebook of successful tactics and descriptive adjectives, phrases, and analogies.
2. Observe other directors.
3. Share/exchange ideas with other directors.
4. Think outside the box and experiment.
5. Be proactive and design lessons with specific intelligences in mind.

Using Analogy and Metaphor

A powerful technique that relates to both visual and linguistic learners is the use of metaphor and analogy. For example, instead of asking students to play with accents, we can ask them to "pounce on each note." Instead of asking for a stronger crescendo to m. 35, we can ask for a "tidal wave of sound to build up and final crest at m. 34." Instead of asking for a lighter texture, we can ask the ensemble "to play like a group of dancing ballerinas tip-toeing across the stage, rather than like a group of Sumo wrestlers."

Analogy and metaphor evoke non-musical situations, images, actions, and stories to encourage musical playing. This requires students to make their own connections between the imagery and the musical technique, and by doing so creates a strong commitment by the player to musically reflect the metaphor. Some conductors are able to improvise analogies on the podium, while others benefit from pre-planning and having a few at their disposal for a variety of situations. Effective ones should be added to our rehearsal thesaurus for use in a similar situation—but don't overuse them, or else they will likely lose their effectiveness. A few other caveats on their use:

- Avoid using a glitzy metaphor when "play louder" would have been just as effective.
- Keep analogies short and focused. A 5-minute story to evoke "staccato" is inefficient.
- Design metaphors/topical analogies—the current generation of students might find "keep the line as nimble as Harry Potter in a game of Quidditch," more evocative than "keep the line as nimble as Kevin Costner in *Robin Hood*." We might appreciate the second, but our students will likely look at us with blank faces!

Incorporating Special Techniques, or "Tools" into the Rehearsal Process

Another useful approach is to employ special strategies, or "tools." Tools often isolate a specific issue and get students to feel what it is like to play musically, and then incorporate that feeling into its original context. In many cases they are a mini Macro–Micro–Macro process. On the Companion Website is a starter "toolkit" of rehearsal ideas and tools, though eventually experience, creativity, and professional development will be your greatest sources for new techniques.

Tools are especially useful for chronic problems, or for those which have not resolved themselves after a typical Macro–Micro–Macro approach. For example, a typical procedure for incorporating these tools during rehearsal to work with a specific issue could be:

1. *Alert the ensemble to a specific problem*—e.g., "Clarinets, please play with crisper staccato at Letter B. Let's try it again. Everybody at Letter B, please."
2. *Use analogy/metaphor*—e.g., "Clarinets, play your eighth notes as if they are tiny puffs of air." This is often effective in a Macro setting, essentially substituting for the direct instructions of point 1.
3. *Use Macro–Micro–Macro to break the section down and focus on the clarinets*—e.g., "Clarinets only please at Letter B. Let's try it a little bit slower to really concentrate on articulation." Clarinets play. "OK, let's try it at the performance tempo." Clarinets play. "OK, let's put everyone together at Letter B."
4. *Use a tool or special technique.*

In some cases we might start with the Macro–Micro–Macro, or begin with a tool. Generally speaking:

- points 2, 3, and 4 are easily combined—e.g., use an analogy when focusing on the clarinets during the Micro section
- Macro–Micro–Macro and tools take more time than simply giving instructions, but allow more direct and focused rehearsing
- younger players have limited musical maturity and control over their instruments, and thus generally respond less to verbal instructions
- no matter the technique, once an issue has been played correctly, repetition of the correct performance will help solidify its retention.

(See the Companion Website for written explanations and videos for "The Rehearsal Toolkit").

Suggestions for Developing Student Listening Skills

In diagnosing and fixing problems, it is important not to become a musical policeman, endlessly handing out musical violations to the group. Our challenge is to improve the ensemble's performance while simultaneously developing listening skills in our students that teach an understanding of their role in the ensemble. Even though they are playing in a large group, we want them to use their musicianship in the same way as a chamber musician.

Admittedly, in the short run this takes more time than simply giving students the answer to their musical problems. The goal is to balance conductor-centered "policing" with student-centered "self-governance." In the long run, the more our students develop listening skills, the more they will be able to make music on their own without micromanagement from the podium.

Techniques to build ensemble listening skills share two important features. First, they direct students to listen for something specific, whether it is another voice part or a technical aspect of their performance (e.g., "Clarinets, what is happening to your pitch at the end of the phrase?"). Second, they promote self-awareness while playing. For example, if we ask students to play softer than the 2nd clarinets, this demands they hear themselves in relation to another part rather than mindlessly following our instruction to play more softly.

Though it would be impractical to rely exclusively on the techniques discussed below, they should be a regular part of your "Rehearsal Toolkit." Consider the following techniques to develop student listening skills:

- *Ask questions*—Instead of simply telling students what is wrong, insist they listen and evaluate themselves. Ask questions about what they are (or are not) hearing (e.g., "What is happening to the tempo? [rushing] . . . And where does it start to rush?").

- *Find the countermelody or other inner voice*—Direct students' attention to a specific voice in the ensemble and give them opportunities to find it aurally in the context of tutti playing. Have students who play the part model it first, then challenge students to "find" the melody while everyone plays the section in context. This exercise demands that students be aware of other parts and adjust their own playing to hear them.
- *Remove the conductor*—Have the ensemble play a section without a conductor, thus emphasizing everyone's responsibility to maintain good rhythm, blend and balance. (An advanced approach is for the ensemble to rehearse and perform a chorale sans conductor. The conductor offers general guidance, but otherwise principal players lead the discussion during rehearsals.)
- *Ensemble music critics*—Ask the students to provide a constructive assessment of their playing (written or aural) after listening to a recording of the rehearsal. Insist on specific comments and suggestions, not simply generalized admonishments.
- *Interpretation through democracy*—Although we do not want to abdicate interpretative duties to the ensemble, rather than constantly spoon-feed an interpretation to the group we can occasionally provide opportunities to collaborate on decisions regarding phrasing and style (e.g., "Trumpets, the chorale melody you have at letter B needs more horizontal direction. While I work with the flutes, quietly make some decisions regarding the phrasing.") Invite the section to model their interpretation for the entire group. Or, solicit suggestions from the group about how to shape a phrase. Try out a few suggestions with the group and take a vote for the winner.

Pencil Markings

Do not assume students will automatically use their pencils in rehearsal. Show them exactly how they can mark their parts—e.g.:

- circling dynamics
- expression marks, accidentals
- counts (e.g. 1 + 2 + 3 + 4 +)
- "eyeglass" symbol as a reminder to look up at the conductor
- breath marks
- arrows to direct the eyes to where D.S. al Coda/Dal Segno repeats back
- add measure numbers
- add rehearsal marks to break sections into smaller parts (e.g., A, A2, B, B2)
- performance reminders (e.g., ⌇⌇⌇ = hold back, stylistic cues, dynamics)
- fingering reminders
- bowings
- who to listen for . . . timing, balance, pitch, etc.
- V.S. (Volti subito)
- highlight articulation markings to make them stand out
- slash marks to indicate downbeats
- note names for hard-to-read divisi parts
- break up long multi-measure rests into smaller segments and align with aural cues
- indicate pitch tendency (e.g., up/down arrows)

Additional Ways to Enrich the Rehearsal Experience

Commissioning

Beyond the sense of pride students receive from premiering a brand new work, the process of commissioning provides students direct contact with a living composer and his/her creative process. They can discover how compositional decisions are made and how these decisions affect the final product. Admittedly, commissioning can be expensive. We suggest forming a consortium in which several schools pool their resources. Or, commission graduate composers, who are often eager to write for young ensembles.

Composer-in-Residence

This is a wonderful way for students to work with living composers. Try to play a series of works by the composer, and have him visit the school periodically throughout the year.

Guest Clinicians

A simple, inexpensive way to put fresh and varied perspectives in front of your students is to do a "director exchange" program with a local colleague in another school. One day you go to her school and another day she visits yours. Students enjoy the variety, and sometimes it takes another person teaching the same concepts to make a difference. Local college, civic, military, and professional conductors are other great resources. Most would ask for only a small honorarium (if any).

Guest Performers

The benefits to the ensemble of hearing a professional musician and learning the challenges of playing accompaniments are well-worth the occasional expense of bringing in a guest-artist (or, use student and faculty soloists).

Videoconferencing and Teleconferencing

When funds are not available to support residencies or guest artists, use a phone/or video conference to interact with a composer. Even with a minimum of technology (a cellphone and speaker; microphone, webcam, and Skype) the ensemble can perform, ask questions, and receive immediate feedback. In addition to spur-of-the-moment comments, ask students to script questions in advance.

Recording the Ensemble

No matter how often we try to verbally describe how the ensemble sounds, nothing is more effective than recording a rehearsal and playing it back to the group. Mp3 recorders, direct-to-CD recorders, and laptop computers make this inexpensive and portable. We suggest experimenting with two approaches: (1) Record a run-through and play it back at the end of rehearsal or the next day; (2) In the course of a normal rehearsal, record short passages and replay them immediately for instant feedback. Recording rehearsals is also a terrific way to improve our own rehearsal technique, for it reveals what we are missing while on the podium.

Playing Professional Recordings and Videos

If a picture is worth a thousand words, then an aural picture is worth one thousand talkative minutes in rehearsal! Without us even having to comment, nothing models tone, balance, energy, precision, and style better than a high-quality recording. Don't only play music the group is performing; music in a similar style or recordings by great soloists also provide excellent models.

Alternative Seating Arrangements

Using set-ups where students sit near different instruments allows them to more clearly hear other parts and adds a little spice to the rehearsal routine. Examples of alternative seating arrangements include:

1. *The scatter drill*—Everyone sits wherever they like provided the players next to them are NOT in their section.
2. *Rehearsal-in-the-round*—Set up the ensemble in a circle or square, with the conductor in the middle. This allows sections to see and hear others more easily and creates the feeling of a large chamber group.

Student conductors

Giving students a chance to conduct is not only a good way to stretch their musicality, but it also energizes the rest of the ensemble. You will be amazed at the level of eye contact as students watch their friends conduct! Beyond featuring them on concerts, student conductors can be used during warmups or simply to give ourselves an opportunity to hear the ensemble from a new perspective.

Silent Rehearsal

Few techniques galvanize a group's attention and eye contact like the silent rehearsal. The key is for the conductor not to talk at all—use hand signals and flashcards to announce the next starting point, and describe every instruction through gestures and facial expressions. The silence creates a palpable intensity as the conductor strives to be efficient and the group strives to be attentive.

Teaching Students Good Practice Habits

This text spends a fair amount of time outlining strategies of how to rehearse a large ensemble, recognizing that efficient rehearsals lead to accelerated progress. The same applies to individual practice sessions. A recent study by Peter Miksza looked at the practice habits of high school students from Indiana and New Jersey to determine which techniques were associated with achievement on a prescribed etude.[6] Miksza measured the frequency of the following practice techniques:

- repeat measure
- repeat section (repeating something longer than a measure)
- repeat entire etude
- chaining (described as "playing a segment of music and systematically adding segments that appeared either before or after the original segment")
- varying musical elements (articulation, rhythm, pitch)

- non-etude related playing
- singing or whistling
- marking part
- whole–part–whole
- use of metronome

The results showed that there was wide variety in the length of time students spent practicing and whether they practiced strategically (Mikzsa, 371). Repeat section, slowing, whole–part–whole, and chaining were correlated with higher performance achievement. An earlier study of college brass players added marking parts and varying pitch to this list.[7] Both studies found little correlation between time spent playing and performance achievement. In other words, 20 minutes of deliberate and strategic practice could be as productive as one hour of non-directed playing. (*Note*: Because very few of the subjects in Mikzsa's study actually used a tuner or metronome in their sessions, Mikzsa's conclusions should not be taken to mean that use of either is ineffective.)

The implication, of course, is that we must teach students how to practice effectively. Motivating them simply to spend time on the instrument is not enough. Without guidance, young students simply play a piece in its entirety over and over again.[8] Others spend too much time playing the passages they already know, but count it as practice time. Still others focus on difficult passages with no strategy, and thus make little progress.

Long *and* inefficient practice sessions compound the ineffectiveness, as students become frustrated and less likely to practice the next day. "After all," they may fret, "if an hour of practice this time barely made a dent, does that mean I have to spend two hours tomorrow?!"

Consider how other classroom teachers give assignments: Math teachers do not tell their students to "Go home and practice your math." Instead, they assign specific exercises, model techniques in class, and offer strategies for troubleshooting. Music teachers should use the same approach.

1. Since many practice strategies crossover to rehearsal strategies, model good technique whenever possible. Make a point to explain the process to students and how they can use it in their individual practicing.
2. Model inefficient and efficient practice habits for students so they understand what to avoid and what to emulate (*Effective Practice*, 373).
3. Impress upon students that the amount time they practice is less important than the quality of their practice session. A half hour of good practice is preferable to an hour of poor practice.
4. Insist that students practice daily, in small chunks, rather than weekly, in large cram sessions.
5. Give students well-defined goals by assigning specific passages for homework.
6. Suggest specific practice strategies for specific sections.
7. Encourage students to play something correctly more than one time before moving to another section.
8. Require that students own a metronome (and ideally a tuner, too) and use it consistently. The metronome is a win-win device since it does not increase the amount of time spent practicing; it just makes the time spent more effective.
9. Ask students to record themselves practicing and self-evaluate. They will often be surprised by what they hear ("Do I really sound like that?").
10. Use Smart Music software, which offers a wealth of practice tools for students, including pre-recorded accompaniments with options to change tempo and loop measures.

Activities/Assignments for Further Exploration

1. Keep a rehearsal journal: Attend ensemble rehearsals and write down useful phrases and techniques used by the conductor.

2. Role play: Record an ensemble rehearsal. As you listen to the recording, identify musical issues you would rehearse. In other words, what would *you* stop for? Do this first with a score and then without one.

3. For common words such as "short," "loud," "smooth," and "light," find three words or phrases that serve as synonyms.

4. For common musical issues (e.g., lightness, crescendo, etc.) or for specific passages in a work, design several metaphors or analogies to describe how students should play.

5. After identifying a specific rehearsal goal, discuss teaching strategies that engage a variety of intelligences, skill levels, or models of instructional design.

6. Video-record your own rehearsals. What needs improvement? What was effective?

7. Ask a respected music colleague to observe your rehearsal and offer feedback.

Further Reading

Battisti, Frank L. *On Becoming a Conductor: Lessons and Meditations on the Art of Conducting*. Galesville, MD: Meredith Music, 2007.

Boonshaft, Peter Loel. *Teaching Music with Passion: Conducting, Rehearsing, and Inspiring*. Galesville, MD: Meredith Music, 2002.

Gardner, Howard. *Frames of Mind: The Theory of Multiple Intelligences*. New York: Basic Books, 1993.

Gardner, Howard. *Multiple Intelligences: The Theory in Practice*. New York: Basic Books, 1993.

Harris, Fred. *Conducting With Feeling*. Galesville, MD: Meredith Music Publications, 2001.

Lisk, Edward S. *The Creative Director: Alternative Rehearsal Techniques*. Ft. Lauderdale, FL: Meredith Music Publications, 1991.

Nowak, Jerry, and Henry Nowak. *Conducting the Music, Not the Musicians*. New York: Carl Fischer, 2002.

Tomlinson, Carol A. *The Differentiated Classroom: Responding to the Needs of all Learners*. Alexandria, VA: Association for Supervision and Curriculum Development, 1999.

Whaley, Garwood. *The Music Director's Cookbook: Creative Recipes for a Successful Program*. Galesville, MD: Meredith Music Publications, 2005.

Williamson, John E., Kenneth L. Neidig, and Frederick Fennell. *Rehearsing the Band*. Galesville, MD: Meredith Music Publications, 2008.

Chapter 13

Intonation

To Guide Your Reading

What are some strategies to teach students to hear the difference between sharp and flat?

Why do certain instruments naturally play out of tune?

What is temperament?

How can drones be used to improve intonation?

What is the interaction between tone color and intonation?

In what ways can technology help or hinder the development of intonation skills?

What tuning notes are best for tuning the band and orchestra, and why?

What are effective procedures for tuning the band/orchestra?

When we ask students with at least a few years of playing experience if they perceive poor intonation, many say "Yes." Yes, they know they are out of tune! Then why, we might ask, don't they fix it? Some students are unable to tell if they are sharp or flat, and so they continue to play out of tune, powerless to figure out exactly why, or whose pitch is the "correct" one. Other students simply do not know how to physically adjust the pitch. Still others labor under the misconception that their instrument is in tune once they tune their B♭ or their strings. The result is that many ensembles warmup well, play beautiful tuning pitches, and then play their concert literature with poor intonation.

The ability to play in tune involves the interaction of the following skills:

1. An awareness of pitch discrepancy.
2. Physical skills to maintain good pitch and adjust it up or down, as needed.
3. A theoretical understanding of pitch issues, including overtones, temperament, and harmonic context.
4. Knowledge of the pitch tendencies of each note on the instrument.

Developing these skills is not an overnight process, but the time invested at every level of instruction is crucial to help musicians play in tune without micromanagement from the podium.

Developing an Awareness of Pitch Discrepancies

Research suggests that young musicians, particularly middle school students, are ineffective in evaluating themselves in regard to intonation, especially compared to areas such as melodic and rhythmic accuracy. Hewitt (2002, 2005) showed that, at least in the short run, students actually became worse at evaluating their intonation, though they did improve in the long run from middle school to high school to college.[1] Since students' perception of intonation problems still seems to lag behind other areas, it is important for us to guide them to hear the difference between sharp and flat.

For novice musicians, the first step in perceiving intonation is to recognize whether two notes are "in tune" or "out of tune." Many students perceive this without any coaching. Others need to be encouraged to "listen for the beats" and then taught to manipulate their pitch until the beats disappear. (Beats are the dissonances resulting from two waves with slightly different frequencies—the faster the beats, the more out of tune).

The following exercises help develop an awareness of pitch discrepancies:

Exercise 1—Demonstrating the Difference between In Tune and Out of Tune

   Method 1: Take two adjustable tuners or tone generating devices and have both sound A = 440. Using the calibration setting, shift one of the tuners to A = 441. Continue to raise the pitch, one increment at a time, so students hear the beats get faster. Reverse the direction slowly so the beats slow down until the tuners again match pitch. Then, do the same exercise by gradually *lowering* the pitch of one tuner.

   Method 2: Using two trombonists, have Player 1 sustain third space E and Player 2 sustain second space C. While Player 1 sustains the E, Player 2 slowly glisses up to the E. If done slowly enough the players will hear the beats gradually dissipate until they are eliminated. Other brass players can perform this exercise using their main tuning slide. String instruments can duplicate this by sliding their fingertip along the string.

Exercise 2—Vocalizing the Beats with "Wa Wa"

Singing the Beats Exercise (in a small group setting)

1. Have two students play a note in unison.
2. Designate one student to maintain a steady pitch while the other tries to tune to it.
3. Have the students hold the note for eight slow counts.
4. Ask the student who is tuning to sing the speed at which they hear beats occurring. (E.g., slow beats are sung "wa ———— wa ———— wa ———— wa ————"; fast beats are sung "wa – wa – wa – wa –".) Demonstrate this for the students before they try.
5. Taking turns, repeat steps 2–4 so each student has the opportunity to tune and sing beats. If a student does not sing the correct speed, model it for them.

   For use in a large group setting:

• After the two students have sustained the unison pitch, the teacher sings beats at a medium speed (again, use "wa-wa").

- Ask the students to use thumbs-up or thumbs-down to show if the unison pitches had faster or slower beats than what the teacher sang.

The rate of beats will frequently change while the students sustain the pitches. In these cases ask: "Did the beats get faster or slower as the note sustained?"

Exercise 3—Evaluating Intonation
(Pencil and paper required)

1. Group students into pairs.
2. Have each pair play a unison pitch for eight beats.
3. Ask the rest of the ensemble to write down two evaluations: The first should describe the pitch at the beginning of the note; the second should describe the pitch at the end of the note.

Use the following shorthand:

Check minus = very out of tune
Check = slightly out of tune
Check plus = in tune.

4. Share answers with the class after each pair has played.

Tips

- Percussionists participate by matching the pitch of one timpani to another.
- For an impromptu exercise without pencil and paper, have the class use thumbs up/thumb sideways/ thumbs down to show their answers.
- For a greater challenge: Use different instruments to tune to each other; use different octaves; use different intervals.

Exercise 4—Recording, Playback, and Evaluation
Record student performances (in concerts, rehearsals, and lessons) and evaluate as a class.

Defining the "Sound" of Sharp and Flat

After students have learned to recognize in tune and out of tune, the next step is to learn the difference between sharp and flat. A useful analogy is color: Most of us perceive the difference between red and blue instantly without any calculation. It is difficult, however, to verbally describe the distinction; we *just know* it to be true. Lacking technical data we substitute adjectives: Purple is *darker* than blue; red is *brighter* than maroon; mustard yellow is *deeper* than school-bus yellow, etc.

Discerning between sharp and flat (and all of the gradients in between) is analogous, except in this case we perceive *aural* colors. Keep in mind that these colors depend on the accurate perception of a pitch center. For example, if we randomly play two notes in near unison without tuning or establishing an in tune tonal center, there is no way to determine if pitch 1 is sharp to pitch 2, or if pitch 2 is flat to pitch 1. However, in most musical contexts the pitch center is more or less clear because the majority of notes fall within it; outliers are perceived as sharp or flat. And as with colors, descriptive adjectives help focus perception:

Sharp ⇨ bright, high
Flat ⇨ dull, low

The goal is to hear intonation along an aural ROYGBIV spectrum.

Colors: Red — Orange — Yellow — Green — Blue — Indigo —Violet
Pitch: Very flat – Flat – Slightly flat – In tune – Slightly sharp – Sharp – Very sharp

Hearing the "colors" of sharp and flat takes practice. Several of the exercises discussed above can be adapted to develop this skill:

- Exercise 1—Use the pitch-change procedure to demonstrate the difference between sharp and flat as the pitch changes.
- Exercise 3—For each pair of students, assign one to be the reference pitch and ask the rest of the class to evaluate the other student. Use "⬆" for sharp, "⬇" for flat, and "=" for in tune (or use sharp and flat symbols).

If students can recognize when they are out of tune they can become proactive in fixing it. Encourage students to make their best guess. If they temporarily make the problem worse by adjusting the wrong way they will hear the dissonance and beats intensify. If they move the right way they will hear beats slow down and the dissonance resolve. Either way, the key is to do something! Insist, "Don't accept what you hear if you know it's wrong!" Assure students we would rather hear the pitch oscillate as they search for the pitch center than hear prolonged and unchanging problems.

Eventually, though, we want to move away from "miss and fix" playing, in which students play a note, hear it is out of tune, and *then* adjust. The idea instead is to make the adjustment *before* playing the note.

Remember, intonation is not "up for discussion." Emphasize to students that out of tune notes are the same as pressing the wrong key on a piano: It's either the correct note or it's not!

Teaching Students About Acoustics

Overtones and Harmonics

It is important for students to understand how the length of the vibrating column they play directly relates to the pitch that sounds. To make this concept clear we should present it systematically: Sound is created by the ear's perception of how matter—air, strings, wood, water, etc.—vibrates to create waves. No matter how musical instruments are constructed, they all work on the same principle: Pitch is adjusted by manipulating the length of a vibrating column, which changes the length of the waves and the resultant pitches we hear: the longer the wave, the lower the perceived sound. String instruments adjust length by the placement of the fingers on the fingerboard; valved brass instruments adjust the length by the way various valve combinations create different lengths of tubing; trombones adjust with the main slide; woodwind instruments use tone holes to change the length of the tube—put more fingers down to close the holes and thus lengthen the column; on mallet instruments, harps, and keyboard instruments, each pitch is created by a separate vibrating body. In all cases, whether it is columns of air, pieces of wood, or lengths of string, the shorter the length, the higher the pitch.

Though inexperienced musicians may believe their instrument is tuned at the factory, the reality, of course, is that centering the tuning note only puts notes in the neighborhood of being in tune. This is true even on the finest professional instruments. Students may reasonably wonder, "Why don't they just make every note in tune? Why can't my flute be like the piano?" Setting aside physical variables such as reed quality, air support, hand and finger position, and embouchure formation, we should show students that many of the intonation inconsistencies on their instruments are the unavoidable consequence of the intersection between tonality and physics. To understand why this is so, students need a basic understanding of acoustics and temperament.

In addition to the wave that traverses the length of the vibrating body (creating the "fundamental" pitch), we should explain there exists a series of smaller vibrations within the main vibration, each calculable with mathematic precision. These vibrations create "overtones" that simultaneously ring above the fundamental. Demonstrate to students how brass players achieve more than one pitch per valve combination or slide position (often called "partials"); how woodwind players play multiple notes with the same fingering by "overblowing"; and how string players play harmonics by lightly touching the string. The fundamental wavelength stays the same, but the player accesses the pitch of a simultaneously sounding overtone.

Given a fundamental pitch of C, the overtones occur in the following sequence:

FIGURE 13.1 The Overtone Series Based on C

Pure intervals—i.e., the intervals resulting between the pitches in an overtone series (see Figure 13.1)—can be expressed through simple integer ratios. For example, if we divide a string (the fundamental) in half and measure the interval between the original length and the halved-length, we hear a perfect octave. Divide the original into thirds and we hear a perfect twelfth above the fundamental (or, a perfect fifth above the first overtone). Figure 13.2 shows the ratios for each interval.

Students often enjoy seeing the overtone series in action, and string instruments are an ideal way to demonstrate them. Try collaborating with a science teacher to prepare a presentation for physics and music classes. A particularly enjoyable way to demonstrate overtones is through a whirly toy: a corrugated tube of colored plastic that sounds overtones as it is "whirled" in a circle. The faster the whirling, the higher the overtone. Or, use the *Tartini* software included on the Companion Website, which can graph the exact overtones of any pitch played into the computer through a microphone.

FIGURE 13.2[2]   Deriving Pure Intervals from Integer Ratios

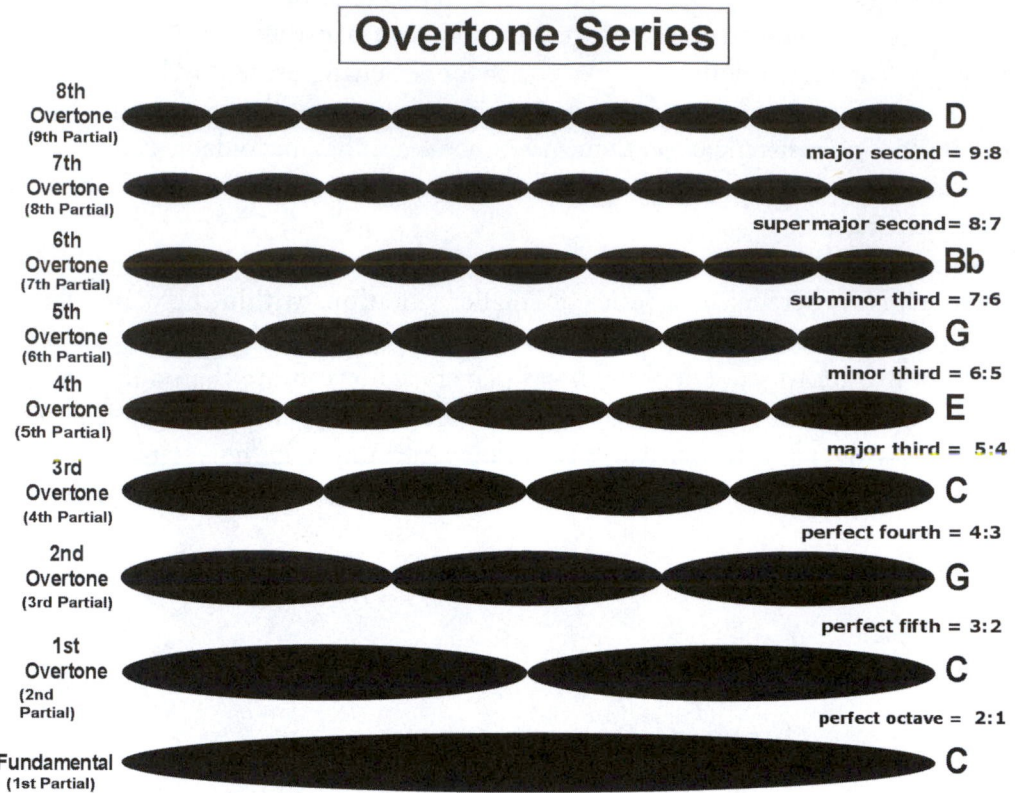

Source: Hermann von Helmholtz and Alexander John Ellis, *On the Sensations of Tone as a Physiological Basis for the Theory of Music* (New York: Dover Publications, 1954), 187.

A Brief Introduction to Tuning and Temperaments

Let us assume we keep dividing a vibrating body into thirds: We start with a C, divide it into thirds to get a G; then divide that G into thirds to get a D, and so on around the circle of fifths—A-E-B-F#-C#-G#-D#-A#-F-C. On paper it seems quite tidy; eventually we should return to the C we first divided into thirds, only in a higher octave. Yet if we calculate our wavelength subdivisions accurately the pitch of this second C is about 24 cents sharper than the first C (approximately one-quarter of semitone). How can this be? If we trace the same path on the piano, don't we land exactly on another C perfectly in tune with the original one? It turns out that acoustically pure fifths (i.e., the ones created by dividing strings into thirds) are ever so slightly wider than the perfect fifths we hear on the piano. If we travel completely around the circle of fifths using pure fifths, when we arrive at the pitch where we began it will be noticeably sharper than the pitch we started with. This difference is called the "Pythagorean comma," named after the famous mathematician who first calculated it.

FIGURE 13.3 The Pythagorean Comma

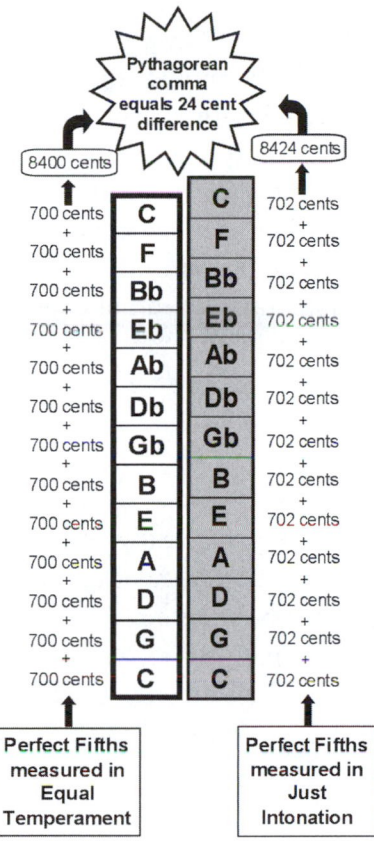

Temperaments were the music theorist's solution to this discrepancy. In a temperament, intervals are modified (or tempered) from the pure form in which they appear in the overtone series.[3] In *How Equal Temperament Ruined Harmony*, Ross Duffin writes, "Typically temperaments tried to balance euphony with utility—to have the most common chords and keys sound good at the expense of the least common chords and keys" (Duffin, 38). Several temperaments were used throughout Western music history, but eventually musicians and theorists settled on *equal temperament*, in which each of the 12 pure fifths are tempered to become slightly smaller, essentially ironing out the comma to create equal semitones. The result is that all 12 fifths played in sequence arrive at the exact pitch class at which they began, though seven octaves higher—no overshooting the mark as with Pythagorean tuning. (Equal temperament is similar, but not identical to the system that inspired Bach to write *The Well-Tempered Clavier*.)

The sound of equal temperament is nearly ubiquitous in modern keyboards and synthesizers. But equal temperament's intervals are intonation compromises to which winds, strings, and voices are not tied. These instruments can adjust pitch using a combination of alternate fingerings, embouchure control, and by slightly changing the length of the vibrating column (à la the trombone slide or finger position on the fingerboard). This allows them to play in "just intonation." Technically speaking, just intonation is not a temperament because its intervals are not tempered and its pitches are not fixed. Instead, it creates pure intervals using the integer ratios seen in Figure 13.2. The ratio 1:1 = unison, 2:1 = octave, 3:2 = perfect fifth, 4:3 = perfect fourth, 5:4 = major third, 6:3 = minor third (Duffin, 32).

Implications for Performance

What does this all mean for performers? Whether they are aware of it or not, many professional musicians approximate just intonation by reacting to the harmonic context of each note they play and making slight adjustments. For example, a G may be played slightly sharper if tuned purely to a C, slightly flatter if tuned purely to an E♭. These same players may switch to equal temperament when playing with fixed-pitch instruments. Of course, "switching" is a figurative term. Most musicians are likely unaware of which tuning system they use. They rely instead on their well-trained ears to tell them what in tune sounds like. Our challenge is to teach our students to behave the same way.

Many young musicians naturally gravitate to the sound of equal temperament. In his 1998 study, Brant Karrick suggests that our predilection for equal temperament is caused by its prevalence in today's music, since pianos, synthesizers, electronic tuners, etc., are all tempered.[4] The noted jazz choir director and educator Gerald Eskelin agrees. He writes:

> Having worked with professional singers, I have to say that most (yes, most) formally trained singers (even those with graduate degrees) have never really experienced pure acoustic pitch relationships. Their ears are corrupted by years of practicing scales and chords with a tempered-tuned piano (or worse, an out of tune piano). Most can't produce a purely tuned perfect fifth—one of the simplest of harmonic relationships. String and wind players have a much better circumstance for learning accurate tuning simply because they do their practicing without a keyboard. Mother Nature is more likely to be heard when she doesn't have to shout through artificial tuning.[5]

The important point is that "in tune" is a relative concept, and so must be one's sense of tuning. It should be no surprise, then, that though every note on a wind instrument has a discrete fingering, the notes are not automatically in tune. How could they be? It depends completely on context! Of course, as public school band and orchestra directors, it is unrealistic and counterproductive to teach the subtleties of a specific type temperament or tuning strategy. Instead, we should:

- help students experience what in tune sounds like with pure intervals
- develop an aural "muscle memory" for pure intervals and break the equal-temperament addiction, especially for thirds and fifths
- demonstrate to our students that every note on their instrument is naturally out of tune relative to the overall tonality and that it is incumbent upon them to listen and adjust.
- teach the musical and acoustic theory behind intonation.
- familiarize students with the specific differences between chords tuned in equal and just temperament—See the Companion Website for a complete list.

At the onset, simply let students hear how pure intervals and chords sound different from tempered ones. Remember, without a frame of reference students may prefer the tempered versions, or at least not recognize there is a difference. (The CD included with this text includes demonstration exercises of the difference between equal temperament and pure intervals.) Over time, students will sensitize to the differences.

Teaching Good Intonation Habits to String Players

Many strings teachers use tapes or dots affixed to the fingerboard (almost as frets) to promote good intonation in the early stages of left hand development. Others believe that using tape causes students to view intonation as a visual skill instead of an aural one, and teaches the inflexible tuning of equal temperament.

The irony of the latter view is that students with a more discriminating sense of pitch are apt to gravitate to the out of tune notes that their classmates play. Their listening skills lead them to attempt to match the sounds they hear, whether the model is right or wrong. However, with the tape in place, students with less experience gain confidence as they learn the proper sounds of relatively in tune pitches (we say relatively in tune because the tape doesn't move according to harmonic context).

Repetitive practice of the fingers' placement is an effective way to prepare for playing with reliable intonation. But the visual aid of the tape should never be seen as absolute. Let students know that it is a guide, and that the final judge will always be aural. Make it a point to reward the removal of the tapes, and point out that you and other professionals do not use them.

Context and Pitch Center—The Unintentional Curse of Equal Temperament Tuners

Tuners are extremely useful devices, but they are not cure-alls for intonation problems.

- Because they are equally tempered they do not adjust for the subtleties of just intonation.
- Tuners teach students that intonation is something to see, rather than something to hear. In the context of performance (as opposed to sitting alone in a practice room), players must learn to use their ears to anticipate and adjust to the correct pitch. This means someone might be exactly in-sync with the tuner but out of tune with the rest of the ensemble. We need to show students that the ultimate arbiter of good intonation is not a machine, but rather our ears.

Sometimes the arbiter is the "pitch center" of the ensemble, even if it drifts away (usually higher) from A = 440. Of course, our long-term goal is to discourage this shift, but at the same time we must insist that if it does happen, everyone must be aware of it. Remember, there are no moral victories with intonation! A student cannot claim that they are in tune and the rest of the ensemble is out of tune.

Particularly in unison playing, or passages where one section hands off a pitch to another section, players must heed the "rule of the majority." Sometimes this means adjusting to be out of tune with the tuner. If, say, 12 flutes are playing slightly sharp, a trumpeter playing in unison cannot be a maverick; he must adjust to the flutes.

Still, tuners have important and legitimate uses:

1. For tuning chord roots, unisons, octaves and tuning notes.
2. As a reference to determine a pitch's general tendency (e.g., very sharp pitches will likely be sharp in all cases, even accounting for the subtle differences between equally tempered and justly tuned notes).
3. As visual reinforcement for students who struggle to hear the pitch.

Technology and Tuners

Technology has been a boon to intonation training. Quality chromatic tuners are now available for as little as $15. Purchase at least a few inexpensive units for use in lessons, chamber music rehearsals, practicing, and sectionals.

From a pedagogical perspective, it is interesting to note that most tuners show sharp and flat along a horizontal plane: Right of center is sharp; left of center is flat. As a more intuitive alternative, flip the tuner sideways (counterclockwise) to show the concept of "sharp = high," "flat = low." Or, tilt the tuner away from the body so it shows "sharp = instrument too short," "flat = instrument too long" (see Figure 13.4).

FIGURE 13.4 Flipping the Tuner

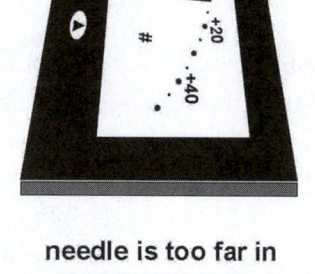

Beyond the typical analog, digital, and strobe tuners, a few other devices are inexpensive but useful.

- *Clip-On Chromatic Tuner*—Look for one that attaches to any wind, brass, or string instrument and measures pitch based on the vibrations of the instrument itself. Since the device only shows the pitch of the instrument to which it is attached, it can be used in ensemble settings. Investing in even one or two can pay dividends for the entire group. Each day (or week), lend it to another player during rehearsal and encourage him to constantly reference it, taking note of consistently out of tune passages and the tendencies of out of tune notes.

- *Tartini* (included on the Companion Website)—*Tartini* software was named after the eighteenth-century Italian composer, and acoustic theorist, Giuseppe Tartini. Developed at New Zealand's University of Otago and programmed by Philip McLeod, *Tartini* is free software for the Windows operating system. With the aid of an inexpensive microphone it offers a full chromatic tuner with a "digital needle," plus the following features:

1. Harmonic structure graph (shows the sounding overtones of any note played, an invaluable tool for explaining harmonics).
2. Volume graphs (tracks the evenness of crescendos and decrescendos and the consistency of long tones).
3. Vibrato contour graph (visually illustrates a vibrato's shape and frequency).
4. Pitch graphs (charts the pitch of any note in real time).

FIGURE 13.5 Tartini—Main Screen

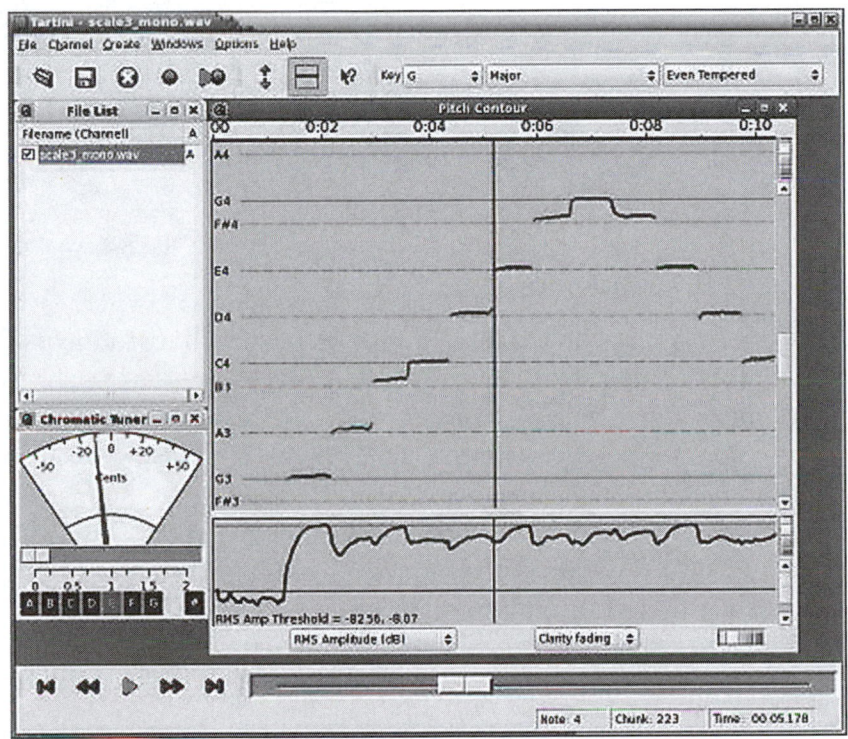

FIGURE 13.6 Tartini—Harmonic Track

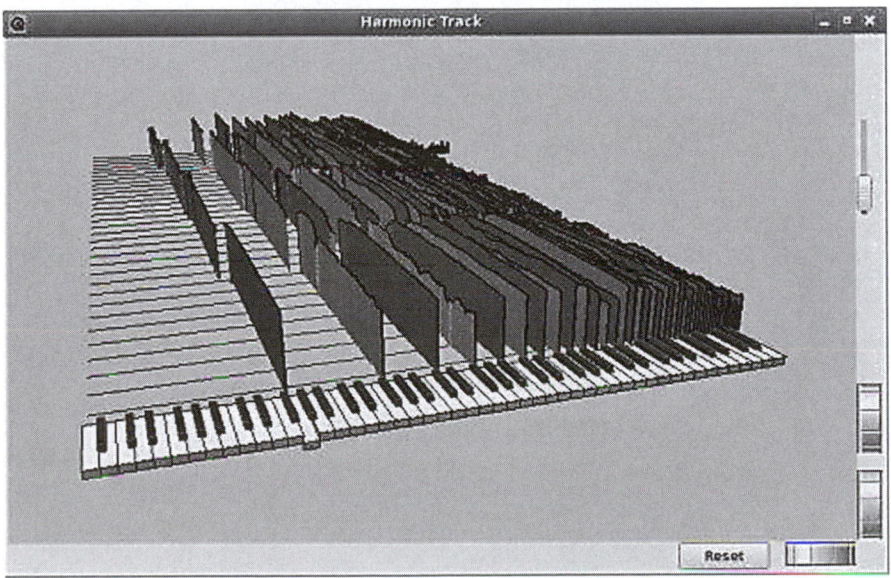

FIGURE 13.7 Tartini—Vibrato View

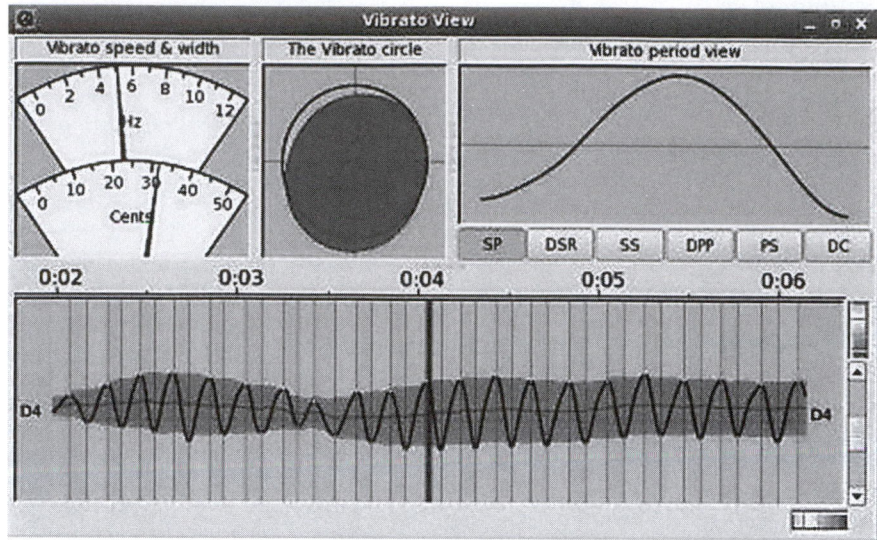

- *Flutini* (free download)—In spite of its name, *Flutini* is usable for all instruments. Most tuners have a needle that shows the pitch of one sound at a time. In contrast, *Flutini* tracks the intonation of all pitches and illustrates them instantly and simultaneously. It thus eliminates the need to isolate and sustain one problematic note to measure its pitch while playing. (See Figure 13.8.) Play something in real time, and *Flutini* shows the average intonation for each note it hears, no matter how fast the tempo (e.g., play a passage with five G4s and it shows the average pitch of that G). *Flutini* was developed by Scott R. Turner. It is based on McLeod's *Tartini* and Graeme Roxburgh and Terry McGee's *Polygraph*, another free pitch analysis program (http://www.mcgee-flutes.com/RTTA.htm).

FIGURE 13.8 Flutini Screen Shot

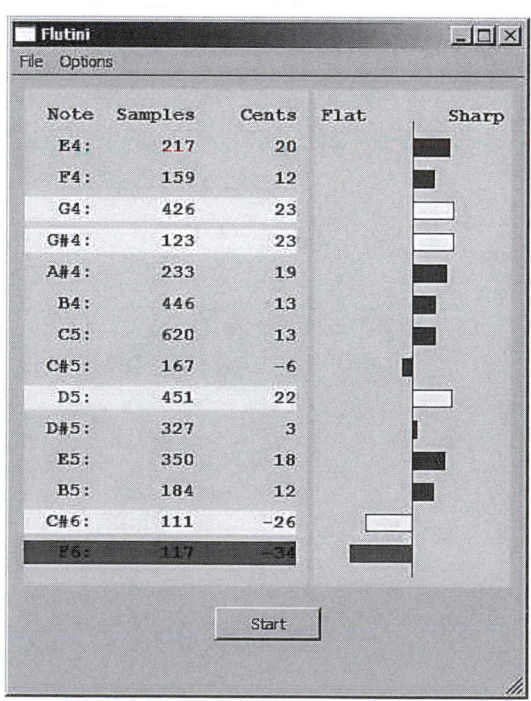

Using Drones and Long Tones to Develop Good Tone and Pitch

Breath control, embouchure, posture, and bow technique directly influence tone. Interestingly, there is evidence that tone improves when students focus on it even if they are not primarily aware of how they are creating it. Long tone (sustained tone) exercises are a useful application of this effect.[6]

Long-tone exercises are effective in group settings, when students focus on finding, matching, and sustaining the pitch center, and in individual settings, when students focus on sustaining a pitch as measured by an electronic tuner. Nearly every ensemble method book contains sustained tone exercises. The exact exercise is unimportant as long as the patterns involve sequential motion and a pitch center. Sustain each note for at least five seconds.

String players will benefit from "free bowing"[7] while sustaining pitches (analogous to the wind players sustaining) and also a more metered approach where four repeated quarter notes are played with a broad stroke. Strategies using this articulated sustain:

1. Students sustain the note until all players match their sound. When the ensemble sound is clear and in tune, move to the next pitch.
2. During the first few notes, students focus on the current pitch, but as they move towards the last few strokes ask them to think of proper placement of the finger for the next pitch.[8]

The Benefits of Using Drones

Drones, as woodwind specialist Harold E. Griswold points out, are a "universal concept of music texture not restricted to geographical, historical, or stylistic boundaries. They are found in many of the world's musics, from the drones on bagpipes in the British Isles to the drones used in today's jazz and rock music."[9] Drones are also an excellent pedagogical tool. They train students to audiate the pitch center, and thus perceive intonation and tonal tendencies whether or not the pitch center is actually sounding.

Intervalic drones of pure fifths and pure triads provide an aural picture, or an intervalic "scaffolding" for the pure intervals of just intonation. Eventually, the drone's scaffolding becomes "imprinted" and students are able to maintain the shape of the pure intervals on their own.

Unison and pure fifth drones also help tune intervals of a scale. No matter what mode is employed, each scale degree creates tension or stability in relation to the pitch center. The stronger a note "pulls" towards a pitch, or a member of the tonic triad, the more unstable and dissonant it is in relation to the tonic (i.e., the drone). The most obvious example is the major scale's leading tone, which pulls inexorably upward. Playing against a drone brings this shifting consonance/dissonance into relief.

Use long tones and drones to practice melodic intervals (scales and melodies) and harmonic intervals (diads and triads). Even in scale work, take care not to play too rapidly against the drone. The goal is to develop an aural "muscle memory." (Singing against the drone helps this, too.) The longer each pitch is sustained, the longer the ear and embouchure has to find the placement of the pure interval. Concentrate on octaves, thirds, and fifths, and allow students to feel and hear the tension of each scale degree.

Eventually they will prefer the pure sound to the tempered one, and they will naturally play just intervals without the scaffolding provided by the drone. As with any exercise, change the key center frequently. Ensembles often warmup on long tones, slow scales and sustained chords anyway, so why not practice them against a drone?

Drone exercises work well in individual, small group, and full-ensemble settings. For the full-ensemble, use speakers that can produce enough sound so the entire group can play and still clearly hear the drone. (Speakers mounted above the group are generally more effective than those placed at head level or below.)

At first this might seem overbearingly loud, but it is imperative that the group not drown out the aural scaffolding they are trying to match. Also, experiment with using instruments in the ensemble to create the drone. Begin with bass voices, but also use mid-range and soprano instruments.

Below are a few drone exercises to consider:

- Sing and play scales (in solo or ensemble situations)—Use the mono (tonic pitch only), diad (open fifth), and triad drones (three pitches, either major or minor) that are included on the CD enclosed with this text. Scales can be (a) in unison; or (b) chorale-style scales (Group 1 starts on the tonic, Group 2 enters on tonic as Group 1 reaches scale degree 3).
- Sing and play long tones to tune intervals or chords: (a) the entire group on the same chord tone (then switch); (b) one-third of the group on the root, one-third on the fifth, one-third on the third (then switch).
- Play unison and perfect fifth drones during sections of the literature that are firmly diatonic. Begin playing a tonic drone before the group enters and keep it going during the entire section, making sure it is loud enough to be heard. Have either the entire group play, or separate the melody and accompaniment voices. Repeat at least twice before removing the drone.

The tracks on the enclosed CD include:

1. Comparisons of equal temperament and pure intervals
2. Pure-fifth drones (two voices in the mid-range) for all 12 chromatic pitches
3. Pure-fifth drones (multiple voices access a full range) for all 12 chromatic pitches
4. Major triad drones for all 12 chromatic pitches
5. Minor triad drones for all 12 chromatic pitches

Other Factors that Affect Intonation

The Interaction of Pitch and Tone Color/Timbre—"Fix the Tone Before You Fix the Intonation!"

The famous nineteenth-century German physicist Hermann von Helmholtz suggested that intonation was mostly a function of the fundamental pitch, while the upper partials only contributed to tone color. Today, however, music educators generally agree that good tone quality and good pitch are mutually inclusive, interconnected, and dependent on each other (Millsap, 53). Indeed, recent research shows that overtones play a significant role in pitch perception.[10] Since the frequency and strength of overtones create tone color, it is more than cosmetic; it directly influences our perception of the pitch itself (Geringer and Worthy, 136, 147).

Here is another way of looking at it: Most woodwind and brass instruments are designed to resonate with good tone and intonation at a specific tube length. Play with a poor tone, and likely the slides or joints will need adjustment to play in tune. But though the instrument can be played in tune with slides pulled too far out or in, the tone color will never resonate optimally. If the slides are at the optimal length, only playing with good tone—with overtones in tune and resonating at the ideal strength—enables the instrument to be played in tune.

FIGURE 13.9 Interaction of Timbre, Resonance, and Pitch

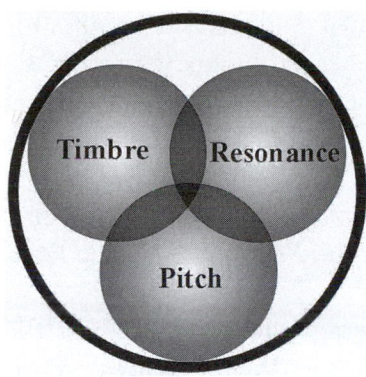

Some research demonstrates that listeners cannot focus on pitch and timbre without one factor being influenced by the other.[11] This perception differs based on the musician's experience. Compared to university music majors, "the association of bright [tone] quality with perceived sharpness and dark [tone] quality with flatness was particularly pronounced for the high school and non-music major instrumentalists" (Grainger, Worthy, 145–146).

This research has implications for teaching intonation. Tones of beginning performers in ensembles often vary widely in quality, and these differences may lead students to conclude that perceived pitch differences may be addressed immediately and adequately by adjusting tube length (Geringer and Worthy, 147). Particularly at beginning levels of ensemble playing, we may attempt to tune a poor quality tone by adjusting the length of the instrument, when in fact, the source of the perceived intonation mismatch may have little to do with the frequency of the note.

Since inexperienced players may not perceive the difference between poor tone and poor intonation, it is incumbent upon the teacher to show them. In a different study Worthy suggests that improving a student's tone quality should take priority over improving accuracy of pitch.[12]

Learning to Compensate for the Effect of Dynamics and Articulations

Many intonation problems exist because students do not understand how to control pitch when they accent, crescendo, or decrescendo. Except for flute, all wind instruments have a tendency to go flat when they play louder and sharp when they play softer. This has less to do with the acoustics of the instruments themselves and more to do with what happens to the embouchure during dynamic changes: the louder we play, the harder it is to maintain the same tension and focus, and as a result the embouchure's aperture tends to open, causing pitch to go flat. In contrast, during soft playing we often pinch the aperture closed in an effort to maintain tone, thus causing the pitch to creep sharp. Note that these tendencies are reversed on the flute: crescendos make the pitch go sharp; decrescendos make the pitch go flat. This is true whether the flutist plays softer as part of a decrescendo or because he is running out of air. In any case, make students aware of these tendencies and teach them the physical skills necessary to compensate.

For string players, it is important to consider how *forte* is accomplished. Sound must always be drawn out, never pushed out. Use natural arm weight in place of pressure. A loud sound produced by pressing down hard on the string will have an adverse effect on pitch. For all players, practice dynamics exercises on long tones while striving to maintain a centered pitch.

Charting Individual Intonation Tendencies

Every instrument has natural intonational tendencies throughout its playing range, both sharp and flat. If students have accurate information they can anticipate problems and compensate for deficiencies, or at least make a best-guess adjustment based on their personal tendency.

Several texts on the market chart pitch tendencies for each wind instrument:

Al Corky Fabrizio, *Guide to Understanding and Correction of Intonation Problems* (Hal Leonard).
Robert Garofalo, *Improving Intonation in Band and Orchestra Performance* (Meredith Music Publications).

Share these with students and encourage them to memorize the tendencies for each note. Quiz them frequently in rehearsal—e.g., "Saxophones: We're out of tune on the D. What's the tendency of that pitch?" By constantly reinforcing this information we emphasize that good pitch is their responsibility.

Since each instrument brand and student embouchure creates variations from these norms, another approach is to have students chart their own tendencies. The process of playing each note against a tuner allows one to experience and compensate for tendencies first-hand and not rely on what a book says.

 Figure 13.10 (showing an intonation chart in the treble clef) and Figure 13.11 (an intonation chart in the bass clef) include a line for p, mf, and f dynamics. Why? Because playing a note in tune in a practice room with a tuner is good, but notes in context are rarely played at "tuning note" volume (mf). Students should see and hear the effect dynamics have on their pitch and learn how to compensate. Have students keep the completed chart in their folder and encourage them to reference it often.

Tuning the Ensemble

Choosing a Tuning Note

There are numerous methods for tuning an ensemble which is less an indication that nobody knows what is best than a testament to the existence of many effective solutions. Remember, using a tuning note really only tunes *one note*. Still, it provides an important base line to put instruments in the ballpark. The most common options for tuning pitches are B♭, F, and A. Since no pitch is ideal for all instruments, we recommend using more than one as a reference tuning note.

Concert B♭

Advantages: Tried and true, the good ol' B♭ is an excellent note for many wind instruments. It works well for those playing in a B♭ transposition, including clarinets, bass clarinets, tenor saxophone, and trumpet, and for C instruments with a B♭ fundamental, such as trombone, euphonium, and BB♭ tuba. Wind band repertoire is frequently pitched in the key of B♭ or a related key. Additionally, it allows the trumpets, trombones, euphoniums, and tubas to tune to an "open note" (shortest instrument length of tubing), thus removing any additional variables.

Disadvantages: B♭ is not a good note for flutes, E♭ saxophones, and string instruments, and less experienced brass players may not be able to play their middle B♭ comfortably with a characteristic tone. Many young brass players' parts (except for the first parts) are frequently not this high.

FIGURE 13.10 Intonation Tendency Chart—Treble Clef

FIGURE 13.11 Intonation Tendency Chart—Bass Clef

Concert F

Advantages: Like the B♭, F allows brass players to tune an open pitch without manipulating slides or valves. But because it is lower than the B♭ it encourages a warmer, darker sound from the ensemble. Young brass players can play their middle F comfortably with a characteristic tone. Young brass players' parts often have a tessitura close to F.

Disadvantages: For saxophones, concert F produces a notoriously stuffy tone.

Concert A

Advantages: The standard pitch for orchestra tuning is also a good note for flutes (A) and clarinets (written B) to tune to. Indeed, the majority of woodwind concert A's are reliably in tune.

Disadvantages: Concert A does not allow brass players to tune the open length of their instrument, and it is particularly poor for trombones (who would be in 2nd position).

Ensemble Tuning Procedures

For Bands

There are five basic tuning styles:

- professional style
- concerto
- brass and woodwinds
- bottom-up
- principals lead

Each style is not mutually exclusive, and in fact they usually cross-pollinate to create new variations. Nevertheless, we can identify a few principles that link them. First, the player (or machine) who establishes the pitch must sustain with a clear and characteristic sound, even if that means the lead trumpet stands in for the oboe or a euphonium for the tuba. Second, give each instrument a chance to tune a stable note on the instrument, even if that means sounding multiple pitches. Also, the tuning pitch must sustain long enough to allow everyone to internalize it before they start tuning to it. Third, depending on the length of the rehearsal, the entire tuning procedure should take no more than two minutes (not including warmups), which means we must work to develop each student's ability to tune themselves rather than manually tune player by player. Fourth, insist that students plant their pitch inside the fundamental provided, then slowly expand their tone so that it blossoms in tune, without trying to overpower the original pitch. Finally, the tuning procedure should never atrophy into a perfunctory ritual, which means we must constantly remind students why we tune and how we tune. *Do not use the tuning procedure as an opportunity to take attendance, hand-out papers, etc.*

Tuning Styles (Mix and match as Needed)

Note: Reserve the use of the tuner only for the player who provides the tuning pitch. Other students must use their ears, not their eyes, to adjust the pitch.

Professional style
1. Using a tuner, principal oboe plays A-concert
2. All winds tune
3. Principal oboe plays B♭ concert
4. All winds tune

Concerto

For pieces with a prominent part for a fixed-pitch instrument (piano, mallets, harp, etc.), the soloist should provide the tuning pitch for the oboe (or whomever plays the sustained pitch)

Brass and Woodwinds Separately
1. Using a tuner, principal tuba establishes F concert or B♭ concert
2. All brass players tune to the tuba (low instruments first, then high)
3. Using a tuner, principal oboe establishes A-concert for the woodwinds
4. All woodwinds tune to the oboe (low instruments first, then high)

   Note: Like the professional style, this is a fast and efficient procedure, and it encourages players to hear themselves as part of the woodwind or brass family

Bottom-up
1. Using a tuner, principal tuba establishes F-concert
2. In order of low to high instruments (bass, tenor, alto, soprano voices), all players tune to the tuba

Principals lead
1. Using a tuner, principal tuba establishes B♭ concert
2. In order of low to high instruments, all principal players tune to the tuba
3. Each section then tunes to their principal player

   Note: By establishing a characteristic tone for each instrument, every student has a model to imitate

4. Younger students in particular will have more success evaluating their pitch if they compare it to a tone with the same range and timbre

For Orchestra

For orchestras, the convention is a concert A. Two are given by the oboe—one for the strings, and then one for the winds (including brass).

1. If there is no oboe player, or he has an unreliable sound, use the most reliable wind player, preferably a clarinet or trumpet.
2. Though not the convention in professional orchestras, consider giving the winds a B♭ or F in addition to the A.

The Tuning Toolkit

As with other rehearsal issues, it is useful to have a variety of techniques to use for intonation. Here are a few ideas:

- *Tuning in trios*—Ask students to match their pitch to the players, sitting on their left and their right. Tell them, "If each trio across the ensemble is in tune, everyone is in tune!"
- *On/Off*—It is often difficult to hear one's individual pitch while the entire ensemble is tuning. To help students isolate their own sound, encourage them to stop playing and then re-articulate the tuning note. A variation on this is to have the tuning pitch sound and then allow two seconds of silence before inviting the rest of the ensemble to play. This method makes it easier for students to discriminate whether they are sharp or flat by highlighting the difference between the tuning pitch and their pitch (as opposed to *adding* their pitch to the tuning note while it sounds, which may obscure the differences). Also consider having students close their eyes to heighten their awareness of sound.
- *Fade in/Fade out*—As the reference pitch sustains, have individuals enter the texture softly, crescendo, and then fade out. Like the On/Off tool this helps students distinguish their own sound.
- *Loud last*—The sound of a large trumpet section may obscure the tuning pitch for woodwinds (all they hear is trumpet.). As a solution, invite the flutes to tune before the trumpets enter.
- *Humming/Singing*—Sometimes the best way to tune is to ask the human voice to find the correct pitch without the mechanical and physical challenges of an instrument getting in the way. Have students hum the pitch with their mouths closed and then play it. Or, have half the group sing the note while the other half tunes to the human drone. Emphasize that instruments serve as amplifiers of what we hear, hum, and sing.
- *Electronically amplified tuning pitches*—Particularly for younger players, experiment with an electronically amplified drone (unison or perfect fifth). The idea is to make the pitch center accurate and easy to find, even amidst a large ensemble tuning at the same time.
- *Mid-rehearsal re-tunes*—As instruments and rooms become warmer, pitch centers slide. A quick retuning recalibrates the pitch center.
- *Isolate a section*—To isolate the pitch of a specific section, say, the alto saxophones, have the full ensemble sustain the pitch and then release every group except the altos. The sudden juxtaposition of the tutti sound with a section's sound helps highlight pitch discrepancies.

Activities/Assignments for Further Exploration

1. Besides the exercises described in this chapter, devise other ways to help students hear beats and pitch discrepancies?
2. In your own words, describe the difference between equal temperament and just intonation.
3. Fill out the intonation tendency chart for your own instrument. Were you surprised by any of the results?
4. Practice singing and playing scales/intervals against a drone. Write a lesson plan that uses drones to improve intonation for a piece you are studying.
5. Have the entire class sing/play the progression I-VI-I while one or more students sustain the third of the tonic chord. Ask them to pay close attention to how this pitch needs to be adjusted as it shifts from third ⇨ fifth ⇨ third.

Further Reading

Benade, Arthur H. *Fundamentals of Musical Acoustics*. New York: Oxford University Press, 1976.

Campbell, Murray, Clive A. Greated, and Arnold Myers. *Musical Instruments: History, Technology, and Performance of Instruments of Western Music*. Oxford: Oxford University Press, 2004.

Duffin, Ross W. *How Equal Temperament Ruined Harmony (and Why You should Care)*. 1st ed. NY: W.W. Norton, 2007.

Fabrizio, Al. *A Guide to the Understanding and Correction of Intonation Problems*. Ft. Lauderdale, FL: Meredith Music, 1994.

Garofalo, Robert Joseph. *Improving Intonation in Band and Orchestra Performance*. Ft. Lauderdale, FL: Meredith Music Publications, 1996.

Helmholtz, Hermann von, and Alexander John Ellis. *On the Sensations of Tone as a Physiological Basis for the Theory of Music*. New York: Dover Publications, 1954.

Isacoff, Stuart. *Temperament: How Music Became a Battleground for the Great Minds of Western Civilization*. New York: Vintage, 2003.

Jeans, James Hopwood, Sir. *Science and Music*. New York: Dover Publications, 1968.

Chapter 14

Directing Other Ensembles

To Guide Your Reading

In what ways can a marching/pep/parade band program be successful and also support an indoor band program?

What are some strategies to administering and conducting a musical theater pit orchestra?

In what ways can sound reinforcement enhance a jazz band's stage performance?

How does one overcome the challenge of incorporating chamber music into the curriculum?

How can students be taught to rehearse themselves in chamber groups?

How does one arrange the seating for musical theater pits, jazz ensembles, and chamber ensembles? What are the different ways a parade band can be lined up?

Most band and orchestra directors have responsibilities beyond their primary ensemble, including marching band, pep band, parade band, jazz ensemble, musical theater pit, and chamber groups. Fortunately, the fundamental skills needed to rehearse and lead an orchestra or band translate surprisingly well to these ensembles. Just think of each one as representing a different musical dialect rather than an altogether different language. A detailed study of each ensemble is beyond the scope of this text, but some of their philosophical, conducting, and teaching challenges are worth a brief discussion.

Marching Bands/Pep Bands/Parade Bands

Running a marching band program is a complicated operation, roughly akin to an outdoor musical theater production. The band director functions as the producer and stage director, coordinating disparate and often competing elements into a coherent production. First: music, drill, uniforms, costumes, and props must be secured. Then, wind instruments, drum line, percussion pit, and color guard rehearse separately and later in unison. Ultimately every element comes together into a multi-layered tableau.

Some directors thrive on the diversity of these artistic elements and their integration. They run competitive marching programs supported by impressive fundraising and dedicated parent helpers. They write the music and drill themselves or hire specialists. They employ large staffs to help teach the drill, drum line, and color guard. They travel regularly to band camps, competitions, and football games. And they field a musical, kinesthetic, dynamic production with students who love the music, the physical challenge, the showmanship, the camaraderie, and the competitive experience.

Some directors take a different approach. Perhaps their school doesn't offer the necessary funding; or the school is too small to consistently field a large band; or the school doesn't have a tradition of competitive bands; or the band director would rather direct energy on the indoor concert bands during the fall. Whatever the reason, these programs operate differently. They may have parent helpers, but there is much less emphasis on fundraising. The directors likely write the drill themselves or purchase commercial drill and music arrangements. They likely employ smaller staffs, play mostly at home football games, and travel rarely. Yet still their program may capture some of the musical and non-musical benefits of other competitive programs.

On Competition and the Non-Musical Benefits of Group Music-Making

Whether or not musical ensembles should compete has long been debated. While some directors loath the idea of performing music for awards and recognition, others thrive on making competition a regular part of their activities. The debate is fraught with contradiction and ambiguity, and ultimately a case may be made for either side.

On the one hand, the act of making music is not a competitive endeavor, at least in the professional world. The Chicago Symphony does not compete against the New York Philharmonic; there is no inter-orchestra competition to determine who plays the best Beethoven. Although a musical performance reflects a certain level of achievement, it is not a triumph, or a "win." We don't "defeat" Mozart if we play his music well (though perhaps he can defeat us if we perform miserably).

On the other hand, there are components of musical study that are unavoidably competitive, such as auditions and concerto competitions. These activities have clear winners and losers. The winners receive glory, recognition, and opportunity. The losers do not, and their only reparation is to practice more and live to enter another contest. This type of competition is not unique to music, of course. It's the way most disciplines with limited opportunities sort out the talent pool. We compete to get into college, to play on the baseball team, and to get a job. From natural selection to capitalist marketplaces; from silver-back gorillas pounding their chest to humans placing personal ads, competition and the rewards success brings are timeless strategies to motivate people to be their best.

In competitions with inherent artistry and skill involved, it can be difficult to divorce the beauty of the game from the lure of the contest. Still, even the sheer act of competing offers ancillary benefits beyond trophies, certificates, and the competition itself:

- the excitement of performing in front of crowds
- the thrill of victory
- the value of teamwork
- the importance of putting the group ahead of the individual
- how to deal with personal and group disappointment (losses, bad calls, poor umpiring, etc.)
- how to handle personal and group success (personal achievements, group victories, etc.)
- how to show class in the face of defeat
- how to show class in the euphoria of victory.

Indeed, some research suggests that music students in competitive situations value the non-competitive aspects the most. Schmidt (2005) found "that students may respond best to the intrinsic or cooperative aspects of instrumental music, rather than its extrinsic or competitive aspects."[1] That implies competition may be extremely beneficial, assuming teachers focus on teamwork and cooperation rather than on winning trophies.

This resonates with how many directors view competition. In competitive marching bands, directors rate contests quite low in their musical benefit and high in personal benefits to students.[2] In contrast, school principals look quite favorably upon contests for their ability to improve public relations. How interesting it is that principals support such an expensive and time intensive activity even though some of their own teachers devalue its music educational benefits—all the more reason to maximize competition's *positive* benefits.

Seen in this light, perhaps instead of fretting that marching band offers an inferior musical experience, we should embrace what it *does* offer, especially to those students who do not participate in team athletics. Of course, some directors are understandably uncomfortable about turning music into a sport. They reason that music is a worthwhile activity precisely because it *doesn't* need competition to give it meaning.

The challenge is to maximize competition's benefits without compromising musical ideals. On the one hand, if we enter a competition, ought we *compete*? We don't want to teach the idea of winning at all costs, but perhaps we do a disservice if we fail to prepare students for success and failure, however unmusical we believe these competitive skills are. And when they do succeed, why not tastefully celebrate? The New York Philharmonic may not, but shouldn't students enjoy their victories?

On the other hand, after months of rehearsals with music-making as a goal unto itself, it seems frivolous to suddenly morph from composer's advocate into judge's advocate, or worse, judge's sycophant. We might say, "Violins, if you play it like that, the judges will deduct points from our score"; "We came in second place overall, took home first place trophies in drum-line and color guard, and second place in marching, music, and special effects—good job!" Are we merely "teaching to the test" if we insist on details just because the judges will look for them? It takes a deft hand to motivate using competition but still build an environment in which music has meaning even without an opponent.

Ultimately, every director should grapple with the issue of competition and develop a reasoned philosophy without simply bowing to tradition, experience, or convenience. Remember, students embrace the values of their teachers. If the teacher emphasizes winning as the most important goal, it is likely the students will as well. If trophies are shifted to the periphery of music-making, students will follow in suit.

For directors who wish to cultivate the non-musical benefits of competition, consider the following:

- Supplement trophy-driven festivals with clinics by quality musicians and conductors—Bringing in a clinician before or after a festival gives the best of both worlds: a trophy for administrators to celebrate and a positive musical experience for students to learn from.
- Apply marching band-inspired leadership to indoor ensembles—A wind ensemble can reap the same benefits as a marching band from section leaders (squad leaders) and student conductors (drum majors). The dynamics that fuel camaraderie, leadership, and cooperation on the football field have the same effect in the concert hall.

A detailed discussion of the skills needed to administrate and direct marching bands is outside the scope of this text. Other texts expertly cover the topic. We recommend:

The Complete Marching Band Resource Manual: Techniques and Materials for Teaching, Drill Design, and Music Arranging, by Wayne Bailey

The Marching Band Director: A Master Planning Guide, by Bill Raxsdale

The Dynamic Drum Major, by George N. Parks

The System: Marching Band Methods, by Gary E. Smith

Techniques of Marching Band Show Design, by Dan Ryder

The Marching Band Program: Principles and Practices, by Bentley Shellahamer, James Swearingen, and Jon Woods

The Dynamic Marching Band, by Wayne Markworth

American Band: Music, Dreams, and Coming of Age in the Heartland, by Kristen Laine

Figures 14.1 and 14.2 show two possible parade band set-ups. Figure 14.1 essentially sets up the winds and percussion in score order; Figure 14.2 moves the woodwinds to the back and trombones to the front of the formation.

FIGURE 14.1 Parade Formation #1

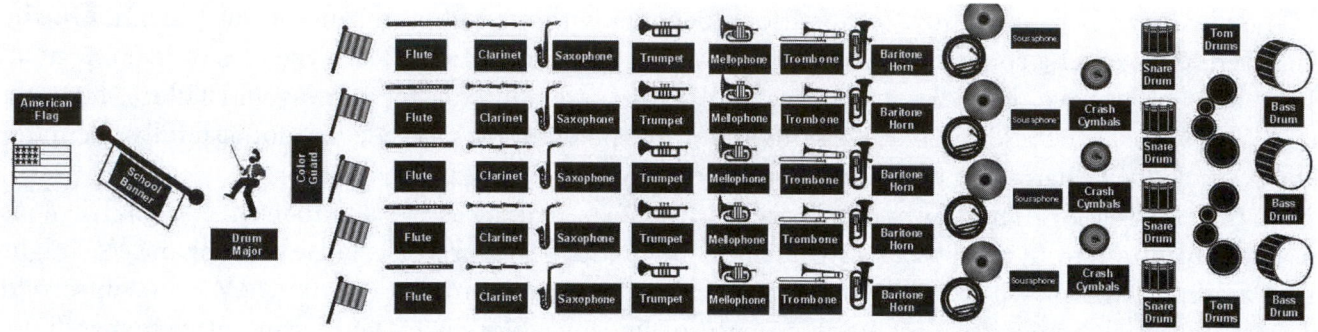

FIGURE 14.2 Parade Formation #2

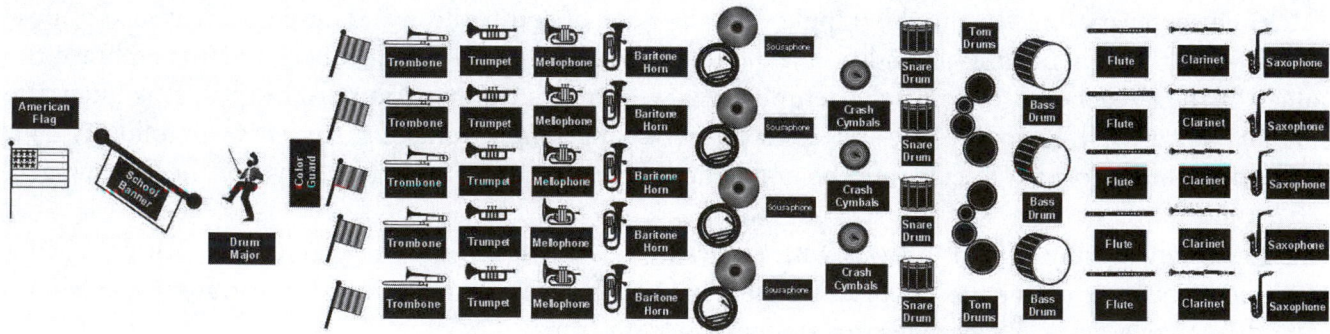

Musical Pit Orchestra

Like the marching band, the pit orchestra is a collaborative effort among many creative personalities. Director, music director, vocal director, choreographer, set designer, costume designer, and lighting designer all have individual roles but must work together towards the final production. (At the public school level, some of these positions are combined, but usually there are at least two or three faculty members working together.)

Conducting a pit can be extremely satisfying, but the conductor must temper his ego and the desire to control every aspect of the show. Don't suppress every creative instinct, but understand the pit orchestra's dual role: sometimes it's the star, and sometimes it's a supporting cast member. By all means, make your opinions and needs heard. But recognize when your role is to make the rest of the production better, even if that means doing something inconvenient.

Every show has a slightly different instrumentation. Seek the strongest, most dedicated, musically independent, and patient players available, whether by audition or invitation. In the chaos and stress of a tech-week rehearsal (the rehearsal a week before opening night during which lights, costumes, scenery, blocking, and music are finally coordinated) there is no time to deal with unreliable, undisciplined, and unprepared players. Whenever possible, recruit from within the school's music program, but also ask the drama director to establish a budget for hiring additional players. A "ringer" is only insulting to a student if we bypass someone who is capable of playing the part. If no student can reasonably play the lead trumpet part, we create a situation in which someone is bound to fail in a very public manner. Instead, invite a student to play as an "assistant"—doubling parts when possible and covering if the principal player (i.e., the "ringer") is absent.

Performing in a pit ensemble is a huge responsibility. Ask students to sign a "contract" that details the rehearsal schedule, sets limits on how many rehearsals may be missed because of other conflicts, and holds them responsible for returning their music in good condition. Make sure students understand the extent of their commitment, especially for tech-week, which usually entails rehearsals that last 3–5 hours each night. It is a draining, meticulous process during which changes are made and decisions solidified—attendance must be mandatory.

Design the schedule so pit rehearsals become more frequent as opening night nears. Here's an example:

3–4 months out: 1 rehearsal every two weeks (if you can acquire the music this far out in advance)
2 months out: 1 rehearsal per week
1 month out: 1–2 rehearsals per week, with at least one for adding the cast
1 week out: tech(nical) and dress rehearsals every night of the week
0 weeks out: Showtime! (typically 2–3 performances)

Especially because it is often unsatisfying to rehearse without vocalists, play recordings of each song at the first or second rehearsal (preferably multiple recordings of the same song). The bulk of the initial rehearsal is typically spent simply playing through the book. This tends to be a tedious process, as negotiating repeats, cuts, and da capos is tricky. (*Caveat emptor*: Beware that some Broadway cast recordings are different from the published version.)

In professional productions woodwinds players usually double. This means a single book (i.e., part) contains a mixture of woodwind instruments, and one person is expected to switch, or double, as needed. Though MTI (Music Theatre International) and its counterparts often commission arrangements for school groups, it is inevitable that we will encounter books with doublings. Usually these are labeled as "Reed 1," "Reed 2," etc. Unless we have students with the skills to play multiple instruments, we have several options:

1. Use the instrument which plays the bulk of the book and leave out the other parts. (Feasible if the orchestration includes copious doublings.)
2. Add as many instruments as needed to play the book. (Recommended if each part is satisfying on its own. If the flute barely plays, we're asking a student to give up a large chunk of time for a very small role.)
3. Re-score doublings for other instruments as "inserts." (Highly recommended.)

Admittedly, option 3 is time consuming. Since most sets include only a condensed score we may have to compare the orchestration manually. Lay each book on a table and follow the score from book to book, notating important passages for instruments that we do not have in the ensemble. Then re-write the parts. For example, depending on the range and difficulty, a re-score of Reed 1 might become an insert for Reed 2.

Be creative when re-scoring. For instance, it is usually more desirable to have a soprano saxophone solo played by the clarinet than not played at all.

Common re-scoring techniques include the following:

1. *Transfer to "like" transpositions*—Oboe to flute, trumpet/soprano sax to clarinet, bass clarinet to tenor sax. Adjust the range as needed.
2. *Woodwinds as stand-ins for chordal string passages*—One flute and two clarinets substitute nicely for upper strings playing sustained chords.
3. *Piano covers all*—A quality pianist can cover a multitude of omissions.
4. *"Synthesize" rather than cut*—A good keyboard synthesizer covers background string passages quite convincingly. It also stands in well for the bass part.

Conducting the Pit Orchestra—Tips and Strategies

As with operas and concerti, a pit involves special skills compared to typical concert conducting.

1. *Annotate piano/vocal scores with details about orchestration*—Most shows provide only a piano/vocal score for the conductor with minimal details about the scoring. Obviously, this makes rehearsals and cues difficult. If you know the arrangement is identical to the recorded cast album, make specific annotations in the score before the first rehearsal. Mark which instruments play inner lines, and newly notate (using pencil!) other lines that are not printed, but which you discover through the recording or during the first rehearsal. Save valuable rehearsal time by numbering all measures and have students do the same.
2. *Mark the parts*—Considering the number of cuts, inserts, and jumps most shows entail, it is absolutely, positively essential that players mark their parts to indicate a clear roadmap. Encourage the use of symbols and arrows (rather than words) to quickly convey important information.
3. *Mark the score*—Mark the conductor score meticulously. Indicate vamps, repeats, cuts, jumps, fermatas, tempo changes and important cues (music and dialogue). Be clear, but avoid cluttering the score with unnecessary markings. Use sticky notes for special reminders and cardboard clip tabs (available at office supply stores) to easily flip back multiple pages of the score for D.C. and D.S. parts.
4. *Use erasable pencils*—Any un-erased marks at the end of the show will likely incur a fine from the music rental company. Let students know from the beginning that they are responsible for damaged or permanently marked books.
5. *Maintain eye contact with the on-stage performers*—Conducting musical theatre involves simultaneously conducting two ensembles: pit orchestra and choir (plus soloists). Rehearse the pit with the intention of making them self-sufficient. This frees us to make strong eye contact with the on-stage performers. For cues and cutoffs, raise the left hand high as an alert for an upcoming cue (2–4 beats before the event), and then use a large preparation to actually give the cue (or release).
6. *Use a metronome*—Singers and dancers depend on steady tempos that are consistent from day to day. Imagine a dancer who has to jump on beat one and land on beat two. If the tempo is too slow, they

will land early. Too fast, they land late. Practice hitting the correct tempo for each song in the order it is performed, and mentally sing a part of each song before showing the preparation beat. Also, there is no shame in having multiple metronomes on the conductor stand silently blinking the correct tempi for several different songs.

7. *Be consistent yet supportive*—Even with agreed-upon tempi, there should be give-and-take between orchestra and singer. Though we are the music director, ultimately our job is to support the musical needs of the cast and the show, not to stubbornly insist things are done the way we want them. James H. Laster, Professor Emeritus of Music at Shenandoah University, calls this, "Flexibility under the guise of consistency."[3]

8. *Use the "Float and Drop" technique for rubato passages*—Most conductors are taught downbeats are usually prepared. An exception to this rule is during accompanimental conducting, when sometimes we must start without establishing the tempo. This "Float and Drop Technique" is often used during rubato passages when we follow a performer who stretches the tempo. The key is to float slowly upward with the baton as time is stretched. When the baton reaches eye level, freeze it or slowly continue floating upward. Do not start any downward motion until the rubato is over, at which point head straight down to the next beat. (To avoid being late to that downbeat, do not prep upward first—head directly downward.) During this gesture our attention must be on the performer, not the pit or the score. Through a combination of eye contact, body language (breathing gestures, etc.), and prior agreement, we can usually predict exactly how the tempo resumes.

9. *For repeated measures*—If a passage has a predetermined number of repeats, help the group keep track by counting down with fingers in the left hand. Counting down rather than up simplifies things, since the pit will know that "one finger" is always the last time through the section.

10. *Show vamps with the left hand*—If a section repeats *indefinitely* as the conductor awaits a cue from onstage (e.g., a line of dialogue, a character's entrance, etc.), conduct with the right hand and keep the left hand up with an index finger pointing to the ceiling. To signal that it is time to go on, lower the left hand, then give a large preparation to cue the measure after the vamp (Laster, 117).

11. *Use different planes for pit and cast cues*—Cues for the pit should be lower than cues for the cast. The latter should be shoulder level or above. Cues for the cast can be prepared by raising the left hand as a "warning" a few beats before the entrance and then giving the actual cue with a one or two-handed gesture. Be sure to make eye contact with the cast; even if they are not looking directly at you they can spot your cue with their peripheral vision.

12. *For scene transition music, show the last note with a clear gesture to avoid a sloppy cut-off*—Conduct the transition music with right hand only; wait for a cue that gives you at least a few seconds to end the music; bring the left hand up to indicate the transition is about to end (optional: show a slight decrescendo); find the nearest appropriate stopping point, even if it is in the middle of a phrase; use both hands to cue the last note, which should be played as a light accent, as if it is the last note of the piece (even if it occurs in the middle of a phrase).

13. *For silent measures, make a clear distinction between passive and active beats*—*Mark all measures.* In measures where nothing happens in the orchestra part (e.g., Grand Pause, recitative-like passages), we still need to account for every measure by "marking" each one. Otherwise, we are bound to confuse someone who is counting rests. To mark measures in which the orchestra does not play we have two options: (a) Float through the pattern using a "passive" beat without a click. Switch to an "active" beat, with a click, to prep an entrance; (b) Show the beginning of each measure by indicating "beat 1" with a large, inactive downbeat (a large, "dead beat"). Some conductors like to show this with an inactive prep and then a touch of the tip of the baton on their finger or the score. In a passage where this seems excessive, explain it to the entire group ("I won't be conducting measure 54"; OR "Measure 54 no

longer exists; you can cross it out" OR "The next thing you see will be measure 55.") Have everyone mark their parts appropriately.

14. *"Stir the pot" to alert the group to get ready for the next song*—To remind the pit a song is approaching after a long stretch of dialogue (e.g., 10–20 seconds before the beginning of the next song), use an inconspicuous "stirring" gesture from the wrists, as if stirring a pot of soup with each hand. This signals the players to bring their instruments to "ready" position.

15. *Always be clear*—Pit books are filled with rests, confusing cuts, da capos, and distractions from the stage and audience. Nothing defeats a pit orchestra faster than an unclear conductor. Make the performers' jobs easier by placing each beat in a distinct place on the conducting plane.

16. *Train the ensemble to recover from mistakes and mishaps*—Even the most meticulously rehearsed show will experience problems. Perhaps a light cue will not work; perhaps a singer will miss an entrance or enter too early. Help prepare the pit to handle these mini-emergencies by practicing them during rehearsal. Try this: change tempos unexpectedly; cut music off early; whisper out a rehearsal letter while the ensemble is playing and then cue that measure.

Occasionally we need to help the pit adjust to a cast member's mistakes; other times the pit will hear the mistake and jump instinctively (Laster, 130). Indeed, one of the reasons playing in a pit is a valuable experience for our students is that it develops their ability to be musical and professional under unpredictable and unusual circumstances.

Setting-Up the Pit Orchestra

Space is almost always at a premium in a pit orchestra, so expect things to be cramped. Though ultimately the right set-up is the one that makes the most sense for the music and the show, Figure 14.3 illustrates two common models. Be sure to invest in extra stand lights, bulbs, power strips, and extension cords— always have a few more than you think you need. Also recommended:

- For safety, tape down loose wires
- Add colored plastic gels over the stand lights to dull their glare.

Attire for pit orchestras is traditionally all black: black pants/long skirt, black shirt/blouse/sweater, black socks, black dress shoes.

FIGURE 14.3 Pit Orchestra Set-ups

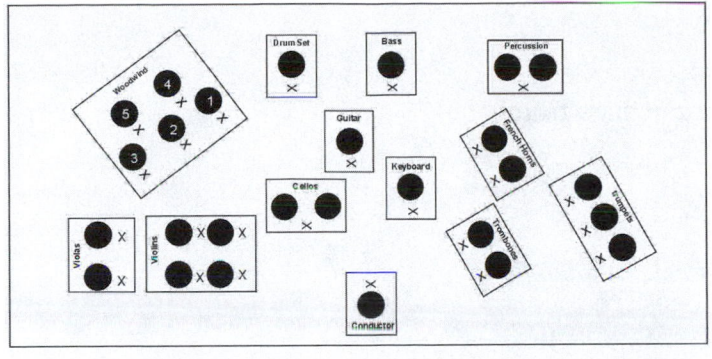

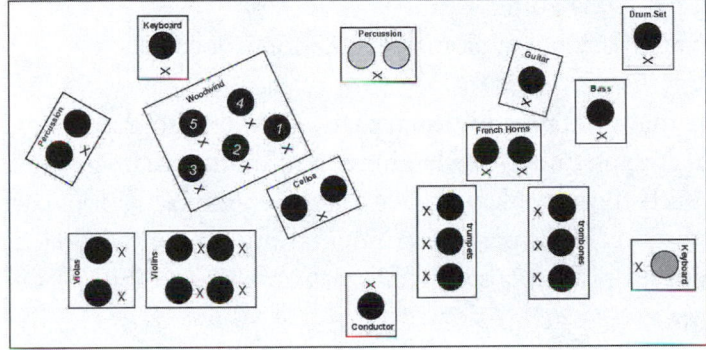

Jazz Ensemble

For music teachers who have never played in a jazz ensemble, directing one can be a daunting task. Fortunately, in spite of the mysteries it holds for the uninitiated—swing, jazz articulation, improvisation, rhythm sections, etc.—jazz is different in degree, not in kind, from traditional Western classical music. Even a musician who has never heard a big band can detect issues of intonation, precision, balance, notes, and rhythm. And jazz improvisation has direct analogues in classical music. Medieval/Renaissance vocal music, instrumental dance music, organ improvisation and classical cadenzas all use techniques that appear in some form in jazz, only with a different set of scales, harmony, and syntax. Moreover, Baroque and Classical ornamentation is uncannily similar to jazz's collection of shakes and turns. For a non-jazzer, then, directing a jazz ensemble is largely an issue of understanding and experiencing its performance practice. For example:

- immerse yourself in recordings
- attend jazz ensemble rehearsals at other schools and colleges
- take an improv(isation) lesson with a local professional
- practice jazz style and improvisation with a play-along book and recording (e.g., the Jamey Aebersold series)
- attend summer jazz workshops
- join a community jazz band

The study of jazz is a massive topic, and complete discussion is well beyond the scope of this text, but let's examine some of the basics issues.

The instrumentation of a typical big band has become relatively standardized in educational settings.

Wind Section
2 Alto saxophones
2 Tenor saxophones
1 Baritone saxophone
4 Trombones (includes one bass trombone)
4 Trumpets

Rhythm Section
Drum set
piano
guitar(electric)
bass (double bass or electric bass guitar)
optional, but common: auxiliary percussionist, vibraphone, vocalist.

Advanced arrangements may contain additional parts, including soprano saxophone, clarinet, bass clarinet, flugelhorn, and flute. Arrangements for beginner and intermediate groups sometimes include flute, clarinet, and bass clarinet parts that double other voices, or generic B♭, F, or C parts. Like a wind ensemble, traditional jazz ensembles use "one on a part" instrumentation. Students who play instruments outside the core jazz instrumentation often pick up a secondary instrument, as Table 14.1 shows.

TABLE 14.1 Secondary Instruments

Students who play these instruments . . .	. . . often play these instruments in a jazz ensemble
Clarinet/Bassoon	Saxophone
French horn	Trumpet
Euphonium	Trombone or valved trombone
Tuba	Bass trombone

Alternatively, have students play their non-core instrument using one of the regular core parts.

TABLE 14.2 Core and Non-core Parts

Non-traditional jazz ensemble instruments . . .	. . . play these parts
Flute/Oboe	Trumpet (must transpose part)
Clarinet	Trumpet or tenor sax
Bass clarinet	Tenor saxophone or trombone (must transpose part)
Bassoon	Trombone
French horn	Trumpet parts 3 or 4 (must transpose part)
Euphonium (or valved trombone)	Trombone
Tuba	Bass or bass trombone (transpose down an octave)
Xylophone/Marimba/Vibraphone	Piano or guitar (play chords)

Directors can write parts for these non-traditional instruments and/or purchase charts for flexible instrumentation e.g., *Kendor Konvertibles* (Kender Music); *Jazz Combo Paks* (Hal Leonard Publishing).

Standard and non-standard instruments are ideal for organizing jazz combos, which typically include a rhythm section (bass, drums, optional harmony instrument) and one to four other instruments.

Set-up

The jazz ensemble essentially functions as a large chamber group. Although the winds set-up in straight, parallel rows, it is vital that rhythm section players be able to see each other. A typical jazz ensemble set-up is shown in Figure 14.4.

FIGURE 14.4 Jazz Ensemble Set-up

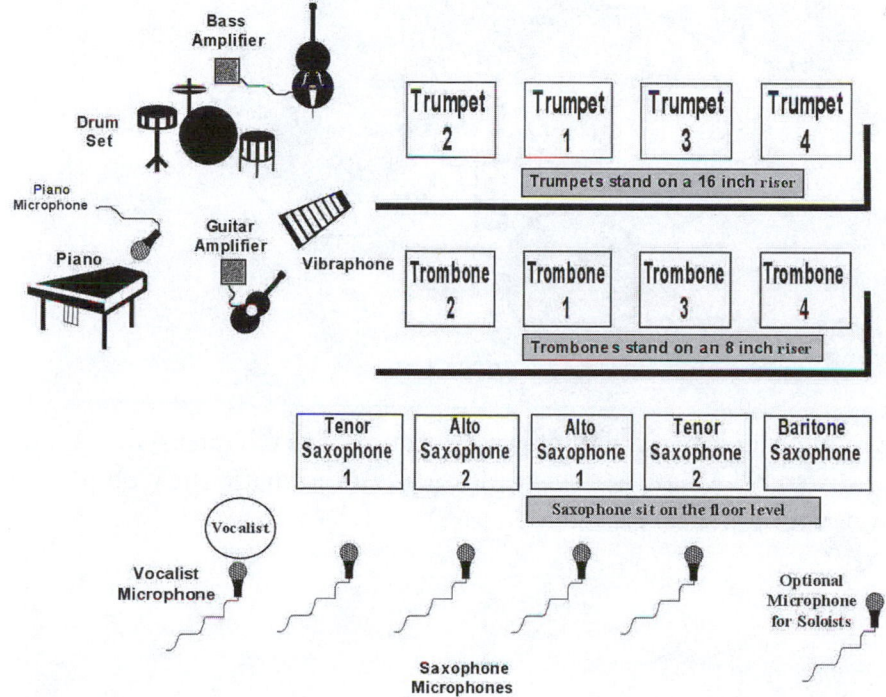

- Since they receive the bulk of open solos, Tenor saxophone 1 and Trumpet 2 are closest to the rhythm section.
- Notice the placement of the lead alto saxophone, trumpet, and trombone: As in an orchestral wind section, this set-up puts lead players in the center of the group.
- Seat winds in tiers so all parts are easily heard: saxophones on the floor, trombones bit higher, and trumpets always standing. If risers are not available, try putting the trombones on stools.
- The rhythm section sits as a combo that supports and drives the rest of the band. The pianist typically sits with his back towards the audience, allowing eye contact with the set-player and bassist. This placement also allows the piano to project into the winds and audience.
- The lowest parts (Trumpet 4, Trombone 4, Baritone saxophone) are placed one in front of the other so they can easily hear each other.
- Vocalists typically perform in front of the rhythm section to help them feel more connected to the groove.

Figure 14.5 shows the basic drum kit set-up.

FIGURE 14.5 Drum Kit Set-up

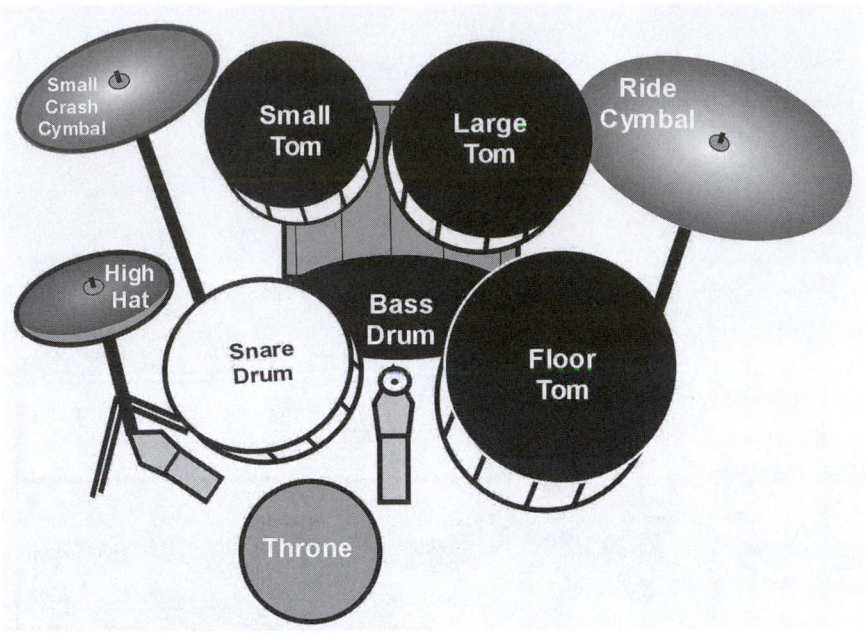

  Improvisation should be an integral part of jazz education. See Chapter 4 for a general discussion, and consult the resources listed below jazz-specific pedagogy. (Additionally, the Companion Website contains several videos demonstrating improvisation exercises.)

Suggested Resources

David Baker, *Jazz Pedagogy*
Jerry Coker, *The Teaching of Jazz*
Richard Dunscomb/Willie Hill, *Jazz Pedagogy*
Tom Ferguson/Sandy Feldstein, *The Jazz/Rock Ensemble*
Lissa A. Fleming, *Getting Started with Jazz Band*
Robert Henry, *The Jazz Ensemble*
Steve Houghton, *A Guide for the Modern Rhythm Section*
John Kuzmich/Lee Bash, *Instrumental Jazz Instruction*
Richard Lawn, *The Jazz Ensemble Director's Manual*
MENC – *Teaching Jazz: A Course of Study*
Hal Sherman, *Techniques & Materials for the Stage Band*
Hal Sherman, *The Rhythm Section*
Roger Schuler, *So You Want To Lead A Jazz Band?*
Gordon Vernick, et al., eds., *Teaching Jazz: A Course of Study*
Jack Wheaton, *How To Organize & Develop The Stage Band*
www.moiaje.org
www.jazzstandards.com
www.uncjazzpress.com

Chamber Music

Chamber music develops a unique set of musical and interpersonal skills. It requires a brand of individualism that is compatible with teamwork; it holds students accountable for their part, provides repeated opportunities to play independently, and returns expressive freedom as a reward. Though these are skills we instill in large ensembles, there are too few opportunities to practice them there, and it is far too easy for students to "hide" within their section.[4]

In chamber music there is no place to hide. Its intimate nature allows students to take more control of musical decisions than they can in large ensembles. Players (often) rehearse themselves, diagnose ensemble issues, and prescribe solutions. Interpretation generates through a democratic process. The group develops an overall vision, individuals propose ideas, and everyone negotiates which ideas to accept and reject. Instead of relying on a conductor to spoon-feed a single viewpoint, students practice conceptual understanding; they apply concepts and techniques for themselves—how to shape a phrase, when to crescendo, how to apply rubato, how to start and stop together, etc. In short, chamber music is a vehicle for developing a group aesthetic that depends upon interpersonal skills, teamwork, and personal responsibility (Latten, 46).

Strategies for developing a chamber music program include:

- Use non-classical ensembles. Dixieland combos, jazz combos, and funk-rock groups allow mixed instrumentation and are a great forum to explore improvisation (Latten, 46).
- Use small group lesson time to rehearse.
- Meet before or after school on a rotating basis.
- Find alternative rehearsal spaces. Sometimes we must think outside the box—literally! Teachers' offices, practice rooms, unused classrooms, instrument storage rooms, dressing rooms, costume closets, etc. are all worth considering. Since most chamber groups are 3–5 players they usually aren't too loud (be sure to check with your administration regarding rules for leaving students unattended.)
- Look to the community for performance venues. Community centers, nursing homes, senior citizen centers, churches and synagogues are often receptive to having school chamber ensembles perform. It's a win-win-win scenario: the community receives great music, the students receive appreciative audiences, and the music program receives greater visibility.
- Use chamber ensembles for student compositions. With fewer instruments to track, chamber ensembles are excellent vehicles for composition and arranging assignments (Latten, 47). Chamber groups can read and rehearse student compositions with the composer present, and later perform them on a special recital, or before a regular concert.

Chamber Music Rehearsal Skills

Rehearsal skills taught in the large group setting will not automatically transfer to the student-run rehearsal. We can help guide students through the process:

- Set up the group so everybody can make eye contact with each other. Encourage the group to do so during beginnings, endings, cues, and passages when instruments are paired.
- Model how each instrument can be used to help cue other players and keep an ensemble pulse—e.g., instrument raises up and down with the breath; head motion with eye contact.
- Encourage the ensemble to move regularly during the piece. ("Since there is no conductor, everybody has to conduct each other!")

- Provide recordings or video performances of the work, if available. Let students see the "forest" before they concentrate on the "trees".
- Show students how to record rehearsals and listen to themselves immediately afterwards for quick feedback.
- Encourage students to ask the same questions of themselves as we would of a large ensemble. Coax everyone to listen, diagnose, and rehearse on their own. Challenge the group to answer questions while they play, and consider having pre-printed questions to answer after each run-through.

> *"Are we all matching articulation?"*
> *"Are we following the dynamics and expressive marks on the page?"*
> *"Can I hear everyone else in the group?"*
> *"Do I know who has the melody? Is it me?"*
> *"Who am I playing with? Am I in tune with them?"*
> *"Are we playing together?"*

If the answer is "No!" then the group knows something needs to be addressed.

- Let the group know everybody has the right to make a suggestion or ask a question.
- Require everyone in the ensemble to have a pencil. Encourage players to write reminders about what their ensemble-mates play—e.g., "with flute"; "clarinet has ♩♩♩"; "viola has pick-up."
- Help groups regulate their pacing so the flow becomes: Play–Play–Talk rather than Talk–Talk–Play.
- Be creative and exhaustive in seeking appropriate literature. There's much more out there than you think.
- Consider the following sources:

> *Brass*: Robert King Music
> *Woodwind*: Musicians Publications
> *Strings*: Boston Music Company
> *Percussion (including music for percussion and winds)*: Steve Weiss Music
> *For mixed ensembles*: Kjos-*Standards of Excellence Festival Ensembles* (Books 1 and 2) by Chuck Elledge
> and Bruce Pearson, Kendor Music
> *For any ensemble*: Shattinger Music Company, J.W. Pepper, New England Sheet Music
> (For further resources, see the reading list at the end of the chapter.)

- Try independently owned music stores, which often specialize in chamber music and stock more than the large houses do. Some send music on approval, and they often bring crates of music to large conventions, so allow time to browse!

- Check Sibelius.com, an online clearinghouse for web-published music available free or inexpensively.

Instrumental combinations to look for include:

- string quartets
- string ensembles of all shapes and permutations
- flute ensembles (two players and up)
- B♭ clarinet quartets

- mixed clarinet quartet (including a bass)
- saxophone quartet (2 alto, 1 tenor, 1 baritone OR 1 soprano, 1 alto, 1 tenor, 1 baritone)
- woodwind quartet (flute, oboe, clarinet bassoon OR oboe, clarinet, horn, bassoon)
- woodwind quintet
- woodwind choir
- trumpet ensemble (two players and up; quartets especially common)
- horn ensemble (two players and up; quartets especially common)
- trombone ensemble (two players and up; quartets especially common)
- brass quartet (ex. two trumpets, horn, trombone OR two trumpets, two trombones)
- brass quintet
- brass choir (various groupings of brass, often with multiple parts per instrument)
- percussion ensembles (mallet only, non-pitched only, mixed, body and prop percussion)

- Many arrangements come with alternate parts. If not, adapt for your instrumentation: adjust ranges, notate new transpositions, or ask players to transpose (see Table 14.3).

TABLE 14.3 Adapting Instrumentation (Be sure to account for transpositions)

These instruments can substitute for each other's parts	
Flute/Oboe	Violin
Bass Clarinet	Bassoon
Bassoon/Bass Clarinet	Cello/Bass
Clarinet/Soprano saxophone	Trumpet
Mallets	Flute/Oboe/Violin
Tuba	String bass
Trombone/Euphonium	Cello

Figures 14.6, 14.7, 14.8, and 14.9 illustrate set-ups for some of the most common chamber ensembles.

FIGURE 14.6 Brass Quintet

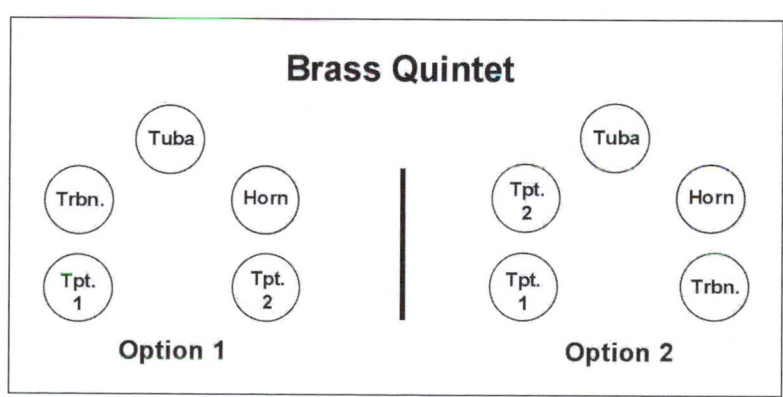

FIGURE 14.7 Woodwind Ensembles Set-ups

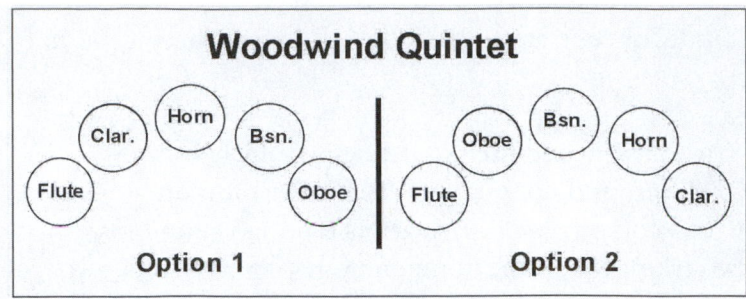

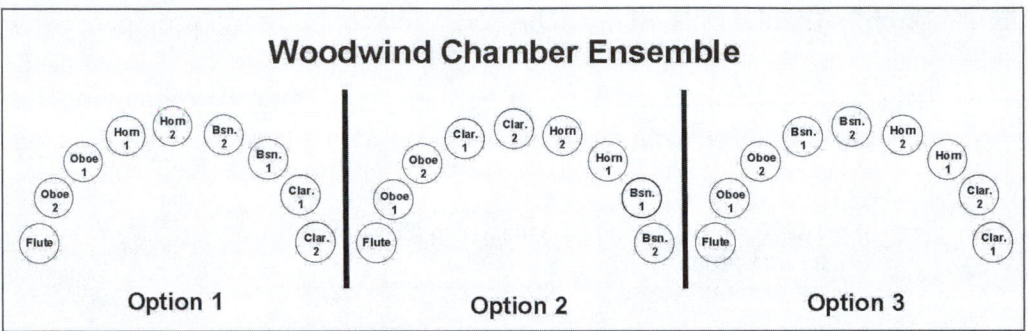

FIGURE 14.8 String Quartet Set-ups

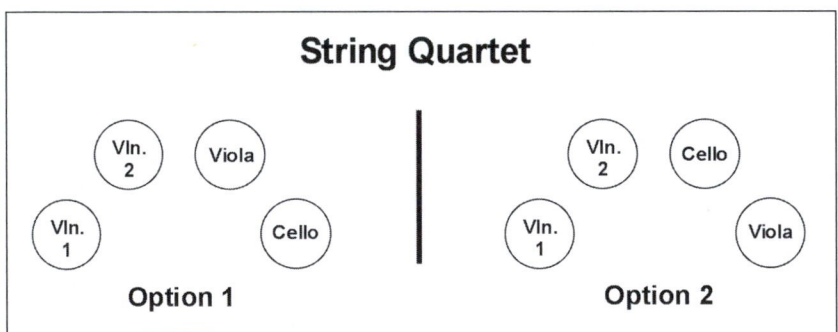

FIGURE 14.9 Saxophone Quartet Set-ups

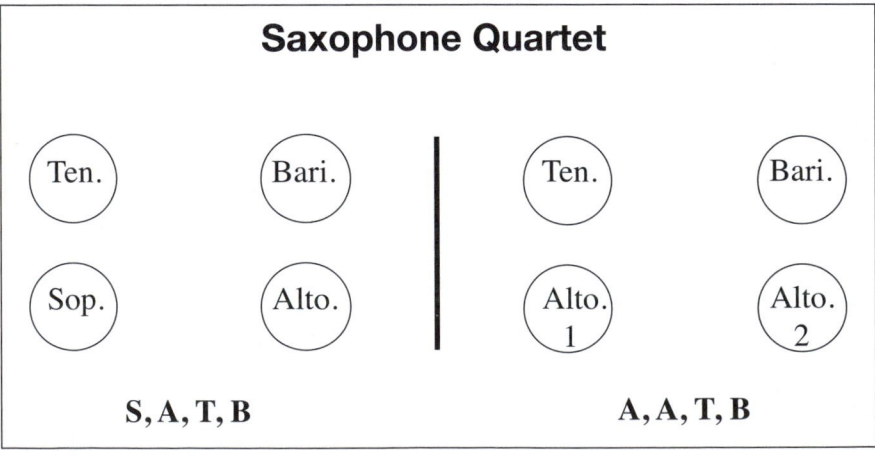

Activities/Assignments for Further Exploration

1. Write a personal philosophy for marching band OR chamber music OR jazz ensemble. What are the educational and musical goals of studying it? What does it offer that other ensembles do not provide?

2. Find repertoire excerpts to practice pit orchestra conducting techniques, such as:

   - passive beats versus active beats
   - the "float and drop" technique
   - marking measures
   - getting out of vamps
   - fade-outs (for transitions)
   - cues for the cast versus cues for the pit.

3. Brainstorm ways to facilitate students working together in chamber groups. In what creative ways can we encourage them to develop interpretations, self-assess their progress, devise their own solutions, and be aware of each other's part while they play?

Further Reading

Marching/Parade Band

Bailey, Wayne, and Thomas Caneva. *The Complete Marching Band Resource Manual: Techniques and Materials for Teaching, Drill Design, and Music Arranging*. Philadelphia, PA: University of Pennsylvania Press, 2003.

Laine, Kristen. *American Band: Music, Dreams, and Coming of Age in the Heartland*. New York: Gotham Books, 2007.

Markworth, Wayne. *The Dynamic Marching Band*. Three Rivers, MI: Accent Publications, 2008.

Raxsdale, Bill. *The Marching Band Director: A Master Planning Guide*. New Berlin, WI: Jenson Publications, 1985.

Ryder, Dan, and Karen Ryder. *Techniques of Marching Band Show Designing*. Austin, TX: Dan Ryder Field Drills, 2005.

Smith, Gary E., and Tom Keck. *The System: Marching Band Methods*. Savoy, IL: Gary Smith, 2007.

Spencer-Pierce, William. *Marching Band Arranging: Methods-Materials-Techniques*. United States: Creative Media Consulting, 2008.

Musical Theater

Laster, James. *So You're the New Musical Director!: An Introduction to Conducting a Broadway Musical*. Lanham, MD: Scarecrow Press, 2001.

Jazz Ensemble

Baker, David. *David Baker's Jazz Pedagogy: A Comprehensive Method of Jazz Education for Teacher and Student*. Van Nuys, CA: Alfred Pub. Co., 1989.

Caniato, Michele. *The Jazz Ensemble Companion: A Guide to Outstanding Big Band Arrangements Selected by Some of the Foremost Jazz Educators*. Lanham, MD: Rowman & Littlefield Education, 2009.

Coker, Jerry. *The Teaching of Jazz*. Rottenburg, N., West Germany: Advance Music, 1989.

Dunscomb, J. Richard, and Willie Hill. *Jazz Pedagogy: The Jazz Educator's Handbook and Resource Guide*. Miami, Fla: Warner Bros. Publications, 2002.

Lawn, Richard. *The Jazz Ensemble Director's Manual: A Handbook of Practical Methods and Materials for the Educator*. Oskaloosa, Iowa: C.L. Barnhouse, 1995.

MENC, the National Association for Music Education (U.S.). *Teaching Jazz: A Course of Study*. Lanham, MD: Rowman & Littlefield Education, 2007.

Miles, Richard B., and Ronald Carter. *Teaching Music Through Performance in Jazz*. Chicago: GIA Publications, 2008.

Chamber Music

Loft, Abram. *How to Succeed in an Ensemble: Reflections on a Life in Chamber Music*. Portland, OR: Amadeus Press, 2003.

Scott, William. *A Conductor's Repertory of Chamber Music: Compositions for Nine to Fifteen Solo Instruments*. Music reference collection, no. 39. Westport, CT: Greenwood Press, 1993.

Secrist-Schmedes, Barbera. *Wind Chamber Music: For Two to Sixteen Winds: An Annotated Guide*. Lanham, MD: Scarecrow Press, 2002.

Winther, Rodney. *An Annotated Guide to Wind Chamber Music: For Six to Eighteen Players*. Donald Hunsberger Wind Library. Miami, FL: Warner Bros. Publications, 2004.

Chapter 15

Special Topics: Motivation

Motivation is a complex branch of human psychology. Unlike other animals, which are motivated by the primal need for survival, humans add to that a complex social existence in which our desire and will to complete a task is influenced by a host of factors[1]—everything from our childhood memories to the current weather. Vernon and Louise Jones (2004) propose the following three components of human motivation:

1. The degree to which someone values the rewards associated with completing the task.
2. The degree to which someone believes they can accomplish a task.
3. The degree to which someone works/participates in an environment conducive to completing the task.

Rewards—Intrinsic and Extrinsic Motivation

Let us begin by focusing on the first factor: the rewards for studying music. In an ideal world, students behave and participate because they care about the study of music. They practice at home, arrive to class on time, focus during rehearsal, and seek additional opportunities, all because they want to, and because they have, at least to some degree, an interest in music. They are *intrinsically motivated* because studying music is its own reward. The reality, of course, is that students are not always intrinsically motivated for instrumental music study. They are always motivated to do *something*, just not necessarily what we will teach in the classroom.

Types of Extrinsic Motivators

In the absence of intrinsic motivation for musical study, it is possible to rely on external factors to induce motivation. When students are motivated by tangible or intangible rewards, they are said to be extrinsically motivated. Grades, prizes, trophies, certificates, tokens, points, verbal or gestural praise, special privileges and other rewards for doing well are examples of extrinsic motivators.

Extrinsic motivation is often manufactured through competition, nicely summarized by the phrase, "Competition breeds excellence." Seen through the guise of behaviorism, it creates external rewards and reinforcement that motivates people to perform better—whether it be for the thrill of competing, the prizes, the prestige, or the pride that accompany success. We can use nearly any measurable thing—intangible or tangible—as long as the stimulus it provides has this effect.

Some examples of extrinsic motivators are:

- Sticker chart of accomplishments (e.g., coming to lessons, having all your equipment)
- Awards given out in front of peers (e.g., trophies, certificates, and pins)
- Displaying group awards to the rest of the school
- Special privileges (e.g., choose the movie for bus trips, choose the last piece to be rehearsed/sightread)
- Having student accomplishments announced during school-wide announcements
- Acknowledging things that students do correctly
- Praising students
- Token economies (students earn points or "music tokens" for good behavior and accomplishment, which can be turned in later for privileges or small prizes).

Extrinsic motivation programs that use tokens are a favorite of economists and educational foundations. In several schools in New York City and Dallas, for example, students are paid for doing well on Advanced Placement exams. In some schools in Washington, D.C., checks are distributed for good grades, attendance, and behavior. Much of the initial data shows success. An increased number of New York students took Advanced Placement tests after the program was instituted; in Dallas, a higher rate of students enrolled in college.[2]

Debating the Use of Extrinsic Motivators

One of the major criticisms of extrinsic motivators is that they undermine *intrinsic* motivation. Alfie Kohn, the author of *Punished by Rewards: The Trouble With Gold Stars, Incentive Plans, A's, Praise, and Other Bribes*, warns, "The more rewards are used, the more they seem to be needed. The more often I promise you a goody to do what I want, the more I cause you to respond to, and even to require, these goodies."[3] Though the external item may fuel motivation in the near-term, eventually the need is habitual, stifling an intrinsic desire to learn.

Research by renowned psychologist Edward L. Deci suggests that students unfortunately become conditioned to receiving rewards for learning, and their interest in learning without the rewards decreases.[4] Psychologists have also shown a direct correlation between rewards and how much students dislike what they are rewarded for. For example, one study showed that third-graders eventually spent less time reading if they were rewarded for doing so with tokens such as toys and candy.[5] In this way, schools may condition students to dislike learning the very subjects they teach (Edwards, 21). The reason may be because children often resist being controlled, and they can sense that extrinsic rewards are attempts to do this, even if the rewards are pleasurable.[6]

A counterargument maintains it is unfair and impractical to expect students to learn all the time merely because they want to, or because they know it is good for them. Educational psychologist Ennio Cipani writes:

> According to that logic, one should not need special diets, programs, or incentives to lose weight, exercise more, or stop smoking, drinking, speeding on the highways, leaving work early, being inaccurate on their tax returns, having unprotected sex, and so forth.[7]

Cipani examines research that show student motivation decreases after extrinsic motivators have been removed. He counters that the control groups in these studies—i.e., the students who received no rewards—*also* decreased over time, sometimes more dramatically than the drop-off in the experimental group (the one that received rewards).

If one chooses to use extrinsic motivators, consider using rewards that relate to the activity. This is the flip side of "logical consequences." Instead of offering candy or money, find music-related items:

- Sheet music of popular music for students who complete method book assignments early.
- An opportunity to solo with the band or conduct during rehearsal for those who make honor bands.
- Reeds and special valve oils for students who care for their instruments, arrive prepared, and help keep the classroom organized

Using Verbal Praise as an Extrinsic Motivator

Rather than tangible rewards, verbal praise can also be effective (and cost-efficient!), though admittedly research is inconclusive whether it increases or decreases intrinsic motivation (Kohn, 98). However, praise is a powerful reinforcer. Consider the following strategies when using verbal praise:

1. Praise specific actions rather than general qualities—"John, you phrased that passage beautifully" is more motivating than "John, you're a great player." Indeed, the more specific the praise the more likely the student will focus on the content of our praise rather than simply on our approval (Kohn, 108). Recognize challenges that were difficult to achieve, and offer comments and suggestions for further improvement.

    EXAMPLES

    "John: Bravo for tackling a very difficult solo. You made some great improvements in your technique, and I appreciate the dynamic contrast in the opening section. For the next session you should work on making the articulation cleaner . . ."
    "Sarah: Thank you for being more attentive in class. I definitely saw a difference this week, and I appreciate the effort. Next week let's try to get even better, especially between pieces."

2. Give only sincere praise—Most people, even young children, quickly sense if praise is designed to control their behavior rather than express sincere and specific appreciation (Kohn, 109). If we praise minimal effort, we devalue significant effort.[8]
3. Praise in a way that avoids competition—Research shows that phrases such as "You performed the best in the class at . . ." undermine intrinsic motivation (Kohn, 110).
4. Some praise is better done in private than in public—Research suggests that public praise of a single person may weaken motivation of the individual and the entire group: (a) It implies that person has "won" a competition; (b) It does not improve the student's standing with the group, and in fact may diminish it; and (c) It can be perceived by the group as an attempt to control their behavior (Kohn, 110). On a student-by-student basis, consider whether public or private praises will have the best effect.

On the Power of Encouragement

Perhaps even more important than praise is constant encouragement, something essential for self-confidence and self-esteem. Students need to know we believe in them and in their ability to succeed.

Dreikurs believes misbehavior is directly caused by low confidence:

Every misbehaving or deficient child is discouraged. As long as he has confidence in his ability, he will use constructive means to find a place in the home or in school . . . Discouragement is the root of mistaken approaches.[9]

It is important to recognize the crucial difference between encouragement and praise. *Encouragement* expresses our belief that a student will succeed in a task, though they have not yet done so. It thus boosts self-esteem, which in turn strengthens motivation. Encouragement should be used liberally and consistently. *Praise* expresses our approval for a task that has already been completed. It boosts self-esteem and confidence as long as the student believes he has achieved something worthwhile.

Developing, Strengthening, and Using Intrinsic Motivation

Intrinsically motivated students participate in an activity because they perceive that it directly satisfies their needs. They consider the rewards of the learning activity, and not arbitrary prizes, as valuable in and of themselves.[10] For these reasons we recommend using extrinsic motivation in moderation, and working to move towards intrinsic motivation.

Here are some strategies:

Show Connections
Students are often unaware how their school studies relate to their personal interests. Whether it is the result of boredom, previous school experience, peer influence, or the image of education as depicted in popular culture, students become conditioned to assume that school has no connection to their other interests in life.

- Draw a parallel between musical and other arts, e.g.:

  - the shifting timbres of a musical passage compared to different shades of color one sees in paintings of a sunrise or sunset. Bring in examples (paintings or photos) to make the point more tangible.
  - themes in a piece of music compared to characters in a play or movie
  - trills, percussion effects, fortepianos, and other gestures compared to special effects in a movie
  - projection and "selling the character" in music and drama.

- Draw analogies between music and sports, e.g.:

  - blocking for a running back $\Longleftrightarrow$ playing the accompaniment
  - preparation with a tennis racquet $\Longleftrightarrow$ preparation with a mallet/bow/breath
  - inhale/exhale for karate chop $\Longleftrightarrow$ inhale/exhale for a forte accent
  - just like in football, don't be "offsides" $\Longleftrightarrow$ listen to the "snap count" and play together!
  - handing off a musical line $\Longleftrightarrow$ baton exchange: it must be smooth!

- Use analogies and comparisons with other types of music, including pop music, soundtracks, and video games scores.
- Design activities to resonate with student interests—There is no shame in occasionally programming literature students are already familiar with, whether it is pop arrangements, movie medleys, or music that sounds like them. Instead of merely allowing the group to let their musical hair down, do not

jettison the more subtle aspects of phrasing, balance, intonation, etc. By holding students accountable on repertoire they are intrinsically motivated to play we develop an expectation about how music—any music—is made.

Consider instituting a "show and tell" during which students bring in their favorite music and share it with the class. The crucial point is to insist that students speak musically and critically. Prompt a dialogue with the class; try questions such as: "Why do you like this music? Does your interest come from similarities or differences to other music? What are the moments that are predictable? Unexpected? " Do not judge their interests, but also do not allow them to offer generic answers such as "Because I like it," or "Because it's cool." Push them to answer: Why? What *specifically* do you like or dislike?

Create Variety
Intrinsic motivation intensifies when students perceive a task to be unique. For example:

- rotate warmup activities to work on different skills; demand more from the ones already learned (e.g., new scale patterns, more complex rhythms, an alternate chorale, etc.)
- find repertoire that challenges students technically and musically
- look for new, unusual, and innovative fundraisers.

Give Students Ownership
We can invest students with ownership for musical and non-musical aspects of the program.

Musical
- Give students a voice in interpretative decisions. In rehearsal, for example, experiment with multiple ways to phrase a melody, and elicit students to suggest their own. If students own the interpretation they are more likely to participate in its success.
- Rotate solos and/or first parts so that students who work hard but are not the fastest to advance have the chance to shine in rehearsal and performance.
- Program student compositions and feature student soloists.

Non-Musical
Elect band officers; give students leadership roles in the day-to-day operations of the class.

Challenge Students to Succeed
As much as students complain that they do not want work to do, the reality is that problem solving is motivational. Psychologists call this effect *cognitive disequilibrium*, a natural motivation to solve problems and understand how the world works (Burden, 147). Music teachers can harness this type of intrinsic motivation as long as they do not confuse healthy cognitive disequilibrium with sheer difficulty. Literature that is far beyond students' technical abilities will likely demoralize students, not motivate them.

Challenge Systems for Seating

A common motivational strategy is to allow students to challenge players seated ahead of them in one-on-one competitions for advancement. Although this motivates a certain type of student, it also: (a) turns the collaborative, communal aspect of music-making into an every-man-for-himself arena; (b) may diminish student motivation; and (c) can cause animosity between students and teachers. In this system one student's triumph is unavoidably associated with another's personal and public failure (Bollinger, 34). Though it is legitimate to adjust seating assignments based on student improvement or regression during the year, we recommend basing it on scheduled playing tests for the entire ensemble rather than guerrilla-warfare playing challenges.

Belief: Success Breeds Success

It should be no surprise that in the long run students enjoy activities at which they succeed and dislike ones at which they fail. In other words, providing challenges is only part of motivation. Students need and thrive upon success. In fact, research tells us that students learn more when they complete tasks (Jones and Jones 2004, 195), assuming the tasks are not *too* easy.

There are many ways to instill the feeling of success:

- Play at least some music that is easy enough for the ensemble to sound good on in a short amount of time. Initially choosing some music that has more block scoring will help weaker students with rhythm.
- Instead of leaving every section unfinished until the next rehearsal, practice a section of music over and over until it is correct.
- Give performances outside of the classroom when the group genuinely sounds good.
- Give a performance to much younger children. The seniority of the older students makes them feel successful.
- Have students perform for one another when they have reached mastery levels.
- Use the concept of limits to give students a greater chance of success when creating composition projects and playing improvisation exercises (See Chapter 4).

Activities/Assignments for Further Exploration

1. Identify examples of extrinsic and intrinsic motivators outside the music classroom. In your experience, which are effective and which are not?

2. Debate the merits of the following two statements:

   "Extrinsic motivators are effective and a natural part of life."
   "Extrinsic motivators do more harm than good in the long run."

3. What was the best compliment you ever received? What made it so satisfying?

4. Besides the topics discussed in this chapter, can you think of other factors that affect motivation? Which of these can we influence?

Further Reading

Deci, Edward L., and Richard M. Ryan. *Intrinsic Motivation and Self-Determination in Human Behavior* (Perspectives in Social Psychology). New York: Plenum, 1985.

Kohn, Alfie. *Punished by Rewards: The Trouble with Gold Stars, Incentive Plans, A's, Praise, and Other Bribes.* Boston: Houghton Mifflin Co., 1999.

Laming, D. R. J. *Understanding Human Motivation: What Makes People Tick?* Malden, MA: Blackwell Pub., 2004.

Unit 3

Administrative Issues

Chapter 16

Recruiting, Organizing, and Starting the Band and Orchestra

To Guide Your Reading

What factors should we consider when deciding when to begin offering the study of instruments?

What are the advantages and disadvantages of starting students in Grades 3–5 versus Grade 6?

How can exposure and recruiting concerts familiarize potential students with instruments?

In what ways can we communicate with parents and teachers thought the recruiting process?

What factors should we consider when determining whether to initially offer a core instrumentation or a majority of all instruments?

What are some strategies we can use to control and balance our instrumentation?

What is the purpose of musical aptitude testing?

Describe the Instrumental Fitting Process? What is an effective way to run it so we efficiently match students with the instrument that is best for them?

How does one deal with limited resources of instruments?

What elements should we consider when choosing a method book for beginning band and orchestra?

What are the advantages of using "traditional" method books? Or "sound–to–symbol" method books?

What are the "habits of musicianship"?

How do we successfully switch a student to a new instrument?

What strategies can be used to retain students once they have began studying an instrument?

Building Programs from the Bottom Up

When observing a successful high school program it is easy to forget that the groundwork for their achievement is done in the elementary and middle schools. These programs are often called "feeders," though this is something of a pejorative misnomer. Elementary and middle school programs do not exist to "feed" or sustain "higher" programs. They are simply an initial and crucial step in a sequential process that continues through high school and beyond.

The beginning levels are when we shape the good habits we expect students to have as they mature. How many times have directors wished their students had a better knowledge of history and theory; sang regularly, and without reticence; showed a keen awareness of pitch, etc? If these are not instilled throughout their early education, they may never be. A student who has never been asked to sing during an instrumental lesson or rehearsal will likely resist it in high school.

But before any instrumental music learning can commence, students must enroll in the program. Beginning orchestra and band classes are typically not required, unlike, say, mathematics or history classes. As a result, we must proactively attract participants. With so many activities competing for young people's attention—in-school athletics, dance classes, karate, Little League, video games, the internet etc.—we cannot assume students and parents will discover the pleasures and benefits of music education on their own. In addition, renting, purchasing, and maintaining an instrument is an expensive venture to which parents must be willing to commit.

The recruiting process has dual roles: First, it should assign students an instrument that gives them the greatest chance of long-term success. Second, it is the best opportunity to directly build balanced instrumentation and insure that future years enjoy the same. Having poor balance at the beginning level will reap havoc at the middle and high school levels.

When Should the Study of Band and Orchestra Instruments Begin?

How early should instrumental music study begin? When we see great child performers in music, dance, athletics, etc., should we then conclude that one of the secrets to creating successful musicians is to begin as early as possible? Why not start practicing in early childhood, pushing our offspring to become the next Yo-Yo Ma while they tote around an instrument twice their size? Research that shows it takes 10,000 hours of practice to truly become an expert in any subject would seem to encourage an extra head-start.[1] Yet although musical study can practically begin in the womb, most young children lack the maturity and physical characteristics to begin instrumental study, and indeed, pushing them to take up an instrument before they are ready will severely limit their progress and perhaps poison future success.

Most school programs begin band and orchestra study between Grades 4–6. The argument for Grade 4 is similar to the "head-start" argument: Begin early and get a jump on other programs who wait. For string instruments there is some logic to this since instruments are available in a variety of sizes to suit a variety of hand sizes (e.g., half size, three-quarter size, etc.). But band instruments are generally "one size fits all," and so there may be diminishing returns to starting in third or fourth grade, particularly for smaller students. For example, students with petite fingers will have difficulty covering the tone holes of a clarinet. Others will have trouble reaching the sixth and seventh slide positions on trombone. In any case, research has overwhelmingly shown that students who start in the sixth grade perform at the same level as those who start earlier by the time they all reach the seventh or eighth grades.[2]

Some string programs begin the year before the band to get a head-start. Fourth graders may choose a string instrument simply because they would rather not wait another year to play a band instrument. But once the same students have the opportunity to start in band a year later, first-year frustrations and the beckoning of a shiny new instrument entice some to switch. On the other hand, initial success and reluctance to buy or rent another instrument may discourage new band recruits. Either way, orchestra and band enrollments are often affected by factors other than what is most appropriate for students musically and physically.

In her study, "Influence of Starting Grade and School Organization on Enrollment and Retention in Beginning Instrumental Music," Linda Hartley offers the following comparisons between programs that start in third, fourth, and fifth grades and those that start in sixth grade (Hartley, 305):

Frequency of Rehearsals/Lessons

- Programs that meet daily have higher retention rates than those that do not. Daily meetings are typically not possible in fourth and fifth grades since music classes tend to be weekly pull-outs or electives, rather than a regular part of the schedule.
- Some research suggests that students starting in fourth and fifth grades become more easily frustrated and drop-out at higher rates than sixth-grade beginners.

Retention Rate

- Though other factors come into play, overall retention and long-run ability (two to three years after starting) do not seem to be affected by the starting grade of instruction.
- Attrition rates seem highest when students switch buildings, as when they move from elementary school to middle school, and from middle school to high school. This highlights how important it is for directors in the higher grades to make early contact with students to build good relationships and help them make the transition (Hartley, 315).

Competition with Other Activities

- Some programs begin in fourth and fifth grades to avoid competition with other activities that crowd the field by sixth grade. The evidence supporting the effectiveness of this tactic is inconclusive (Hartley, 314).

Building a Balanced Instrumentation

What are the ideal numbers for a beginning instrumental class? We cannot offer absolutes, but use the percentages in Figures 16.1, 16.2, 16.3, and 16.4 as a guide.

Keep in mind the following:

1. Despite our best efforts, some students will not continue beyond the first year.
2. With our guidance, a percentage of students will switch to oboe, bassoon, bass clarinet, saxophone, horn, tuba, percussion, and bass (depending, of course, on the core of instruments we offer for beginners).

To further understand why we must carefully plan our instrumentation we need to take a look at the significant differences between the way beginning, intermediate, and advanced music is scored. Music written for beginning ensembles has only three or four voice parts, so the heavy doubling that is common often hides instrumentation problems. But as the music's grade levels increase, the harmonies, textures, and orchestration becomes more complex. By high school, the music has more than three times as many

FIGURE 16.1 Recommended Percentages for Recruiting a Large Range of Band Instruments

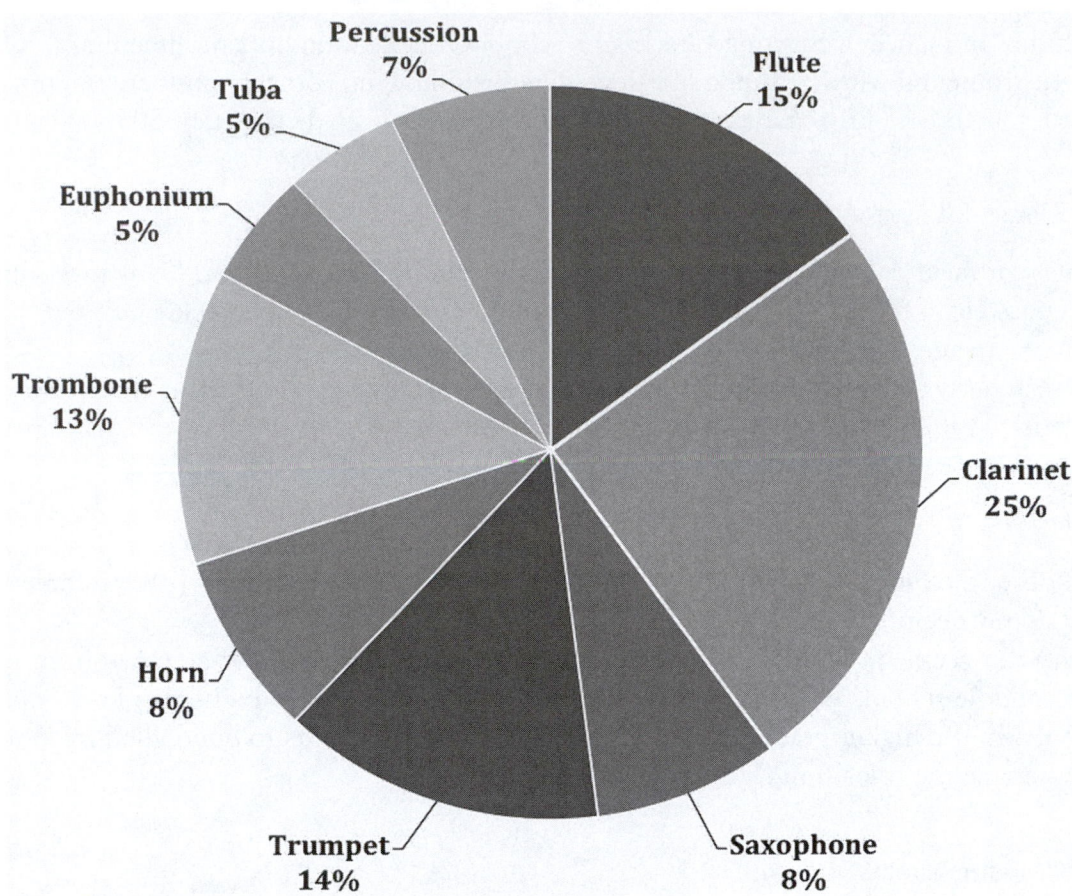

FIGURE 16.2 Recommended Percentages for Recruiting a "Core" of Band Instruments

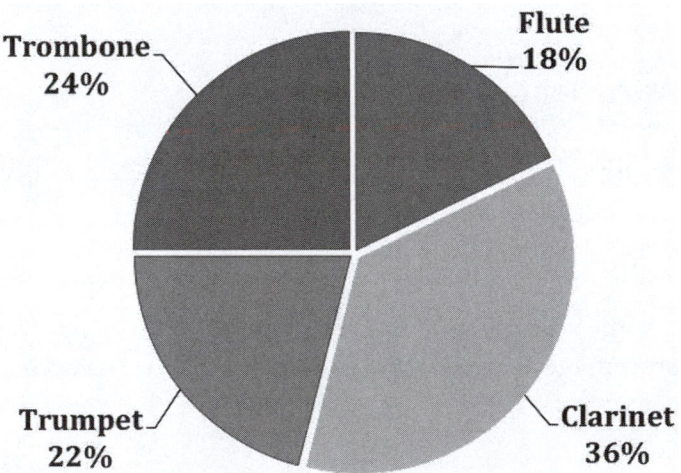

FIGURE 16.3 Recommended Percentages for Recruiting a "Core" of String Instruments

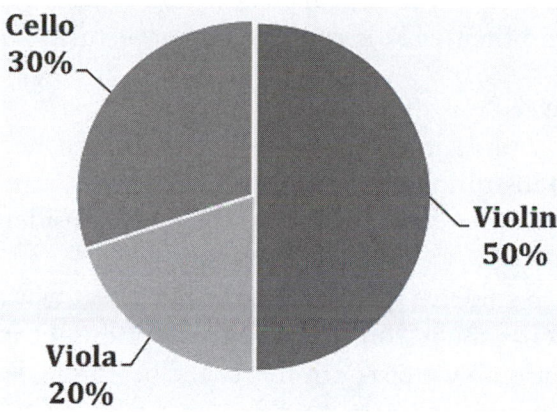

FIGURE 16.4 Recommended Percentages for Recruiting All String Instruments

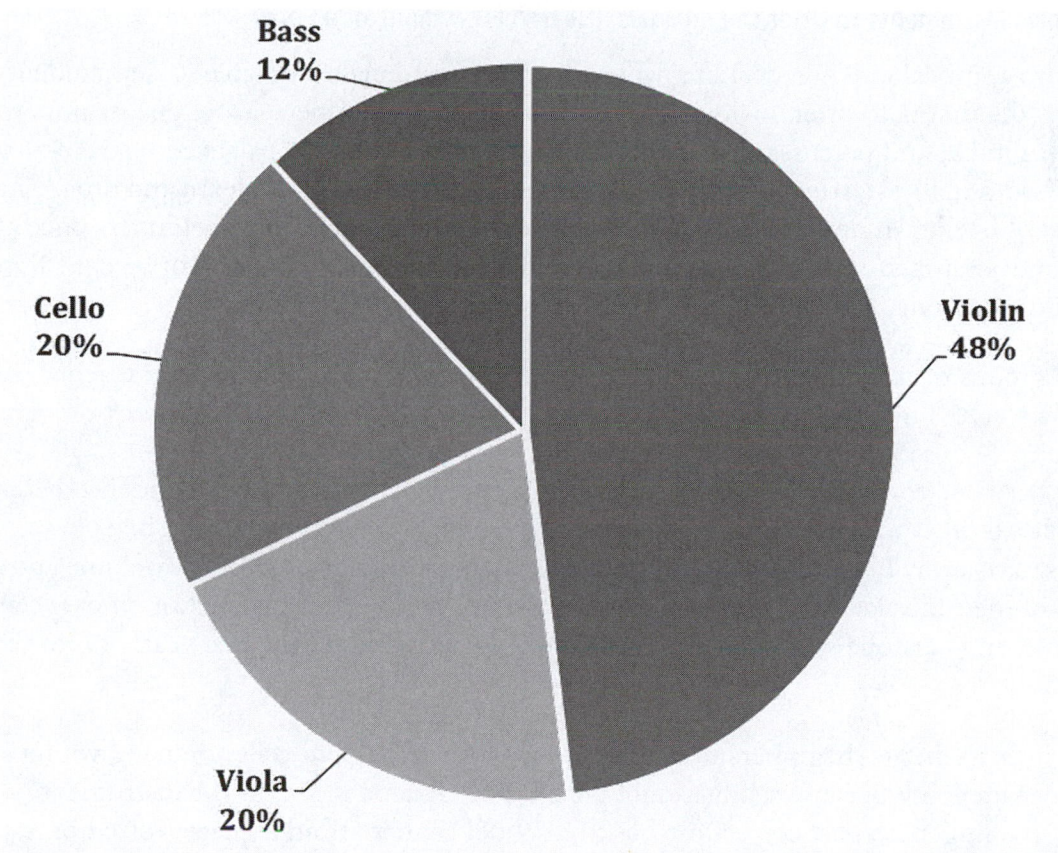

parts to be covered, and at this point early instrumentation imbalances are exacerbated. Trying to perform a mature musical work with say, one horn, is akin to using one actor to stage a play that has four roles.

Clearly, recruiting new players has a long term effect on students' musical experiences, as unbalanced ensembles will spend an inordinate amount of time compensating for problems caused by having too few of one instrument, and way too many of another. Consider a band program that has three elementary schools. Two oboes in each band could forward six oboes to the sixth grade band; six percussionists in each band leave the middle school band with a whopping 18 players. But as long as schools collectively have a balanced instrumentation there is leeway for imbalances within an individual school.

Effective recruiters understand their work is part of a bigger picture. They:

- see themselves as a team player
- communicate with other beginning level teachers to insure their collective instrumentation does not create an overload of certain instruments
- strive to create a balanced instrumentation for their group and consider the implications for groups at subsequent levels
- take the time to carefully help students choose an instrument that works best for them
- do not allow everyone to choose the instrument he wants without regard to maintaining balance
- understand that instrumentation must be controlled at the beginning level for ensembles to run properly at the intermediate and advanced levels
- keep a spreadsheet that tracks instrumentation across the distinct for each grade level so trends and concerns are highlighted before they become unmanageable.

Choosing Which Instruments to Offer to Beginners: (Nearly) Everything, or a Core?

There are two approaches when deciding which instruments to make available to new students. For band instruments, the first is to offer a wide variety, including: flute, clarinet, saxophone, trumpet, trombone, baritone horn, tuba, and percussion. This allows the teacher to create a balanced instrumentation across the board. Additionally, starting all of these instruments allows everyone to learn and progress at the same pace instead of having students later switch to new instruments and become beginners once again.

The second approach streamlines the number of instruments to a small core—e.g., flute, clarinet, trumpet, and trombone. The reasoning behind this approach is as follows:

1. Limited groups of instruments mean fewer fingerings and embouchure-types a teacher has to simultaneously teach. This is especially important for districts that do not provide for homogeneous pull-out lessons.
2. Teacher has time to observe students' work habits, musicianship, and independence before deciding who is placed on especially challenging instruments such as French horn and oboe.
3. Teachers have a way to control the numbers of popular instruments, such as saxophone and percussion.
4. Because of their physical size, expense, and limited availability, the introduction of bass clarinet, tenor saxophone, and baritone saxophone can be delayed until the end of the first year, or into the second or third year.

For string instruments, beginners usually start on violin, viola, and cello. Starting young students on bass can be challenging because many cannot physically manage the size of the instrument or the stretch required by the fingers to play correct pitches. If a school cannot afford a quarter-sized bass or smaller, a more unorthodox option is to take a full size cello and retune the strings to match that of a string bass, only an octave higher. This enables the student to stand while playing and use string bass fingerings.

Caveat: Since the shape of the cello's body is different from that of the bass, students will need to relearn proper playing techniques when switching to an actual bass.

To retune a cello to a string bass one octave higher:

- retune the G string up a whole step (to A)
- retune the C string up a major third (to E)

- keep the D string on D
- retune the A string down a whole step (to G)

> It is best to have the following string instrument sizes in the school inventory:
>
> Elementary school—quarter, half, and three-quarter sizes
> Middle school—half, three-quarter, and full sizes
> High school—full sizes.

Using Auditions After Recruiting the Core

Starting with a core of instruments can be a first step to preventing gluts of popular instruments—especially percussion. Some programs unintentionally create an artificial divide between those who cannot play mallets ("drummers") and those who can ("percussionists"), a distinction that intensifies as students mature and entrench their "specializations."

Instead after recruiting a core that does not include percussion, announce that a certain number of percussion slots will be offered at the end of the first semester, and that students who are already studying piano, string, or wind instruments may audition.

This strategy can also be used to choose saxophonists, another instrument that is popular with students well out of proportion to its need in a concert band. Since clarinet to saxophone is a natural transfer, consider only offering clarinet at the onset, with the understanding that these students will have the opportunity to audition to switch to saxophone later in the year.

Both of these strategies require a bit of planning. For the first concert, consider bringing in more advanced students to cover the saxophone and percussion parts. Also, check with the local music dealer to confirm that students can transfer payments on a rent–to–own instrument (i.e., so a clarinetist can switch to saxophone with little or no penalty).

Whether one chooses to start a core or a nearly complete instrumentation, the most important thing is to create a balanced group that supports the needs of the older ensembles.

The Process of Recruiting

Unfortunately, we cannot simply announce that band and orchestra are starting and wait for students to arrive at our doorstep. We must undertake a recruiting process during which music teachers, students, and parents gather information and use it to make an informed decision.

What Students Need to Know

- Instruments available from which they may choose
- Instruments that match their preferences
- Benefits of participating
- Responsibilities of participating (practice time, etc.)

What Parents Need to Know

- Benefits of allowing their child to participate
- Financial commitment
- What they must do to help their child succeed

What Music Teachers Need to Know

- How many students wish to participate
- How many new students the school's resources can support
- The ideal balance of instrumentation given the number of students interested
- Each student's musical aptitude
- Each student's preference and aptitude for a specific instrument

The Eight Steps of the Recruiting Process

The recruiting process described below is designed to achieve the above goals systematically and effectively. The steps are as follows:

1. Exposure concerts
2. Recruiting concert
3. Letter home to parents
4. Parent informational meeting
5. Aptitude testing (before or at the beginning of the instrument fittings)
6. Classroom teacher interviews
7. Instrumental fittings and assignments
8. Follow-up letter to parents (immediately after instruments have been assigned).

1. Exposure Concerts

The first step in recruiting is to "hook" students on the idea of studying an instrument. Concerts and presentations throughout the school year help familiarize students with us, the instruments, and the program in general. If we develop positive relationships with the students early on, the more trusting and eager the students will be when it comes time to choose an instrument.

There are several types of exposure concerts that can be used throughout the school year:

- in-class presentations with your current students
- inviting younger students to regular concerts
- concerts during school time (e.g., in-school assemblies—have a high school ensemble perform to model the characteristic sounds of each instrument)
- student chamber group performances, particularly of instruments we need to emphasize (e.g., tuba and string bass)
- performances by local professional chamber groups.

For those schools that offer recorder in general music classes, the general music teacher can be a wonderful advocate during the recruiting process.[3]

2. Recruiting Concerts

Two weeks prior to the fitting process, make a formal presentation to potential new students. At this point they should learn about the instrumental program, what instruments are available, what is expected of them once they begin studying an instrument, and how and when the upcoming fitting process will take place.

Perhaps the most powerful recruiting tools available are current instrumental students. They enable potential students to make a real connection to successful students close to their own age (and who may also be older siblings and friends). The recruits also get to see how quickly the first year ensemble members are able to make music—less than a year after beginning study.

Also enlist the help of high school musicians or the current first-year students to make brief presentations about their instruments. This helps recruits choose an instrument based on what it sounds like rather than simply what it looks like. Presentations should include a brief explanation of how the instrument works, its musical role in the ensemble, and a short musical example. Familiar music from television, movies, and pop artists can be an excellent tool to excite students about perennially less-popular instruments such as the viola, string bass, tuba, and trombone.

During the demonstration, exploit the distinctive qualities of each instrument. For example, have your viola section stand and play a beautiful line that shows their tone and richness. Then repeat the section with everyone, pointing out how much that viola tone adds to the overall section. The ultimate goal is to match students with an instrument that instills a desire to make that particular sound well.

However, the presentation is also the ideal time to lay the groundwork for instrumentation limitations: every instrument is important, but only so many people can play each one. Use football or baseball teams as an analogy: A baseball team can't have 10 pitchers, and a football team can't have 12 quarterbacks. By the end of the concert, potential students should know the name, sound, and role of every member of the team.

Also remember that the quarterback doesn't have to be a boy! Though the cause and depth of instrumental gender association is disputed (Fortney, *A Study of Middle School Student's Band Choices*, 29), trumpet, trombones, and drums are generally considered masculine, while flute, clarinet, and violin are considered feminine. (Saxophone and cello tend to be gender neutral.) We can thwart these common associations by having boys demonstrate upper woodwinds and strings and girls demonstrate low brass and percussion (Bazan, *An Investigation of the Instrumental Selection Processes Used by Directors*, 19).

In some cases you may want to emphasize, de-emphasize, or even omit instruments in the presentation. For example, if trombones have been particularly unpopular in the past, make a special pitch to show how much fun it instrument is. If flute players always seem to recruit themselves, perhaps extra advertising is unnecessary.

3. The Letter Home

After the final exposure and recruiting concert, send a letter home with the students explaining the beginning music program. It should include detailed information about participating, as well as what will be happening in the future with regards to the fitting process. Here is a sample letter:

Dear Prospective Band Parent,

Today your child attended a band and string ensemble assembly. Its main purpose was to introduce students to the instruments that will be taught in next year's Elementary Instrumental Music program. As a parent, you will play a very important role in the future success of your child's music making, should he/she decide to join the program.

With this in mind, I would like to take this opportunity to invite you and your family to Smithtown Elementary's annual Band and Orchestra Open House, on Monday, May 17, at 7:30pm.

Studying music through learning an instrument is a uniquely rewarding experience— many of its benefits are well-celebrated: the discipline it develops through practicing; the skills of teamwork it develops through rehearsing and performing with others; the sense of pride it engenders after a performance of great music; and the opportunity to discover one's own culture and those of others through a creative medium shared by nearly every culture, religion, and country.

We believe music is one of society's greatest inventions. It is a form of artistry that is both scientific and aesthetic. It can simultaneously be studied like a science and enjoyed as an entertainment. Listening to music is an important part of its appreciation, but PERFORMING it is even more meaningful, and we're proud that Smithtown Elementary school supports these programs.

In fact, you and your child may have already decided, "Yes, I want to study an instrument!" But we realize you may have many questions: Which instrument should my child play? How much of a financial commitment will I have to make? Where can I rent or purchase an instrument? How and when are the lessons and rehearsals scheduled?

Before the end of the school year we will test or "audition" each student who has returned the attached sign-up form by June 10. Our goal is to match each student with the instrument that gives him/her the greatest chance for success. In addition, our goal is to develop a balanced instrumentation, which is essential to create a superior ensemble and a positive experience for everyone.

The band instruments available to study are:

- Clarinet, Trumpet, and Trombone (we will need many of these instruments)
- Flute, Alto Saxophone, French Horn, Euphonium, Tuba, and Percussion (a limited number of each of these will be selected).

The string instruments available to study are:

- Violin, Viola, Cello, String Bass.

I hope you will join us in the Band Room at 7:30pm on May 17. Refreshments will be served, and you'll have the opportunity to hear performances by some of our current students in the 4th, 7th, and 10th grades!

If you have any questions, please feel free to contact me either by email or phone.

Musically yours,

Mr. Tom Johnson
Band and Orchestra Director
Smithtown Elementary School

Overview of the Smithtown Elementary Instrumental Music Program

The Three Parts of the Program

1. Daily individual practice (6 days per week, 30 minutes per day).
2. One group lesson weekly during school.
3. Concert Band rehearsals twice-weekly during school.

Student Responsibilities

1. Practice for 30 minutes 6 days/week.
2. Treat their instrument, lesson book, and music with care and respect.
3. Attend all lessons and rehearsals on time and properly prepared.
4. Use a positive "can do" attitude.

Parent Responsibilities

1. Provide an instrument in good working order.
2. Be encouraging and supportive.
3. Help child to plan ahead for practice time. Help them set a schedule and stick with it.
4. Verify and sign the practice sheet the night before a lesson.

Music Teacher Responsibilities

1. I will teach students proper ways to handle and care for their instruments.
2. I will teach students the proper ways to play their instrument.
3. I will provide students with information about various aspects of music history, music theory, and performance practice.
4. I will help every student become the best player he/she can be while developing his/her passion and love of music.
5. I will provide opportunities for students to perform in individual, small group, and large group settings.
6. I will help students create, perform, appreciate, and critique music.
7. I will encourage students to find the beauty in music and to interpret it in expressive ways.

Sign Up Sheet for Instrumental Music Program

Fill out the top portion <u>only</u> and return to your classroom teacher <u>by June 10th</u>

Student's Name: _____

Parent's Name: _____

Phone:_____

Address: _____

Classroom Teacher: _____

My child currently takes piano lessons_____. Number of years: _____

We own the following instruments: _____

Is this instrument currently in use?_____

All late sheets will be put on a waiting list.

<u>Please do NOT write below here – for teacher use only.</u>

This will be completed by the teacher and student together.

Flute	Clarinet	Saxophone	Trumpet	French Horn
Trombone	Euphonium	Tuba	Percussion	

1st choice _____

2nd choice_____

3rd choice _____

(We will use this scoring sheet to help choose the best instrument for each student.)

4. Parent Informational Meeting

At the open house, be sure to outline the advantages of learning an instrument and performing music. It is important that parents understand that participating carries challenges and rewards: that, yes, it is a subject which involves discipline, teamwork, and creativity, but that it also teaches lifelong skills; that it allows students to balance their core classes with a field that demands artistry and self-expression; that it offers a type of education no other area can duplicate; and that anyone can participate, grow, and benefit from participation, regardless of their background and aptitude.

As with the exposure concerts, an open house is a fantastic opportunity to showcase current students of all ages. Many directors also invite a representative from a local music store to bring demonstration instruments and explain rent–to–own programs (but be sure to research your school's policy on working with local businesses).

5. Aptitude Testing

Aptitude testing is a powerful way to identify the strengths and weaknesses of potential music students. The results help us guide beginners towards a suitable instrument and provide insight about how best to teach them. They also direct our recruiting towards the students who need our encouragement, because there may be little relationship between musical aptitude and positive attitudes about music (Nierman and Veak, 1997, 387.) Contrary to what one might believe, students do not naturally gravitate towards activities in which they have high aptitude. As many as 50 percent of high-aptitude students are never identified as such during their school careers, never realize they have talent, and never pursue musical study (Gordon, *Music Aptitude and Related Tests*, 5). How many great violists, composers, and theorists are simply never given the necessary encouragement? Whereas older students will likely identify themselves through their self-motivated musical achievements, younger students rarely have that opportunity, and in these cases our personal attention and invitations can make the difference (Gordon, 6).

Music Aptitude versus Achievement

It is important to understand the difference between musical aptitude and musical achievement. Aptitude is a measure of one's potential to learn. Achievement, in contrast, is a measure of what one has actually learned. Technically speaking, one cannot achieve beyond one's aptitude, though one can fall short of fulfilling its promise. Though it has been long-debated, most researchers agree that aptitude is formed by a combination of innate abilities (i.e., heredity) and environmental influences (e.g., exposure to music at an early age). But what they do not agree on is which factor is more important (Gordon, *Introduction to Research*, 4, 9). Edwin Gordon writes:

> What seems to be the case is that regardless of the level of music aptitude children are born with, they must have favorable early informal and formal experiences in music in order to maintain that level of potential. Further, unless they have favorable early informal and formal environment experiences with music, that level of music aptitude will never fully be realized in achievement (Gordon, *Introduction to Research*, 9).

However heredity and the environment interact, genetics account for only so much; a child's early musical experiences are crucial for developing long-term potential. Aptitude stabilizes by age nine. Learning can still take place, but it is done within the confines of aptitude (Gordon, *Introduction to Research*, 10). This means that by the time students reach the age for public school band and orchestra programs their aptitude is locked-in. But, to understand how to teach each student to their full potential we must know the nature of their aptitude.

Music Aptitude Tests

It is important to recognize that aptitude tests are not designed to exclude weak students from participation. Even students with low aptitude still have the ability to fulfill their potential in a meaningful, musical way, assuming we are prepared to teach to their needs. And while it is true that all students with high achievement have high aptitude, it is NOT true that all students with high aptitudes automatically demonstrate high achievement (Gordon, *Learning Sequences in Music*, 42).

As directors, we must make clear to parents and administrators that our objectives in measuring aptitude are: (1) to identify exceptionally gifted students; and (2) effectively to teach to everybody's strengths, weaknesses, and individual differences. Students with lower musical aptitude may require more help developing melodic, tonal and rhythmic skills, while students with high aptitude can benefit from enriched activities in the same areas (Gordon, *Musical Aptitude Profile Manual*, 56–65).

We need to stress again that Musical Aptitude Profiles should not be used to exclude students from studying music. With proper instruction, all students—those with low and high aptitude—can benefit from developing their musical abilities.

Several aptitude tests are commercially available. For example, GIA's Musical Aptitude Profile (MAP) may be administered to students nine years old and older in three 50-minute periods.

Timbre Preference Testing

Edwin Gordon's research has shown that beginning instrumental students who choose an instrument corresponding to their timbre and range preferences stay with instrumental programs longer and achieve more than students who begin on an instrument in conflict with their natural preferences (Gordon, *Music Aptitude and Related Tests*, 15–16). Unfortunately, merely asking students what instrument they like is not reliable. Even after a demonstration concert they may still choose based on how the instrument looks, what instrument their friends play, or what instrument Lisa Simpson plays. And once the newness of the experience fades, no matter how excited a student initially is to play flute, if they do not enjoy the experience they are unlikely to want to continue.

The "Instrument Timbre Preference Test," (ITPT) published through GIA, offers a possible way to determine student likes and dislikes. The test takes about twenty minutes and involves comparing seven distinct timbres. The melodies stay exactly the same— only the timbre and range change. By synthesizing sounds (thus removing any chance of familiarity with instrument tone colors) and strictly controlling the other variables, the test isolates the listener's preference for timbre and provides information to help students choose an appropriate instrument. It should be noted that this test does not identify aptitude or achievement, though Gordon points out many students with high music aptitudes never choose an instrument, possibly because they have never identified an instrument they would like (Gordon, *Music Aptitude and Related Tests*, 15–16).

To be fair, research in support of the ITPT is mixed. Fortney-Boyle-DeCarbo (1993) confirmed that timbre is an important consideration for many students when choosing instruments (Fortney, 38). However, other research has questioned the reliability and validity of the ITPT. Colwell and Abrams note that the test may be of limited value by itself (without music aptitude tests to correlate data) (Colwell and Abrams, 27). Their study found that 52 percent of students who chose instruments based on the test dropped out of band after a year, a rate they say is "roughly equal to the norm" (Colwell and Abrams,

28). In his 1996 study, David Williams found that listeners correctly identified the intended instrument of the synthesized timbre only 50 percent of the time, creating doubt that the test offers a valid analogy to acoustic instruments.[4] Gordon would counter that an exact match defeats the purpose, and that synthesized sounds help objectively measure a preference without complicating the decision with the extra-musical factors that an exact identification would encumber. Williams also found that only 20 percent of current players preferred the timbre associated with their instrument, a statistic Williams calls "distressing" (Williams, 275).

Nevertheless, the ITPT concept is reasonable—nobody enjoys an activity he finds annoying, and so it follows that students who like listening to their instrument are more likely to want to practice it. The ITPT can be used with the Instrumental Fitting Process (see below) to expose students to the sound of each instrument and gage how much they enjoy each one.

6. Classroom Teacher Interviews

Meet with classroom teachers two weeks before the instrumental fitting process. Beyond the empirical data collected from MAPs and ITPTs, classroom teachers offer insight regarding non-musical aptitude, study habits, and reliability. General music teachers can provide information about previous musical achievement (e.g., recorder). Many band and orchestra directors use this information to identify the most talented, hard-working students, and then make a special pitch to them for challenging instruments, such as horn and oboe. ("Scott . . . Mrs. Smith tells me you are doing very well in her class, and that you just did a terrific project on Astronomy! If you're interested, I have a really important instrument I'd like to invite you to try in band next year.") As with MAPs, this strategy should only be used to identify potential recruits, and never as a way to exclude students from participating. *Caveat*: Some schools restrict what information teachers may share with each other, especially about academics and health. Ask your supervising administrator first!

Developing good relationships with classroom teachers is important even if we do not glean information about their students. Be collegial, supportive, open-minded, and flexible. From a humanistic perspective the advantages are obvious; from a professional perspective, we need their cooperation to encourage our students to come to lessons and allow us to make recruiting presentations during their class. Quite simply, if we support their teaching they are more likely to support ours.

7. The Instrumental Fitting Process

On the Consideration of Physical Characteristics

There is a long tradition of using a checklist of physical characteristics to match students with instruments—thin lips for flute; slender fingers for violin and viola; lips that are full in proportion to the size of the brass mouthpiece; long arms for trombone; long fingers for saxophone; even teeth for woodwind and brass instruments; big person for big instrument; small person for small instrument, etc. But there is also evidence these stereotypes are inaccurate. A classic study from 1935, replicated in 1983, found that they were poor predictors to future success on an instrument. As noted British music educator Janet Mills summarizes: "The slenderness of students' fingers bore hardly any relation to their success on violin. Indeed, one could predict a violinist's success just as readily by considering the evenness of their teeth!" (Mills, *Instrumental Teaching*, 90–91, 99).

Mills observed a wide-range of stereotype-debunking success stories:

I found high-flying instrumentalists with all sorts of supposedly undesirable features: short-armed trombonists, thick-lipped trumpeters, left-handed cellists, thin-lipped asthmatic oboists, buck-teethed bassoonists, clumsy percussionists, and so on. These students had been given a chance to play a particular instrument, despite their physical characteristics not fitting in with the theories, and were making very good progress (Mills, 99).

Instead of pseudoscience, Mills offers pithy advice: "Give them some lessons and see how they get on." (Mills, 88). In other words, one of the best indications that a student may have an aptitude for a particular instrument is their initial tone production and basic hand coordination. This is precisely what the "Instrumental Fitting Process" below is designed to test. How students initially succeed with their instruments is crucial for their future success and retention, as students who perceive themselves to be successful at tasks are less likely to disengage from them.

Still, when beginning in the fourth grade the consideration of physical characteristics makes some sense, since many students are not physically, aurally, and emotionally mature. These are kin to the height requirements on a roller coaster, or the importance of being able to reach the pedals on a go-kart.

Running the Fitting Process

Running the fitting process can be overwhelming, especially for the new teacher. Some choose to run it completely on their own, which allows for complete control over the entire process. However, a group effort speeds the entire process and allows each teacher to offer expertise in their major instrument.

Before students try the instruments it is important to explain to them:

- the importance of finding the best fit to help insure their success
- that a balanced instrumentation is crucial for everyone's success
- why some instruments are considered specialty instruments
- the challenges of playing each instrument
- how the testing process will be conducted

THE PROCESS

Arrange for students to come into the music room in groups no larger than five. This allows us to offer personal attention and still maintain control of the rest of the group. Allow 40 minutes for each group to complete the testing. (Keep in mind, if we manage the entire fitting process on our own it may take a week to fit one hundred students.) With some exceptions (discussed later), every student should try each instrument so we can identify the best match. Students should also be tested for their ability to match pitches by singing back melodies sung by the teacher. Though strong listening skills are important to all instruments, the horn, trombone, and tuba have particularly strong needs for pitch discrimination for initial success. To help make sure nothing is dropped or damaged, minimize how long the students (especially young ones) hold the instruments on their own, if at all, and let them do so with our hands close by. After each instrument is tried the teacher writes down a score (0–10) and adds notes as needed (e.g. 'able to reach 3 partials') on the score sheet (page 294).

SUPPLIES FOR RUNNING THE FITTING PROCESS

The following supplies are needed to effectively run the fitting process.

Woodwind, brass, and percussion

- One of each wind instrument that will be offered.
- Five mouthpieces for each instrument
- Five clarinet, five alto saxophone reeds (of the same strength we plan to start students on)
- Liquid sterilizer and paper towels for cleaning mouthpieces (use rubbing alcohol or mouthpiece sanitizing spray, available through most music stores)
- Two pairs of drum sticks (one for teacher, one for student) and a drum pad

String instruments

- One of each sized violin—full, three-quarter, half
- One of each viola—15-inch, 14-inch, 13-inch
- One cello—full, three-quarter, half
- One bass—three-quarter, half
- One violin bow, one viola bow, one cello bow, one bass bow
- A variety of sponges and rubber bands to be used as a shoulder pad for violins and violas.
- Rosin
- Rock stop for cello and bass
- Stool for the string bass

General Supplies:

- Tables for setting instruments on at each testing station

FITTING BRASS INSTRUMENTS

Complete the brass fitting process in band score order: trumpet, horn, trombone, euphonium, and tuba. It is easier for a first time player to start with a relatively tight embouchure and then move to a looser embouchure. For each instrument, equip every student with a mouthpiece and teach the entire group how to produce a buzz. Do this first without the mouthpiece, then with the mouthpiece, and finally with the entire instrument.[5] Because novice players do not have the muscle control needed to make subtle lip adjustments, keep technical explanations to a minimum. Demonstration and analogy are our best allies. For instance, to get the students to make a trumpet embouchure we can tell them to pretend they are sucking on a very sour lemon. For many, this will instantly flatten the chin, tighten the lips at the corners, and draw their lips together without curling them over the teeth.

IDENTIFYING GOOD BRASS-PLAYING TRAITS

As with all wind instruments, the embouchure is the most critical issue. The most common traits that are shared by good brass embouchures are:

- flat chin
- firm corners
- flat cheeks (no puffing)
- horizontally centered mouthpiece.

In addition, look for the following instrument-specific characteristics:

Trumpet

Student should be able to:

- go back and forth between C below the staff and second line G; at minimum the student needs to be able to play the second line G
- maintain a flat chin and keep the cheeks from puffing outwards

French Horn

Student should be able to:

- accurately sing back melodies sung by the teacher
- discriminate higher and lower pitches when the teacher demonstrates on the French horn (e.g., "Which of these notes sounds lower?")
- go back and forth from first line E and second line G
- maintain a flat chin and keep the cheeks from puffing outwards
- naturally place the mouthpiece more on the upper lip than the lower

Euphonium/Baritone Horn

Student should be able to:

- go back and forth from bass clef second line B♭ and fourth line F; at minimum the student needs to be able to play the F
- maintain a flat chin and keep the cheeks from puffing outwards

Trombone

Student should be able to:

- accurately sing back melodies sung by the teacher
- discriminate higher and lower pitches when the teacher demonstrates on the trombone (e.g., "Which of these notes sounds lower?")
- at minimum, play a fourth line F
- demonstrate basic coordination to move the slide comfortably
- maintain a flat chin and keep the cheeks from puffing outwards

Tuba

Student should be able to:

- accurately sing back melodies sung by the teacher
- discriminate higher and lower pitches when the teacher demonstrates on the tuba
- play a B♭ below the staff, or at a minimum, the F just below the staff

FITTING PROCESS FOR WOODWIND INSTRUMENTS

Unlike brass instruments, which require a similar set of skills, each woodwind instrument has a unique set of ideal traits.

Flute

Students should be able to do the following:

- Demonstrate good finger coordination skill. Try the following finger coordination test, which does not actually use a flute: Have the students place their hands up as though they were playing the flute. Label the fingers 1–3 on each hand (index finger = 1, middle finger = 2, and ring finger = 3). Ask students to touch their fingers to their thumbs using different fingers in arbitrary combinations (e.g., "Left hand—1 and 2, Right hand—2.") A rapid succession will help identify those students who demonstrate good finger coordination skills.
- Sustain a long steady airstream (no wind puffing).

Clarinet

Student should be able to do the following:

- maintain a flat chin
- keep the cheeks from puffing outwards
- play low and high range notes (with the teacher's help). Set up the clarinet backwards with the mouthpiece properly in the student's mouth and the keys rotated 180 degrees. This allows the teacher to stand in front of the student and finger the instrument. Start on thumb F and walk down the F major scale, to F below the staff. Then add the register key to produce a first space C. This gives a basic idea of the student's natural clarinet embouchure.

Saxophone

Student should be able to do the following:

- maintain a flat chin
- keep the cheeks from puffing outwards

FITTING PROCESS FOR PERCUSSION INSTRUMENTS

Student should be able to do the following:

- demonstrate a steady tempo by clapping a steady beat at different tempos set by the teacher
- using drum sticks, play back rhythms and stickings performed by the teacher
- demonstrate hand coordination by performing a slow sticking pattern (e.g., paradiddle)

FITTING PROCESS FOR STRING INSTRUMENTS

Violin and Viola

While holding the instrument in playing position the student should be able to reach the finger board with the left hand without the arm touching the ribs of the instrument.

Cello

While sitting on the front four inches of the chair, with the endpin pull out approximately 6 inches the student should be able to:

- reach both arms around the cello as if hugging it
- reach a minor third between the first and fourth fingers

String Bass

In standing position, with the instrument leaning into the body and the left knee supporting the instrument from behind the student should be able to:

- reach into first position with the left hand
- reach a whole step between the first and fourth fingers

Assigning Instruments

After the student has tried each instrument we help them select their three top choices. Using their performance ratings that we wrote down, review with the student which instruments they had the most success on. Also share the results of any MAPs we administered.

We can subtly influence their attitude by projecting a positive demeanor. If someone struggled on an instrument, be encouraging, and do not emphasize his problems. For cases in which he showed success, share your excitement (e.g. "Johnny, wow you did a great job on the trombone, tuba, clarinet but the trumpet and flute seemed more difficult for you.").

Then ask the student to select his top three choices. Once everyone has been through the fitting process instruments will be assigned based on the student's interest, initial success, aptitude, and overall balance needs.

Whenever possible, assign students their number one choice. But remember that the reason we have students choose their top three is to retain flexibility. This goes beyond creating proportional numbers. We also need to place at least one natural leader on each instrument; a section of "followers" and no leaders will always struggle. A natural leader is someone that demonstrates potential for success on the assigned instrument, is strong in their academics classes, works hard, and is an independent performer—all information we gather from our teacher interviews, the instrument fitting process, and aptitude testing.

STRATEGIES FOR DEALING WITH THE POPULARITY OR UNPOPULARITY OF CERTAIN INSTRUMENTS

Some instruments create recruiting challenges because they are burdened with stereotypes and poor public relations: Flutes are extremely popular with girls because they are easy to carry and are perceived as being feminine. Trumpets appeal to boys because they seem more macho than flutes and clarinets. Trombones often seem too large and less fun than their treble-clef colleagues. Violas struggle with the stereotype of being a large violin that never gets the melody. Cellos and string basses have unwieldy cases. If recruiting these instruments becomes a problem, try the following:

- De-emphasize popular instruments during exposure concerts.
- Make unpopular instruments seem cool through the tunes that are demonstrated and the students/ teachers who demonstrate them.
- Make one-on-one pitches to students. Don't lie, but instead highlight points that are not obvious— e.g.,"It's important to have someone really smart on the trombone, and I think you'd be great in that role"; "The tuba player has to be a leader. It has to be someone we can rely on, so I only ask a few students to play it."
- Pitch the parents, too. Many like to know that playing a less popular instrument gives greater opportunities to shine. This may seem disingenuous, but it's no lie to say: "String bass players are always in demand."
- Point out convenience and financial advantages. Since it is common for schools to own tubas, euphoniums, bassoons, baritone saxophones, and string basses, playing these can be made attractive by pointing out: (1) The possibility of having an instrument both at home and at school; (2) The opportunity to rent an instrument from the school for a fraction of what local music stores charge.

As discussed earlier, use athletic analogies. For example: A baseball team can't have 10 first basemen and no outfielders. Sometimes it seems like the heroes in soccer are the forwards who score goals, but if you ask soccer experts they'll tell you the goalkeepers are the real stars.

8. Post Instrument Fitting

Sending the Follow-up Letter

Once students have been fitted and assigned instruments it's time to involve the parents again.

Advise parents that rent–to–own arrangements are usually in their financial interest because (a) they build equity, and (b) if for any reason their child stops playing they are not obligated to finish out the contract. Keep in mind that most parents have never purchased an instrument. To help them make smart purchases, ask them to bring our letter with specific recommendations to the music store, along with this list of questions:

- Is there a warranty or maintenance program? (even for leased instruments)
- Does the leasing program provide new or used instruments? (avoid used instrument programs)
- What is the policy on switching instruments mid-lease? (look for programs that allow switching)
- Does the leasing program build equity towards the purchase of the instrument? (preferred)
- At the lease's end, can you pay extra and upgrade to a higher quality instrument? (very useful so students are not playing beginner instruments in high school)

If students intend to use an instrument they already own, ask to inspect it first to ensure it works properly.

Dear Parent,

Congratulations! Your child _____ will be playing the _____
in the Smithtown Elementary Instrumental Music Program.

Getting Started:
All students must acquire an instrument by September 13. This can be done through the following means:

- You already own an instrument.
- You rent/lease an instrument *see below*
- Since most music stores do not rent French Horns, baritones, or tubas, Smithtown Elementary has these instruments available for a minimal yearly maintenance fee. I will be contacting the students who chose to play these instruments to help make these arrangements.

Instrument Quality and Condition:
For your child to be successful he/she must have an instrument in top playing condition. If you already own an instrument you must have its playing condition checked by a professional. What may look good to you may still not work best for your child. Contact me if I can be of any help in this matter.

Rental Programs:
Enclosed is a list of area music dealers. I have also included a list of instrument brands that people have had success with in the past. Look for instruments that will help your child be successful, rather than obtaining an instrument for the lowest price possible that will continually need repairs.

**Be careful about purchasing an instrument over the Internet. Cheap instruments are typically made very poorly. You get what you pay for!

If you are renting an instrument please use the following plan as a guide:

1. Thoroughly read the contracts and select a dealer.
2. Fill out the appropriate contract and return it to the dealer along with the deposit as soon as possible. An early response (prior to mid July) will ensure that a quality instrument is available for your child in September.
3. Request that the dealer deliver the instrument, lesson book, and music stand to Smithtown Elementary by the first week of September. Your child will receive instructions regarding assembly, care and maintenance of the instrument at his/her first lesson. To prevent inadvertent damage, no matter how tempting it may be, do not attempt to assemble or play the new instrument before receiving formal instruction at school.

Additional Required materials before September 4

The additional required supplies below can be purchased at any music retailer. Make sure to get those items that pertain to your instrument:

For all Band and String students:

- *The Do-It! Band Method*, Book 1 (be sure to get the specific book for your instrument)
- An instrument in good working condition
- Wire music stand
- An instrument case ID tag
- Pencil

For Woodwind Instruments:

Flute: handkerchief for cleaning the inside of the instrument, flute head joint tuning rod (should come with the instrument)
Clarinet, Alto Saxophone: four #2 strength Vandoren reeds, reed case for four reeds, cork grease, cloth swab, mouthpiece cap and ligature, a mouthpiece brush

For Brass Instruments:

Trumpet, Baritone Horn, and Tuba: valve oil, tuning slide grease, mouthpiece brush, snake brush
French Horn: rotary oil and tuning slide grease, mouthpiece brush, snake brush
Trombones: tuning slide grease, slide cream, mouthpiece brush, snake brush, a small water spray bottle (must be able to fit inside of instrument case).

For Percussion:

Bells, snare drum, mallet bag, Vic Firth rubber bell mallets, Vic Firth SD1 snare drum sticks, Drum pad

For String Instruments:

Violin, Viola: rosin, clean polishing cloth
Cello, Bass: rosin, rock stop, clean polishing cloth

Recommended Instrument Manufacturers

Flute: Armstrong, Artley, Gemeinhardt, Yamaha, Selmer
Clarinet: Armstrong, Artley, Buffet, Leblanc, Vito, Yamaha, Selmer
Saxophone: Bundy/Selmer, Yamaha
Trumpet: Bach, Conn, Holton, Yamaha
Trombone: Bach, Conn, Holton, King, Yamaha
Percussion: Yamaha, Vic Firth, Pearl (Pearl has a complete Learning Center Kit that includes a carry bag and rolling cart)

Area Music Dealers

Please note that Smithtown Elementary does not endorse a particular dealer and you are not required to use one from this list. Whomever you do use, be sure to review their rental policies before entering into a contract.

Barry's Music Shop   Van Melder Music Center
1368 Route 43   387 Route 18
Pleasant Street, NY 17513   Moore Side, NY 17514
(876) 555-4321   (876) 555-4321

Ashley's   Top Hat Music
845 Dawn Drive   584 Michlewski Road
Middle Hill, NY 17515   Moore Side, NY 17514
(876) 555-4321   (876) 555-4321

I am looking forward to working with your child! If you have any questions please do not hesitate to contact me at tomjohnson@smithtown.edu or 555-5555.

Sincerely,

Mr. Tom Johnson
Band and Orchestra Director
Smithtown Elementary School

Working With the Local Instrument Rental Store

Communicate well in advance with the local instrument store to insure all instruments and supplies are ready when students need them. Items to discuss include:

- brand of instruments to stock
- a list of supplies each student will need
- the method book(s).

Consider requesting that all new instruments be delivered to the school and not given directly to the families. Before their first lesson, students are likely to try playing as soon as they bring it home, which creates the potential for mishandled and damaged instruments.

After new instruments are delivered we can insure they are unwrapped, ready to play, and include all required supplies. Further, we should test-play every instrument to identify possible manufacturer problems (e.g., pad issues on woodwinds, valve problems on brass instruments such as pads issues on woodwind instruments). Unfortunately some less than reputable retailers do not rent instruments that are in top playing condition.

Handling Discontented Parents and Students

Since students are directly involved in selecting their top choices, most will be pleased with their assigned instrument. But on the occasion a parent contacts us we can refer to our notes from the fitting process. Once the parent hears his child was more successful on the instrument they were assigned than on the instrument she initially wanted, most are satisfied. Unfortunately, some still insist on a specific instrument, frequently because they already own it. At this point we are best off letting the student play it, as long as both the parent and child understand that their child will need to work hard to overcome any initial difficulties.

Recruiting in Areas with Limited Resources

In many communities, families cannot afford to rent or own instruments and school districts have scant resources to supply them to all who are interested.

Try contacting retailers to see if they can donate damaged instruments from their rental inventory. Many stores will restore these to playing condition before giving them to the school.[7] Publish an announcement in local newspapers asking for instrument donations from families who have an instrument no longer being played. (Check with the school administration to see if there are policies regarding donated items. Some schools require a formal process to be followed.) Always thank companies and families in writing with a picture of the students playing the donated instruments (including big smiles!), and in concert programs. Be sure to tell them that your superintendent's office has been made aware of the donation. If possible, request that your administrators write a thank you note, as well.

Also, ask your teachers or PTA if anyone would like to sponsor a student's rental. Be sure that there is insurance on the rental and run the donation through your school's activity fund. Some districts have an organization that acts as a fiduciary for charitable contributions. Meet with them to explore avenues for instrument donations.

Finally, explore private and public grants. Sources for grant information include:

*   The Children's Music Workshop: http://www.childrensmusicworkshop.com
*   Foundation Center: http://www.fdcenter.org
*   Music Educators National Conference: http://www.menc.org
*   Mr. Holland's Opus Foundation: http://www.mhopus.org
*   National Endowment for the Arts: http://www.nea.gov
*   VH1 Save the Music Foundation: http://www.vh1savethemusic.com
*   American String Teachers Association:http://www.astaweb.com

(List from Mixon, 22)

When recruiting in impoverished areas, keep in mind that students are often motivated more by the teacher than by the task[6]. Put simply, if students like the music teacher they are more likely to try an instrument. This makes the personal recruiting touch ever important. Classroom teachers can be powerful advocates for us, too, so develop good relationships with them. Also take the time to be visible in school activities and get to know students before asking them to join. Make a phone call to parents, or try to meet them in person, to outline for them the requirements of the program, time and financial commitments, and benefits for their children.

Consider emphasizing non-traditional ensembles rather than concert band and orchestra. Percussion, rock, mariachi, and jazz create powerful cultural relevancy, especially in communities with high percentages of minorities (Mixon, 18). Specialized method books make these ensembles easier than ever to organize.

- *Simplemente Mariachi, A Standards-Based, Comprehensive Mariachi Method*, Northeastern Publications.
- *Standards of Excellence – Jazz Ensemble Method*, Kjos Music.
- *Row-Loff Productions* – an excellent publisher of beginning and intermediate percussion ensemble music.

A limited number of instruments and erratic home lives may preclude students from practicing at home. Kevin Mixon, an experienced urban school teacher, recommends finding places for students to practice in school and inviting them to come during free periods, lunchtime, before/after school, etc.

Organizing Beginning Instruction

Scheduling

Once students have been assigned instruments we need to organize them into beginning classes. No matter how our school schedules these—every day, every other day, pull-out lessons, etc.—a good portion of initial contact with students should be in "like-instrument" settings. This allows us to focus on the individual pedagogy of each instrument. Separate lesson groups for each instrument is ideal, though it may require more staffing than is available. At the very least, schedule students into groups divided by woodwinds, brass, percussion, upper strings, and lower strings. After the first few months, when students gain proficiency, transition to a schedule that includes larger, mixed groupings, such as all woodwinds/all brass/percussion, and later, the entire ensemble.

Choosing a Method Book

Today music teachers have a plethora of options for beginning instrumentalists, as nearly every music publisher offers a method book. Despite the shiny covers, glossy pages, and full color photos, no book is perfect, and no matter which we use we should be prepared to supplement it with additional material. Consider the following when choosing a book.

1. *Quality and clarity of illustrations or photos demonstrating proper embouchure and playing position.* Prose descriptions are useful, but ultimately students return to visual images for reminders about the basics of playing. Look for examples that clearly show proper technique, and better yet, also show an example of improper technique, as it is important for students to learn what something *is* by knowing what it *isn't*.
2. *Variety of musical examples.* Look for a method book that presents tunes in a variety of keys, modes, meters, and styles. We should teach minor at the same time as major; compound meters at the same time as duple meter, etc. One of the reasons advanced students often shy away from ⁶⁄₈ meter, for example, is that they were underexposed to it during their first years of study. (Music teachers inadvertently teach their students that ⁶⁄₈ is "difficult" by avoiding it.) Further, consider the type of melodies that are included. Especially during the early stages, look for familiar melodies and ones that are easy to sing. These will be important as we teach students to audiate sounds before they perform them on their instruments.
3. *Integration of theory and history.* How effectively does the method book integrate theory and history into its coverage of notation and technique?

Some of the most popular method book series are:

Band Methods

Accent on Achievement, John O'Reilly and Mark Williams, Alfred Music Publishing.

Band Expressions, Robert W. Smith, Susan Smith, Michael Story, Garland Markham and Richard Crain, Alfred Music Publishing.

Belwin 21st Century Band Method Book, Jack Bullock and Anthony Maiello, Alfred Music Publishing.

Best in Class, Bruce Pearson, Neil A. Kjos Music Co.

Ed Sueta Band Method, Ed Sueta, Ed Sueta Music Publications.

Essential Elements 2000, Tim Lautzenheiser, John Higgins, Charles Menghini, Paul Lavender, Tom Rhoades and Don Bierschenk, Hal Leonard Publishing Corp.

First Division Band Method, Fred Weber, Alfred Publishing.

Standard of Excellence, Bruce Pearson, Neil A. Kjos Music Company.

Yamaha Advantage, Sandy Feldstein and Larry Clark, Playtime Publishing.

String Methods

Adventures in Music Reading, William Starr, Alfred Music Publishing.

All for Strings, Gerald Anderston and Robert Frost, Neil A. Kjos Music Co.

Artistry in Strings, Robert Frost and Gerald Fischbach, Neil A. Kjos Music Co.

Essential Elements 2000 for Strings, Michael Allen, Robert Gillespie, Pamela Tellejohn Hayes, and arr. John Higgins, Hal Leonard Publishing Corp.

New Directions for Strings, Joanne Erwin, Robert D. McCashin, Kathleen Horvath, Brenda Mitchell, and Elliot Del Borgo, and Soon Hee Newbold, FJH Music Company Inc.

Orchestra Expressions, Kathleen Brungard, Michael Alexander, Gerald Anderson, and Sandra Dackow, Alfred Music Publishing/Belwin Division.

Using Traditional versus Sound–to–Symbol Method Books

In earlier chapters we discussed so-called "traditional" method books that emphasize notation and the mechanical aspects of playing. Based on a 1988 study, 88–99 percent of the melodies in these books were in major tonalities, and only two of nine included singing.[8] Though these non-sound-to-symbol books do not carry our highest recommendation, it should be also said that they have much to offer. First, their ancillaries tend to be very well-developed. Play-along CDs and DVDs are usually included or inexpensively available, teacher's manuals are filled with useful resources, and some have supplemental student workbooks for history and theory. A few have works for full ensemble that are sequenced directly with the method book. Additionally, many of the most popular beginning method books work in conjunction with *SmartMusic* software.

Second, many are visually quite attractive, which tends to motivate young students to use them.

Third, given their pedagogical approach, they are thoughtfully sequenced, and are adaptable to a sound–to–symbol philosophy, assuming we supplement with other exercises.

Sound–to–symbol methods books are less popular but worth exploring. They include the *Jump Right In* series and *Do It!*. *Jump Right In* strictly follows Gordon's *Music Learning Theory*, and thus looks quite different from traditional books. Instead of basic notation and simple long tones, we see tonal and rhythmic patterns without traditional notation.

The *Do It!* series bridges the gap between traditional and sound–to–symbol books. Details about notation, time signatures, key signatures, etc., are separated in their own section and are not discussed within the text. Beginners see notation from the start, but the first line they play is a simple, singable melody with accompanying lyrics. As does *Jump Right In, Do It!* introduces improvisation early, and by supplying lyrics constantly emphasizes the importance of singing before playing.

Ironically, though they are relatively new, *Jump Right In* and *Do It!* hearken back to some of the earliest group instrumental method books used during the first part of the twentieth century. *The Universal Teacher* (1923) included lyrics for many of its melodies, implying that students may have sung first and then played. To encourage home practicing, the Universal Teacher also relied on familiar tunes, an approach echoed by Suzuki, Kodály, and Gordon (Sheldon, 48).

Duke and Byo's "Habits of Musicianship" Method Book

To some extent, any beginning method book is as good as we make it. As renowned music education professors Robert Duke and James Byo point out, the melodies in a method book are only the vehicle through which we apply an approach to teaching. Books don't teach; teachers teach! It's the approach, whether it be sound-to-symbol, traditional notation-focused teaching, or something else, that can make a dramatic difference in how students learn. Here Duke and Byo describe a common scenario in beginning classrooms:

> Get students to make a sound, any sound, on their instruments; then teach them to play 7 or 8 notes; teach them to start notes with the tongue; teach them to play a few different rhythms in common time; teach them to play softly when there's a *p* and loudly when there's an *f*; tap their feet to the beat of the music (or some approximation of the beat); count rhythms using some syllabic coding system; clap rhythms as they count; follow the conductor; breathe only at phrase endings; match one or two pitches to an electronic tuner. Are all these good goals? Sure they are. Anything missing? Lots. Music's missing. And expression. And beauty of sound. And melodic intonation.[9]

Granted, getting absolute beginners to play musically with good tone and intonation is easier said than done. But it may be even harder if that's not our goal in the first place, and if instead our objective is to teach students how to play different notes in an effort to speed through the method book. Perhaps, as Duke and Byo suggest in their beginning band method book *The Habits of Musicianship*, we should change that paradigm and make good tone, musicianship, and beautiful playing the priorities. This would allow the nitty-gritty details of technique to follow in due course as a result of playing musically, successfully, and beautifully.

One of the overriding principles in this approach is to take the time to establish good playing habits in beginners from the *very first day of instruction*. The goal is to always make a good sound with good technique, even if that means the introduction of a new fingering, rhythm, or term is delayed a few days. Duke and Byo describe this approach as establishing the "habits of musicianship." The below summary of these principles can be applied to both beginning band and orchestra students (Duke and Byo, *Habits*):

- Slow down, and allow beginning students to develop good habits before they develop bad ones. Of course, it's not really slowing down, since in the long run it will save the student the agony of having to unlearn bad habits of technique, pitch, and tone.
- Show students the difference (through their own playing and through the teacher's modeling) what good tone sounds like. For students who do not achieve good habits even at the slower pace, this gives them something to work towards during their own practicing.

- Listen to students individually and in small groups as often as possible. Not only does this allow us to evaluate student progress, but it allows the student to hear his progress, too, instead of always blending imperceptibly into the group's sound.
- Minimize conducting and cues from the podium; give students the responsibility for keeping the pulse and knowing when to come in.
- Teach a broad range of meters and tonalities from the beginning (e.g., $\frac{6}{8}$, not just $\frac{4}{4}$, minor, not just major). Young students typically have trouble with compound meters and unfamiliar tonalities not because they are difficult, but because they are unfamiliar.
- Emphasize legato playing without bow change or the tongue (except for trombone) in order to establish good embouchure habits (à la long tones) and connected musical lines without breathing after every note.
- Play every example musically and beautifully. Avoid using the criteria, "Well, we can get through that example!" as an indication of when to move on to the next line or exercise. Repeat and refine to establish the sound and the habit of musical playing.

Duke and Byo's approach is applicable to nearly any beginning method book. But to facilitate their ideas they offer a free book (with teacher's score and parts) through the Center for Music Learning at the University of Texas at Austin (http://cml.music.utexas.edu). The downloadable scores and parts are useful on their own or as a supplement to another text. It is well worth exploring, as is the rest of the research and resources available from the center's website.

Teaching Instruments to Beginners

Our Companion Website at www.routledge.com/textbook/970415992107 contains video demonstrations for brass, woodwind, percussion, and string instruments, presented by professional players and leading music teachers.

After the First Year: Switching Students to New Instruments

By necessity or by design, some students change their instrument during the first few years of playing. Switching usually falls into two categories: (1) Switching to improve the overall balance of the ensemble; (2) Switching to an instrument that was not offered during the first year (e.g., bassoon).

Switching to improve balance should be the exception rather than the rule, as we should strive to create balanced instrumentation through the recruiting process. Keep in mind that younger students often have more success when switching, partly because they have less to "unlearn," and partly because they have more time to "catch up" to the proficiency level of their peers. Once students reach high school, switching is difficult because most either own their own instruments (and thus do not want to invest in another instrument), or they feel a strong attachment to their present one.

Because of these challenges, unbalanced instrumentation problems usually last for years. However, a motivated young high school student can make quick progress since he will already read notation, know basic breathing and articulation techniques, and have more physical and mental maturity than most young beginners.[10]

The second type of switching occurs for the instruments that are delayed—usually one year—until students develop basic finger, bowing, embouchure technique, reading ability, and aural skills (e.g., oboe, bassoon, horn, tuba, viola, string bass).

In selecting a student to switch, keep in mind we need someone who is committed, patient, and willing to work. Since they will often be playing alone, at least initially, choose someone with strong rhythm skills who enjoys playing independently and in front of others.

Our first instinct may be a first or second chair caliber player who has already demonstrated high achievement. A potential problem with this is that it depletes the leaders in that section. On the other hand, if we choose a low performing student (to preserve the top players), he will likely have just as much difficulty on the new instrument, thus defeating the purpose of switching someone in the first place. This leaves us a small pool of players in the middle.

Some directors ask for volunteers. This allows motivated students to self-select, though there is no guarantee these students are physically suited for the new instrument. As suggested earlier in this chapter for saxophones and percussionists, another tactic is to hold auditions. This makes the new instrument seem desirable and gives the teacher an opportunity to identify the best candidate. An "audition" also makes the new instrument seem selective and coveted, whereas a request for "volunteers" implies looking for someone to make a sacrifice.

At this point we still have to contend with a number of questions: Do we have the support of the parents who may have already purchased an instrument? Is the student a good "fit" for the new instrument?

The following table shows the best candidates for making switches to new instruments.

TABLE 16.1 The best candidates for making switches to new instruments

New instrument	Instrument to recruit from
Oboe	Flute, Clarinet, Saxophone
Bassoon	Flute, Clarinet, Saxophone
Clarinet	Saxophone
Horn	Trumpet and Flute
Euphonium	Trumpet
Tuba	Trumpet and Euphonium
Percussion	Any Instrument
Bass	Cello

Now the hard work begins! Though the student may be on par musically with the rest of the ensemble, obviously their physical skills will trail. Some strategies to help students make a successful transition:

- Commit to several private lessons with the student to teach the basics of the instrument, embouchure, fingerings, etc.
- Work from a beginning method book with an easy-to-read fingering chart.
- Assign the student a mentor from the ensemble; for younger students ask a high school student to donate some lesson time.
- Encourage the student to take private lessons.
- Be patient and supportive.
- Ask the class for their support. Remember, some students thrive on a new challenge, but others might self-consciously feel they have "regressed" in front of their peers.
- Simplify parts of the concert repertoire as necessary (i.e., "water down" parts). Give the student every opportunity to immediately feel successful. For example, have them play harmonically comple-mentary half notes periodically throughout the piece. This lets them be a contributing and successful

part of the group without challenging them to the point of frustration. (This is probably not allowed at a ratings festival, of course.)

Retention

Even after the most successful recruiting, some attrition is inevitable. At the beginning levels, students frequently cite required practice time, perceived instrument difficulty, and academic problems as reasons for dropping. Dropping because of academic concerns is exacerbated if instrumental classes are not built into the schedule, and thus students must be pulled from their regular coursework.[11] Interestingly, parents and teachers rank fear of failure as being more influential than activity conflicts in decisions to drop (Gamin, 44). At the high school level, students commonly cite academic conflicts and concerns about time management, including other activities, such as sports and after school clubs (Stewart, 67).

Although music dealers sometimes blame music teachers, most students and teachers do not blame the quality of the educational experience for dropouts. But this is basically an admission of helplessness on the part of teachers—"It's not MY fault!"—when in fact they do have some control over retention (Gamin, 53).

- Encourage, encourage, encourage! It goes a long way towards giving students the confidence to overcome their fears of failure.
- If feasible, push for beginning instrumental classes that do not conflict with other academics.
- Work with students to manage their practice time.
- Maintain good relationships with classroom teachers and communicate frequently to preempt problems with pull-out lessons.
- Cultivate the attractive features of instrumental programs that match those of popular activities (i.e., student leadership opportunities, travel, variety of music/activities/performance venues), assuming it does not dilute the quality of music education.
- Stay sensitive to students' non-musical commitments and be aware of other event calendars, especially when designing the year's schedule. Many athletic and fine arts calendars are published nearly a year in advance, making it possible to avoid double-booking students.
- Encourage private lessons. Private instrumental study has been shown to correlate with staying in band, though this could be because the students already value instrumental study more than their peers who do not study.[12]
- Perform! Most school concert bands and orchestras perform infrequently, particularly during the first few years of study. But students enjoy knowing that their rehearsals and lessons are working towards a goal. Be creative and consider short performances, performances of just the melody lines with younger students, joint performances, small-group performances, and performances for administrators and other classes (Stewart, 69).
- Start a mentor program in which older students work with younger ones on the same instrument.
- Set up opportunities for older students to perform for younger students, especially on instruments such as oboe, bassoon, horn, trombone, and tuba.
- Feature those instruments with fewer students on concerts with chamber music.
- For directors in the upper grades, visit the beginning instrumental program to teach small group lessons. If high school directors develop working relationships with students before they arrive, they will be more likely to continue playing once they graduate middle school.
- Offer to conduct the elementary/middle school ensemble in a rehearsal or concert.
- On a concert, include one or two combined pieces for Grades 5–8 and/or 9–12.

- Have a "vertical concert," which includes instrumental students from elementary through high school. This demonstrates to younger students and their parents the range of experiences they will experience as members of the program.
- Re-recruit students who have dropped out of the program. Sometimes these students simply need encouragement or a new challenge.
- Self-evaluate: If you were to put yourself in the students' shoes would you be excited and motivated during your own rehearsals?
- Keep students out of scheduling conflicts and work directly with coaches and other teachers to determine the best place for the student during overlapping events. If the ace pitcher is a member of your flute or violin section, send them off to the game with a blessing and well wishes. Announce at the concert: "We are all rooting for Sarah tonight as she pitches in the tournament." OR "Tom is hitting different pitches tonight at the baseball playoff game against Hickory Hills High, but we will miss his sound here."

If possible, attend a few games, too! Remember, we teach the total child, and they need sound bodies as well as sound ears. If we show a willingness to compromise, the coach will be more forgiving when our principal oboe has a concert during his practice. Too often we take a stubborn stance. Instead, begin with an email that the coach can read when she is not en-route to a game. Ask the coach, "Did you know that John is also a wonderful clarinet player? He is very talented in many areas. I know how dedicated he is in practicing his instrument. He must be a great asset to your team! We have a concert on the 23rd and I notice you have practice. I could really use him at 7:00. Is there a way we can work this out so he doesn't feel like he is letting either one of us down?"

Still, unsolvable conflicts will occur. Remember, however, that one of the fastest ways to drive students away from the music program is fail them for having another interest. If a student does miss a concert because of these conflicts, offer them the opportunity to play a solo or chamber performance in lieu of the concert (consider having a policy on missed performances in the grading system). In general, use conflict as a teaching tool for life. Students will eventually make choices, and we should set the model for how to make them.

Activities/Assignments for Further Exploration

1. Devise ideal recruiting numbers for each school's ensembles assuming you teach in a district that has the following set-up:

    (Have your professor suggest enrollment numbers for each program.)

    3 elementary schools, 1 middle school, 1 high school
    5 elementary schools, 2 middle schools, 2 high schools
    11 elementary schools, 4 middle schools, 3 high schools

2. Suppose you were about to give a recruiting concert for young students: Write a lesson plan that includes: (a) a sample script for your presentation of each instrument; (b) a list of demonstration tunes you would choose for each instrument.

3. Discuss the advantages and disadvantages of using the following instruments as a core or delaying their introduction. What are some strategies for introducing them?

   Oboe, bassoon, saxophone, percussion, euphonium, tuba, viola, string bass

4. What strategies would you use to regulate the numbers of extra-popular instruments? To encourage unpopular ones?

5. Evaluate a beginning method book according to the criteria discussed in this chapter. What are its advantages? Disadvantages?

6. Discuss the differences between "traditional" and "sound–to–symbol" style method books.

Further Reading

Colwell, Richard, and Thomas Goolsby. *The Teaching of Instrumental Music*. Upper Saddle River, NJ: Prentice Hall, 2002.

Cook, Gary. *Teaching Percussion*: with DVD. Belmont, CA: Thomson Schirmer.

Griswold, H. Gene. 2008. *Teaching Woodwinds*. Upper Saddle River, NJ: Pearson/Prentice Hall, 2006.

Hamann, Donald L., and Robert Gillespie. *Strategies for Teaching Strings: Building a Successful String and Orchestra Program*. New York: Oxford University Press, 2004.

Johnson, Keith. *Brass Performance and Pedagogy*. Upper Saddle River, NJ: Prentice Hall, 2002.

Mixon, Kevin. *Reaching and Teaching All Instrumental Music Students*. Lanham, MD: Rowman & Littlefield Education, 2007.

Ryan, Charlene. *Building Strong Music Programs: A Handbook for Preservice and Novice Music Teachers*. Lanham, MD: Rowman & Littlefield Education, 2009.

Walker, Darwin E. *Teaching Music: Managing the Successful Music Program*. New York: Schirmer Books, 1998.

Chapter 17

Planning and Managing the Concert

To Guide Your Reading

What types of activities need to be completed before the concert takes place?

How do we choose appropriate concert attire?

What factors go into choosing a concert time and call time?

Why are program notes important, and how does one write and present them effectively?

What are the components and format of a printed concert program?

What are the key points to a smoothly run concert?

How can we best manage the movement of ensembles on and off stage?

How does one bow appropriately?

What is proper on-stage concert etiquette for our students?

Concerts are among our most public presentations. In one evening they showcase months of preparation for an audience of family, students, teachers, and administrators, all of whom are likely to form opinions on the quality of our teaching from what they hear and see, regardless of whether it actually reflects what we do in the classroom. But unlike our rehearsals, concerts usually involve multiple ensembles, often of multiple ages, working with unfamiliar procedures and a host of new variables. Without proper management they can be hectic, unnecessarily long, and unenjoyable for all involved.

Concert preparation begins well before the concert itself, and a systematic approach ensures that no details will be forgotten. Use the schedule below as a template for knowing what to do and when to do it.

Concert Preparation Schedule

Beginning of the School Year

Checklist

Choose a date.
Sign-out facilities.
Choose a starting time for each concert.
Choose a call time for the students.
Choose attire.

Choose a Date

Cross-reference as many other calendars as possible to avoid conflicts with religious holidays, school-wide trips, standardized tests, and athletic games (especially playoffs).

Sign-out Facilities

Secure the use of the performance hall at the beginning of the school year. Note that some school systems require facilities to be reserved in the year *prior* to its use. Make copies of all paperwork, and always verify the reservation with the administration even after it has been approved. If the venue was mistakenly double-booked, most conflicts can be resolved with enough lead time. Finally, contact the head custodian to confirm that the facilities will be cleaned, ready, and temperature adjusted.

Choose a Starting Time for Each Concert

7:00pm or 7:30pm are optimal starting times. 6:00/6:30pm tend to conflict with parent work schedules, dinner, and athletic schedules. Unless it only runs one hour, an 8:00pm concert will end too late, especially on school nights. (However, some schools start at 8:00pm to accommodate students on sports teams who have late "away" games.)

Choose a Call Time

Plan on allowing 30–45 minutes for pre-concert tuning and warmup procedures, and schedule the call-time accordingly. Call times that are too early have diminishing returns; students lose focus waiting to perform, potentially giving way to discipline problems.

Choose Attire

Most professional orchestras require their players to have a variety of concert dresses in their wardrobe, since not every performance is given at 8pm in an air conditioned concert hall. Their options range from dressy casual to tuxedos. School ensembles only need one or two possibilities, but should choose by answering the same questions as do the professionals: Where is the performance venue? Who are we performing for? What impression are we trying to convey to the audience? How formally do we wish to present the ensemble? How much can we expect our students (or the district, if the administration is willing) to spend? What will the temperature be in our performance venue?

SAMPLE OPTIONS

Conductor's Attire

Same as the students or one level higher (Exception: Only wear a tuxedo if the group is wearing dark suits or formal attire.)

Formal Attire

Boys: Tuxedo jacket, tuxedo shirt, black bow-tie; black tuxedo pants or back dress slacks; black socks, black shoes

Girls: Black dress (below the knees) OR black dress slacks; black or white blouse (director must choose the same color for everyone); black socks or sheers, dress shoes

"Professional" Attire

Boys: Black sports coat, tuxedo shirt with bow-tie OR white dress shirt*, dark-colored tie (director must choose the same color for everyone); black dress slacks; black dress socks, black dress shoes

Girls: Black skirt that rests below the knee; black or white blouse*(director must choose the same color for everyone), black socks or sheers

*a uniform color theme can also be used for the shirts and blouses

"Classy" Casual

Everyone: Collared shirt of a uniform color; pants of a uniform color (e.g., khaki); shoes of uniform color (e.g., black), socks of a uniform color (always dark); possibly a uniform color tie for the boys

Informal Casual

Everyone: blue denim jeans (no holes!), clean sneakers (no holes!), white socks, a colored t-shirt

Or

Printed t-shirts in school colors (e.g. school logo or music logo)

One Month Ahead

Checklist

Send special invites to administrators, school board members, and faculty.

Arrange for concert chaperones (parents and/or faculty).

Arrange for concert to be recorded.

Special Invites to Administrators, School Board Members, and Faculty

It is in the music program's best interest to have administrators, board members, and faculty attend our concerts and witness for themselves the achievements of the music program. These colleagues are more likely to attend if they receive a personal invitation. Email is appropriate, but a hand written note, phone call, or face-to-face meeting is much more personal.

Arrange for Concert Chaperones (Parents and/or Faculty)

Adult chaperones may be used to:

- supervise students if we need to leave the presence of the ensemble
- supervise students in the audience while they are watching other students perform
- monitor the auditorium doors to prevent people entering the concert hall while an ensemble is performing
- monitor the hallways to prevent disruptions

Arrange for Concert to be Recorded

If the school does not have built-in recording equipment and/or a staff member who is familiar with its operation, find an A/V savvy student or parent to help out. If a fully integrated, professional system is beyond the means of the district, near-professional-level equipment is relatively inexpensive and can run through a laptop. Standalone digital sound recorders (e.g., M-Audio, Zoom, Edirol, Marantz) are extremely portable, affordable, and surprisingly powerful. Consider video recording the concert, too, which can be synchronized with the recording using consumer-grade video software (e.g., iMovie, Pinnacle). (However, be aware of copyright restrictions regarding the distribution of these recordings. See Chapter 21.)

Two Weeks Ahead

Checklist

Advertise
Set ensemble meeting location
Send concert reminder letter
Plan the length of the concert
Plan the performance order
Write program notes
Design the concert program

Advertise

Many local newspapers publish free public service announcements for school events. Remember to include: school name, ensemble name(s), concert title, concert date, time, and location, and ticket information. If the concert is a fundraiser, state its goal. Be sure to check with your administration, as some districts require that all press releases go through a particular office (e.g. business office, printing department, etc.).

For a more cyber-friendly approach, post concert information on the music department and the general school website. Additionally, advertise using Facebook and other social networking sites. By inviting online "friends" we can inexpensively target a large audience. (Be aware that some school districts have strict policies about staff members posting school related information on social networking sites.)

Set Ensemble Meeting Location

If the concert includes multiple ensembles it is important to plan where each one meets, especially for a school with only one rehearsal room. Reserve spaces that can comfortably host a large number of students, such as the concert stage, cafeteria, or gymnasium. Select a location that:

- is close to the performance venue. When students travel too far they tend to lose focus.
- has room for the same set-up that will be used on-stage (otherwise we risk unnecessary confusion at the start of the concert)
- contains minimal distractions; avoid locations near sporting events and other activities.

Concert Reminder Letter for Students

Letters (or emails) sent home to parents should contain all the important details regarding the concert. A copy of this letter should also appear on the music department website. Include:

Time, date, and location
Concert attire
Concert procedures and expectations
Concert admission cost
Call time
Meeting locations
Concert starting time
Attendance policy

Plan the Length of the Concert

Audiences will judge our concerts not only by the music but also by the overall concert experience, of which length plays a major role. A satisfying concert length is 60–90 minutes, with elementary concerts on the short end of this range. Keep in mind that the audience's attention typically wanes when concerts exceed 90 minutes, and young children, who are typically in attendance at elementary school concerts, have even shorter spans.

Plan the Performance Order

It is important to create a smooth flow from one group to the next, especially when different schools and age groups perform. We suggest:

- smaller ensembles before larger ensembles
- less-experienced ensembles before more experienced ensembles
- younger student ensembles before older student ensembles
- soft ensembles before loud ensembles (e.g., 9th grade string ensemble before the 100-member concert band).

Program Notes

Whether written by us or adapted from the notes in the score, most audience members appreciate learning something about a work before they hear it. Program notes need not be long. Effective ones provide important background information, prepare the ear for the unfamiliar (without ruining the surprise), and whet the appetite for what is about to come. Ineffective notes speak vaguely or in a dry narrative that means little unless one reads the notes as the piece is played (e.g., "first the trumpets play the melody, then the flutes with eighth-note accompaniments, then the whole ensemble plays the main theme. . ."). Consider having students write program notes as part of an assignment. Include the best ones in the program, or publish a separate packet. (For more strategies on writing program notes see Chapter 8.)

Design the Concert Program

Professional and informative programs are relatively easy to create using word processing software. Include the following:

Concert title
Date
Ensemble names
Director names
Student names (ordered by instrument, then either by seating order or alphabetical order)
Acknowledgments (administrators, board members, custodial staff, parent helpers, faculty helpers, music staff throughout the school district)
Upcoming dates/events
Student honors (honor ensembles, section leaders, scholarship awards, graduating seniors) indicated by asterisks and denoted at the bottom of the page
For each piece: title, year composed, composer, years of birth/death
Soloists
Announcements

One Week Ahead

Checklist

Assign student helpers
Design a seating plan (if regular plan does not fit on-stage)
Contact custodians
Print concert programs
Confirm audio/visual and non-musical items needed

Assign Student Helpers

Tasks that students can help with include:

- stage set-up and changes
- passing out programs
- ushering

- the Look-out: listens to the previous ensemble's performance to tell the conductor when it is time to line-up the next group
- post-concert cleanup

DESIGN A SEATING PLAN

We may need to adjust regular seating plans to fit on-stage. Try to keep the concert set-up similar to the rehearsal set-up, and have at least one dress rehearsal on-stage to acclimate to any differences. Make a set-up diagram for use during the concert that shows the shape of each row and the exact number of chairs and stands in each one. Make transitions easier by specifying what needs to be added or subtracted from each row to change the set-up for the next group. Distribute copies of this chart to the set-up crew and post a copy in the stage wings.

CONTACT CUSTODIANS

The custodial staff is always our ally. Contact them at least one week prior to the concert to remind them of any special needs (e.g., moving risers from off-site storage, clearing non-music equipment off the stage, thermostat settings, etc.). Never take their work for granted! Always thank them publicly and personally.

PRINT CONCERT PROGRAMS

Submit early so you can request a proof copy and spot glitches before printing the entire batch. Also, pass around a copy to the ensemble so they can check if their name is included and properly spelled.

CONFIRM AUDIO/VISUAL AND NON-MUSICAL ITEMS NEEDED

Since the school auditorium is shared by many groups, confirm that the stage will be clear, the sound system set-up, and the lights appropriately focused for the entire stage. (This is especially important directly after a theater production has closed.)

Day of the Concert

Checklist

Reserve seats.
Set up the stage and warmup rooms.

RESERVE SEATS

Treat administrators, board members, and other special guests with extra class by reserving their seats. Also consider reserve seating for ensembles while they are not performing. Add courteous signs that read "Reserved for the Band, Thank You."

Note: If seating is available, we recommend requiring students from different ensembles to watch each other's performance. For many this is the only time they will hear their peers perform. Additionally, it motivates younger ensembles to aspire to the level they hear in advanced ensembles.

SET UP THE STAGE AND WARMUP ROOMS

Have everything set up and ready to go for the first performing ensemble well before call time. Remember to ensure the following have been done:

- Be sure the venue has been cleared and cleaned.
- Set concert programs out for ushers.
- Remind custodians of the concert time to make sure doors are unlocked.
- Control the performance environment (thermostat, lighting board, sound board).
- Confirm lights are focused.
- Set-up recording equipment.
- Use tape to secure loose wires, particularly in areas where people could trip.
- Ensure you have blank media (CD, DVD, etc.) on which to record.
- Post directional signs (where each ensemble meets, auditorium, warmup meeting location and times, public restrooms for audience members).
- Designate areas to store cases and personal belongings (Keep hallways clear!).

Managing the Concert

For the concert to run smoothly we need to know exactly what should happen at every point in the evening. Carry a note card as a script or "cue card". By using this kind of cheat sheet we can focus on music-making instead of management.

Sample Director's Cue Card

Setting Up for the Concert

- Confirm that concert programs are in the front of auditorium.
- Unlock doors.
- Gather my equipment: baton, tuner, scores, announcements card.

Warmup Room "To Do"

- Line-up order to enter the stage.
- Lock room; remind students not to leave valuables in the warmup room.

Beginning of Concert

- Bring down house lights.
- Make opening announcements.

On Stage

- Bring lights up.

- Check that everyone has all equipment.
- Soloists to acknowledge:
  - for *Festivo*: Angie, Fred, Barbara
  - for *Portsmith Overture*: Harris, Jim, Jennifer

- List of announcements for the audience:

  - reminder about silent auction fundraiser
  - congratulations to students who made All-County
  - meet your student in the main lobby (not backstage) after the concert.

Talking to the Audience

Concerts offer a captive audience for our announcements, but be careful not to tax their patience. Instead, talk in small spurts between ensembles and pieces, and consider putting routine information in the concert program or in a PowerPoint presentation that continuously loops before the concert.

TOPICS TO ADDRESS

- Concert etiquette (when to clap, cell phones off, etc.)
- Emergency exits
- Upcoming dates (class trips, money due dates, deadlines for paperwork)
- Extra-curricular programs available for students (e.g., summer camps)/
- Requests for parent help (e.g., chaperoning, fundraising)
- Student achievements (e.g., honors bands)
- Special events
- Thank-yous (administration, parents, custodians, music teachers, chaperones, etc.)
- Information about private lessons

Note: In the unfortunate case that a student's name was inadvertently left off the concert program acknowledge this error to the audience and recognize the student.

Tuning Backstage

Many directors tune each student individually before a concert. For less experienced groups (especially for string students) this can be helpful, but since there is usually a delay and a temperature difference between the warmup room and stage, it is rendered meaningless. We recommend using the group's regular tuning procedure and encouraging students to get together as a section before going on-stage.

    With an orchestra, do not underestimate the importance of careful and accurate tuning of the open strings. For large ensembles it is useful to enlist the help of local professionals or advanced high school students to speed the process of individually tuning each instrument before the concert. (This may require staggered arrival times for the performers.) Begin with the oldest students and allow them to warmup supervised in an extra room as the youngest players tune. Use one common tone source for the concert A. Otherwise the pitch tends to slide from one student to another, the result being a wide range of supposedly "in tune" instruments.

Getting On and Off Stage

An ensemble's entrance onto the stage is its first opportunity to impress the audience with its professionalism. No matter the age of the ensemble, the entrance should be efficient and organized. Excessively long transitions, particularly between ensembles, needlessly lengthen the concert and make the audience restless. For set-up changes, have a crew with a seating chart ready in the wings.

Although members of American professional orchestras traditionally enter the stage leisurely and begin to warmup in their seats, for reasons of efficiency and organization it is advantageous for young students to enter formally in a line and settle into their chairs. Have each row line up in the outside hallway to avoid a disorganized shuffle. With multiple ensembles, one should enter from one side of the stage while another exits the other side. Have the students line up in an order that allows them to move to their seats efficiently. For example, the row furthest away from the stage entrance should enter first. For each row, the player who sits furthest from the entrance point should lead the row's entrance (see Figure 17.1). Younger ensembles should practice this before the day of the concert. Exceptionally large ensembles can enter from both sides of the stage. For even faster entry, set-up chairs with a narrow aisle down the center of the ensemble, which allows students to enter from the left, right, or center of the set-up.

FIGURE 17.1 Getting an Ensemble onto the Stage Efficiently

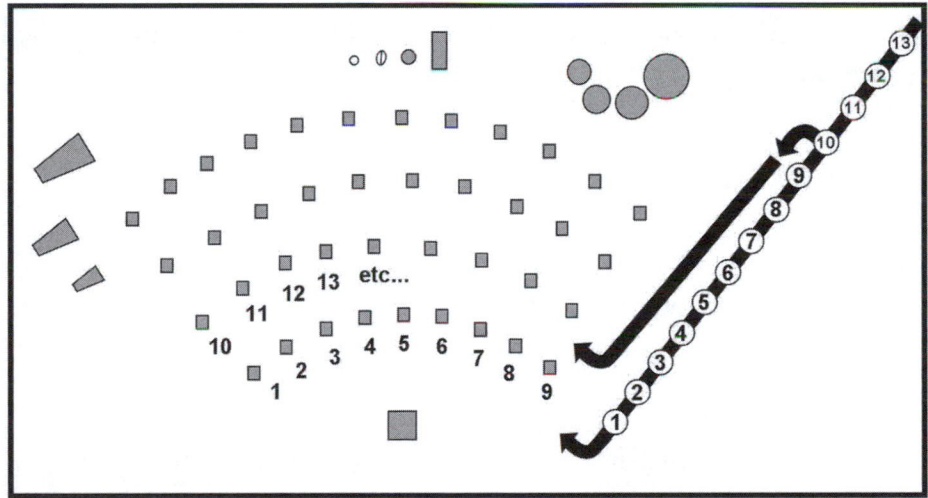

Make safety a priority. Turn up the stage lights so students can easily see where they are walking. Remind students to be careful with their instruments as they walk through the rows, keeping instruments close to their body while walking to reduce the chance of accidental damage. Remind tuba and string bass players to be careful of the bell and neck while walking through narrow doorways.

Older ensembles should have one or more percussionists check that all percussion needs are ready well before starting time. When there is more than one ensemble performing make prior arrangements for the first group's percussionists to help the second group set-up (provide both groups with a chart).

Instruct students to enter silently, carrying only their instruments and essential equipment. There should be no talking, and the first playing should be after the tuning note sounds (or, if tuning is done offstage, until so instructed). After sitting, ask the group to be certain that they have ample room for instruments, bows, slides, and bells, and to signal a problem by raising their hand (not by yelling for help or rushing off-stage in a panic!).

The process of leaving the stage should be as organized as the entrance—a controlled, row-by-row exit is far faster and safer than a mass exodus.

Tuning On-Stage

Once on-stage, if the ensemble has not played within 30 minutes it should take a moment to warmup and tune. Tuning on-stage is particularly important when the temperature of the warmup room and stage are noticeably different.

After the group is completely settled, if you use a concertmaster, have him enter preferably from stage right, and bow. If you do not use a concertmaster, use a visual cue to signal when the tuning note should start—e.g., dim the house lights, brighten the stage lights, close the back doors of the auditorium. Using a visual cue avoids the need to whisper from off-stage: "Psst! Play the tuning note!" Practice this prior to the concert. If needed, briefly re-tune the ensemble between pieces.

For orchestras, after the concertmaster enters the stage and bows, he should play the tuning A (or signal for a wind instrument to play it). He should then nod to direct students to move to D, G, C, and finally, E. Position yourself directly off-stage during this process—listen and watch very carefully! If a student has slipped from pitch, enter the stage quickly from behind and help tune the instrument. Leave the stage once again for the official conductor entrance. Do not be shy about taking time to re-tune individuals! Too much preparation has occurred to jeopardize a student's success because their instrument has slipped out of tune. Fix the problem with a smile and without apology. The audience will appreciate your efforts to put the student at ease, and everyone will appreciate the good intonation.

Posture and Instrument Positions for the Ensemble

Teach the ensemble how to hold their instrument when not playing. There are two main positions we should show: "Rest position"—used when sitting; "Standing position"—used when entering and exiting the stage or while standing to acknowledge applause.[1]

REST POSITION

- *Flutes/Oboe/Clarinet*—Instrument flat across the legs, preferably with the left end of the instrument slightly more towards the knee than the right end.
- *Saxophone*—Bell rests on the leg so the mouthpiece is to the player's left and pointing up to the ceiling.
- *Bassoon*—Instrument along the right side of the body, with the bassoon sitting straight up. *Note*: laying it flat across the lap will leak water from the U-tube into the unlined side of the bore, which could possibly cause wood rot.
- *Trumpet*—Bell rests on the left knee and instrument is held vertically with the left hand.
- *Horn*—Instrument on the lap, across the body, with the mouthpiece pointing upwards towards the ceiling.
- *Trombone*—Instrument rests vertically on the slide's end pin with the instrument between the legs.
- *Euphonium*—Instrument resting across the lap with the bell pointing to the left.
- *Tuba*—Resting across the body on the lap with the bell pointing to the left.
- *Violin/Viola*—Bow in the right hand; instrument resting vertically on the left thigh.
- *Cello*—Instrument in playing position; bowed relaxed in right hand.
- *Bass*—Neck leans back to the left shoulder while remaining vertically on its end pin.
- *Percussion*—Stand straight with arms to the side with stick or mallets in the right hand.

STANDING POSITION

- *Flutes/Oboe/Clarinet*—Held vertically with the right hand.
- *Saxophone*—Rotated to the left so its body is horizontal to the ground.
- *Bassoon*—Held in front of the body as if about to play.
- *Trumpet*—Left hand holds the valve casing as normal, while the right hand holds the edge of the bell.
- *Horn*—Held with the right hand, bell tucked underneath the arm.
- *Trombone*—Both hands hold the instrument as normal but with the bell pointing towards the ground.
- *Euphonium*—Instrument cradled across the body with the bell pointing towards ten-o'clock.
- *Tuba*—Instrument cradled across the body with the bell pointing towards ten-o'clock.
- *Violin/Viola*—Bow in the right hand, instrument in the left hand, peg-side on top about as high as the belly button.
- *Cello*—Bow in right hand, instrument standing vertically on its peg while held in the left hand.
- *Bass*—Bow in left hand, instrument standing vertically on its peg while held in the right hand.
- *Percussion*—Stand straight with arms to the side.

When the group stands everyone should face the audience—i.e., players whose seats face the center of the ensemble should turn outward to face the audience.

Entering the Stage for Conductor

The conductor should enter and exit after the group has settled and tuned, carrying only a baton (or have it sitting on the podium). Do not bring your music out with you. Instead, during the set-up, have a student bring it out, preset the stand to your desired height, and open the first score. Walk confidently but not too quickly when entering. Make eye contact with the audience as if to say, "Welcome to our concert. It's so nice to have you here," as opposed to staring at the stage floor as you head for the podium. Have the group rise one of two ways:

1. Automatically, when the conductor enters the stage (i.e., as a sign of unity and respect). Have a student who can see you enter, such as the concertmaster, lead the group in rising.
2. At the conductor's cue (i.e., to defer the audience's applause to the group as if to say, "Applause? For me? This applause is for you, the ensemble!")

After they stand, acknowledge the ensemble before bowing, preferably from the podium, or right next to it. The standard gesture is an outstretched arm, as if you are putting your arm around somebody. When entering with a soloist, trail slightly behind and allow him/her to take a bow without you while you applaud. In general, the conductor should bow after everyone else has been acknowledged.

Bowing Before the Piece

Applause is the audience's way of saying, "Thank you for being here tonight" or "Thank you for that performance." In response, we need to say, "You're welcome" through bows and acknowledgments. Before beginning the bow subtly acknowledge the audience by turning your head to the left and right as though briefly scanning the audience. A professional bow begins with the hands clasped in front of the waist or hanging naturally at the body's side. The body then bends at the waist with the crown of the head pointing towards the audience. Bend at a 45-degree angle and remain in this position just long enough to say to yourself: "Thank you . . . Thank you very much," or "I am wearing nice shoes tonight!" Do not look at the audience when bowing, as this looks awkward and unprofessional.

Beginning and Ending the Piece

Before lifting your hands to the conducting ready position, visually check in with players, particularly the timpanist and those players who begin the piece. With works that use a large percussion contingent, have each percussionist make eye contact and nod to show you they are ready. When you lift your hands into conducting-ready position, students who play at the beginning should raise their instruments from rest to ready. These movements should be immediate, but they need not be abrupt or robotic.

At the end of the piece the music to "enter silence" gracefully and appropriately. The conductor's hands and the player's instruments should stay up until the last note has decayed. Lower the hands in a way that reflects the style of the ending.

Keep in mind that audiences use our hands and body posture as cues for when to applaud. To discourage clapping between movements, keep the baton hand casually raised after the last note of the previous movement, just long enough to signal the audience to hold their applause. Especially if not listed in the program, it is appropriate before beginning the piece to remind the audience how many movements they will hear.

Bowing and Acknowledgments After the Piece is Over

Acknowledge players by asking them to stand in this order: soloists, sections, the composer (if in attendance), and the entire group. Use a classy gesture for these acknowledgements, such as an open hand, palm-up, rather than a stiffly pointed finger. The conductor should bow after every piece, but only after the other acknowledgments.

Avoid asking the group to stand after every piece. Generally, choose the project piece and the final work. Also, never cut off an audience's applause. If applause continues, bow again, exit the stage, pause for one or two seconds, re-enter the stage, acknowledge the group, and bow again. If you decide to stay on-stage between pieces, intersperse bows and group acknowledgments until the applause wanes, then turn to the group to begin preparing for the next piece, or introduce it to the audience.

For acknowledging players within the ensemble, alert soloists and the entire group beforehand that you will invite them to stand. At the end of concerts, an especially effective technique is to invite the back row to stand first and work towards the front. By pausing a few seconds between rows every parent can see their child.

In a piece with a soloist, acknowledge him/her immediately after the applause begins and allow him to bow. Then acknowledge soloists in the ensemble—all before you take your bow. Always allow the soloist to exit the stage first and then quickly re-enter for encore bows. For the encore bows, the conductor can either stay in the wings, take a bow after the soloist, or trail a few steps behind the soloist and applaud.

Occasionally we may want to show a greater level of appreciation to the audience, such as during a standing ovation. The further we bend our body and the longer we remain in this position, the more appreciation we show. For older ensembles, consider shaking the hands of players in the front rows.

Concert Etiquette for Students

Teach students the proper way to behave before, during, and after the performance. Consider rehearsing these prior to the concert. Our expectations should include:

- Leave valuables at home.
- Turn off all cell phones after entering the building.
- Play only your own instrument in the warmup room.
- Always act professionally; no horseplay in the warmup room or on stage.
- Be silent when lined up to go on stage.
- When on stage, raise your hand if you need something.
- Do not wave to the audience.
- Do not call attention to yourself onstage by loudly playing melodies from the concert literature or your favorite songs.
- Girls in skirts should keep their knees together.
- Do not talk on stage.
- Keep your eyes on the conductor.

Aural Program Notes—Teaching Audiences What We Teach Our Students

An effective alternative to written program notes is to present aural notes and introduce excerpts from the piece. These are especially useful for unfamiliar works, contemporary pieces, or works with overt programmatic meaning, musical symbolism and motivic development. The simplest approach is to play brief excerpts in the way promotional CDs give an overview of a long piece by jumping around. At the very least this associates music with our written labels of "first theme," "second theme," etc.

For a more in-depth, effective, and enjoyable demonstration, break sections down so the audience can hear how the piece is put together. Consider this: Students often admit they like a work better at the end of the rehearsal process than at the beginning. Why? Even if we never explain anything, they become well-acquainted with its inner-workings through the practice process. They have heard us break down each section and put it back together. Through repeated hearings they have made sense of the composer's style and the work's harmonic world. And throughout the entire rehearsal process they have gained perspective on the work's overall form. In other words, students have had a chance to absorb exactly the sort of information our audiences need.

Aural notes can accelerate and summarize this process during the concert. Choose one or two pieces and keep each presentation under three minutes. Pick the most compelling aspects of the work and demonstrate them with the encouragement: "Listen to this!"

- *Introduce themes and motives*—Play the theme (or a snippet of it) without the accompaniment; this is especially effective when the themes have extra-musical associations.
- *Show one or more transformations of the theme*—Play augmentations, diminutions, fragmentations, stretti, etc., so the audience recognizes themes when they are transformed.
- *Build the layers*—For thick textures that are difficult to make sense of after one hearing, introduce each layer and build the texture part by part.
- *Break down harmonies*—For harmonies audience members might find "weird" or "ugly," show them why it sounds that way. For example, for a polytonal chord, play each of its component triads separately, and then combine them again.
- *De-compose and Re-compose*—Composers often play off our expectations by adjusting and elaborating musical conventions. But if audiences do not recognize the underlying convention, it is difficult to appreciate compositional creativity. Using aural notes we let audiences hear the original version and then the composer's "doctored" version. For example, play a section without added dissonances, and

then play as-written. Or, temporarily re-write rhythmic surprises to demonstrate the expected version, and then add the surprise back in.

- *Identify unusual instruments*—Do a brief "Show and Tell" of special instruments such as slapstick, water gong, English horn, muted tuba, etc.

Aural Program Note Samples: Demo Excerpt Sheets

Give students a sheet of "Demo Excerpts" with self-explanatory descriptions. The conductor should memorize the excerpts so the flow between speech and music is seamless.

In the example below, sentences in italics are what the conductor says to the audience; no need to print these lines on the student excerpt sheets.

EXAMPLE: CHESTER, OVERTURE FOR BAND, WILLIAM SCHUMAN

1. *Chester was a patriotic anthem from the American Revolution. This entire overture is based on it. We first hear it as a reverent chorale:*
   Everybody: m. 1–4

2. *Its first transformation is into an aggressive version of itself that we hear twice as fast in the woodwinds:*
   Everybody: m. 46–49

3. *If you're wondering what that dissonant chord accompanying it is, you can easily play it at home! By the way, dissonance, the opposite of consonance, is when two or more notes grind together. It's sort of like musical "friction." To create this chord, just use your entire forearm and simultaneously play every white note on the piano. When the band does it, it sounds like this:*
   Brass/low winds/snare: m. 38—sustain the chord until I release it.

4. *Sometimes the original melody is a little less obvious, as in this version:*
   Everybody: m. 101–107
   First time: As written

5. *But that's basically just the main theme with some rhythmic tricks. Here's the same section in slow motion, without those twists.*
   Second time: Out of time, like a chorale, without syncopations

6. *There's a harmonic twist, too. The trumpets and trombones are each playing in different keys!*
   Third time: Trumpets hold their first note (*the trumpets are in one key . . .*)
   Fourth time: Trombones hold their first note (*. . . and the trombones are in another . . .*)

7. *Combine those two keys together, and it sounds like this:*
   Fifth time: Trumpets and trombones hold their first note

8. *After all these variations, Schuman finally gives us the theme as we might have heard it during the American Revolution, though in this version the trumpet replaces the fife:*
   Trumpet and Snare only: m. 212–215

9. *We hope you enjoy our performance of William Schuman's* Chester, Overture for Band!

Activities/Assignments for Further Exploration

1. For a piece you are currently conducting or playing, write program notes and design an aural program note presentation.
2. Practice entering the stage, bowing, and exiting. Have your classmates critique you.
3. Collect sample programs from at least two ensembles. Take note of effective formatting features. Ask the directors if they would send you the word processing template they use.

Further Reading

Green, Barry, and W. Timothy Gallwey. *The Inner Game of Music*. Garden City, NY: Anchor Press/Doubleday, 1986.

Hagberg, Karen A. *Stage Presence from Head to Toe: A Manual for Musicians*. Lanham, MD: Scarecrow Press, 2003.

Holoman, D. Kern. *Writing About Music: A Style Sheet*. Berkeley: University of California Press, 2008.
Ristad, Eloise. *A Soprano on Her Head: Right-Side-Up Reflections on Life and Other Performances*. Boulder, Colorado: Real People Press, 1981.

Wingell, Richard. *Writing About Music: An Introductory Guide*. Upper Saddle River, NJ: Pearson Prentice Hall, 2009.

Chapter 18

Promotion and Advocacy

To Guide Your Reading

What should we consider when deciding if and how to fundraise?

What ethical issues are involved in fundraising?

What is the difference between individual and group fundraising activities, and what are the advantages and disadvantages of each?

What is the role of a parent booster organization?

How does one write an effective press release?

What are the components of an effective flyer?

What other forms of writing can be used to promote the music program?

What are ways to regularly showcase a music program to the community?

Why is music education advocacy important?

How can music advocacy be couched through its inherent benefits and peripheral benefits?

Fundraising

It is unlikely the school budget will cover all costs of running an instrumental music program, particularly extra-curricular aspects such as trips and competitions. The cost of transportation, lodging, registration fees, etc., can quickly rise to thousands of dollars. It is almost a given that bands and orchestras will need to raise money to cover some of these expenses.

Before engaging in fundraising activities, check with the school's administration for guidelines and expectations. Determine exactly what the district typically provides and what the band/orchestra is expected to purchase itself. Whenever possible, avoid fundraising for basic curricular needs (e.g. instruments, music, repair costs, etc.), otherwise we signal to the administration that we do not need their full financial support.

Also explore restrictions. For instance, some districts prohibit the sale of raffle tickets because it resembles illegal gambling. Out of professional courtesy, research the fundraising programs of other school organizations to avoid duplicates. If the swim team and the band are both selling fruit, each will poach the other's markets, putting students and customers in an awkward position.

Individual and Group Fundraising

There are two broad approaches to fundraising: *individual-focused* activities; and *group-focused* activities. In individual-focused activities, each student essentially works for himself in selling a product or service, and the profits are put into an individual account. Everyone may work as hard as he needs to: If John must raise all $700 for a trip to Florida, he has the opportunity to sell as much product as he can to reach that goal. If his family has the means to pay or he has a part-time job, he may choose to work less.

In contrast to the citrus-dominated sales of years past, today's fundraising catalogs offer endless options. Among the most popular are:

- citrus fruit
- candy
- gift wrap
- gift packs (everything from candles to gourmet foods)
- discount cards
- cookie dough
- magazine subscriptions
- popcorn canisters
- calendars
- entertainment coupon books
- fundraising programs through restaurants (McDonald's, Krispy Kreme).

Food is among the most common products. According to the Center for Science in the Public Interest, a 2000 survey found that 80 percent of PTAs sell food; 76 percent sell chocolate, 67 percent sell high-fat baked goods, and 63 percent sell non-chocolate candy. It's reasonable to assume music program sales have a similar profile.[1]

"Health Food" versus "Junk Food"

There is always a market for lollipops and cookie dough, but it is worth reflecting upon whether we want to sell candy to children when many schools are removing junk food from their menus and vending machines. As fundraising expert Frank Sennett points out, we risk acting unethically, or worse, hypocritically, if we peddle candy in the face of rampant childhood obesity.[2] Sennett suggests turning a candy-boycott into marketing leverage:

> [T]ell potential donors something like this: "We've kicked the junk food habit. Please help keep us healthy by participating in the fun, calorie-free event." The beautiful part of this appeal is that it gives members of the school community another altruistic reason to contribute . . . all the while thinking of their donation as a blow against obesity, too (Sennett 4).

A natural solution is to offer a natural product. Beyond fresh fruit, try:

- dried fruit and vegetable snacks (such as "Just Fruit")—perfect for snacking
- low fat pizzas and baked goods
- granola bars and other high-protein snacks
- bottled water
- gourmet spices.

Sample Individual Fundraisers Involving Services

Many of the best fundraising options involve selling services rather goods. Here are two examples:

- *Odd jobs*—Set up a program by which students (either individually or in small groups) are hired by local families and businesses to do minor tasks such as painting, leaf raking, snow shoveling, and cleaning. Design an announcement on school letterhead so prospective customers understand that the proceeds help the music program. Or, advertise the program internally, by word-of-mouth, and by referrals from family, friends, and colleagues.
- *Chamber music for hire*—Similar to the Odd Job program, but in this case the students provide a musical service in the form of brass quintets, string quartets, flute trios, and other small ensembles. It's a great way to jump-start a chamber music program. In return for live music, local businesses can be encouraged to offer a small honorarium or donation.

Be sensitive to fundraiser burnout. With any of these programs we risk turning our students (and their parents) into zombie salespeople, descending upon friends, neighbors, and office colleagues for patronage. Not only does this put students in the uncomfortable position of directly soliciting money, but it can be incredibly time-consuming.

An alternative to these student-focused activities are large-scale group events, with the proceeds placed into a general account for the band/orchestra. Profits often go towards purchasing items that benefit everybody, such as transportation, contest-fees, etc, or to help defray everyone's cost for a trip (e.g., in a group of 75, a $1000 group profit would decrease the individual cost by about $13)

Sample Large Group Fundraisers

Here are a few ideas for large group fundraisers:

- *Bake sales*—Perhaps the most venerable group fundraiser of all, they still have the potential to do quite well. For variety, try a low-fat, low-calorie version.
- *Car washes*—Another classic, these are easy to organize, inexpensive to run, and great for group bonding. Frank Sennett suggests finding local car collectors to display their vehicles as "eye candy" for potential customers (Sennett, 98).
- *School variety show*—Showcase the known (and unknown!) talents of students and faculty. Charge admission at the door, or ask for donations.
- *Auctions and tag sales*—Most families have interesting but unused "stuff" clogging their attics and basements. Ask music parents to donate as much as they can, and then sell it in an auction or tag sale. These have the potential to raise thousands of dollars, though it's necessary to wait a few years for the next generation of families to enter the program with a new crop of valuable stuff they are willing to donate. In *Beyond the Bakesale*, Jean C. Joachim suggests auctioning memberships (discounted from local businesses) and services (donated by parents and professionals)[3]— e.g., memberships and gift

certificates from health clubs, golf courses, gyms, etc.; donated services for lessons in dancing, photography, painting, music, sports, etc. *Note*: As with any donations, be sure to send "Thank you" notes to those who donate.

- *Faculty/Local Celebrity/Local Dignitary Auctions*—Although many will be too shy to participate, some faculty and celebrities may be willing to donate small items and fun opportunities (a meal with a teacher, a trip to a museum or concert, a chance to play one-on-one basketball, a day as the County-chairperson, etc.).
- *Silent auctions*—Solicit parents and local businesses to donate items or gift certificates, and allow them to display their company name prominently around the item. Combine small items into gift-baskets (e.g., holiday baskets, cheese selections, etc.). During a predetermined bidding period, all items up for auction are displayed on tables, allowing guests to decide the items they wish to bid for. Bidding may either be done publicly, meaning people write their bid on a sheet of paper in front of each item, or privately, meaning bids are written down and placed into a receptacle. Silent auctions are readily combined with a dinner event, allowing guests to eat and browse at their leisure.
- *50/50 raffles*—This is a simple yet effective activity in which the prize is half of the money paid into the raffle. If each ticket costs $2 and 100 people buy tickets, the winner and the school each collect $100.
- *Corporate catering*—As part of their community outreach, many upscale chain restaurants (e.g., Carabbas, Outback) cater fundraising events with substantial discounts for non-profit organizations. For example, if the restaurant charges $4 per plate, the music organization can charge a reasonable $10 per dinner. This yields a substantial profit for the school with a quality-meal that is no more expensive than it would be in the restaurant.
- *Program ads*— Some districts allow school organizations to sell advertisements in their programs. For a reasonable price local businesses can thus reach a captive audience of parents and children.
- *Dinner dances, adult proms, name-that-tune, and karaoke nights*—Using the jazz ensemble, concert band, orchestra, chamber groups, and student bands as entertainment, organize a classy event that includes food, entertainment, and fun. Profits come from ticket sales, and costs can be kept to a minimum with pot-luck food donations by parents. Ticket prices often range from $15–30 per head.

    Caveat: Be sure to investigate copyright issues (performing copyrighted music for a profit) before embarking on this type of event.
- *Large-scale scavenger hunts*—Charge an entry fee per car, provide a map and clues, and send guests on a journey around town to find local sites and businesses. If possible, recruit local businesses to be included as "treasures" in return for raffle prize donations. Teams can prove they've solved every clue by taking digital pictures with a camera or cell phone. It's fun and relatively inexpensive (Sennett, 50).
- *Spelling bees*—Invite local dignitaries, administrators, and celebrities to participate in an adult spelling competition and charge admission. Or, stage a competition with students and raise money by soliciting pledges for each word spelled correctly (say, $1 per word). (This is basically a spelling version of the classic Bowl-a-Thon.)
- *Gift wrapping services*—Malls often allow school groups to set up tables during the holiday season so shoppers can have their gifts wrapped (for a small fee) right after purchasing them.
- *Sports tournaments*—Instead of the standard basketball or softball tournament, try frisbee golf in a local park or table tennis. Charge $10–15 per entrant. Enlist the help of local businesses and social groups to design and sponsor holes (Sennett, 64).
- *Concession stands*—Many high schools, colleges and universities allow non-profit groups to run concession stands at football games.
- *Antique appraisals*—Enlist the help of a local expert to appraise antique items. Charge an entrance fee for people to bring things in, but don't take a percentage of the profits if the items are later sold.

- *Instant CDs*—A few years ago Mark Custom Recording, based in Clarence, New York, began selling recordings from music conventions on the day after the performance. For small-scale jobs, the turnaround can be even quicker. Near pro-level recording is possible on well-equipped laptops or with school-owned equipment. To make it work, pre-print jewel case inserts, borrow laptops for burning multiple disks, and excite the audience with the possibility of walking away that night with the CD in hand.

    Note: Be sure to obtain copyright permissions before selling any recordings.
- *Recycle*—As an environmentally friendly service, offer to collect and recycle old cell phones and printer cartridges for a small fee or donation. Or, use a company that specializes in recycling fundraisers, such as FundingFactory.com.
- *Fun-houses, Halloween haunts, and hazes*—Set up a haunted house in the local gym or on a nearby farm. Charge admission for each "victim"!

Generally speaking, proceeds from student-focused fundraisers go into individual accounts, while proceeds from group activities go into general accounts. It can be challenging to use individual sales for the benefit of the group; students may be unmotivated since they will only see a small portion of the profits. For group activities, directors often divide profits depending on how long each student worked on the project— work more hours, make more money. One problem with this solution is determining what activities are "billable" hours. Is preparing for the event worth just as much as participating in it? Who logs the hours?

Whenever possible, avoid handling the money yourself. Recruit parent volunteers to serve as accountants, or ask the parent organization to appoint a fundraising chairperson, even if this person's job is simply to collect and count the money. At the very least, this saves us from time-consuming paperwork, and in a worst-case scenario it saves us from accusations of impropriety.

After the fundraiser is complete, find opportunities to send "Thank you" notes, especially to donors and parents who helped organize it. Remember: by referencing past generosity, "thank you" notes set up philanthropy in the future. Short, handwritten note-cards are more personal than emails.

A constant challenge in fundraising is keeping students motivated, and part of that is a function of our attitude and approach. If students and parents believe in the end goal and have fun doing it, motivation will take care of itself. As Frank Sennett writes:

> [I]f you treat school fundraising as drudgery, the community will agree with you. But if you get excited about FUNdraising [sic] and maximize each event's potential for education, outreach, and plain old good times, the buzz likely will prove infectious—while participation levels and receipts soar to new heights (Sennett, xvii).

Parent Organizations

Among the music program's strongest fundraising allies are the parents of the students in our ensembles, especially when organized into Band Parent Organizations (BPAs) or Music Booster Organizations (MBOs). Booster organizations are often in place when directors arrive at a school, but if not they are relatively easy to organize. After obtaining administrative approval, poll the parents about the possibility of an MBO and determine whether there is any history you need to consider (failed attempts, disbanded organizations, etc.). Inform parents about the need for an organization and your desire to create one. At an open meeting for parents and administrators, discuss the potential for a booster club; decide whether to have a band/orchestra-only organization or an MBO that services the entire music/fine arts department.

It is also useful to create a temporary leadership committee to write bylaws and cultivate interest among other parents.

The best resource for designing bylaws are the MBOs of other schools. Among other things, bylaws should explicitly describe:

- a statement of the organization's missions and objectives
- the makeup of the executive board and responsibilities of each member (e.g., president, vice-president, secretary, treasurer)
- requirements for membership in the group
- procedure for elections
- descriptions of committees
- procedure for changing the bylaws

Although an MBOs' primary responsibility is to fundraise, it should only do so for items we do not expect the district to purchase. Avoid using booster funds to purchase instruments, music, general supplies, chairs, stands, and facilities upgrades. Otherwise, we signal to the administration that their support is unnecessary or superfluous. To avoid conflicts and the perception of impropriety, have an MBO officer handle all monies and transactions. And under no circumstances should booster funds be used to supplement the band director's salary, as this creates a serious conflict of interest wherein the director is essentially employed by the organization that is tasked with supporting his program.

It is common, however, for MBO's to fund the activities of marching bands and parade bands, including:

- staff instructors (colorguard, marching, drumline, pit percussion)
- custom drills and music arrangements
- transportation and entrance fees for competitions and festivals
- special props (flags, fabrics for costumes)
- special instruments (sousaphones, marching quads)
- equipment (wheels for pit percussion instruments, drum major stands)

Ideally, however, MBOs should concentrate on funding special opportunities for students, such as:

- commissions for new works
- guest artists
- masterclasses
- trips
- attending professional concerts
- private lesson scholarships
- summer music programs

MBOs can also provide support for the program in non-financial ways, such as organizing chaperones for trips, helping to move pit percussion equipment (e.g., driving the truck), and providing manpower to record and videotape concerts.

As with any organization that earns and spends money, MBOs need organized budgets. The music director and board should work together at the end of the school year to develop next year's priorities and goals. What is most needed? What amount is reasonable to ask the organization to raise? This budget will likely need to be voted on by the entire MBO. After all, it is the parents who will be doing a good deal of the work!

It is crucial to cultivate a healthy relationship between the music director and the parent organization. Both sides should respect each other, but ultimately the MBO needs to understand it is a service and advisory organization. Directors must not allow the MBO to dictate the needs, mission, or policies of the music program. If irreconcilable differences develop and the MBO becomes "out of control," work firmly, patiently, fairly, and ethically to adjust the direction of the parent group before student education suffers and teacher jobs are put in jeopardy.

These situations are fraught with political, personal, and professional minefields, however, so enlist the counsel of administrators, other teachers, and fellow directors. In extreme cases the director may need to disband the group and rebuild in a few years, after tensions have abated. To help monitor issues within the MBO, the director or one music department staff member should attend all meetings. If there is any sign of concern, keep the school administration advised.

Promoting Events with Writing

Most school concerts have a built-in audience of friends and family, and thus need little advertising beyond an announcement and a letter or email home. But special events and fundraisers need a bit more help; we can't expect a huge audience to show up automatically. The most common ways to publicize are:

- *Email*—Compile a list of previous audience members and customers and send a friendly message announcing new events. In this age of spam, it is important to make the list voluntary— include a mailing list sign-up sheet at concerts, and include a space for email addresses on registration forms. If people enjoy the product, they won't mind an occasional message.
- *Calendar announcements for local newspapers and radio*—Local stations and NPR affiliates often make free announcements for schools and other non-profit organizations. Newspapers may have an arts section or community calendar.
- *Press releases*—A press release is a short written statement distributed to the media. Music programs can use them to announce concerts, fundraisers, and special guests. Occasionally newspapers will use them as the basis for a short article covering the event. Press releases should follow a standard format and succinctly cover the "who, what, where, and why" of the event. Avoid long sentences filled with jargon. Keep in mind that newspaper editors are more likely to use the release if it is nearly article-ready, with little editing needed.

Sample Press Release 1

For Immediate Release: May 10, 2010
Contact: John Bocal
Director of Bands
Acme High School
(555) 555-5555
johnbocal@acme.edu

Acme High School Band to perform final concert of the year

Mapleville, NY—On Thursday, June 14, 2010, the Acme High School band program will present its final concert of the year at 7:30pm in the Acme High School Auditorium. The concert will feature the Wind Ensemble and Concert Band.

Band director John Bocal is proud of what his students have accomplished this year. "Our season began back in the heat of August," he said, "and it's been extremely gratifying to see how the students have improved."

This year the Acme band program sent 22 students to the Orange County All-County honor band, and more students than ever before to the All-State Festival in Rochester, NY. Five students represented Acme in Rochester, all chosen on the basis of their solo performances in March's solo festivals hosted in nearby Oaktown.

Thursday's concert will feature classic music for concert band, such as Gustav Holst's *First Suite in E♭*, and Percy Grainger's *Irish Tune from County Derry*. "These are among the masterpieces of our literature, and contain some of the most beautiful music ever written," Mr. Bocal said.

The band is trying something new, too, as the senior class has chosen the final piece of the concert: John Phillip Sousa's *Washington Post March*. The band performed the march during the fall parade season, and it was the unanimous choice with which to end the concert with a bang.

Admission for Thursday's concert is free.

For more information, visit: www.acmehighband.org

Sample Press Release 2

For Immediate Release: November 20, 2010
Contact: Sandra Bow
Director of Orchestras
Acme Middle School
(555) 555-5555
sbow@acmemiddle.edu

Acme Middle School Orchestra to hold holiday gift-wrapping fundraiser

Mapleville, NY—With the holiday season upon us, the Mapleville Middle School Orchestra will be holding its annual gift-wrapping fundraiser at the Birchway Mall from December 10–15. For a small fee, orchestra students and their parents will wrap any presents that are brought to the table, regardless of whether they were purchased at the mall.

Sandra Bow, the orchestra director, says this is the fourth year in a row the orchestra has set up shop in the mall. "It was first suggested by one of the orchestra parents, and since then it's become one of our most popular fundraisers," she said. Ms. Bow said the music program uses the proceeds of the fundraiser to defray the cost for orchestra festivals, and also to bring in professional musicians to hold masterclasses.

The gift-wrapping tables will be set up at the North end of the mall, just down the hallway from the Primespot Department Store. Small packages cost $4 to wrap; large packages, $6. A variety of wrapping papers will be available for Christmas and Hannukah, including some without a holiday pattern. Bows will be available for an extra $1.

The gift-wrapping tables will be open from 4-8pm each day.

For more information, visit acmemiddleschoolorch.org

Contact: sbow@acmemiddle.edu

Phone: (555) 555-5555

- *Social Networking sites*—Sites likes Facebook have created a new way to reach people. Students can easily send invites to their "friends," and clickable advertisements (similar to the ones Google places on the sides of searches and websites) can be targeted towards specific audiences. Fees are calculated "per click"—the more people view and click, the more the advertisement costs. But at only pennies each, these ads are affordable and efficient.

  Note: Technology is constantly evolving, so always check to see what options are available and affordable. Also, be sure to have a student or parent set up and maintain the account in the group's name. Avoid using your personal account for any communication.
- *Flyers*—Although social networking sites have made old fashioned flyers somewhat obsolete, they are still a great way to announce events around the school and the community.

  - Find a student or parent with computer graphics expertise to design a logo for the ensemble and/or the music program. The logo need not always headline the announcement, but its inclusion adds a professional touch and consistency from flyer to flyer. Check with the district offices to obtain clearance to use the school's name or logo.
  - Design a template that is easily modified and re-used. A slick template is better than a hastily-designed original.
  - Don't expect people to read the entire flyer. After reading the main visual image or headline, people spend barely a second before deciding whether to read the rest.[4] Make these visual hooks catchy and to the point.
  - Make important details such as the date, time, and place easy to spot (Callen, 62).
  - Use bullet points rather than full sentences to highlight information; keep wordiness to a minimum (Callen, 62).

With all advertising:

- determine if there are policies that require releases to go through a central district office to insure format and consistency
- proofread carefully for spelling, grammar, punctuation, and accuracy
- proofread again, and then ask someone else to proofread!

Advocacy—A Brief Introduction

The topic of advocacy for music education is a vast subject, and a complete discussion is beyond the realm of this text. We offer here a few thoughts as a means to spur discussion and further exploration. Music educators seem locked in a never-ending battle to justify music's value. Some of this is practical: If we do not justify music programs' large budgets, they may fall prey to cuts; and if we do not justify music's place in the curriculum, core subject initiatives may crowd it out. Advocacy should lead others to understand why music is important, why instrumental study is an irreplaceable way to access music's benefits, and why it needs to be taught alongside physics and literature. Moreover, learning how to advocate for music should be more than an exercise in flag-waving and lobbying. It should be an introspective endeavor that informs and guides our own teaching.

For perspective, let us consider the argument for teaching science in our schools, a subject whose importance seems unassailable. Dennis Overbye writes in the New York Times:

> Science . . . is something that people do to look for truth. That endeavor, which has transformed the world in the last few centuries, does indeed teach values. Those values, among others, are honesty, doubt, respect for evidence, openness, accountability and tolerance and indeed hunger for opposing points of view. These are the unabashedly pragmatic working principles that guide the buzzing, testing, poking, probing, argumentative, gossiping, gadgetry, joking, dreaming and tendentious cloud of activity . . . that is slowly and thoroughly penetrating every nook and cranny of the world . . . It requires . . . just the hypothesis that nature can be interrogated and that nature is the final arbiter.[5]

Overbye's argument is notable both for its elegance and its dual tact. It extols science for what makes it unique— the unbiased search for knowledge—and also for its peripheral benefits—the values and thought processes it teaches. Music advocacy can take a parallel approach. Eleven years earlier in the *New York Times*, music critic Paul Griffiths wrote an equally elegant defense of music education. He began with the peripheral benefits:

> Music teaches the ability to listen, which is fundamental to education. And all the evidence suggests that listening to music and performing music help a child in acquiring other skills. Music seems to hook into parts of the brain that have to do with mathematical and language abilities. On a more practical level, a child involved in a musical performance is confronted with challenges that will be of lifelong benefit: how you present yourself in public, how you argue a case, how you interpret a document, what evidence you accept and what you question, where you draw the limit between what you are told and what you want, how you work with others toward a common goal.[6]

Griffiths concluded with music's inherent benefits:

> the values of giving expression to a thought or a feeling without going through words, the values of phrasing that expression so that it can be understood by others, the values of asserting the importance of things (musical works) that have no physical existence or monetary worth, the values of stimulating and training the experience of sound and of what sound can mean (Griffiths, 37).

Keep in mind that effective advocacy is not only about promoting the music program during times of economic and curricular crisis. "Maintenance advocacy" involves proactively showcasing the music program's benefits and achievements on a consistent basis. For example:

- Find opportunities to showcase the most talented students for school events (e.g., school awards ceremonies, school board meetings, etc.)[7].
- Cultivate outreach performances in the community (e.g., county fairs, events hosted by local politicians, nursing homes, veterans associations) (Bollinger, 27).
- Send monthly newsletters to parents and administrators with updates about the music program and the students' achievements.
- Include school administration and school board members' names on concert programs (typically they are listed on the back page).
- Hold an open rehearsal and invite administrators to attend.
- Send copies of programs from concerts, festivals, and competitions to administrators.
- Invite administrators to attend sessions with guest artists, composers, and clinicians.

Activities/Assignments for Further Exploration

1. Poll the class about their favorite fundraisers. Which did they think were the most effective? Which motivated them to participate?

2. Brainstorm ideas for individual and group-focused fundraisers.

3. Contact two local music teachers and ask to see a copy of the bylaws for their music booster organizations. Share these with the class and compare.

4. Write a sample press release for the following scenarios:

   Upcoming holiday concert
   Car wash fundraiser
   Hosting a marching band competition

5. As a class, discuss the following questions:

   What are music's inherent benefits?
   What are music's peripheral benefits?
   Which do you think are more important?
   Why should we be studying music in schools?

6. If you were asked to make a presentation to the board of education defending music's budget and its place in the curriculum, what would you say? Would your argument change if the same presentation was made to a faculty meeting of non-music teachers? Parents? Students?

Further Reading

Elliott, David James. *Music Matters: A New Philosophy of Music Education*. New York: Oxford University Press, 1995.

Jorgensen, Estelle Ruth. *Transforming Music Education*. Bloomington, IN: Indiana University Press, 2003.

Lautzenheiser, Tim, and Charles Thomas Menghini. *Band Director's Communication Kit*. Milwaukee, WI: Hal Leonard, 2000.

Lautzenheiser, Tim. *Music Advocacy and Student Leadership: Key Components of Every Successful Music Program: A Collection of Writings*. Chicago: GIA Publications, Inc., 2005.

Music Educators National Conference (U.S.). *Music Booster Manual*. Reston, VA (1902 Association Dr., Reston 22091-1597): Music Educators National Conference, 1989.

MENC, the National Association for Music Education (U.S.), NAMM, the International Music Products Association, and National School Boards Association. *Music for all Students: A Leadership Guide for Planning a Music Education Advocacy Day with State Legislatures*. Reston, VA: MENC, the National Association for Music Education, 2000.

Reimer, Bennett. *A Philosophy of Music Education: Advancing the Vision*. Upper Saddle River, NJ: Prentice Hall, 2003.

Reimer, Bennett. *Seeking the Significance of Music Education: Essays and Reflections*. Lanham, MD: Rowman & Littlefield Education, 2009.

Chapter 19

Communication

To Guide Your Reading

What are effective ways to communicate with parents via phone, email, and in person?

What are common pitfalls during these communications?

How do the conventions of writing email change depending on the situation?

How can we keep track of our communications with students, parents, and administrators?

In what ways can we communicate en masse?

What topics and materials are usually included in student handbooks?

There is a common tendency to talk to parents only when we absolutely need to, usually if a child has become a discipline issue. In reality, we should call as much to convey the good news ("David did very well on his playing test; he's really made improvement this semester") as the bad. And we should make contact with parents throughout the school year. Even if they do not initiate it, most appreciate when a teacher takes extra time to keep them involved and informed.

Reasons to Contact Parents

Positive: to convey achievement or improvement.
Preventative: to identify issues that are likely to become problems.
Reactionary: to address current problems and identify areas which need immediate improvement.

Make parent contact positive and productive by approaching the conversation compassionately, professionally, and logically. Remember, it is about helping the student become more successful, not about placing blame.

No matter what happens, always—ALWAYS!—be courteous and in control. Quite simply, parents are more likely to be supportive if they are treated with respect. Here are some useful phrases with which to build your conversation:

Generic Phrases

I want what is best for your child.
How may I help?
Is there anything I can do at school to help your child?
I have been frustrated by . . .
It is important that . . .
I am concerned with . . .
Johnny is not progressing . . .
Johnny would benefit from . . .
Jane needs to take more responsibility for . . .

Student Disrupts Class

Sarah needs to follow directions in class.
Johnny initiates discussion with those around him when he should be listening to class instruction.
He/she creates a class distraction by . . .

Student Shows Improvement

Jane has shown consistent progress since the beginning of the current quarter.
Jane has shown significant improvement over the past month.
Jane has been showing more self-confidence.

Student is Doing Very Well

Johnny is a pleasure to have in class.
Johnny is very enthusiastic toward the subject matter.
Jane is very cooperative.
Jane works very well with others.
Johnny is very conscientious.

Student Has Lateness/Absence Problems

Jane's excessive absences are limiting her progress and that of her section and ensemble.

Be sure to appropriately prepare *before* having the conversation: Review the student's record and all previous contact regarding the issue with the student, parents and administrators. Then, use an organized, systematic plan for the phone call.

Sample Script: Making the Phone Call

1. Greet, state your name, position, and school where you teach.
   "Hello, this is Mr. Sax, the band director at Acme High School."

2. Ask for the student's parent by either their last name . . .
   "May I please speak to either Mr. or Mrs. Jones?"

. . . or, by asking for a parent of the student.
"May I please speak to one of John's parents?"

3. If someone else had initially answered the phone, reintroduce yourself once the parent picks up, even if you hear the first person say who is on the phone.

4. Start the conversation in a positive and non-confrontational manner.
"I am calling to share with you a situation John is having in his band class. I am confident there is something that we can do together to get John on the right track."

5. Present the situation and the student's specific behavior.
"John has forgotten his instrument four times over the past two weeks."

6. Explain how the behavior impedes his progress in class.
"Every time he comes to band without his instrument he is unable to participate. If this continues he will fall further and further behind."

7. Explain what behavior is expected from all students. Help the parent understand we are not singling out her child.
"All students are required to bring their instrument daily in order to be successful."

8. Wait and let the parent respond without interruption, even if you disagree with a point they make. The only exception to this is if a parent unreasonably repeats herself or rambles off-task. In these cases, politely interrupt in order to get the conversation moving forward again.
"I appreciate your concerns, Mrs. Jones, but for the purpose of this particular call, let's stay focused on the issue regarding John's instrument."

9. Restate or paraphrase what the parent has said. This indicates you have been listening and accurately understand what you heard.
"What I hear you saying is John is having a hard time remembering to take his instrument in the morning because he cannot find it when he is leaving in the morning."

10. Discuss solutions: First offer a concrete suggestion to help the student improve the situation. Additionally, invite the parents to share suggestions.
"A great idea that works for many students is have John place his instrument by his sneakers the evening before his next band class."

11. Ask the parent if there is anything that can help his child in our class.

12. Offer a way to contact you if any future questions or concerns.
"Here is my office phone number: 555-1234. Please feel free to call me if you have any questions or concerns."

13. End the conversation.
"Thank you for your time and help. Have a good evening."

Meeting with Parents In Person

There will be times when we or parents request a face-to-face meeting regarding a child's progress, grade, behavior, seating assignment, etc. In these cases it is important to make the parent feel welcome in a non-threatening atmosphere. Do not sit behind a desk, which implies a confrontational situation by placing a barrier between teacher and parent. Rather, move the chair so it is near the parent, thus fostering cooperation. Listen patiently while the parent is talking. Maintain eye contact and refrain from taking notes (which suggests a litigious attitude). As with the phone call, wait until the parent has finished before replying. Always remain calm, at least on the outside, even if the information being shared is inaccurate.

Avoid the following, which create confrontation and hostility:

- accusing the parent
- placing blame
- lecturing the parent
- using phrases such as: *"Your child"*, *"You"*
- losing composure and acting disrespectfully
- becoming defensive
- unnecessarily interrupting the parent.

Once a parent feels attacked, accused, offended, or the need to "save face," productive conversation shuts down. Keep in mind that a defensive parent:

- will not support you or help to change the situation
- may complain to the administration and/or fellow parents
- can become *offensive*.

It is important to diffuse these situations quickly. If appropriate, admit any wrongdoing. A parent will rarely argue if he feels his point of view is understood. Explain to the parent that you are there for the child, have only his best interests in mind, and want to help him become successful.

However, just as you have no right to disrespect parents, they have no right to aggressively disrespect you. If you cannot regain control of the situation, it may be in your best interest to politely and firmly end the conversation and request that the parent makes appointment with the school's principal. Then, contact your principal *as soon as possible* and explain exactly what transpired. An administrator is more likely to be supportive if he receives the facts before the parent calls.

Email Etiquette

With email supplanting written mail and phone conversations as the primary means for business communication, it is important to maintain high writing standards and professionalism. With "snail mail" even the most casual messages usually conform to minimum writing conventions; nobody puts a stamp on as much as a "thank you" note without a brief salutation and sign-off. But email communications run the gamut from formal business letters to extremely short messages resembling cell phone texts and Tweets: no salutation, punctuation, or capital letters. For school-related communication, emails should nearly always fit into the formal category. What follows are a few strategies for writing professional emails:

- Always include a salutation at the beginning of the email.
- In most cases a comma after the salutation is appropriate. A colon (e.g., Dear Mr. Smith:) may be used for communications to vendors.
- In descending order of formality:

Dear Mr. Smith	Use for new acquaintances, parents, Administrators, School Board Members
Dear Harold,	Use for established acquaintances, staff, other teachers, students, select administrators with whom you are already on a first-name basis
Harold,	Same as above
Hi Harold,	Use for close colleagues, friends

- Always include a sign-off/signature at the end of the email. In descending order of formality:

Sincerely, John Bocal Director of Bands (Acme High School)	Use for new acquaintances, parents, administrators, members of the school board (Not needed for intra-school correspondence)
Sincerely, John Bocal	Use for established acquaintances, staff, other teachers, students, select administrators with whom you are already on a first-name basis
Sincerely, John Bocal (Director of Bands) Or Best, Mr. Bocal (Director of Bands)	Use for students, parents (Not needed if you have already established your position in a previous email)
Mr. Bocal	Use for students
Best/Best wishes, John Bocal	Use for established acquaintances, staff, other teachers, administrators with whom you are already on a first-name basis, parents
John	Use for established acquaintances, other teachers, administrators with whom you are already on a first-name basis, or conversations that have been in progress for a few emails
JB	Use for other teachers, close friends, or conversations that have been in progress for a few emails

- In conversations that go back and forth with short messages, it is appropriate to omit the salutation and use "John" or "JB" as the signature after the first few emails, but only if these conversations are with another teacher or close colleague.
- Always use a subject heading. Make it brief and to-the-point; each word need not be capitalized, though that is also appropriate. Below are some examples:

Subject: Room Reservation Request
Subject: Ideas for next year's marching band show
Subject: Attendance Info from Last Week
Subject: Question about next week's workshop
Subject: Rehearsal Schedule

Do not use:

- all-caps
- emoticons
- non-standard abbreviations such as "gr8" or "R U"
- colored fonts
- hard-to-read fonts
- background patterns or pictures (they make the email harder to read).

- Always proofread the email before pushing "Send", and be sure to check for inadvertent "Reply-alls"!
- Be courteous and polite.
- Be aware that emails can easily be misconstrued. It is difficult to judge emotion, inflection, and sarcasm through text, especially when one writes conversationally.
- Avoid emailing about non class-related items.
- Do not 'friend', email or instant message with students via your personal account on social networks. Even the most innocent communication may be perceived as being inappropriate. Instead, have a student or parent establish an ensemble page on the network(s). Be sure to monitor all information posted. Maintain your online correspondence with students and parents exclusively through your school account.

Sample Email 1: The Right Way

Dear Barbara,

I would like to submit a room reservation request for the auditorium on April 3, 2010, from 3:30–6pm. The band is bringing in a guest bassoon player and we will be hosting a recital and masterclass during that time.

Please let me know if you have any questions.

Thank you,

John Bocal
Band Director

Sample Email 1: The Wrong Way

I need the auditorium from 3:30–6pm on April 3.

JB

Sample Email 2: The Right Way

Sarah,

Thank you for your email regarding next week's rehearsal. Yes, I will need a note in order to consider making that an excused absence for you. You can either give it to me after our next rehearsal or simply leave it on my desk with your name on it.

Best,

Mr. Bocal

Sample Email 2: The Wrong Way

that absence won't be excused WITHOUT A NOTE.

Sample Email 3: The Right Way

Dear Dr. Clarino,

Last week the fine arts faculty met to discuss budget priorities for next year. I believe we made excellent progress and came up with some creative solutions. I have attached our proposal to this email.
     Please let me know if you have any questions, and I look forward to your comments.

Sincerely,

John Bocal
Band Director

Sample Email 3: The Wrong Way

Chuck,

Here's the budget. Hope u r well.

JB

Sample Email 4: The Right Way

Dear Mr. Parlance,

It was a pleasure speaking with you yesterday evening about Frank's progress in band. I have every confidence Frank's performance in class will improve once he establishes a regular practice schedule. If you have any questions or concerns, please feel free to contact me, either by email (johnb@acme.nc.us) or phone (555-5555).

Sincerely,

John Bocal
Band Director
Acme Middle School

Sample Email 4: The Wrong Way

good talking last night. contact me if you need to.

Keeping a Log

To be thorough, we should track every conversation we have with students, parents, and administrators regarding discipline and behavior. By charting progress, the steps we have taken, and our efforts to keep parents informed, we help insure systematic and consistent communication. We also create a transcript should we encounter disputes or discrepancies.

For example, if John consistently arrives late, after applying our first few consequences we may decide to call his parents: "*Good evening, Mr. Johnson. This is Ted Sax, John's band director. I wanted to relay some recent attendance problems I've been experiencing with John. When he's in class he's usually motivated and attentive. However, although I've talked with him about it, I've been frustrated by his late arrivals this past week, which have been disrupting rehearsals after they begin.*"

Depending on our policies we may tell Mr. Johnson what the next steps are. What do we expect of John and what are the consequences if the situation does not improve? Ideally, John will begin arriving to class on time. But if he does not, his grade may be reduced, or we may refer him to school-wide discipline procedures. Students and parents may claim some variation of "I didn't know this was a problem," or "I didn't know this is what would happen."

Along with our clearly posted discipline policy, our log is a tool to justify our actions and show what steps we previously took to address the problem without any "he said/she said" bickering. Administrators appreciate this information because it makes it easier for them to support teachers in the face of conflicting information from an unhappy parent.

If not kept on a computer, we recommend using a notebook or set of index cards, with one full side or card per student (to avoid mixing information for different students.) At the top of each card, write the student's name, year, instrument, interests, activities, parent/guardian names, contact phone numbers and emails. Record each communication with the date, time, and a brief summary of what was discussed, including comments from both parties.

Sample Student Log

Frankie Markowitz – Junior – Oboe

Studies privately with Sarah Connor

Soccer team, loves math & videogames, active in Key Club

Sarah & Irving, (h) 341-555-1212, markowitzg@acme.com

9/14: 8pm – Spoke to Mr. Markowitz to comment on Frankie's improvement over the summer

9/23: Verbally warned Frankie during class about disruptions and spoke to him after class to remind him of class rules; he mentioned he was not getting much sleep but would try harder

10/21: 6pm – Spoke to Mr. Markowitz to inform him of Frankie's in-class disruptions; Mr. Markowitz said he would follow up with his son

10/25: Gave Frankie a referral for repeatedly disrupting the rehearsal

10/29: 6:30pm – Spoke to Mrs. Markowitz to tell him Frankie had shown improvement; Mr. Markowitz requested I follow-up again in a few weeks

---

Communicating with Parents *En Masse*

It is important to be able to communicate information to parents quickly and efficiently. The ubiquity of email makes this much simpler than it used to be, but it's not the only method.

- *Letters and newsletters*—Classy and time-tested, snail mail is also the slowest and most expensive. Use it for "welcome back letters," "thank you" notes, the occasional newsletter, and important announcements.
- *Phone trees*—Beyond email, phone trees are a fast way to get the word out. When the first parent receives a phone call, she calls her assigned family, who then calls their assigned family, and so on. Unlike email, phone trees depend on families expecting a phone call so the information doesn't become caught in voicemail.
- *Websites*—Music departments commonly have a page hosted through the school's website. If necessary, find a student or parent to design it, but do so in a way that makes it easy to add information and make simple changes. When the student webmaster graduates, we still want easy access! Websites are valuable for:

  - calendars
  - newsletters
  - information about private teachers, music stores, and recommended instruments

– class schedules and assignments
– announcements about student achievements.

Websites can also be used to display student work. For example, Wendy Buehl, orchestra teacher at Oregon Middle School in Oregon, Wisconsin, posts student blogs that describes the week's activities and what was learned (Block, 18). This allows students to reflect on their music-making and practice their writing. It also serves as advocacy for the program, as other teachers, parents, and administrators get a peek inside the classroom. (Block, 18)

Regarding email: Collect separate email lists for parents and students (sometimes these addresses will be the same, as children often use a family account). But use mass emails sparingly—mostly for concert reminders and occasional newsletters. Otherwise our messages will be ignored as another piece of spam.

Student Handbooks

The student handbook is an important resource for students and parents to learn about all aspects of the music program. Printed versions of the handbook should contain the most essential information, including:

- mission and philosophy statement
- classroom rules and procedures
- grading policy
- attendance policy
- calendar of events
- required supplies and materials
- director's school contact information
- ensemble and course descriptions (e.g., marching band, pep band, concert band, chamber ensembles, jazz band, pit orchestra)
- concert attire
- home practice requirements
- information about instrument, equipment, and music care

The back page of the printed handbook should contain a parent and student contract form. Students and parents sign and date this document as acknowledgment that they have read and understood the information in the handbook. Should we ever be challenged on any aspect of the program, this form allows us to show that both the student and parent were fully aware of their responsibilities.

For online versions of the handbook consider also adding:

- practice records
- private lesson information
- audition requirements for honor ensembles
- fundraising announcements
- uniform guidelines
- travel guidelines
- ensemble officers
- uniform fees
- lockers/instrument storage information
- school-owned instruments
- scheduling information

Activities/Assignments for Further Exploration

1. Write the following sample emails.

    Inviting superintendent/board members to attend a concert.
    Announcing to parents the details of an upcoming fundraiser.
    Setting up an after school appointment with a student.
    Placing an order for music with the local music shop.
    Soliciting donations for a silent auction from a local store.
    Offering congratulations to students after a concert.
    Responding to a request for a meeting with the Fine Arts Chairperson.
    Reserving a bus from a private company for travel to a competition.
    Requesting the help of the school's A/V specialist to record a concert.
    Reporting on the progress of a student to . . .

    - the Assistant Principal
    - the parent
    - the student.

2. Discuss and consider proper etiquette for other forms of communication, including:

    - phone calls and voice messages
    - personal introductions
    - hand-written thank-you notes.

3. Stage a mock conversation with a parent. Have one classmate play the part of the parent and another the part of the teacher. Choose a reason for the conversation and have each "actor" plan their back story before engaging.
4. Find two examples of well-designed school music program websites and share them with the class. What makes the sites well-designed? What could be improved?
5. Search the internet for student handbooks. Find one for middle school and one for high school that you think are particularly well-presented and comprehensive. Share these with the class and discuss the most/least effective features of each.

Further Reading

Carnegie, Dale. *How to Win Friends and Influence People*. New York: Pocket Books, 1982.

Chan, Janis Fisher. *E-mail: A Write it Well Guide: How to Write and Manage E-mail in the Workplace*. Oakland, CA: Write It Well, 2008.

Covey, Stephen R. *The Seven Habits of Highly Effective People*. New York: Free Press, 2004.

Chapter 20

The Music Budget

To Guide Your Reading

What are the standard components and operating procedures of a school music budget?

What are purchase orders and how are they used?

What are effective strategies for researching equipment and supplies?

How does one write budget requests?

What does it mean to put an item out for "bid"?

Budget Lines and Codes

Budgets are divided into categories, or budget "lines," each designated for purchasing particular items or services. Every budget line is referenced by a specific numeric code. The typical budget contains at least three lines:

- *Equipment code*—Durable items such as instruments, sound equipment, podiums, risers, etc.
- *Supply code*—Items considered to be non-durable, inexpensive (under $100), and frequently replaced. These may include drum heads, strings, reeds, and valve oil. If there is no separate code for sheet music/ instructional materials, it is usually covered under this code (i.e., it is considered non-durable and inexpensive).
- *Contractual services code*—Purchases that hire a person or company to perform a service. Examples include instrument repairs, piano tuning, fees for performing at a festival, state or county organizational participation fees, and clinicians or guest performers.
- *Other possible codes*—Textbooks, sheet music, instructional materials.

Music budget managers have a variety of responsibilities, including these:

- Deciding how the *total funds are divided among each budget line*—How much for supplies? How much for contractual services? Note that in some schools, once the funds are divided they cannot be transferred between lines. Thus, if the budget line for purchasing music runs out, money available in the repair budget line cannot move over. In schools with this restriction it is vital to accurately estimate needs for each line in advance.

- Dividing funds *within* each line—For instance, sheet music funds must be shared amongst each ensemble director, according to their needs. Repair codes are often not divided at all, and are used on an "as needed" basis.
- Controlling which vendors are engaged based on pricing or service quality.
- Making final decisions on all purchases. In order to economize, budget managers may need to adjust requests or decline them based on whether they are judged to be valid or reasonable.
- Managing budget paperwork. This includes following district procedures for purchases; keeping records of every purchase request and receipt; keeping and balancing the records for each code.

Purchase Orders

The majority of school purchases are done with a *purchase order* (or P.O., as it is commonly referred to). A purchase order is essentially a promise from the school to make a payment for goods or services. Schools use purchase orders to:

- create an approval process to control purchases
- help monitor the delivery of goods and services from suppliers
- ensure that suppliers deliver exactly what was requested
- report the procurement status of goods and services to the school's administration.

Most vendors accept purchase orders because they recognize that schools reliably pay their bills. Still, always contact potential vendors to make sure they accept them. If not, work with the district's financial office to find an alternate means of payment. This is usually possible, but may involve extra paperwork, and most districts discourage it as the regular procedure for ordering.

Each school district has its own procedures for submitting purchases orders. But whether submitted digitally or with paperwork, the same basic information is required:

- description of item or service
- quantity of items
- current price
- shipping and handling charges
- vendor's product code
- vendor's address and phone number
- catalog page number (unless online)
- brand and model number
- budget code that the purchase will come out of

Always plan ahead for P.O. purchases, because in most cases they are not processed immediately. Heed this adage: "An emergency for you does not mean an emergency for someone else!" Exceptions are occasionally granted, but do not expect to be able to change procedures to meet your needs or compensate for your lack of planning.

A special type of purchase order is called an "open" or "standing" P.O. In this format the vendor essentially extends a pre-set line of credit to the school. Typically secured at the beginning of the school year, the open P.O. earmarks a requested amount of money from a department's appropriate budget code. Once established, the department no longer needs approval from the financial office for requests— simply call the vendor and make a purchase against that P.O. number.

Open purchase orders are typically set up with:

- sheet music vendors
- instrument repair vendors
- piano tuning services

Some schools allow teachers to make their purchase directly with the vendor using an open purchase order. Other schools still require teachers go through a budget manager. Either way the open P.O. is a convenient and speedy way of ordering materials that are needed regularly and quickly. Keep in mind that some vendors will warn before a P.O. is overdrawn, though some *do not*. Beware of overspending!

After goods and services are provided companies will usually bill the business office directly or include an invoice with the shipment. File a copy of these forms and immediately forward the originals to the business office/budget manager to process payment.

Income and Expenses

Even if a separate budget manager oversees school-wide music finances, good planning is the responsibility of every director. Keep in mind that district funds can not usually be carried over to the next fiscal year, and thus must be "spent out." This may seem wasteful, but it is important to find productive ways to use all available funds (without overspending, of course), lest the administration perceive the surplus money as justification for a budget reduction. Music Booster Organizations can carry funds from year to year, so use their accounts to save for special projects and emergencies.

Once you have determined how much money the district provides, make a separate budget to guide your total spending. Note that smaller districts will sometimes budget a lump-sum to the program, putting the burden on the director to divide it appropriately into his own budget lines. Among others, consider the following questions: How much music will you buy, and how much can you borrow or use from your library? Which instruments can be repaired, and which absolutely need to be replaced? How much will parent organizations help fund initiatives? How will you divide music funds among several ensembles?

Income usually comes from the following sources:

- School district
- Music boosters (via fundraising and gifts)
- Student-led fundraising
- Concert admission
- Grants

Expenses usually fall under the following categories:

- Music for all groups—band, orchestra, marching, jazz, chamber, solo.
- New instruments

- Replacement instruments (for broken or stolen instruments)
- Non-instrumental equipment (risers, podium, stands, etc.)
- Travel (buses for marching band, contests, field trips, etc.)
- Awards (special awards for the end of the year)
- Printing and publicity (programs, fliers, etc.)
- Repair and Maintenance
- Uniform purchase and/or maintenance (replacement uniforms or parts of uniforms, dry cleaning, etc.)
- Fees (for competitions and festivals)
- Consultants (guest conductors, performers, lesson teachers, etc.)
- Staff (particularly for the marching band)
- Contingency (reserve funds to cover extra or unexpected expenses)

Writing Budget Requests

Most administrations ask for budget requests during the spring semester. The following items should be included in a complete request:

- Brief letter thanking the administration for previous support and outlining crucial budgetary needs for the next year.
- Itemized budget proposal (see Figure 20.1).
- Rationales justifying requests for budget line increases or specific equipment/services (see the following text for examples).

When submitting requests and rationales, it is not enough to simply list a need and its cost. We must also present a logical and compelling rationale. And we must remember that many of the people reading the request will not be musicians. Our principal, superintendent, or department supervisor may have difficulty grasping the difference between, say, tenor trombones and bass trombones, or plastic and wood clarinets. We must point out why the percussion needs of marching bands are different from those of concert bands and orchestras; that even well-maintained instruments need regular maintenance; that some items need replacement even if they do not look "broken" (e.g., worn drum heads); that although we may have an extensive library, the repertoire is constantly expanding; that larger instruments (i.e. bassoons, bass clarinets, baritone saxophones and upright basses) are essential to the sound of the ensembles and we cannot expect students to purchase them.

Even well-intentioned supporters of our program cannot help if they do not understand *how* to help! Thus, it is our responsibility to educate administrators as to what it takes to run a successful program and emphasize how the request meets the educational needs of our students. If administrators are convinced that education will be compromised without the item they are more likely to grant a request. Effective rationales should have the following components:

1. A specific dollar amount for the request; avoid listing ranges (e.g., $4000–8000), as it signals to the reader that we have not adequately researched.
2. A clear description of the item or what the budget line supports
3. An explanation of why the item or line is needed (e.g., to replace an un-repairable instrument; to meet the demands of a growing enrollment, etc.)

4. An explanation of how the item or line will support the goals of the program and/or school (e.g., to provide an instrument suitable for playing outdoors; to allow the ensemble to play advanced literature, etc.)

Sample Requests and Rationales

Sample 1: *Bass Clarinet,* Selmer Intermediate Bass Clarinet (Wood Body), Model TK3—$3500

The bass clarinet is a standard instrument in the Concert Band (up to three students play it) and is often used in the Orchestra (1 player). With the increased enrollment in the Middle School program and retention into the High School program, we consistently have three or more bass clarinet players, yet we own only two instruments. Because bass clarinet players switch from the regular Bb clarinet (which they still play in marching band), it is not reasonable to expect them to purchase a second instrument. The Selmer Intermediate model is highly recommended for its excellent sound and durability.

Sample 2: 20 Manhasset Music Stands @ $25 = $500

With increased enrollment in ensembles and an increasing number of ensembles using rehearsal spaces simultaneously, we have a considerable shortage of music stands. Ensembles regularly use large numbers of stands in the band room, orchestra room, stage, and practice rooms. Like classroom desks, stands are essential for learning, but unlike desks, a few stands become un-usable each year through normal wear-and-tear. This is a purchase that benefits the entire music department.

Sample 3: Yamaha Baritone Saxophone, Model XYZ3—$3200

Currently the school owns two working baritone saxophones and an older instrument that is beyond repair. However, we have three ensembles that regularly need this instrument (Wind Ensemble, Concert Band, and Symphonic Band) with as many as six players currently sharing instruments. This makes it difficult for players to practice since the instrument is constantly being played. This purchase would essentially replace the third instrument we can no longer use.

Sample 4: Bach Bass Trombone, Model 2YZ—$1100

Many pieces at the high school level require the ability to play notes that standard tenor trombones cannot play effectively. We believe it is unreasonable to ask students to purchase another instrument in addition to the tenor trombone they have already purchased. Many of our trombones are older, smaller bore trombones without an F attachment, which makes them usable for beginners but inadequate for advanced players performing literature with true bass trombone parts. This new instrument would replace an older instrument and allow players to create the full-bodied tone our repertoire demands.

Sample 5: Electric Violin, Meisel Model AB3—$2000

The string teaching and performing world is currently undergoing a great paradigm shift. Alternative styles of music such as jazz, fiddle, and rock are becoming part of the mainstream. Many public schools are including these styles in their programs and students are choosing to attend jazz and fiddle summer camps in ever greater numbers. A quality electric violin will allow our violin students to participate in these exciting musical activities.

Sample 6: Music Budget Line—Increase of $300, for a Total of $2500

In instrumental music, sheet music largely serves as the textbook. Though we borrow music from other schools and use our own library when possible, the repertoire is continually expanding, and purchasing new sheet music is essential to teach our curriculum. This request is based on the need to furnish music for the newly added 9th grade orchestra, and also to absorb the price increase recently imposed by publishers.

Researching Needs for Equipment, Supplies

Few directors are bona fide experts on every instrument and piece of equipment. Yet when a new piece of equipment must be ordered, we are expected to know what to order and from where to order it. Before we discuss effective strategies, a few warnings about what *not* to do:

1. Do not assume a previous purchase should be duplicated. If you can confirm that the last French horn bought is a quality instrument, for example, then it makes sense to purchase another. Otherwise, don't make the same mistake twice.
2. Do not rely on recommendations from glossy catalogs, slick websites, and customer service representatives. Though these are usually reputable companies who care about their product, remember that they are naturally motivated to make a profit. Some may make recommendations based on price and popularity, neither of which are reliable indications of quality.
3. Do not guess in order to save time. Instrument and equipment purchases are long-term investments, and time well spent in the short term will save repair costs in the long run and provide tone and intonation. Like many instruments already in our inventories, the goal is to purchase an instrument that will still be used in 30 years.

So, how can a clarinet-playing band director make an intelligent decision about buying a cello? Factor in answers to the following questions:

1. Do you need a beginning level instrument (recommended for elementary and middle school levels) or an intermediate/entry-level professional instrument (recommended for advanced middle school and high school programs)?
2. How will this instrument fit into the overall inventory of the school? Is the instrument intended for indoor or outdoor use? For example, if the school already owns a high-quality bass clarinet, perhaps a less-expensive model is appropriate. If every oboe the school owns is plastic, perhaps it would be wise to invest in a wood instrument. If a clarinet is needed to allow students to keep their personal Grenadilla instruments inside, perhaps less expensive plastic instruments are ideal.
3. What special features are needed on the instrument? Low E♭ or low-C bass clarinets? F-trigger for a trombone? How many octaves for the marimba? Today's catalogs offer a dizzying array of options, and we need to know what is available, and how it interfaces with what we need.

Further Recommendations

- Survey other band directors: Call colleagues in your area and ask their opinion.
- Use the expertise of local private teachers, or make contact with the studio teachers from your college program. These professionals can offer insight for the features, tone, and reliability of student models.
- Do not rule out the possibility of a high-quality used instrument (or "pre-owned"), especially if you have access to an advanced player who can test its quality before purchase.

Putting Items Out for Bid

Once approved for purchase, public schools require large-ticket items costing over several thousand dollars to be submitted for public bid, often from at least three vendors.

Items typically submitted for bid include:

- new instruments
- marching band uniforms
- risers
- storage cabinets and lockers
- large quantities of music stands and chairs.

Though certainly much more tedious and time-consuming than simply shopping from a catalog, the bidding process is important to help schools receive the best possible price. Bidding works like this: The district releases a "Request for Price Quote or Proposal," or an "Invitation to Bid." This document is posted publicly (e.g., department website) and sent to specific vendors. The bid request contains the exact specifications of what is being requested, details about shipping costs, and stipulations about submitting the quote (see Figure 20.2 for an example). Vendors may substitute a similar item for something listed, which is generally legal as long as the alternate is labeled and described. If we require a specific item, brand, or model we must state in our bid request "no substitutes allowed." For their part, districts often reserve the right to choose parts of a bid by item (i.e., choosing some, but not all, of the items requested), or to award contracts based on what best meets their needs.

One key to an effective bid request is to be as specific as possible. Do not list "B♭ trumpet," "Intermediate model B♭ trumpet," or even "Yamaha intermediate B♭ trumpet," but rather "Yamaha Model YLC-10 B♭ trumpet." Any detail not supplied by the bid-requester will be filled in by the bidder, possibly with an inferior item. Remember, purchase departments seek the best product for the best price, but we cannot expect them to understand the difference between a plastic clarinet and a wood clarinet, or the difference between a three and four-valve euphonium. (Note that marching band uniform bid requests are notoriously long, often numbering 5–10 pages with details about fabrics, measurements, manufacturing techniques, and accessories).

Be diligent in keeping records. Make copies of purchase orders before submission, and keep bills and receipts after receiving goods or services. If questions ever arise concerning money matters, hard evidence is our best advocate.

FIGURE 20.1 Sample Budget Request

Acme High School Band
100 School Drive
Meldan, Wyoming

Band Budget Request: 2010–2011 School Year   **Date:** Feb. 15, 2010
Submitted by: John Bocal

Instructional Materials/Music

Concert band	$400.00
Marching band	$200.00
Jazz band	$300.00
Orchestra	$400.00
Chamber ensembles	$300.00
Subtotal:	$1,600.00

Capital Expenses/Equipment

Instruments

Renard Model 333 Protege Oboe	$2,449.00
Selmer 1430LP Bb Bass Clarinet	$1,649.00
Yamaha YBH-301S Baritone	$2,324.00
Musser M635B Classic Chimes	$2,870.00
Yamaha Standard Model AVC5	$2,095.00

Non-instrumental equipment

Classic 50® Music Stand $49x10 =	$490.00
Conductor's podium	$442.00
Subtotal:	$13,169.00

Travel

Marching band	$2,000.00
Solo festival	$500.00
Large ensemble festival	$1,000.00
Attend Symphony Concert	$500.00
Subtotal:	$4,000.00

Repair & Maintenance

Instrument repair	$3,000.00
Supplies (Pads, oil, tools):	$300.00
Subtotal:	$3,300.00

Consultants/Services

Fees

Marching band competitions	$300.00
Large ensemble contest	$200.00
Guest artists	$1,000.00
Subtotal:	$1,500.00
Total:	$35,322.00

FIGURE 20.2 Sample Bid Request

Washington School District

Washington High School Music Department

6 West Main Street, Washington, North Carolina 55155
Main Office (555) 555-1112 – FAX (555) 555-1113

June 1, 2011

Dear Vendor,

The Washington School District has sent this quotation request for the musical equipment listed below. Please respond only for the items that you sell. You may quote equivalent makes and models but none of lesser quality. Bids will be awarded based on the best quality for the best price. The Washington School district reserves the right to reject any and all quotations. We assume, unless stated otherwise, that you will accept orders for any individual items quoted.

Please submit both the unit and total costs for each item. The quotations must include shipping and handling, or list a separate shipping and handling cost.

If you have any questions regarding the specifications of our request, please contact me. The deadline for these quotations is Monday, June 22, 2011 at 9am.

Thank you for your service.

Sincerely,
Tom Johnson
Washingtonville High School
Music Dept. Chair
tjohnson@wsd.k12.nc.us
(555) 555-1111

Quantity	Item Description	Unit Price	Total Cost
2	Yamaha Bass Clarinet, Model YCL221, w/ case		
1	Fox Renard Bassoon, Model 240, w/ case		
3	Bach Trumpet, Model TR2071/ w case		

FIGURE 20.3 Sample Bid Compilation/Comparison

Bid Results

(winning bids shown in gray)

Quantity	Item	John's Music	Music Box	Music Central
1	Yamaha Eb soprano clarinet - ebonite	$ 2,855.00	$2,755.00	$ -
1	Manhasset storage cart	$ 310.00	$ 345.00	$ 261.00
1	Fishman P-100 Bass Pick-up	$ 135.00	$ 130.00	$ 112.00
1	Fender standard jazz bass	$ 910.00	$ -	$ 402.00
1	LP Giovanni Bongos natural finish	$ 247.00	$ 330.00	$ 241.00
2	Deg tuba rest	$ 136.00	$ 150.00	$ 119.80
1	Briefcase Style Mallets Case	$ -	$ 50.00	$ 43.12
1	Enduro Cymbal Case with foam	$ 96.00	$ 100.00	$ 107.00
1	Enduro Pro Percussion Cases with foam for snare drum(8"x14")	$ 72.00	$ 90.00	$ 74.64
1	Enduro Pro Percussion Cases with foam for large concert tom (11"x14")	$ 77.00	$ 90.00	$ 72.03
1	Companion Case (36" X 14 ½ " X 9") with foam	$ 160.00	$ 225.00	$ -
2	Tuba/Sousaphone wall mount	$ -	$ 120.00	$ 528.00

Activities/Assignments for Further Exploration

1. Research the best option to purchase the following items:

   - oboe
   - concert tuba
   - double bass
   - recording equipment
   - make up your own!

2. For the above items, write a sample rationale and budget request.

3. Interview a local band or orchestra director about how his school budget operates. Who controls the funds? What are the challenges of the system and how does he manage them? What does he know now that he wishes he knew when he first began teaching?

Further Reading

Hartman, William T. *School District Budgeting*. Lanham, MD: Scarecrow Press, 2003.

Kratz, Robert N., Charles Alvin Scott, and Harry T. Zechman. *A Primer on School Budgeting*. Lanham, MD: Scarecrow Press, 2001.

Ryan, Charlene. *Building Strong Music Programs: A Handbook for Preservice and Novice Music Teachers*. Lanham, MD: Rowman & Littlefield Education, 2009.

Walker, Darwin E. *Teaching Music: Managing the Successful Music Program*. New York: Schirmer Books, 1998.

Chapter 21

Copyrights

To Guide Your Reading

What misconceptions do many people have about what is legal under copyright law?

Why were copyright laws enacted?

What is "fair use" and what are its limits?

To what extent does the law allow music educators to make copies of copyrighted music?

Do music educators receive copyright law exemptions regarding recordings and live performances?

Are arrangements and adaptations covered by copyright law?

How does one find out specific information regarding copyrighted material and request permissions?

Understanding Copyright Law

Copyright is one of the most complex and misunderstood aspects of music education. The reality is that many teachers either knowingly or inadvertently break the law on a regular basis. It is an easy crime to commit; after all, there is no law enforcement officer policing our classroom, and our crime leaves no evidence of hurting its victim. In fact, from the teacher's perspective, the crime may seem to help people more than it hurts. Here are a few common justifications of copyright infringement:

- I'm doing this to help my students.
- I didn't know it was wrong.
- Copying parts doesn't hurt anybody.
- The publishers make so much money. My little infringement isn't going to hurt them.
- My budget is limited, so I need to save money wherever I can.

Of course, copyright holders do not share our justifications, and usually, neither does the law. Copyright laws were created to insure that those who reproduce, arrange, or perform artistic works compensate or secure permission from those who created the work in the first place. Put simply, without copyright laws there would be few consequences for stealing, and without compensation there would be little incentive for artists to create their art.

Some argue that copyright laws are unnecessarily restrictive, and indeed a copyright law reform movement has arisen to advocate for change. Among the goals of its various interest groups: limit the duration of copyright protection (thus putting works into the public domain more quickly); require copyright registration (to reduce the number of works protected and allow less restricted exchange of information); impose proportional fines and punishments (to insure violators do not receive punishment in excess of the damage they do to society); and create new ways for authors to license their work (to make it easier for others to use copyrighted works without threat of litigation).[1]

The way they are currently set up, copyright laws automatically protect nearly everything published after 1923 that is original, results from a spark of creativity, and is in fixed and tangible form. This means that even if something is not officially on file with the U.S. copyright office it is still likely protected. Of course, many music copyrights are held by businesses, not individuals. Music publishing houses essentially buy artistic rights from the composer, arranger, and performer in exchange for an agreed upon royalty— for every unit of the product for which the company is paid for, it will pay a portion of it back to the artist.

Usually this payment is a small percentage of the product's price, which the company justifies to cover its costs for editing, producing, manufacturing, packaging, marketing, and distributing the product. But the reality remains that artists are not paid unless their music publisher is first.

Interestingly, recent advances in music notation programs, desktop publishing, and internet marketing have encouraged some composers and performers to move away from this model. With software, a good printer and a website, it is feasible to self-publish and sell music directly to the public without a middleman. In the book-publishing world this practice is often derogatively called "vanity publishing"; but in music publishing it has become a way for composers to control the entire process, as well as make available pieces that publishers might reject as commercially unviable. With this new publishing model, copyright laws are as vital as ever.

Though seemingly daunting and inflexible, the law does permit exceptions and special dispensations for education. These are often listed under the umbrellas of "For educational use" and "Fair use." What follows below is a brief explanation of some of educators' specific rights and responsibilities under the law. Keep in mind the following generalities:

- *Ignorance of the law is not a defense of the law.* As convenient as it sounds, we cannot flout the law with the intent of claiming, "But I didn't know!" if we are caught.
- *"Fair use" and "For educational purposes" are not free passes.* Though the law makes dispensation to facilitate teaching, it does not allow education to be used as a blanket shield against copyright infringement. A teacher who is cited for copyright infringement must be able to show that he made a good-faith, reasonable effort to comply with fair-use guidelines.
- *Working in a school does not offer protection for prosecution.* If a copyright holder decides to pursue an infringement, individual teachers can be held liable.
- *Music publishers* do *pursue copyright violators.* "Cease-and-desist" orders are their first line of offense; if the matter is decided in court, fines in small cases can run from $750–30,000. More serious infringements have the potential of as much as $250,000 in fines plus five years' imprisonment.
- *"Out-of-print" does not necessarily mean something is in the public domain and thus free of copyright restrictions.* Permission may still be required to make copies. Always check with the publisher first. A standardized permission request letter is available on the MENC website.

- *Music by dead composers is not necessarily free from copyright restrictions.* Copyrights can be inherited by members of the composer's estate. Further, the rights to many editions are owned by the publisher, not the composer, and these rights last for 95 years after the music was published.
- *Illegally downloaded music and recordings are illegal*—even if used within the allowances and exemptions detailed on page 352–353.

When contacting publishers to request permission, keep in mind the following:

- Copyright information is usually located on the inside title page. If it is unclear who owns the copyright, consult one of the three performing rights organizations that deal with U.S. copyright: ASCAP (http://www. ascap.com); BMI (http://www.bmi.com); and SESAC (http://www.sesac.com).
- Publishers usually complete permissions requests via email or fax. A standardized request form is available from the MENC website.
- Remember, the law is constantly changing and evolving. The information provided in this chapter should not be treated as legal advice.
- If you have questions about copyright, what is protected, what is appropriate, etc.—Ask! Three valuable sources of information are: National Music Publisher's Association (http://www.nmpa.org); Music Publisher's Association of the United States (http://www.mpa.org); and United States Copyright Office (http://www.copyright.gov).

With the growth of downloadable music, digital recordings, peer-to-peer sharing, blogs, web video, and the rest of the internet, questions of copyright are becoming more and more complicated. A good resource to find answers is James Frankel's excellent book, *The Teacher's Guide to Music, Media, and Copyright Law.* Frankel suggests that a teacher asks herself the following questions to decide whether a use is permissible, an infringement, or a fair use (Frankel, 123–124):

- Am I infringing on any of the exclusive rights afforded by copyright?
- If I am, is my use considered a fair use?
- If it is not considered a fair use, is there a way I can teach the same concept without infringing?

Based on the 1976 Copyright Act, the following situations with music are considered "fair use," and thus allowed under the law.

Note: The information below appears in U.S. House of Representatives Report 94–1476, which, like all U.S. Government documents, carries no copyright.

Copying Music

Permissible uses:

1. Emergency copying to replace purchased copies which for any reason are not available for an imminent performance provided purchased replacement copies shall be substituted in due course.
2. For academic purposes other than performance, multiple copies of excerpts of works may be made, provided that the excerpts do not comprise a part of the whole which would constitute a performable unit such as a section, movement or aria but in no case more than 10 percent of the whole work. The number of copies shall not exceed one copy per pupil.

3. Printed copies which have been purchased may be edited OR simplified provided that the fundamental character of the work is not distorted or the lyrics, if any, altered or lyrics added if none exist.
4. A single copy of recordings of performances by students may be made for evaluation or rehearsal purposes and may be retained by the educational institution or individual teacher.
5. A single copy of a sound recording of copyrighted music may be made from sound recordings owned by an educational institution or an individual teacher for the purpose of constructing aural exercises or examinations and may be retained by the educational institution or individual teacher. (This pertains only to the copyrights of the music itself and not to any copyright that may exist in the sound recording.)

The following situations are not considered fair use, and are thus *prohibited*:

1. Copying to create or replace or substitute for anthologies, compilations or collective works.
2. Copying of or from works intended to be "consumable" in the course of study or teaching such as workbooks, exercises, standard tests and answer sheets and like material.
3. Copying for the purpose of performance (except in case of an emergency, assuming the item is purchased in due course).
4. Copying for the purpose of substituting for the purchase of music except for points 1 and 2 of the previous section.
5. Copying without inclusion of the copyright notice which appears on the printed copy.
6. Charging students for the costs of copying under "fair use."

For non-musical printed works, such as copyrighted books and periodicals, the law is similar.

Single Copying For Teachers

A single copy may be made of any of the following by or for a teacher at his or her individual request for his or her scholarly research or use in teaching or preparation to teach a class:

1. A chapter from a book.
2. An article from a periodical or newspaper.
3. A short story, short essay or short poem, whether or not from a collective work.
4. A chart, graph, diagram, drawing, cartoon or picture from a book, periodical, or newspaper.

Multiple Copies For Classroom Use

Multiple copies (not to exceed in any event more than one copy per pupil in a course) may be made by or for the teacher giving the course for classroom use or discussion; provided that:

1. The copying meets the tests of brevity and spontaneity as defined below; and,
2. Meets the cumulative effect test as defined below; and,
3. Each copy includes a notice of copyright.

Brevity, spontaneity, and cumulative effect are defined as follows:

Brevity

1. *Poetry:* (a) A complete poem if less than 250 words and if printed on not more than two pages, or (b) from a longer poem, an excerpt of not more than 250 words.
2. *Prose:* (a) Either a complete article, story or essay of less than 2,500 words, or (b) an excerpt from any prose work of not more than 1,000 words or 10 percent of the work, whichever is less, but in any event a minimum of 500 words. (Each of the numerical limits stated in "1" and "2" above may be expanded to permit the completion of an unfinished line of a poem or of an unfinished prose paragraph.)
3. *Illustration:* One chart, graph, diagram, drawing, cartoon or picture per book or per periodical issue.
4. *"Special" works:* Certain works in poetry, prose or in "poetic prose" which often combine language with illustrations and which are intended sometimes for children and at other times for a more general audience fall short of 2,500 words in their entirety. Paragraph "2" above notwithstanding such "special works" may not be reproduced in their entirety; however, an excerpt comprising not more than two of the published pages of such special work and containing not more than 10 percent of the words found in the text thereof, may be reproduced.

Spontaneity

1. The copying is at the instance and inspiration of the individual teacher.
2. The inspiration and decision to use the work and the moment of its use for maximum teaching effectiveness are so close in time that it would be unreasonable to expect a timely reply to a request for permission.

Cumulative Effect

1. The copying of the material is for only one course in the school in which the copies are made.
2. Not more than one short poem, article, story, essay or two excerpts may be copied from the same author, nor more than three from the same collective work or periodical volume during one class term.
3. There shall not be more than nine instances of such multiple copying for one course during one class term. (The limitations stated in "2" and "3" above shall not apply to current news periodicals and news-papers and current news sections of other periodicals.)

Performing, Recording, and Arranging Copyrighted Works

Performances of copyrighted works are also protected by law. Contrary to popular opinion, purchasing music does not grant the right to use it in any performance situation. Fortunately, there are a number of exemptions that apply to the everyday activities of music educators:

- *School Concert Exemption*—School ensembles, students, and teachers, can put on a performance of a non-dramatic literary or musical work at a school concert as long as no money changes hands. That is, nobody can gain any direct or indirect commercial advantage; no fee or compensation can be paid to the performers, promoters or organizers; and no admission charge can be levied. (*Note*: There is even an exception to this: there can be an admission charge, but all of the proceeds must be used only for educational or charitable purposes.) The performance may not take place if the copyright owner objects in writing seven days before the performance.

- *The Face-to-Face Exemption*—To qualify for this exemption, the performance must be initiated by instructors or pupils and must occur within the context of the "face-to-face teaching activities" of a nonprofit educational institution, in a classroom or similar place devoted to instruction (e.g., a library, studio or workshop). It should be noted that there is no specific restriction, in this case, on the type or amount of a copyrighted work that may be performed. This exemption is limited, and *does not* apply to:

  - performances by actors, singers, or instrumentalists brought in from outside the school to put on a program
  - performances, whatever their cultural value or intellectual appeal, that are given for the recreation or entertainment of any part of their audience
  - performances in profit-making institutions such as for-profit dance or music studios
  - performances in an auditorium or stadium during a school assembly, graduation ceremony, class play, or sporting event, where the audience is not confined to the members of a particular class (Only performances "in a classroom or similar place devoted to instruction" fit this provision; performances at shopping malls and the like are certainly not covered).

- *The Distance Education Exemption*—The law does permit performance or display of a musical work by a transmission (distance education) in an amount comparable to that which is typically displayed in the course of a live classroom session. Because the law places the onus of developing and implementing a copyright policy on the transmitting body or institute (the school system), this really only applies to teachers who work in schools that have developed the technical and legal structures to deal with this issue. For example, storage and dissemination of the work must be tightly controlled. Also, this exemption does not apply to works developed directly for distance learning or for recordings that were made illegally. At any rate, to come within the distance education exemption, the performance or display must be:

  - made by, at the direction of, or under the actual supervision of an instructor
  - an integral part of a class session offered as a regular part of the normal teaching of a public school or an accredited nonprofit educational institution
  - essential to the teaching content of the transmission; and made solely for and, to the extent technologically feasible limited to reception by, students officially enrolled in the course for which the transmission is made.

- *Music for Worship Exemption*—Performance of non-dramatic literary or musical works or of dramatico-musical works of a religious nature, in the course of services at places of worship or at a religious assembly, is permitted.

Distributing Recordings

Beyond the reference copy, recordings of school concerts may not be distributed, even if the copies are only given to students free-of-charge. To legally distribute such recordings it is necessary to obtain a compulsory license for each work on the recording from its U.S. copyright holder. These licenses are priced on a per-copy basis, the amount determined on a per-selection basis or by-the-minute. The most well-known clearing house for these licenses is the Harry Fox agency (http://www.harryfox.com), which streamlines the process for obtaining them. However, the Harry Fox agency markets itself to those who wish to produce at least 500 copies. Obviously, if the plan is to make only 200, paying the fee for 500 copies is not very cost-efficient. In these cases it may be best to bypass the convenience of Harry Fox and request permission directly from the music publishers.

Making Derivative Works

"Derivative works" generally include arrangements of a copyrighted work. Outside of the allowance for editing and simplification (see earlier), arrangers must obtain permission from the publisher, even if the work is not available. In other words, if, say, a Billy Joel song is not available in an arrangement for string orchestra, the teacher cannot legally make his own for the class without permission from the copyright holder.

Activities/Assignments for Further Exploration

1. It is sometimes argued that copyright laws are needlessly strict and unfair to the consumer, especially one who has already paid for the item. What do you think?
2. Over the next week, count how many copyright violations you see. Why do you think these occur? Are they avoidable? Would avoiding them compromise the quality of education? Can you design an alternate way of presenting the copyrighted material that does not break the law?
3. Take a piece you are studying in private lessons or in large ensembles: Investigate what the cost would be for a compulsory recording license for each one (Research for both fewer than 500 copies and more than 500 copies).
4. Find a song that has been arranged for band, orchestra, or jazz ensemble. Investigate who owns the rights to the original song. Who would need to be contacted for permission to make a further arrangement? To perform the piece on a for-profit concert? To include the piece on a recording?

Further Reading

Axford, Elizabeth C. *Song Sheets to Software: A Guide to Print Music, Software, Instructional Media, and Web Sites for Musicians.* Lanham, MD.: Scarecrow Press, 2009.

Crews, Kenneth D., Kenneth D. Crews, and Dwayne K. Buttler. *Copyright Law for Librarians and Educators: Creative Strategies and Practical Solutions.* Chicago: American Library Association, 2006.

Frankel, James. *The Teacher's Guide to Music, Media, and Copyright Law.* New York: Hal Leonard, 2009.

Joseph, Linda C. *Net Curriculum: An Educator's Guide to Using the Internet.* Medford, NJ: CyberAge Books, 1999.

Woody, Robert Henley. *Music Copyright Law in Education.* Bloomington, IN: Phi Delta Kappa, 1994.

Chapter 22

Managing Sound Levels

Protecting Your Ears and Those of Your Students

To Guide Your Reading

What is the scientific way to measure sound levels?

How do the sound levels of music compare to those of other everyday sounds?

What are the factors that determine if sounds will damage human hearing?

What does current research say about sound levels in music education environments?

Besides hearing loss, what are other types of noise-induced hearing problems?

How can we protect our own hearing and that of our students?

Human ears have evolved to handle a wide range of naturally occurring sounds, some quite loud. Our ears include an emergency feature for aurally dangerous situations—the temporary deafness or muted sensation some experience is how the ear rests after being overexercised. But the intensity of man-made sounds has pushed our natural protective mechanisms to their limits. In an increasingly loud world, one with hyper-amplified sound, tightly tuned drum heads, and in-the-ear headphone buds, it is imperative we consider the effect sound has on our hearing health and that of our students.

First, a brief explanation of how we measure sound intensity: the decibel. A decibel (dB) is a logarithmic unit that measures sound intensity, though it also has applications in electronics and communications. A zero dB sound is at the threshold of human hearing, and we are capable of perceiving changes as small as +/− one dB. Note that what matters in dB levels is the difference between two levels, not the actual reference level. A three dB increase corresponds to a doubling of sound intensity though this is not the same as loudness.[1] It should be noted that the logarithmic scale of decibels means the actual dB number can be deceiving if used as an indicator of "loudness." The doubling of intensity with a 3 dB increase does not mean the ear perceives the sound to be twice as loud. For loudness, think of dB as steps on a measurement scale, like temperature. 80 dB is 10 dB louder than 70, just as 80 degrees Fahrenheit is 10 degrees hotter than 70 degrees.

Decibel levels correlate with distance from where the sound is produced. Sound grows less intense as one moves away from the source—double the distance, and the decibels decrease by about six decibels.

This has direct applications within the ensemble. Percussionists and other players who sit near the drums or directly in front of directional brass hear significantly more intense sound than those situated further away. For example, a timpani might be 100 decibels for its player, 96 decibels for the trumpets, and only 84 decibels for the flutes and conductor sitting in the front of the ensemble.

These differences in dB may not cause dramatic differences in loudness, but the accompanying changes in intensity have crucial implications for auditory health. Any sound over 85 decibels will eventually cause hearing loss. Interestingly many sound environments in modern society reach or exceed this level:

Decibel Level

- Firearm 140+ dB
- Jet engine 140 dB
- Jackhammer 130 dB
- Sporting event 127 dB
- Live music concert 120+ dB
- Jet plane takeoff 120 dB
- Band practice 120 dB
- iPod and other mp3 players at maximum volume 120 dB
- Health club and aerobics studio 120 dB
- Movie theater 118 dB
- Motorcycle 95–120 dB
- Chainsaw pneumatic drill 100 dB
- Lawnmower 90 dB
- Subway 90 dB
- Busy street 80 dB
- Alarm clock 80 dB
- Vacuum cleaner 70 dB
- Conversation 60 dB
- Dishwasher 60 dB
- Moderate rainfall 50 dB
- Quiet room 40 dB
- Whisper, quiet library 30 dB

(American Speech-Language-Hearing Association, as quoted in *USA Today*[2])

Although they are more pleasant to listen to (usually!), musical instruments regularly reach dangerous levels, too.

The figures in Table 22.1 are not exact, of course. Not all trombonists play the same volume, and the ear's perception of the sound depends on how concentrated the sound waves are directed into the ear. If we compare a stadium and a practice room, the sound intensity is in fact higher in the practice room for the same source sound power level, because sound waves reflected from the walls reach the ear along with the direct sound. In the stadium only the direct sound reaches the ear.

Sheer volume is only part of the story. Length of exposure to sound is a major factor. Simply put, the louder a sound, the faster it causes hearing damage.

The unavoidable conclusion is that music is a loud business, capable of permanently damaging our ears. Instrumental music education is not immune to its effects. A recent study by researchers at the University of North Carolina at Greensboro measured sound levels experienced by students during a high school

TABLE 22.1 Sound Levels of Music

Sound Levels of Music[1]

Normal piano practice	60–70 dB
Fortissimo singer, 3'	70 dB
Chamber music, small auditorium	75–85 dB
Piano, playing loudly	84–103 dB
Violin	82–92 dB
Cello	85–111 dB
Oboe	95–112 dB
Flute	92–103 dB
Piccolo	90–106 dB
Clarinet	85–114 dB
French horn	90–106 dB
Trombone	85–114 dB
Timpani and bass drum	106 dB
Walkman on 5/10	94 dB
Symphonic music peak	120–137 dB
Amplified rock music, 4–6'	120 dB
Rock music peak	150 dB

1 "Decibel (loudness) comparison chart," Hearnet, http://www.hearnet.com/at_risk/risk_trivia.shtml (accessed October 11, 2009).

TABLE 22.2 Permissible Noise Level Exposure

Daily Permissible Noise Level Exposure[2] from the US Occupational Safety and Health Administration (OSHA)

Hours per day	Sound level
8	90 dB
6	92 dB
4	95 dB
3	97 dB
2	100 dB
1.5	102 dB
1	105 dB
.5	110 dB
.25 or less	115 dB

2 "Daily Permissible Noise Level Exposure," Occupational Safety and Health Administration, http://www.osha.gov/pls/oshaweb/owadisp.show_document?p_table=STANDARDS&p_id=10625 (accessed October 8, 2009).

marching band camp. Preliminary results indicate that on the first day of data collection, 15 of the 16 subjects experienced noise doses in excess of 500 percent, or 400 percent above the dosage recommended by the National Institute of Occupational Safety and Health (NIOSH). (100 percent is NIOSH's maximum allowable daily sound dosage.) On the second day of data collection 15 of 16 subjects experienced noise doses in excess of 300 percent, or 200 percent above the recommended dosage. In a specific example, a student playing the snare drum experienced the highest levels of noise on both days at 3,925 percent on day one and 1,866 percent on day two. A member of the color guard experienced the lowest levels of noise on both days, at 27 percent on day one and 23 percent on day two.[3]

In a similar study, Joseph Keefe, a former drummer in the Duke University Marching Band, showed that Duke band members were exposed to sounds in excess of 100 dB for hours at a time.[4] According to OSHA's standard, those levels would damage hearing in as little as 25–30 minutes.

It is easy to dismiss these figures as statistical hyperbole. After all, people listen to loud music all the time. They attend rock concerts that far exceed safe levels; their mp3 players are capable of producing sound at 115 dB (remember, the ear buds transmit directly into the ear canal, so the intensity is at a much higher level than if one were listening to the bud from across the room.); and high-powered marching bands are ubiquitous. Yet we do not hear many complaints— people expose themselves to these sounds willingly.

Should we really be concerned? Well, consider that factory and construction workers operating loud equipment are often required to wear protection and limit their exposure, but that musicians exposed to the same sound levels often wear nothing: Why shouldn't we be concerned? If our classes were slowly making students blind, wouldn't we care?

Although hearing loss caused by extremely loud sounds (e.g., 120+ dB) may be instant and painful, often the problem creeps in gradually and pain-free, and only over time will someone notice it. Though hearing loss brought on by sudden auditory trauma is sometimes temporary, *most damage is permanent and irreversible.*

Further, ears cannot develop a tolerance to loud sounds. If someone believes he can "tough it out" or has become "used to" loud sounds, it likely means he has already experienced hearing damage. Regrettably, hearing loss in young musicians may be quite prevalent. Another study at the UNC-Greensboro School of Music found that 52 percent of undergraduate music students show declines in high-frequency hearing consistent with acoustic overexposure.[5] The loss was largest in percussion, brass, and woodwind players, but it existed to some extent in all populations, including string players and vocalists. Though the study's authors noted that other environmental sound exposure could have contributed to the loss, it is hard to ignore music's influence when practice room levels easily reach 85 dB[6] and ensemble rehearsal rooms even higher.

Music teachers are also at high risk. Still another report from UNC-Greensboro found that average sound-level exposures of high school band directors were over 90 dB, and that daily sound doses were 261 percent of NIOSH's recommendations.[7] The overall hearing health of current and former music teachers has not been well-studied, but anecdotal evidence suggests hearing loss is common,[8] and that several music careers have been cut short because of it.

High-level sound exposure is associated with a variety of problems, including:

- *Hearing loss*—Sometimes temporary, but quite often permanent.
- *Tinnitus*—This is a ringing in the ears that can range from a faint high-pitched sound to a debilitating multi-toned ringing. Tinnitus is often caused by infections, head-trauma, and drug interactions, but noise-induced tinnitus is quite common in rock musicians and is often, though not always, associated with hearing loss. Though there are effective therapies, there is no known cure. People often experience a temporary ringing after listening to extremely loud sounds, but there is no way to effectively predict which sounds will cause permanent tinnitus.
- *Hyperacusis*—This is defined as a collapsed tolerance for everyday sounds, usually those within a certain frequency. Hyperacusis sufferers have an overly strong sensitivity to sounds other people tolerate without trouble. In its severest forms hyperacusis and tinnitus are debilitating conditions, though recent therapies have shown promise. (Dr. Pawel J. Jastreboff has been a pioneer in treating hypercacusis through his "Tinnitus Retraining Therapy," which uses a variety of techniques—including white noise—to retrain the brain, neurological system, and the ear.)

- *Misophonia*—Frequently confused with hyperacusis, misophonia is a conditioned response that causes the subject to dislike loud sounds. Its symptoms are similar to those of hyperacusis, though its treatment involves behavioral retraining to associate loud sounds with pleasure, rather than pain.

Fortunately, hearing problems are preventable.

- *Educate students about safe sound levels, proper protection, and the potential problems.*
- *Invest in "musicians' ear plugs" and encourage students to do the same.* Custom-molded musicians' ear plugs come with filter discs that allow the wearer to change the amount of protection by changing the disc (usually 5 dB, 15 dB, 25 dB). These are available for $100–200 from most audiologists and hearing centers. They offer a clearer and more accurate sound than disposable plugs.
- *Keep disposable ear-plugs on-hand.* Quality foam earplugs are available in bulk from online dealers for as little as $15/pair. Pharmacies and grocery stores sell them in small quantities. Decibel protection ranges from 5–30 dB, depending on the material. (The maximum protection is always printed on the packaging.)
- *Do not be ashamed or "too proud" to wear hearing protection when necessary.* A bit of temporary self-consciousness in the short-term is well-worth a long and effective career in music and lifelong hearing health.
- *Model good hearing protection behavior.* Reduce the stigma of wearing hearing protection by using it yourself when appropriate. Students should see protecting themselves as common, typical, necessary, and obvious.
- *Insist that students wear protection when appropriate.* Players especially susceptible to hearing loss include:

  - drum lines and drum set players, especially when playing indoors
  - piccolo players, especially in the right ear
  - ensemble players who regularly sit or stand near the percussion or in front of trumpets and trombones
  - all ensemble members during indoor marching band rehearsals or other loud rehearsal and performance situations.

- *If you are concerned that sound levels in your rehearsal and/or performance space are potentially dangerous, consider notifying your administration and union and request that professional sound measurements be made.*
- *For indoor facilities, request sound absorbing acoustical treatments.* Cloth-covered or painted fiberglass boards placed strategically on the walls can considerably reduce volume levels. These are available from the Wenger Corporation or through an acoustic consulting firm.
- *If necessary, consider less expensive solutions.* With the permission of the school administration, carpeting and cloth drapes make a difference, and can even be installed by a group of motivated music parents. Egg crate foam (the kind found in some mattress pads) is a cheap and effective alternative to professional acoustical treatments, though not as visually pleasing.
- *Schedule an audiology test so you can determine your base level of hearing.*

Activities/Assignments for Further Exploration

1. If you have access to a decibel meter, take the measurements of various sounds, both inside and outside the music building (e.g., parties, movies, conversations, construction, practice rooms, concerts). Notice the dramatic effect of proximity.
2. What instrumentalists are typically exposed to the highest sound levels? Why?
3. Noise-induced hearing problems are regularly experienced in the professional music world (classical and rock). Research a few examples of this and what musicians have done to protect themselves from potential hazards.
4. What other professions and everyday activities involve high sound levels? Is hearing protection typically utilized?

Further Reading

Baguley, David, and Gerhard Andersson. *Hyperacusis: Mechanisms, Diagnosis, and Therapies*. San Diego: Plural Pub., 2007.

Bauman, Neil G. *Help! I'm Losing My Hearing: What Do I Do Now?: A Basic Guide to Hearing Loss (and Other Ear Problems)*. Stewartstown, PA: GuidePost Publications, 2005.

Jastreboff, Pawel J., and Jonathan W. P. Hazell. *Tinnitus Retraining Therapy: Implementing the Neurophysicological Model*. Cambridge, UK: Cambridge University Press, 2004.

Vernon, Jack A., and Barbara Tabachnick Sanders. *Tinnitus: Questions and Answers*. Boston: Allyn and Bacon, 2001.

Websites

American Tinnitus Association: http://www.ata.org

Hearing Loss Association of America: http://www.hearingloss.org

Chapter 23

Special Topics: Leadership, Mentors, and Professional Development

On Leadership—"The Servant as Leader"

To some extent, all teachers are leaders. Taken in the strictly autocratic sense of the word, music teachers lead through the agenda and policies they put in place: the curriculums they set determine what is covered in class; the teaching strategies they employ guide students to learn; the rules and procedures they employ influence the classroom's learning environment; and the technique, musicianship and inspiration they display on the podium lead to great music-making. These are well-trod and legitimate characterizations of leadership, but their view is somewhat limited. The best teachers also respond and adapt to the needs of their students. They lead not only by their authority but by serving as role models, too, and they inspire excellence in those they lead. If the writings of Machiavelli epitomize the autocratic style, the essays of Robert Greenleaf perfectly represent this newer, more holistic viewpoint. Greenleaf's views on leadership promote the idea of "the servant as leader," in which the leader's primary responsibility is to serve others and strengthen the community. The "servant-leaders," as they are often referred to, have had a wide-reaching influence, from CEO's to clergymen to teachers. Band and orchestra directors, with their organizational, educational, and motivational responsibilities, can also learn a great deal from Greenleaf's blueprint. Larry Spears, longtime champion of Greenleaf's ideas, outlines ten crucial characteristics of the servant-leader:[1]

1. *Listening*—The ability to listen intently and receptively to others and then clarify what they are saying.
2. *Empathy*—The ability to recognize the unique strengths of each individual and the patience to not reject a person even if one must reject that person's *actions*.
3. *Healing*—An understanding of how to heal relationships and emotional wounds.
4. *Awareness*—A pursuit of overall awareness and self-awareness, both of which help the servant-leader handle issues concerning ethics and values.
5. *Persuasion*—An ability to convince rather than command through building a group consensus.
6. *Conceptualization*—An ability to think beyond "day-to-day realities" and envision the big picture for a program or institution. As Spears observes, "in a corporation trustee members must be conceptual and visionary, staffs need to be operational, and servant-leaders need to have a healthy dose of both" (Spears, 7).
7. *Foresight*—An ability to learn from the lessons of the past and understand the realities of the present in order to anticipate results in the future.

8. *Stewardship*—Having a commitment to serve others, and to do so with honesty and persuasion.
9. *Commitment to the growth of people*—A commitment that involves helping others improve themselves, respecting their ideas and thoughts, and involving the group in decision-making (basically, this is an extension of empathy).
10. *Building community*—An ability to use the resources of a large institution (e.g., a school and its music program) to build a sense of community.

Taking Over Smoothly from Your Predecessor

Your first step as a new teacher is to contact the previous director and gather information about the scope and sequence of the entire program, including:

- fundraising
- returning students and instrumentation
- student leadership positions
- previous year's concert calendar
- audition procedures
- past programs/repertoire
- competitions, festivals, and trips
- classroom rules and procedures
- band/orchestra handbook
- booster organization.

When taking over a new position you will undoubtedly have your own ideas, philosophy, and vision for the program, some of which may conflict with those of your predecessor. You may also hear rumors and gossip. But under no circumstances should you disparage the policies, actions, or achievements of your predecessor. Be gracious and diplomatic, regardless of the situation. Especially in the first year, make major changes selectively, and favor those that will likely offer positive results quickly.

If there are aspects of the program with which you disagree philosophically—e.g., competitions, audition procedures, etc.—remember that these may be long-standing traditions. Immediate, wholesale changes can cause dissent and distrust from students, parents, and administration, which will predispose them to disagree with even the most well-reasoned alternative. In *The Conductor as Leader*, Ramona Wis observes, "Asking them to get to know us and accept all new traditions and practices simultaneously means we have stripped them of their foundation altogether."[2] Supporting a tradition through at least one cycle of students will earn trust and give you the credibility to implement changes. Patience establishes the new teacher as an insider who understands the tradition, rather than as an outsider who dismisses everything without consideration.

Some undesirable situations require gradual change. For example, if an ensemble is used to playing only pop literature on every concert, an abrupt shift to an all-classical repertoire will be jarring. Instead, introduce appropriate repertoire little by little—perhaps one piece on the first concert, two on the next few concerts, etc.

It is reasonable to expect a certain degree of transitional friction because of the loyalties students and parents develop naturally with longstanding teachers. Do not take this dissent personally. Realize that each year in the position represents a new class of students who did not know the previous system, and another year for upperclassmen to develop a renewed sense of security.

Bear in mind that some things *must not* remain the same. Change must occur in the face of discipline, attendance, and motivation problems. As Ramona Wis advises,

> Just as members of the organization desire security, they also expect that we will lead them forward, which means some things must change . . . Even those in unruly ensembles desire, down deep, for someone to provide structure and direction so they don't have to walk into chaos every day (Wis, 52–53).

On the Challenges of Being a New Music Teacher

Not everything about teaching music deals with music itself. Though armed with a broad, not necessarily in-depth course of study, graduating music education majors enter the teaching ranks and face an enormous array of responsibilities unique to the music educator, e.g.:

* equipment maintenance
* inventories of music and instruments
* maintaining uniforms
* working with parent booster organizations
* providing music for community events
* public performances
* solo and ensemble festivals
* travel with large groups
* tour planning.

Non-musical responsibilities can be overwhelming to the new music teacher, especially when combined with the challenges of classroom management. They threaten a profession plagued with teacher shortages and high turnover. In 1993–94, 193,000 teachers entered the teaching profession (all disciplines, not just music), which was counterbalanced by 213,000 who left within the next 12 months.[3] In an era of increasing student enrollments and teacher retirements, teacher retention is a critical issue (Ingersoll, 523–524). Overall the music profession does well: 94 percent of music teachers stay in the profession. But those most likely to leave include women, minorities, and teachers in the under-30 and 30–39 age brackets (i.e., new teachers).[4]

Many of those who leave the profession cite job dissatisfaction as the primary reason (Ingersoll, 522). Dissatisfaction has many causes, including:

* lack of support from school administration
* student discipline problems
* lack of teacher influence in decision-making
* low salaries
* lack of student motivation.

There is some evidence that teaching-related stress ameliorates over time, or that at least some eventually learn how to manage it. In a study of over 100 music teachers, Hedden (2005) showed a notable decrease in stress between 1996 and 2003.[5] Perhaps teachers learn to cope using experience, time management skills, and classroom management techniques, or perhaps stress' manifestations evolve over time and teachers become tragically unaware of the effects (Hedden, 67).

Mentoring Programs

In response to these challenges, most school districts have instituted new-teacher induction programs. Smith and Ingersoll (2004) report that there is a strong link between participation in induction programs and reduced rates of turnover, and that among the most effective of them—at least in terms of reducing teacher turnover—is mentoring.[6]

Think of mentoring programs as an extension of student teaching. Mentors can help with all of the ins and outs of teaching and working in a new district, such as:

- district procedures and expectations ("how things are done")
- information about the union
- classroom management advice
- dealing with parents
- lesson planning and pacing
- choosing appropriate literature

Some evidence suggests that new teacher induction programs may not have the same positive effects on music teachers as they do on non-music teachers.[7] One way to maximize their effect may be to pair young teachers with very experienced mentors.[8] If your district does not have a formal mentoring program, let your building principal know you are interested in being paired with an experienced, veteran teacher.

Other New Teaching Induction Strategies

Beyond mentor relationships and school-sponsored orientation programs, new teachers should explore a variety of strategies to comfortably and successfully integrate into the profession.

- Observe classes taught by music colleagues at all levels. Also, seek out respected teachers from other districts. Ask your administrators if you can "shadow" the teacher for a half-day. Many administrators allow this as part of professional development. If not, consider taking a personal day.
- Observe classes taught by non-music teachers. There is much we can learn from classroom teachers about lesson planning, classroom management, and assessment (among other things), and it is a great way to jump-start ideas about interdisciplinary projects.
- Eat lunch in the main faculty lounge, even during a busy day.
- Join professional organizations and become involved in conferences, committee work, honor bands, audition selection committees, etc.
  (Keep in mind, too, that some states require music teachers to be a paying member of MENC or the state bandmasters association in order for students to be eligible for honor ensembles sponsored by those organizations.)
- Regularly read journals of professional organizations (e.g., MENC's *Music Educator's Journal*).

Activities/Assignments for Further Exploration

1. Think of some of the most effective teachers you have known. What made them effective?
2. Make a list of policies, procedures, and traditions that can be easily and quickly changed when entering a new program. Make a list that requires patience and/or a gradual approach.
3. Does the success of the previous director affect the lists from #2? Should we take a different approach depending if this success was real or perceived?
4. What are some ways a new teacher can develop security, comfort, and trust with students, parents, and administrators?
5. Discuss potential strategies for responding to those who resist change.
6. If you have previously been in a mentoring relationship, what did you learn from it? In what ways could it have been improved?

Further Reading

Greenleaf, Robert K., Don M. Frick, and Larry C. Spears. *On Becoming a Servant-Leader.* 1st ed. San Francisco: Jossey-Bass Publishers, 1996.

Greenleaf, Robert K., and Larry C. Spears. *The Power of Servant-Leadership: Essays.* San Francisco, Calif: Berrett-Koehler Publishers, 1998.

Lautzenheiser, Tim. *The Joy of Inspired Teaching.* Chicago: GIA Publications, 1993.

Wis, Ramona M. *The Conductor As Leader: Principles of Leadership Applied to Life on the Podium.* Chicago: GIA Publications, 2007.

Endnotes

Preface

1 Aniruddh D. Patel, *Music, Language, and the Brain* (Oxford: Oxford University Press, 2008), 513.

Chapter 1

1 Leonard Bernstein, *The Unanswered Question: Six Talks at Harvard* (Cambridge, MA: Harvard University Press, 1976), 54.
2 Daniel J. Levitin, *This is Your Brain on Music* (New York: Penguin Publishing, 2007), 128.
3 Aniruddh D. Patel, *Music, Language, and the Brain* (New York; Oxford: Oxford University Press, 2008), 177.
4 A. D. Patel, J. R. Iversen, and J. C. Rosenberg, "Comparing the Rhythm and Melody of Speech and Music: The Case of British English and French," *Journal of the Acoustical Society of America*, 119, Part 1 (May 2006), 3034–3047.
5 Patel summarizes the differences: "Spoken French had significantly lower pitch interval variability than spoken English, and music mirrored this pattern. That is, French musical themes had significantly lower interval variability than English themes. Put another way, as the voice moves from one syllable to the next in speech, the size of each pitch movement is more uniform in French than in English speech" (ibid., 223).
6 R. A. Miranda and M. T. Ullman, "Double Dissociation between Rules and Memory in Music: An Event-Related Potential Study," *NeuroImage* 38, no. 2 (2007), 331–345.
7 Steven Pinker, *How the Mind Works* (New York: Norton, 1997).
8 Steven Pinker, *The Language Instinct* (New York: William Morrow and Co., 1994).
9 Frank Smith, *Reading Without Nonsense* (New York: Teachers College Press, 1985), 50.
10 Eric Bluestine, *The Ways Children Learn Music: An Introduction and Practical Guide to Music Learning Theory*, 2nd ed. (Chicago, IL: GIA Publications, 2000), 88.
11 Micheál Houlahan and Philip Tacka, *Kodály Today: A Cognitive Approach to Elementary Music Education* (Oxford; New York: Oxford University Press, 2008), 23.
12 John Feierabend, "Integrating Music Learning Theory into the Kodály Curriculum," in *Readings in Music Learning Theory*, ed. Darrel L. Walters and Cynthia Taggart Crump (Chicago: GIA Publications, 1989), 264.
13 Jean Sinor, *Kodály Handbook* (Morristown, N.J.: Silver Burdett & Ginn, 1988), 38.
14 B. H. Creider, "Music Learning Theory and the Suzuki Method," in *Readings in Music Learning Theory*, ed. Darrel L. Walters and Cynthia Crump Taggart (Chicago: GIA Publications, 1989), 260.

15 John D. Kendall, *The Suzuki Violin Method in American Music Education: What the American Music Educator Should Know About Shinichi Suzuki* (Washington: MENC, 1973), 13–15.

16 Edwin Gordon, *Buffalo Music Learning Theory: Resolutions and Beyond* (Chicago: GIA, 2006), ix.

17 This is precisely why Suzuki delays the introduction of notation for up to three years. (Contemporary editions of his method often accelerate this, partly as an accommodation to the traditional timetable of learning to read music.)

18 Edwin Gordon, *Learning Sequences in Music: A Contemporary Music Learning Theory*, 2007 ed. (Chicago: GIA Publications, 2007), 4.

19 Zoltán Kodály and Ferenc Bónis, "Pentatonic Music," in *The Selected Writings of Zoltán Kodály* (London; New York: Boosey & Hawkes, 1974), 221.

20 Zoltán Kodály, "A Hundred Year Plan," in *The Selected Writings of Zoltán Kodaly*, ed. Ferenc Bónis (London: Boosey & Hawkes, 1974), 161.

21 Beth Landis and Polly Carder, *The Eclectic Curriculum in American Music Education: Contributions of Dalcroze, Kodály, and Orff* (Washington: Music Educators National Conference, 1972), 1–2.

22 Warren Haston, "Teacher Modeling as an Effective Teaching Strategy," *Music Educators Journal* 93, no. 4 (2007), 26.

23 Patricia Ann Grutzmacher, "The Effect of Tonal Pattern Training on the Aural Perception, Reading Recognition, and Melodic Sight-Reading Achievement of First-Year Instrumental Music Students," *Journal of Research in Music Education* 35, no. 3 (1987), 177–178.

24 Scott Shuler, "Music Learning Sequence Techniques in Instrumental Performance Organizations," in *Readings in Music Learning Theory*, ed. Darrel L. Walters and Cynthia Crump Taggart (Chicago: GIA, 1989), 210.

Chapter 2

1 Émile Jaques-Dalcroze, *Eurhythmics, Art, and Education* (New Dalcroze York: B. Blom, 1972), 97.

2 Ibid. 82; hereafter cited in text as Dalcroze.

3 Beth Landis and Polly Carder, *The Eclectic Curriculum in American Music Education: Contributions of Dalcroze, Kodály, and Orff* (Washington: Music Educators National Conference, 1972), 10.

4 Jo Pennington, *The Importance of Being Rhythmic: A Study of the Principles of Dalcroze Eurhythmics Applied to General Education and to the Arts of Music, Dancing and Acting* (London; New York: G. P. Putnam's Sons, 1925), 7.

5 We use the terms beat, pulse, and counts interchangeably.

6 Daniel J. Levitin, *This is Your Brain on Music: The Science of a Human Obsession* (New York: Dutton, 2006), 174–175.

7 Dalcroze, 110. The complete eurhythmics program encompasses three areas: rhythmic movement, solfege, and piano improvisation, thus echoing the body/ear/voice trio of music making activities (Pennington, 12).

8 Daniel L. Kohut, *Instrumental Music Pedagogy: Teaching Techniques for School Band and Orchestra Directors* (Champaign, Ill: Stipes Pub, 1996), 19.

9 Edwin Gordon, *Buffalo Music Learning Theory: Resolutions and Beyond* (Chicago: GIA, 2006), 9; hereafter cited in text as Gordon.

10 Bruce Dalby, "Toward an Effective Pedagogy for Teaching Rhythm: Gordon and Beyond," *Music Educators Journal* 92, no. 1 (2005), 54–55; hereafter cited in text as Dalby.

11 Edwin Gordon, *Rhythm: Contrasting the Implications of Audiation and Notation* (Chicago: GIA Publications, 2000), 96.

12 In their recent music theory and ear-training textbooks, Philip Tacka and Micheál Houlahan have appropriated Takadimi syllables for use with the Kodály system.

13 Richard Hoffman, William Pelto, and John W. White, "Takadimi: A Beat-Oriented System of Rhythm Pedagogy," *Journal of Music Theory Pedagogy* 10 (1996), 14.

14 Don P. Ester, John W. Scheib, and Kimberly J. Inks, "Takadimi: A Rhythm System for All Ages," *Music Educators Journal* 93, no. 2 (2006), 63.

15 David Newell, *Teaching Rhythm: New Strategies and Techniques for Success* (San Diego, CA: Neil A. Kjos Music Co, 2008), 28, 31.

16 Ruth Zinar, "Reading Language and Reading Music: Is There a Connection?" *Music Educators Journal* 62, no. 7 (1976), 72.

17 Diana Nicholson, "Music as an Aid to Learning" (Ph.D. diss., New York University, 1972).

18 I. Hurwitz, P. Wolff, B. Bortnick, and K. Kokas, "Non-Musical Effects of the Kodály Music Curriculum in Primary Grade Children," *Journal of Learning Disabilities*, vol. 8 (1975), 167–174.

19 Catherine Moritz "Relationships between phonological awareness and musical rhythm subskills in kindergarten children and comparison of subskills in two schools with different amounts of music instruction" (unpublished dissertation, Tufts University, 2007).

20 Ron Butzlaff, "Can Music Be Used to Teach Reading?" *Journal of Aesthetic Education* 34, no. 3/4, Special Issue, "The Arts and Academic Achievement: What the Evidence Shows" (2000), 167–178.

21 Michael Normal, "Developing Thinking Musicians in Instrumental Music," in *The Development and Practical Application of Music Learning Theory*, ed. Maria Runfola and Cynthia Crump Taggart (Chicago: GIA Publications, 2005), 213.

22 Gerald Eskelin, *Lies My Music Teacher Told Me: Music Theory for Grownups* (Woodland Hills, CA: Stage 3 Pub, 1994), 117.

Chapter 3

1 Eric Bluestine, *The Ways Children Learn Music: An Introduction and Practical Guide to Music Learning Theory* (Chicago, IL: GIA Publications, 2000), 35.

2 Charles A. Elliott, "Effect of Vocalization on the Sense of Pitch of Beginning Band Class Students," *Journal of Research in Music Education* 22, no. 2 (1974), 127.

3 Kathy A. Liperote, "Audiation for Beginning Instrumentalists: Listen, Speak, Read, Write," *Music Educators Journal* 93, no. 1 (2006), 46.

Chapter 4

1 Jeffrey Agrell, *Improvisation Games for Classical Musicians: A Collection of Musical Games with Suggestions for Use: For Performers, Instrumental Teachers, Music Students, Music Therapists, Bands, Orchestras, Choirs, Chamber Music Ensembles, Conductors, Composers, Pianists, Percussionists, and Everybody Else (Even Jazz Players)* (Chicago: GIA Publications, 2008), 30–31.

2 William Russo, Jeffrey Ainis, and David Stevenson, *Composing Music: A New Approach* (Chicago: University of Chicago Press, 1988), 230.

3 Eleni Lapidaki, "Learning from Masters of Music Creativity: Shaping Compositional Experiences in Music Education," *Philosophy of Music Education Review* 15, no. 2 (2007), 108.

Chapter 5

1 Michael L. Mark, *A Concise History of American Music Education* (Lanham, MD: Rowman & Littlefield Education, 2008), 2; hereafter cited in text as Mark, 2008.

2 James A. Keene, *A History of Music Education in the United States* (Hanover, NH: University of New England Press, 1982), 285.

3 National Research Council of Music Education (NRCME), "High School Credit Courses in Music," *Music Supervisors Journal* 15, no. 5 (May 1929), 29–37.

4 Frank L. D'Andrea, "Music Education Looks Back," *Music Educators Journal* 31, no. 3 (January 1945), 30, 34, 59.

5 Michael L. Mark, "The Evolution of Music Education Philosophy from Utilitarian to Aesthetic," *Journal of Research in Music Education* 30, no. 1 (Spring 1982), 18; hereafter cited in text as Mark, 1982.

6 Charles Leonhard, "Philosophy of Music Education," *Music Educators Journal* 32, no. 1 (September–October 1965), 59.

7 Marie McCarthy and J. Scott Goble, "Music Education Philosophy: Changing Times," *Music Educators Journal* 89, no. 1 (September 2002), 21.

8 Constantijn Koopman, "Music Education: Aesthetic or Praxial," *Journal of Aesthetic Education* 32, no. 3 (Autumn 1998), 2–3.

Chapter 6

1 Madeline Hunter, *Enhancing Teaching* (New York: Macmillan, 1994), 35.

2 Jeanne Ellis Ormrod, *Educational Psychology: Developing Learners.* 2nd ed. (Upper Saddle River, NJ: Merrill, 1998) 587; hereafter cited in text as Ormrod.

3 J. S. Bruner, "The Act of Discovery," *Harvard Educational Review* 31, 1 (1961), 21–32.

4 Eleni Lapidaki, "Learning from Masters of Music Creativity: Shaping Compositional Experiences in Music Education," *Philosophy of Music Education Review* 15, 1 (Fall 2007), 101.

Chapter 7

1 Alliance for Excellent Education, "Teacher Attrition—A Costly Loss to the Nations and to the States," August (2005), 1, 3; hereafter cited in text as *Alliance*.

2 Rudolf Dreikurs et al., *Discipline Without Tears,* 2nd ed. (New York: Hawthorn Books, 1974), 90; hereafter cited in text as Dreikurs.

3 T. E. Apter, *The Confident Child: Raising Children to Believe in Themselves* (New York ; London: W. W. Norton, 2007) 125; hereafter cited in text as Apter.

4 Beverly H. Johns and Valerie G. Carr, *Techniques for Managing Verbally and Physically Aggressive Students* (Denver: Love Pub. Co, 1995), 156; hereafter cited in text as Johns and Carr.

5 Charles H. Madsen, and Clifford K. Madsen, *Teaching: Discipline; Behavioral Principles Toward a Positive Approach* (Boston: Allyn and Bacon, 1970), 74; hereafter cited in text as Madsen.

6 A. H. Johnstone, and F. Percival, "Attention Breaks in Lectures," *Education in Chemistry* 13 (1976), 49–50.

7 Joan Middendorf and Alan Kalish, "The 'Change-Up' in Lectures." *National Teaching and Learning Forum* 5, no. 2 (January 1996), 4.

8 Joseph Lanza, *Elevator Music: A Surreal History of Muzak, Easy-Listening, and Other Moodsong* (New York: St. Martin's Press, 1994), 48–49; hereafter cited in text as Lanza.

Chapter 8

1 Colleen Conway, "Curriculum Writing in Music," *Music Educators Journal* 88, no. 6 (2002), 55.

2 J. S. Bruner, *The Process of Education,* Cambridge, MA: Harvard University Press, 1977.

3 Robert A. Duke, *Intelligent Music Teaching: Essays on the Core Principles of Effective Instruction* (Austin: Learning and Behavior Resources, 2005), 34.

4 *The School Music Program: A New Vision: The K-12 National Standards, PreK Standards, and What They Mean to Music Educators*, ed. Music Educators National Conference (U.S.) (Reston, VA: Music Educators National Conference, c1994).

5   Aurelia W. Hartenberger, "Connecting Assessment to Standards through Core Conceptual Competencies," in *Assessment in Music Education: Integrating Curriculum, Theory, and Practice*, ed. Timothy S. Brophy (Chicago: GIA Publications, 2008), 72.

6   J. S. Bruner, *The Process of Education* (Cambridge, MA: Harvard University Press, 1977).

7   David Elliot, "Music Education and Assessment: Issues and Suggestions," in *Assessment in Arts Education*, ed. Philip Taylor (Portsmouth, NH: Heinemann, 2006), 41.

8   Richard Colwell, "Music Assessment in an Increasingly Politicized, Accountability-driven Educational Environment," *Assessment in Music Education: Integrating Curriculum, Theory, and Practice*, ed. Timothy S. Brophy (Chicago: GIA Publications, 2008), 7.

9   Michael R. Peterson, and The American School Band Directors Association, *The New ASBDA Curriculum Guide* (Miami, FL: Warner Brothers Publications, 1997), 14.

10 Greg Dimitriadis, Lois Weis, and Cameron McCarthy, introduction to *Ideology, Curriculum, and the New Sociology of Education*, ed. Lois Weis, Cameron McCarthy, and Greg Dimitriadis (New York: Routledge, 2006), 5.

11 Michael Apple, *Ideology and Curriculum* (London: Routledge and Kegan Paul, 1979), 29.

12 Charles R. Hoffer, "Issues in the Assessment of K-12 Music Instruction," in *Assessment in Music Education: Integrating Curriculum, Theory, and Practice*, ed. Timothy S. Brophy (Chicago: GIA Publications, 2008), 31.

13 Katherine Luongo-Orlando, *Authentic Assessment: Designing Performance-Based Tasks* (Markham, ON: Pembroke Publishers, 2003).

14 Joseph P. McDonald, "Dilemmas of Planning Backwards: Rescuing a Good Idea," *Teachers College Record* 94, no. 1 (1992), 152–169.

15 Dannelle D. Stevens and Antonia Levi, *Introduction to Rubrics: An Assessment Tool to Save Grading Time, Convey Effective Feedback, and Promote Student Learning* (Sterling, VA: Stylus Pub, 2005), 19.

16 Douglas C. Orzolek, "Navigating the Paradox of Assessment in Music Education," in *Assessment in Music Education: Integrating Curriculum, Theory, and Practice*, ed. Timothy S. Brophy (Chicago: GIA Publications, 2008), 40.

17 Maud Hickey, "Assessment Rubrics for Music Composition," *Music Educators Journal* 85, no. 4 (1999), 26.

18 Dee Hansen, "Lectern: Writing in the Music Classroom," *Teaching Music* 16, no. 4 (2009), 29.

19 Stanley L. Schleuter, *A Sound Approach to Teaching Instrumentalists: An Application of Content and Learning Sequences,* 2nd ed. (New York: Schirmer Books, 1997), 188–189.

20 See: Michael P. Hewitt, "Self-Evaluation Tendencies of Junior High Instrumentalists," *Journal of Research in Music Education* 50, no. 3 (2002), 215–226; and Michael P. Hewitt, "Self-Evaluation Accuracy among High School and Middle School Instrumentalists," *Journal of Research in Music Education* 53, no. 2 (2005), 148–161.

21 Lissa F. May, "Factors and Abilities Influencing Achievement in Instrumental Jazz Improvisation," *Journal of Research in Music Education* 51, no. 3 (2003), 254.

22 M. Scriven, "Evaluation of Students," unpublished manuscript, 1974, quoted in Barbara Gross Davis, *Tools for Teaching,* 1st ed. (San Francisco: Jossey-Bass Publishers, 1993), 282.

23 Jeanne Ellis Ormrod, *Educational Psychology: Developing Learners*, 2nd ed. (Upper Saddle River, NJ: Merrill, 1998), 388.

24 Claire Wehr McCoy, "An Exploratory Study of Grading Criteria Among Select Ohio Ensemble Directors," *Contributions to Music Education* (1988), 15–19; Claire Wehr McCoy, "Grading Students in Performing Groups: A Comparison of Principals' Recommendations with Directors' Practices," *Journal of Research in Music Education* 39, no. 3 (1991), 181–190.

25 "Grading Practices in Music," *Music Educators Journal* 84, no. 5 (1998), 38.

26 Paul R. Lehman, "Getting Down to Basics," in *Assessment in Music Education: Integrating Curriculum, Theory, and Practice*, ed. Timothy S. Brophy (Chicago: GIA Publications, 2008), 23.

Chapter 9

1 Acton Eric Ostling, *An Evaluation of Compositions for Wind Band According to Specific Criteria of Serious Artistic Merit* (Ann Arbor, MI: University Microfilms International, 1979).

2 Stephen Budiansky, "The Problem with Band Repertoire in Music Education" (paper presented at the bi-annual meeting of the World Organization for Symphonic Bands and Ensembles (WASBE), Cincinnati, Ohio, July 2009).

3 Stephen Budiansky, "The Kids Play Great. But That Music", *The Washington Post* (http://www.washingtonpost.com/wp-dyn/articles/A46383-2005Jan29.html) January 2005, B3.

4 Stephen Budiansky and Timothy W. Foley, "The Quality of Repertoire in School Music Programs: Literature Review, Analysis, and Discussion," *Journal of the World Association for Symphonic Bands and Ensembles* 12 (2005), 17–39.

5 Allen P. Britton, "American Music Education: Is it Better than we Think? A Discussion of the Roles of Performance and Repertory, Together with Brief Mention of Certain other Problems," in *Basic Concepts in Music Education, II*, ed. Richard C. (Niwot, CO: University Press of Colorado, 1991), 175–188.

6 Daniel J. Levitin, *The World in Six Songs: How the Musical Brain Created Human Nature* (New York: Dutton, 2008), 3.

7 R. Bernard Fitzgerald, "CMP Seminar on Comprehensive Musicianship," *Music Educators Journal* 52, no. 1 (1965), 56.

8 Cynthia M. Colwell, "Integration of Music and Core Academic Objectives in the K-12 Curriculum: Perceptions of Music and Classroom Teachers," *Update: Applications of Research in Music Education* 26 (2008), 33–41.

9 Joseph A. Labuta, *Teaching Musicianship in the High School Band* (Ft. Lauderdale, FL: Meredith Music Pub, 1997), 126.

10 The American School Band Directors Association, *The New ASBDA Curriculum Guide* (Miami, FL: Warner Brothers Publications, 1997), 83.

11 Ken Stephenson, *What to Listen for in Rock: A Stylistic Analysis* (New Haven, CT: Yale University Press, 2002), 253.

12 Hypermeter is a large-scale meter that we perceive in addition to the printed one. For example, in Johann Strauss' *On the Beautiful Blue Danube*, although the printed meter is $\frac{3}{4}$, we can perceive a hypermeter of $\frac{4}{4}$ in which each $\frac{3}{4}$ measure serves as a macrobeat.

Chapter 10

1 Jan LaRue, *Guidelines For Style Analysis*, 1st ed. (New York: W. W. Norton, 1970), 1.

2 Erich Leinsdorf, *The Composer's Advocate: A Radical Orthodoxy for Musicians* (New Haven: Yale University Press), 1981.

3 Michael Votta, "I Know It's Wrong, But I'm Not Sure How to Fix It—Strategies for Improving Aural Skills on the Podium" (paper presented at the Midwest Band and Orchestra Clinic, December, 2008).

Chapter 11

1 Donald E. Bollinger, *Band Director's Complete Handbook* (West Nyack, NY: Parker Pub. Co., 1979), 65–66, 397.

Chapter 12

1 Ennio Cipani, *Classroom Management for all Teachers: Plans for Evidence-Based Practice,* 3rd ed. (Upper Saddle River, N.J.: Pearson Merrill/Prentice Hall, 2008), 12.

2 Regena Turner Parrish, "Effects of Two Instructional Methods on High School Band Students' Sight-Reading Proficiency, Music Performance, and Attitude," *Update—Applications of Research in Music Education* 17, no. 1 (1998), 14–20.

3 Michael Votta, "I Know It's Wrong, But I'm Not Sure How to Fix It—Strategies for Improving Aural Skills on the Podium" (paper presented at the Midwest Band and Orchestra Clinic, December, 2008).

4 Carol Ann Tomlinson, Kay Brimijoin, and Lane Narvaez, *The Differentiated School* (Alexandria, Virginia: Association for Supervision and Curriculum Development, 2008), 4–5.

5 Howard Gardner, *Frames of Mind: The Theory of Multiple Intelligences* (New York, NY: Basic Books, 1993).

6 Peter Miksza, "Effective Practice: An Investigation of Observed Practice Behaviors, Self-Reported Practice Habits, and the Performance Achievement of High School Wind Players," *Journal of Research in Music Education* 55, no. 4 (2007), 359–375; hereafter cited in text as Effective Practice.

7 Peter Miksza and Charles Punnett Schmidt, *Relationships Among Impulsivity, Achievement Goal Motivation, Practice Behavior, and the Performance Achievement of High School Wind Players* (Ph.D. diss, 2007, ISBN 9780549151258 0549151257).

8 Gary McPherson and James Renwick, "A Longitudinal Study of Self-Regulation in Children's Musical Practice," *Music Education Research* 3, no. 2 (2001), 169–186.

Chapter 13

1 Michael P. Hewitt, "Self-Evaluation Tendencies of Junior High Instrumentalists," *Journal of Research in Music Education* 50, no. 3 (2002), 215–226; Michael P. Hewitt, "Self-Evaluation Accuracy among High School and Middle School Instrumentalists," *Journal of Research in Music Education* 53, no. 2 (2005), 148–161.

2 Hermann von Helmholtz and Alexander John Ellis, *On the Sensations of Tone as a Physiological Basis for the Theory of Music* (New York: Dover Publications, 1954), 187.

3 Ross W. Duffin, *How Equal Temperament Ruined Harmony (and Why You Should Care)*, 1st ed. (New York: W.W. Norton, 2007), 38.

4 Brant Karrick, "An Examination of the Intonation Tendencies of Wind Instrumentalists Based on Their Performance of Selected Harmonic Musical Intervals," *Journal of Research in Music Education* 46, no. 1 (1998), 124.

5 Gerald Eskelin, *Lies My Music Teacher Told Me: Music Theory for Grownups* (Woodland Hills, CA: Stage 3 Pub, 1994), 32.

6 Millsap, Tonya Anne. "The Daily Implementation of Sequential Sustained Tone Exercises as a Means of Improving the Ensemble Intonation and Tone Quality of Second-Year Middle School Bands," Ph.D. diss., University Microfilms International (MI) Ann Arbor, MI, 1999. Millsap examined the effect of long tone exercises on the physical technique, tone, and intonation of middle school band students. She organized the exercises sequentially from simple to complex intervalic and chordal relationships, and recorded the effects when practiced by the ensemble for 5–7 minutes per rehearsal. After only ten weeks she found statistically significant improvement in ensemble intonation, ensemble tone quality, and individual tone quality, assuming the instructor guided the students through with exercises with feedback on blend, balance, embouchure formation, and breath support (Millsap, 98). Interestingly, she found no statistically significant improvement in individual embouchure, breath control, or pitch discrimination. This suggests it is effective to give students time to focus their attention predominantly on pitch and tone. In a sense they are their own best teachers, making improvement regardless of how quickly their breath support and embouchure improves.

7 Free bowing refers to the unsynchronized bowing style employed by Leopold Stokowski with the Philadelphia

Orchestra. The rich, homogeneous results of the technique are associated with the "Stokowski sound," or "Philadelphia sound," for which the orchestra became well-known.

8 Here is an application of this technique to help less experienced players look ahead: Students play two beats and then rest two beats. During the rest, players place their fingertip on the next pitch but do not sound it until both rests have been counted.

9 Harold E. Griswold, "How to Teach Aural Skills with Electronic Tuners," *Music Educators Journal* 74, no. 5 (1988), 50.

10 John M. Geringer and Michael Worthy "Effects of Tone-Quality Changes on Intonation and Tone-Quality Ratings of High School and College Instrumentalists," *Journal of Research in Music Education* 47, no. 2 (1999), 136.

11 Carol L. Krumhansl and Paul Iverson, "Perceptual Interactions between Musical Pitch and Timbre," *Journal of Experimental Psychology: Human Perception and Performance* 18, no. 3 (1992), 739–751.

12 Michael D. Worthy, "Effects of Tone-Quality Conditions on Perception and Performance of Pitch among Selected Wind Instrumentalists," *Journal of Research in Music Education* 48, no. 3 (2000), 254.

Chapter 14

1 Charles P. Schmidt, "Relations among Motivation, Performance Achievement, and Music Experience Variables in Secondary Instrumental Music Students," *Journal of Research in Music Education* 53, no. 2 (2005), 144.

2 George L. Rogers, "Attitudes of High School Band Directors and Principals Toward Marching Band Contests." *Journal of Research in Music Education* 33, no. 4 (1985), 265–266.

3 Laster, James, *So You're the New Musical Director!: An Introduction to Conducting a Broadway Musical* (Lanham, Md: Scarecrow Press, 2001), 129.

4 James E. Latten, "Chamber Music for Every Instrumentalist," *Music Educators Journal* 87, no. 5, Special Focus: Interdisciplinary Curriculum (2001), 46.

Chapter 15

1 Paul R. Burden, *Classroom Management and Discipline: Methods to Facilitate Cooperation and Instruction* (New York: Longman, 1995), 146.

2 Lisa Guernsey, "Rewards for Students Under a Microscope," *New York Times* (2009), 1. March 2, 2009, Science section.

3 Alfie Kohn, *Punished by Rewards: The Trouble with Gold Stars, Incentive Plans, A's, Praise, and Other Bribes* (Boston: Houghton Mifflin Co., 1999), 17.

4 Edward L. Deci, Richard Koestner, and Richard M. Ryan, "Extrinsic Rewards and Intrinsic Motivation in Education: Reconsidered Once Again," *Review of Educational Research* 71, no. 1 (2001), 1–27.

5 Barbara A. Marinak and Linda B. Gambrell, "Intrinsic Motivation and Rewards: What Sustains Young Children's Engagement with Text?" *Literacy Research and Instruction* 47, no. 1 (January 1, 2008), 9–26.

6 Edward L. Deci and Richard M. Ryan, *Intrinsic Motivation and Self-Determination in Human Behavior*, ed. Richard M. Ryan (New York: Plenum, 1985), 248.

7 Cipani, Ennio, *Classroom Management for all Teachers: Plans for Evidence-Based Practice*, 3rd ed. (Upper Saddle River, NJ: Pearson Merrill/Prentice Hall, 2008), 19.

8 Apter, T. E. *The Confident Child: Raising Children to Believe in Themselves*, New York; London: W. W. Norton, 2007, 133.

9 Rudolf Dreikurs, "Understanding the Child, a Manual for Teachers," monograph, 1951, as quoted in Rudolf Dreikurs, Bernice Bronia Grunwald, and Floy C. Pepper, *Maintaining Sanity in the Classroom: Classroom Management Techniques,* 2nd ed. (New York: Harper & Row, 1982), 353.

10 James S. Cangelosi, *Classroom Management Strategies: Gaining and Maintaining Students' Cooperation*, 2nd ed. (New York: Longman, 1993), 218.

Chapter 16

1 Daniel J. Levitin, *This is Your Brain on Music: The Science of a Human Obsession* (New York, NY: Dutton, 2006), 197.
2 Linda A. Hartley, "Influence of Starting Grade and School Organization on Enrollment and Retention in Beginning Instrumental Music," *Journal of Research in Music Education* 44, no. 4 (1996), 305.
3 Glenn E. Nierman and Michael H. Veak, "Effect of Selected Recruiting Strategies on Beginning Instrumentalists' Participation Decisions," *Journal of Research in Music Education* 45, no. 3 (1997), 387.
4 David Williams, "A Study of Internal Validity of the Instrument Timbre Preference Test," *Journal of Research in Music Education* 4, no. 3 (Fall 1996).
5 Because the mouthpiece hides the lips it is essential that we see how the students form their embouchure while buzzing without a mouthpiece. Once we add the mouthpiece the lips are hidden.
6 Kevin Mixon, "Building Your Instrumental Music Program in an Urban School," *Music Educators Journal* 91, no. 3 (2005), 22.
7 Point out to your string players that Stradivarius violins are hundreds of years old and full of scrapes and scratches from years of playing. Old is not bad when it comes to a violin! "What a story those nicks could tell about the other musicians who played before them . . ."
8 R. V. Brittin and D. A. Sheldon, "An Analysis of Band Method Books: Implications of Culture, Composer, and Type of Music," *Bulletin—Council for Research in Music Education* no. 161/162 (2004), 52–53.
9 Robert A. Duke and James L. Byo, "Introduction," in *The Habits of Musicianship: A Radical Approach to Beginning Band* (Austin, Texas: Center for Music Learning, 2009), 2, http://cml.music.utexas.edu/Habits/Habits.htm
10 George L. Rogers, "Concert Band Instrumentation: Realities and Remedies," *Music Educators Journal* 77, no. 9 (1991), 38.
11 Rachel M. Gamin, "Teacher Perceptions regarding Attrition in Beginning Instrumental Music Classes During the First Year of Study," *Contributions to Music Education* 32, no. 2 (2005), 53.
12 Jennifer L. Stewart, "Factors Related to Students' Decisions to Continue in Band," *Contributions to Music Education* 32, no. 1 (2005), 67. Surprisingly, one study found a negative correlation between the length of time students studied privately and their attitudes toward performing and sight-reading by themselves (Stewart, 67). Perhaps this could be because of constant criticism received during lessons. Although obviously this is a natural part of intensive one-on-one study, it suggests we should vet the teachers we recommend to our students to ensure they have a positive experience.

Chapter 17

1 Karen A. Hagberg, *Stage Presence From Head to Toe: A Manual for Musicians* (Lanham, MD: Scarecrow Press, 2003), 57–58.

Chapter 18

1 Joy Johanson and Margo G. Wootan, "Sweet Deals," February 2007, Center for Science in the Public Interest, www.cspinet.org/schoolfundraising.pdf

2 Frank Sennett, *FUNdrasin: 50 Proven Strategies for Successful School Fundraisers* (Thousand Oaks, CA: Corwin Press, 2008), 3.

3 Jean C. Joachim, *Beyond the Bake Sale: The Ultimate School Fund-Raising Book*, 1st ed. New York: St. Martin's Griffin, 2003, 209.

4 Barry Callen, *Perfect Phrases for Sales and Marketing Copy: Hundreds of Ready-to-use Phrases to Capture Your Customer's Attention and Increase Your Sales* (New York: McGraw-Hill, 2008), 61.

5 Overbye, Dennis. "Elevating Science, Elevating Democracy," *New York Times.* January 26, 2009. Section D1.

6 Paul Griffiths, "Don't Blame Modernists for the Empty Seats," *New York Times*, March 22, 1998, Classical View, 37.

7 Donald E. Bollinger, *Band Director's Complete Handbook* (West Nyack, N.Y.: Parker Pub. Co., 1979), 27.

Chapter 21

1 James Frankel, and Technology Institute for Music Educators, *The Teacher's Guide to Music, Media, and Copyright Law* (New York: Hal Leonard, 2009), 151–154.

Chapter 22

1 The formula is (10*log (I1/I2)).

2 Brophy Marcus Mary, "For iPod users, a budding problem—MP3 earphones raise hearing-loss concerns," *USA TODAY* March 5, 2006, 10D.

3 Jennifer Stewart Walter, "Sound Exposures of High School Marching Band Members During Band Camp: A Pilot Study." Accepted for publication by the *Journal of Band Research.*

4 Joyce Cohen, "Marching band—a threat to hearing?—Thousands of students may be at risk," *USA TODAY* October 17, 2007, 10D.

5 Susan Phillips, Sandra Mace, Donald Hodges, and Julie Shoemaker "Environmental Factors in Susceptibility to Noise-induced Hearing Loss in Student Musicians," *Medical Problems of Performing Artists*, 23 (2008), 20.

6 Susan Phillips and Sandra Mace, "Sound-level Measurements in Music Practice Rooms" (2008) (Under Review —*Music Performance Research*).

7 Patricia Sink and Sandra Mace, "A Preliminary Analysis of Sound-Level Exposures of Fulltime Choral, General, And Instrumental Music Educators During Typical Work Days" (paper presented at the North Carolina Music Educators Association conference, Winston-Salem, NC, November, 2004).

8 Gary White, "Hazards of Striking Up the Band," *The Ledger*, 16 October 2007, accessed online: http://www.theledger.com/article/20071016/NEWS/710160347?Title=Daily-Exposure-to-Thunderous-Sounds-Can-Damage-Music-Directors-Hearing

Chapter 23

1 Larry C. Spears, "Introduction," in *The Power of Servant-Leadership*, by Robert Greenleaf, ed. Larry C. Spears (San Francisco: Berrett-Koehler Publishers: 1998), 1–16.

2 Ramona M. Wis, *The Conductor As Leader: Principles of Leadership Applied to Life on the Podium* (Chicago, IL: GIA Publications, 2007) 52.

3 Richard M. Ingersoll, "Teacher Turnover and Teacher Shortages: An Organizational Analysis," *American Educational Research Journal* 38, no. 3 (2001), 514.

4 Carl B. Hancock, "Music Teachers at Risk for Attrition and Migration: An Analysis of the 1999–2000 Schools and Staffing Survey," *Journal of Research in Music Education* 56, no. 2 (2008), 130–144.

5 D. G. Hedden, "A Study of Stress and Its Manifestations Among Music Educators," *Bulletin—Council for Research in Music Education*, no. 166 (2005), 57–68.

6 Thomas M. Smith and Richard M. Ingersoll, "What are the Effects of Induction and Mentoring on Beginning Teacher Turnover?" *American Educational Research Journal* 41, no. 3 (2004), 706.

7 Janice N. Killian, "The Effect of Personal and Situational Factors in the Attrition and Retention of Texas Music Educators," *Journal of Music Teacher Education* 16, no. 1 (2006), 41–54.

8 Colleen M. Conway, "An Examination of District-Sponsored Beginning Music Teacher Mentor Practices," *Journal of Research in Music Education* 51, no. 1 (2003), 6–23.

References

Assessment in Arts Education. Edited by Philip Taylor (foreword by Joe Kincheloe) Portsmouth, NH: Heinemann, c2006.

Agay, Denes. *Best Loved Songs of the American People.* 1st ed. Garden City, NY: Doubleday, 1975.

Agrell, Jeffrey. *Improvisation Games for Classical Musicians: A Collection of Musical Games with Suggestions for use: For Performers, Instrumental Teachers, Music Students, Music Therapists, Bands, Orchestras, Choirs, Chamber Music Ensembles, Conductors, Composers, Pianists, Percussionists, and Everybody Else (Even Jazz Players).* Chicago: GIA Publications, 2008.

Alliance for Excellent Education. "Teacher Attrition—A Costly Loss to the Nations and to the States." August (2005).

American School Band Directors Association. *The New ASBDA Curriculum Guide: A Reference Book for School Band Directors.* Miami, FL: Warner Bros. Publications, 1997.

Apple, Michael. *Ideology and Curriculum.* London: Routledge and Kegan Paul, 1979.

Apter, T. E. *The Confident Child: Raising Children to Believe in Themselves.* New York; London: W. W. Norton, 2007.

Azzara, Christopher D., and Richard F. Grunow. *Developing Musicianship Through Improvisation. 1. C Instruments (treble clef).* Chicago: GIA Publications, 2006.

Bailey, Derek. *Improvisation: Its Nature and Practice in Music.* New York: Da Capo Press, 1993.

Bailey, Wayne. *The Complete Marching Band Resource Manual: Techniques and Materials for Teaching, Drill Design, and Music Arranging.* Philadelphia: University of Pennsylvania Press, 2003,

Bauman, Neil G. *Help! I'm Losing My Hearing: What do I do Now?: A Basic Guide to Hearing Loss (and Other Ear Problems).* Stewartstown, PA: GuidePost Publications, 2005.

Bazan, D. E. "An Investigation of the Instrument Selection Processes Used by Directors of Beginning Band." *Contributions to Music Education* 32, no. 1 (2005): 9–31.

Beidler, Peter G. *Why I Teach.* Kansas City, MO: Andrews McMeel Pub., 2002.

Bernstein, Leonard. *The Unanswered Question: Six Talks at Harvard.* Cambridge, MA: Harvard University Press, 1976.

Bernstein, Leonard. *The Infinite Variety of Music.* New York: Simon and Schuster, 1966.

Blanchard, Bonnie, and Cynthia Blanchard Acree. *Making Music and Enriching Lives: A Guide for all Music Teachers.* Bloomington, IN: Indiana University Press, 2007.

Block, Debbie Galante. "A New Kind of Show-and-Tell." Teaching Music (January 2009): 18.

Bluestine, Eric. *The Ways Children Learn Music: An Introduction and Practical Guide to Music Learning Theory.* 2nd ed., rev. and enl. ed. Chicago, IL: GIA Publications, 2000.

Bollinger, Donald E. *Band Director's Complete Handbook.* West Nyack, NY: Parker Pub. Co., 1979.

Borg, James. *Persuasion: The Art of Influencing People.* 2nd ed. Harlow, UK: Pearson Prentice Hall, 2007.

Boyer, René, Washington University (Saint Louis, MO), Theses, and Music. *Perspectives for Developing Principles and Guidelines in the Construction of the General Music Curriculum for American Elementary Schools: An Eclectic Approach.* St. Louis, 1978.

Breaux, Annette L., and Todd Whitaker. *Seven Simple Secrets: What the Best Teachers Know and Do.* Larchmont, NY: Eye On Education, 2006.

Brittin, R. V., and D. A. Sheldon. "An Analysis of Band Method Books: Implications of Culture, Composer, and Type of Music." *Bulletin—Council for Research in Music Education* no. 161/162 (2004), 47–56.

Brophy Marcus, Mary. "For iPod Users, a Budding Problem—MP3 Earphones Raise Hearing-loss Concerns," *USA TODAY (Arlington, VA)* 2006, p. 10D.

Brophy, Timothy S., and Kristen Albert. *Assessment in Music Education: Integrating Curriculum, Theory, and Practice.* Chicago: GIA Publications, 2008.

Bruner, J. S. *The Process of Education.* Cambridge, MA: Harvard University Press, 1977.

Bruner, J. S. "The Act of Discovery." *Harvard Educational Review* 31, 1 (1961), 21–32.

Budiansky, Stephen. "The Kids Play Great. But That Music". *Washington Post* (http://www.washingtonpost.com/wp-dyn/articles/A46383-2005Jan29.html) January 2005.

Burden, Paul R. *Classroom Management and Discipline: Methods to Facilitate Cooperation and Instruction.* New York: Longman, 1995.

Butzlaff, Ron. "Can Music be used to Teach Reading?" *Journal of Aesthetic Education* 34, no. 3/4, Special Issue: "The Arts and Academic Achievement: What the Evidence Shows" (2000), 167–178.

Callen, Barry. *Perfect Phrases for Sales and Marketing Copy: Hundreds of Ready-to-use Phrases to Capture Your Customer's Attention and Increase Your Sales.* New York: McGraw-Hill, 2008.

Cangelosi, James S. *Classroom Management Strategies: Gaining and Maintaining Students' Cooperation.* 2nd ed. New York: Longman, 1993.

Carder, Polly, and Beth Landis. *The Eclectic Curriculum in American Music Education: Contributions of Dalcroze, Kodály, and Orff.* Rev. ed. Reston, VA: Music Educators National Conference, 1990.

Cipani, Ennio. *Classroom Management for all Teachers: Plans for Evidence-Based Practice.* 3rd ed. Upper Saddle River, NJ: Pearson Merrill/Prentice Hall, 2008.

Cohen, Joyce. "Marching band—a threat to hearing?—Thousands of students may be at risk," *USA TODAY* (Arlington, VA) 2007, p. 10D.

Colwell, Richard, and Frank Abrahams. "Edwin Gordon's Contribution: An Appraisal." *The Quarterly Journal of Music Teaching and Learning 2*, nos. 1 & 2: *The Work of Edwin Gordon* (Spring/Summer 1991): 19–36.

Colwell, Richard, and Music Educators National Conference (U.S.). *MENC Handbook of Research Methodologies.* Oxford; New York: Oxford University Press, 2006.

Colwell, Richard, and Music Educators National Conference (U.S.). *Handbook of Research on Music Teaching and Learning: A Project of the Music Educators National Conference.* New York: Schirmer Books ; Toronto; New York: Maxwell Macmillan Canada; Maxwell Macmillan International, 1992.

Condron, Stephanie. "Music Teachers are Ordered to Wear Earmuffs." *Mail Online* (http://www.dailymail.co.uk) January 2009.

Conway, Colleen. "Curriculum Writing in Music." *Music Educators Journal* 88, no. 6 (2002), 54–59.

Conway, Colleen M. "An Examination of District-Sponsored Beginning Music Teacher Mentor Practices." *Journal of Research in Music Education* 51, no. 1 (2003), 6–23.

Conway, Colleen, Erin Hansen, Andrew Schulz, Jeff Stimson, and Jill Wozniak-Reese. "Becoming a Teacher: Stories of the First Few Years." *Music Educators Journal* 91, no. 1 (2004), 45–50.

Crawford, Donna K., Richard J. Bodine, and Robert G. Hoglund. *The School for Quality Learning: Managing the School and Classroom the Deming Way.* Champaign, IL: Research Press, 1993.

Creider, B. H. "Music Learning Theory and the Suzuki Method." In *Readings in Music Learning Theory*, ed. Darrel L. Walters and Cynthia Crump Taggart. Chicago: GIA Publications, 1989.

Dalby, Bruce. "Toward an Effective Pedagogy for Teaching Rhythm: Gordon and Beyond." *Music Educators Journal* 92, no. 1 (2005), 54–60.

D'Andrea, Frank L. "Music Education Looks Back." *Music Educators Journal* 31, no. 3 (January 1945), 30, 34, 59.

Dániel, Katinka Scipiades, Zoltán Kodály, and Barbara Gross Davis. *Kodály Approach Method Book.* 2nd ed.. Champaign, IL: M. Foster Music Co., 1979.

Davis, Barbara Gross. *Tools for Teaching.* 1st ed. San Francisco: Jossey-Bass Publishers, 1993.

Deci, Edward L. and Richard M. Ryan. *Intrinsic Motivation and Self-Determination in Human Behavior.* Ed. Richard M. Ryan. New York: Plenum, 1985.

Deci, Edward L., Richard Koestner, and Richard M. Ryan. "Extrinsic Rewards and Intrinsic Motivation in Education: Reconsidered Once again." *Review of Educational Research* 71, no. 1 (2001), 1–27.

Delzell, Judith K. "The Effects of Musical Discrimination Training in Beginning Instrumental Music Classes." *Journal of Research in Music Education* 37, no. 1 (1989), 21–31.

Dimitriadis, Greg, Lois Weis, and Cameron McCarthy, eds, *Ideology, Curriculum, and the New Sociology of Education.* New York: Routledge, 2006.

Don P. Ester, John W. Scheib, and Kimberly J. Inks. "Takadimi: A Rhythm System for all Ages." *Music Educators Journal* 93, no. 2 (2006), 60–65.

Dreikurs, Rudolf, Pearl Cassel, and David Kehoe. *Discipline Without Tears: How to Reduce Conflict and Establish Cooperation in the Classroom.* 2nd ed. New York: Hawthorn Books, 1974.

Dreikurs, Rudolf, Bernice Bronia Grunwald, and Floy C. Pepper. *Maintaining Sanity in the Classroom: Classroom Management Techniques.* 2nd ed. New York: Harper & Row, 1982.

Duffin, Ross W. *How Equal Temperament Ruined Harmony (and Why You Should Care).* 1st ed. New York: W. W. Norton, 2007.

Duke, Robert A. *Intelligent Music Teaching: Essays on the Core Principles of Effective Instruction.* Austin, TX: Learning and Behavior Resources, 2005.

Duke, Robert A. and James L. Byo. "Introduction." In *The Habits of Musicianship: A Radical Approach to Beginning Band.* Austin, TX: Center for Music Learning, 2009. http://cml.music.utexas.edu/Habits/Habits.htm

Edwards, Clifford H. *Classroom Discipline and Management.* 4th ed. New York: Wiley, 2004.

Elliott, Charles A. "Effect of Vocalization on the Sense of Pitch of Beginning Band Class Students." *Journal of Research in Music Education* 22, no. 2 (1974), 120–128.

Eskelin, Gerald. *Lies My Music Teacher Told Me: Music Theory for Grownups.* Woodland Hills, CA: Stage 3 Pub., 1994.

Farrell, Susan R. *Tools for Powerful Student Evaluation: A Practical Source of Authentic Assessment Strategies for Music Teachers.* 2nd ed. rev: ed. Ft. Lauderdale, FL: Meredith Music Publications, 1997.

Feierabend, John. "Integrating Music Learning Theory into the Kodály Curriculum." In *Readings in Music Learning Theory,* ed. Darrel L. Walters and Cynthia Crump Taggart. Chicago: GIA Publications, 1989.

Fitzgerald, R. Bernard. "CMP Seminar on Comprehensive Musicianship." *Music Educators Journal* 52, no. 1 (1965), 56–57.

Fortney, Patrick M., J. David Boyle, and Nicholas J. DeCarbo. "A Study of Middle School Band Students' Instrument Choices." *Journal of Research in Music Education* 41, no. 1 (1993): 28–39.

Frankel, James, and Technology Institute for Music Educators. *The Teacher's Guide to Music, Media, and Copyright Law.* New York: Hal Leonard, 2009.

Franken, Robert E. *Human Motivation.* 3rd ed. Pacific Grove, CA: Brooks/Cole Pub. Co, 1994.

Gamin, Rachel M. "Teacher Perceptions regarding Attrition in Beginning Instrumental Music Classes during the First Year of Study." *Contributions to Music Education* 32, no. 2 (2005), 43–64.

Gardner, Howard. *Frames of Mind: The Theory of Multiple Intelligences.* New York.: Basic Books, 1993.

Geringer, John M. "Effects of Tone-Quality Changes on Intonation and Tone-Quality Ratings of High School and College Instrumentalists." *Journal of Research in Music Education* 47, no. 2 (1999), 135–149.

Gingras, Michèle. *Clarinet Secrets: 52 Performance Strategies for the Advanced Clarinetist.* Lanham, MD: Scarecrow Press, 2004.

Gordon, Edwin. *Learning Sequences in Music: A Contemporary Music Learning Theory.* 2007 ed. Chicago: GIA Publications, 2007.

Gordon, Edwin. *Buffalo Music Learning Theory: Resolutions and Beyond.* Chicago: GIA, 2006.

Gordon, Edwin. *Music Aptitude Profile.* Chicago: GIA Publications, 2001.

Gordon, Edwin. *Rhythm: Contrasting the Implications of Audiation and Notation.* Chicago: GIA Publications, 2000.

Gordon, Edwin. *Introduction to Research and the Psychology of Music.* Chicago: GIA, 1998.

Gordon, Edwin. *Learning Sequences in Music: Skill, Content, and Patterns: A Music Learning Theory.* 1997 ed. Chicago: GIA, 1997.

Gordon, Edwin. *Music Aptitude and Related Texts.* Chicago: GIA Publications, 1992.

Gordon, Thomas, and Noel Burch. *T.E.T., Teacher Effectiveness Training: The Program Proven to Help Teachers Bring Out the Best in Students of all Ages.* New York: Three Rivers Press, 2003.

Greenleaf, Robert K., Don M. Frick, and Larry C. Spears. *On Becoming a Servant-Leader.* 1st ed. San Francisco: Jossey-Bass Publishers, 1996.

Greenleaf, Robert K. *The Power of Servant-Leadership: Essays.* Edited by Larry C. Spears. San Francisco, CA: Berrett-Koehler Publishers, 1998.

Griffiths, Paul. "Don't Blame Modernists for the Empty Seats." *New York Times, March 22,* 1998, Classical View.

Griswold, Harold E. "How to Teach Aural Skills with: Electronic Tuners." *Music Educators Journal* 74, no. 5 (1988), 49–51.

Grunow, Richard E., Edwin E. Gordon, and Christopher D. Azzara. *Jump Right In: The Instrumental Series—For Winds and Percussion.* Chicago: GIA Publications, Inc., 2001.

Grunow, Richard E., Edwin E. Gordon, and Christopher D. Azzara. *Jump Right In: The Instrumental Series—For Recorder.* Chicago: GIA Publications, Inc., 1999.

Grunow, Richard E., Edwin E. Gordon, Christopher D. Azzara, and M. E. Martin. *Jump Right In: The Instrumental Series—For Strings.* Chicago: GIA Publications, Inc., 2002.

Grutzmacher, Patricia Ann. "The Effect of Tonal Pattern Training on the Aural Perception, Reading Recognition, and Melodic Sight-Reading Achievement of First-Year Instrumental Music Students." *Journal of Research in Music Education* 35, no. 3 (1987), 171–181.

Guernsey, Lisa. "Rewards for Students Under a Microscope." *New York Times*, March 2, 2009, Science section.

Gumm, Alan. *Music Teaching Style: Moving Beyond Tradition.* Galesville, MD; Milwaukee, WI: Meredith Music Publications; Exclusively distributed by Hal Leonard, 2003.

Haack, Paul, and Michael V. Smith. "Mentoring New Music Teachers." *Music Educators Journal* 87, no. 3 (2000), 23–27.

Hagberg, Karen A. *Stage Presence from Head to Toe: A Manual for Musicians.* Lanham, MD: Scarecrow Press, 2003.

Hancock, Carl B. "Music Teachers at Risk for Attrition and Migration: An Analysis of the 1999–2000 Schools and Staffing Survey." *Journal of Research in Music Education* 56, no. 2 (2008), 130–144.

Hansen, Dee. "Lectern: Writing in the Music Classroom." *Teaching Music* 16, no. 4 (2009), 28–30.

Harris, Jr., Frederick. *Conducting With Feeling.* 1st ed. Galesville, MD: Meredith Music Publications, 2001.

Hartenberger, Aurelia W. "Connecting Assessment to Standards through Core Conceptual Competencies." In *Assessment in Music Education: Integrating Curriculum, Theory, and Practice,* ed. Timothy S. Brophy. Chicago: GIA Publications, 2008.

Hartley, Linda A. "Influence of Starting Grade and School Organization on Enrollment and Retention in Beginning Instrumental Music." *Journal of Research in Music Education* 44, no. 4 (1996), 304–318.

Haston, Warren. "Teacher Modeling as an Effective Teaching Strategy." *Music Educators Journal* 93, no. 4 (2007), 26–30.

Haston, Warren A. *Comparison of a Visual and an Aural Approach to Beginning Wind Instrument Instruction,* Ph.D. diss, Northwestern University, U.S., 2004.

Haugland, Susan L., *Crowd Control: Classroom Management and Effective Teaching for Chorus, Band, and Orchestra.* Lanham, Md; Reston, VA: Rowman & Littlefield Education, 2007.

Hedden, D. G. "A Study of Stress and its Manifestations Among Music Educators." *Bulletin—Council for Research in Music Education*, no. 166 (2005), 57–68.

Hewitt, Michael P. "Self-Evaluation Accuracy among High School and Middle School Instrumentalists." *Journal of Research in Music Education* 53, no. 2 (2005), 148–161.

Hewitt, Michael P. "Self-Evaluation Tendencies of Junior High Instrumentalists." *Journal of Research in Music Education* 50, no. 3 (2002), 215–226.

Hewitt, Michael P. "The Effects of Modeling, Self-Evaluation, and Self-Listening on Junior High Instrumentalists' Music Performance and Practice Attitude." *Journal of Research in Music Education* 49, no. 4 (2001), 307.

Hickey, Maud. "Assessment Rubrics for Music Composition." *Music Educators Journal* 85, no. 4 (1999), 26–33.

Hoffman, Richard, William Pelto, and John W. White. "Takadimi: A Beat-Oriented System of Rhythm Pedagogy." *Journal of Music Theory Pedagogy* 10 (1996).

Holt, John Caldwell. *Learning all the Time.* Reading, MA: Addison-Wesley, 1989.

Houlahan, Micheál, and Philip Tacka. *From Sound to Symbol: Fundamentals of Music.* New York: Oxford University Press, 2009.

Houlahan, Micheál, and Philip Tacka. *Kodály Today: A Cognitive Approach to Elementary Music Education.* Oxford; New York: Oxford University Press, 2008.

Hullfish, William Rouse. *A Comparison of Response-Sensitive and Response-Insensitive Decision Rules in Presenting Learning Materials in Music Theory by Computer-Assisted Instruction.* Buffalo, NY: State University of New York at Buffalo, 1970.

Hunter, Madeline. *Enhancing Teaching.* New York, New York: Macmillan, 1994.

Hurwitz, I., P. Wolff, B. Bortnick, and K. Kokas. "Non-Musical Effects of the Kodály Music Curriculum in Primary Grade Children." *Journal of Learning Disabilities* 8 (1975), 167–174.

Ingersoll, Richard M. "Teacher Turnover and Teacher Shortages: An Organizational Analysis." *American Educational Research Journal* 38, no. 3 (2001), 499–534.

Jaques-Dalcroze, Émile. *Eurhythmics, Art, and Education.* New York: Arno Press, 1980.

Jaques-Dalcroze, Émile. *Rhythm, Music and Education.* London: Dalcroze Society, 1967.

Jeans, James Hopwood, Sir. *Science and Music.* New York: Dover Publications, 1968.

Joachim, Jean C. *Beyond the Bake Sale: The Ultimate School Fund-Raising Book.* 1st ed. New York: St. Martin's Griffin, 2003.

Johanson, Joy and Margo. G. Wootan, "Sweet Deals," February 2007, Center for Science in the Public Interest, www.cspinet.org/schoolfundraising.pdf

Johns, Beverly H., and Valerie G. Carr. *Techniques for Managing Verbally and Physically Aggressive Students.* Denver, CO: Love Pub. Co, 1995.

Johnstone, A.H. and F. Percival. "Attention Breaks in Lectures." *Education in Chemistry* 13 (1976)

Jones, Vernon F., and Louise S. Jones. *Comprehensive Classroom Management: Creating Communities of Support and Solving Problems.* 7th ed. Boston: Pearson/Allyn and Bacon, 2004.

Jones, Vernon F., and Louise S. Jones. *Comprehensive Classroom Management: Motivating and Managing Students.* 3rd ed. Boston: Allyn and Bacon, 1990.

Jorgensen, Estelle Ruth. *The Art of Teaching Music.* Bloomington, IN: Indiana University Press, 2008.

Jorgensen, Estelle Ruth. *Transforming Music Education.* Bloomington, IN: Indiana University Press, 2003.

Jorgensen, Estelle Ruth. *In Search of Music Education.* Urbana, IL: University of Illinois Press, 1997.

Jorgensen, Estelle Ruth. *Philosopher, Teacher, Musician: Perspectives on Music Education.* Illini Books ed. Urbana, IL: University of Illinois Press, 1993.

Jørgensen, Harald, and Andreas C. Lehmann. *Does Practice make Perfect?: Current Theory and Research on Instrumental Music Practice.* Oslo, Norway: Norges musikkhøgskole, 1997.

Karrick, Brant. "An Examination of the Intonation Tendencies of Wind Instrumentalists Based on their Performance of Selected Harmonic Musical Intervals." *Journal of Research in Music Education* 46, no. 1 (1998), 112–127.

Kartje, Jean V. "O Mentor! My Mentor!" *Peabody Journal of Education* 71, no. 1, Mentors and Mentoring (1996), 114–125.

Keene, James A., *A History of Music Education in the United States.* Hanover, NH: University of New England Press, 1982.

Kendall, John D. *The Suzuki Violin Method in American Music Education: What the American Music Educator Should Know About Shinichi Suzuki.* Washington: MENC, 1973.

Killian, Janice N. "The Effect of Personal and Situational Factors in the Attrition and Retention of Texas Music Educators." *Journal of Music Teacher Education* 16, no. 1 (2006), 41–54.

Kodály, Zoltán, and Ferenc Bónis. *The Selected Writings of Zoltán Kodály.* New York: Boosey & Hawkes, 1974.

Kohn, Alfie. *Punished by Rewards: The Trouble with Gold Stars, Incentive Plans, A's, Praise, and Other Bribes.* Boston: Houghton Mifflin Co., 1999.

Kohut, Daniel L. *Instrumental Music Pedagogy: Teaching Techniques for School Band and Orchestra Directors.* Champaign, IL: Stipes Pub, 1996.

Koopman, Constantijn. "Music Education: Aesthetic or Praxial." *Journal of Aesthetic Education* 32, no. 3 (Autumn 1998), 1—17.

Krueger, Carol J. 2007. *Progressive Sight Singing.* New York: Oxford University Press, 2007.

Krumhansl, Carol L., and Paul Iverson. "Perceptual Interactions between Musical Pitch and Timbre." *Journal of Experimental Psychology: Human Perception and Performance* 18, no. 3 (1992), 739–751.

Kuhn, Wolfgang E. *Instrumental Music, Principles and Methods of Instruction.* 2nd ed. Boston: Allyn and Bacon, 1970.

Labuta, Joseph A. *Teaching Musicianship in the High School Band.* Revised ed. Ft. Lauderdale, FL: Meredith Music Pub, 1997.

Laine, Kristen. *American Band: Music, Dreams, and Coming of Age in the Heartland.* New York: Gotham Books, 2007.

Lampl, Hans. *Turning Notes into Music: An Introduction to Musical Interpretation.* Lanham, MD: Scarecrow Press, 1996.

Landis, Beth and Polly Carder. *The Eclectic Curriculum in American Music Education: Contributions of Dalcroze, Kodaly, and Orff.* Washington: Music Educators National Conference, 1972.

Lanza, Joseph. *Elevator Music: A Surreal History of Muzak, Easy-Listening, and Other Moodsong.* New York: St. Martin's Press, 1994.

Lapidaki, Eleni. "Learning from Masters of Music Creativity: Shaping Compositional Experiences in Music Education." *Philosophy of Music Education Review* 15, no. 2 (Fall 2007), 93–117.

LaRue, Jan. *Guidelines for Style Analysis.* 1st ed. New York: W. W. Norton, 1970.

Laster, James. *So You're the New Musical Director!: An Introduction to Conducting a Broadway Musical.* Lanham, MD: Scarecrow Press, 2001.

Latten, James E. "Exploration of a Sequence for Teaching Intonation Skills and Concepts to Wind Instrumentalists." *Journal of Band Research* 41, no. 1 (2005), 60–87.

Latten, James E. "Exploration of a Sequence for Teaching Intonation Skills and Concepts to Wind Instrumentalists." Ph.D. diss., University Microfilms International (MI) Ann Arbor, MI, 2003.

Latten, James E. "Chamber Music for Every Instrumentalist." *Music Educators Journal* 87, no. 5, Special Focus: Interdisciplinary Curriculum (2001), 45–53.

Lehman, Paul R. "Grading Practices in Music." *Music Educators Journal* 84, no. 5 (1998), 37–40.

Leinsdorf, Erich. *The Composer's Advocate.* London: Yale University Press, 1982.

Leonhard, Charles. "Philosophy of Music Education," *Music Educators Journal* 32, no. 1 (September–October 1965), 58–61, 177.

Levitin, Daniel J. *The World in Six Songs: How the Musical Brain Created Human Nature.* New York: Dutton, 2008.

Levitin, Daniel J. *This is Your Brain on Music: The Science of a Human Obsession.* New York: Dutton, 2006.

Liperote, Kathy A. "Audiation for Beginning Instrumentalists: Listen, Speak, Read, Write." *Music Educators Journal* 93, no. 1 (2006), 46–52.

Lisk, Edward S. *The Creative Director: Alternative Rehearsal Techniques.* Ft. Lauderdale, FL: Meredith Music Publications, 1991.

Lunongo-Orlando, Katherine. *Authentic Assessment: Designing Performance-Based Tasks*. Markham, ON: Pembroke Publishers, 2003.

Lustig, Nora. *Shielding the Poor: Social Protection in the Developing World*. Washington, D.C: Brookings Institution Press, 2001.

Lysons, Kenneth. *Understanding Hearing Loss*. London: Jessica Kingsley, 1996.

MacKenzie, Robert J. *Setting Limits in the Classroom: How to Move Beyond the Dance of Discipline in Today's Classrooms*. 2nd edition Roseville, Calif: Prima Pub, 2003.

Madsen, Charles H., Clifford K. Madsen. *Teaching Discipline; Behavioral Principles Toward a Positive Approach*. Boston: Allyn and Bacon, 1970.

Madsen, Clifford K., and John M. Geringer. "Discrimination between Tone Quality and Intonation in Unaccompanied Flute/Oboe Duets." *Journal of Research in Music Education* 29, no. 4 (1981), 305–313.

Marinak, Barbara A. and Linda Gambrell. "Intrinsic Motivation and Rewards: What Sustains Young Children's Engagement with Text?" *Literacy Research and Instruction* 47, no. 1 (January 1, 2008), 9–26.

Mark, Michael L. *A Concise History of American Music Education*. Lanham, MD: Rowman & Littlefield Education, 2008.

Mark, Michael L. "The Evolution of Music Education Philosophy from Utilitarian to Aesthetic." *Journal of Research in Music Education* 30, no. 1 (Spring 1982), 15–21.

Markworth, Wayne. *The Dynamic Marching Band*. Three Rivers, MI: Accent Publications, 2008.

May, Lissa F. "Factors and Abilities Influencing Achievement in Instrumental Jazz Improvisation." *Journal of Research in Music Education* 51, no. 3 (2003), 245–258.

McCarthy, Marie and J. Scott Goble. "Music Education Philosophy: Changing Times." *Music Educators Journal* 89, no. 1 (September 2002), 19–26.

McCoy, Claire Wehr. "Grading Students in Performing Groups: A Comparison of Principals' Recommendations with Directors' Practices." *Journal of Research in Music Education* 39, no. 3 (1991), 181–190.

McCoy, Claire, Wehr. "An Exploratory Study of Grading Criteria Among Select Ohio Ensemble Directors." *Contributions to Music Education* (1988), 15–19.

McDonald, Joseph P. "Dilemmas of Planning Backwards: Rescuing a Good Idea." *Teachers College Record* 94, no. 1 (1992), 152–169.

McGill, David. *Sound in Motion: A Performer's Guide to Greater Musical Expression*. Bloomington, IN: Indiana University Press, 2007.

McMahon, Colin. "NYC to Try Buying Good Parenting—Cash Grant Initiative Modeled on Mexico's," Chicago Tribune, 27 May 2007.

McNamara, Barry E. *Learning Disabilities: Appropriate Practices for a Diverse Population*. Albany, NY: State University of New York Press, 1998.

McPherson, Gary, and James Renwick. "A Longitudinal Study of Self-Regulation in Children's Musical Practice." *Music Education Research* 3, no. 2 (2001), 169–186.

Medhus, Elisa. *Hearing is Believing: How Words Can Make Or Break Our Children*. Novato, CA: New World Library, 2004.

MENC Task Force for National Standards in the Arts. *The School Music Program: A New Vision*. Lanham, MD: Rowman and Littlefield Education, 1994.

MENC Task Force on Band Course of Study. *Teaching WindandPercussion Instruments: A Course of Study*. Reston, VA: Music Educators National Conference, 1991.

Middendorf, Joan, and Alan Kalish. "The "Change-Up" in Lectures." *National Teaching and Learning Forum* 5, no. 2 (January 1996).

Mikszia, Peter. "Effective Practice: An Investigation of Observed Practice Behaviors, Self-Reported Practice Habits, and the Performance Achievement of High School Wind Players." *Journal of Research in Music Education* 55, no. 4 (2007), 359–375.

Mikszia, Peter. "Relationships among Impulsiveness, Locus of Control, Sex, and Music Practice." *Journal of Research in Music Education* 54, no. 4 (2006), 308–323.

Miksza, Peter, and Charles Punnett Schmidt. *Relationships Among Impulsivity, Achievement Goal Motivation, Practice Behavior, and the Performance Achievement of High School Wind Players*, Ph.D. diss., ISBN 9780549151258 0549151257, 2007.

Mills, Janet. *Instrumental Teaching*. Oxford; New York: Oxford University Press, 2007.

Millsap, Tonya Anne. "The Daily Implementation of Sequential Sustained Tone Exercises as a Means of Improving the Ensemble Intonation and Tone Quality of Second-Year Middle School Bands." Ph.D. diss., University Microfilms International (MI) Ann Arbor, MI, 1999.

Miranda, R. A., and M. T. Ullman. "Double Dissociation between Rules and Memory in Music: An Event-Related Potential Study." *NeuroImage* 38, no. 2 (2007), 331–345.

Mixon, Kevin. "Building Your Instrumental Music Program in an Urban School." *Music Educators Journal* 91, no. 3 (2005), 15–23.

Moore, Marvelene C., Angela L. Batey, and David M. Royse. *Classroom Management in General, Choral, and Instrumental Music Programs*. Reston, VA: MENC, the National Association for Music Education, 2002.

Moritz, Catherine. "Relationships between phonological awareness and musical rhythm subskills in kindergarten children and comparison of subskills in two schools with different amounts of music instruction." Unpublished dissertation, Tufts University, 2007).

Mott, Gregory. "The iPod and the Fury—A Reality Check of the Recent Reports on Mobile Music and Hearing Loss." *Washington Post* (http://www.washingtonpost.com/wp-dyn/content/article/2006/01/16/AR2006011 601100.html), January 2006.

Myers, David G. *Exploring Psychology*. 6th ed. New York: Worth Publishers, 2005.

National Research Council of Music Education. "High School Credit Courses in Music." *Music Supervisors Journal* 15, no. 5 (May 1929), 29–37.

Nelsen, Jane, Lynn Lott, and H. Stephen Glenn. *Positive Discipline in the Classroom: Developing Mutual Respect, Cooperation, and Responsibility in Your Classroom*. Rev. 3rd ed. Roseville, CA: Prima Publishing, 2000.

Newell, David. *Teaching Rhythm: New Strategies and Techniques for Success*. San Diego, CA: Neil A. Kjos Music Co, 2008.

Nicholson, Diana. "Music as an Aid to Learning." Ph.D. Diss., New York University, 1972.

Nierman, Glenn E., and Michael H. Veak. "Effect of Selected Recruiting Strategies on Beginning Instrumentalists' Participation Decisions." *Journal of Research in Music Education* 45, no. 3 (1997), 380–389.

Olmstead, Andrea. *Juilliard: A History*. Urbana, IL: University of Illinois Press, 1999.

Ormrod, Jeanne Ellis. *Educational Psychology: Developing Learners*. 2nd ed. Upper Saddle River, NJ: Merrill, 1998.

Orzolek, Douglas C. "Navigating the Paradox of Assessment in Music Education." In *Assessment in Music Education: Integrating Curriculum, Theory, and Practice*. Ed. Timothy S. Brophy. Chicago: GIA Publications: 2008.

Ostling, Acton Eric. *An Evaluation of Compositions for Wind Band According to Specific Criteria of Serious Artistic Merit*. Ann Arbor, MI: University Microfilms International, 1979.

Overbye, Dennis. "Elevating Science, Elevating Democracy." *New York Times*. 26 January 2009. Section D1.

Parisi, Joseph, and Stephen Young. *The Poetry Anthology, 1912–2002: Ninety Years of America's Most Distinguished Verse Magazine*. Chicago: Ivan R. Dee, 2002.

Parks, George N. *The Dynamic Drum Major*. Oskaloosa, Iowa: C.L. Barnhouse, 1984.

Parrish, Regena Turner. "Effects of Two Instructional Methods on High School Band Students' Sight-Reading Proficiency, Music Performance, and Attitude." *Update—Applications of Research in Music Education* 17, no. 1 (1998), 14–20.

Patel, Aniruddh D. *Music, Language, and the Brain*. New York; Oxford: Oxford University Press, 2008.

Patel A. D., Iversen J. R., and Rosenberg J. C., "Comparing the Rhythm and Melody of Speech and Music." *Journal of the Acoustical Society of America* 119, Part 1 (May 2006), 3034–3047.

Pennington, Jo. *The Importance of Being Rhythmic: A Study of the Principles of Dalcroze Eurhythmics Applied to General Education and to the Arts of Music, Dancing and Acting*. London; New York: G.P. Putnam's Sons, 1925.

Peterson, Michael R., and The American School Band Directors Association, *The New ASBDA Curriculum Guide*. Miami, FL: Warner Brothers Publications, 1997.

Phillips, Susan, Sandra Mace, Donald Hodges, and Julie Shoemaker. "Environmental Factors in Susceptibility to Noise-induced Hearing Loss in Student Musicians," *Medical Problems of Performing Artists*, 23 (2008), 20.

Phillips, Susan and Sandra Mace. "Sound-level Measurements in Music Practice Rooms" (2008) (Under Review— *Music Performance Research).*

Pinker, Steven. *How the Mind Works.* New York: Norton, 1997.

Pinker, Steven. *The Language Instinct.* New York: William Morrow and Co., 1994.

Poe, Delena Browder. *Teaching Comprehensive Musicianship through the Junior High School Band Program.* M.M.E. thesis, Virginia Commonwealth University, 1984.

Priest, Thomas. "Creative Thinking in Instrumental Classes." *Music Educators Journal* 88, no. 4 (2002), 47–58.

Raxsdale, Bill. *The Marching Band Director: A Master Planning Guide.* Hal Leonard, 1985.

Ribner, Neil, and California School of Professional Psychology. *The California School of Professional Psychology Handbook of Juvenile Forensic Psychology.* 1st ed. San Francisco: Jossey-Bass, 2002.

Richardson, Sheryl Lott. "Music as Language." *American Music Teacher* 53, no. 6 (2004), 21–25.

Richmond, Virginia P., and James C. McCroskey. *Power in the Classroom: Communication, Control, and Concern.* Hillsdale, N.J: L. Erlbaum, 1992.

Robinson, Mitchell. "To Sing Or Not to Sing in Instrumental Class." *Music Educators Journal* 83, no. 1 (1996), 17–47.

Rogers, George L. "Concert Band Instrumentation: Realities and Remedies." *Music Educators Journal* 77, no. 9 (1991), 34–39.

Rogers, George L. "Attitudes of High School Band Directors and Principals Toward Marching Band Contests." *Journal of Research in Music Education* 33, no. 4 (1985), 259–267.

Rohwer, Debbie, and Jeremy Polk. "Practice Behaviors of Eighth-Grade Instrumental Musicians." *Journal of Research in Music Education* 54, no. 4 (2006), 350–362.

Runfola, Maria, and Cynthia Crump Taggart. *The Development and Practical Application of Music Learning Theory.* Chicago, GIA Publications, 2005.

Russo, William, Jeffrey Ainis, and David Stevenson. *Composing Music: A New Approach.* Chicago: University of Chicago Press, 1988.

Ryder, Dan. *Techniques of Marching Band Show Design.* Wylie, Texas: Dan Ryer Field Drills.

Schleuter, Stanley L. *A Sound Approach to Teaching Instrumentalists: An Application of Content and Learning Sequences.* 2nd ed. New York: Schirmer Books, 1997.

Schmidt, Charles P. "Relations among Motivation, Performance Achievement, and Music Experience Variables in Secondary Instrumental Music Students." *Journal of Research in Music Education* 53, no. 2 (2005), 134–147.

Schuler, Scott. "Music Learning Sequence Techniques in Instrumental Performance Organizations." In *Readings in Music Learning Theory,* ed. Darrel L. Walters and Cynthia Crump Taggart. Chicago: GIA Publications, 1989.

Schuller, Gunther. *The Compleat Conductor.* New York: Oxford University Press, 1998.

Sennett, Frank. *FUNdraisin: 50 Proven Strategies for Successful School Fundraisers.* Thousand Oaks, CA: Corwin Press, 2008.

Shehan, Patricia K. "Effects of Rote Versus Note Presentations on Rhythm Learning and Retention." *Journal of Research in Music Education* 35, no. 2 (1987), 117–126.

Shellahamer, Bentley, James Swearingen, and John Woods. *The Marching Band Program: Principles and Practices.* Oskaloosa, Iowa: C.L. Barnhouse, 1986.

Sheppard, Philip. *Music Makes Your Child Smarter.* Iver Heath, UK: Artemis Editions, 2005.

Simon, William L., Dan Fox, and Reader's Digest Association. *Reader's Digest Popular Songs that Will Live Forever.* Pleasantville, NY: Reader's Digest Association, 1982.

Sink, Patricia and Sandra Mace. "A Preliminary Analysis of Sound-Level Exposures of Fulltime Choral, General, and Instrumental Music Educators During Typical Work Days." Paper presented at the North Carolina Music Educators Association conference, November, 2004, in Winston Salem, NC.

Sinor, Jean. "The Ideas of Kodály in America." *Music Educators Journal* 83, no. 5 (1997), 37–41.

Sinor, Jean. *Kodály Handbook.* Morristown, NJ: Silver Burdett & Ginn, 1988.

Smith, Frank, *Reading Without Nonsense*. 2nd ed. New York: Teachers College Press, 1985.

Smith, Gary E. *The System: Marching Band Methods*. Smith Walbridge Band Products, 2006.

Smith, Thomas M., and Richard M. Ingersoll. "What are the Effects of Induction and Mentoring on Beginning Teacher Turnover?" *American Educational Research Journal* 41, no. 3 (2004), 681–714.

Stephenson, Ken. *What to Listen for in Rock: A Stylistic Analysis*. New Haven, CT: Yale University Press, 2002.

Stevens, Dannelle D., and Antonia Levi. *Introduction to Rubrics: An Assessment Tool to Save Grading Time, Convey Effective Feedback, and Promote Student Learning*. Sterling, VA: Stylus Pub, 2005.

Stewart, Jennifer L. "Factors Related to Students' Decisions to Continue in Band." *Contributions to Music Education* 32, no. 1 (2005), 59–74.

Taylor, Philip, ed. *Assessment in Arts Education*. Portsmouth, NH: Heinemann, 2006.

Tomlinson, Carol Ann, Kay Brimijoin, and Lane Narvaez, *The Differentiated School*. Alexandria, VA: Association for Supervision and Curriculum Development, 2008.

Walter, Jennifer Stewart. "Sound Exposures of High School Marching Band Members During Band Camp: A Pilot Study." Accepted for publication by the *Journal of Band Research*.

Williams, David. "A Study of Internal Validity of the Instrument Timbre Preference Test." *Journal of Research in Music Education* 4, no. 3 (Fall 1996), 268–277.

VanderCook College of Music. *Masters' Projects: Summer Session 1993*. 1993.

Von Helmholtz, Hermann, Alexander John Ellis, and ed. and tr. *On the Sensations of Tone as a Physiological Basis for the Theory of Music. Uniform Title: Lehre Von Den Tonempfindungen. English*. 2nd English ed., translated, thoroughly rev. and corrected, rendered conformal to the 4th (and last) German ed. of 1877, with numerous additional notes and a new additional appendix bringing down information to 1885, and especially adapted to the use of music students, by Alexander J. Ellis. With a new introd. (1954) by Henry Margenau, ed. New York: Dover Publications, 1954.

Votta, Michael. "I Know It's Wrong, But I'm Not Sure How to Fix It—Strategies for Improving Aural Skills on the Podium." Paper presented at the Midwest Band and Orchestra Clinic, December, 2008.

Wade, Bonnie C. *Thinking Musically: Experiencing Music, Expressing Culture*. New York: Oxford University Press, 2004.

Walters, Darrel L., and Cynthia Crump Taggart. *Readings in Music Learning Theory*. Chicago, IL: GIA Publications, 1989.

Walvoord, Barbara E. Fassler, and Virginia Johnson Anderson. *Effective Grading: A Tool for Learning and Assessment*. 1st ed. San Francisco: Jossey-Bass Publishers, 1998.

White, Gary. "Hazards of Striking Up the Band." *The Ledger* (http://www.theledger.com/article/20071016/NEWS/710160347?Title=Daily-Exposure-to-Thunderous-Sounds-Can-Damage-Music-Directors-Hearing), 16 October 2007.

Wis, Ramona M. *The Conductor As Leader: Principles of Leadership Applied to Life on the Podium*. Chicago, IL: GIA Publications, 2007.

Wolbers, Mark. "Singing in the Band Rehearsal." *Music Educators Journal* 89, no. 2 (2002), 37–41.

Wong, Harry K., and Rosemary T. Wong. *The First Days of School: How to be an Effective Teacher*. Mountain View, CA: Harry K. Wong Publications, 2005.

Worthy, Michael D. "Effects of Tone-Quality Conditions on Perception and Performance of Pitch among Selected Wind Instrumentalists." *Journal of Research in Music Education* 48, no. 3 (2000), 222–236.

Zinar, Ruth. "Reading Language and Reading Music: Is There a Connection?" *Music Educators Journal* 62, no. 7 (1976), 70–74.

Index